THE McKAY HOME IN SALT·LAKE CITY

THE
PRESIDENT'S
OFFICE

This belongs to Shirley Suter Ferguson
794 Portola Drive
San Leandro, Calif

Gospel Ideals

May this book help to inspire
you with the truthfulness
of our wonderful Gospel.
Every thing in this book is
true – and will be helpful
to your lovely family in
acquiring the learning
and understanding of things
they should know about.
May our heavenly fathers
choisest blessings attend you
is my prayer –
Love –
Mom.

July 23rd 1958

Gospel Ideals

SELECTIONS

FROM THE DISCOURSES

OF

David O. McKay

NINTH PRESIDENT OF
THE CHURCH OF JESUS CHRIST
OF LATTER-DAY SAINTS

AN IMPROVEMENT ERA PUBLICATION

1953

Printed by

in the United States of America.

PREFACE

With President McKay's approval and gracious co-operation, this book, *Gospel Ideals*, has been prepared for presentation to the unnumbered thousands who will read these words of counsel and advice and consolation and encouragement from a beloved President.

President McKay is an exceptional literary figure. He is familiar with the best, the most inspirational literature of the world. His oral and written discourses mark this literary quality. He uses the English language effectively. An educator at the time he was called into Church service as an Apostle of the Lord, he has prepared his utterances with care. He approaches important problems and attacks pertinent issues with precision and force. His speeches and writings are analytical. Their author has practised what he no doubt taught as a teacher of English: unity and clarity.

The eighty volumes of conference reports alone, from which part of these paragraphs were compiled, are indicative of the wealth of material from which selections were taken. A minimum of change has been made in bringing the material up-to-date and adapting it to book use. Every effort has been made to keep the compilation true to the author in form as well as in spirit.

The President was in Europe when this book was put on the press. Even before that, his arduous duties did not permit his giving this compilation detailed attention—and if errors and inaccuracies appear on these pages, the editors take full responsibility for them.

The mission and message of the Church of Jesus Christ (which transforms the lives of men and society by means of simple gospel principle) is basic to all of President McKay's utterances. Any section of *Gospel Ideals* will offer aid to all who seek to find light in a troubled world. There is comfort for those who need comfort, courage for those who need courage, guidance for those who need guidance, peace for those who need peace, and spiritual challenge for those who need challenge.

With a conviction that this book will aid in the building of a better world, the management and editorial staff of *The Improvement Era* present this volume to President David O. McKay on the eightieth anniversary of his birth.

ACKNOWLEDGMENTS

Compiling and publishing a volume of this kind demands dedicated service from those who work with it. Many there are who never receive commendation beyond a passing thanks for the work they do. Their satisfaction lies in knowing that they have given their best and have aided in making a contribution to the countless readers whose lives are touched by the book. The work of others can be more readily recognized.

To Dr. John A. Widtsoe goes the credit for initiating this work. The line of communication between the President of the Church and the people was dear to his heart. Even though he passed away before publication was completed, Dr. Widtsoe guided the formative stages of this book and proposed and planned its final presentation to honor President David O. McKay on the occasion of his eightieth birthday anniversary.

Dr. G. Homer Durham ably and discriminatingly did the initial selecting, arranging, and titling. He devoted untold hours to reading, weighing, integrating, and compiling the great wealth of material from President McKay's addresses and written words.

The editorial staff of *The Improvement Era* further planned, selected, edited, designed, and checked and rechecked materials from manuscript to final form, and worked closely with artists, engravers, printers, and photographers, to all of whom appreciation is here expressed.

Doyle L. Green, Marba C. Josephson, Elizabeth J. Moffitt, Albert L. Zobell, Jr., and Iris Parker, particularly deserve highest commendation for their devotion and painstaking diligence in the long and demanding labor of giving attention to every detail.

Especial thanks is given Clare Middlemiss, secretary to President David O. McKay, for her wholehearted co-operation in making available materials for this work and checking much of its contents.

Much thanks and credit are also due Elbert R. Curtis, general superintendent of the Y.M.M.I.A. and general manager of *The Improvement Era;* Bertha S. Reeder, general president of the Y.W.M.I.A. and associate manager of the *Era,* and John D. Giles, the *Era's* business manager, for their continued interest, encouragement, and support.

But the real substance was provided by the President himself, in words that he has written and spoken during nearly five decades. One cannot read these pages without sensing that President McKay has had a long and providential preparation for the high office he holds. The constancy of his counsel and the conviction of his testimony of truth will give guidance and comfort, encouragement and conviction for this, his own day, and far into the future.

RICHARD L. EVANS

Key to Abbreviations and Notes on Sources

Abbreviations for references used in this volume are listed below.

AA	*Ancient Apostles*, by David O. McKay. (Deseret News Press, 1918.)
CAUU	*Commencement Address,* "Education: The Paramount Purpose of a Free People," University of Utah, June 1951.
CR	Annual and Semi-Annual *Conference Reports.*
D. & C.	Doctrine and Covenants.
DNCS	"The Church Section" of *The Deseret News.*
FS, ms.	Funeral Sermons from the personal files of President McKay.
GM	*The Utah Historical and Genealogical Magazine.*
I	*The Juvenile Instructor* and its successor, *The Instructor.*
IE	*The Improvement Era.*
MS	*Millennial Star.*
P. of G. P.	The Pearl of Great Price.
RSM	*The Relief Society Magazine.*
YWJ	*The Young Woman's Journal.*

Numbers preceding colons after book titles or abbreviations refer to chapter or section; those following, to verse or verses.

Numbers preceding colons after abbreviations of magazine titles refer to bound volume numbers; those following to page or pages.

When references to the same source follow each other closely and uninterruptedly, *ibid.* is used instead of repeating the book title.

---

*No longer published.

Contents

"*I testify to you that God our Heavenly Father lives, that he communicates with his servants, that he has established in this dispensation of the world his great work, the only plan of salvation whereby mankind may be saved, the only means by which peace may be established in the world.*"

—David O. McKay

The Improvement Era
Volume 24:404

Book I

THE GOSPEL OF JESUS CHRIST

" 'What think ye of Christ?'
. . . To the Church, and to
the world, I repeat this question as being the most vital,
the most far-reaching query
in this unsettled, distracted
world."

—DAVID O. McKAY

Conference Report,
April 1951, p. 92.

Chapter 1

The Power of the Gospel

THE GLAD TIDINGS

The Guide to Higher Things. We declare that the gospel, the glad tidings of great joy, is the true guide to mankind; and that men and women are happiest and most content who live nearest to its teachings.

" . . . the voice of the Lord is unto all men, and there is none to escape; and there is no eye that shall not see, neither ear that shall not hear, neither heart that shall not be penetrated.

"And the voice of warning shall be unto all people, by the mouths of my disciples, whom I have chosen in these last days." (D. & C. 1:2, 4.)

What the sun in the heavenly blue is to the earth struggling to get free from winter's grip, so the gospel is to sorrowing souls yearning for something higher and better than mankind has yet found.—*CR,* October 1947, p. 121.

The "Good News." "Good tidings of great joy"—the gospel of Jesus Christ is that good tidings. The term *gospel* means, literally, "good news," and such is the news that emanates from above. There have been but few men in the world's history who have been so in tune with the heavens that they could receive directly from God the Father that good news; but there have always been, in every dispensation, opportunities for men to receive that good news, and these prophets who were in tune with the infinite and who heard first and directly that good news have had imposed upon them the responsibility to convey that good news to others of their fellow men, that they who are concerned with the things of the world might receive the glad message and be brought back into the environment of peace, harmony, and good will. In this dispensation, that same responsibility has been given to man.—*CR,* April 1910, p. 106.

THE GOSPEL AND JOYOUS LIVING. The principles of the gospel are the surest, safest guide to mortal man. Christ is the light to humanity. In that light man sees his way clearly. When the light is rejected, the soul of man stumbles in darkness. No person, no group, no nation can achieve true success without following him who said:

"I am the light of the world: he that followeth me shall not walk in darkness, but shall have the light of life." (John 8:12.)

It is a sad thing when individuals and nations extinguish that light—when Christ and his gospel are supplanted by the law of the jungle and the strength of the sword. The chief tragedy in the world at the present time is its disbelief in God's goodness and its lack of faith in the teachings and doctrines of the gospel.

To all who believe in a living, personal God and his divine truth, life can be delightful and beautiful.

As a matter of fact, it is glorious just to be alive. Joy, even ecstasy, can be experienced in the consciousness of existence. There is supreme satisfaction in sensing one's individual entity and in realizing that that entity is part of God's great creative plan. There are none so poor, none so rich, sick, or maimed who may not be conscious of this relationship.—CR, April 1940, p. 115.

THE POWER OF THE GOSPEL

THE GREATEST FORCE IN LIFE. Religion is the most potent power in life. Spiritual development and moral integrity are fundamental in the lives not only of the Latter-day Saints but also of all who would build a community that will contribute to the safety and advancement of our republic or of any other nation. President Calvin Coolidge truly said that "the government of a country never gets ahead of the religion of a country. There is no way by which we can substitute the authority of law for the virtue of man. Of course, we can help to restrain the vicious and furnish a fair degree of security and protection by legislation and police control, but the real reforms which society in these days is seeking will come as a result of our religious convictions or

they will not come at all. Peace, justice, humanity, charity—
these cannot be legislated into being. They are the results
of a divine grace."—*CR, April 1934, p. 22.*

POWER TO SOLVE WORLD PROBLEMS. The responsibility
of showing to the world that the gospel of Jesus Christ will
solve its problems rests upon the men who make the claim,
who believe that the declaration made by the Prophet Joseph
is true. We heard from Brother Stephen L Richards that
the Church is so constituted that every human need may be
supplied. I believe in his statement. I believe, too, that every
*world problem may be solved by obedience to the principles
of the gospel of Jesus Christ.*—*CR, April 1920, p. 116.*

The solution of the great world problems is here in the
Church of Jesus Christ. Ample provision is made not only
for the needs of individuals, but also for the nation and groups
of nations. I realize that it is a great claim. I grant that
we may seem to be arrogating to ourselves superior wisdom,
but we are not. It is simply the application of God's plan to
the world problems. You who hold the priesthood have greater
responsibility today, now that you live in this creative moment
in the world's history, than ever the Church has had before.
I repeat it. If we make the claim to hold the truth, it is obliga-
tory upon every Latter-day Saint so to live, that when the
people of the world come, in answer to the call, to test the
fruit of the tree, they will find it wholesome and good.

The Lord help us to be able to prove to the world that
we possess just what the world today is longing for, and
when they see it, may they know, as you know, as I know,
that the everlasting gospel is a light to the world. May
it ever be upon the hill a light to the nations, a savior to
them, and a solution of all the world problems, I pray, in the
name of Jesus Christ.—*CR, April 1920, pp. 118-119.*

PEACE BY CONFORMING TO THE GOSPEL. Though we are
living in perilous times, you and I can rejoice because the
gospel is among men. The Church is established in this free
country, nevermore to be thrown down or given to another
people. Nations may rise, and nations may destroy each
other in strife, but this gospel is here to stay, and we must
preach it and proclaim it, that peace may come, for it is only

through obedience to the gospel of Jesus Christ that peace will come permanently upon the earth.—*DNCS*, January 2, 1952, p. 4.

THE POWER OF GOD "UNTO SALVATION" AND ETERNAL LIFE. The gospel of Jesus Christ, as revealed to the Prophet Joseph Smith, is in very deed, in every way, the power of God unto salvation. It is salvation *here*—here and now. It gives to every man the perfect life, here and now, as well as hereafter.

Life is the dearest thing to us in all the world. Nothing else do you cherish as you cherish your life. You who would give your life today for someone else would give it in order to save the life of one who is dearer to you than your own life. So life is the one thing we hold to. It is the one thing we desire here and hereafter.

WHAT IS ETERNAL LIFE? In that glorious prayer of intercession offered by Jesus, our Redeemer, just before he crossed the brook Cedron and received the traitor's kiss that betrayed him into the hands of the soldiers, we find these words, "And this is life eternal, that they might know thee the only true God, and Jesus Christ, whom thou hast sent." (John 17:3.) To know God and his Son is eternal life. There is the key. Life eternal is what I desire. I desire it more than I desire anything else in the world—life eternal for me and mine and all the world. And there in the words of the Redeemer I have the secret given to me in a simple sentence: "to know God and Jesus Christ, whom thou hast sent, is eternal life."

But how shall I *know* him? That is the next question. How may I know him? Has he, at any time, or on any occasion, answered that question? If so, I want the answer, because it is vital. In searching the record as it is given to us by men who associated daily with the Lord, I find upon one occasion that men out in his audience cried out against him. They opposed his works as men today opposed you, my fellow missionaries, when you were out in the field. And one voice cried out and said in effect, "How do we know that what you tell us is true? How do we know that your profession of being the Son of God is true?" And he answered in just a simple way; and note the test: "If ye will *do the will* of my Father, which is in heaven, ye shall know whether the doctrine is of God or whether I speak of myself." (See John 7:17.)

That test is most sound. It is most philosophical. It is the most simple test to give knowledge to an individual of which the human mind can conceive. Doing a thing, introducing it into your very being will convince you whether it is good or whether it is bad. You may not be able to convince me of that which you know, but you know it because you have lived it. That is the test which the Savior gave to those men when they asked him how they should know whether the doctrine was of God or whether it was of man.

THE ESSENCE OF THE GOSPEL. But in considering his answer another question arises. If ye will *do the will*—what is the *will?* We can see what conditions will bring eternal life. We have the spoken statement that if we will do his will, we shall know; but now comes the question, what is the will? And therein, my brethren and sisters, is the whole essence of the gospel of Jesus Christ — just as plainly as Jesus stated and defined what is eternal life or how we should know it, just as plainly as he laid down that test, just as plainly has he expressed what his will is.

I am not going to take time—it would not be wise, even if I could—to narrate all the principles that constitute that will; but they are so simple that, as the scriptures say, a wayfaring man, though a fool, need not err therein.

The Church of Jesus Christ of Latter-day Saints bears testimony to the world that this will of God has been made manifest in this dispensation, that the principles of the gospel, the principles of life have been revealed. They are in harmony with the principles which Christ taught in the Meridian of Time. . . .

So we might go on with our principles. But then you can sum it up in this, my fellow workers, that after obeying the principles and the ordinances of the gospel the will of God is to serve your fellow men, benefiting them, making this world better for your being in it. Christ gave his all to teach us that principle. And he made the statement, "Inasmuch as ye have done it unto one of the least of these my brethren, ye have done it unto me." (Matt. 25:40.)

—*CR, October* 1915, pp. 70-72.

FAITH, GRACE, AND WORKS. The fallacy that Jesus has done all for us, and live as we may, if on our deathbed, we only believe, we shall be saved in his glorious presence, is most pernicious. Jesus Christ, the Savior of the world, has given us the means whereby man may obtain eternal happiness and peace in the kingdom of our Father, but man must work out his own salvation through obedience to the eternal principles and ordinances of the gospel.

For centuries men have been blinded by the false teaching of "belief alone sufficient"; and today there is manifest on every hand the sorry plight into which this and other perverse doctrines have thrown the pseudo-Christian sects. The world is in sore need at the present time of the gospel of individual effort—the gospel of faith and works. He who will not grasp this means provided him, will sink beneath the waves of sin and falsehood.—MS, 85:762 (1923).

Love of God and of his righteousness is shown not in words but in works.

Eternal life is God's greatest gift to man, and the Lord in turn is glorified in man's immortality. Eternal life is the result of knowledge, and knowledge is obtained by doing the will of God.—MS, 85:761-762 (1923).

It is the height of folly for men to try to persuade themselves that Christ has done everything for them, that he has thrown a rope around them, as it were, and will pull them to safety in spite of themselves.—MS, 85:761 (1923).

THE GOSPEL CRUCIBLE. If America is the "melting pot," the gospel of Jesus Christ is the crucible in which hate, envy, and greed are consumed, and good will, kindness, and love remain as inner aspirations by which man truly lives and builds.—CR, October 1942, p. 70.

When things do not harmonize with the truths of the gospel, we can pass them by or at least hold them in abeyance until either their truth or falsity be established.—CR, October 1931, p. 10.

I love the gospel. It is truly the power of God unto salvation and to happiness here and now. I wish all men and women could accept it and cherish its ideals and apply them in their daily lives. What a happy world we might be living in if we only would be kind and considerate of one another, as the gospel teaches.—*DNCS*, September 6, 1952, p. 3.

CHAPTER 2

PRINCIPLES OF SALVATION

FAITH

THE FIRST PRINCIPLE. What does it mean to keep the faith? It means, first, that we accept Jesus Christ, not merely as a great teacher, a powerful leader, but as the Savior, the Redeemer of the world. Now there is much associated with that, for I know that many students are reading comments from reputably great educators who say that in order to be a Christian it is not necessary to accept Christ as the literal Son of God, it is not necessary to believe in the miraculous conception, it is not necessary to believe in the literal resurrection from the grave. But he who keeps the faith will accept Jesus Christ as the Son of God, the Redeemer of the world. I would have all men keep that faith. I think it is fundamental to man's happiness, fundamental to his peace of mind. I think it is the cardinal principle of the Church of Jesus Christ.—*CR*, October 1928, pp. 36-37.

THE WORLD'S GREAT NEED. The world's greatest need is an unwavering faith in a divine Providence.—*DNCS*, July 9, 1952, p. 2.

Faith is more potent in human endeavor even than judgment or experience.—*IE*, 50:507 (1947).

. . . so faith [is] the great need of the world today, faith that there is a God in heaven, who is real, not just a force, but a Father who hears prayers and answers them, the Father of our Lord and Savior, Jesus Christ, his beloved Son. While we stand here bearing witness to that, already we can hear in imagination the leaders of whole nations denouncing faith in God the Father. Communism is anti-Christ! That alone condemns it as idiotic.—*DNCS*, July 9, 1952, p. 2.

MAN MUST WALK BY FAITH. I am not unmindful of the scripture that declares, "For by grace are ye saved through faith; and that not of yourselves: it is the gift of God." (Eph. 2:8.) That is absolutely true, for man in his taking upon

himself mortality was impotent to save himself. When left
to grope in a natural state, he would have become and did
become "carnal, sensual, and devilish by nature." But the
Lord through his grace appeared to man, gave him the gospel
or eternal plan whereby he might rise above the carnal and
selfish things of life and obtain spiritual perfection.

But he must rise by his own efforts, and he must walk
by faith.—CR, April 1938, p. 18.

THE APPLICATION OF FAITH. "What doth it profit, my
brethren, though a man say he hath faith, and have not
works? can faith save him?" (James 2:14.)

In this significant passage, James decries the impotency
of faith as a merely intellectual perception and implies the
importance of the application of truth to daily life and conduct. He teaches that "faith is dead and useless unless it
expresses itself in a true life and true Christian activities."
There has been, and is today, too much discrepancy between
belief and practice, between the proclamation of high ideals
and the application of these ideals to daily life and living.
—CR, October 1937, p. 100.

A young man who was in the great battle of the Philippines told me that before that battle, the highest number that
attended a religious service was forty-seven. After that three-
day battle, however, the attendance jumped to 274. At one
service there were five hundred present. It would seem that
with most people it takes something out of the ordinary, a
great calamity, or the realization of the nearness of death,
to make them realize that their faith in God and in an hereafter must find expression in daily acts, but unless such expression springs from a sincere heart, it will have little or no
avail.—IE, 48:69 (1945).

FAITH A PERSONAL MATTER. Faith in God cannot of
course be other than personal. It must be yours; it must be
mine; and, to be effective, must spring from the mind and
heart. Every man will do well to pray with Emerson: "O God,
make me willing to be willing to do thy will." The responsibility, therefore, of making the world better belongs to you,
and to you, and to a million others professing his name.—IE,
47:13 (1944).

REPENTANCE

AN UNQUESTIONED PRINCIPLE. There are many people in the world who doubt that the ordinance of baptism is essential to salvation; but it is inconceivable to think that anyone can even question the essentiality of repentance. Every principle of the gospel when studied carefully reveals a harmony with truth that is simply sublime. Each seems to be all comprehensive, either leading into or embracing other principles. Thus, faith in a perfect being, inspiring one to live righteously, seems to include repentance. So forgiveness may encompass charity; charity, love; and so on. This harmony, or rather this oneness of all fundamental principles of the gospel is indicative of their being elements of eternal truth. Truth being "the sum of existence" is all comprehensive: faith, repentance, charity, forgiveness, and every other element of truth will of necessity show a close relationship not only to each other but also to the whole, of which they are a part.

It is difficult, therefore, to designate any one principle as being the most important. One student may name this, and another name that as being chief, the choice of each being determined by the amount of study and attention given to the favorite principle. When comparing eternal principles, it is more nearly correct to say that each is equal to any other.

This thought, however, does not lessen the significance of the great Thomas Carlyle's forceful remark about repentance. "Of all acts," he says, "is not, for man, repentance the most divine? The deadliest sin, I say, were that same supercilious consciousness of no sin; that is death; the heart so conscious is divorced from sincerity, humility, and in fact, is dead."

A PRINCIPLE OF PROGRESS. What progress can there be for a man unconscious of his faults? Such a man has lost the fundamental element of growth, which is the realization that there is something bigger, better, and more desirable than the condition in which he now finds himself. In the soil of self-satisfaction, true growth has poor nourishment. Its roots find greater succor in discontent.

> "Our pleasures and our discontents
> Are rounds by which we may ascend."

Heaven pity the man who is unconscious of a fault! Pity him also who is ignorant of his ignorance! Neither is on the road to salvation. "The greatest of faults is to be conscious of none." (Thomas Carlyle.)

The first step to knowledge is a realization of the lack of it; and the first step towards spiritual growth is the belief in a higher and better life, or conversely, a realization of the meanness of one's present state. Repentance is the turning away from that which is low and the striving for that which is higher. As a principle of salvation, it involves not only a desire for that which is better, but also a sorrow—not merely remorse—but true sorrow for having become contaminated in any degree with things sinful, vile, or contemptible.

It is not uncommon for people to have remorse for mistakes made, for follies and sins committed, but to have no turning away from such frailties and evils. They may even feel penitent; but "penitence," we are told, "is transient, and may involve no change of character or conduct." Repentance. on the other hand, "is sorrow for sin with *self-condemnation*, and complete turning away from the sin." It is, therefore, more than mere remorse; "it comprehends a change of nature befitting heaven."

AN ESSENTIAL TO SALVATION. Every principle and ordinance of the gospel of Jesus Christ is significant and important in contributing to the progress, happiness, and eternal life of man, but there is none more essential to the salvation of the human family than the divine and eternally operative principle, repentance. Without it, no one can be saved. Without it, no one can even progress. Its sublimity and essentiality stirred the Prophet Alma's soul when he exclaimed:

"O that I were an angel, and could have the wish of mine heart, that I might go forth and speak with the trump of God, with a voice to shake the earth, and cry repentance unto every people!

"Yea, I would declare unto every soul, as with the voice of thunder, repentance and the plan of redemption, that they should repent and come unto our God, that there might not be more sorrow upon all the face of the earth." (Alma 29:1-2.)

Ignorance and sin are man's worst enemies. They are barriers to salvation. Only through repentance and obedience to the gospel can these be eradicated. In the repentant man's soul these evils are supplanted by light and knowledge. From him who will not repent "shall be taken even the light which he has received; for the Spirit of the Lord will not always strive with man." (See D. & C. 1:33.)

It is the duty of the elders of the Church (1) to apply to their own lives this eternal principle, and then (2) to go forth and speak with the power of God, and cry repentance unto every people.—*MS*, 86:24-25 (1924).

THE CHANGE THAT IS REPENTANCE. To repent—this we should note carefully—is to feel regret, contrition, or compunction for what one has done or omitted to do. It means to change one's mind in regard to past or intended actions or conduct on account of regret or dissatisfaction. It means to conquer selfishness, greed, jealousy, faultfinding, and slander. It means to control one's temper. It means to rise above the sordid things, which carnal nature would prompt us to do to gratify our appetites and passions, and to enter into the higher or spiritual realm.—*CR*, September-October 1950, p. 110.

To repent is to change one's mind or one's heart with regard to past or intended action, conduct, etc., on account of regret or dissatisfaction.—*CR*, April 1948, p. 65.

THE ORDINANCE OF BAPTISM

A PRINCIPLE AS WELL. Baptism is one of the "first principles and ordinances of the gospel." As an established rite of the Church, it is classified clearly as an *ordinance*. Though in strict analysis it may not be considered a principle in the sense that faith and repentance and love are principles, yet it becomes such, inasmuch as it is law established by divine power. It is merely as an ordinance, however, that it is generally considered.

Even in this more obvious, and, we may say, superficial aspect, baptism always connotes fundamental principles of spiritual growth. Three of these are sincerity, simplicity, and purity:—sincerity, "the mother of a noble family of virtues"; simplicity and purity, "the two wings with which man soars above the earth and all temporary nature."

THE VIRTUE TEST. These three virtues everyone should possess who desires to have administered unto him this sacred rite. Sincerely should he go before his Maker, and with contrite and penitent heart, acknowledge his weakness and errors, and manifest a desire to live a new life. He should have no selfish ends to serve. He should sincerely "desire to come into the fold of God," to be numbered with his people, and "to bear others' burdens that they may be light." Only in this manner can the eternal principle of true repentance be made manifest.

Purity lies in the affection. It "unites with and enjoys God." It is the pure in heart that shall *see* God. No person of impure heart, though baptized a hundred times, can approach him.

Simplicity is manifest in the intent. Prompting the soul to obedience, it drives from it all desire for ostentation, publicity, personal honor, or earthly emoluments. In the worthy intent is manifest only the simple desire to comply with one of God's commandments.

SIMPLICITY OF THE ORDINANCE. Nor is it in the *intent* alone that the virtue of simplicity is associated but in the administration of the ordinance as well. Of this every account of baptism in sacred history bears evidence. Take, for example, the baptism of Jesus in the Jordan; the baptism of Queen Candace's servant by Philip; of the jailor by Paul and Silas; of Cornelius and his household by Peter; of Helam and others by Alma, etc. All these instances seem to have been characterized by simplicity and sacredness. There is no evidence of set periods of preparation, of pompous ceremony, and of irrelevant rites. Faith in the Lord Jesus Christ, repentance from sin, as shown in sincerity and purity of life, and a desire to become affiliated with God's people were the only preparatory requirements.

It is well for the elders of the Church to hold to the simplicity of this gospel ordinance. Avoid associating with it any ceremonies that will in the least degree rob it of this virtue. Already there are some who think a prayer, "dedicating the water," is an essential part of the ceremony; others, who think a preparatory service must be held; and still others who insist upon leading each applicant into the water, and then "leading" him out again, evidently a useless waste of time and energy, particularly when many applicants are present.

All such details are non-essentials, neither adding to nor taking from the efficacy of the ordinance. There is danger lurking, however, in the possibility of these excrescential ceremonies becoming so firmly attached to the principle itself that in time they may not be separated from it. Proper instructions to the applicant should always precede baptism, and the importance of the obligations he is about to assume impressed upon him; and, of course, prayer is appropriate and fitting on all sacred occasions.

PURPOSE AND SUBLIMITY OF BAPTISM. Jesus was baptized of John "in order to fulfil all righteousness"; but the Pharisees and lawyers rejected the counsel of God against themselves, being not baptized of him.

To Nicodemus Jesus said, "Except a man be born of water and of the Spirit, he cannot enter into the kingdom of God." (John 3:5.)

To the members of the Church, Paul and Peter wrote, "For ye are all the children of God by faith in Christ Jesus. For as many of you as have been baptized into Christ have put on Christ." (Gal. 3:26-27.) "The like figure whereunto even baptism doth also now save us . . . by the resurrection of Jesus Christ." (I Peter 3:21.)

In these three instances we have set forth clearly the threefold purpose of the ordinance of baptism, viz.:

(1) A rite established by God himself and associated with the eternal principle of righteousness, compliance with the law, therefore, being established to man's salvation.

(2) An initiatory ordinance—the gateway leading to membership in the fold of Christ.

(3) A beautiful and sublime symbol typifying the burial of the "former" man with all his weaknesses and impurities, and the coming forth into a newness of life.

The ordinance of baptism is a law of God, obedience to which, in sincerity, in purity, in simplicity, brings inevitably the promised blessing of the Comforter, a divine Guide, whom they can never know, who "change the ordinance and transgress the law." Though men may scoff at it, ridicule it, and doubt its efficacy, baptism remains ever, even in its simplicity, not only one of the most beautiful symbols known, but also one of the most effective laws operating for the salvation of man. In baptism, then, as in all other things, all men should follow him who said: "I am the light of the world: he that followeth me shall not walk in darkness, but shall have the light of life." (John 8:12.)—MS, 85:328-330 (1923).

SALVATION FOR THE DEAD

The Sectarian Dilemma. Since repentance and baptism by water as well as by the Spirit are essential to salvation, how shall the millions who have never heard the gospel, who have never had an opportunity either to repent or to be baptized enter into the kingdom of God? Surely a God of love can never be satisfied if the majority of his children are outside his kingdom, dwelling eternally either in ignorance, misery, or hell. Such a thought is revolting to intelligent minds. On the other hand, if these millions who died without having heard the gospel can enter into the kingdom of God without obeying the principles and ordinances of the gospel, then Christ's words to Nicodemus were not the statement of a general and eternal truth, and Peter's words on the Day of Pentecost had not a universal application, even though he said plainly, "For the promise is unto you, and to your children, and to all that are afar off, even as many as the Lord our God shall call." (Acts 2:39.)

Now the gospel of Jesus Christ teaches that *all* mankind may be saved by obedience to the laws and ordinances thereof. Nor is the term "all" restricted in meaning to include only a chosen few; it means every child of a loving and divine Father. And yet, hundreds of millions have died without ever having heard that there is such a thing as a gospel plan.

All nations and races have a just claim upon God's mercies. Since there is only one plan of salvation, surely there must be some provision made whereby the "uncounted dead" may hear of it and have the privilege of either accepting or rejecting it. Such a plan is given in the principle of salvation for the dead.

THE APOSTOLIC TEACHINGS. Peter tells us that after the Savior was put to death in the flesh, " . . . he went and preached unto the spirits in prison,

"Which sometime were disobedient, when once the long-suffering of God waited in the days of Noah, . . ." (I Peter 3:19-20.) Thus did Christ preach the gospel ". . . also to them that are dead, that they might be judged according to men in the flesh, but live according to God in the spirit." (I Peter 4:6.)

It is evident that if Christ preached the gospel again to people who had rejected it, they who have never heard it should in justice have the privilege of hearing it.

This principle of salvation for the dead was not only understood in the days when the Savior taught among men, but also the necessity of the dead's being baptized, as Jesus said they must be in order to enter into the kingdom of God. Since this ordinance had not been administered to them when they were living on the earth, it seemed proper to administer it to them by proxy.

Paul referred to this practice of baptism in his argument in favor of the resurrection. He said, "Else what shall they do which are baptized for the dead, if the dead rise not at all?" (I Cor. 15:29.) The psuedo-Christian world, unenlightened by revelation, has stumbled over the meaning of this simple text, and not a few commentators have tried to explain away its true applicability to all mankind of the Savior's teachings. Truly, " . . . there is none other name under heaven given among men, whereby we must be saved." (Acts 4:12.) All ordinances performed by the priesthood of the Most High are as eternal as love, as comprehensive and enduring as life, and through obedience to them, all mankind, living and dead, may enter into and abide eternally in the kingdom of God.—MS, 85:680-682 (1923).

GENEALOGICAL RESEARCH. One of the most significant phases of this great work is the operation of the Spirit of the Lord upon the hearts of men and women who are not members of our Church, impelling them to use their time and means in gathering genealogical records, binding them in books, and thus making them accessible to those who have the authority to do the work for those who have passed beyond. Many are the interesting incidents that are related showing

how these records fall into the hands of members of the
Church. I think this phase is most significant and proves to
us conclusively that this is the day in which the Lord expects
his Church at least to inaugurate the great work of turning
" . . . the heart of the fathers to the children, and the heart of
the children to their fathers. . . . " (Malachi 4:6.)—GM, 25:59
(1934).

CHAPTER 3

REVELATION AND COMMUNICATION WITH GOD

DIVINE REVELATION

WORSHIP OF THE TRUE GOD. You will remember that in the first section of the Doctrine and Covenants the Lord refers to the tendency of the world to have different gods. They set up unto themselves their gods which are after the fashion of the world. Has there ever been a time in the history of the world when men worshiped so many different gods after the fashion of the world—the god of wealth, the god of industrialism, the god of unionism, the god of greed, of selfishness, the god of sensuality? Why, it seems to me that every form of idol is now worshiped in preference to God the Eternal Father, and men sacrifice everything for their earthly deities.

GOD COMMUNICATES WITH MAN: I testify to you that God our heavenly Father lives, that he communicates with his servants, that he has established in this dispensation of the world his great work, the only plan of salvation whereby mankind may be saved, the only means by which peace may be established in the world. Peace can come only when men will acknowledge God as their Creator, as their Father, and when they will obey the principles of the gospel of Jesus Christ, when they will have in their souls individual righteousness, a desire to reverence God, a desire to serve their fellow men, a desire to bless the other man instead of bringing, at the expense of the other man, some benefit to themselves. The lines are being more sharply drawn, every day of our lives, as never before; and we can look over the world and know for a surety the distinction between the peace of the gospel of Jesus Christ and the conflict and envy so manifest in daily strife. We must preach repentance, as the Prophet Joseph through inspiration declares in so many of his revelations, and preach, too, the restoration of the gospel of Jesus Christ.

REVELATION BASIC TO THE WORK OF THE CHURCH: AN
EXAMPLE. I know that the Lord communicates with his servants. I have not doubted this as a fact since I was a boy and
heard the testimony of my father regarding the revelation
that came to him of the divinity of the mission of the Prophet
Joseph. I feel impressed to relate that circumstance and add
his testimony to the one that I am now giving. He accepted
a call to a mission about 1880. When he began preaching
in his native land and bore testimony of the restoration of
the gospel of Jesus Christ, he noticed that the people turned
away from him. They were bitter in their hearts against
anything Mormon, and the name of Joseph Smith seemed to
arouse antagonism in their hearts. One day he concluded
that the best way to get these people would be to preach just
the simple principles, the atonement of the Lord Jesus Christ,
the first principles of the gospel, and not bear testimony of
the restoration of the gospel. It first came simply, as a passing
thought, but yet it influenced his future work. In a month
or so he became oppressed with a gloomy, downcast feeling,
and he could not enter into the spirit of his work. He did not
really know what was the matter, but his mind became ob-
structed; his spirit became clogged; he was oppressed and
hampered; and that feeling of depression continued until it
weighed him down with such heaviness that he went to the
Lord and said: "Unless I can get this feeling removed, I shall
have to go home. I cannot continue my work with this feeling."

It continued for some time after that, then, one morning,
before daylight, following a sleepless night, he decided to retire
to a cave, near the ocean, where he knew he would be shut
off from the world entirely, and there pour out his soul to
God and ask why he was oppressed with this feeling, what
he had done, and what he could do to throw it off and continue
his work. He started out in the dark towards the cave, and
he became so eager to get to it that he started to run and was
hailed by an officer who wanted to know what was the matter,
as he was leaving the town. He gave some noncommittal
but satisfying reply and was permitted to go on. Something
seemed to drive him; he had to get relief.

He entered that place and said: "Oh, Father, what can
I do to have this feeling removed? I must have it lifted or

I cannot continue in this work"; and he heard a voice, as
distinct as the tone I am now uttering, say: "Testify that
Joseph Smith is a Prophet of God."

Remembering, then, what he tacitly had decided six
weeks or more before and becoming overwhelmed with the
thought, the whole thing came to him in a realization that
he was there for a special mission, and that he had not given
that special mission the attention which it deserved. Then
he cried in his heart, "Lord, it is enough," and went out from
the cave.

As a boy, I sat and heard that testimony from one whom
I treasured and honored as you know I treasured no other man
in the world, and that assurance was instilled in my youthful
soul. The inspiration and testimony of God has come since,
and today I testify to you that God lives, and that he is guiding this Church, that he has inspired those at the head, and
that he will continue to inspire them and lead them through
this turmoil and unrest in the world, caused by unrighteousness, wickedness, and lack of faith in God.

Brethren and sisters, let us thank our Heavenly Father
today for the testimony that the Lord Jesus Christ has placed
in our souls.—*IE*, 24:404-406 (1921).

THE PERSONALITY OF GOD. The Prophet Joseph Smith,
but a youth, did not argue upon the personality of God; he
did not speculate upon that eternal source of energy and intelligence from which all life gets its being; he merely stated
the truth. Nearly a hundred years later Charles A. Dinsmore
through thought and reason confirmed this truth as follows:

"Religion standing on the known experience of the race,
makes one bold and glorious affirmation. She asserts that
this power that makes for truth, for beauty, for goodness, is
not less personal than we. This leap of faith is justified because God cannot be less than the greatest of his works; the
cause must be adequate to the effect. When, therefore, we
call God personal, we have interpreted him by the loftiest
symbol we have. He may be infinitely more; he cannot be
less. When we call God a spirit, we use the clearest lens we
have to look at the everlasting. As Herbert Spencer has
well said, 'The choice is not between a personal God and

something lower, but between a personal God and something higher.' "*

Thus anchored in the faith, our young people have the foundation of spirituality, and the teachings of materialistic philosophy cannot dislodge them. Next to this belief in a supreme Being is the testimony they have that God is revealed through his Son Jesus Christ, the one perfect being who is the light and life of the world.—CR, April 1934, p. 23.

THE REALITY OF COMMUNICATION. The reality of God the Father, the reality of Jesus Christ, the risen Lord, is a truth which should possess every human soul. God is the center of the human mind as surely as the sun is the center of this universe, and once we feel his Fatherhood, once we feel his nearness, sense the divinity of the deity of the Savior, the truths of the gospel of Jesus Christ follow as naturally as the day the night, and as night the day.—CR, October 1925, pp. 106-107.

A fundamental truth is this, that direct communion between the Spirit of God and the spirit of men may be a reality. With all my soul I echo the appeal of my brother, Stephen L Richards, that we may lead the youth into that realm in which they will sense that communion. The promise of the Lord to his Apostles is a reality:

"And I will pray the Father, and he shall give you another Comforter, that he may abide with you for ever." (John 14:16.)

"But when the Comforter is come, whom I will send unto you from the Father, even the Spirit of truth, which proceedeth from the Father, he shall testify of me." (Ibid., 15:26.) —CR, October 1935, pp. 101-102.

AN ILLUSTRATIVE TESTIMONY. As surely as you can tune in on the radio and hear voices from afar, so sure am I that God our Father lives, and the soul of man can commune with him through the Holy Spirit. I give you that as my testimony; I know it.—CR, September-October 1950, p. 112.

---

*"Religious Certainty in an Age of Science." Quoted in *Christianity and Modern Thought.* New Haven: 1924.

ALL PRIESTHOOD MEMBERS ENTITLED TO GUIDANCE. The
most precious thing in the world is a testimony of the truth.
I repeat, truth never grows old, and the truth is that God
is the source of your priesthood and mine; that he lives, that
Jesus Christ, the great high priest, stands at the head of this
Church, and that every man who holds the priesthood, if
he lives properly, soberly, industriously, humbly, and prayer-
fully, is entitled to the inspiration and guidance of the Holy
Spirit. I know that is true.—CR, April 1948, p. 172.

ASPIRATION AND INSPIRATION DEFINED. There is a difference between aspiration and the inspiration that comes from
prayer. Both relate to desire; but aspiration is merely subjective, while inspiration includes divine help.—DNCS, November 14, 1936, p. 3.

MAN'S RELIGIOUS OUTLOOK

"As some tall cliff that lifts its awful form,
Swells from the vale, and midway leaves the storm,
Though round its breast the rolling clouds are spread,
Eternal sunshine settles on its head."
                        Goldsmith, *The Deserted Village*.

THE PROPHET'S REVELATIONS AS FACT. Many years ago
Joseph Smith, a mere boy between fourteen and fifteen years
of age, declared that in answer to prayer, he received a revelation from God. His declaration was simple but positive, and
he was surprised when men doubted the truth of his assertion.
To him his claim was but the statement of a fact; to the Christian world, it was a lightning flash that shattered their
religious structure from turret to foundation.

Two important elements in his first message were these:
(1) that God is a personal Being and will communicate his
will to men; and (2) that no creed in Christendom had the
true plan of salvation. Indeed, all were an "abomination in
the sight of God. The professors of them were corrupt,
teaching for doctrine the commandments of men, having a
form of godliness, but denying the power thereof." (See P. of
G. P. Joseph Smith 2:19.)

For boldness of assertion, for rejection of prevailing
orthodoxy, as a challenge to professed ministers, this claim
of a fair-haired, blue-eyed youth stands without parallel

since the days of Jesus of Nazareth. Not even Luther's defiance at Worms is excepted, for his inspired effort, at first, was only to purify the church of corrupt practices, while Joseph Smith rejected the creeds as unauthoritative and many of their doctrines as absolutely false.

GENERAL PRINCIPLES. The stand of the Church in regard to the first principles of the gospel, as given to Joseph the Prophet, is, from a biblical point of view, invulnerable, and his claim most reasonable, that divine authority to officiate in the ordinances is necessary. For many years professors of Christendom assailed the Church on its adherence to the essentiality of these principles and ordinances—particularly on its claim that baptism by immersion is necessary to salvation, but all attacks have proved futile. Of course, these principles, in one form or another, were taught by all the different sects, and yet, no one church taught all of them as being absolutely essential to salvation; and even had it done so, the Son of God, through Joseph Smith, denied its authority to administer them. Each succeeding year of the past century has tended only to vindicate the Prophet's teachings in regard to these two great questions—the harmony of the doctrines of the Church with the Bible; and the necessity of divine authority to officiate in things pertaining to God.

But the inspiration and the boldness of the Prophet's teachings, and their subsequent effect upon the religious and philosophic minds, may best be seen by reference to some of the more advanced, and, I may say, obscure principles, of the plan of salvation. Take, for example, predestination.

EFFECT ON THE DOCTRINE OF PREDESTINATION. At the time Joseph Smith received his revelation, some of the creeds of Christendom were teaching that,

"Election to eternal life is not founded on foresight of faith and obedience, but is a sovereign act of God's mercy, whereby according to the counsel of his own will some men and angels are predestined into everlasting life, and others foreordained to everlasting death"; and, "these angels and men thus predestined and foreordained are truly and unchangeably designed, and their number is so certain and definite that it cannot be either increased or diminished." (Westminster Confession.)

In direct contradiction to this false doctrine, the boy-prophet declared that "all mankind may be saved by obedience to the laws and ordinances of the gospel."

He taught that,

"To every man is given an inherent power to do right or to do wrong. In this he has his free agency. He may choose the right and obtain salvation, or he may choose evil and merit abomination; but one man is not predestinated to do evil and another to do good."

" . . . whosoever will come may come and partake of the waters of life freely; and whosoever will not come the same is not compelled to come; but in the last day it shall be restored unto him according to his deeds." (Alma 42:27.)

CREEDS OF CHURCHES MODIFIED. Nearly half a century passed before the ministers of some of the churches became bold enough so to modify their creeds as to reject that paragraph on predestination; but they eventually did so. Here is one example:

The Presbyterians, in their General Assembly, May 22, 1902, adopted, by a vote of 600 to two, the unanimous report of a revision committee which had been at work on the subject for two years. The *Outlook* (May 1902), commenting upon the significance of this revision, summarizes as follows:

"The most important thing in this explanation is the definite declaration that the ordination vows of officers requires the adoption of the Confession of Faith *only as containing the system of doctrine taught in the Holy Scriptures.*"

Thus any officer is left free to reject any part of the Confession of Faith which, in his judgment, is not taught in the Holy Scriptures. One of the particular parts rejected is named by the *Outlook* in these words:

"Following this broad statement are two overtures. The first *disclaims any fatalistic inference from the doctrine of Predestination, and asserts clearly that God loves all mankind and desires not the death of any sinner, and that no man is condemned except on the ground of his sin.*"

If any plainer revision of the Presbyterians' creed on the pernicious doctrine of predestination is needed, it can be found in the statement of Reverend Henry Van Dyke:

"The Presbyterian Church, today [May 1902], does not believe that some men are created to be saved, and others to be damned; and to guard against misapprehension on the subject, it wishes to say clearly and unmistakably that God has not put any barrier between any human soul and salvation."

So Joseph Smith proclaimed before Henry Van Dyke was born, at the time, too, when every Presbyterian officer took a vow that God did predestine some to be saved and others to be damned.

INFANT BAPTISM. Closely allied with the doctrine of predestination was the equally false teaching that unbaptized infants were condemned to eternal punishment. Said the old school of Presbyterianism:

"Infants come into the world, not only destitute of knowledge, righteousness, and true holiness, but with a nature inclined to evil and only evil."

The Prophet Joseph said:

"But little children are holy, being sanctified through the atonement of Jesus Christ; . . ." (D. & C. 74:7.)

Little children need no repentance, neither baptism.

"And he that saith that little children need baptism denieth the mercies of Christ, and setteth at naught the atonement of him and the power of his redemption." (Moroni 8:20.)

Three-quarters of a century later, creeds, the ministers of which had said the boy-prophet's revelations were from the devil, concluded that this doctrine, too, was right—devil or no devil.

The Westminster creed was modified by the assembly, referred to above, to deny what it had declared for centuries, and to confirm the view expressed by the Prophet Joseph. It now declared that,

"All who die in infancy are chosen of God and saved by Christ through the spirit." (Explanation of Westminster Confession, 1902.)

This is confirmed by Henry Van Dyke, who says:

"Presbyterians today believe that all who die in infancy are saved by Jesus Christ."

PRE-EXISTENCE. One hundred years ago, theologians seldom, if ever, referred to the doctrine of pre-existence of spirits,

let alone accepting it as part of the solution of the eternal plan
of redemption. When writers or philosophers mentioned it, it
was designated the Platonic opinion; and those who favored it,
as Platonists. This because Plato, with a spark of inspiration,
taught that pre-existence and the closely associated doctrine
of "reminiscence" are connected with the doctrine of immortality.

Even Wordsworth found it necessary to offer a half
apology for referring to this doctrine in his inspired poem,
"Intimations of Immortality." In the light of poetic revelation
he wrote:

> "Our birth is but a sleep and a forgetting:
> The Soul that rises with us, our life's Star,
> Hath had elsewhere its setting,
> And cometh from afar:
> Not in entire forgetfulness,
> And not in utter nakedness,
> But trailing clouds of glory do we come
> From God, who is our home."

Subsequently, when in the shadowy realm of popular
opinion, learning that his doctrine "had given pain to some
good and pious persons," he protested that he "meant not
to inculcate such a belief" (pre-existence). However, with
a glimmer of the light still in his mind, he adds: "But let us
bear in mind that, though the idea is not advanced in revelation, there is nothing there to contradict it, and the fall of
man presents an analogy in its favor."

Now, undoubtedly, the boy-prophet had not even read
Plato, and the presumption is that he had never read Wordsworth or any other advocate of this phase of the doctrine of
immortality; and yet, when God revealed it to him, note how
unqualifiedly he declared the truth:

"I [Christ] was in the beginning with the Father, and
am the Firstborn;

"Ye were also in the beginning with the Father; . . . "
(D. & C. 93:21, 23.)

And again:

"Now the Lord had shown unto me, Abraham, the intel-
ligences that were organized before the world was; and among

all these there were many of the noble and great ones."
(Abraham 3:22.)

Though God has taught it to his children from the
days of Adam down, yet one hundred years ago this was a
bold, strange doctrine. And even today ministers of religion,
if not entirely rejecting it, rather shy at it. But the leaven
is working, and great minds, accepting the doctrine, are now
proclaiming it in their theories of the immortality of man.

In discussing "The Permanence of Personality," Lodge,
in *Science and Immortality*, says:

"This doctrine—*the theory* of a larger and permanent
personality of which the *conscious self is only a fraction in
process of individualization* * * * as a working hypothesis, il-
luminates many obscure facts, and serves as a thread through
an otherwise bewildering labyrinth. It removes a number of
elementary stumbling blocks which otherwise obstruct an
attempt to realize vividly the incipient stages of personal
existence; it accounts for the extraordinary rapidity with which
an individual proceeds; and it eases the theory of ordinary
birth and death."

And then, after commenting upon the subject of "Disloca-
tion of Memory," he continues:

"The analogy pointed to is that whereas we, living men
and women, while associated with this mortal organism, are
ignorant of whatever experience *our larger selves may have
gone through in the past*—yet when we wake out of this
present materialized condition, and enter the region of larger
consciousness, we may gradually realize in what a curious
though legitimate condition of ignorance we now are; and
may become aware of our fuller possession, with all that has
happened here and now fully remembered and *incorporated
as an additional experience into the wide range of knowledge
which our larger entity must have accumulated since its
intelligence and memory began*. The transition called death
may thus be an awakening rather than a sleeping; it may be
that we, still, involved in mortal coil, are in the more dreamlike
and unreal condition."

THE NOTION OF HELL. When Joseph Smith as a boy
attended any of the churches in his neighborhood, he un-

doubtedly heard the furies of hell pictured in thrilling elo-
quence.

And to all this and much more must be added "dreadful
shrieks issuing from dungeons and prisons into which special
victims were thrown for special enormities."

To unspeakable horrors many men and women were
predestined, there to burn and burn and never to be consumed
forever and ever!

That is the doctrine of the damned which Joseph Smith
heard from man.

This is what he heard from God:

" . . . the only ones on whom the second death shall have
any power;

"Yea, verily, the only ones who shall not be redeemed in
the due time of the Lord * * * * [are] those sons of perdition
who deny the Son after the Father has revealed him.

"Wherefore, he saves all except them— . . . " (D. & C.
76:37-38, 43-44.)

The Lord revealed to him all the different degrees of
glory in which men receive judgment in accordance with the
deeds done in the body, and he

" . . . saw the glory and the inhabitants of the telestial
world, that they were as innumerable as the stars in the firmament of heaven, or as the sand upon the seashore;

"And heard the voice of the Lord, saying: These all shall
bow the knee, and every tongue shall confess to him who sits
upon the throne forever and ever;

"For they shall be judged according to their works, and
every man shall receive according to his own works, his own
dominion, in the mansions which are prepared." (Ibid., 76:
109-111.)

"He will judge them not according to what they have not,
but according to what they have; those who have lived without
law will be judged without law, and those who have a law
will be judged by that law, we need not doubt the wisdom and
intelligence of the Great Jehovah. He will award judgment
or mercy to all nations according to their several deserts, their
means of obtaining intelligence; the laws by which they are
governed." (Times and Seasons, Vol. III, p. 759.)

MODERN VIEW OF CHRISTENDOM. The modified view of modern Christendom is probably best expressed in an article entitled, "What Has Become of Hell?" by Reverend George W. Shimm, and printed in the *North American Review,* 1900. After asserting that all churches had practically ceased to speak of hell as a place of eternal punishment, he concludes:

"It cannot be that all the redeemed in the future will be equally happy, and that all the lost will be equally wretched; for there are varying degrees of capacity. There must be infinite grades of happiness there, as there must be a vast difference between those who are driven into outer darkness.

"When men's eyes are opened, they may see that the loss of what they might have been and their degradation through sin, is indeed the visitation of penalty. Judgment consists quite largely in deprivation. Such a judgment has begun here, and it points to the awful issues of the future, when the days of earthly probation shall have ended.

"Men are condemned by themselves. They must recognize at some period that they prepared themselves for their own place and for their own condition."

And so we might refer to tithing, organization of the Church, the principles of co-operation, and even the United Order and show what a marked change of sentiment has taken place in regard to them during the last half century; but space will not permit.

The world will not admit, nor do we ask it to admit, that all these modified views regarding man's place in the universe have been brought about solely by the influence of the Prophet Joseph Smith. God's Spirit is ever ready to guide away from error the sincere seeker after truth; and undoubtedly, hundreds of honest men and women have rejected in their hearts the errors pointed to above without ever having known the truths as revealed to the Prophet. However, the marks of his influence upon religious thought are manifest upon every hand, and whether men acknowledge it or not, the light that came from heaven a century ago is dissipating the darkness that has enthralled the minds of men for ages.

As we look through the vista of one hundred years and see the boy-prophet standing alone in the midst of a tempestuously religious world, declaring that God had spoken to him, and that there was not an authorized Church of

Christ upon the earth; when we know that to make good his claim, he must give to the world something superior to that produced by the philosophy of the ages and the best wisdom of man; when we realize how impotent he was to do this, if dependent upon his own learning and wisdom—we cannot help concluding, since he has given to the world something which has stood the acid test of time and criticism, and which stands today in brilliancy and sublimity, superior to anything proclaimed by human wisdom—that surely he was indeed the chosen Prophet of the latter day.—*IE*, 23:506-513 (1919-1920).

CHAPTER 4

JESUS THE CHRIST

THE POWER THAT CHANGES HISTORY. Nearly two thousand years ago a little group of men faced a future that was just as threatening and foreboding to them as that which the world faces today. The men in that group were Simon Peter, Thomas, Nathanael of Cana in Galilee, James and John, sons of Zebedee, and two others of his disciples. A short time before that gloomy period Jesus had said to them:

"Let not your heart be troubled: ye believe in God, believe also in me." (John 14:1.)

He promised them the Comforter who would testify of the Christ, who would bring all things to their remembrance, who would show them things to come.

Notwithstanding all those promises and divine exhortations, the disciples, following the crucifixion of their Lord, were depressed in their feelings. Their hopes were shattered. Their future, so far as Christ's triumph on earth was concerned, seemed all but blighted. They had been called and set apart to be fishers of men, and to Peter had been given the keys of the kingdom. Notwithstanding all this, in that hour of despondency, Peter turned to his old vocation, and said: "I go a fishing," and the others replied, "We also go with thee." (See John 21:3.)

They were in that state of mind when the resurrected Christ said to the discouraged leader of the Twelve: "Simon, son of Jonas, lovest thou me more than these?" Peter answered, "Yea, Lord; thou knowest that I love thee." Said the Lord, "Feed my sheep." I have my own interpretation of what "these" means. Keep in mind, will you please, that it was his vocation—what he would get. He had there before him the products of his morning's fishing, for he had fished all night and caught nothing. "Simon, son of Jonas, lovest thou me more than these?" "Yea, Lord, thou knowest that I love thee." "Feed my sheep." (See John 21:15-17.)

On that occasion Peter became conscious of his responsibility not only as a fisher of men but also as a shepherd of the flock. It was then that he sensed finally and completely the full meaning of the divine injunction, "Follow thou me."

With that never-failing light, those twelve humble men succeeded in changing the course of human relations. —*CR*, April 1948, pp. 66-67.

"WHAT THINK YE OF CHRIST?" "What think ye of Christ?" was the question Jesus put to a group of Pharisees when they, with scribes and Sadducees, sought to entrap, to confound the Great Teacher by asking him entangling questions. He silenced the Sadducees in their attempt to ensnare him with regard to paying tribute to Caesar. He satisfied the scribes regarding the first and great commandment. He put to silence the Pharisees regarding their anticipated Christ.

To the Church, and to the world I repeat this question as being the most vital, the most far-reaching query in this unsettled, distracted world.

Great minds in all ages who have contributed to the betterment of mankind have been inspired by noble ideals.

History is replete with men, who, as Wordsworth expresses it, "By the vision splendid, were on their way attended."

The highest of all ideals are the teachings and particularly the life of Jesus of Nazareth, and that man is most truly great who is most Christlike.

What you sincerely in your heart think of Christ will determine what you are, will largely determine what your acts will be. No person can study this divine personality, can accept his teachings without becoming conscious of an uplifting and refining influence within himself. In fact, every individual may experience the operation of the most potent force that can affect humanity. Electricity lightens labor in the home, imprisons alike on a disc the warbling tones of the mockingbird and the convincing appeal of the orator. By the turn of a switch, it turns night into day. The possibilities of the force resulting from the breaking up of the atom seem to be limitless either for the destruction or the blessing of life. Other and greater forces are already glimpsed.

None, however, is so vital, so contributive to the peace and happiness of the human family as the surrendering of our selfish, animal-like natures to the life and teachings of our Lord and Savior, Jesus Christ.—*CR*, April 1951, pp. 92-94.

THE GREAT IDEAL. Christ came to redeem the world from sin. He came with love in his heart for every individual, with redemption and possibility for regeneration for all. By choosing him as our ideal, we create within ourselves a desire to be like him, to have fellowship with him. We perceive life as it should be and as it may be.

The chief Apostle Peter, the indefatigable Paul, the Prophet Joseph Smith, and other true followers of the risen Lord recognized in him the Savior of the individual, for did he not say, "This is my work and my glory—to bring to pass the immortality and eternal life of man?"—not the sacrificing of the individual for the perpetuation of the socialistic or communistic state.

Members of the Church of Jesus Christ are under obligation to make the sinless Son of Man their ideal—the one perfect Being who ever walked the earth.

Sublimest Example of nobility.
Godlike in nature.
Perfect in his love.
Our Redeemer.
Our Savior.
The Son of our Eternal Father.
The Light, the Life, the Way.

I know he lives and his power is potent; that he is the Son of God, and that he has restored in this dispensation the complete plan of salvation.—*CR*, April 1951, p. 98.

THE INFLUENCE OF A SINGLE LIFE. J. A. Francis wrote a tribute to Christ, as follows: "I am far within the mark when I say that all the armies that ever marched and all the navies that were ever built, and all the parliaments that ever sat, and all the kings that ever reigned, put together, have not affected the life of man upon this earth as powerfully as has this one, solitary life."—*CR*, April 1950, p. 179.

TRUST IN THE LORD. Absolute trust in the Lord will awaken a desire, at least, to try to live in accordance with

Christ's teachings, chief of which is to love, not hate one another.—CR, October 1941, p. 55.

CHRIST AND CHRISTMAS. Christmas is a fitting time to renew our desires and to strengthen our determination to do all that lies within our power to make real among men the message heralded by the angels when the Savior was born. Let us glorify God by seeking the good, the true, the beautiful! Let us strive to establish peace on earth by exercising that same good will toward one another which God has shown toward us!—MS, 85:802 (1923).

In northern climes particularly, Christmas is the happiest season of the year. At first thought, it is strange that it is so. The days are short and gloomy; the nights, cold and long; trees are leafless, and the landscape barren or covered with snow. Excepting the fur-clad and a few other hardy animals, all nature lies asleep. No warbling songsters fill the air with music; no flowers nor brilliant foliage gladdens the eye. The rippling streams that lured the heart in summer are frozen and still. The pine-covered hills are uninviting, if not quite inaccessible. Everything is gone which made springtime joyous, the summer delightful, and the autumn glorious! Notwithstanding all this, Christmas, in the depth of winter, is full of happiness and cheer.

This is because in Christian lands the yuletide festivity is impregnated with the Spirit of the Christ. At that time more than at any other, we think of others and try to express either in word or deed our desire to make others happy. Herein lies the secret of true happiness. "He that will lose his life for my sake and the gospel's shall find it," is sound philosophy, which the true Christmas spirit helps us to understand.

Love for God and for one another should be the Christmas theme. Such was the divine announcement by the heavenly host that first heralded the "glad tidings of great joy!"

"Glory to God in the highest, peace on earth, good will toward men!"

How simple the words! How deep, how comprehensive their significance! At Christmas, we celebrate his birth in whose mission on earth (1) God is glorified; (2) earth is promised peace; (3) all men given the assurance of God's good will toward them!

If every man born into the world would have as the beacon of his life these three glorious ideals—how much sweeter and happier life would be! With such an aim, everyone would seek all that is pure, just, honorable, virtuous, and true—all that leads to perfection; for these virtues he would glorify who seeks to glorify God. He would eschew that which is impure, dishonorable, or vile. If every man *desired* to show good will toward his fellow men and strove to express that desire in a thousand kind sayings and little deeds that would reflect unselfishness and self-sacrifice, what a contribution each would make toward universal peace on earth and the happiness of mankind!—*MS*, 85:801-802 (1923).

"ALL MEN SEEK THEE!" What a glorious condition will be in this old world when it can be truthfully said to Christ, *"All men seek thee!"* Selfishness, envy, hatred, lying, stealing, cheating, disobedience to parents, cruelty to children and to dumb animals, quarreling among neighbors, and fighting among nations—all will be no more when it can be truthfully said to the Redeemer of mankind, *"All men seek thee!"*—*AA*, p. 23.

THE PRINCIPLES HE TAUGHT

SIMPLE MORAL TRUTHS. What are the moral ideals and the spiritual teachings of the Man of Nazareth? Down through the centuries there have come ringing these words: "I am the light of the world: he that followeth me shall not walk in darkness, but shall have the light of life." (John 8:12.)

Do Christians really believe this? If so, they are hearing his other ringing words: "But seek ye first the kingdom of God, and his righteousness; and all these things shall be added unto you." (Matt. 6:33.)

His teachings are simple, and sometimes they seem so simple that we toss them aside.—*CR*, October 1935, p. 100.

The world needs fundamentals, eternal verities that never change. It needs to adopt the teachings of the man into whose hands the soldiers drove the iron spikes, "the only world conqueror who came with clean hands."—*CR*, October 1935, p. 99.

NEGATION OF THE RULE OF FORCE. To all who accept Christ as the risen Lord, there can be no question as to the error of the doctrine that "might makes right," that all who are weak must yield to those who are strong, or that any man possessing either political or financial power has the right to use human beings as mere things or chattels to be disposed of as any other pieces of property.—*CR*, April 1939, pp. 111-112.

RIGHT THINKING. No principle of life was more constantly emphasized by the Great Teacher than the necessity of right thinking. To him, the man was not what he appeared to be outwardly, nor what he professed to be by his words: what the man *thought* determined in all cases what the man was.

His teachings regarding man's duty to himself as well as man's duty to his neighbor are pervaded with the truth that thought in all cases determines the man's right to happiness or his condemnation for sin.—*MS*, 85:520 (1923).

THE PEACE OF CHRIST

THE INVITATION. How utterly foolish men are to quarrel, fight, and cause misery, destruction, and death when the gifts of a divine and loving Father are all around us for the asking—are already in our possession if we would but recognize them. Christ's invitation is still extended to all peoples:

"Come unto me, all ye that labour and are heavy laden, and I will give you rest.

"Take my yoke upon you, and learn of me; for I am meek and lowly in heart: and ye shall find rest unto your souls.

"For my yoke is easy, and my burden is light." (Matt. 11:28-30.)

THE PATH TO PEACE. When Jesus was talking to his disciples immediately preceding his betrayal, explaining to them that he would have to leave them, he said: " . . . ye believe in God, believe also in me." (John 14:1.) He desired them to understand, as he wants the whole world to know, that only through him can man find the life abundant. Those were not mere words of defiance which Peter uttered as he and John stood prisoners before the high priests. He proclaimed an eternal truth when he said: " . . . for there is none other name under heaven given among men, whereby we must be saved." (Acts 4:12.) That truth is reiterated in the Doctrine and Covenants—" . . . all men must repent and believe on the name of Jesus Christ, and worship the Father in his name, and endure in faith on his name to the end, or they cannot be saved in the kingdom of God." (D. & C. 20:29.)

I like to associate with that word *saved* the power that man gets in this life to rise above his animal instincts and passions, power to overcome or resist social evils that blight men's and women's souls and shut them out not only from the peace of the world, but also from membership in the kingdom of God. Men may yearn for peace, cry for peace, and work for peace, but there will be no peace until they follow the path pointed out by the living Christ.—*CR*, April 1948, p. 68.

THE ACCEPTANCE OF THE SON OF GOD AS THE SAVIOR OF MANKIND. The world wants peace, the winning of which seems to be more difficult than the winning of the war.

No peace, even though temporarily obtained, will be permanent unless it is built upon the solid foundation of eternal principles.

The first of these the Lord gave to Moses on Mount Sinai—"Thou shalt worship the Lord thy God." Consider what that means. When we sincerely accept God as our Father and make him the center of our being, we become conscious of a new aim in life. No longer is the chief end of daily life merely to nourish and to pamper the body as all animals do. Spiritual attainment, not physical indulgence, becomes the chief goal. God is not viewed from the standpoint of what we may get from him, but what we may give to him. Only in the complete surrender of our inner life may we rise above the selfish, sordid pull of nature. Divine and eternal as an element in the acquisition of peace is Christ's admonition: " . . . seek ye first the kingdom of God, and his righteousness; . . . " (Matt. 6:33.)

Of equal importance is the acceptance of the Son of God as the Savior of mankind.—*CR*, April 1948, p. 67.

HOW PEACE COMES. The peace of Christ does not come by seeking the superficial things of life, neither does it come except as it springs from the individual's heart. Jesus said to his disciples: "Peace I leave with you, my peace I give

unto you: not as the world giveth, give I unto you. ... " (John
14:27.) Thus the Son of Man, the executor of his own will
and testament, gave to his disciples and to mankind the "first
of all human blessings." It was a bequest conditioned upon
obedience to the principles of the gospel of Jesus Christ. It is
thus bequeathed to each individual. No man is at peace with
himself or his God who is untrue to his better self, who trans-
gresses the law of right either in dealing with himself by
indulging in passion, in appetite, yielding to temptations
against his accusing conscience, or in dealing with his fellow
men, being untrue to their trust. Peace does not come to
the transgressor of law; peace comes by obedience to law; and
it is that message which Jesus would have us proclaim among
men.—*CR*, October 1938, p. 133.

"PEACE IS WITHIN YOU." Peace, as Jesus said of the king-
dom of God, " ... cometh not with observation:
"Neither shall they say, Lo here! or, lo there! ... "
(Luke 17:20-21.)
Behold, the source of peace is within you.
This fact is emphasized throughout the teachings of
Jesus, most particularly in the Sermon on the Mount. Each
Beatitude names a virtue and contributes to the perfect state
of peace for the individual. The opposite attitude or condition of mind shows the source of confusion and strife.
The *poor in spirit* are they who are conscious of their
destitution—not of worldly possessions but of heavenly riches.
Those who experience this condition run counter to them who
arrogantly manifest pride in personal accomplishments or
acquired possessions.
Those who *mourn* are they who weep not because of
loss of wealth or of earthly emoluments but who sense their
own deficiencies in spiritual possessions. That feeling runs
counter to the calloused, the indifferent, and the self-satisfied.
Meekness is closely allied to the poor in spirit, but in
addition to consciousness of a dearth of spirituality, meekness
connotes a reserved dignity—a reservoir of self-control. A
meek person may be quiet, unrevengeful, and not pusil-
lanimous. Jesus said of himself: " ... I am meek and lowly
in heart: ... " (Matt. 11:29) and as he stood before Pilate,
saying: "My kingdom is not of this world: ..." (John

18:36) the Roman governor beheld one who possessed all the attributes of greatness, and caused him to declare: "Behold the man!" (John 19:5.) The unmeek are proud, resentful, revengeful.

Those who *hunger* and *thirst after righteousness* have hearts and minds yearning for the truth. Those who are opposite seek the lust of the flesh, the lust of the eye, and bask in the pride of life.

Those who *show mercy* will obtain mercy. "Forgive and ye shall be forgiven." The opposite of mercy is hardheartedness, cruelty.

The *pure in heart* are those who are sincere. Inward purity stands in contrast with painted hypocrisy. One who cherishes his virtue is always in the best of company. He lives nearest the Eternal. Surely it is he who will see God. —*IE*, 48: 104 (1945).

TRUE CHILDREN OF GOD. The *peacemakers* are truly the *children of God*. They stand in direct opposition to the quarrelsome and contentious.—*IE*, 48:104 (1945).

THE DIVINITY OF JESUS CHRIST

MERE BELIEF IN JESUS AS A GREAT MAN INSUFFICIENT. A mere belief in Jesus as a great teacher or even as the greatest man that ever lived has proved inadequate in combating the ills of the world. Among many writers and many thinking people, there is quite a general agreement as to the *greatness* of Jesus. By one, for example, he is designated as "the peerless personality in history"; by another (Renan) "whatever may be the surprises of the future, Jesus will never be surpassed." Colonel Robert G. Ingersoll once wrote: "When a boy in Peoria, Illinois, I may have said silly things about Jesus, but now I regard him as the one perfect man." "Christ stands for the highest development of man," writes Keable, "and try as we will, we cannot see any other intelligent mind than man's in the universe. To other forces that we dimly sense, we cannot attribute personality, but to the Christ we can and must. He is our God. We are not ashamed of him, and the less so as he is a man."

Manifestly the need of the world, and particularly in the present crisis, is more than a mere acceptance of the Man of Galilee as the greatest of all men. What is really essential is *faith in him as a divine Being—as our Lord and Savior.* It is such faith as the Apostle Peter experienced when he declared: "Thou art the Christ, the Son of the living God." (Matt. 16:16.) It is such faith as called forth Paul's testimony as he stood a prisoner before Agrippa and bore witness that Christ had appeared to him, and said: "I am Jesus whom thou persecutest: . . . " (Acts 9:5.) It is the faith that enabled the doubting Thomas to say: "My Lord, and my God." (John 20:28.)

It is such faith as must have sustained the eleven Apostles and at least seventy disciples who met Christ after the resurrection. In their minds there was absolutely no doubt of his personality. They were witnesses of the fact. They knew because their eyes beheld, their ears heard, their hands felt the corporeal presence of the risen Redeemer.

It is that unwavering faith which brought forth this glorious vision given to the Prophet Joseph Smith:

"And now, after the many testimonies which have been given of him, this is the testimony, last of all, which we give of him: That he lives!

"For we saw him, even on the right hand of God; and we heard the voice bearing record that he is the Only Begotten of the Father—

"That by him, and through him, and of him, the worlds are and were created, and the inhabitants thereof are begotten sons and daughters unto God." (D. & C. 76:22-24.)

Those who have such assurance in their hearts accept him as "The Way, the Truth, and the Life," as the one safe guide in this perplexing universe.—*IE*, 47:12 (1943).

JOB'S ASSURANCE. "For I know that my redeemer liveth, and that he shall stand at the latter day upon the earth:

"And though after my skin worms destroy this body, yet in my flesh shall I see God:

"Whom I shall see for myself, and mine eyes shall behold, and not another; though my reins be consumed within me." (Job 19:25-27.)

Thus was spoken the heartfelt assurance of Job, expressed in humiliation when everything else was taken from him and even his body utterly wasted in affliction.

If a few more million men in the world could feel that testimony—the testimony of the reality of our Redeemer— selfishness would be less manifest, war among nations would be eradicated, and peace would reign among mankind. Do you believe that, my fellow workers?—*CR, April 1951, p. 92.*

THE TESTIMONY OF PETER AND JOHN. I feel it an honor to be associated with men and women who believe in the reality of Christ, our Redeemer. I should like to express what I mean by that, and so shall call attention to two incidents in scripture—one, the experience of two of the ancient Apostles, and the other the testimony of the Prophet Joseph Smith. The Apostles one day, after the death and resurrection of their Lord, were preaching in the temple, and the Sadducees and officers came and arrested them and put them in prison. The next day Peter and John were brought before the high priest, before Annas and before Caiaphas, some of the very men who had been the means of crucifying the Lord. "And when they had set them in their midst they asked" (referring to the miracle which Peter and John had performed the day before by healing the impotent man at the gate), "By what power or by what name have ye done this?

"Then Peter, filled with the Holy Ghost, said unto them, Ye rulers of the people, and elders of Israel,

"If we this day be examined of the good deed done to the impotent man, by what means he is made whole;

"Be it known unto you all, and to all the people of Israel, that by the name of Jesus Christ of Nazareth, *whom ye crucified, whom God raised from the dead,* even by him doth this man stand here before you whole.

"This is the stone which was set at nought of you builders, which is become the head of the corner." (See Acts 4:7-11.)

To Peter and to John on that occasion Christ, the Redeemer, was a reality. They had associated with him in the flesh; they had sat in his company; they had seen his miracles; they had listened to his divine teachings; they had stood by, John, at least, when the Master was nailed to the cross. They had associated with him for approximately forty days after his resurrection from the tomb. And now clothed with the power which the Lord had given them, they faced the very men who had crucified their Redeemer and said: " . . . by him whom thou didst crucify is this man made whole." To them, Jesus was not an imaginary being; his life was not an idealism nor a mere mental conception. Christ, I repeat, was a reality. He was indeed the very Son of God, the divine Redeemer of the world.

THE TESTIMONY OF JOSEPH SMITH. Now listen to another testimony and this within the age of a few of the men—I wish there were many—who are here assembled today: "When the light rested upon me I saw two Personages, whose brightness and glory defy all description, standing above me in the air. One of them spake unto me, calling me by name, and said, pointing to the other: '—This is My Beloved Son: Hear Him!' " The Prophet Joseph's object in going to the Lord on that occasion was to inquire of him which of all the sects professing to be followers of the Redeemer was right. This, then, was his answer: "I was answered that I must join none of them, for they were all wrong; and the Personage who addressed me said that all their creeds were an abomination in his sight; that those professors were all corrupt; that: 'they draw near to me with their lips, but their hearts are far from me; they teach for doctrines the commandments of men, having a form of godliness, but they deny the power thereof.' " (See P. of G. P., Joseph Smith 2:17-19.)

THE MEANING OF THESE TESTIMONIES. To him who accepts Jesus of Nazareth as the very Son of God, to him who believes with all his soul that Jesus lives today, that he can influence and that he does influence the world, to him, I say, who accepts that truth, Christ's teachings as well as his personality become a reality. You cannot profess to be truly a Christian and refuse to live up to the principles that Christ taught and obeyed.—CR, April 1918, pp. 77-79.

I ask you if the Christians who profess to be Christians in reality believed in the doctrines and the teachings of the Redeemer as he gave them, should we have today the carnage, the bloodshed, the infamy that is now depopulating the Christian nations? I do not; I do not.

I will tell you what I am inclined to think: That many who profess Christianity are accepting Christ as an ethereal

being and are inclined to look upon his teachings as impractical. They do not fully realize *that before the world can be
saved, they must accept his teachings; they must walk in his
paths as individuals and as nations; they must accept as a
veritable truth his saying: "I am the light of the world: . . . "*
(John 8:12.)—*CR*, April 1918, p. 79.

The Coming of the Son of Man. God has spoken. The
day of Israel is here, and the coming of the Son of Man is
not far off. How many years it matters not. It is nearby. We
must do our part and prepare for it.—*CR*, October 1918, p.
49.

The World's Greatest Need. " . . . because thou hast
seen me, thou hast believed: blessed are they that have not
seen, and yet have believed." (John 20:29.)

So spoke Jesus to Thomas who had just confidently exclaimed: "My Lord and my God!"—an acknowledgment indicating that doubt in the mind of Thomas had been supplanted
by absolute certainty.

It is in this sense of unwavering trust that I refer to faith
in Christ as the most important need of the world—a *belief*
that determines a man's religion. It is more than a mere
feeling. It is power that moves to action and should be in
human life the most basic of all motivating forces. It was in
this sense that an eminent doctor of medicine, who had but
recently lost his mother in death, admonished his students to
keep their faith: "Those of you who have discarded faith will
live to regret it. There are times such as this when science
is entirely inadequate. I commend you to think seriously
about these matters. They give comfort and solace which
can be obtained in no other way. Many have discarded religion because it appears unscientific. I believe that you will
find in the last analysis that it is scientific."—*IE*, 47:12 (1943).

A Personal Witness. Brethren, I know as I know I am
looking into your faces that the gospel of Jesus Christ is true
and that he is my Savior, as real as he was when Thomas
said, with bowed head, "My Lord and my God!" (John 20:28.)
—*CR*, April 1949, p. 182.

Chapter 5

The Conquest of Death

THE RESURRECTION AND FUNDAMENTAL PRINCIPLES OF THE GOSPEL

The event we celebrate today [Easter] connotes the fundamental principles of the gospel of Jesus Christ. In general these are:

THE FATHERHOOD OF GOD. No man can accept the resurrection and be consistent in his belief without accepting also the existence of a personal God. Through the resurrection Christ conquered death and became an immortal soul. "My Lord and My God" was not merely an idle exclamation of Thomas when he beheld his risen Lord. The Being before him was his God. Once we accept Christ as divine, it is easy to visualize his Father as being just as personal as he; for, said Jesus, "He that hath seen me hath seen the Father."

Inseparable with the idea of a divine personal Being is the acceptance of him as the Creator of the world. True Christianity does not look upon the universe as the result of mere interaction of matter and motion, of law and force, but, on the contrary, it regards all creation as the product of a divine Intelligence "who made the world and all things therein." As one writer puts it: "This is what Christianity means by a personal God. It believes that all existence has its roots in a conscious and intelligent purpose and that this purpose is good."

SONSHIP OF JESUS CHRIST. The gospel teaches that Christ is the Son of God, the Redeemer of the world. No true follower is satisfied to accept him merely as a great Reformer, the ideal Teacher, or even as the one perfect Man. The Man of Galilee is, not *figuratively*, but *literally*, the Son of the living God.

THE IMMORTALITY OF THE HUMAN SOUL. Belief in the resurrection connotes also the immortality of man. Jesus passed through all the experiences of mortality just as you and

I. He knew happiness; he experienced pain. He rejoiced as well as sorrowed with others. He knew friendship. He experienced also the sadness that comes through traitors and false accusers. He died a mortal death, even as every other mortal. Since his spirit lived after death, so shall yours and mine. So shall that of your soldier boy who gives his life on the battlefield.

THE BROTHERHOOD OF MAN. One of the two great, general principles to which all other principles are subsidiary is this: "Love your neighbour as yourself," (see Matt. 19:19) and correlated with it, the promise: "Inasmuch as ye have done it unto one of the least of these my brethren, ye have done it unto me." (*Ibid.*, 25:40.)

The gospel "bids the strong bear the burdens of the weak, and to use the advantages given them by their larger opportunities in the interest of the common good, that the whole level of humanity may be lifted and the path of spiritual attainment be opened to the weakest and most ignorant," as well as to the strong and intelligent.

THE STANDARDS OF LIFE. Finally, since Jesus was the one perfect man who ever lived, as he, in rising from the dead, conquered death, and is now Lord of the earth, how utterly weak, how extremely foolish is he who would wilfully reject Christ's way of life, especially in the light of the fact that such rejection leads only to unhappiness, misery, and even to death.

What a more delightful world this would be if, for example, man earnestly strove to apply Christ's advice that if he rememberest that his brother hath ought against him, go to him. (see *ibid.*, 5:23-24.) Or, again his admonition to seek first the kingdom of God and his righteousness (see *ibid.*, 6:33), which means, simply, be not so anxious about worldly things as to make them of superior worth to spiritual attainment.

The Savior condemned hypocrisy and praised sincerity of purpose. Keep your heart pure, and your actions will be in accord therewith. Social sins—lying, stealing, dishonest dealing, fornication, and the like—are first committed in thought. Jesus taught that an unsullied character is the noblest aim of life.

Herein, brethren, lies the true source of the testimony: "I know that my Redeemer lives." No man can sincerely resolve to apply in his daily life the teachings of Jesus of Nazareth without sensing a change in his nature. The phrase "born again" has a deeper significance than many people attach to it. This changed feeling may be indescribable, but it is real.

Happy the person who has truly sensed the uplifting, transforming power that comes from this nearness to the Savior, this kinship to the living Christ. I am thankful that I know that Christ is my Redeemer.

Easter is a sacred day, a day of thanksgiving and divine worship. It is not a day just for rejoicing because of the opening of springtime, not merely an opportunity to display beautiful hats and fine clothing—it is an occasion for the expression of gratitude to God for having sent his only begotten Son into the world, to be "the way, the truth, the life," to declare the eternal truth that " . . . whosoever believeth in him should not perish, but have everlasting life." (John 3:16.)

When Christians throughout the world have this faith coursing in their blood, when they feel a loyalty in their hearts to the resurrected Christ, and to the principles connoted thereby, mankind will have taken the first great step toward the perpetual peace for which we daily are praying. Reject him, and the world will be filled with hatred and drenched in blood by recurring wars. . . .

Brethren and sisters: As Christ lived after death so shall all men live, each taking his place in the next world for which he has best fitted himself. The message of the resurrection, therefore, is the most comforting, the most glorious ever given to man, for when death takes a loved one from us, our sorrowing hearts are assuaged by the hope and the divine assurance expressed in the words:

"He is not here: he is risen." Because our Redeemer lives, so shall we. I bear you witness that he does live. I know it, as I hope you know that divine truth.

May all mankind some day have that faith, I pray in the name of Jesus Christ.—CR, April 1944, pp. 123-125.

THE QUESTION OF THE AGES

LIMITATIONS OF THE SCIENTIFIC ANSWER. Death brings us face to face with the question of the ages—"If a man die, shall he live again?"

The answer given to that question by science is neither yes nor no because science is limited to a study of phenomena of experience. No one on earth, it claims, ever experienced immortality; but even science leans to the affirmative in the answer by demonstrating the most striking of scientific facts that nothing can be destroyed; that matter is indestructible, so also is energy. "One can change the form of both, but can annihilate neither of them."

Among the generalizations of science, evolution holds the foremost place. It claims: "Man is a creature of development; that he has come up through uncounted ages from an origin that is lowly." Why this vast expenditure of time and pain and blood? Why should he come so far if he is destined to go no farther? A creature which has traveled such distances and fought such battles and won such victories deserves, one is compelled to say, to conquer death and rob the grave of its victory.—FS, ms., May Anderson, June 14, 1946.

Is there something within which is superior to this old house of clay? Or are we mere mechanisms that become lifeless clay when the heartbeats stop? Even my reason will not let me doubt the existence of something within which is superior, which controls, which lives in this body. Physically our sight, our hearing, our smell, our tasting are limited to certain distances. In the rainbow, for example, we see only the violet on one side, and the red on the other. We cannot see anything beyond, but you know and I know that there are vibrations beyond the red, and vibrations beyond the violet. The vibrations are either too rapid or too slow for us to interpret, and so we are limited in our vision. We can hear a sound just so far away. If we were up in the Arctic Circle, we could hear it twenty miles away. You know and I know that something within our intelligence can become cognizant of a thought or of a fact two hundred fifty miles away. You cannot hear it with your physical ear nor see it with your physical eye, but you get the knowledge of it. "But there is a spirit in man: and the inspiration of the Almighty giveth them understanding." (Job 32:8.)

Philosophy and science can lead us only to the probability of immortality, and there is a vast step from probability to certainty. "The starry heavens above, and the moral law within" may well have thrilled the great philosopher [Kant] of the last century with ever-growing reverence and awe, but beyond the starry heavens, and behind the moral law lie the sublimer regions of faith which fill us with deepest reverence, and which alone can give us solid comfort in life and in death. —FS, ms., Mrs. William R. Calderwood, February 23, 1949.

CONCEPTS OF DARWIN AND JAMES. Living in deeds, living in writings, living in monuments, living in the memory of friends is not immortality; neither living in the lives of our children and our grandchildren to the latest generation. There are those who say that is the only immortality that man will have. But the author of evolution, Charles Darwin, shrank from that thought as he contemplated the greatest descent or origin in his mind of the human family, his theory, as you know. He finally came to the point that there will come a time when the human family will end. If that theory is right, all sentient beings known as man cannot live. And so he wrote: "It is an intolerable thought that man and all other sentient beings are doomed to annihilation after such long, continued, slow progress."

I mention it now merely to say that to live through one's children, even though their characteristics and thoughts will go on forever and forever so far as the world is concerned, is not immortality, and it is not the immortality that Jesus had in mind when he said: "And whosoever liveth and believeth in me shall never die." (John 11:26.) He had in mind something within which transcends the limits of this physical surrounding.

I remember when Brother George Q. Morris and I were in the university on Second West. Reading in James' Psychology, a reference dealing with the stream of consciousness, we came to a point where William James said that it is thought on thought that continues this stream. It is thought catching upon thought, and he added: "Coming to closest possible quarters with the facts, it is difficult for me to detect in the activity, any purely spiritual element at all."

I don't know whether George remembers it, but that gave

me a shock. Here was a man for whom we had such respect
and confidence, giving us psychology from the physiological
standpoint, who couldn't find any evidence of the something
else in there but the thought. But at the end of the chapter,
William James said: "If thought itself is not the thinker, the
only pathway that I can discover for bringing in a more
transcendental thinker would be to deny that we have any
direct knowledge of the thought as such. The latter's existence
would then be reduced to a postulate, an assertion that there
must be a *knower* correlative to all this known; and the
problem who that knower is would have become a meta-
physical problem."

A day or so after that we read in the literature class this
encouraging thought from Dryden:

"Dim as the borrow'd beams of moon and stars
To lonely, weary, wand'ring travellers,
Is Reason to the soul: and as on high
Those rolling fires discover but the sky,
Not light us here; so Reason's glimmering ray
Was lent, not to assure our doubtful way,
But guide us upward to a better day."
Dryden, *Religio Laici.*

And that "day" is the faith which Christ gave to Martha
or awakened in her soul when Lazarus slept as Nephi [L.
Morris] sleeps today. And he said, "Thy brother shall rise
again." Martha said, "I know that he shall rise again in
the resurrection . . ." and Christ answered, "I am the resurrection, and the life: he that believeth in me, though he were
dead, yet shall he live." (John 11:23-25.) And that same Jesus,
after his voice was silenced by death, so-called, arose and
appeared to his loved ones, to his associates, his disciples.

That was Nephi L. Morris' faith; shall I say it was his
knowledge. I have here a quotation, in part, and I should
like you to hear in imagination Nephi L. Morris' voice as he
gave it once before, I think, on Easter: "And last of all,
we are witnesses of these things. And in his humble name
may I to this great congregation—bear the testimony of all
Latter-day Saints that the Bible is the word of God; that
Jesus Christ was resurrected from the grave, and that through
obedience to him and a comprehension and intelligent observa-

tion of the plan of life and salvation, we too shall be resurrected from the grave, into which we shall sometime fall, by the matchless power by which he alone is able to change and fashion our bodies like unto his glorious being."

Well, we'll say to James, the psychologist, in the light of that testimony and the testimony of our own hearts, we know who that *Knower* is—the spirit within. "But there is a spirit in man: and the inspiration of the Almighty giveth them understanding." (Job 32:8.)—FS, ms., Nephi L. Morris, April 7, 1943.

"DEATH IS NOT THE END." A few years ago, as a grave was being dug for a national hero who had practically given his life for his friend, an unknown person stepped into the grave, took the shovel, threw out a few shovels full of dirt, and, handing the shovel back to the gravedigger, said: "So this is the end!" He climbed out of the unfinished grave and left without making his identity known. An account of the incident was given wide publicity in the daily press of the United States.

I think there is nothing which is more unexpressive of the truth than that expression when applied to death: "This is the end!" Accurately speaking, it applies only to one fact, and that is this: Death is the end only of one's mortal existence. It is true that—

"The boast of heraldry, the pomp of power,
And all that beauty, all that wealth e'er gave,
Awaits alike the inevitable hour
The paths of glory lead but to the grave."
                    Thomas Gray, *Elegy in a Country Churchyard.*

But the grave receives only the earthly tenement of the intelligence, mind, and spirit, that the power of death cannot touch.—FS, ms., May Anderson, June 14, 1946.

THE UNIVERSAL YEARNING FOR IMMORTALITY. At some time or other every human being faces that thing which we call death. When I was but a boy, I sensed that deeply in the cry of a mother who sat by the side of the casket that contained her little boy. Several of us boys had been playing with firecrackers on Twenty-eighth Street in Ogden. We did not know then that one of our playmates had powder in his pocket. At that time we used to celebrate and show our loyalty by firing firecrackers and shooting off bombs. Unfortunately, in a moment of thoughtlessness, this young boy broke what we called a "lighter," and while it still had sparks in it, he put it in his pocket where the powder lay, and an explosion occurred. His clothes were set on fire which we, his associates, tried to extinguish as best we could; but he was very severely and fatally burned.

Two or three days later his playmates sat in the funeral services. I chanced to be near enough to the mother and to President Charles F. Middleton to hear President Middleton say: "Don't cry, Ann! Don't cry! You'll meet your boy again." And then—you will have to imagine, for I cannot express it—a cry came from that mother's soul in these words: "Oh, if I only knew!" That is all. I did not know its significance then. I could just respond to the cry. But since, I have read in that cry the answer to the longings of the human heart. No parent can lay aside a child without longing, without wishing, that the child might come again, or that the parent might speak with the child again. You cannot lay aside your darling wife without longing for a continuation of the association that has been so heavenly to you. The bereaved wife experiences the same yearning at the departure of a devoted husband. Isn't it so throughout life? Everybody to a greater or lesser degree longs for immortality.—DNCS, December 13, 1941, p. 5.

No husband can kneel at the side of a departed wife; no wife can kneel at the side of a departed husband; no child can part with a loving parent without being filled with an ardent desire to meet that loved one again somewhere in a better world where the pangs of parting are unknown.

> ". . . Whence this pleasing hope, this fond desire,
> This longing after immortality?
> Or whence this secret dread, and inward horror,
> Of falling into naught? Why shrinks the soul
> Back on herself, and startles at destruction?
> 'Tis the divinity that stirs within us;
> 'Tis Heaven itself, that points out an hereafter,
> And intimates eternity to man."
> Addison, *Cato*, Act 5, Sc. 1.
> —FS, ms., Frank Evans, August 21, 1950.

THE MEANING OF IMMORTALITY

THE PERSISTENCE OF PERSONALITY AFTER DEATH. Living in posterity is not immortality. Some say there will come a time when not a grandchild can be found living on earth. It may be that we can see the time when even these virtues will not be perpetuated.

In what, then, does true immortality consist? It consists in the persistence of personality after death. The Savior's heartbeats were silenced, his body placed in the tomb; but his personality, the eternal part, lived and moved and had its being in the eternal beyond to which his persecutors were unresponsive and dead.—FS, ms., Rudger Clawson, June 25, 1943.

I believe with all my soul in the persistence of personality after death. I cannot believe otherwise. Even reason and observation demonstrate that to me.

Some of you have heard me give experiences that illustrate this thought. As I have stood by the bedside of dying men, women, and children, these illustrations have been proved. Not a week has passed since I received what I thought was another illustration of that fact.

I spoke at the funeral service of a mother in Logan only recently. That good mother, before she died, as she lay on the bed of illness, was wont to inquire about her brother. Nearly every night she would say, "How is he getting along?" mentioning his name, but, suddenly, one day that brother left his mortal existence almost instantly. That afternoon as the sister awoke from sleep, she made no inquiry as to the condition of her brother, didn't ask about him, but stated, "I have seen William and Mother together. How happy they seem. They wanted me to go with them, but I was not ready. How happy they will be."

She knew he was gone. Nobody had said a word to her, but a consciousness had come to her that her brother William was with her mother, who had been dead for many years. The sister, however, was not quite ready. In two more days she, too, joined them. Her body was weakened by disease, suffering; her physical strength was wasted, but the spirit was responsive to another environment to which her loved ones, in the prime of physical life and health, were unresponsive.

I have seen one young man particularly responsive to that environment when he was dead to us who stood by ready to bless him, and his vocal chords could be used, for he spoke, his lips seemed to say, and distinctly I heard him say, "Yes, Father, I recognize you. May I come back?" and at the conclusion of these words his cousin, Sister Bertha Wright, said, "Administer to him, Brother McKay."

I said, "It is too late, he is gone," But yet his heart was beating, his vocal chords were expressing words, but I was as conscious and sure as that I am standing here, that he was unresponsive to us. He was responding to another environment to which we were unresponsive, to which we were dead. Not five minutes passed before his heartbeat stopped, and then we said he was dead. His spirit was free, even before the heartbeat stopped. His father had been dead for fifteen years.

I am not giving this as argument but merely as an illustration of the fact that the spirit when free from the body which is subject to disease, is whole, possessing the loving characteristics and beautiful virtues that were so well-known in the loved one here, and so this is my witness and testimony to you today.—FS, ms., Mrs. Bertha Harmon Lee, August 18, 1937.

THE SPIRIT OF MAN IS ETERNAL. Nearly two thousand years ago a man who took upon himself mortality was crucified on the cross, his heartbeats were stilled, his loved ones grieved, and his body was silently placed in the tomb. No matter how many critics try to explain it away, those things are facts! Eighteen hundred years later that Being appeared to the Prophet Joseph Smith, personally—not just in a dream, not in imagination, but in reality. And if one Being who took upon himself mortality, born of mortal woman, can pass through those stages, so can each one of you. And while the Savior's body lay in the tomb, his personality, his spirit preached to the spirits in prison, who had been disobedient in the days of Noah hundreds of years before.

Personality is persistent, and that is the message of comfort, that is the real way in which death is conquered. Death cannot touch the spirit of man.—FS, ms., Robert S. Richards, October 1, 1951.

This old body is just a house, as physical as the house in which we are meeting today. We can analyze and find most of it is fluid; a few chemicals go to make up this old chemical house; but in a few years it begins to decay; the brain ceases to function. We can analyze that brain, with its gray matter, its white matter, and we know what it is, and we can see the explosion that takes place when thought is produced, and yet each of us knows that there is something within which is greater than the thought.

It is the spirit, the soul that is within us that bears witness to the immortality of the soul.—FS, ms., Mrs. Martha H. Rolapp, September 8, 1942.

The Immortality of the Soul. Life is full of partings. Parents are saying good-bye to boys drafted into the army. Missionary farewells are being held weekly. We say good-bye to our boys and girls who go back to college. Nearly every parting is associated with sadness. The suddenness of parting intensifies the sadness, but in all these temporary partings there is the hope of a reuniting, which, to an extent, alleviates sorrow caused by separation. The point I wish to make is that this parting, caused by death, though sudden and somewhat extended, is no less free from the realization of another meeting—the hope of a mother to meet her soldier boy on his return; the hope of a mother to meet her missionary son when he comes back with an honorable release; the hope of parents to meet their son after he has perhaps completed a college course—this hope is no more real than the hope we have of reuniting with husband, father, friend, and business associate.

Death may have power over the body, for we are, in this life, open to accident and disease; and death may take advantage of these conditions, but there his power ends. Death cannot touch the spirit. Our friend who lies silent here is just as whole in personality, possessing all his qualities of manliness as he lived pure and possessed those qualities here in life.

If there is any truth that is taught through the gospel of Jesus Christ, it is the truth of the immortality of the soul. —FS, ms., James H. Riley, August 7, 1946.

I last saw Brother Andrew Jenson a few weeks ago as he was entering the office. On one side gently assisting him was

his son; on the other, his daughter. It was evident that his
body was becoming enfeebled; his mind and intellect were
as alert as ever. As I continued to my office, I was reminded
of ex-President John Quincy Adams' reference to his bodily
enfeeblement and the expression of his faith in immortality.
One day as Mr. Adams was walking down a street in Boston,
a friend accosted him and said: "Mr. Adams, how are you?"
Confident that he would live after his body had ceased to
function in the physical world, the venerable man replied:
"Thank you, sir! John Quincy Adams himself is well, sir,
quite well. I thank you. But the house in which he lives
at present is becoming dilapidated. It is tottering upon its
foundations. Time and the seasons have nearly destroyed it.
Its roof is pretty well wornout. Its walls are much shattered,
and it trembles with every wind. The old tenement is becoming almost uninhabitable, and I think John Quincy Adams will
have to move out of it soon; but he, himself, is quite well, sir,
quite well."—FS, ms., Andrew Jenson, November 22, 1941.

CHARACTER ENDURES. "And all wept, and bewailed her:
but he [Jesus] said, Weep not; she is not dead, but sleepeth.

"And they laughed him to scorn, knowing that she was
dead.

"And he put them all out, and took her by the hand, and
called, saying, Maid, arise.

"And her spirit came again, and she arose straightway:
and he commanded to give her meat." (Luke 8:52-55.)

You recognize this as a quotation taken from Luke's account of the raising of the twelve-year-old daughter of Jairus,
a ruler of the synagogue. I have quoted it today because it
contains two elements appropriate to this sacred occasion:

The first is, that the little maiden through sickness had
met what we must all meet some day. Either through sickness, accident, or old age, death eventually comes to all.

The second is reference to the fact of the dual nature
of each individual: " . . . her spirit came again."

The important question with each of us today, as it
should be always, is: How well prepared are we to meet that
eventuality in life, that inescapable experience called death?

One man, contemplating this, tried to imagine what we could take with us when the end came:

"Supposing today were your last day on earth.
　　The last mile of the journey you've trod;
After all of your struggles, how much are you worth?
　　How much can you take home to God?

"Don't count as possessions your silver and gold,
　　Tomorrow you leave these behind;
And all that is yours to have and to hold,
　　Is the service you've rendered mankind."

When I first read that, I could not agree with him nor do I today, unless he includes in that rendering of service, the development of spiritual gifts and attainments—the character that we have developed, the virtues which have been ours through righteous living in this mortal stage, and the credit of service to others.—FS, ms., Mrs. Adele Cannon Howells, April 17, 1951.

DEATH—A DOORWAY TO LIFE. Truly, "He [man] cometh forth like a flower, and is cut down: . . ." (Job 14:2) but "He that . . . believeth on him that sent me, hath everlasting life, and shall not come into condemnation; but is passed from death unto life." (John 5:24.)

This stage of existence is progress towards death. That which we call death is the door into the life of living.—FS, ms., Henry A. Gardner, May 12, 1948.

A SLEEP. What we call death Jesus referred to as sleep. "Lazarus sleeps," he said to his disciples. "The damsel sleepeth," were his comforting words to the bereaved and sorrowing parents of a little girl. Indeed, to the Savior of the world there is no such thing as death—only life—eternal life. . . .

With this assurance, obedience to eternal law should be a joy, not a burden, for life is joy, life is love. It is disobedience that brings death. Obedience to Christ and his laws brings life.—CR, April 1939, p. 115.

THE PURPOSES OF RELIGIOUS FUNERAL SERVICES. The purpose of these services is to pay tribute to our departed brother, [President George Albert Smith], and, secondly to bring solace, and peace to the sorrowing hearts of the bereaved. We have listened to tributes as great, I think, as could be paid to any great leader.

May I now say a word about the second purpose of a funeral service: to bring solace and comfort to sorrowing hearts. This is done by three principal means.

First, in contemplation of the fact that he, whose departure strains the heartstrings, has lived a useful, noble life. What consolation that will bring to any bereaved father, mother, or child.

Second, comfort in the consciousness that loved ones were true and loyal, as his children and kinfolk, and that particularly during illness they did everything humanly possible to administer to his needs, to alleviate his pain, and to give him comfort.

And third, comfort in the assurance of the immortality of the human soul; the assurance that their father is just away.—CR, April 1951, pp. 181-182.

THE EVIDENCE FOR THE RESURRECTION

CHRIST'S APOSTLES WITNESSES OF THE RESURRECTION. Let us ask ourselves, and ask sincerely, is it a fact that the crucified Jesus did appear after his death as a resurrected being? Accept this as an actuality, and you have at least presumptive evidence of the truth of his teachings regarding the sacredness of the individual as a child of God.

That the literal resurrection from the grave was a reality to the disciples, who knew Christ intimately, is a certainty. In their minds there was absolutely no doubt. They were witnesses of the fact. They knew because their eyes beheld, their ears heard, their hands felt the corporeal presence of the risen Redeemer.—CR, April 1939, p. 112.

VALUE OF THE APOSTOLIC WITNESS. Nearness to the event gives increased value to the evidence given by the Apostles. A deeper value of their testimony lies in the fact that with Jesus' death the Apostles were stricken with discouragement and gloom. For two and a half years they had been upheld and inspired by Christ's presence. But now he was gone. They were left alone, and they seemed confused and helpless.

Only John stood by the cross. Not with timidity, not with feelings of doubt and gloom and discouragement is a skeptical world made to believe. Such wavering, despairing minds as the Apostles possessed on the day of the crucifixion could never have stirred people to accept an unpopular belief and to die martyrs to the cause.

I urge the youth of the Church, students particularly, carefully to consider the testimony of these eyewitnesses, whose honesty is not questioned even by skeptical criticism.—CR, April 1939, pp. 112-113.

MARK'S TESTIMONY. We have no evidence that Mark joined the Church while the Savior was on the earth. Undoubtedly the Savior was in Mark's home. Mark was probably the youth who rushed into the Garden of Gethsemane and warned Jesus that the soldiers were coming. At any rate we are justified in assuming that he was acquainted with the Master.

Mark does not himself recount any appearance of the risen Lord, but he testifies that the Lord would meet his disciples. From Mark we hear the glorious proclamation of the first empty tomb in all the world. For the first time in the history of man the words, "Here lies," were supplanted by the divine message, "He is risen." No one can doubt that Mark was not convinced in his soul of the reality of the empty tomb. To him the resurrection was not questionable—it was real; and the appearance of his Lord and Master among men was a fact established in his mind beyond the shadow of a doubt. To the proclaiming of this truth he devoted his life, and if tradition can be relied upon, he sealed his testimony with his blood.

LUKE'S TESTIMONY. Another who records the testimony of eyewitnesses was Luke, a Gentile, or, as some think, a proselyte of Antioch in Syria, where he followed the profession of physician. (See Col. 4:14.) Even some of his most severe modern critics have placed him in the first rank of an historian, and his personal contact with early Apostles makes his statements of inestimable value.

What he wrote was the result of personal inquiry and investigation and was drawn from all available sources. Particularly he interviewed and recorded the declarations of those "who from the beginning were eyewitnesses and ministers of the word." He avers that he "accurately traced all things from the very first," so that he might "write them in order." This means that Luke obtained the testimony of these "eyewitnesses" directly from themselves and not from previous narratives.

According to all trustworthy testimony, we have the gospel of Luke as it came from his hand. In Chapter 24, Luke testifies to the divine message: "Why seek ye the living among the dead?

"He is not here, but is risen: ... " (Luke 24:5-6.)

With equal assurance as to their accuracy we can accept his statements and witness in regard to Peter's and Paul's and other Apostles' testimony regarding the resurrection. "To whom also he [Christ] shewed himself alive after his passion by many infallible proofs, being seen of them forty days, and speaking of the things pertaining to the kingdom of God." (Acts 1:3.) Who can doubt Luke's absolute confidence in the reality of the resurrection?

It is true that neither Mark nor Luke testifies to having personally seen the risen Lord, and therefore, some urge that their recorded testimonies cannot be taken as firsthand evidence. That they do not so testify, and yet were convinced that others did see him, shows how incontrovertible was the evidence among the Apostles and other disciples that the resurrection was a reality.

PAUL'S TESTIMONY. Fortunately, however, there is a document which does give the personal testimony of an eyewitness to an appearance of Jesus after his death and burial. This personal witness also corroborates the testimony not only of the two men whom I have quoted but of others also. I refer to Saul, a Jew of Tarsus, educated at the feet of Gamaliel, a strict Pharisee, and before Saul's conversion a bitter persecutor of all who believed in Jesus of Nazareth as having risen from the dead.

And now in the oldest authentic document in existence relating or testifying to the resurrection of Christ, we find Paul saying this to the Corinthians:

"For I delivered unto you first of all that which I also

received, how that Christ died for our sins according to the
scriptures;

"And that he was buried, and that he rose again the
third day according to the scriptures:

"And that he was seen of Cephas, then of the twelve:

"After that, he was seen of above five hundred brethren
at once; of whom the greater part remain unto this present,
but some are fallen asleep.

"After that, he was seen of James; then of all the apostles.

"And last of all he was seen of me also, as of one born
out of due time.

"For I am the least of the apostles, that am not meet to
be called an apostle, because I persecuted the church of God."
(I Cor. 15:3-9.)

THE TESTIMONY OF MODERN REVELATION. In addition
to the ancient Apostles, we have the testimony of the Prophet
Joseph Smith who gives in an unequivocal description the
following stirring testimony in relation to his first vision:

" . . . When the light rested upon me I saw two Personages, . . . standing above me in the air. One of them spake
unto me, calling me by name and said, pointing to the other—
'This is My Beloved Son. Hear Him!' " (P. of G. P., Joseph
Smith 2:17.)

THE LATTER-DAY SAINT BELIEF. Thus the Church of
Jesus Christ of Latter-day Saints stands with Peter, with
Paul, and with James, and with all the other Apostles in accepting the resurrection not only as being literally true but
also as the consummation of Christ's divine mission on earth.
Other great religious leaders among the nations of the world
since history began have taught virtue and temperance, self-
mastery and service, obedience to righteousness and duty;
some have taught a belief in one supreme ruler and in an
hereafter; but only Christ broke the seal of the grave and
revealed death as the door to immortality and eternal life.
—CR, April 1939, pp. 113-115.

THE GREAT CONFIRMATION. The latest and greatest confirmation that Jesus rose from the grave is the appearance of

the Father and the Son to the Prophet Joseph Smith, eighteen hundred years after the event that today Christendom is celebrating. It is highly appropriate, therefore, that the Church should join in the annual festival commemorating the resurrection of Christ, the most significant, the most memorable event in the history of mankind.—*CR*, April 1944, p. 120.

THE MESSAGE TO MAN. If Christ lived after death, so shall men, each one taking the place in the next world for which he is best fitted. Since love is as eternal as life, the message of the resurrection is the most comforting, the most glorifying ever given to man; for when death takes a loved one from us, we can look with assurance into the open grave and say, "He is not here," and "He will rise again."—*CR*, April 1939, p. 115.

A PERSONAL TESTIMONY. It is just as easy for me to accept as a divine truth the fact that Christ preached to the spirits in prison while his body lay in the tomb as it is for me to look at you from this pulpit. It is true. And it is just as easy for me to realize that one may so live that he may receive impressions and direct messages through the Holy Ghost. The veil is thin between those who hold the priesthood and divine messengers on the other side of the veil.—*CR*, April 1948, p. 172.

A PERSONAL HOPE. By the power of the priesthood, whatsoever is bound on earth is bound in heaven. This is an eternal promise. I refer to William McKay and Ellen Oman, my grandparents, also to my father and mother, my brothers and sisters over there now.

I hope to meet them and recognize them and love them as I recognized and loved them here. And I base that upon knowledge that is as real as my speaking to you. It has come through inspiration from on high, and I base it also upon the biblical scripture that as Christ's body lay in the tomb his spirit went to preach to the spirits in prison which were disobedient at one time, in the days of Noah.—*DNCS*, June 18, 1952, p. 3.

THE SIGNIFICANCE OF EASTER

" . . . Ye seek Jesus of Nazareth, which was crucified: he is risen; he is not here: behold the place where they laid him." (Mark 16:6.)

Those lines when written had no reference whatever to Easter. They were a simple statement concerning the resurrection of Jesus Christ—one of the two greatest events in the history of mankind.

Easter is a spring festival that has been adopted from the pagan celebration given in honor of Astarte or Eostro, a Saxon goddess corresponding to the Ashtaroth of Syria.

All that men say of Eastertide as the season of new life and new hope may be appropriately connoted with this ancient pre-Christian festival. True, spring and resurrection are happily associated, not that there is anything in nature exactly analogous to the resurrection, but there is so much in springtime which suggests the *awakening* thought. Like the stillness of death, Old Winter has held in his grasp all vegetable life, but as spring approaches, the tender, life-giving power of heat and light compel him to relinquish his grip, and what seemed to have been dead, gradually awakens to a newness of life, revivified, refreshed, invigorated after a peaceful sleep.

But the re-awakening of physical life or even the rehabilitation of spiritual ideals is not the real significance of Easter as celebrated by the early Christians when they adopted the pagan spring festival.

They commemorated the coming forth from the tomb of their crucified Lord, the resurrected Christ.

To sincere believers in Christianity, to all who accept Christ as their Savior, his resurrection is not a symbolism, but a reality.

As Christ lived after death, so shall all men, each taking his place in the next world for which he has best fitted himself.

With this assurance, obedience to eternal law should be a joy, not a burden, for compliance with the principles of the gospel brings happiness and peace.

To this truth, may each recurring Easter morning give

new emphasis and fill our souls with divine assurance that
Christ is truly risen and through him man's immortality assured.

May the day soon dawn upon the world when reliance
upon brute force and belief in the false ideal that *might makes
right* will be supplanted by the higher ideals that radiate the
charitable, peace-loving spirit of the risen Lord!—*DNCS,*
April 16, 1952, pp. 2, 3.

CHAPTER 6

SOME GOSPEL QUESTIONS

IS CHRISTIANITY COMING OR GOING?

TRUE CHRISTIANITY. True Christianity—by which I mean the sublime truths of life as taught by the Savior of men, and his authorized Church—had not been upon the earth for many centuries. That organization men rejected by killing the servants whom Christ authorized to preach his gospel. Following their death, men substituted for the heaven-inspired Church an organization which gave glittering promises of truth and salvation, but which it could not fulfil. Pomp and ceremony in worship were substituted for simplicity. True Christianity promised love, service, peace, brotherhood. The spurious Christianity has spread hate, selfishness, discord, and international enmity. So when men say, "Christianity is going" or "Christianity has failed," it is well to understand that they refer to that which has paraded as Christianity for so many centuries and not Christ's Church itself, not to his doctrines, which are eternal truth itself. "For they have strayed from mine ordinances," says the Lord, "and have broken mine everlasting covenant.

"They seek not the Lord to establish his righteousness, but every man walketh in his own way, and after the image of his own God, whose image is in the likeness of the world, . . . " (D. & C. 1:15-16.)

THE NEW CHRISTENDOM—RESTORED IN THE WEST WITH A GLOBAL MESSAGE. But true Christianity, the plain, simple, but sublime doctrine of the Redeemer is "coming"; indeed, has already come. His Church is established among men in western civilization, "never more to be overthrown or given to another people." That Church was not established by man nor by legislative enactment; but by the Redeemer himself. It is, therefore, his Church—the Church of Jesus Christ, destined to transform the lives of men in all nations, and eventually to link together in the endless chain of salvation the whole human race. It is the science of living, of living completely, and the more men know about it, the more they introduce its doctrines into their everyday life, the more they love it, and the more eager they become to declare to their fellow men its Godlike virtues.

And this gospel shall be preached ". . . unto them that dwell on the earth, and to every nation, and kindred, and tongue, and people,

"Saying with a loud voice, Fear God, and give glory to him; for the hour of his judgment is come." (Rev. 14:6-7.) —MS, 85:536-538 (1923).

ISRAEL, THE JEWS, AND ZIONISM

JEWISH-CHRISTIAN RELATIONSHIPS. Twenty-three hundred years ago the prophet looking down through the vista of time saw this day. He saw Israel scattered among all nations. He saw them become a hiss and a byword, but added, "Nevertheless, when that *day cometh, . . . that they no more turn aside their hearts against the Holy One of Israel, . . .*"—note he does not say when they accept him as their Redeemer, nor necessarily declare to the world that he was the Messiah to come to their people—the prophet words it most significantly; viz., "*when . . . they no more turn aside their hearts against the Holy One of Israel, then will he remember the covenants which he made to their fathers.*" (I Nephi 19:15.)

Brethren, isn't it a significant thing that today there is a change in the hearts of the descendants of Israel in regard to the Holy One of Israel?

In 1918, while I was visiting the California Mission, President Joseph E. Robinson put in my hand a book entitled, *Jesus, the Jew,* written by a prominent Jew of Sacramento. In the first chapter of that book we get a picture of the enmity and bitterness of the Jews when the author was a boy. Their hearts were not turned, even at that late date, much toward the Holy One but most bitterly against him. He said in substance: "I remember, when a boy, that one of my classmates brought into the class a book containing the name of Jesus. I remember how wrought up and excited the rabbi became when he was made aware of its presence in the schoolroom. 'Sacrilege! Sacrilege!' he indignantly cried. Then the rabbi proceeded to denounce the Holy One. He said: 'How can

any Jew who realizes what that name has brought upon his
people even touch a book containing the name of Jesus?' He
told how the Jews had been persecuted, how they had been
made outcasts and wanderers, how they had been driven from
pillar to post, over the face of the earth; how their beards
had been torn from their roots, their teeth drawn from their
jaws; how they had been whipped at the post, put upon the
rack, and their bones drawn joint from joint; how they had
been outraged, ravished, and killed, all on account of Jesus"—
and by the Christians. That is one picture, when that man
was but a boy—when you were boys, my fellow workers in
the priesthood.

THE BOOK OF MORMON AND A CHANGE OF HEART.
Here is another picture given by a prominent Jew, Isadore
Singer, the editor of the *Jewish Encyclopedia*: "When I was
a boy, had my father, who was a very pious man, heard the
name of Jesus uttered from the pulpit of our synagogue, he
and every other man in the congregation would have left
the building, and the rabbi would have been dismissed at
once." That is illustrative of the spirit among the descendants
of Israel when the Book of Mormon came forth among the
children of men. Even at that time no man, it seems to me,
acting upon his ordinary judgment, would dare say that the
time would come when they would accept that Holy One,
but here, two thousand years before, a prophet of God said
the day would come when they would no more turn their
hearts aside from the Holy One, and that then he would
remember the promises he made to their fathers.

Now the question is: Has that day come? That same
man who heard his teacher say, "Sacrilege! Sacrilege!" because
a boy happened to bring a book containing the name of Jesus,
said:

"I began to study his teachings. I found what his teachings were—purity, humility; 'Blessed are the poor in spirit.'
'Blessed are they that mourn.' 'Blessed are the pure in heart,
for they should see God; blessed are the meek, for they shall
inherit the earth; blessed are they that hunger and thirst
after righteousness, for they shall be filled.' " And then he
proceeds to show how Israel today is indebted to Jesus, the
Jew. In one chapter entitled, "Is the Messiah yet to come?"

he says: "The enlightened Jew says no, but the Messianic age is what the Jews today are looking forward to."

And here in that connection let me just read one verse from that same Mr. Singer: "I regard Jesus of Nazareth as a Jew of the Jews, one whom all Jewish people"—all Jewish people!—"are learning to love. His teaching has been an immense service to the world in bringing Israel's God to the knowledge of hundreds of millions of mankind. The great change in Jewish thoughts concerning Jesus of Nazareth I cannot better illustrate than by this fact—" and then he relates the instance of his childhood, as I have read it.

"Now, it is not strange in many synagogues to hear sermons preached eulogistic of this Jesus, and nobody thinks of protesting. In fact, we are all glad to claim Jesus as one of our people."

ORIGINS OF THE MODERN STATE OF ISRAEL. Boys of latter-day Israel, does it not seem that the time has come when "their hearts no more turn against the Holy One?" It seems to me that it has. Then, if so, great events are to take place. God has said he will remember his promises. What are they? Turn to the tenth chapter of II Nephi [10:7], and there you will find that "When the day cometh that they shall believe in me, . . . they shall be restored in the flesh, . . ." unto their own land.

In the month of December 1917, General Allenby, of the British Army, took possession of the holy city, Jerusalem. To-day the Holy Land is practically freed from the domination of the Turk, and it is under the rule of the Gentile. It was significant that during that very month one of the leaders of the British Parliament, announcing the taking of Jerusalem, also suggested that it should be made the home of the Jews. In the next paragraph in II Nephi [10:8] the prophet also added this significant reference: " . . . and the nations of the Gentiles shall be great in the eyes of me . . . in carrying them forth to the lands of their inheritance." As soon, practically, as the announcement was made by Mr. Arthur J. Balfour, I think, that Jerusalem should be held for the Jews, a prominent Jew in this country wrote an article in one of the magazines saying, "We don't want to go back to Jerusalem. The Holy Land is of such strategic value that should the Jews gather there and build a Jewish republic, and the nations go to war later, we shall be crushed as Belgium was crushed in this war"; but he was answered by the leaders of the Zionist movement, one of whom was Israel Zangwill, the author of that most patriotic American play, *The Melting Pot,* and they said this: "Place the Jewish republic under the protection of some such nations as Great Britain and the United States," and in harmony with that sentiment, June the 26 of this year [1918], prominent Jews held a convention in Pittsburgh in which it was stated publicly and authoritatively that at that time fifty thousand Jews were with General Allenby working for the freedom of the Holy Land; and the Jews who stood up in that convention, said: "We dedicate the rest of our lives to the rebuilding of Jerusalem."

AN EVENT IN THE DRAMA OF HISTORY. It has been said by someone that we cannot see great events when we are close to them, and it may be that we are too close to the fulfilment of these prophecies to get their full significance. However, I am sure this morning that we get at least glimpses of their significance. This is one thought, then, which I desire to give to the boys and girls of Zion—that "The providence that watches over the affairs of men works out of their mistakes at times a healthier issue than could have been accomplished by their own wisest forethought."

I grant you that the Gentile nation, Great Britain, did not go over there to get Jerusalem free for the Jews. In this great war she wanted to protect her possessions and interests in the Far East. That was simply a strategic movement in this great war, but out of it what has come? I myself heard within the last month a prominent Jew of our own state express to an audience his appreciation of what is now dawning for his people. "Under the storm and the cloud today, and today the hard peril and pain, tomorrow the stone shall be rolled away for the sunshine shall follow the rain." God's providence will bring out of this great conflict blessings to humanity of which they scarcely dream.

But in order that they might have them and acknowledge them, there is a responsibility upon the people of the earth. Liberty is offered them; and the perfect law of liberty, the gospel of Jesus Christ, is offered them. In this day, the greatest in the world's history, a day toward which prophets looked with longing hearts, you and I are witnesses of the fulfilment, at least in part, of God's promises. You and I, then, have the responsibility if there is anything at all in the testimony we bear, of giving to this people, not only the Jews, but also to the world, the gospel, the perfect law of liberty. —CR, October 1918, pp. 45-48.

THE SACRAMENT OF THE LORD'S SUPPER

A SACRED CHRISTIAN ORDINANCE. The partaking of the sacrament of the Lord's Supper is one of the most sacred ordinances of the Church of Jesus Christ. Associated with it are principles fundamental in character building and essential to man's advancement and exaltation in the kingdom of God. Too few communicants attach to this simple though sublime rite the importance and significance that it merits. Unfortunately, the *form* of worship is frequently an outward compliance without the true soul acknowledgment of its deep spiritual significance.

One reason why thinking men and women are rejecting the pseudo-Christian sects of the day is because of the discrepancy between the pretensions and the daily acts of so-called Christian believers. It is very easy to go to Church, to sing hallelujah, and to cry, "Lord, Lord!"; but it is not so easy to do that which the Lord requires.

When churchmen's acts do not conform to their pretensions, non-churchmen accuse them of hypocrisy, one of the gross sins condemned most vehemently by the Savior.

Members of the Church of Jesus Christ should strive very earnestly to reflect in their daily conduct those ideals which on Sunday they profess to cherish.

In the partaking of the sacrament, there is danger of people's permitting formality to supersede spirituality. When such is the case, the ordinance may prove to be a curse instead of a blessing.

The blessing on the bread, which is offered in behalf of everyone who partakes of the sacrament, reveals clearly the relation that each one assumes to the Lord, and the obligations each one takes upon himself. Reverence and the sacredness of a promise are the first two principles therein emphasized.

REVERENCE ENJOINED. The address, "O God, the Eternal Father," is an acknowledgment on the part of the congregation that the Lord is present; at least that his Spirit is in possible communication with the spirit of each one who sincerely seeks him. Charles Lamb once said, "If Shakespeare were to come into this room, we should all rise up to meet him; but if Christ were to come into it, we should all fall upon our knees." This reverent attitude should be maintained during the administration of the sacrament. Though the congregation does not kneel, it should maintain perfect order.

Everybody present should think of the virtues of Christ's life, for the sacrament is "blessed and sanctified" that each may partake of it "in remembrance" of the Son of God.

PROMISES ATTESTED. There are few things in life more sacred than one's word of honor. Truthfulness, honesty are fundamental virtues, without which it is impossible to build a noble character. Charles E. Jefferson aptly says, "All virtues are important, but some are more essential than others. There are virtues whose absence leaves the character ragged and marred, and there are others whose absence leaves the soul a hollow shell." The man who disregards a promise, who treats lightly and with contempt his word of honor, has a soul that is but "a hollow shell."

All who partake of the sacrament, *witness*, that is, give evidence of, or *attest* before "God, the Eternal Father," that they are willing to do certain things. In England, when a man witnesses a signature to an important legal document, the barrister before whom the signature is attested may require the man to solemnize his word or oath by touching the Bible. Of course, that is mere folly, but it originally signified that a promise made in the presence of that which is holy would be more sacredly kept than a promise or oath not so made. However, a promise given man to man is sufficiently binding. Then surely that which is witnessed before God is of such a nature that it never should be broken.

THREE COVENANTS. In this solemn presence, therefore, every partaker of the sacrament gives evidence of his willingness to assume three very great obligations, the first of which, and to which he becomes bound in sacred honor, is: *To take upon himself the name of the Son.*

To be called worthily by his name is to become a son of God, to be numbered one in the brotherhood of Christ. "Beloved, now are we the sons of God, and it doth not yet appear what we shall be: but we know that, when he shall appear, we shall be like him; for we shall see him as he is.

"And every man that hath this hope in him purifieth himself, even as he is pure." (I John 3:2-3.) The second is: *That he will always remember him.*

Remembrance is the act of having what is known, consciously before the mind. The promise, then, is that *at all times* he will bear in mind with gratitude and reverence Him whose life was the epitome of purity, kindness, love. Under all conditions, he is to eschew evil, and to cherish virtue, and to supplant hatred with compassion and benevolence. The third obligation is: *To keep his commandments.*

Were we to particularize, the commandments of God might be designated as many. Indeed, they touch every phase of man's being. But Jesus, himself, summed them all up as follows:

" ... love the Lord thy God with all thy heart, and with all thy soul, and with all thy mind, and with all thy strength: ...

"And ... thy neighbour as thyself. ... " (Mark 12:30-31.)

This is what every man who partakes of the sacrament expresses a willingness to do!

Who can measure the responsibility of such a covenant? How far-reaching! How comprehensive! It excludes from man's life: profanity, vulgarity, idleness, enmity, jealousy, drunkenness, dishonesty, hatred, selfishness, and every form of vice. It obligates him to sobriety, to industry, to kindness, to the performance of every duty in church and state. He binds himself to respect his fellow men, to honor the priesthood, to pay his tithes and offerings, and to consecrate his life to the service of humanity.

RESULTANT BLESSING. The all-comprehending reward named as the result of compliance with the three obligations assumed is the guiding and inspirational companionship of God's Holy Spirit. This is to the spirit of man what the sunshine is to the material world. It is the light that leads to eternal life. The operation of the law of cause and effect is as constant in the spiritual realm as it is in the physical world, and the keeping of each promise made in relation to the sacrament brings its resultant blessing, as surely as the sun brings light.

Order, reverence, attestation in divine presence to enter the fold of Christ; to keep his virtues and his life ever in mind; to love the Lord wholeheartedly; and to labor even at the sacrifice of self for the brotherhood of the human family—these and all kindred virtues are associated with the partaking of the Lord's Supper.—*MS*, 85:776-778 (1923).

THE STATUS OF CHILDREN WHO DIE IN INFANCY

HEIRS OF THE CELESTIAL KINGDOM. The Church of Jesus Christ promulgates the doctrine that little children are redeemed and sanctified through the atonement of our Lord and Savior. If they die before reaching the age of accountability, they become heirs of the celestial kingdom of heaven. Such is the sublime teaching set forth by the Prophet Joseph Smith as early as the year 1832.

THE ERRONEOUS DOCTRINES OF DEPRAVITY AND INFANT BAPTISM. At that time, and even a number of years later, the old school of pseudo-Christianity taught the pernicious doctrine that, "Infants come into the world, not only destitute of knowledge, righteousness, and true holiness, but also with a nature inclined to evil and only evil." With minds poisoned by this false idea, ministers taught, and trusting but misguided parents believed that unchristened infants that died were condemned to eternal punishment. Such a doctrine is worse than pernicious; it is horrible!

Equally erroneous, and wholly unjustifiable by the Holy Scriptures, is the doctrine of infant baptism. The Savior refuted the false idea of eternal punishment for unchristened infants, also the necessity of infant baptism when in the love of his heart he said: "Suffer the little children to come unto me, and forbid them not: for of such is the kingdom of God." (Mark 10:14.)

In harmony with this sublime and reasonable declaration, the Church of Jesus Christ today affirms that "All children are redeemed by the blood of Jesus Christ," and that when they die, they "will be enthroned in the presence of God and the Lamb," where they will enjoy "the fulness of that light, glory, and intelligence, which is prepared in the celestial kingdom."

CHILDREN IN THE RESURRECTION. The question frequently arises as to whether a child that died in infancy will remain a child in the hereafter, and whether in the resurrection the spirit will take up the same body that it tabernacled in the flesh.

The doctrine of the Church in this respect was very clearly set forth by the late President Joseph F. Smith in an editorial in *The Improvement Era,* June 1904, wherein he stated, "The body will come forth as it is laid to rest, for there is no growth or development in the grave. As it is laid down, so will it arise, and changes to perfection will come by the law of restitution. But the spirit will continue to expand and develop, to the full stature of man."

Parents, therefore, who have been parted from their children by death may rest assured that, if worthy through obedience to the principles of the gospel, they will not only meet their children in the spirit world, but will also recognize them and know them as they knew them in this life. Parents, too, have even a greater comfort in the fact that their little ones whose lives on earth were cut short will continue to grow and develop, and receive every blessing to which their inheritance and faithfulness will entitle them.—*MS,* 86:616-617 (1924).

Book II

THE CHURCH OF JESUS CHRIST OF LATTER-DAY SAINTS

"The greatest event of the nineteenth century was the appearing of two heavenly Beings to the boy Prophet Joseph Smith, revealing the personal identity respectively of God the Eternal Father and of his Son Jesus Christ."

—David O. McKay
Millennial Star
Volume 85:408

CHAPTER 7

THE MISSION OF THE PROPHET
JOSEPH SMITH

THE RESTORATION OF THE GOSPEL

THE GREATEST EVENT OF THE NINETEENTH CENTURY. Nearness to an event tends to minimize its full significance and importance. Though the world is still near the great events that made the nineteenth an epoch-making century, yet so far-reaching and significant were the wonderful discoveries and inventions of the latter half of that century that they overwhelm us even in their nearness.

In this first quarter of the twentieth century we are looking at these momentous realities only as observers, who, standing at the foot of a high mountain, see it only in part. Its majestic slopes, towering peaks, and relative position to surrounding ranges are hidden from view. Yet even our limited vision fills us with astonishment. What mighty things have been accomplished! What mightier possibilities of the future! Who, for example, can measure the material benefits to society of the steam engine, the cotton gin, the automobile, the telegraph, the telephone; or who can even imagine the ultimate effect upon the human race of William Harvey's discovery, or that of Louis Pasteur? Space prevents even the mentioning of other events of equal significance and far-reaching benefits.

But none of them has answered man's greatest need and man's most yearning desire. Not one has yet revealed that for which man has sought for ages. That need—that ever-present yearning in man's heart—is to know God, and man's relation to him. The microscope has not revealed him; the telescope has not discovered him; even radio has not yet penetrated his abiding place—only one event of the nineteenth century claims to give to the human soul this answer. If in that event man finds the truth for which the human race has ever sought, then it truly merits the distinguishing tribute of the greatest event of the nineteenth century!

That event was the appearing of two heavenly Beings to the boy Prophet Joseph Smith, revealing the personal identity respectively of God the Eternal Father and of his Son Jesus Christ.—*MS*, 85:408 (1923).

PRAYER—THE KEY. About 1820, religious excitement led Joseph Smith to seek the right church, the proper mode of worship, the right way to live. The desire to know impelled the youth to seek the Lord in earnest prayer. One result of the answer to his prayer was the organization of the Church in Peter Whitmer's home on Tuesday, April 6, 1830. In that organization may be found the comprehension of the whole plan of man's salvation.

Now I wish to consider that organization as one evidence of his inspiration. Joseph Smith had neither support nor encouragement of any prominent men. He had no wealth. He had around him no influential legislators nor men who were styled the wisest thinkers of the time—elements surrounding these others that would be contributing factors in achieving success.—*IE*, 45:13, 54 (1942).

JOSEPH SMITH—HIS SOURCE OF KNOWLEDGE. Many years ago Joseph Smith, a mere boy between fourteen and fifteen years of age, declared that, in answer to prayer, he received a revelation from God. His declaration was simple but positive; and he was surprised when men doubted its truth. To him his claim was but the statement of a simple fact; to the Christian world it proved to be a lightning flash that, striking, weakened their religious structure from turret to foundation.

Two important elements in his first message were these: first, that God is a personal Being, who communicates his will to man; and second, that no creed in Christendom had the true plan of salvation.

The result of this declaration was his immediate ostracism from the religious world. In a very short time he found himself standing alone.

Alone—and unacquainted with the learning and philosophy of his day!

Alone—and unschooled in the arts and sciences!

Alone—with no philosopher to instruct him, no minister

to guide him! In simplicity and kindness he had hastened to them with his glorious message; in scorn and derision they had turned from him saying it was all of the devil; that there were no such things as visions or revelations in these days; that all such things had ceased with the Apostles; and that there would never be any more of them.

Thus he was left alone to embark upon the ocean of religious thought, having rejected every known vessel with which to sail and never having built one or even having seen one built himself. Surely if an impostor, the bark he could build would be indeed a crude one.

On the other hand, if that which he built possesses an excellence and superiority over that which the learned professors and philosophers had given to the world during the preceding hundreds of years, men will be forced, at least, to say in surprise, whence hath this man his wisdom!

It would appear, then, that though he seemed alone, he was alone only as was Moses on Sinai; as Jesus on the Mount of Olives. As with the Master, so with the prophet, his instructions came not through man-made channels but direct from God, the source of all intelligence. He says: "I am a rough stone. The sound of the hammer and chisel were never heard on me until the Lord took me in hand. I desire the learning and wisdom of heaven alone."

The result of this divine guidance was an assurance of the righteousness of what he taught and a fearlessness in proclaiming it. When Joseph Smith taught a doctrine, he taught it authoritatively. His was not the question whether it agreed with man's thoughts or not, whether it was in harmony with the teachings of the orthodox churches or whether it was in direct opposition. What was given to him he gave to the world irrespective of its agreement or disagreement, of its harmony or its discord with the belief of the churches, or the prevailing standards of mankind; and today, as we look through the vista of over one hundred years, we have a good opportunity of judging of the virtue of his teachings, and of concluding as to the source of his instruction.

It is interesting as well as profitable, too, to know how the advanced thought of today harmonizes with what he taught so authoritatively three-quarters of a century ago. The guiding spirit of his life was manifest right in the beginning and harmonizes with his wonderful declaration that God had spoken to him. In his own words it is this: "Whatever God requires is right, no matter what it is, although we may not see the reason thereof until long after the events transpire."

His claim to revelation from God, if established, leaves no doubt as to his authority to organize the Church of Jesus Christ upon earth, and to administer authoritatively the principles and ordinances thereof. Thus at the very inception of this great latter-day work was laid the immovable corner-stone of Christ's Church in this dispensation, viz., the authority to officiate in the name of Jesus Christ in things pertaining to his Church.

Each succeeding year of the past century has tended to vindicate, and the contending creeds of Christendom today confirm, the Prophet's teachings in regard to the necessity of divine authority to officiate in the things pertaining to God.

Not only did he receive guidance and instruction from the divine Head, but, once received, defended it with invincible resolution, and his "reliance on truth, on virtue and in God were most unfaltering."—*MS*, 85:88-90 (1923).

"WHENCE HATH THIS MAN HIS WISDOM?" When Joseph Smith received his first revelation, 1820, he was a mere youth. He was unschooled, untrained. Ten years later he organized the Church of Jesus Christ of Latter-day Saints. He was not yet thirty-nine years of age when he was martyred.

The harmony of his teachings with those taught by the Savior and his Apostles; the reasonableness of his assertion that men must be called of God to officiate in things pertaining to God; the complete organization of the Church; its government, laws, and wonderful adaptation to the needs and to the advancement of the human family—these and many other phases of this great latter-day work, when even only partly understood, lead thinking persons to ponder upon the source of the Prophet's wisdom.

The boldness of his assertions was remarkable. Many of these were in direct opposition to the belief of the orthodoxy of his day. He contradicted doctrines advocated by learned divines—a rash thing for an unlearned youth to do unless he had an assurance that he was right. If he had this assurance, whence did it come? Have time and intelligent thought vindicated him or condemned him?—*MS*, 85:104-105 (1923).

Other men with noble aspirations, with power and popularity, failed utterly in attempting to establish their ideals. Joseph Smith was favored intellectually by inspiration. Brother Joseph knew he was chosen of Almighty God to establish in this dispensation the Church of Jesus Christ which he, as Paul, declared to be the power of God unto salvation—social salvation, moral salvation, spiritual salvation.

You, the youth of Israel, bear the responsibility first of comprehending the significance and magnitude of this, the Lord's work; and, secondly, the responsibility of carrying it to a world now war-torn, but in which there are millions of honest hearts, yearning for better conditions than those under which they live.

If the people of today were to ask, as men did in the Savior's time, "Whence has this man wisdom?" we unhesitatingly declare: "He received it from on high."

> "Praise to the man who communed with Jehovah!
> Jesus anointed that Prophet and Seer.
> Blessed to open the last dispensation,
> Kings shall extol him, and nations revere."
> —*IE*, 45:55-56 (1942).

HARMONY OF THE PROPHET'S TEACHINGS WITH THOSE OF JESUS. Nobody can study critically and intelligently the restored gospel of Jesus Christ without being deeply impressed with the harmony of the teachings with those given by the Lord and Savior himself when he was on the earth with his disciples. Consider, for example, the Prophet's revelation concerning the Creator—God as an intelligent Being, one who is, as Jesus taught, "Our Father in heaven. . . . "

Joseph Smith's doctrine that Jesus Christ is the Only Begotten of the Father, the Savior of the world, is identical with the teachings of Jesus himself and his Apostles.

So also is his doctrine of the persistence of personality after death.

On these three fundamentals of religion, there can be little or no doubt about the harmony of the teachings of the restored Church with those of the Savior—the doctrine of God; his doctrine of sin and salvation; and the doctrine of immortality.

The same harmony is found in the teachings of other principles of the gospel such as faith, repentance, baptism, laying on of hands for the gift of the Holy Ghost, ordination to the priesthood, his teachings on "knowledge, temperance, godliness, brotherly kindness, charity," etc.—*IE*, 48:14-15 (1945).

THE SACRED GROVE. Meeting in these lovely surroundings I have been reminded of the quotation that "groves were God's first temples." I have felt that in this grove, we are in one of these temples. I cannot imagine any man's irreverently defacing one of these trees—pillars of that temple—any more than I can imagine a man's entering a house dedicated to God and desecrating the hardwood finish or other decorations of the Church. Truly, he is a vandal who would do such a thing. I mention this merely to emphasize the sacredness of these surroundings, the sacredness of this hallowed place.

Of all groves in the world, this, I think, may be designated as the most sacred, for it was here that the Father appeared in person and introduced his Beloved Son to the Prophet Joseph Smith, and you have witnessed that you know that event to be true. That knowledge is the greatest possession that can come to you.—*DNCS*, September 12, 1951, p. 2.

A PERSONAL TESTIMONY. I know that the gospel was restored through the Prophet Joseph Smith, by the Father and the Son, who are as real today in connection with the other world as my loved ones and yours.—*CR*, April 1949, p. 182.

THE PROPHET'S WORK IN ESTABLISHING THE CHURCH

PATTERNED AFTER CHRIST'S TEACHINGS. Charles A. Ellwood, author of *Man's Social Destiny*, declared that the religions of the future cannot be based upon historical Christianity, but must, in order to avoid misunderstanding, "go back to the teachings of Christ as recorded in the gospel."

Is it not significant that a man as young as was Joseph Smith, unlearned in regard to the social systems of his age or of any age in the United States, should have understood what leading thinkers realize today as the great need in religious government and instruction?

"The Church of Jesus Christ was organized in accordance with the order of the Church as recorded in the New Testament," said Joseph Smith. The practical and beneficent workings of this organization prove its divine authenticity.

REVELATION—THE BASIS. One outstandingly distinguishing feature of this Church is divine authority by direct revelation. The appearing of the Father and the Son to Joseph Smith is the foundation of this Church. Therein lies the secret of its strength and vitality. This is true, and I bear witness to it. That one revelation answers all the queries of science regarding God and his divine personality. Don't you see what that means? What God is, is answered. His relation to his children is clear. His interest in humanity through authority delegated to man is apparent. The future of the work is assured. These and other glorious truths are clarified by that glorious first vision.

MAN'S SOCIAL AND SPIRITUAL NEEDS SUPPLIED. Following such a declaration of divine guidance, the world may justifiably expect to find in the organization of the Church superior opportunities to supply the social and spiritual needs of man.

Now, you can prove that such is the case—that fraternity, education, judicial procedure, social and economic advantages are superior to those found in any other organization. We do not say that ourselves. Economists and sociologists so declare.

THE DIVINE AUTHENTICITY OF THE BOOK OF MORMON

FIVE TESTS. I was interested—and I will just present this briefly—in applying to this book, the coming forth of the Book of Mormon, a test that was given many, many years ago by a philosopher to a ruler who asked for direct evidence of the divinity of the Bible. This man said, "If an alleged fact will bear five marks, you can pretty well conclude that it is right, that its authenticity is established."

Let us apply these five marks to the Book of Mormon. They are: first, that the claim should be a sensible fact. By that he means that it is something that should appeal to one or more of the five senses. Second, there should be witnesses to the fact. Third, those witnesses should be reputable men or women, so that their testimonies would be unquestioned. Fourth, there should be monuments or memorials to that place; and fifth, those monuments or memorials should date back to the time of the incident.

First, a sensible fact: The Prophet Joseph claimed that the Book of Mormon was translated from plates on which were engravings placed there fourteen hundred years before that event. Plates are tangible things. They could be felt. Therefore the first claim is established, so far as the first test is concerned.

Second, there should be witnesses to it. In the Book of Mormon, we can read the testimony of Oliver Cowdery, of David Whitmer, and of Martin Harris, who said they saw those plates and signed this declaration.

The second mark—and they signed their names, Oliver Cowdery, David Whitmer, Martin Harris. Not only those three, but later eight others saw the plates.

Now the third mark is whether those men were reputable. Did they tell the truth? Or were they conniving with somebody to create a hoax upon humanity?

No person can with accuracy accuse any of those witnesses of unreliability, and each was true to his testimony to his death.

The next mark: monuments or memorials: The Book of Mormon itself is the memorial. The date when the plates were brought forth, the date when the manuscripts were taken to the printer may be verified, and when a few years ago, the monument to Moroni was erected there at Palmyra, I heard one of the justices in New York state bear testimony to the witness that he as a boy heard his father tell about when these men, Oliver Cowdery and Martin Harris, particularly Oliver Cowdery, carried the manuscript to the printing office which stands today there on the streets of Palmyra, where nearby stands the monument to Moroni, and we participated in its dedication a few years ago. That those monuments (or the fifth mark) date back to the event is evidenced by the testimony of this justice, and others, who remember, through their parents and their grandfathers, and the events themselves.

It is a physical fact, a sensible fact, there were witnesses to it, the reliability of those witnesses is established, there are monuments and memorials to it, and those monuments and memorials date back to the event itself.—*DNCS*, July 9, 1952, p. 2.

THE THREE WITNESSES

Oliver Cowdery. Oliver Cowdery was a young schoolteacher. He signed his name to his testimony under oath, for God commanded him to do it. That is more sacred than putting your hand on your Bible and swearing to tell the truth. In the course of events, Oliver Cowdery did not sustain the Prophet in certain Church procedures, and fell out of harmony with his leader, the details of which we cannot take time to consider here. He was excommunicated from the Church. Had there been collusion, then would have been the time to confess and proclaim it and by so doing expose any chicanery or fraud. This he did not do.

Following his excommunication Oliver Cowdery practised law. During the ten years he was away from the Church he maintained that his testimony was true; for example, on one occasion an opposing lawyer accused him of having signed his name to a document stating that an angel appeared to him and showed him the plates from which the Book of Mormon was translated. Oliver Cowdery replied:

"May it please your honor and gentlemen of the jury, this I say, I saw the angel and heard his voice—how can I deny it? It happened in the daytime when the sun was shining bright in the firmament; not in the night when I was asleep. That glorious messenger from heaven, dressed in white, standing above the ground, in a glory I have never seen anything to compare with—the sun insignificant in comparison—and this Personage told us if we denied that testimony there is no forgiveness in this life nor in the world to come. Now how can I deny it—I dare not; I will not!"

To the end of his earthly life, Oliver Cowdery was true to the testimony of the visit of the angel, to his having seen the plates from which the Book of Mormon was translated.

THE TESTIMONY OF DAVID WHITMER TO JAMES H. MOYLE. David Whitmer, too, was excommunicated because he was out of harmony. Did he ever deny his testimony? There is one encyclopedia which falsely states that he did. There is ample evidence that he maintained the truth to the last. I am going to give you the evidence of one whom I knew personally— Elder James H. Moyle, father of Henry D. Moyle.

Several months before Elder Moyle's death, Sister McKay and I were guests at a party given by Brother Henry D. Moyle whose father, during the evening, addressed the company and gave us directly his experience with David Whitmer. The following in substance is the testimony we heard Elder Moyle give on that occasion:

"From my boyhood I had read the Book of Mormon, and during my study of the same, found in it nothing but that which is virtuous, pure, and ennobling—a great and wonderful history of a people who lived on this continent in former ages. I was always interested in utilizing such opportunities as were given me to demonstrate its divinity, to know whether or not I might be deceived, and whether my parents, grandparents, and friends were likewise deceived. Therefore on my way home from school in 1885, I took advantage of the opportunity to visit David Whitmer, another of the Three Witnesses, then an old gray-haired man, bowed in years and expecting almost any time the summons to call him thence to his eternal reward.

"As I left the train in the little village of Richmond, Missouri, I inquired of those whom I met: What kind of man is David Whitmer? From all I received the same response, that he was a good citizen, an honest man, and that he was highly respected in the community. I went to his humble home, and I told him of my origin, my belief, and as a young man starting out in life I wanted to know from him, older than my grandfather, what he knew about the Book of Mormon, and what about the testimony he had published to the world concerning it.

"He told me in all the solemnity of his advanced years, that the testimony he had given to the world, and which was published in the Book of Mormon, was true, every word of it, and that he had never deviated or departed in any particular from that testimony, and that nothing in the world could separate him from the sacred message that was delivered to him.

"I still wondered if it was not possible that he could have been deceived. I wondered if there was not something in the psychological operation which some offer as the cause of these miraculous declarations and by which he could have been deceived—although there were three witnesses present besides the Prophet Joseph Smith, who saw and heard the same mighty and solemn truths; so I induced him to relate to me, under such cross examination as I was able to interpose, every detail of what took place.

"He described minutely the spot in the woods, the large log that separated him from the angel, and that he saw the plates from which the Book of Mormon was translated, that he handled them, and that he did hear the voice of God declare that the plates were correctly translated. I asked him if there was any possibility for him to have been deceived, and that it was all a mistake, but he said: 'No.' I asked him, then, why he had left the Church. He said he had not, but the Church had left him.

"He said that his faith in the fundamental principles of the gospel, which had been revealed prior to the year 1835, had never been changed; that he was still devoted to them and believed in them just as much as he ever did, and was trying to live those principles and exemplify them in his life. He said he knew Joseph Smith was a prophet of God, and that through him had been restored the gospel of Jesus Christ in these latter days. To me this was a wonderful testimony." (Elder James H. Moyle.)

MARTIN HARRIS. After many years' absence from the Church, Martin Harris went west and in one of the general conferences of the Church bore his testimony in the Salt Lake Tabernacle. In my early childhood and youth I heard my mother testify that she and Father heard Martin Harris bear testimony to the divinity of the Book of Mormon.

The last five years of his life were spent at Clarkston near Cache Junction, Utah. His body is buried at that place, and a granite tombstone is erected on which he is designated as one of the Three Witnesses to the Book of Mormon. Many of you, as I, have visited the farm, part of which he mortgaged for three thousand dollars in order to pay for the printing of the Book of Mormon.

There you have your witnesses and their reputability. —*DNCS*, September 12, 1951, p. 4.

CHAPTER 8

THE NATURE AND MISSION OF THE CHURCH

WHAT IS THE CHURCH?

AN INSTITUTION FOR SERVICE. The Church is a means of rendering in order and wisdom mutual service. Jesus Christ is its author and the divine head. He himself, while in mortality, was the personification and exemplification of brotherhood and spirituality, and it is he who says to you and to all the world, "Learn of me, and listen to my words; walk in the meekness of my Spirit, and you shall have peace in me." (D. & C. 19:23.)—CR, October 1936, p. 105.

MORE THAN A PROTESTANT BODY. At one time it grieved me to know that this Church was not numbered among Protestant churches. But now I realize that the Church of Jesus Christ is more than a protest against the errors and evils of Catholicism. This Church was established in the only way in which the Church of Jesus Christ can be established—by direct authority from God. Thus founded, it invites the whole world to come to a Church recognized by God himself, and which offers every advantage that the human mind, the emotions, and desires may contemplate in the fulfilling of the individual mission on this earth. "It is an ever-broadening wave of direct personal influence, destined ultimately to touch and transform all men, so that they, like Jesus, shall become Godlike." "Mormonism," as true Christianity, "subdues selfishness, regulates the passions, subordinates the appetites, quickens the intellect, exalts the affections. It promotes industry, honesty, truth, purity, kindness. It humbles the proud, exalts the lowly, upholds the law, favors liberty, is essential to it, and would unite men in one great brotherhood."—CR, April 1927, p. 105.

MORE THAN AN OFFSHOOT OF SOCIAL FERMENT. Suppose that the Son of Man said to mankind in the present age, "What seek ye?" What would be the answer? Many would say: We seek pleasure; some, wealth; others, fame and power; but the most thoughtful would answer, We are seeking the light of the ages, as mankind has ever sought. We are seeking a social Utopia. We want a society in which we may be re-relieved of some of the ills of mankind, free from the troubles and toils of life.

With every progressive age of the world, intellectual, noble-minded leaders have sought for a better way of living than that which was current. The good life, a social Utopia, has been the quest of the ages. To sense the need of reform has been easy; to achieve it has been difficult and often well-nigh impossible. Ideas and suggestions proposed by the wisest of men have seldom been practical, often fantastical; yet in most cases the world in general has been made better by the disseminating of new ideas, even though the experiments proved failures at the time. In this respect the century just past has been no exception.

The first half of the nineteenth century was marked by a general feeling of social unrest. Observant people became dissatisfied with social and economic conditions, and thinking men sought for remedial changes. In France, early in the century, the fanciful theories of Charles Fourier were circu-lated. He attempted to outline the future history of our globe and of the human race for eighty thousand years. Today his books aren't even read. Robert Owen founded a com-mercial society at New Harmony, Indiana. Although sup-ported by a fortune he had amassed by intelligent and frugal efforts, and although he was encouraged by the Duke of Kent, who became his patron, his scheme for the betterment of mankind came to naught in 1827. He returned to England where he tried several similar experiments with the same result.

George Ripley, a Unitarian minister, conceived a plan of "plain living and high thinking." He had as his associates such able men as Nathaniel Hawthorne, Charles A. Dana, afterward Assistant Secretary of War in the United States, and John S. Dwight. Ripley's impulse was really religious rather than economic, and "was due to a kind of monastic desire for withdrawal from a sordid world rather than a desire for a new society." He and his associates became the founders of what was known as the Brook Farm, a "Great Experiment" as it was called, to make the world an agreeable place to live in. It came to an end in 1846.

"Some of these Colonies" writes Phillip Russell, "were religious in purpose, others educational, and still others economic; but all, including Brook Farm, were social symptoms—rashes and growths indicating a sick and strained America."

It has been charged by a cynical writer that the Mormon Church was but one more excrescence of the fermenting body politic of this religious-social reaction. But in considering the Church as a social organization having as one object, at least, the amelioration of social ills, and the advancement of mankind, it is well to keep in mind at the outset these other facts:

First: That Joseph Smith undoubtedly had never heard of Fourier's phalanxes, the Owen experiment, nor any other scheme, religious or economic, for the bettering of social conditions;

Second: That the six original members were practically unknown, were financially poor, and had no political or social standing; and

Third: That Joseph Smith did not organize the Church by man's wisdom but by divine direction, "in accordance with the order of the Church as recorded in the New Testament."

This organization has survived financial panics, social upheavals, and religious turmoil, and today conforms to the best concepts of sociologists as a means of supplying the highest needs of mankind.—CR, April 1930, pp. 78-80.

A COMPLETE SOCIAL UNIT. Do you tell me that that young boy comprehended out of his own wisdom such a complete social unit?

One day a man, standing on the deck of a ship sailing from the north of Africa to Singapore, addressed a Mormon elder and said: "You say your Church is divine. Then there must be found in it the answer to every human need."

"Yes," said the young man, "you are right. It should be found."

In the conversation that followed they named as essential needs the following:

1. Brotherhood and fraternity.
2. Educational opportunities.
3. A judicial system.
4. Opportunity for social betterment.

In the Church the priesthood quorums and auxiliary organizations offer fellowship, brotherhood, and religious instruction to men, women, and children.

What about education? Turn to one of those early revelations and find that that boy—may I keep calling him so?—later said: "We are saved only as fast as we gain knowledge and wisdom." And again: "No man can be saved in ignorance." Then glimpse the opportunities for education in our schools, in the quorums, in the auxiliaries, for the education of the young, the middle-aged, and the old.

Another was the judicial features. Included in this are the ward teachers, whose duty it is to visit the members of the Church to see that no iniquity exists, no backbiting or evil speaking; it is their duty, furthermore, to see that people are not in want of food or clothing, and to report to the bishopric and the Relief Society, and have that want, if found, supplied. That is really their first duty; but they are also arbitrators. What did Joseph Smith know about arbitration? You and I now hear a great deal about it. Woodrow Wilson tried to establish a court of arbitration for the purpose of preventing war.

Over a hundred years ago that principle was placed in the Church, and you will find it in the Doctrine and Covenants, written a few years after that boy was ridiculed.

The next step in the judicial system is the bishopric's trial, the high council, the traveling high council [the Council of the Twelve Apostles], the final appeal to the First Presidency—a perfect judicial unit.

The last mentioned by this traveler was the need of economic and social advantages. In this matter tithing and fast offerings might be named as means to supply the financial needs. Then picture the division of the Church into wards and stakes, a ward a church in miniature, a stake a church in miniature. An organization established not by Joseph Smith, but by God the Father; for I cannot, friends, believe that that young obscure boy, uneducated, with the meagre advantages for learning such as then existed in his community, could of his own wisdom establish an organization which has stood the test of over a century, when these other wise attempts by honest and sincere men failed! To it all I have but one answer, and that is that that boy, who will be associated with this countryside for all time, did receive inspiration from on high.—*DNCS*, August 31, 1935, p. 6.

A MODEL OF GOVERNMENT. Considered politically the world is upset at the present time in its opinion as to the best form of government. We are just witnessing the downfall of monarchies. Rising from these monarchial ruins have come democracy as exemplified chiefly in Great Britain in her dominions and in the United States and the dictatorship of the proletariat as in Soviet Russia. It is apparent that men are seeking for a better form of government than most nations now have. Will they find it in the government by a dictator or in the government by the people, or in a combination of both?

One clear writer, Mr. Kirkpatrick, the sociologist, says that "Efficiency and progress are favored when the government is such that the local community has a great deal of responsibility of its own affairs and the central government has final authority to introduce those institutions and rules of procedure that have been shown to be permanently useful."

Now, my fellow workers and thinking honest men of the world, take that fundamental definition of government and see how admirably the Church of Jesus Christ conforms to it. A careful analysis of the organization of the Church reveals the fact that it embodies all the strength of a strong central government and every virtue and necessary safeguard of a democracy.

First, it has the authority of priesthood without the vice of priestcraft, every worthy man being entitled to a place and a voice in the governing quorums.

Second, it offers a system of education, universal and free in its application—the safety valve, the very heart and strength of a true democracy.

Third, it offers a judicial system that extends justice and equal privileges to all alike applicable to the poor and to the millionaire.

Fourth, in its ecclesiastical groupings of stakes and wards and branches and districts, efficiency and progress are enhanced inasmuch as every local group attends to its own affairs, and yet each is so closely united with the central government that every mode of procedure proved useful and beneficial to the people can be adopted without delay for the good of the entire group.

Truly, from the standpoint of enhancing efficiency and progress, the Church of Jesus Christ has that form of government which the nations today are seeking.

This is because it is patterned after that order which Christ himself established. On the sixth day of April 1830, the Prophet Joseph stated that the Church was organized after that order given in the New Testament.—*CR*, April 1930, pp. 80-81.

THE CHURCH AND THE SOCIAL ORDER. Brethren, the Church of Jesus Christ of Latter-day Saints has in it all that the world would require. I am not associating political government with our religious government; I am merely pointing out that system of organization established by the revelations of God to man.

The Church, established by divine inspiration to an unlearned youth, offers to the world the solution of all its social problems. It has stood the test of the first century successfully. In the midst of brilliant concepts of men in this twentieth century, who seek conscientiously for social reforms and who peer blindly into the future to read the destiny of man, the Church shines forth as the sun in the heavens around which other luminaries revolve as satellites of minor importance. Truly, it is the creator and preserver of man's highest values; its real task, the redemption of our human world. "It is the light of truth radiating everywhere in the world, and this light cannot fail to reveal to man, sooner or later, the divine ideals by which man should live."

God help us and qualify us for the mission of carrying to the world this light. May we labor even more zealously than heretofore for the establishment of a social order in which God's will shall be done on earth as it is in heaven— a kingdom of God which shall foster the brotherhood of man and acknowledge the Fatherhood of God.—*CR*, April 1930, pp. 82-83.

The Church of Jesus Christ of Latter-day Saints, accepting Christ as the revelation of God to man, believes that Jesus in his life and teachings reveals a standard of personal living and of social relations, which, if fully embodied in individual lives and in human institutions, would not only ameliorate the present ills of society but also bring happiness and peace to mankind.

If it be urged that during the past two thousand years so-called Christian nations have failed to achieve such a goal, we answer that all failure to do so may be found in the fact that they have failed to apply the principles and teachings of true Christianity.—*CR*, October 1937, p. 100.

THE CHURCH FOSTERS THE PRACTICAL THINGS OF LIFE. The Latter-day Saints are truly a people who aid one another in the productive life, a life that tends towards the salvation of the human being. By that salvation I do not mean just a place in the hereafter where all our cares and worries may cease, but a salvation that applies to the individual, to the family, and to society here and now. Through the gospel of Jesus Christ, and the perfect organization of the Church as revealed in this dispensation to the Prophet Joseph Smith, we are aiding one another *spiritually* by taking advantage of the many opportunities for service in the Church. We are fostering *brotherhood* by activity and association in priesthood quorums, in auxiliary associations, and in our social gatherings and ward reunions. We are aiding the young people in securing *wholesome pleasures*, by giving them sweet and wholesome enjoyment under the direction of the priesthood, as it serves particularly in the Mutual Improvement Associations of the Church as well as in other organizations and in the amusements under the direction of the authorities of the ward. The Church is aiding in *temporal matters*, and a practical benefit is resulting to the people today through the united efforts of the membership of the Church. In such ways, and many others, the Church fosters the practical things of life.—*CR*, April 1915, p. 103.

THE CHURCH FITS MEN FOR THE STRUGGLES OF LIFE. I am grateful for membership in a church whose religion fits men for the struggle with the forces of the world and which enables them to survive in this struggle.—CR, April 1914, p. 87.

THE MOST DISTINGUISHING FEATURE. If at this moment each one of you were asked to state in one sentence or phrase the most distinguishing feature of the Church of Jesus Christ of Latter-day Saints, what would be your answer? It occurs to me now that my answer would be this:

Divine authority by direct revelation.

There are those who claim authority through historical descent, others from the scriptures, but this Church stands out as making the distinctive claim that the authority of the priesthood has come directly from God the Father and the Son, by revelation to Joseph Smith.

Founded upon that principle, accepting it as absolute gospel, we have clearly defined in our minds some fundamental principles:

First, that God is a personal Being; that he has a spirit-personality.

The acceptance of divine authority by direct revelation also reveals to us the fact that Jesus Christ is the only begotten Son in the flesh, for the Father in appearing to Joseph Smith stated in definite words, "This is My Beloved Son. Hear Him!"

Correlated with that revelation is another fundamental fact, that the Lord is interested in his people, that the whole human family is related as his children, and he loves them, and that he has authorized men to officiate among the children of the world, to bring them back into his presence.

The Father and the Son appeared to Joseph Smith and restored authority to establish the kingdom of God on earth, and this is my testimony.

I also testify that divine authority rests in rich abundance upon him whom the Lord has chosen to stand at the head of this work at the present time. I am deeply grateful for the opportunity I have had to sit in council with President Grant and President Clark. I wish every person in this Church might have had the same opportunity to look into President Grant's noble spirit as I have; to know him as I have had the privilege to know him; to glimpse his unbounded generosity, his love for mankind, and particularly for those who are true and loyal to the Church; to realize how fearlessly he stands for right. If you realized these virtues more fully, I am sure that when you kneel down to pray there would be a note of thanksgiving in your heart and in your words which perhaps there has not been heretofore.

I would like to pay a tribute to President Clark, a man of sterling integrity, who loves his work above everything else in this world. He is loyal and true, sound and clear in judgment, a valiant servant of the Lord.

I should like you to know that there is a spirit of unity and oneness in the council of the First Presidency, the spirit for which Christ prayed just before he went into the Garden of Gethsemane: "That they all may be one; as thou, Father, art in me, and I in thee, that they also may be one in us: ... " (John 17:21.) And as he prayed on that occasion, so I pray now that that spirit of oneness may characterize the leading councils of the Church; nay, may I say, continue to characterize the leading councils of the Church, for I believe that there has not been a time in the history of our Church when there was more unity among these councils than at the present time. I pray that that spirit of oneness may spread throughout all the Church, that it may be characteristic of presidencies of stakes and high councils, bishoprics, ward teachers, and particularly of the quorums and auxiliaries of the Church, that they may all be one, to quote the Savior, as he and his Father are one. God help us to achieve this principle, that our faith in God and in his work may be unwavering, and our loyalty never doubted.—CR, April 1937, pp. 121-122.

THE SOURCE OF CHURCH VITALITY

THE SECRET OF GROWTH—INDIVIDUAL TESTIMONY. People today wonder wherein lies the secret of the growth, stability, and vitality of the Church of Jesus Christ. Those who are prejudiced when they come in our midst are convinced that there is something within the Church which those not of us do not comprehend. Recently a young lady from the East spent a few weeks among us, visiting friends. Evidently her mind was previously filled with prejudice against the people of Utah, particularly against the Church. But she went around with some of her friends who were actively engaged in Religion Class work, some who were actively engaged in Primary and others in Sunday School. One day when they returned from some of this regular work, she made this remark: "Well, there must be something in this Church or so many intelligent men and women would not be so actively engaged in it. Why, I almost feel that I want to enter in the work myself."

You, no doubt, have met people who, seeing perhaps some such demonstration as this of the strength of Israel, wonder how it is that this Church manifests such vitality and growth. The secret is this, that every true Latter-day Saint possesses individually the assurance that this is the work of God, the same power that gave Peter and John strength to stand before their accusers and declare openly and boldly in the Sanhedrin that "Jesus whom ye crucified is the power by which this man was made whole," that his name is the only name given among men by which they can be saved.

The secret lies in the testimony possessed by each individual who is faithful in the membership of the Church of Jesus Christ, that the gospel consists of correct principles. —CR, October 1912, p. 120.

THE NATURE OF INDIVIDUAL TESTIMONY. This testimony has been revealed to every sincere man and woman who has conformed to the principles of the gospel of Jesus Christ, obeyed the ordinances, and become entitled to and has received the Spirit of God, the Holy Ghost, to guide him. Every individual stands independent in his sphere in that testimony, just as these thousands of incandescent lamps which have made Salt Lake City in recent years so brilliant at night, each one of which stands and shines in its own sphere, yet the light in it is produced by the same power, the same energy, from which all the other lights receive their energy. So each individual in the Church stands independently in his sphere, independently in the knowledge that God lives, that the Savior is the Redeemer of the world, and that the gospel of Jesus Christ has been restored through the Prophet Joseph Smith.

Now it is given unto some, says the Lord in the Doctrine and Covenants, to know by the Holy Ghost that

Jesus is the Son of God and Savior of the world. It is to these I refer who stand firm upon the rock of revelation in the testimony that they bear to the world. But the Lord says further there are others to whom it is given to believe upon the testimony of others' words, that they may also receive salvation if they continue faithful. To all these, however, there comes the testimony also of daily experience. The Latter-day Saints throughout the world find confirmation of their testimony in every performance of duty. They know that the gospel teaches them to be better individuals, that obedience to the principles of the gospel makes them stronger men and truer women. Every day such knowledge comes to them, and they cannot gainsay it; they know that obedience to the gospel of Jesus Christ makes them better and truer husbands, true and honored wives, obedient children. They know that obedience to the principles of the gospel makes them in every respect ideal home builders; the ideal is there; they sense it in their minds; they cannot gainsay it; they know it; and they know that transgression of these principles will have the opposite effect upon their individual lives and upon their home life. They know that obedience to the gospel fosters true brotherhood and fellowship among mankind; they know that they are better citizens by virtue of obedience unto the laws and ordinances. So, as they go through their daily acts and apply religion in their vocation, the truth of the gospel becomes exemplified in their lives. Thus, with the testimony of the Spirit, the testimony of reason, and the testimony of daily experience, the Latter-day Saints throughout the world must stand impregnable.—*CR*, October 1912, pp. 120-121.

THE MISSION OF THE CHURCH

To Establish the Kingdom of God. Let us here and now express gratitude for the Church of Jesus Christ with quorums and auxiliaries specially organized to combat evil. It was established by divine revelation of God the Father and his Son Jesus Christ. Its glorious mission is to proclaim the truth of the restored gospel; to uplift society that people may mingle more amicably one with another; to create in our communities a wholesome environment in which our children may find strength to resist temptation and encouragement to strive for cultural and spiritual attainment; to make ineffective the influence of designing men who would make profit out of their fellows who are fallen so low as to be slaves to their appetites and passions—and who would fill their purses through the weaknesses of addicts to gambling, and the pitiable courtesan outcasts. The gospel is a rational philosophy that teaches men how to get happiness in this life and exaltation in the life to come.

The mission of the Church is to establish the kingdom of God upon the earth, which, in the words of Thomas Nixon Carver, "is not a mythical but a real kingdom. It is a body of people dominated by ideals of productivity, which is mutual service. We do not strive for the things which satisfy but for the moment and then leave a bad taste. We strive for the things which build us up and enable us and our children to be strong, to flourish, and to conquer. We strive to make ourselves worthy to receive the world by fitting ourselves to use the world more productively than others. We believe that obedience to God means obedience to the laws of nature, which are but the manifestations of his will; and we try by painstaking study to acquire the most complete and exact knowledge of that will, in order that we may conform ourselves to it."—CR, October 1948, p. 122.

GOD IS AT THE HELM. My brethren and sisters, as I contemplate the growth of the mission of the Church of Jesus Christ, I feel to exclaim with Browning: "God's in his heaven—all's right with the world!" Men and nations make errors and will be punished therefor, but ultimately the Lord will overrule the acts of men for the triumph of truth.—CR, October 1938, p. 130.

The Lord is not just an absent, faraway influence. He is a kind Father, solicitous of the welfare of his children, and ready and willing to hear and answer their call. The answer may be negative, as sometimes a wise parent gives a negative answer to the pleadings of a child, but he is ever ready to hear and to answer.

His Beloved Son stands at the head of this Church. It is his Church. Oh, may the world realize that in the very near future, open their minds to study the needs of the war-torn world, and see that those needs may be supplied by obedience to the principles of the revealed word of God.

This is Christ's Church. God help us all that we may be faithful members therein, and so live that others, seeing our good deeds, may be led to glorify our Father in heaven. —*CR*, October 1952, p. 129.

THE KINGDOM OF GOD A REALITY. What was the burden of Christ's teaching when he came among men? The first great proclamation was the announcement that the kingdom of God is at hand. "Repent for the kingdom of God is at hand." The forerunner, John the Baptist, preached that. He preached the coming of the Lord. He showed the position which the Lord would hold in that kingdom, and the Savior bore witness to it and preached the same. And what was the kingdom? Not a mythical, but a real kingdom; not only a feeling within, but also an outward expression of righteousness! *It was divine government among men.* That was what the Savior had in mind, the establishing of a divine government among men.—*CR*, October 1919, p. 76.

TO TRANSFORM SOCIETY. There are those in the world who say that jealousy, enmity, selfishness in men's hearts will always preclude the establishing of the ideal society known as the kingdom of God. No matter what doubters and scoffers say, the mission of the Church of Jesus Christ is to eliminate sin and wickedness from the hearts of men, and so to transform society that peace and good will will prevail on this earth.—*CR*, April 1941, p. 109.

SEEK FIRST THE KINGDOM. From among the sublime teachings of the Savior in the Sermon on the Mount, I quote the following:

"But seek ye first the kingdom of God, and his righteousness; and all these things shall be added unto you." (Matt. 6:33.)

This admonition and promise I have chosen for my theme at this time because it seems so aptly to epitomize generally the timely instructions given at this conference. Then, too, it expresses the ideal to which every man who holds the priesthood has subscribed. Again, if heeded, it will be the greatest and best safeguard to our sons who are called to serve their country. And, finally, I firmly believe that if rulers of nations followed that admonition, contention and war would be banished from among men.

What the kingdom of God is, is answered by the Prophet Joseph Smith as follows:

" . . . Whenever there has been a righteous man on earth unto whom God revealed his word and gave power and authority to administer in his name, and where there is a priest of God—a minister who has power and authority from God to administer in the ordinances of the gospel and officiate in the priesthood of God, there is the kingdom of God; . . . " (Joseph Fielding Smith, *Teachings of the Prophet Joseph Smith*, p. 271.)

Seeking first the kingdom means subordinating to the principles of the gospel all other aims and pursuits.

WHAT THE KINGDOM OF GOD IMPLIES. The term implies divine rule in the hearts and wills of men and in society. Man acknowledges a power and authority superior to his own. "It is not the arbitrary rule of a despotic Deity, but is based upon man's voluntary submission of his will to that of God's." On one occasion Jesus said, "The kingdom of God is within you." That is true, for it is in the heart of man that membership in the outward kingdom has its origin. Devotion and loyalty that spring thus from the heart "for the common Father of all mankind is the strongest and only universal bond that can bind all men together." Only such a group looking as one mind to heaven for guidance can eventually transform human society.

The kingdom of God implies also a universal brotherhood in which all men acknowledge God as their supreme Ruler and cherish the desire to obey his divine will.

THE PURPOSE OF THE CHURCH. The mission of the Church is to prepare the way for the final establishment of the kingdom of God on earth. Its purpose is, first, to develop in men's lives Christlike attributes; and, second, to transform society so that the world may be a better and more peaceful place in which to live.—*CR*, April 1941, p. 106.

SPECIFIC OBJECTIVES. The consummation of God's purposes is put in these words: " . . . this is my work and my glory —to bring to pass the immortality and eternal life of man." (Moses 1:39.) This divine purpose may be achieved by using the Church as a means of accomplishing the following specific objectives in the achievement of which lies a sufficient challenge for the brightest minds in the world:

First, *physical strength, virility, cleanliness.* When therefore you hear harping critics say that the Church Authorities overemphasize the Word of Wisdom, you may know that they have not studied very deeply the significance of the Word of Wisdom. Fundamentally, physical strength and virility are essential factors in the progress of humanity.

Second, *economic security.* When you hear a young man say we lay too much stress on tithing, you may know he does not realize the relation of tithing and fast offerings to the economic security of every man, woman, and child in the Church.

Third, *social justice.* Go into any quorum and see who are meeting there—your lawyers, your doctors, your farmers, all meeting on a social plane. In the Church of God every man and woman has equal privileges to every other man and woman.

Fourth, *spiritual enlightenment.* Cultivating the fruits of the Spirit which are love, joy, peace, kindness, longsuffering, and gentleness.

Now, if ever, is the time to make practical the gospel of Jesus Christ and to strive to live up to the principles of true Christianity.

The anchor of the young people is in the realization that the Church is established as a means of consummating God's purposes; and they realize, too, even if they have not thought it out as they will some day, that there is nothing in the world to compare with the Church of Jesus Christ as an effective organization in alleviating the ills of mankind.

And now, young people, thus anchored in the faith, and thus organized, we ask you to join the organizations in your wards, to heed the advice of the President of the Church, to affiliate with your quorums, with your auxiliary organizations, in your fast meetings, and there in these local groups express your thoughts, express your doubts, seek after the truth, apply measures that will appeal to those of your associates, and when you prove those measures to be effective and satisfying to the soul, then can the central organizations take those measures and adapt them to the whole as a universal benefit. In that way, and in that way only, will progress and efficiency be fostered. Don't stand out on the sidelines, and say, "This quorum is not doing its work," but get into the quorum and help it do its work. That is the way which God intends people to work in this Church, and it offers to you one of the best opportunities in the world.—CR, April 1934, pp. 23-24.

THE IDEAL OF MORMONISM. The first duty of the citizens of the kingdom is to live exemplary lives.

But as I have said, the betterment of the individual is only one aim of the Church. The complete ideal of Mormonism is to make upright citizens in an ideal society.—CR, April 1941, p. 107.

CHAPTER 9

THE CHURCH: A WORLD-WIDE INSTITUTION

TO ALL NATIONS

THE DIVINE COMMISSION. On a momentous occasion two thousand years ago eleven men assembled near a mountain in Galilee—eleven humble, obscure men who had been chosen and ordained Apostles of the Lord Jesus Christ. According to appointment these men met the resurrected Christ who made what to them must have been a startling declaration. They had been with their Master not yet three years and had been expressly enjoined by him to go not in the way of the Gentiles, to enter no city of the Samaritans, but to go rather to the lost sheep of the house of Israel. (See Matt. 10:5-6.) At this meeting, however, as his final parting instructions, he opened their eyes to the universality of the gospel by giving them this divine commission:

"Go ye therefore, and teach all nations, baptizing them in the name of the Father, and of the Son, and of the Holy Ghost:

"Teaching them to observe all things whatsoever I have commanded you: and, lo, I am with you alway, even unto the end of the world." (Matt. 28:19-20.)

In the restricted experience of these eleven disciples, the idea of preaching Christ and his saving doctrine to any but members of their own race germinated very slowly. Indeed, the Savior of men found it necessary to give another direct revelation to Peter, the chief Apostle, before even he fully realized that the Gentiles "should hear the word of the gospel, and believe."

THE SPREAD OF CHRISTIANITY. However, as the light of truth dawned in their hearts, these earnest followers set about to give the gospel to the world—" . . . simple men, with only the wind to bear them over the seas, with only a few pence in their pockets, and a shining faith in their hearts. They fell far short of their ideal; their words were twisted and mocked; and false temples were built over their bones, in praise of a Christ they would have rejected. And yet, by the light of their inspiration many of the world's loveliest things were created, and many of the world's finest minds inspired."

APOSTASY AND THE PROTEST. Three hundred years passed, and Christianity became the dominant religion of the most powerful nation in the world, and the persecuted became the persecutors. Pride and worldliness supplanted humility and faith. The church became corrupt. Doctrines of men supplanted the commandments of God; spiritual darkness enshrouded the nations of the world.

Later, courageous, God-fearing men began to protest against the evil practices of a corrupt clergy. The dawn of a spiritual awakening appeared, but none either claimed or received divine authority to reestablish the Church. Roger Williams, pastor of the oldest Baptist Church in America, resigned his position, because, said he, "There is no regularly constituted church on earth, nor any person authorized to administer church ordinances, nor can there be until new apostles are sent by the Great Head of the church for whose coming I am seeking."

RESTORATION. That authority came early in the nineteenth century by the personal appearance of the risen Lord. Again was given the divine injunction for authorized servants to be " . . . sent forth to the east and to the west, to the north and to the south," (D. & C. 42:63) that "every man might speak in the name of God the Lord, even the Savior of the world;

"That faith also might increase in the earth;

"That mine everlasting covenant might be established;

"That the fulness of my gospel might be proclaimed by the weak and the simple unto the ends of the world, and before kings and rulers." (Ibid., 1:20-23.)

THE WORLD-WIDE DESTINY UNFOLDS. Though the Church is still young and has had to struggle through persecution, mobocracy, drivings, poverty, misrepresentation by egotists, uninformed preachers, apostates, and by a prejudiced public sentiment, it is moving steadily forward toward its world-wide destiny. Almost immediately after the organization of the Church, the proclamation of the restored gospel began.

The land of China has been dedicated for the proclaiming of the gospel to her 450,000,000 people. Letters of appeal are coming from India. There are those who are praying that the way will soon be cleared for missions in Hungary, Italy, and Russia. Besides the three missions already established in South America, other countries in that land are beckoning for the gospel as Macedonia beckoned Paul and his companions.

As the Savior said to the eleven in Galilee and to all whom they appointed, so he says to his authorized servants today: Go ye therefore and make disciples of all nations, teaching them to observe all things whatsoever I have commanded. (See Matt. 28:19-20.)

Where, however, each missionary of old could speak to one person, the representatives of Christ today can speak to millions. A sentence uttered in an ordinary tone of voice can encircle the globe in less than a minute. The marvels and inventions of science today make it possible to spread the gospel as never before in the history of the world.

And what a message the Church has for this distracted world! "Its appeal," as Kent says of true Christianity, "is universal—to the rich and the poor, the strong and the weak, the learned and the ignorant. It proclaims God to be not only the one supreme Ruler of the universe, but the Father of each individual, a God of justice, yet a God of love, constantly watching over and guiding even the humblest of his children."

The Church, with its complete organization, offers service and inspiration to all. It is "pre-eminently a social religion." In quorums and auxiliaries it "aims by training the individual conscience and will, to establish a closely knit, world-wide fraternity." It is in no sense ascetic. Instead of taking men out of the world, it seeks to develop perfect, Godlike men in the midst of society, and through them to solve the problems of society."—*DNCS*, December 20, 1947, p. 4.

It matters not in what part of the globe the meeting is held, whether in the islands of the sea, in Japan, in Syria, in the Scandinavian countries, in England, Germany, France, Holland—wherever one meets a group of Latter-day Saints whose faith in the gospel of Jesus Christ is unwavering, there one finds the spirit of oneness, the spirit of love, the spirit of willing sacrifice for the good of humanity. God bless the Latter-day Saints all over the world that they may continue in that same spirit.—*CR*, April 1925, p. 11.

AN ENSIGN TO THE NATIONS

A LIGHT UNTO THE WORLD. "And even so I have sent mine everlasting covenant into the world, to be a light to the world, and to be a standard for my people, and for the Gentiles to seek to it, and to be a messenger before my face to prepare the way before me." (D. & C. 45:9.)

The Church of Jesus Christ of Latter-day Saints was scarcely one year old when that declaration was made through inspiration by the Prophet Joseph. He himself was but twenty-six years of age. It is a marvelous declaration, great in its pretension, comprehensive in its scope: " . . . mine everlasting covenant" (the gospel), is sent "into the world, *to be a light to the world, and to be a standard for my people, and for the Gentiles to seek to it, . . .* " (D. & C. 45:9.)

On Bedloe Island, at the entrance of New York harbor, there stands the Statue of Liberty, a light to the nations. What it has meant to thousands and hundreds of thousands of the downtrodden of Europe has been most graphically expressed by Israel Zangwill in that impressive production, *The Melting Pot.* I shall give a few words. David the emigrant, the little Russian Jew, is speaking:

"All my life America was waiting, beckoning, shining, the place where God would wipe away tears from off all faces. To think that the same great torch of Liberty which threw its light across all the seas and lands into my little garret in Russia is shining also for all those other weeping millions of Europe, shining wherever men hunger and are oppressed, shining over the starving villages of Italy and

Ireland, over the swarming, starving cities of Poland and
Galicia, over the ruined farms of Romania, over the shambles
of Russia. When I look at our Statue of Liberty, I just seem
to hear the voice of America crying: Come unto me, all ye
who are weary and heavy laden, and I will give you rest,
rest."

What that Statue of Liberty symbolizes to the oppressed
and downtrodden of Europe, the gospel of Jesus Christ is to
the world. Mormonism, so-called, has reared an ensign to the
nations and, with words as comprehensive as those I have
read in the revelation, invites the world to peace, to rest, to
contentment.

> "High on the mountain top
>   A banner is unfurled;
> Ye nations, now look up;
>   It waves to all the world;
> In Deseret's sweet, peaceful land—
>   On Zion's mount behold it stand!
>
> "Then hail to Deseret!
>   A refuge for the good,
> And safety for the great,
>   If they but understood
> That God with plagues will shake the world
>   Till all its thrones shall down be hurled."

And to whom does that ensign now wave? To what sort
of world does the beacon light of the everlasting gospel extend
its invitation? A new world, or rather a world struggling
to make itself new! The terrible war that has just passed was
but the birth pangs—and now the world is ready to be reborn.
"We stand at a creative moment in human history," says
Sherwood Eddy. "Never before has the whole world had the
chance to make all things new, old customs and contentions,
old rules and ruts, old traditions and enslavements have been
broken forever. We are living in the birth pangs of a world
struggling to be reborn, and the issues of our time will reach
into eternity."—CR, April 1920, pp. 114-115.

NOTHING TO CONCEAL. The Church of Jesus Christ has
nothing to conceal. It neither teaches nor practises anything

of which it is ashamed. It stoops to no secretive methods to obtain converts. Carrying the responsibility of proclaiming the fact that the gospel of the Redeemer in all its simplicity and power is restored to man, the Church seeks by every legitimate means to declare this message to the whole world. —MS, 85:728 (1923).

A WORLD-WIDE CHRISTIAN RELIGION. A more important question for us today is this: "Are the so-called Mormons true Christians and does the Church of Jesus Christ of Latter-day Saints contain the elements of a world-wide Christian religion?" It is my sincere belief and testimony that the Latter-day Saints commonly called Mormons are Christians in the truest and fullest sense of the term, and that this Church is world-wide in its comprehensiveness, in organization, and in its blessing and salvation of the human family. As true Christianity should and as it did in the days of the Savior, Mormonism combines the essential elements in the teachings of Israel's prophets, priests, and sages; and in accepting the Jehovah of the Old Testament as the Savior of mankind, it fulfils the noblest aspirations of the Hebrew race, thereby indicating a world-wide scope so far as Israel's people and Israel's God are concerned.

All that is "virtuous, lovely, or of good report, or praiseworthy" in the teachings of all the great religious teachers of mankind, teachings that today are influencing hundreds of millions of God's children, are comprehended in the ethical teachings of the Church of Jesus Christ.

Mormonism is an authoritative religion, yet at the same time the most thoroughly democratic Church on earth—a combination that is well worthy of serious thought. It emphasizes the universal bonds of human brotherhood. It seeks by training the individual conscience and will to establish a closely knit, world-wide fraternity. It glorifies humanity and all normal human relations. It is a spiritual force emanating from God himself.—CR, April 1927, pp. 104-105.

THE RESPONSIBILITIES OF WORLD-WIDE ACTIVITY. Most earnestly do I hope that we shall never lose the great conviction that the world is our field of activity. Can you think of anything more potent in moving a people to action?

But what a responsibility this entails of leading good men and good women all over this world to know God, and to know what their mission is on earth! Fathers and mothers, fellow workers, do you fully realize today what it means to assume the responsibility of carrying the message of peace and good will to all men? The base of our operations must be here at home. Neglect your duty here, and all you undertake abroad will be compromised because people can rightfully ask: What do you do at home? What life are you living at home? Every elder who goes abroad to preach this gospel must first live the gospel to the best of his ability and have a conviction in his heart that he is preaching the truth. True, at first this testimony may be somewhat indefinite; but all our children have it to some extent. They breathe it as they breathe the mountain air, but they often neglect to define it, to express it in the plane of consciousness. It is the duty of presidents of stakes, bishops of wards, to make definite in the minds of missionaries this testimony of the truth. Through study, service, humility, and prayer, this testimony will increase.—*CR*, April 1927, p. 106.

THE FUTURE OF THE CHURCH. What of the future? "Come and see." "Life abundant, beauteous, laughing life," more brotherhood, securer peace, better social relations are some of the fruits of Mormonism as seen by the eye of faith.

"Th' increasing prospect tires our wand'ring eyes,
Hills peep o'er hills, and Alps on Alps arise!"

—Pope, *Essay on Criticism*.

Can you not see many nations yet to hear the truth—Jew as well as Gentile! India and China both awakening, Russia but in the throes of the birth of a new nation, a new religious freedom it must be. God will overrule it, for that people must hear the truth, and the truth in simplicity. Truly there is much for the Church to do in the coming century! —*CR*, April 1930, p. 82.

We are grateful for the blessings of the Lord to his Church in all the world, and for the assurance of his divine guidance and inspiration.—*CR*, April 1952, p. 11.

THE UNITING OF CHRISTIAN CREEDS

THE NECESSITY OF UNITING. There is permeating Protestant Christendom today, a keen realization of the necessity
of uniting all creeds into one great Christian church. The
petty differences and distinctions now existing among the
various creeds professing the name of Christ are recognized
as barriers to the fulfilment of the hope that Christianity shall
become the world-wide religion.

But the question of how to break down these differentiat-
ing barriers is yet unanswered, and the difficulties encountered
in trying to accomplish the desired unity seem insurmount-
able.

"The conviction," says *The Christian Century*, "that our
denominational system is fundamentally defective is well
known. The sincere desire of its editors and many of its
contributors is to help in finding a remedy for these defects,
and to assist communities on which the futility of their denominational organizations has forced the issue of finding a
remedy, is also well known. It is not surprising that the
mail brings many letters to this office from eager and more
or less distressed spirits whose bewilderments and perturbations
we would fain dispel. We sometimes long for ready formulas
by which these seekers might be shown the way. But evils
so serious do not yield to light and easy remedies."

One such letter containing a sincere appeal for help is
as follows:

"I have been reading with profit in your paper what
you say concerning community churches. We are about ready
to unite here; but we technically do not know how to do it.
We are bothered: how to break away from our denomination
at large; or how to remain tied loosely to it; what to do with
benevolent monies, etc., etc. Can you direct me how to find
out, or have you any suggestions for us? We must build singly
if not together; but I am anxious to unite our two churches.
I would be willing to lose my job if necessary in order to bring
this about. However, the spirit is ripe; but how shall we
begin? Would it be best to continue some denominational
attachment? We would be most grateful for any help you
can furnish in this great work.—*A Subscriber*."

To these questions *The Christian Century* says: "We

don't know." Neither does it offer a solution of the problems of the contribution and the disbursing of funds; of the securing of ministers; of the sort of church the community proposes to form, etc., etc. Nor will these problems be solved until the cause that produced so many conflicting sects shall have been recognized and removed.

MARKS OF THE GREAT UNITED CHURCH. Once this reason for the existing disunion throughout Christendom is recognized, and with it the acceptance of the fact that Jesus Christ, the author of our salvation, is the only one who has the authority and right to establish his Church among men—once the ministers of the sectarian churches of so-called Christianity are absolutely honest with themselves and mankind, and will acknowledge the fact that they have not been divinely authorized to officiate in the name of Jesus Christ nor to administer any ordinances in his Church—once they accept the dictates of reason, and the teaching of the scriptures, both of which give the conviction that a man must be called of God to officiate in the ordinances of the gospel—then, and not till then, will the great difficulty be overcome of establishing one great united Christian church upon the earth.

Such a church will be called the Church of Jesus Christ.

Such a church will be the same in all essential principles and ordinances as that which Christ established when he was upon the earth.

Such a church will have apostles, prophets, pastors, teachers, evangelists, deacons, and other necessary helps in government.

In that church there will be never a question as to the source of the finances necessary for its temporal needs; never a question as to who shall receive the funds nor as to how and by whom they shall be dispersed. All this will be in accordance with the law of God.

In that church there will never be a question as to the relation of one official to another, no matter how great its numbers nor how unlimited its subdivisions; perfect order and harmony will always exist because the organization is of divine origin.

In that church men will not preach for money nor divine for hire; but every worthy man will be a priest, a servant of the people, a preacher and teacher of righteousness; every worthy woman will have an opportunity to render service in a perfectly organized capacity.

In that church the millionaire and the man of humble earnings, the professional man, the artisan, and the laborer will all meet on common ground, and study, in equality and brotherhood, the divine principles of happiness, progress, and eternal life.

In that church the poor need not and should not suffer from a lack of sufficient food, clothing, and shelter, because ample provision will be made for the physical, the temporal, as well as the spiritual salvation of every human being.

In short, the Church of Jesus Christ, the universal church, will acknowledge the fatherhood of God and make not only possible but practical the universal brotherhood of man.

That church is already upon the earth, established by God the Eternal Father and his Son Jesus Christ, by whose divine authority men are now commissioned to officiate in all the ordinances of the gospel. The necessity of its having been so established by direct revelation was shown to the Prophet Joseph Smith in the words of the Savior who declared that the contending "creeds were an abomination in his sight."

Until the authority of the Redeemer is acknowledged, in vain will so-called Christian sects seek for unity; and in vain will they strive to regain the power they once held over the minds and hearts of the children of men. In vain, also, will they fight against the Church of Jesus Christ, which is destined to grow until it fills the whole earth, until every knee shall bow and every tongue confess that Jesus is the Christ.—*MS*, 85:248-250 (1923).

THE ROAD TO UNION. Another difficulty, and one frequently entertained by unprejudiced minds, is the idea that "one church is as good as another. They are all trying to do the will of God, and will eventually lead to his kingdom." The thought is summarized in the timeworn phrase, "All roads lead to Rome."

On one occasion, when Paul was about to be scourged, he said to the centurion, "Is it lawful for you to scourge a man that is a Roman, and uncondemned?"

Hesitating before administering his first blow, the scourger called the chief captain, who asked:

" . . . art thou a Roman?"

"Yea."

"With a great sum obtained I this freedom."

"But," answered Paul, "I was free born." (See Acts 22:25-28.)

This incident shows two means of obtaining Roman citizenship. There were many in Rome, who, not entitled to citizenship by birth, could neither purchase it nor obtain it by any other means.

By traveling any of the many roads leading to that great medieval city, they could reach it, enter it, and even participate in some of its advantages and far-famed glory; but before they could become citizens, they had to comply with the prescribed conditions.

So it is with the church and kingdom of God. All churches and all creeds contain some good which lead toward the kingdom of our Father; but to become a citizen of that kingdom everyone must conform to the requirements made by the King. Indeed, there is only *one way* in which entrance into the Church of Jesus Christ may be obtained, and that is the way marked out by Jesus Christ, the Lord. "I am the way, the truth, and the life: no man cometh unto the Father, but by me." (John 14:6.)

The means of obtaining citizenship in the Church of Jesus Christ are very explicit; so clear, indeed, that it is surprising that so many seemingly intelligent and well-read people will arrogate to themselves the thought that they can gain entrance by other and various means.

There is only one who has the right to prescribe the means of human salvation. Surely he spoke not meaninglessly when he said what is necessary to citizenship in his kingdom.

Note how explicit are his words: "Except a man be born again, he cannot *see* the kingdom of God." (*Ibid.* 3:3.) In explanation of this seemingly enigmatical saying to Nicodemus, the Master continued:

"Except a man be born of water and of the Spirit, he *cannot* enter into the kingdom of God." (*Ibid.* 3:5.)

Evidently Peter, the chief Apostle, attached significance to this requirement as an essential means of gaining not only citizenship in the Church, but also salvation in the kingdom of God, for, when the multitude pricked in their hearts cried out, "Men and brethren, what shall we do?" he answered and said:

"Repent, and be baptized every one of you in the name of Jesus Christ for the remission of sins, and ye shall receive the gift of the Holy Ghost." (Acts 2:38.) Thus are given the four requirements, the four essential principles and ordinances, obedience to which are essential to membership in Christ's Church: viz., faith, repentance, baptism, and the reception of the Holy Ghost. . . .

There are many roads being pointed out as leading to the kingdom of God, but there is only one gate through which entrance and citizenship therein may be obtained. Christ plainly pointed this out when he was among men; and he has again revealed it through the Prophet Joseph Smith. The way is simple and easy to find, and as infinitely sublime as it is eternal.

There are many roads in so-called heathen and Christian lands leading sincere people *toward* the church and kingdom of God, but those who would participate in the privileges and blessings of citizenship therein must obey the principles and ordinances of the gospel of Jesus Christ.

" . . . wide is the gate, and broad is the way, that leadeth to destruction, and many there be which go in thereat:

"Because strait is the gate, and narrow is the way, which leadeth unto life, and few there be that find it."—(Matt. 7:13-14.)—*MS*, 85:168-170 (1923).

CHAPTER 10

MISSIONARY WORK

THE CALL TO MISSIONARY SERVICE

A WORLD-WIDE COMMISSION. We are living in what may be the most epoch-making period of all time. Scientific discoveries and inventions, the breaking down of heretofore approved social and moral standards, the uprooting of old religious moorings, all give evidence that we are witnessing one of those tidal waves of human thought which periodically sweep over the world and change the destiny of the human race. I call attention to world conditions because the mission of the Church of Jesus Christ is world-wide.—CR, October 1947, p. 116.

The world is full of honorable men and women who, as those men who accosted Peter on the day of Pentecost, desire to know what to do—what to believe.—CR, October 1937, p. 115.

PHILOSOPHY OF THE MISSIONARY SYSTEM. Nearly every member of the Church understands that there are two general ecclesiastical divisions of the Church of Jesus Christ; one made up of the organized stakes and wards; the other, of the missionary work.

It is of this second division I wish to speak.

Many of us fail to realize the value and potent possibilities of this great branch of Church activity.

1.—As an example of voluntary service in the cause of the Master, it is unexcelled.

2.—As an incentive to clean living among youth, as a contributing factor to character building, its influence is immeasurable.

3.—As an educative force and uplifting influence upon our communities, its effect is clearly manifest.

4.—As a contributing factor to a better understanding among nations and to the establishing of international friendship, it wields a significant influence.

5.—As it is the purpose of the Almighty to save the individual, not to make him a mere cog in the machinery of the state, the missionary service works most harmoniously in the consummation of this eternal plan!

"Remember the worth of souls is great in the sight of God;

"And if it so be that you should labor all your days in crying repentance unto this people, and bring, save it be one soul unto me, how great shall be your joy with him in the kingdom of my Father!

"And now, if your joy will be great with one soul that you have brought unto me into the kingdom of my Father, how great will be your joy if you should bring many souls unto me!"(D. & C. 18:10, 15-16.)—*CR*, Sept.-Oct. 1949, p. 117.

THE CHRISTIAN MESSAGE FOR ALL NATIONS. Springing out of this sense of responsibility to bear witness to all people, is the desire to Christianize the world. Some Protestant ministers do not like to consider Mormons Christians. Be that as it may, the fact remains that the paramount desire in every Latter-day Saint's heart is to make all people Christians, and that is a conviction second only in power and urgency to the testimony that God has spoken in this dispensation. "Go ye . . . and teach all nations, . . . " said the Savior to his disciples. (Matt. 28:19.) "For the promise is unto *you, and to your children, and to all that are afar off,* even as many as the Lord our God shall call." This Peter said on the day of Pentecost. (Acts 2:39.) " . . . proclaim these things unto the world, . . . " said the Prophet Joseph (D. & C. 1:18) through inspiration in this age, "That faith also might increase in the earth;" (*ibid.* 1:21) "That mine everlasting covenant might be established." (*Ibid.* 1:22.)

I know of no other religious conviction that has affected the daily life of a people more potently than this desire to have every nation hear the message of this latter-day gospel of peace. Very few indeed are the homes in the Church that have not been influenced by it.—*CR*, April 1927, pp. 102-103.

IS THE MISSIONARY PROJECT REALISTIC? But does the world need Christianizing? Our Protestant brethren say, "Why don't you send your elders out to the heathen, why go to Christian nations?" As I have said, our mission is to the whole world. We believe so-called Christian nations need the message as well as the so-called heathen lands, and Christian ministers by their own statements confirm this belief; for example: In an issue of *The Literary Digest* under a glaring heading, "Tolling the Knell of Protestantism," one Reverend Herbert Parrish wrote that it is his conviction that "the sooner Protestantism disappears from American life the better. Its narrow sectarian spirit, fostering division, incapable of a large synthesis of values, of unity, unfits it to represent our national religious life. . . . As a moral guide it is superficial, depending on the exterior force of state legislation to effect the redemption of the race. As a mystical experience it is sentimental, without intelligence, and with narrow vision. As a teaching force it is vague, negative and uncertain. As an organization it is illogical and chaotic." (*The Literary Digest*, April 12, 1927, p. 34.) That I consider a very severe arraignment of Protestantism by a Protestant pastor. I do not know him nor do I know by what authority he speaks.

Probably a more trustworthy and authentic authority is Harry Emerson Fosdick, one of the leading thinkers in our nation today, who, commenting on the need of modern religious leadership, writes:

"No society ever has been healthy whose religious life was unhealthy. Even those who are impatient of contemporary formulations of faith, those who are outside the churches, and alienated from their denominational loyalty, should still be deeply concerned about the fortunes of religion. A society which, providing for the future, builds great factories, immense railroad systems, and even innumerable schools, but does not care whether the future has a wholesome religious life, is playing a fatally short-sighted game.

"In view of this fact the situation which we face is serious. *Much of our contemporary Christianity is not making people better, but worse. It accentuates bitterness, brings out meanness, sanctions ignorance and bigotry, divides those who might otherwise be brotherly, and lapses from its high possibilities into a force for spiritual deterioration and decay.*"

Are not these statements and others that might be given, sufficient answer regarding the need of working for the Christianizing of the world?—*CR*, April 1927, p. 104.

PERSONAL DEVELOPMENT NOT THE END. At the dinner table today friends commented upon the number of our missionaries in different parts of the world. What a culture they bring into our community! One guest had two sons in Germany. He mentioned another in France, and another in one of the missions in the United States. Another guest mentioned two in Norway, one in France, one in Argentina, and so they are in different parts of the world.

What a wonderful thing it is; but, brethren, missionaries are called not for individual blessings. They are called to preach the gospel, to represent the Church. The blessings come inevitably as they do their duty, and it is most unfortunate if a young man leave your ward to represent the Church who does so unworthily. It injures him, breaks his parents' hearts, reflects upon the ward, and it might blight some souls who otherwise would come into the Church.—*CR*, October 1948, p. 175.

HOW TO PREACH CHRISTIANITY. The best way to preach, my dear fellow workers, is by example. Are you following Christ's admonition to pray to the Father and teach your children to pray, that godliness, reverence for God and his work, every day may be impressed upon the hearts of your children? That should be in every home. Pray not only for yourselves, but also for your enemies. Are you charitable in your homes and your organizations for those who are not of the same opinion as you? We talk about service to others. Too often when service is mentioned, we think of some physical aid that we might render. I tell you a better service can sometimes be given to others by speaking well of them, or, if you cannot speak well of them, by refraining from speaking of them at all.—*CR*, October 1919, pp. 78-79.

A PERSONAL VISTA. A short time ago, I stood in a little room in Wales, in which my mother was born 102 years before, the room so small that the six-foot bed covers the entire width, and its length is barely two feet longer than it is wide, and the old rafters just two feet above my head, so about eight feet high. But my thoughts on that occasion have been sacred to me. I share one or two with you.

I thought, as Sister McKay and I stood in that small bedroom, how different life would be now if two humble elders had not knocked at that door a hundred years ago! And how different life would be if my mother's father and mother had not accepted that message! I looked around the village and found descendants of others who heard it at that time, descendants of some who ridiculed my grandfather and grandmother for having accepted the truth; and they made light of their religion, scoffed at them and ostracized them for having accepted Mormonism. I realized how unenlightened those neighbors were when they condemned my grandparents.

I recalled, as we stood there, what my grandmother said to me in Ogden, when she told me as a student in my teens, about the experience she had when she left Cefn Coed. My mother's sister, Aunt Lizzie, the youngest of the children, had just been born, when the eldest son was called away by death. My grandmother there in Ogden said, "I condemned the Lord in my heart for having taken our one main help on the journey ahead of us, and I said in my heart, 'Lord, if you had to take any of my children, why didn't you take this little helpless baby and leave us the oldest son to help us on the journey across the ocean and across the plains?' " When she told me that, she said, "I was wrong in my judgment. God knew best, and I should have trusted him. You see today how blessed I am, living here with the comfort I have of Lizzie, my youngest child, now the mother of three boys, and my comfort in my old age. God looked farther into the future than I could."

I remember that statement, as I fancied I could hear the cry of my mother, born two years before. Incidentally, acceptance of that gospel meant much to me. Father's folk were way up in the north of Scotland. It was only through the gospel that Father and Mother met. So I expressed gratitude, as I sensed it probably never so keenly before, as we stood in that little room, six by eight.—DNCS, September 6, 1952, p. 4.

COSTS AND BENEFITS. A young man was called from this city to go on a mission to the Pacific Islands. He responded and gave his message to the world as best he could. A few weeks ago he came into my office and said: "I have been home a year, and I have succeeded during that year in paying all but $100.00 of the $600.00 debt I had when I returned. In another two months I will have it all paid, and my tithing in full besides."

"Well, was it worth it?" said I.

"Twice as much," he promptly replied. "I would not have missed that experience for anything."—CR, April 1927, p. 103.

I met a young man when I was coming home from the Eastern States Mission who had spent all his earnings in that mission, and also several hundred dollars beside, which a banker in his home town had furnished him, merely upon the young man's promissory note. He has paid his note since coming home, and although he has been in ill health part of the time, he rejoices in his missionary service. I met a mother on the train whose son was then in the mission field. She said she was having a difficult time to pay the taxes and other expenses and to keep her son in the field, and sympathetically I suggested that perhaps he might better be released. She turned in her seat suddenly and said: "Brother McKay, I would rather work these fingers to the bone than to have my boy come home before his duty is performed."—CR, April 1927, p. 103.

QUALIFICATIONS AND CALLING OF MISSIONARIES

TRUE CHRISTIAN BEHAVIOR. Every elder should be a Christian gentleman always. A gentleman—who is he? "Whoever is open"—nothing to hide, no downcast look because of the consciousness of guilt; "whoever is loyal"—loyal to the truth, to virtue, to the Word of Wisdom—"true, of humane and affable demeanor, honorable himself and in his judgment of others, faithful to his word as to law, and faithful alike to God and to man—such a man is a true gentleman," and such a man the elder of this Church should be who goes out to Christianize the world.—CR, April 1927, p. 106.

INSTRUCTIONS TO BISHOPS AND PRESIDENTS OF STAKES. I plead with you bishops and presidents of the stakes to be more careful in your inquiries unto the worthiness of the missionaries whom you recommend. Will you, before calling them or interviewing them, just look over the missionary recommendation which you are going to sign? Do not just put it in the hand of the missionary and let him fill the blanks, but you note the significance of these questions. If he is married, please inquire into the condition of his family. Is he divorced or is she divorced? Please state why and see whether or not he or she is worthy to go out and preach the sacredness of the marriage covenant and the ideals of the Church in regard to home building.

Under morality, answer sincerely before you put this in the hands of the member of the Council of the Twelve. Are you satisfied, after thorough investigation, that he or she conforms to Church standards, aye, in chastity. The world has difficulty in believing that young men in our Church grow to manhood as chaste and pure as virgins. I have had them say they did not believe it; they did not believe that any young men could do that. But I tell them such is the fact, and that it is the standard of the Church for young men as well as for young women, to keep themselves unspotted from the world. In the Church there is but the single standard of morality and that applies to young men as well as to young women. See to it that prospective missionaries realize what this means, no matter what false teaching they have had in psychology or in other classes about "inhibitions," and so on. The standard of the Church is right; it is divine; it contributes to manhood and virtuous womanhood, happy homes, perpetuity of the nation.

Are you satisfied through investigation that he or she conforms to the Church in the observance of the Word of Wisdom? And note this, in integrity. Is there anybody in the ward who will say: "Well, he has cheated me. He is not worthy. If that is the kind of men they have to send out, well then, I am done with the Church."

These pointed questions are put in the recommend purposely, and they mean something, because those who go out to represent the Church are chosen. They are set apart. They are leaders. They are teachers. They are ambassadors of truth. Please, when you bring these young men and young women to the members of the Council of the Twelve and place in the hands of the Council of the Twelve this written recommendation with your signature, be sure that you have made a thorough investigation, because it is embarrassing, very embarrassing, to the young man to be rejected as a representative.—CR, October 1948, pp. 175-176.

STANDARDS FOR CALLING MISSIONARIES. There are certain standards by which we should be guided in calling our missionaries: First, call no young man or young woman for the purpose of saving him or her. The young man is getting wayward, and you think a mission would do him good. It would. But that is not why you are sending him out. Choose the young men and young women who are worthy to represent the Church, see that they are sufficiently mature, and, above all, that they have good character.

THE PHYSICALLY HANDICAPPED. Again there is the problem of the physically handicapped; of course you would like them to go, but think how they will interfere with their companions. Elders should go two by two, and so should sisters, and no one of them should be hampered in his or her activity with somebody who is not equal to the responsibility of missionary work.

IMPORTANCE OF CHARACTER. But the most important standard is character. Let each one whom you interview sense the fact that he is going out as a representative. Some of the brethren have urged that each ward should have in the mission field a certain percentage of the ward membership. That is not an ideal. If you have no one who is worthy and financially able to represent the Church, do not send anybody out, but sit down with these young men and young women and say, "If you accept this call willingly, you go out as a trusted representative of the Church and of the Lord Jesus Christ." And to be trusted, young men, is a greater compliment than to be loved, and you cannot violate that trust. You are obligated to keep that trust between now and the time you go to the missionary home. Maintain the Church standards with your companions who will want to give you a farewell party. We have heard of some missionaries who have been called who have joined in with their fraternity friends in action that reflected discredit upon themselves and upon the missionary cause.

Tell the young man, "From now on, from this very moment, you are a trusted representative of this ward, of your parents, and of the Lord Jesus Christ."—*CR*, April 1950, pp. 176-178.

PHYSICAL STRENGTH A REQUISITE. Missionary work is strenuous, the change of climate, often the worry that takes possession of some of our young men at first, sometimes homesickness, discouragement set in. Unless they are physically strong, they break under it. . . . That, too, hinders the work in the mission field. That applies also to those who are past middle age, to elderly couples that would like to go out. They seem strong, capable to do work here at home, but when they get out in the field under different circumstances, not a small number of them fail to meet the vicissitudes and the responsibilities of the mission. So now, before your elderly couple will be sent out to the field the mission president will be communicated with; and if he can use them, all right; if not, we shall ask that they remain in the home fields, in the organized stakes.

Now we recognize, bishops, that you are going to have difficulty in satisfying some of these young men who may be physically handicapped. Physicians may declare a weakness in the eyes, probably in the heart. The young men will say, "Well, we can work hard, and we should like to go," and sympathetically you say, "All right." They feel as though they will be deprived of a privilege, and no doubt they will in a sense, but let us emphasize the importance of the work here at home. It is just as important, the home missionary work, and they can be here under their normal surroundings, and be near any help, medically, which they might need. So let us try to impress them with the fact that they can serve the Lord here at home to the extent of their physical, intellectual, and spiritual ability, and probably better than going out into the world under conditions that might be too strenuous for them.—*CR*, April 1949, pp. 177-178.

Because of the call to military duty the number of missionaries in the field is not so large as one year ago. The missionaries are returning and reporting for military duty by the scores every month. Reports of uprightness in the lives of these returned missionaries indicate that by example they will still continue to be good missionaries while serving their country.

I think I shall take time to give you just an extract from one of these reports. A letter dated September 4, 1951 from a major says this:

"This is quite a group we have. With the exception of two fellows it is made up entirely of returned missionaries. This morning we all ate together in the enlisted men's mess hall, and not a single one of them had coffee, even though boiling pitchers full were set at each table. I noticed a peculiar look on the mess sergeant's face as he scratched his head in bewilderment when thirty-two soldiers all took milk."

It is only a little incident, but it speaks volumes for the loyalty of our missionaries who are entering the service in their determination to maintain the standards of the Church. God bless them!—*CR*, October 1951, pp. 4-5.

WOMEN AND MISSIONARY SERVICE. It is surprising how eagerly the young women and some married women seek calls to go on missions. We commend them for it, but the responsibility of proclaiming the gospel of Jesus Christ rests primarily upon the priesthood of the Church.

In this connection, we advise that mothers who have dependent children, that means children who are in their teens or unmarried, should not be called on missions even though the grandparents are willing to take care of the children. No nobler work in this world can be performed by any mother than to rear and love the children with whom God has blessed her. That is her duty, and that is far greater than going out into the world to proclaim the gospel because somebody else can do that who does not bear the responsibility of rearing and loving the children who call her mother.—*CR*, April 1951, p. 81.

THE MISSIONS AT MID-CENTURY (1949)

THE MISSION PRESIDENTS. The men who preside over our missions are chosen generally from the rank and file of the Church. They are businessmen, contractors, ranchers, college professors, lawyers, physicians and surgeons, dentists, and members of other professions. When the call comes to any such, no matter what his responsibilities or circumstances, seldom if ever does he offer an excuse but, as Samuel of old, replies: "Speak; for thy servant heareth," (I Samuel 3:10) even though such acceptance means a financial sacrifice and sometimes the loss of political preferment.

THE MISSIONARIES. The missionaries, generally, are young men and women, ranging in age from twenty to thirty years, with a sprinkling among them of more experienced men and women.

It is well to say here that the direct responsibility of preaching the gospel rests upon the priesthood of the Church— not upon the women, though the efficiency of the latter in cottage meetings, in Primaries, and Sunday Schools, and in other phases of missionary work, is of the highest order, and their willingness, even eagerness, to labor is not excelled by that of the young men.

Who are these youths chosen to represent the Church? They, too, as their mission presidents, come from the rank and file. They are farmers, artisans, factory workers, bank clerks, secretaries in business firms, and followers of other vocations. Some who are married leave their wives and their children who help to support them in their work. All of them look forward to the time after their return when they, with congenial loving companions, may build happy homes.

As already stated, each pays his or her own expenses, in most cases, of course, with the assistance of parents. True Christianity is love in action. There is no better way to manifest love for God than to show an unselfish love for your fellow men. This is the spirit of missionary work. Our hearts respond to the cry of the poet:

"O brother man! fold to thy heart thy brother.
Where pity dwells, the peace of God is there;
To worship rightly is to love each other,
Each smile a hymn, each kindly deed a prayer."

—John Greenleaf Whittier, "Brotherhood."

These men go out in the spirit of love, seeking nothing from any nation to which they are sent: no personal acclaim, no monetary acquisition. Two or three years ago, many of these missionaries were honorably discharged from military duty. Not a few had saved their government allowance to pay their expenses in the mission field if and when they should be called.

INFLUENCE OF MISSIONARY SYSTEM UPON YOUTH. I once read one of the most impressive letters of a mother to a son that I think has ever been written. It contained only three words, except the signature: "Quinn, keep clean," and was signed, "Lovingly, Mother."

Young men in the army, therefore, who looked forward to serving as missionaries and saved their money for that purpose, cherished higher ideals than their "buddies" who sometimes prodigally spent their earnings in saloons, gambling dens, and brothels.

In more than one instance, Latter-day Saint soldiers sent home their earnings to their parents to be deposited in the savings bank to bear their missionary costs after the war. And we know of two or three young men each of whom added in effect: "If I do not come home, use the money to pay the expenses of some other young man to go out as a missionary."

These young men are instructed that they go out as representatives of the Church, and that a representative of any organization—economic or religious—must possess at least one outstanding quality, and that is: trustworthiness. . . .

These ambassadors . . . carry . . . one of the greatest responsibilities of their lives.

THE MISSIONARY MESSAGE. Now, what is the outstanding message that they have to give to Christian, as well as to non-Christian countries? There must surely be something distinctive to justify their presence in all parts of the world.

First, their message is that Jesus Christ is the Son of God, the Redeemer and Savior of mankind. To these missionaries—"Jesus is not a legendary figure in history," to paraphrase a question asked by Hall Caine to the Christian world:

" . . . he is not merely a saint to be painted in the stained glass of church windows, a sort of sacred fairy not to be approached and hardly to be mentioned by name. But he is still what he was in the flesh, a reality, a man of like passions

with ourselves, a guide, a counselor, a comforter, a great voice
calling to us to live nobly, to die bravely, and to keep up our
courage to the last."

The second distinctive message is this: Every missionary
should clearly understand, and so declare in unmistakable
words, the relationship of this Church to other Christian organizations—that it is neither an outgrowth nor a division of any
of them. True, the Church is generally classed with the
Protestants; but Protestantism began with the great dissenters
—Martin Luther, Philip Melanchthon, Ulrich Zwingli, John
Knox, and others. These great reformers denounced corrupt
practices in the Roman church, particularly the selling of
indulgences wherein delinquents could make satisfaction by
money contributions, a practice carried on under one pretext
and another until it became a regular financial expedient for
increasing papal revenue.

It was extended even to souls in purgatory.

The great men whom I have named rebelled against
this evil and others, and organized churches in protest.

Accordingly, when the second Diet of Spires in 1529 passed
a resolution

" . . . disallowing further religious innovations in the
Lutheran states, whilst prohibiting the profession of the
Zwinglian and Anabaptist forms of the reformed faith, the
Lutheran minority protested, and this protestation was signed
by fourteen cities as well as by the elector of Saxony, the land-
grave of Hesse and four other provinces. Hence the name
Protestant as a designation of the evangelical party."

Protestantism under many different names, spread over
Europe and later among the American colonies, and freedom
to worship as one sincerely wished became more and more
the prescribed right of the individual, but in the hearts of
many a true believer in Jesus of Nazareth, there remained an
abiding belief, a feeling that the authority to represent him
had been taken from the earth, and that there

" . . . can be no recovery out of that apostasy till Christ
shall send forth new apostles to plant churches anew."

This in effect is what the Lord told the Prophet Joseph
Smith when as a fourteen-year-old lad he inquired which

of all sects was right and which he should join. Joseph was told to join none of them. . . .

A few years later, specifically, April 6, 1830, Joseph Smith received by the spirit of prophecy and revelation instructions from the Savior "to organize his Church once more here upon the earth."

Thus was established by direct revelation and divine authority from the Eternal Father and Jesus Christ who founded the Church in the Meridian of Time, the Church of Latter-day Saints, which is set up as a forerunner, if you please, to the establishing of the kingdom of God upon the earth. In the words of President John Taylor,

" . . . with such an organization there is a chance for the Lord God to be revealed. There is an opportunity for the law of life to be made manifest, a chance for God to introduce the principles of heaven upon the earth and for the will of God to be done upon earth as it is done in heaven." (*J. D.* 18:140, October 10, 1875.)

With these two great fundamental truths as the heart of their message, namely, (1) the divinity of the mission of the Lord Jesus Christ, the Savior of the world, and (2) the restoration of his gospel in this age, the missionaries are to the best of their ability, fulfilling the injunction to preach the gospel to every creature, baptizing him in the name of the Father and of the Son and of the Holy Ghost, teaching him to observe all things whatsoever the Lord has commanded.

This, then, brethren, is a world-wide Church organized preparatory to the establishing of the kingdom of God on earth by means of which " . . . the Lord God may be revealed, and an opportunity for the laws of life to be made manifest."

AMBASSADORS OF GOOD WILL. These thousands of missionaries and men who hold the priesthood everywhere are ambassadors of good will, the ultimate purpose of whose service is to change the hearts of men everywhere from selfishness and greed to tolerance, compassion, and brotherhood.

May the heart of every missionary be inspired by the Spirit of his Lord, whose authorized servant he is, to the end that selfishness and violence now so powerful in the world will

be replaced by loyal service, truth, and brotherhood!—*CR,*
Sept.-Oct. 1949, pp. 118-123.

THE NOBLEST CALLING IN LIFE. It is difficult, if not quite
impossible, for one to say of anything with absolute certainty:
"This is the best," or "This is the worst." If one so expresses
one's self, another with greater intelligence and more experience may say with much more accuracy that something else
is best or some other thing the worst. It is, therefore, the better
part of wisdom not to dogmatize, nor to speak with too much
assurance of things about which there may be a divergence of
opinion, and upon which one person's judgment will be as
weighty as another's. It is somewhat presumptuous, therefore,
to point out specifically the *noblest* calling in life; for as soon
as it is named, someone may prove conclusively that we have
used the superlative degree inadvisedly.

However, whatever its name, it is evident that man's
noblest work must be impregnated with the greatest of all
forces, love. Furthermore, this power must be directed not
for selfish purposes nor to achieve personal ends. Though
self-preservation is the first law of nature, a calling that has
in view only the preservation of self cannot be called noble,
a term that excludes all sordidness, and includes greatness
of mind and generosity of soul.

The noblest calling in life, then, must be one in which
the attribute of love will manifest itself not for self, but for
others. It must be that calling which most nearly emulates
true motherhood, the mightiest of all forces in human society.
Indeed, if motherhood were not a "distinct and individual
creation," we could pause here and have all true men agree
that it is the noblest, purest calling in life; and that which
makes motherhood is the Christlike element of giving her
life for another. "A father may turn his back on his child;
brothers and sisters may become inveterate enemies; husbands
may desert their wives, wives their husbands; but a mother's
love endures through all."

The element, then, that makes true motherhood divine
must also permeate that call or vocation which may be distinguished by the term *noblest. The most worthy calling in life,
therefore, is that in which man can serve best his fellow man.*
It isn't preaching; it isn't teaching; it isn't medicine; it isn't

engineering nor any other vocation common among men.
Each of these, though offering opportunities for service, may
be followed by men actuated by the most selfish and sordid
of motives.

The noblest aim in life is to strive to live to make other
lives better and happier. Browning sounds the keynote in
Paracelsus, when he says: "There is an answer to the passion-
ate longings of the heart for fulness, and I knew it. And the
answer is this: Live in all things outside yourself by love and
you will have joy. That is the life of God; it ought to be our
life. In him it is accomplished and perfect; but in all created
things, it is a lesson learned slowly against difficulty."

Such is the divine message given to the Prophet Joseph
in the words: "Remember the worth of souls is great in the
sight of God." (D. & C. 18:10.) Such is the philosophy expressed by the Redeemer in the seemingly paradoxical statement, " . . . he that loseth his life for my sake shall find it."
(Matt. 10:39.) The meaning of this becomes clear in the
light of another passage which says, "Inasmuch as ye have
done it unto one of the least of these my brethren, ye have
done it unto me. (*Ibid.* 25:40.)

To no other group of men in all the world is given a
better opportunity to engage in the noblest calling in life
than that which is afforded the elders in the Church of Jesus
Christ of Latter-day Saints. To establish salvation and peace
to the extent of their individual efforts, their lives are dedicated; to make the world a better and a fitter place for man,
their talents and means are consecrated.

Just to be associated with men striving toward such an
aim is a joy; and to assist them in their quest, an inspiration.
Unselfishly, they are trying to serve their fellow men in love.
Thus far, at least, they are true followers of the Master; for
"at the very heart of the Christian faith, the most sublime
of its teachings, and to him who penetrates its deepest sense,
the most human is this: To save lost humanity the invisible
God came to dwell among us, in the form of man, and willed to
make himself known by this single sign: Love."

God bless the elders, and women as well, who, if not
with perfect love, at least with a desire to bring joy and peace
to others, are engaged in the noblest calling in life!

Worthy servants of Christ, you are! Teachers! Followers of the true Teacher, the great Exemplar of all! On with your noble work! There is none greater; none more righteous! Yours is the joy promised by the Savior.—MS, 86:216-217 (1924).

CHAPTER 11

OBLIGATIONS OF MEMBERS

THE SIGNIFICANCE OF ENTRY INTO THE CHURCH

SEEKING TRUTH AND RESISTING EVIL. One expression in the document [the *Address . . . to the World* of 1907] remains in my mind, and I feel to touch upon it, because I believe that it contains much food for thought, as does every sentence in that declaration. It is implied therein that the Latter-day Saints are members of the Church "for the fostering of spiritual life, and the achievement of moral and charitable ends"; in other words, for the developing of the religious sentiment, the true religious spirit. This may be done in two ways: first, by *seeking* the *truth* and *living in harmony* with it; and second, by *resisting every influence, every power, that tends to destroy or to dwarf in any way the religious sentiment.*

When the Latter-day Saint stood at the water's edge, before being buried with Christ in baptism, he had within him an implicit faith that the Church of Jesus Christ is established upon the earth, and that this organization is the best in the world today for the fostering of spiritual life, for the attaining of true religious development, for the salvation of his soul. I repeat that this implicit faith was within him; and with that, there was a true repentance, and that repentance carried with it a desire to leave off everything in the past life that was contrary to the teachings of the gospel or the Church he was about to join. His old life, and the sins, if there were any connected with it, he truly repented of. He looked forward to the time when he would be born anew in the kingdom of God. . . .

That is where we all stood at one time. Those were our feelings, our faith, our hope. We stood that day forgiven of past evils and follies. Now, the whole mission—the life, if you please, of soul development—was before us, and we had thus bestowed upon us the light that emanates from the Father, to lead us that our feet might not stumble, that the truths of his holy gospel might sink into our hearts—the truths that will give us knowledge, that our souls might be saved in intelligence. The Holy Ghost was to bring all things to our remembrance, to show us things to come, to testify of the Father; and as we seek that light, and live in accordance with the duties that are placed upon us by that obligation, we are seeking the true religious development; we are fostering the true religious growth.

But what is the other element which we must consider? Along with this new life, with this seeking for truth, there should be a *strong power of resistance.* Someone has said that when God makes the prophet, he does not unmake the man. I believe that, though being born anew, and being entitled to new life, new vigor, new blessings, yet the old weaknesses still remained with us. The evil one was eager and ready to attack and strike us at our weakest point, and he has been striking on it ever since. Why? That he might thwart the very purpose for which we entered the Church of Jesus Christ. That is his mission.

Our temptation may have come in the form of the old appetite which we had satisfied for years. It may have been, and I doubt not that it was, in the form of some bodily temptation—some longing. It may have been the love of the old pipe which we determined—if we were sincere—to put aside when going into the waters of baptism. O when that longing came, after we were in the Church or kingdom, who was it that said: "Though you pretend to throw that aside, take it only once more; this once will not hurt." There was the necessary moment of resistance. How many of us stood as Christ our leader and said: "Get thee behind me!" This element of resistance in regard to our bodily longings—satisfying the passions, applies to every member of the Church of Jesus Christ. In some way the evil one will attack us; in some way he can weaken us; in some way he will bring before us that which will weaken our souls and will tend to thwart that true development of the spirit within, the strengthening of the inner man, the strengthening and growth of the spirit, that time cannot kill, but which is enduring and lasting as the eternal Father of that spirit. And the things which will tend to dwarf this spirit or to hinder its growth are things which the Latter-day Saints are called upon to resist.—*CR,* April 1907, pp. 10-12.

RESPONSIBILITIES OF CHURCH MEMBERSHIP

LEARNING AND ACTING. What is this responsibility which rests upon every member of the Church? I turn to the 107th section of the Doctrine and Covenants, and there find enumerated the duties of the various organizations of the priesthood, and I read in the ninety-ninth verse the following:

"Wherefore, now let every man *learn* his duty, and *to act* in the office in which he is appointed, in all diligence."

Two principles in that admonition stand out as the duty of the officers to whom this revelation was given: first, the *learning*, the knowing what one's duty is; second, *to act* in all diligence in the performance of duty. To know one's duty, to learn the truth, is the duty of every Latter-day Saint, of every man and woman in the world, including those outside of this Church.

All mankind, I believe, are being impelled, lifted upward by that Spirit which makes them desire the truth. In the political world even, you find great men who have been searching for political truth, for truths that would relieve political situations. In the world of morality you find great reformers reaching out for truths that will alleviate harmful social conditions. The same sentiment is found in the financial world. Scientific men are among the foremost searchers after truth.

We are told about the Power which impelled Columbus to go out into the ocean. In response to that feeling inspired within him to demonstrate a truth of which he felt confident, he could not content himself; he had to give expression to it. There is a natural feeling which urges men and women towards truth; it is a responsibility placed upon mankind. That responsibility rests upon Latter-day Saints in a greater degree than upon their fellow men.

If you turn to the 88th section, you will find the following admonition:

"And as all have not faith, seek ye diligently and teach one another words of wisdom; yea, seek ye out of the best books words of wisdom; seek learning"—how? "even by study," but not alone by study, as the world searches for it, "and also by faith." (D. & C. 88:118.)

WHAT HAVE WE LEARNED? The Latter-day Saints have learned the truth that the everlasting gospel has been restored. And what does this knowledge bring to them? It brings to all who have honestly and sincerely obeyed the principles of repentance and baptism the gift of the Holy Ghost, which enlightens their minds, quickens their understanding, and imparts unto them a knowledge of Christ.

The Latter-day Saints have a guide, a help, a means to assist in their acquisition of truth, in their desire to know what their duty is, that the world does not possess. And this guide is necessary; man cannot find out truth—he cannot find out God by intellect alone. It has been said that no man can find out God by a microscope. Reason alone is not a sufficient guide in searching for truth. There is another, higher, more sure guide than reason.

That guide is faith—that principle which draws our spirit into communion with the higher Spirit which will bring all things to our remembrance, show us things to come, and teach us all things. To acquire that Spirit is the responsibility of the Latter-day Saint who would know truth.

MERE KNOWLEDGE INSUFFICIENT. But knowing a thing or merely feeling an assurance of the truth is not sufficient. " . . . to him that knoweth to do good, and doeth it not, to him it is sin." (James 4:17.) Now, where are we? Think of the instructions that have been given during this conference. You and I know now, as probably we have never realized before, what the duty of the individual Latter-day Saint is, and what the duty of the various organizations is.

THE NECESSITY OF PERFORMANCE. This thought brings us to consider the second duty mentioned in this revelation by the Prophet Joseph Smith: "Wherefore, now let every man learn his duty, and to *act* in the office in which he is appointed, in all diligence." (D. & C. 107:99.) The man who knows what his duty is and fails to perform it, is not true to himself; he is not true to his brethren; he is not living in the light which God and conscience provides. That is where we stand, and it comes right home to you; it means me. When my conscience tells me that it is right to go along in a specified line, I am not true to myself if I do not follow that.

Oh, I know we are swayed by our weaknesses, and by influences from without; but it is our duty to walk in the straight and narrow path in the performance of every duty! And mark this: Every time we have opportunity and fail to live up to that truth which is within us, every time we fail to express a good thought, every time we fail to perform a good act, we weaken ourselves, and make it more difficult to express that thought or perform that act in the future. Every time we perform a good act, every time we express a noble feeling, we make it more easy to perform that act or express that feeling another time.—CR, October 1906, pp. 112-113.

THE OBLIGATION OF TEACHING. Luther once said: "Count it one of the highest virtues upon earth to educate faithfully the children of others, which so few, and scarcely any, do their own." The obligation of teaching is placed by the Church first upon the parents. Fathers and mothers are accepted absolutely as teachers, and the responsibility thereof has been placed upon them by divine command. But beside these there is an army of men and women, and boys and girls, who have accepted the responsibility of teaching. In the priesthood quorums alone the number runs into the thousands. Among these there are selected not a few thousand to act as instructors of the youth.—CR, April 1914, p. 87.

"EVERY MAN, EVERY WOMAN, MUST BEAR . . . RESPONSIBILITY." I do not know whether I have succeeded in expressing the feelings of my heart so that you understand them; but I wish to leave this thought: that every man, every woman, must bear a part of the responsibility of this Church. Feeling that does not necessarily make him imagine that it is resting upon him only. There is no man so unimportant that he can sink without making even a bubble or a ripple in the great ocean of life. At the same time his importance is so great that his actions go a long way towards establishing the power, the dignity, the advancement of God's kingdom on earth.

Then, no matter where we are, if we are in the hills one week from today or tomorrow, wherever circumstances or business affairs may call us, be it in the canyon or elsewhere, and we are tempted, on a cold morning, to break the Word of Wisdom by drinking two or three cups of tea or coffee, let us feel then the responsibility of right. Let each one say to himself, "The responsibility of membership in the Church is upon me; I will not yield. What though nobody sees me, I know and God knows when I yield, and every time I yield to a weakness I become weaker myself and do not respect myself."

If you are in business, and your companions say, "Come, let us go in and have a drink on this bargain, or this sale," let your answer be, "No, no!" What though your thirsty appetite makes you long for it, be men, be Latter-day Saints, and say, "No; the responsibility of membership in the Church rests upon me."

When you are tempted to stay away from that seventies' meeting, from that elders' meeting, from that deacons' quorum and you shrink from going there, because you feel you will not be interested, say, "I will go; the duty of a Latter-day Saint is upon me; the responsibility of membership in that quorum is upon me, and I must go and help make that meeting interesting."

And so, if you carry that feeling in all the duties of a Latter-day Saint, you will come to the conclusion that every time you stand by the truth, you are more of a man, you are more in harmony with God's Spirit. He loves to dwell in such tabernacles; he will guide you into all truth; he will make your soul to rejoice; and you will know this gospel is true. "He that heareth these sayings of mine and doeth them" is the one that is likened unto the wise man. "Not every one that saith unto me, Lord, Lord, shall enter into the kingdom of heaven; but he that doeth the will of my Father which is in heaven." (Matt. 7:21.)

"But be ye doers of the word, and not hearers only, . . . " (James 1:22.)—*CR*, October 1906, p. 115.

COURAGE TO ENTER NEW REALMS. The first time that it was my privilege to stand on the brink of the Grand Canyon of the Colorado, I was overwhelmed with a sense that I was not comprehending the magnitude of that great gorge. I had learned that it was over a mile down to what appeared to be a little winding stream, the mighty Colorado, and that the opposite wall was said to be thirteen miles away, but I could not comprehend the majesty and sublimity of that mighty chasm.

I think I had a similar feeling this morning when I tried to visualize the potential audience that listened over the Church of the Air to your congregational singing, for there were probably ten million people in that potential audience. I am sure I cannot comprehend the significance of that great service. One thing though is clearly defined in my mind, and that is this: That we have greater responsibility than ever to learn and to live the gospel of Jesus Christ. We have greater tasks before us. The final work is not all done yet. You and I have the responsibility of taking advantage of these new and great opportunities to preach the gospel, of making real new visions, and of bringing into the lives of Latter-day Saints and members of the world more blessed opportunities to know the way of truth.

We need courage to enter into those new realms; we need courage to meet our present situations and conditions, and that is why I have chosen the text, "Be of good courage, and he shall strengthen your heart, all ye that hope in the Lord." (Psalm 31:24.)—*CR*, April 1936, pp. 57-58.

BUILD, DON'T MURMUR. Now, my brethren and sisters, as in the world so in the Church, we have two classes; we have the builders, and we have the murmurers. Let each ask himself in which class shall I be placed? We are called upon to perform duties. High councilors with presidents of stakes are asked to build up their stakes and do other work in the Church. They introduce some plan of action, and many times the majority will say: Yes, we will do that; let us perform the duties that the presidency of the stake and the high councilors call us to do.

But somewhere we shall hear a murmurer, a faultfinder, who will say, No, you cannot do that. They scoff as Laman and Lemuel did and say you cannot do it. Misjudging motives, some soon find themselves with Laman and Lemuel, instead of with Nephi who expresses the voice of God. It may be in an auxiliary board. Instructions go out from the general board or from the stake board, requiring for the success of the movement the united energy of all. Most of the people interested in that association will join hands to build; they will join hands to be with the benefactors that the children might receive the light of the Holy Spirit, that they might get the knowledge that is revealed in this Church; but somewhere there will be murmurers; there will be faultfinders. Look out for them.

Let us watch ourselves and be true to the examples set by the Church and the brethren and sisters who have sacrificed their lives, their all, to build the Church and to advance the principles taught therein. This warning is sometimes expressed in this way: "Speak not against the authorities." What does it mean? Be not a murmurer; that is what it means. It is one of the most poisonous things that can be introduced into the home of a Latter-day Saint—this murmuring against presidents of stakes, high councilors, Sunday School superintendents, presidents of high priests' quorums, seventies, elders, priests, teachers, and deacons. They are called unto their position, what for? To benefit themselves? No, not once can you point to an instance in this Church where a man was called for his personal benefit. He was admonished, before he was called to the position, whatever it was, that he should serve somewhere and serve somebody in this Church or in the world; it was to bless somebody, some class, humanity at large.

That is the mission of every man, from the President of the Church down to the latest convert in the Church. Every officer holds his position to build up, to bless; and, as President Joseph F. Smith has said, to establish righteousness, purity, and virtue among mankind. That is the motive, and yet because of his weakness, because, perhaps, of some little fault that we see in an officer, we begin to murmur and find fault.

Better stop murmuring and build. Remember that one of the worst means of tearing down an individual is slander. It is one of the most poisonous weapons that the evil one uses. Backbiting and evil speaking throw us into the class of malefactors rather than the class of benefactors.—CR, April 1909, pp. 66-67.

Speaking of the Church as a whole, I have often thought that we have chosen the wiser part in answering a faction that left the Church in early days, inasmuch as we did not choose to tear them down or to attack them in public or private. They call themselves the Reorganized Church. As I listened to one who has come out here presumably to teach the truth and heard him revile and ridicule President Brigham Young and other leading brethren of the Church, I felt to say, what good does it do to tear down? Why not build up? Tell us about what you have, and let the people then judge which is the better; it is much the wiser course. When a man begins to tear down, revile, and persecute, he is doing that which injures instead of building up. Our mission should be to build.

But you ask, would you not condemn evil? Yes, by obeying and building up the laws of right. The question in building is this: Is it right? Is that thing necessary to be done? If so, then let us do it.—CR, April 1909, pp. 67-68.

In the Church of Jesus Christ, there are no masters and no servants, but all working for everyone and each one for all.—AA, p. 60.

THE COVENANTS OF "THE LORD'S SUPPER"

THE SACRAMENT MEETINGS OF THE CHURCH. "It is expedient that the church meet together often. . . ." (D. & C. 20:75.) We meet in the house of God not as mere acquaintances, suspicious of one another, but as brethren in the brotherhood of Christ. We meet in the presence of him who has said, "Love one another." I look forward to the time when the membership of our quorums will approach their quorum meetings in anticipation of that brotherhood and experience that fraternal feeling which strengthens the soul and which inspires all to render greater service to their fellow men.

I believe in meetings. I feel impressed to emphasize what the Lord has designated as the most important meeting in the Church and that is the sacrament meeting. In this very text which I have read, given to Joseph Smith by revelation, the Lord refers to that special meeting. "It is expedient that the church meet together often," not for these general purposes to which I have made brief reference, but for the specific purpose of partaking of the sacrament. He has prescribed for us only a few set prayers, two of which are the blessing on the bread and water.

Now, what does it signify? You will find first that the sacrament is a memorial of Christ's life and death.

A second significance or a second principle associated with the administering of the sacrament is the bond of brotherhood.

We meet in the brotherhood of Christ, all on the same level, each expressing confidence in the other and all in one another. Oh, the strength of brotherhood! Sin divides us. Righteousness unites. The partaking of the sacrament indicates also how communion with Christ may be secured. It cannot be obtained by Sunday righteousness and weekday indulgence. It implies that we will remember Christ always. If we show the Lord's death in the sacrament, we must show the Lord's life in the world.

And the third great significance is the promise that it is a means of receiving divine guidance. "If a friend is one who summons us to our best, then is not Jesus Christ our best friend and should we not think of the sacrament as one of the chief appeals to us to be our best? The Lord's Supper looks not back to our past with a critical eye, but to our future with a helpful one."

May I call attention to the great obligation which every member of the Church assumes when he first partakes of the sacrament on the Lord's day. Think of the prayer revealed in this dispensation: "O God, the Eternal Father." What an invocation! An acknowledgment of God as our Creator; the giver of all good; the bestower of all blessings; in whom is all power and all glory; and yet, our *Father*, and we his children! The Fatherhood of God and the brotherhood of man! "We ask thee in the name of thy Son, Jesus Christ," who is interceding for us, through whom all blessings are obtained—"to bless and sanctify this bread to the souls of all those who partake of it."

Bless the bread! It is only bread. There may be a mystery about the sacrament, but that mystery does not consist in the changing of the bread to the actual body of the Christ. As President Brigham Young has said, the thought is a repulsive one. But it is a symbol, and we ask God to bless it to the souls of all those who partake of it, who *witness*—oh, there is the point!—*CR*, October 1929, pp. 10-13.

OBLIGATIONS AND BLESSINGS IN PARTAKING OF THE SACRA-
MENT. My brethren and sisters, do we always stop to think,
on that sacred Sabbath day when we meet together to partake
of the sacrament, that we witness, promise, obligate ourselves,
in the presence of one another, and in the presence of God, that
we will do certain things? Note them.

The first: We are willing to take upon ourselves the name
of the Son. In so doing we choose him as our leader and our
ideal; and he is the one perfect character in all the world.

The second: That we will always remember him. Not just
on Sunday, but on Monday, in our daily acts, in our self-
control. When our brother hurts us, we are going to try to
master our feelings and not retaliate in the same spirit of
anger. When a brother treats us with contempt, we are going
to try to return kindness. That's the spirit of the Christ, and
that's what we have promised—that we will do our best to
achieve these high standards of Christianity, true Christian
principles.

The third: We promise to " . . . keep his commandments
which he has given. . ."—tithing, fast offerings, the Word of
Wisdom, kindness, forgiveness, love. The obligation of a
member of the Church of Jesus Christ is great, but it is as
glorious as it is great, because obedience to these principles
gives life, eternal life. On the other hand, the man who seeks
to live by violating the principles is deceived by the adversary
and goes the way to death.

To partake of the sacrament unworthily is to take a
step toward spiritual death. No man can be dishonest within
himself without deadening the susceptibility of his spirit.
Sin can stun the conscience as a blow on the head can stun
the physical senses. He who promises one thing and deliberately fails to keep his word adds sin to sin. On natural
principles such a man "eats and drinks condemnation to his
soul."

We die in this world before our hearts stop beating, as
we live and partake of eternal life before we pass into the
other world; for this is part of life eternal, and true life consists in obedience to the principles of the gospel. We promise
every Sabbath day to keep those principles.

And what is the blessing? " . . . that they may always have
his Spirit to be with them." What a divine guidance! And I

testify to you that divine inspiration is a reality. Men and women who obey the principles of life and salvation, sincerely repent of their sins, and as sincerely strive to live in accordance with the principles of the gospel, are guided and inspired by the Holy Ghost, and are shown things to come. I testify that that guidance is with this Church and has been since the Prophet Joseph Smith established it. I bear you witness, too, that this Church is the power of God unto salvation, the gospel of Jesus Christ. (See D. & C. 20:77.)

To sum up then, the operation of the law of cause and effect is as constant in the spiritual realm as it is in the material world. You obey the principle, and you receive the blessing, and the keeping of each promise made in relation to the sacrament brings the results and the blessings as surely as the sun brings light.

Order, reverence, attention to divine promises—the promise to enter into the fold of Christ, to cherish virtues mentioned in the gospel of Christ, to keep them ever in mind, to love the Lord wholeheartedly, and to labor, even at the sacrifice of self, for the brotherhood of man—these and all kindred virtues are associated with the partaking of the sacrament. It is good to meet together and especially to renew our covenants with God in that holy sacrament.

> "Help us, O God, to realize
> The great atoning sacrifice,
> The gift of thy Beloved Son,
> The Prince of Life, the Holy One."
> —CR, October 1929, pp. 14-15.

One of the greatest benefits derived from meeting together is the experiencing of new and uplifting thoughts and feelings. These thoughts and feelings are not always those expressed by the speaker. Words do not convey thought—they only call up thought; but those who, while listening, experience new thoughts or noble feelings always derive one of the greatest blessings that come to those who meet together.—CR, April 1908, p. 93.

QUALITIES TO BE CULTIVATED BY LATTER-DAY SAINTS

THE LIFE OF THE INTELLECT AND OF THE SPIRIT. Let us seek to live intellectually. I welcome with all my heart the hundreds and the thousands of boys and girls who are participating in the realm of education in the auxiliary associations and in the Church schools. What are they learning to do but to live—to live completely and abundantly; and in the living to serve—serve their fellow men! He lives most who sees or hears,

> " . . . tongues in trees, books in the running brooks,
> Sermons in stones and good in every thing."
>   Shakespeare, *As You Like It*. Act. ii, sc. 1, 1. 15.

He lives most who sees beyond these trees, these stones, these running brooks, and sees God and goodness in it all, who sees an overruling Providence in all this world and recognizes God's children as brothers and sisters, in every one of whom there is something good, ever striving, to lift the man up out of the sensual world into the realm of true religion.

I believe that there is in every human soul a something good calling for something better, very much as that something in life mentioned by Lowell when he said, referring to spring,

> "Every clod feels a stir of might,
> An instinct within it that reaches and towers,
> And groping blindly above it for light,
> Climbs to a soul in grass and flowers."
>   James Russell Lowell, *The Vision of*
>   *Sir Launfal: Prelude.*

So there is in the human soul that divine element which is calling, striving, urging the person up to a higher, to a better life.

Boys and girls should do right because it is right. The day is past when you can threaten them with punishment hereafter. The world has passed by the fears of a fire and eternal torment. They can be appealed to, however, upon the sound principles of true religious living. It is the best because it works best. It is the best because it makes us happy and better here and now. We are better citizens; we are better friends; we are better football players; we are better students; we are better sons; we are better daughters; we are better everything; and the world should know it.

When we take the opposite view, as many of our boys unfortunately are doing, and seek life in immediate pleasures, transitory pleasures, indeed, we find only disappointment and eventually death, for to be carnally minded is death, but to be spiritually minded is life and peace.

"Live while you live, the epicure would say,
And seize the pleasures of the present day;" [That is one view.]
"Live while you live, the sacred preacher cries,
And give to God each moment as it flies." [The other.]
"Lord, in my view let both united be;
I live in pleasure when I live to Thee."

> Dr. Philip Doddridge, *Epigram on His Family Arms.*
> —*CR*, October 1920, pp. 42-43.

STUDY THE HISTORY OF THE CHURCH. There are many people in the world who condemn us because they are ignorant of the real facts concerning the Church. The great comfort to us, however, is that we know the purpose of the Church; we know its history—a little of it; not, however, so much as we should know, we younger people. We ought to study it more. There is inspiration in the history of this Church. There is inspiration and truth in reading the sayings of the Prophet Joseph and those associated with him in the early days. Read it; study it; do not censure because of ignorance.

When we read the history of the Church, we are forced to acknowledge the fact that it has blessed humanity. When we study the principles, we find that they are the saving principles, as revealed by the Lord and Savior Jesus Christ. What more do we want? There is nothing done, there is nothing taught, under the guidance and inspiration of the Lord but tends to the upbuilding and advancement of the human race, and that tends to the amelioration of the evils that afflict humanity.—*CR*, April 1909, p. 66.

STUDY MODERN REVELATION. If we were to pay more attention to such advice and devote more study to the modern revelations as contained in the Doctrine and Covenants, we should grow in appreciation of the magnitude of the great work that has been established in this dispensation. It is

often said that the Church is the greatest thing in the world—
it is—but the more we give attention to it, and realize how
well adapted it is to our individual life, to our home life, to
our social life; when we study it from the standpoint of our
environment, from the standpoint of scientific discoveries, our
hearts are made to rejoice for God's goodness unto us in having
given to us the privilege of knowing the gospel of Jesus Christ.

Nearly every passage in the Doctrine and Covenants
is replete with admonitions, full of inspiration and wonderful
revelations to men. Sometimes those revelations are couched
in but few words, but by careful study one sees how closely
related they are to all truth. Take, for example, the wonderful revelation, simply expressed, in regard to government by
the priesthood: "No power or influence can or ought to be
maintained by virtue of the priesthood, only by persuasion, by
long-suffering, by gentleness and meekness, and by love unfeigned." (D. & C. 121:41.)

Just think of that use of the word *unfeigned*. Love pretended has no influence. Love unfeigned always has the power
to reach the heart.

To continue: "Reproving betimes with sharpness, . . .
and then showing forth afterwards an increase of love toward
him whom thou hast reproved, lest he esteem thee to be his
enemy." (*Ibid.* 121:43.)

Why, it is a wonderful admonition and lesson in regard
to the government, not only in quorums of priesthood in the
Church offices but also in our home life and in all phases
of association in society!

Consider, again, the suggestion in regard to the worth of
souls, "Remember the worth of souls is great." Also the
revelation in regard to the true riches, "Seek not for riches
but for wisdom," and so on, and the riches of the world will
be added also.

Such things are the real things in the world. And so we
might continue; revelation after revelation as given in the
Doctrine and Covenants, if studied and paid attention to by
the Latter-day Saints, will establish faith in their hearts and
make them rejoice at this great and wonderful organization
placed among men for their salvation.—*CR*, October 1913,
p. 104.

THE ABUNDANT LIFE. The Church accepts as literally true the saying of Jesus:

" . . . I am come that they might have life, and that they might have it more abundantly." (John 10:10.)

We believe, however, that this abundant life is obtained not only from spiritual exultation, but also by the application to daily life of the principles that Jesus taught.

These principles are few and simple and may, if desired, be applied by every normal person. The first of these, and the foundation upon which a true Christian society is built, is:

Love the Lord thy God with all thy heart, mind, and strength. (See Mark 12:30.)

A belief in a supreme Being who lives, and loves his children—a belief that gives power and vigor to the soul—an assurance that he can be approached for guidance, and that he will manifest himself to those who seek him.

Another is: *The acceptance of the truth that life is a gift of God, and therefore divine.* The proper use of this gift impels man to become the master, not the slave, of nature. His appetites are to be controlled and used for the benefit of his health and the prolongation of life. His passions mastered and controlled for the happiness and blessing of others and the perpetuity of the race.

A third principle is: *Personal integrity.* By this I mean, plain, everyday honesty, sobriety, and respect for others' rights, such as will win the confidence of one's fellows. This recognition applies to nations as well as to individuals. It is as wrong for a nation, because it is powerful, to steal from another and oppress it, as it is for an individual to rob and kill his neighbor.

A fourth essential is: *Social consciousness that awakens in each individual the realization that it is his duty to make the world better for his having been in it.* The very heart and spirit of this standard is expressed in the statement of the Prophet Joseph Smith—"If my life is of no value to my friends, it is of no value to me."—*CR*, October 1937, pp. 102-103.

LITTLE ACTS OF KINDNESS. There is no one great thing which we can do to obtain eternal life, and it seems to me that the great lesson to be learned in the world today is to apply in the little acts and duties of life the glorious principles of the gospel. Let us not think that because some of the things named this afternoon may seem small and trivial that they are unimportant. Life, after all, is made up of little things. Our life, our being, physically, is made up here of little heart-beats. Let that little heart stop beating, and life in this world ceases. The great sun is a mighty force in the universe, but we receive the blessings of its rays because they come to us as little beams, which, taken in the aggregate, fill the whole world with sunlight. The dark night is made pleasant by the glimmer of what seem to be little stars; and so the true Christian life is made up of little Christlike acts performed this hour, this minute, in the home, in the quorum, in the organization, in the town, wherever our life and acts may be cast.—*CR,* October 1914, pp. 87-88.

CONVICTIONS OF THE LATTER-DAY SAINTS. The Latter-day Saints are a people of strong convictions; and convictions—convictions of the truth—are the strongest, most potent factors in the world. It has been truly said that no historic event is so important as the advent of a conviction of a new truth. "The power of such conviction in the human soul is to build up institutions, to change the course of events, and to alter the tendencies of human affairs; and among all convictions there are none so strong, permanent, and unconquerable as religious convictions. Ideas," says Paxton, "go booming through the world louder than cannon. Thoughts are mightier than armies."

If I were to couch in definite terms two of the most potent convictions in the hearts of the Latter-day Saints, I would name: First, an abiding assurance that the gospel as taught by the Redeemer when he lived among men and which was later modified, changed, and corrupted by men, has been restored by the Redeemer in its purity and fulness; and second, following naturally the first, a conviction in the heart of every member of this Church that the responsibility rests upon the membership of the Church to preach the restored gospel to every nation, kindred, tongue, and people.—*CR,* April 1927, p. 102.

THE GOSPEL IS OUR ANCHOR.   The gospel is our anchor.
We know what it stands for.   If we live it, feel it, and speak
well of the gospel, of the priesthood, of the authorities in it,
speak well even of our enemies, we shall feel happier ourselves,
and we shall be preaching the gospel of Jesus Christ.   Everybody can do this.   It is possible.   God has not asked us to do
it and then deprived us of the power of performing it.—CR,
April 1910, p. 110.

PURITY OF CHARACTER.   Wordsworth once wrote of
Milton, "Thy soul was like a star and dwelt apart."   It seems
to me, after listening to the brethren testify to the principles
of the gospel and the high standard of living among the
Latter-day Saints, that this people "dwells apart," that they
should be in reality "a peculiar people."

I do not mean that we are not to mingle with our friends
who do not believe as we, neither do I believe that we ought to
be exclusive; but as the Church of God we must "dwell apart."

Now, in what way?   James says that "Pure religion and
undefiled before God and the Father is this, To visit the
fatherless and widows in their affliction, and to keep himself
unspotted from the world." (James 1:27.)   It is in the sense
of keeping ourselves unspotted from the world that I take it
the Church of God should be distinct, in this sense, that the
children of the Church be as a star—pure.—CR, October 1911,
pp. 56-57.

Now, what do we mean by the world?   It is sometimes
used as an indefinite term.   I take it that the world refers to
the inhabitants who are alienated from the Saints of God.
They are aliens to the Church, and it is the spirit of this aliena-
tion that we should keep ourselves free from.   We are told
by Paul not to conform to the fashions of the world.   Titus
was warned not to partake of those things, the evils of the
world, and to "Flee also youthful lusts: but follow righteousness, faith, charity, peace, with them that call on the Lord
out of a pure heart." (II Tim. 2:22.)   Purity of heart—Zion
is the pure in heart, we have been told, and the strength of
this Church lies in the purity of the thoughts and lives of its
members, then the testimony of Jesus abides in the soul, and
strength comes to each individual to withstand the evils of
the world.—CR, October 1911, p. 58.

These evils present themselves insidiously in our daily association. They come in the shape of temptations, as they came to the Savior after his baptism. What were those temptations? When Satan said, " . . . command that these stones be made bread," (Matt. 4:3) he was appealing to the appetite. He knew that Jesus was hungry, that he was physically weak and thought that by pointing to those little limestones which resemble somewhat a Jewish loaf of bread, he could awaken a desire to eat. Failing in that, he received the divine word, " . . . Man shall not live by bread alone, but by every word that proceedeth out of the mouth of God." (*Ibid.*, 4:4.) Satan then tried him in another way. He dared him—an appeal to his pride, to his vanity, quoted scripture to support his temptation, for remember,

"The devil can cite Scripture for his purpose.
An evil soul, producing holy witness,
Is like a villain with a smiling cheek,
A goodly apple rotten at the heart:
O what a goodly outside falsehood hath!"

Shakespeare, *The Merchant of Venice.* Act i, sc. 3, 1. 99.

But the Savior answered him in terms of scripture, "It is written again, Thou shalt not tempt the Lord thy God." (Matt. 4:7.) What was the third? An appeal to his love of power, domain, wealth, "All these things [the kingdoms of the world and the glory thereof] will I give thee," said the tempter, "if thou wilt fall down and worship me." (*Ibid.*, 4:9.) "Get thee hence, Satan: for it is written, Thou shalt worship the Lord thy God, and him only shalt thou serve." (*Ibid.*, 4:10.) Now, nearly every temptation that comes to you and me comes in one of those forms. Classify them, and you will find that under one of those three nearly every given temptation that makes you and me spotted, ever so little maybe, comes to us as (1) a temptation of the appetite or passion; (2) a yielding to the pride and fashion or vanity of those alienated from the things of God; or (3) a desire for the riches of the world, or power among men.

Now, when do temptations come? Why, they come to us in our social gatherings; they come to us at our weddings; they come to us in our politics; they come to us in our business relations, on the farm, in the mercantile establishment, in the dealings in the affairs of life; we find these insidious influences working; and it is when they manifest themselves to the consciousness of each individual that the defense of truth ought to exert itself. There may never come a great opportunity to defend this Church.

"It may not be on the mountain height
    Or over the stormy sea;
It may not be at the battle's front
    My Lord will have need of me;
But if, by a still, small voice he calls
    To paths that I do not know,
I'll answer, dear Lord, with my hand in thine:
    I'll go where you want me to go."

Mary Brown

When that still, small voice calls to the performance of duty, insignificant though it seem, and its performance unknown to anyone save the individual and God, he who responds gains corresponding strength. Temptation often comes in the same quiet way. Perhaps the yielding to it may not be known by anyone save the individual and his God, but if he does yield to it, he becomes to that extent weakened and spotted with the evil of the world.—*CR,* October 1911, pp. 58-59.

DEFENSE OF THE CHURCH A DAILY MATTER. I have never met a member of the Church who would not express himself, and, if occasion arose, who did not so express himself as being willing to defend his membership if this Church were attacked. I have seen boys, apparently indifferent to Church interests, on occasions stand out in expressive defiance of the attack upon the Church.

We frequently arrogate to ourselves the thought that if there were any encroachment upon this Church, we should be ready to stand out and defend it en masse. That feeling, that spirit of defense, is always looking for some exceptional manifestation of opposition, something great that is coming. When such comes, we think we shall be ready to defend the Church, when, perhaps this very day, there has been an encroachment upon our souls which has weakened our power to defend the truth. Trees that can stand in the midst of the

hurricane often yield to the destroying pests that you can
scarcely see with a microscope, and the greatest foes of humanity today are those unseen microscopical microbes that attack
the body.

It is the unseen influences at work in society that are
undermining the manhood and womanhood of today. It is
these unseen influences that come from the world that get us
when we are least prepared to defend ourselves. When we do
not withstand the encroachments of these evil influences, we
weaken the possibility of defending the Church of Jesus Christ.
This is an individual work, and what the individuals are,
that the aggregate is.—CR, October 1911, p. 57.

THE TEST—AN INDIVIDUAL ONE. I was with a party of
friends driving through a beautiful valley, not far from Salt
Lake City. We passed a beautiful wheat field. It was an
impressive sight really, to see that dry farm of wheat, and one
of the party expressed his admiration of the luxuriant growth
in the field and looked at it in general. There it stood apart
from the sagebrush and barren surroundings. But he was
not satisfied with looking at it in the aggregate; the con-
veyance was stopped; and he looked at individual heads of
wheat and exclaimed, "Look what large heads." Just one;
it was the individual stalk that gave him that impression.
That was not enough. He broke the head, shuffled it in his
hand, blew the chaff away, and examined each kernel. "The
kernels," continued he, "are plump and solid."

After all, the test of that wheat field was the individual
kernel of wheat, and so it is in a community, so it is in the
Church. The test, after all, of the efficiency of God's people
is an individual one.—CR, October 1911, pp. 57-58.

I admire that counselor in the presidency of a stake
who, at a political party last fall, when asked to drink the
health and success of that party, left his champagne untouched.
When the chairman came, he said, "You did not respond to
the toast for the success of the party. Aren't you one with
us?"

He said, "Yes, I did."

The chairman said, "There is your champagne untouched."

"But," replied the counselor, "you see the glass of water is empty. I do not drink champagne nor intoxicants, but I am with you in wishing the success of the party."

The man grasped his hand and said, "I admire your strength in living up to your principles." They always do. —*CR*, October 1911, p. 60.

THE POWER OF THE CHRISTIAN LIFE. Men have called Jesus Christ an enthusiast; they have accused him of being a dreamer, an ascetic, a recluse, and other such epithets have they hurled at him, but they are loath ever to say that Christ, the Redeemer, was dishonest or untrue. His life is a life of honesty, honor, uprightness. He was drawn to men who were honest themselves, whose hearts were pure and guileless.

Witness how quickly he saw purity and guilelessness in Nathanael. "Behold," said he, "an Israelite indeed, in whom is no guile!" (John 1:47.) As a negative pole is drawn by the positive, the mutual attraction seemed to be here. Their souls attracted each other, as the dewdrop trickling down the flower in the morning, falls into its brother dewdrop on the flower, absorbed in one whole. So the purity of Christ seemed to absorb, attract, draw to the purity of Nathanael.

Nathanael was honest, upright, pure as a follower of Christ should be. No guileless man can be dishonest. No guileless man can stoop to chicanery and fraud, deceiving a brother.

I say Christ's life and his teachings always bore testimony to the truth. In our day, God has said, through the Prophet Joseph Smith: "God does not walk in crooked paths, neither does he vary to the right hand or to the left. His words are true always, never varying from the straight path, and his words have one eternal round." To the Latter-day Saints, as God's people, he has declared that one of the fundamental principles of their belief is honesty and truthfulness. I rejoice in repeating our thirteenth Article of Faith:

"We believe in being honest, true, chaste, benevolent, virtuous, and in doing good to all men; indeed, we may say that we follow the admonition of Paul—We believe all things, we hope all things, we have endured many things, and hope to be able to endure all things. If there is anything virtuous, lovely, or of good report or praiseworthy, we seek after these things."

Let your light so shine among men that they seeing your good works may be led to glorify our Father which is in heaven. In probably no more effective way can the truth be witnessed before men than for every Latter-day Saint to maintain and foster the confidence of our outside friends in a faithful member of the Church of Jesus Christ.

Now, in order to do that, we must be honest in all things. If we are contractors and agree to put in such and such material in a building, let us put that material in. If we agree to the stipulations of a contract, to put in one hundred and fifty feet of radiation in the building, let us put in one hundred and fifty feet. Those are details, aren't they, but those are the details by which the men with whom you deal will judge your actions. If you are taking to market potatoes of a particular grade, and you so describe that grade, then be sure that an investigation will prove your statements true. I was grieved when I heard a wholesale dealer say that he has opened sacks of produce brought in from the farm and found foreign material, such as rocks and dirt, placed in them to make up weight. I did not ask him for the religion of those men; I asked for no name; but such things are dishonorable; no true member of the Church of Jesus Christ can stoop to such trickery. Let your light shine before men. In this world today there needs to be an ensign, a people standing out in bold relief as an example to the world in honesty and fair-dealing.—CR, Oct. 1910, pp. 48-49.

COURAGE AND FAITH. "Be of good courage, and he shall strengthen your heart, all ye that hope in the Lord." (Psalm 31:24.)

In this promise are two principles that should be cherished by every truly religious man—faith and courage. What is implied in this text? We know with assurance that the Lord is keeping faith with his people; therefore, let none despair but take courage, and their hope shall not be in vain. Faith in God, trust, confidence in our fellow men, the courage of our convictions will enable us eventually to achieve any righteous cause.

Courage is that quality of the mind which meets danger or opposition with calmness and firmness, which enables a man to face difficulties that lie in his pathway to righteous achievement. It is different from fortitude. Fortitude enables us to bear, endure; fortitude is more of a feminine quality. Courage implies facing difficulties and overcoming them.

He who is or should be the guide of our lives was the most courageous of all men. "In Jesus we find bravery at its best; courage at its loftiest; heroism at its climax." True heroism defends the right and faces disaster without cringing. In this regard the Savior was the personification of true courage and heroism. Illustrative of this I need only mention the cleansing of the temple; or his fearlessly speaking the truth when his home folk turned him from Nazareth; or when the five thousand in Capernaum were reduced to only twelve to whom he turned and said, "Will ye also go away?" Never once, however, did the Master despair or turn from his destined course. This is the kind of courage we need in the world today.—CR, April 1936, p. 58.

DAILY CONDUCT. One reason why thinking men and women are rejecting the pseudo-Christian sects of the day is because of the daily acts of so-called Christian believers. It is very easy to go to church, to sing hallelujah, and to cry, "Lord, Lord!" but it is not so easy to do that which the Lord requires.

When churchmen's acts do not conform to their pretensions, non-churchmen accuse them of hypocrisy, one of the gross sins condemned most vehemently by the Savior.

Members of the Church of Jesus Christ should strive very earnestly to reflect in their daily conduct those ideals which on Sunday they profess to cherish.—I, 78:570 (1943).

The boys of our Church who uphold the standards are the ones who are respected and who receive honor from the men of the world as well as from those of the Church.—CR, April 1948, p. 173.

AVOID PROFANITY. Profanity is a vice all too prevalent in America, and though we say it with embarrassment, all too frequently used in the Church.—CR, October 1948, p. 120.

UNITY AND CONCORD. "Holy Father, keep through thine
own name those whom thou hast given me, that they may
be one, as we are.

"Neither pray I for these alone, but for them also which
shall believe on me through their word;

"That they all may be one; as thou, Father, art in me,
and I in thee, that they also may be one in us: that the world
may believe. . . . " (John 17:11, 20-21.)

As nearly all of you readily recognize, I have quoted
from one of the most sublime prayers ever offered among men.
It is an intercessory prayer. The occasion makes the things
prayed for most significant. In it Jesus makes unity pre-
eminent among his followers.

Unity and its synonyms, harmony, good will, peace, concord, mutual understanding, express a condition for which
the human heart constantly yearns. Its opposites are discord,
contention, strife, confusion.—CR, October 1939, pp. 101-
102.

"LET US RESOLVE. . . . " As we depart now, let us make
real the good feelings that have been aroused in our souls.
Let us not permit to evaporate from our minds and feelings
the good resolutions we have formed. First, let us resolve
that from now on we are going to be men of higher and more
sterling character, more conscious of our own weaknesses,
more kind and charitable toward others' feelings.

Let us resolve that we shall practise more self-control
in our homes, control our tempers and our tongues, and control our feelings, that they may not wander beyond the bounds
of right and purity, more seeking the presence of God, realizing how dependent we are upon him for success in the posi-
tions we hold in the Church.

As we leave this conference, let us resolve to be not only
more loyal to our quorums but also more devoted to the
duties assigned us, one of which is attendance at our quorum
meetings, in order to strengthen that group and increase the
power of fellowship and brotherhood, more loyal to our country. This is an election year. Upon you devolves the responsibility of choosing our servants in government, for whoever is elected to preside over this country as President, as

Senators, members of the House of Representatives are your servants, not your rulers. And do not be slothful on the day of election but come out and exercise your right and privilege as a citizen of this great republic. What doth it profit though a man say he hath faith and not works? Here we should prove ourselves loyal citizens.

As we depart, let us be more determined to make beautiful homes, to be kinder husbands, more thoughtful wives, more exemplary parents to our children, determined that in our homes we are going to have just a little taste of heaven here on this earth.

With these resolves in mind, with all my heart I say, fellow workers, God bless you. Cherish in your hearts the testimony of truth, make it as solid and as firm and unwavering as the fixed stars in the heavens. May there come into everyone's heart and in all our homes the true spirit of Christ our Redeemer, whose reality, whose inspiring guidance I know to be real.

God bless you, keep you, and magnify you in the eyes of your associates! May he make more powerful than ever before in the history of this Church the influence of this divine organization, that its potency may be felt throughout the world, and men's hearts turned to serve him as they have never before been influenced, that we may avert the terrible threatening war, and peace be established among the nations of the world, I pray in the name of Jesus Christ.—*CR*, April 1952, pp. 128-129.

Book III

PRIESTHOOD AND CHURCH
PRACTICES

"As long as members of the
priesthood merit the guidance
of Christ by honest and conscientious dealing with their
fellow men, by resisting evil
in any of its forms, by the
faithful performance of duty,
there is no opposing power in
this world which can stay the
progress of the Church of
Jesus Christ."

—DAVID O. MCKAY

The Improvement Era
Volume 48:696.

Chapter 12

Priesthood and Its Work

PRIESTHOOD

RESTORATION OF THE PRIESTHOOD. May 15 marks the anniversary of the restoration of the Aaronic Priesthood. On that day in the year 1829, John the Baptist came to earth as a heavenly messenger and conferred this authority upon Joseph Smith and Oliver Cowdery, saying:

"Upon you my fellow servants, in the name of Messiah I confer the Priesthood of Aaron, which holds the keys of the ministering of angels, and of the gospel of repentance, and of baptism by immersion for the remission of sins; and this shall never be taken again from the earth, until the sons of Levi do offer again an offering unto the Lord in righteousness." (D. & C. 13.)

John, the son of Zacharias, was probably the last among the Jews to hold the keys of the Aaronic Priesthood, which continued among the children of Israel from the time that Moses and the Higher Priesthood were taken from their midst until the coming of Christ in the Meridian of Time. From the standpoint of direct authority, therefore, it is highly fitting that he should be the messenger to restore this authority in this dispensation. He held it not only by right of lineage but also by special ordination when he was eight days old.

PRIESTHOOD DISTINGUISHES THE CHURCH. This question of divine authority is one of the important factors which distinguish the Church of Jesus Christ from the Protestant creeds of Christendom. In plain, unmistakable terms the Church declares that "a man must be called of God, by prophecy, and by the laying on of hands, by those who are in authority to preach the gospel and administer in the ordinances thereof." (Articles of Faith, No. 5.) In this declaration the Church but reiterates the words of one who bore Christ's authority in the Meridian of Time, and who, in writing upon this very question, said, "And no man taketh this honour unto himself, but he that is called of God, as was Aaron." (Heb. 5:4.)

Herein lies one secret of the strength of this great latter-day work. Its origin consists not in the whims, the desires, or the aspirations of men, but in the order and the will of Christ himself, the author of our eternal salvation. If one man could assume the right to speak in the name of the Lord, other men would have the same privilege. These many men, all presuming to say, "Thus saith the Lord," yet not seeing "eye to eye" on important elements of God's kingdom, the inevitable result would be confusion, and sincere men and women would be driven from, not attracted to Christ's Church, yet eventually would be made to suffer for not having obeyed the principles of life and salvation.

Yet the real cause of their failure to accept these eternal principles would be the fact that unauthorized men arrogated to themselves the right to officiate in things pertaining to God. Herein lies the explanation of the discordant condition existing among jarring creeds in the so-called Christian world today. Men who have no right so to do are officiating in the name of Christ. The result, of course, is confusion. Whatever else may be said of the Prophet Joseph Smith, the strength of his position in regard to divine authority must be recognized.

THE MANNER OF THE RESTORATION. The manner of restoring the priesthood in 1829 is strikingly in keeping with Christ's recognition of authority in the early Church. When, for example, the stricken Paul cried, "Lord, what wilt thou have me to do?" the Savior, though he could easily have told him what to do, recognized the authority he had given to man by saying, "Arise, and go into the city, and it shall be told thee what thou must do." (See Acts 9:6.) In the city of Damascus was one Ananias, who had been commissioned to act in the name of Christ, and from him was Paul directed to receive instruction and guidance. So it was when Christ appeared to the Prophet Joseph. He did not confer authority direct but recognized John the Baptist, by whose authority Jesus himself had been baptized, and in the case of the Melchizedek Priesthood, Peter, James, and John, unto whom he had given authority when he established his Church at Jerusalem.

Thus men were made *priests* by him who alone has the right to say who shall officiate in his name. Literally, a *priest* is a mediator between God and man, and priesthood is *power* and authority to administer in the name of the Lord. There is no more justification in a man's arrogating to himself this authority than in his presuming to take upon himself the right to represent, at a foreign court, the British government. Every document such a one would sign in the name of His Majesty the King, Parliament would repudiate as a forgery and would take steps immediately to have the usurper properly punished. Yet in the matters pertaining to the eternal life and happiness of the human family, men usurp the office of priest and mislead with impunity millions of innocent people.

If the world could but realize the full significance of the angel John's coming again to earth, May 15, 1829, multitudes who are praying for the kingdom of God to be established among men would gratefully join in the commemoration of that heavenly manifestation. Their souls would respond to the ecstatic joy that Oliver Cowdery expresses in his description of the event, as follows:

"On a sudden, as from the midst of eternity, the voice of the Redeemer spake peace to us, while the veil was parted, and the angel of God came clothed with glory, and delivered the anxiously looked-for message, and the keys of the gospel of repentance. What joy! what wonder! what amazement! While the world was racked and distracted—while millions were groping as the blind for the wall, and while all men were resting upon uncertainty, as a general mass, our eyes beheld, our ears heard, as in the 'blaze of day'; yes, more—above the glitter of the May sunbeam, which then shed its brilliancy over the face of nature! Then his voice, though mild, pierced to the center, and his words, 'I am thy fellow servant,' dispelled all fear. We listened, we gazed, we admired! 'Twas the voice of an angel from glory, 'twas a message from the Most High! And as we heard we rejoiced, while his love enkindled upon our souls, and we were wrapped in the vision of the Almighty! Where was room for doubt? Nowhere; the uncertainty had fled, doubt had sunk no more to rise, while fiction and deception had fled forever!" (*D.H.C.* 1:43)—*MS*, 85:312-314 (1923).

THE SOURCE OF PRIESTHOOD POWER. Jesus the Christ is the source of the power of the priesthood. As long as members

of the priesthood merit the guidance of Christ by honest
and conscientious dealing with their fellow men, by resisting
evil in any of its forms, by the faithful performance of duty,
there is no opposing power in this world which can stay the
progress of the Church of Jesus Christ.—*IE*, 48:696 (1945).

No man can face an audience of the priesthood of God
without a sense of humility and a prayer in his heart for
guidance from our Heavenly Father.—*CR*, April 1948, p. 170.

WHAT PRIESTHOOD IS

Priesthood is power and authority inherent in the Godhead. In man it is always delegated authority—it cannot be
assumed with efficacy.

PURPOSES OF PRIESTHOOD

PRIESTHOOD MEANS SERVICE. This is true even in its
divine source; as we may infer from the sublime declaration
of the Lord himself: "This is my work and my glory—to bring
to pass the immortality and eternal life of man." (Moses 1:39.)
Emanating from Deity is the service that leads to the redemption of God's children.

Whenever the priesthood is delegated to man, it is conferred upon him not as a personal distinction, although it becomes such as he honors it, but as authority to represent Deity
and an obligation to assist the Lord in bringing to pass the
immortality and eternal life of man.

If priesthood meant only personal honor, blessing, or
individual elevation, there would be no need of groups or
quorums. The very existence of such groups established by
divine authorization proclaims our dependence upon one
another, the indispensable need of mutual help and assistance.
We are, by divine right, social beings.—*DNCS*, April 20,
1935, p. 3.

Our lives are wrapped up with the lives of others. We are
happiest as we contribute to the lives of others. I say that because the priesthood you hold means that you are to serve
others. You represent God in the field to which you are
assigned.—*CR*, Sept.-Oct. 1950, p. 112.

A Fundamental Program for the Priesthood. As the honest people of the world wonder in vain and cry out in uncertainty, "What shall we do?" members of the Church of Jesus Christ who feel secure in the knowledge of the restored gospel should say, "Men and brethren, what *can* we do?"

Some specific things which the priesthood and their families can and should do are these:

First—we can set an example of uprightness; be honest in all our dealings; avoid vulgarity and profanity; demonstrate to our neighbors and to all whom we meet that we live clean, honorable lives.

"Let your light so shine before men, that they may see your good works, and glorify your Father which is in heaven." (Matt. 5:16.)

Second—let us strive for peace and harmony in the home. If we cannot keep quarreling, bickering, and selfishness out of our home, how can we even hope to banish these evils from society?

A true Mormon home is one in which if Christ should chance to enter, he would be pleased to linger and to rest.

Third—having at least striven for a good character, having a home environment that is creditable, we may then consistently discharge our duty as authorized representatives of the Lord Jesus Christ to declare to the world that the conditions that will bring peace and comfort to the individual, to the family, and to the nation, are found in the restored gospel of Jesus Christ. These can be named and understood and as easily practised with resultant contentment and peace as are the evils and vices that bring tribulation.

Summarized, these fundamentals are: An acceptance of Christ as Savior and Redeemer; a moving, soul-consciousness of the existence of God, and that he is our Father in heaven; a daily life consistent with such a knowledge; a love for one's fellow men.

In other words, as the Savior summarized the law and the prophets:

"And thou shalt love the Lord thy God with all thy heart, and with all thy soul, and with all thy mind, and . . . thy neighbour as thyself." (Mark 12:30-31.)—*CR*, October 1947, pp. 119-120.

There is a responsibility resting upon each for the work
of the ministry, for the edifying of the body of Christ, and
that work is to continue until we all come in the unity of the
faith unto the knowledge of the Son of God, unto a perfect
man, even unto the measure of the stature of the fulness of
Christ.

I am inclined to think, however, that much of this work,
both of quorums and auxiliary organizations, is confined largely
among the better and more earnest members of the Church.

We are prone to do our duty, as many men and women
do their work, along the lines of least resistance. Our influence
is felt most strongly among those who need it least. I may
be overstating this. If I am, I am doing so, simply to make a
point; and yet my observation leads me to believe that what
I say is very nearly a fact. Quorum officers, for example,
are wielding their influence, and the need of their quorums is
felt among the most active members of the quorum. Officers
of the auxiliary associations are centering their efforts individually, and as organizations, upon those men and women,
boys and girls, who attend most earnestly and regularly to
their religious duties; and little effort is given to the indifferent,
and the least attention, to those not of us.

I was led to think most earnestly upon this matter when
I heard only a few days ago of a young man not a member of
the Church who has been in Utah for nearly twenty years,
and who had just met a young high councilman of my ac-
quaintance. Although he was with the high councilman
only a short time, he said he had learned more about the
Mormon religion than he had heard during his whole former
stay in Utah.

"Why is it," he asked, "that we do not hear more of this
from you men with whom we associate in daily vocation?"

"Well," said the high councilman, "our meetinghouses
are open, always free; we invite everybody to come to our
meetings; and why have you not availed yourself of this opportunity?"

Said he, "I have attended my own church and consequently did not know you men believed in the doctrines you
have explained to me."

The high councilman who spoke to that nonmember is
a natural missionary. He does not bore his hearers with his

religion; but he proposes it, invites attention to it, and never does he fail to take advantage of the opportunity to tell his companions what the Church offers to humanity, by way of temporal salvation here, and eternal salvation as well.

I was delighted, later, to learn that this nonmember had asked for several more interviews, with a view to joining the Church.

How many such men might be reached, if we, as elders, on whom responsibility to preach the truth rests, would but sense that responsibility? It is ours to teach the truth in plainness, in season and out of season, bearing testimony, not only by words but by our actions.

I would ask, too, if we reach, as well, another set of men and women who come halfway between the regular meeting goers, who are honest and faithful in the Church, and the nonmember. I refer now to that indifferent boy and girl in the Church—and there are all too many of them today, towards whom no gentle hand is outstretched to lead them into ways more fruitful to happiness than the paths in which they now tread. I know of no class of workers in the Church who reach these boys and girls so effectively and so directly as the men and boys to whom has been assigned the duty of ward teacher.

We urge in auxiliary associations that the teachers reach out for the indifferent boy and the indifferent girl. The Mutual Improvement workers are striving to enroll the unenrolled, likewise are the Sunday School, Primary, and religion class workers; but there is not much individual work being done, because it is natural when we see a boy indifferent, one who will answer our inquiry with indifference, to let him alone and say, "Well, you go your own way, if you will not listen to me."

One day I entered a wagon shop and said to a brother who had just taken a cigar out of his mouth,

"I have noticed, lately, that you are getting very fond of cigars."

"Yes, sir," said he, "and I pay for them with my own money."

He became quite haughty and rather resented my suggestion. We frequently will meet that attitude, and we may think it seems all right to say, "You go your way, and I will go mine," but is it? A Mutual Improvement worker may speak to an indifferent girl about her weakness, and the young girl will toss her head and walk away rather resentfully to think the Mutual workers should approach her in any such way whatever. But the very fact that interest was taken, the fact that the attention of the indifferent was called to her weakness will leave seed which in the future will bear good fruit. It is better for her to feel that you are interested than to have her think you have no interest in her.

I shall never forget an answer which a man made at the organization of one of our wards. A branch had been made a ward; the new bishopric had announced in the afternoon meeting that following the sacrament service a special meeting would be called for the purpose of considering ways and means of erecting a house of worship. The meeting was held; committees were appointed; and the next morning the new bishop, meeting a man who had been absent from the business meeting, greeted him and said:

"We held a meeting yesterday, appointed committees with a view of erecting a meetinghouse. I am sorry you weren't there; we missed you."

The man turned to the bishop and said: "That is the first time I have been missed in fifteen years."

He became a member of the building committee and was one of the best workers.

It is not a good thing to let these people feel that they are not missed. They are missed; too many of them, today, are missed from our places of meeting and are found in organizations the influence of which is not conducive to the instilling of the testimony of the truths of the everlasting gospel.

Never before in the history of the Church were there so many insidious influences at work among our people as today. Never before have dangers been so threatening to our youth. I am not a pessimist, neither am I one of those who say our young people are worse now than they used to be; I don't believe they are. I have as much confidence in our boys and girls today as you fathers and mothers had in your sons twenty years ago. Most of the boys of today are just as earnest, they think just as much of their religion in general, and just as much of the truth, as boys did twenty years ago. But there are conditions that are worse than they were twenty years ago. There are more threatening influences enticing our boys and girls from paths of duty, than there were twenty years ago; all of which is evident, without further explanation. It is true some of the boys think that the standard of morality has changed. A young man of seventeen said the other day to his mother who had cautioned him about his company:

"Well, Mother, the standards of morals have changed; they are different from what they were ten years ago."

The standard of morals of the Latter-day Saint boy and girl will never change, must never change. Standards of the outside may change, may be lowered, and that influence may penetrate our social organizations, but our standards must be maintained; our boys and girls should be made acquainted with our standards. On whom rests this responsibility, my brethren and sisters? Upon us all.

Let each one constitute himself, today, a missionary, and sometime during the next week reach out that influence to some boy who is indifferent: go beyond that, say one good word by way of testimony to some man, some nonmember who does not know the truth, who does not know this people, someone who, perchance, has been residing here for many years; and good fruit will result from it.

Applications are made for baptism by those who are already residing here, and I think they are better in many ways than applications of those made ten thousand miles away, to reach whom we spend hundreds and thousands of dollars annually.

The gospel is to be preached to all the world as a witness. Let us not forget our own, those who are in our midst. Let us preach, by voice, as well as by act and example, and if we can reach them all, well and good; and if we are not permitted to do it, we can at least approach the purpose by our acts. The time has come when the Latter-day Saints must cling to the Church organization as the best and safest organization in all the world. No other group of men, no other organizations, in the world, can offer you the safety, the happiness, and security that are offered to you in your quorums and auxiliary associations. Let us stand united, remembering that God has placed his organizations here for the perfecting of the Saints, for the work of the ministry, and that ministry includes everybody.

You ward teachers should not pass a house simply because therein is a nonmember of the Church. You can, at least, ask permission to visit him or leave a tract there. You are not teaching and should not teach or visit only to make a hundred percent report to your bishop, but you should teach with a view to reaching the souls of men, our boys and girls, as well as those who are older, and nonmembers.

Love the work, do your best, then leave the conversion to the workings of the Spirit of the Lord; and know this, that when you have done your duty, the peace and satisfaction that come will more than compensate for any rebuff, resentment, or opposition, that might be manifest. You young teachers may come home and feel that your labor has been in vain. A young teacher said not long ago, "Do we need to go back to the house where the man uses tobacco and says he is going to continue to use it, and his wife favors his using it?" Yes; go back again and again, you do your duty, and leave the rest to the Lord.

In conclusion, brethren and sisters, may I quote these lines which seem to be pertinent:

> "Who does his task from day to day
> And meets whatever comes his way,
> Believing God has willed it so,
> Has found true greatness here below;
> Who guards his post no matter where,
> Believing God must need him there,
> Although but lowly toil it be
> Has risen to nobility.
> For great and low there's but one test.
> 'Tis that each one shall do his best,
> Who works with all the strength he can,
> Shall never die in debt to man."
>
> —*IE*, 23:18-22 (1919).

It is said in Ephesians that Christ gave some apostles and some prophets, some evangelists and some pastors and teachers "For the perfecting of the saints, for the work of the ministry, for the edifying of the body of Christ."

(Eph. 4:12.) The teachers in the Church, holding the Holy Priesthood, have devolving upon them the great responsibility of *perfecting the Saints,* and of *edifying the body of Christ;* therefore, I think it is not too much to say that it is their duty, their *duty,* to carry into every home a divine spirit. No greater responsibility can rest upon any man than to be a teacher of God's children.

When Paul said good-bye to the churches in Asia, knowing that he would never again come back to those branches among which he had labored so incessantly and diligently for several years, he called the elders of Ephesus to him one day, over to Miletus. He did not go over to the church where he had recently spent nearly three years because he wanted to hasten to Jerusalem; but he could not pass them without saying good-bye to them. He sent word to them to meet him at the town of Miletus, where he gave them instructions. Among other things he said: "Take heed therefore unto yourselves, and to all the flock, over the which the Holy Ghost hath made you overseers, to feed the church of God, which he hath purchased with his own blood.

"For I know this, that after my departing shall grievous wolves enter in among you, not sparing the flock." (Acts 20:28-29.) The admonition to these men—and among them were bishops, for the word that is interpreted there "overseers" is used in another place as bishops—was to take heed unto *themselves* first and then to the people over whom they presided. Associated with those bishops were elders, just as we have them in the Church.

That same admonition is applicable to the elders today, who are presiding over the Church as ward teachers. Some of them feel that their calling is of little importance, that there is not much dignity attached to it, when the fact is, that there is no more important work in the Church. We cannot say of any one calling in the Church, that it is of more importance than another because all are devoted to the development, to the instruction, to the salvation of God's children. So it is with the calling of teacher; but if there be any preference given, because of superior advantages in winning these people to salvation, it will go to those men holding the priesthood of God, who come in direct contact with the individual members of the Church. The duty, however,

of each man who has accepted this calling is to first take
heed unto himself.—*CR*, October 1916, pp. 57-58.

Peace—the Message. The future and permanency of
the work is assured so long as the priesthood will keep in mind
the great mission of the Church. It is truly a messenger of
peace. When Christ came to the earth, his advent was heralded
by an angelic chorus singing: "Glory to God in the highest,
and on earth peace, good will toward men." (Luke 2:14.)
This message has been repeated so often it seems trite; and,
yet, if peace and brotherhood could even be approximated, it
would prove the greatest boon that could come to humanity.
—*CR*, October 1938, p. 133.

The Duty to Build Quorums. Members in the Aaronic
Priesthood, and members of the quorums in the Melchizedek
Priesthood, we have a duty to build up our quorums; let us
not tear them down by being absent from priesthood meeting,
or by nonpreparation, or by negligence of duty. Let us feel,
every one of us, that it is our duty to do something to build
up the Church, as the Church's duty is to build on truth
and redeem mankind from sin. Men of the priesthood, let
us be one in the upbuilding; let us belong to the class of benefactors; and let no man, from the high priest to the deacon,
in this great priesthood movement fall into the class of malefactors or murmurers.—*CR*, April 1909, p. 68.

The body of the Church is composed of many members,
yet all one body; and it is healthy, vigorous, strong, and
influential when all the members of that body are working
harmoniously together. You deacons, think of your quorum;
you are members of the body. If you injure your finger, the
whole body suffers; and if a little deacons' quorum, away off
in some remote ward, is inactive, to that extent the body of
this Church is suffering. You who preside over teachers'
quorums, see that the body is in healthy condition. You elders
throughout the Church, and you presidents of elders' quorums,
how is the spirituality of your quorum?

You have the outward form; you have your meetings and
your courses of study; but are the members of the body all in
good condition? If so, happy are you, and you are promoting
the welfare of the Church. You seventies, you are called
upon now to make a special effort each Sunday morning to

put that body of men in proper condition. If any members of these quorums be not in condition for service, the body will suffer to that extent. We want all the members of the Church to be in true working order. If we are true within, we shall grow, and the whole Church then is strong. What matters it though the world turn against us? If we are one, if we are pure, if we are sincere, God is our stay and our inspirer.—*CR,* October 1907, p. 64.

THE QUORUM AND THE SOCIAL ENVIRONMENT. In social environment may be included all our Church influences. As I look at the organization given through the Prophet Joseph Smith to the world in this dispensation, as I occasionally catch a glimpse of the possibilities of the quorums and organizations in this Church, I feel to exclaim, O Lord, my God, how marvelous are thy works! Great is thy wisdom, marvelous are thy ways, and the extent of thy doings none can find out. (See D. & C. 76:2.)

The organization of the Church is so perfect that every man, woman, and child within the Church can find something to do; and therein depends the advancement of the person's spiritual welfare. He has a chance to work in the Church of Jesus Christ, no matter how young a boy or how old a man. Now, think what that means.

You go over, in your minds, the organizations as revealed to us in this dispensation. Go first from the First Presidency, down through the Twelve, the high priests, the seventy, elders, priests, teachers, and deacons, all that line of priesthood! See that mighty army of men, ready to do—what? Called upon to do what? To work for the Lord.

We have heard that not one of those men has been called to the position to honor him, but he has been called into the service of the Lord. What does it mean? It means work; work means knowledge; knowledge means eternal life. Shall we not, as parents, put our boys and girls into that environment? If we do not, are we not unmindful of the call of Christ to suffer the children to come back to him? Are we negligent, as parents, and fail to see that our daughters get to their auxiliary meetings? Think of it. The note has been sounded; are we going to move?—*CR,* October 1909, pp. 91-92.

MOMENTUM AND PROGRESS. When I see the Tabernacle crowded to capacity with our brethren, I have a re-affirmation of the strength of the priesthood. It is a fact, as you know, that if you have a moving body, and you increase the speed, the greater is the momentum. Add weight to that body and increase speed, and the momentum is still greater. That is what is occurring in this Church, a great body of priesthood, moving with an acceleration never before known to the Church. There is nothing that can stop the progress of truth, excepting only our weaknesses or failure to do our duty.

What I have said about the momentum of the body of priesthood is applicable to our great missionary force. Never before have we had so many representatives in the field preaching the gospel of Jesus Christ, and never before in the history of the world was that message more needed.—CR, April 1950, pp. 173-174.

FELLOWSHIP IN THE PRIESTHOOD. One of the most pleasing experiences of this great conference was meeting a bishop who came to the stand and said, "I am here with some of my deacons, whom I should like to have the privilege of meeting you." A true leader accompanying his quorum boys to conference!

Fellowship in the priesthood! If we can get the bishops to fellowship the priests in every ward, and in some way, at opportunities favorable, meet those young men and young women of corresponding age in some social or groups or meetings and win their admiration and confidence, we can avoid some unpleasant things which are occurring in our towns. For those priests and girls determine largely the moral atmosphere of your town. You bishops are the leaders. Your counselors can aid you in associating with the teachers and the deacons.

This companionship applies also to elders.

There are many ways in which we can get these indifferent elders together without inviting them to do things which are difficult. Some of them do not like to pray. They hesitate about standing in public to preach, and some of them would rather go fishing or play golf on Sunday than attend meeting. But, not one of those indifferent elders will refuse an invitation, for example, to come to a funeral of one of the townsfolk, or one of their members, or of one of their members' wives, and if you will come as a quorum and sit together as a quorum, there is one means of fellowship. Our high priests are doing it more than seventies or elders.

I have attended a number of funerals where I have seen reserved seats for high priests, in paying respect to a departed brother. There is group fellowship.

Again, these indifferent men will come to your quorum socials. Make those socials of a high order, and thus you will come in personal contact with them.

We must be mutually helpful. This world would not exist if it were not for the mutual aid we give one another from the time we are born until we are laid away.—*CR,* October 1951, p. 179.

Indifference manifest in the world generally towards the Church should tend only to spur men of the priesthood and teachers in the auxiliaries in the Church of Jesus Christ to more earnest and diligent activity.—*IE,* 49:740 (1946).

CHAPTER 13

THE QUORUMS OF THE PRIESTHOOD

THE QUORUMS OF THE MELCHIZEDEK PRIESTHOOD

OBLIGATIONS OF THE INDIVIDUAL. Priesthood is authority to represent God. A man who is given the priesthood is an authorized representative of the Lord in any particular field to which the individual is assigned. It is the duty of a representative of any individual group or organization to strive to represent that individual group or organization in honor. The best way to be worthy representatives is so to live that each may be susceptible to the promptings of the Lord whom he represents. Now think what that means as to a virtuous life.

" . . . my Spirit shall not always strive with man," (D. & C. 1:33) says the Lord. Everyone, then, who holds this priesthood should live such a life as will entitle him to the inspiration of the Lord. And let me say in this regard that communion with the Holy Spirit is just as real as your connection through the radio with the unheard voices and music that fill the air. The vibrations are there.

It is so with God's Spirit. He is ever ready to guide and instruct those who tune in by upright living and who sincerely seek him. I repeat, it is the duty of every man authorized to represent him so to live as to be responsive to that Spirit.

THE NECESSITY FOR QUORUM ORGANIZATION. Now, I ask you, why did not the Lord leave this great endowment and blessing just as it is? One reason is that he realized that these men need companionship, fellowship, the strength of the group; and so he organized quorums and designated the number in each from the deacon to the seventy.

These groups meet together, first, to instruct and to edify, to improve in knowledge generally, and particularly to instruct in moral and religious knowledge, in faith, in holiness, but also to obtain mutual strength, to act uprightly. These groups supply a need that is felt among mankind generally. In the world that need is satisfied by secret orders.

These we do not need. In their place, we have priesthood quorums which will supply every yearning for fellowship, fraternity, and service if men will but do their duty.

THE NATURE OF THE QUORUM—INDEPENDENT IN ITS SPHERE. These quorums are independent, each one having its assigned sphere. It is the duty of the presidency of each quorum to sit in council and to teach the members their duty. It is their duty to disfellowship, even to withdraw the hand of fellowship from those who may be unworthy of that fellowship. They may teach one another and see that each member does his duty, for example, in the payment of fast offerings and the payment of tithing: The amount is not the presidency's interest but that each one should pay his tithing, that each one is honest in his dealings, that each one is performing his duty in ecclesiastical assignments. . . . Quorums, I repeat, are independent in their sphere, but they are in the Church for service, and it is to that service and the relationship of that service to the ward welfare that I wish now to call your attention.

THE MELCHIZEDEK QUORUM AND THE WARD WELFARE COMMITTEE. The relation of these quorums to the welfare work can best be understood if we have in mind the ward welfare committee. On that committee, as you know, there are eight members, three of whom represent Melchizedek Priesthood quorums. The president of the high priests' quorum, who is also chairman of the personal welfare committee, if he is a member of the ward, is, upon the invitation of the bishop, a member of that ward welfare committee. However, usually, in each ward, there is only a group of high priests. In such cases, not the president of the quorum, but the chairman of that group is, upon the invitation of the bishop, a member of the ward welfare committee. That is true, also, in regard to the seventies and also the elders. If there be an elders' quorum in a ward, the president is a member of the personal welfare committee, and as such, a member of the ward welfare committee.

Now the question is, what right has the bishop to direct these men, who, as quorum officers, are independent, so to speak, in their sphere? The bishop would not presume to preside in any of these quorums, but these quorums are subject to the direction of the bishopric in all welfare work. There are needs of the quorum, we will say. Some members are in financial distress, and they need help. True, it is the duty of the quorum to assist these members; not only the duty, it should be a privilege and pleasure. But that help should not be rendered to quorum members without reporting to the ward welfare committee. You can see at once how by so reporting, duplication of assistance will be avoided.

It is necessary for this ward welfare committee to meet every week to consider reports from the presidency of the Relief Society, from the members of the bishopric itself, from each quorum; for example, the high priest may say: "We have five who are in need of help"; the seventy reporting: "We have a brother whose house has burned down; we desire to rebuild it for him"; the elder may add, "We have an elder who was suddenly taken ill right in the midst of the harvesting of beets; we are going out as a group to help him." That is part of welfare work. All in the ward know what is going on, and the bishop will make such assignments to the elder, to the seventy, to the high priest, or to the deacon, as may be needed to carry on this work within the ward.

Furthermore, the bishop has the right to ask the elders' quorum, for example, "Will you put forth a special effort to increase the payment of fast offerings this month?" Or, "We should like each quorum to put forth special effort, that members of each quorum will have one hundred percent in tithing, in fast offerings, in keeping the Word of Wisdom." Such requests, if and when made, do not interfere in any way with the independence of the quorum, but all are working together in harmony; no group saying, "We have no need of thee; we are going off alone," but all working as the head, the hand, the feet, every organ of the body working in its position, and thus producing life and health and vigor. —*DNCS*, December 7, 1946, pp. 1, 8.

STRENGTH LIES IN THE AUTHORITY OF EACH INDIVIDUAL. The strength of Zion rests in the authority of each individual who holds the priesthood. Each man is responsible for that authority he holds, responsible to magnify it.

You who hold the priesthood and sense that divine authority and are partakers of the divine authority—if you live true to it and magnify that priesthood—I say to you that the gates of hell cannot prevail against you.

No power of communism or atheism can move you from that testimony if you are a partaker of that divine nature. —*DNCS*, August 13, 1952.

PROJECTS FOR THE CHURCH SERVICE COMMITTEE OF EACH QUORUM. For years we have said: Get your inactive member, who will not come to your meetings, but who drives an automobile, to take his auto and get that crippled brother who is now well enough to come to meeting but not able to walk nor to pay his own transportation. Say, "Jim, take your auto and fetch William next Sunday. Will you do it?" I do not know of a man, even if he is not in the Church, to say nothing of one holding the priesthood, who would not respond to such a request. And he will stay at the meeting to help William home.—*DNCS*, April 20, 1935, p. 7.

THE ELDERS' QUORUMS: VISITING QUORUM MEMBERS. A number of years ago in one of the elders' quorums in this city, three young men were called to preside. At their first meeting there were only six men present in the elders' quorum. "Well," they said, "this will not do; let us institute systematic visiting." And so they did.

Those men, as presidents, carrying the responsibility, went out to visit the elders of that quorum. They went into one house and asked the man to take up elders' work, but he said, "No, I will not go to elders' meeting." "May we have a meeting here tonight?" he was asked.

"Yes."

They sang, prayed, spent an hour or so with the man and his wife. At the conclusion of it, the man promised that he would attend elders' meeting. The wife, who was unconverted, and who knew little or nothing of the workings of the Church, who lacked a knowledge of it, because of inactivity, began to cry because her husband's going to meeting would take him away from home. "A mission will be next," she said.

However, that young man promised to go to meeting on this condition: that he would not be asked to take part. "All right," said the brethren. But it was not long before he was willing to take part on the program. They assigned him a subject, and the brother who told me of this incident said it was painful to see what that poor man suffered the first time he stood up before his brethren. Those in the meeting deeply sympathized with the man who was making his first effort in public.

At the conclusion of it the brother said, "You did well."

"No," said the man, "I want another chance; I believe I can do better." He did do better, and he became a strong power in influencing other elders to come out to their meetings.

They went into another home and met a similar spirit of indifference. They asked permission to pray and were told, "No."

They talked to the man a little while, and finally he said, "Well, you may kneel down and pray, if you want to."

"Will you kneel with us?"

"No."

After a little kind persuasion, he knelt down. At the conclusion of the meeting in that home, this second elder, following the brethren to the door, broke down and cried, confessed that he had been away from the influence of the Church, had been in another environment, and said, "Keep with me, work with me, and help me to get back into Church environment."

The president of that elders' quorum is now sitting on this stand, a member of the Presiding Bishopric. He and his fellow workers increased the attendance of the quorum from six to over one hundred during that year.

There is a practical example of *doing*. What was accomplished in this elders' quorum in this city can be done throughout the entire Church.—*CR*, October 1909, p. 93.

QUORUM INACTIVITY. I remember visiting the sugar factory in Sugar City, Idaho. Brother Mark Austin took me through it when every wheel was still; the engine was cold; the chimneys stood like specters; the wheels were unoiled; the sparrows were building their nests in wheels that a few months before had hummed with industry. Men had to be hired to keep the dust off the machinery, to make repairs, to keep the factory from going into decay.

I thought, that is always the result of inactivity. No sugar was manufactured in that inactivity. There were no laborers employed, except those hired to keep the factory from going into decay. But when the power was turned on, then raw products were changed to useful articles, which were carried into the homes, throughout the world.

Sometimes part of the machinery is shut up, closed down, and only one part—that of refining—used. I sometimes think that in our Church we are using just part of the machinery that God has placed in our hands. So many of these quorums are lying in inactivity; dust is accumulating. Shall we not work and bring them into operation? As presidents of quorums, let us meet in council; let us think over what men in our quorums are neglecting their duty.—*CR*, October 1909, pp. 92-93.

THE RESPONSIBILITIES OF PRIESTHOOD OFFICE INCLUDING QUORUM PRESIDENTS

OFFICIAL CAPACITY CARRIES OFFICIAL DUTIES. When a citizen of the United States is called to represent his government in a foreign nation either as consul, minister, or ambassador, he goes to his post not only cognizant of his responsibility as a representative of a whole nation, but also aware of certain duties incumbent upon him as they pertain to the office to which he has been appointed.

So it is with any man called to a position in the Church of Jesus Christ. He should be cognizant of the power that goes with a representative of one so chosen, but he also should see clearly what duties he has to perform in order to discharge the trust imposed upon him when he received his call to serve.

THE STAKE PRESIDENCY. The stake presidency, for example, are set apart to perform certain specific duties. The very fact that they are so chosen implies service to the group over which they are called to preside, and the activities of whose members they have the responsibility of directing.

THE BISHOP MUST KNOW THE DUTIES OF HIS OFFICE. So it is with the office of bishop. One of the first desires, indeed the most paramount desire of one chosen to this office, is to know what the duties of the office are, and it is the bounden duty of each so to inform himself that he may discharge those duties intelligently and effectively.

PRESIDENCY IN THE HIGH PRIESTS' QUORUM. This responsibility of service is equally great and important in the calling of one to preside over the high priests' quorum. His duties also are specific and his responsibilities no less important. Indeed, this thought of service applies to every man who is ordained to the High Priesthood, and everyone so ordained has as his first and foremost obligation the duty of informing himself upon the requirements of his office.

THE OFFICE OF SEVENTY AND THE ELEMENT OF SERVICE. Perhaps the office of seventy more clearly than any other in the Church emphasizes the element of service associated with the priesthood. When a man is ordained to the office of a seventy, he enters the field of missionary service, which is his special calling—a witness to the world of the divinity of Jesus Christ and of the restoration of the gospel in this age. Every seventy should remember that an exemplary life is the most impressive sermon that he can preach. His actions, his words, his very thoughts are either leading men to consider favorably his message or driving them away from it.—DNCS, April 20, 1935, pp. 3 and 7.

THE SPECIAL DUTY OF PRESIDENTS. The quorum is an essential part of the Lord's plan for rendering mutual aid. No other organization in the world is so effectively organized into working groups as the Church of Jesus Christ of Latter-day Saints. What a mighty force for good these quorums would be if the spiritual welfare of each member and his obligation to the Church were considered the special duty of each presiding officer! That is a possibility of achievement.—CR, October 1951, p. 9.

THE QUORUMS OF THE AARONIC PRIESTHOOD. I wonder how many parents have stopped to realize how potent these quorums are in the lives of boys! In the first place, quorum membership awakens in the boy the pride of fellowship and membership. Entrance into that group means that the boy has attained to certain standards of excellence of character, and the more distinctive we can make these entrance requirements, the greater will be the pride in the young boy's heart.

Second, the quorum influence arouses or satisfies the call of the boy for the inspiration of the group. Have you heard of the gang spirit? Have you seen the boys out on the ditch bank gathering in groups in answer to the call of their souls for companionship? Then can you see the wisdom of God in gratifying this natural inclination by grouping the boys under an influence that is educative in the highest sense of the term?

Third, that group throws upon the youth responsibility. Tell a young boy that you trust him, and you have one of the greatest means of guiding him uprightly that can come into your hands. Young boy, I trust you! To be trusted is a greater compliment than to be loved. Boys are few indeed who will not hold inviolate an implicit trust.

Fourth, grouping in a quorum offers service. The Presiding Bishopric, holding a presidency over these young men, have outlined as they have hitherto done, a plan of service into which these young men are invited, not just on Sunday, but on every day of the week.

Finally, into that group is introduced faith in God the Father, in his Son Jesus Christ as the Redeemer of the world, and their service and acts are all done under the cognizance and realization that God is approving their acts. It is sublime. It is divine. Fathers and mothers, let us unite with the priesthood in extending the influence of these groups.

I have mentioned only the Aaronic Priesthood, but our fathers are grouped in like manner. I tell you, this grouping in priesthood quorums has the mark of divinity. It is divine. And Joseph Smith, a young man not twenty-five years of age when he gave that revelation, gave it by the inspiration of God for the salvation of the youth of Zion.—*CR*, April 1928, pp. 104-105.

WHAT IT MEANS FOR A BOY TO RECEIVE THE AARONIC PRIESTHOOD. I pray that we may so sense the value of the priesthood, that every deacon in this Church will realize that when he is given the Aaronic Priesthood he is set apart among his fellows, that he is different from others. He cannot with impunity swear as other boys may swear; he cannot participate in pranks in the neighborhood as other boys may participate; he stands apart. That is what it means to a twelve-year-old boy, and, bishops, that is just what you should explain to them when you choose them to be deacons. Do not just call them up and ordain them, but have a talk with them and let them realize what it means to be given the Aaronic Priesthood. In the boyhood area these boys so chosen and instructed should exert an influence for good.—CR, October 1948, p. 174.

It is our obligation when we accept the priesthood to set an example worthy of imitation by our fellow men. It is not what we say that will influence them. It is what we do. It is what we are.—CR, October 1948, p. 174.

TWO GREAT MESSAGES

To BUILD AN IDEAL HOME; MORE QUORUM ACTIVITY. Among the many great messages that we have received, I should just like to emphasize two. One, of course, is the home. Thirteen thousand men of the priesthood were here last night. Everyone should go back to his home and look around and see wherein he can make it more ideally a Latter-day Saint home.

The other great message is for the priesthood quorums to be more active, to reach out and get the indifferent, approaching them personally, and, as has already been said, "Reproving betimes with sharpness, when moved upon by the Holy Ghost; and then showing forth afterwards an increase of love toward him whom thou hast reproved, lest he esteem thee to be his enemy." (D. & C. 121:43.)—CR, October 1951, pp. 160-161.

CHAPTER 14

WARD TEACHING

THE WORK OF THE WARD TEACHER

GETTING THE VISION OF THE WORK. The other day it was my privilege to drive through the fields in my old home town. I passed through two farms up near the mountain canal. I saw one that had yielded an exceptionally good crop of oats. Notwithstanding the drought, the cold in the spring, and other disadvantages, the farmer had threshed an excellent yield. Just over the fence was another oat field, but a failure, comparatively speaking. I said to the man: "Why, what is the matter? You must have planted poor seed."

"No, it is the same seed that my neighbor has."

"Well, then it was planted too late, and you did not have enough moisture in the ground to bring it up."

"It was sown the same afternoon that he sowed his."

Upon further inquiry, I learned that the first man had plowed his in the fall; then he had disked it carefully in the spring, making a mulch on the surface, and by such tilling had conserved the moisture of the winter. His neighbor, on the other hand, had plowed his late in the spring and had left the furrows unharrowed; the moisture had evaporated. Following the sowing of the seed came four weeks or six weeks of drought, and there was not sufficient moisture to germinate the seed.

The first man had made preparation, the proper kind of preparation, and nature yielded the increase. The second man labored hard, but his preparation was poor; indeed he had made inadequate preparation.

I now can picture in my mind twelve thousand divisions that may be compared in a way to these two fields. In each one are found—not oats, not wheat, not grasses, not things that perish—but living beings as eternal as the Father himself. Over each of these divisions in God's great garden have been placed overseers called teachers, and they are asked to nourish and to inspire God's children. I venture the thought that the great Gardener in looking over his fields can see some that are thriving in righteous activity and others are starving because of the drought of neglected duty, of the chilling atmosphere of vanity, or the blight of intemperance. Why? Perhaps because the gardeners, the overseers, had not made necessary preparations or performed their duty well.

The first thing to do, my brethren, is to look to yourselves, to see whether or not you are prepared to teach. No man can teach that which he himself does not know. It is your duty to teach that Jesus Christ is the Redeemer of the world, that Joseph Smith was a Prophet of God, and that to him in this last dispensation there appeared God the Father and his Son in person. Do you believe it? Do you feel it? Does that testimony radiate from your being when you enter into the home? If so, that radiation will give life to the people whom you go to teach. If not, there will be a dearth, a drought, a lack of that spiritual environment in which the Saints grow.

Second, is your heart free from backbiting, from fault-finding, from hard feelings one to another? It is your duty to see that there is no backbiting, that there is no iniquity existing in the Church. You can teach effectively only that which you yourselves feel. Part of the preparation of a teacher consists in freeing his own heart from those things. In doing so follow the advice of one good writer who says: "In the very depths of your soul dig a grave; let it be as some forgotten spot to which no path leads; and there, in the eternal silence bury the wrongs which you have suffered. Your heart will feel as if a load had fallen from it and a divine peace come to abide with you." With that divine peace in your soul go into the homes and teach the people.

But that condition is but the beginning. Three other things should be kept in mind for thorough preparation. The first is a *knowledge of those whom you are to teach;* the second, *a knowledge of what you are to teach;* and third, *a knowledge,* as much as may be obtained at least by thoughtful consideration and prayer, *of how you are going to teach.*—*CR,* October 1916, pp. 58-59.

WE MUST KNOW THOSE WE TEACH. A visit is not teaching. Reading the outline as prepared by the bishop or the high council or the Church is not teaching. Just repeating some passages of scripture, or merely the telling of something to the members of the family in a home is not teaching.

Teaching is the awakening of thought in the minds of those whom we visit and the convincing of their souls of the truth of the message that we bring to them. There must be giving and receiving, a reciprocal condition. How necessary it is, then, to know those whom we teach! No two families in any district are alike.

I call to mind one group of six families, one member of which is a patriarch in the Church, living in the sunset of a faithful life with his daughter, a teacher in the public schools, and a granddaughter, a student in the high school. On the same block next to him, reside a young couple who have but recently joined the Church. The girl had grown up in our communities, but she had not joined the Church until recently. Two of their little children are also baptized. Across the street reside a widow and her daughter, the daughter a typist in one of the business offices of the city, and the other three families present conditions just as varying.

The message, and particularly the manner of presenting that message, might not be the same when given to one who had spent his life in faithful labor in the Church, as when given to those who are newly converted. As each family is different from another, so each individual in the family differs from others, so our messages and our methods, particularly our methods of presentation, might vary. I cite this just to impress us with this thought, that it is our duty to know those whom we are going to teach. That is the reason, I think, why the Lord says: "The teacher's duty is to watch over the church always, ... " (D. & C. 20:53.) Not just once a month but always a teacher; no hour in the day when you are free from that responsibility! There is no day in the week when you are free and when you should not feel it your duty to do something, if possible, to make that group of members in the Church better and happier.

What you are to teach is the gospel of Jesus Christ. When the bishop gives you any special message—tithing, for example, study that principle, first by "taking heed unto yourself" to see if you can teach it consistently. If it be prayer, "take heed unto yourself" in regard to prayer. Do you get down on your knees before you go out to teach that message? Do you study some boy who is a little questionable in his life to know just what attitude he will take towards prayer? Do you pray for God to inspire you to say something to lead such a one to see the necessity of prayer?

O teachers, yours is an important calling! God help you to be true to it, to feel that part of the responsibility of carrying on God's work, in this the last dispensation, rests upon you.—*CR*, October 1916, pp. 59-60.

You carry the responsibility, teachers, of seeing to it that members of the Church attend sacrament meeting. How can you teach that duty effectively unless you yourself be present, that you may be able intelligently to commend those in your district who are in attendance and to teach those who are absent?—*CR*, October 1916, p. 60.

WARD TEACHING AND INDIVIDUAL WELFARE. In the Church of Jesus Christ every child should be more or less safeguarded; first, by the ward teacher, whose duty it is to " . . . watch over the church always [the "church" meaning members], and be with and strengthen them." (D. & C. 20:53.) Today the perfunctory obligations of the ward teachers are fairly well performed, but the looking after of individuals is woefully neglected. If every teacher, as an appointed representative of the bishopric of his ward, were properly and fully to perform his duty, he would be aware of the activity or inactivity of every child and of every youth in the Church, each teacher watching over the assigned families.—*IE*, 49:740 (1946).

These representatives of the bishop—the ward teachers— are the men who reach the individual, the men upon whom the responsibility rests to convert, to comfort, and to teach. Ward teachers are on the firing line.—*IE*, 41:200 (1938).

TEACHERS TO BE ASSIGNED TWO BY TWO. There is a growing tendency for ward teachers to go singly. We decry this practice. We commend those men who, when they fail to have a partner, are willing to assume the responsibility of visiting the Saints without a companion, but for seventy-five years, and probably longer, it has been the practice of the Church that teachers should go two by two. It is not sufficient for a teacher to say, "I cannot get anybody to go with

me." There are too many young men in the Aaronic Priesthood who hold the office of teacher or priest, and who will
accept an appointment as ward teacher to justify any teacher's
going alone. Call a young man to go with you. Kneel down
with him, as we have been instructed, and then go two by two.

Do this for three reasons: First, because we are instructed
so to do. Second, because it's for your own protection. You
think about that. And third, because you need mutual
strength, mutual guidance in giving correction, where it is
necessary, and in teaching the doctrines of the Church.—*IE*,
48:696 (1945).

DUTIES AND QUALIFICATIONS. The Lord has said what
the teacher's duty is:

"The teacher's duty is to watch over the church always,
and be with and strengthen them;

"And see that there is no iniquity in the church, neither
hardness with each other, neither lying, backbiting, nor evil
speaking;

"And see that the church meet together often, and also
see that all the members do their duty.

"And he is to take the lead of meetings in the absence of
the elder or priest." (D. & C. 20:53-56.)

A careful analysis of these duties discloses the fact that
the ward teacher possesses six leading qualifications; viz., those
of watchman, strengthener, arbitrator, guide, exemplar, and
leader.

The responsibility of seeing that there is no "hardness
with each other, neither lying, backbiting, nor evil speaking,"
is particularly significant. In the performance of this duty
there is manifest the principle of arbitration, expounded by the
Prophet Joseph Smith over a century ago; yet today civilized
nations are just beginning to apply it to the settling of international difficulties and disputes, and that seemingly with
little success.—*IE*, 41:200 (1938).

THE ADMINISTRATION OF WARD TEACHING

CONCERNING REPORTS. If you will turn to your reports,
you will find that the statistics relate more to the labors of the
teacher than to conditions or duties or well-being of those
visited. On a typical report card appear these items:

Husband's name.
Wife's name, etc.
Times attended sacrament meeting.
Number of persons in family.
Number of those present at the visit.
Number of families visited.
Number called on and not at home.
Number not accessible.
Number not called on.

These are statistics which do not cover, excepting in two instances, the specific points that the teacher is required to teach. All this is very good, but is it not possible for us to change our attitude and include some of the fundamentals given by revelation?

FIVE FAMILIES TO A DISTRICT. Let us see: Divide the ward, as it is now, so that each group will contain, let us say, no more than five families. Assign to each group of five families one member of the Melchizedek Priesthood and one member of the teachers' quorum.

THE ORDAINED TEACHER'S ROLE. Let that ordained teacher whose duty it is, take care of the statistics, assist in reporting removals, arrivals, new appointments in quorums, auxiliaries, wards, and missions. He will be glad to do it, and he is capable of doing it.

THE ADULT TEACHER'S ROLE. But the duty of the adult member is to watch over the Church always. For what purpose? To perform the six specific duties God has given him; viz., to guard, to strengthen, to arbitrate, to be exemplary, to admonish, and to lead. When he enters the home, he enters it authoritatively, and the father, or the mother, if the father be absent, respectfully turns over the household to him. The adult teacher will take the lead in ascertaining by such authoritative visits the standing and attitude of each member of every family. Do not say that this is difficult or is making your duties more arduous. It is a necessary service and a privilege.

EACH FAMILY AN INDIVIDUAL CASE. Some families do not need so much attention. You may already know of their circumstances and spiritual condition. You can casually call and find out how they feel and how harmoniously they are living with their neighbors and with the Church. But here is a young man in your district who is indolent, neglectful, sour, spiritually sick. Be with him to comfort him, to strengthen him, not on a formal visit alone, but at every opportunity you can make.

POSSIBLE USE FOR ORDAINED PRIESTS. So much for the teacher. Now what about the priest? It is the duty of the priest "to preach, teach, expound, exhort . . . " (D. & C. 20:46) all to come to Christ. He can hold cottage meetings as some are doing now. Those young priests will come to the house of Brother Brown and say: "We should like to hold a cottage meeting in your house for this district." Having obtained Brother Brown's permission, those young men will invite the non-members and members alike to come to their meeting to be conducted under their direction. They are teaching; that is the duty of the priest, to preach, to exhort, and invite all to come to Christ.

But the adult member of the priesthood and that ordained teacher will act independently of the priest. They will be in sacrament meeting next Sunday and note those who are present at the meeting. They know all of the members in their district, will note the presence or absence of any one of their charges, and when they meet any, they will commend or exhort as occasion merits or demands. A casual remark, such as, "We missed you at sacrament meeting last Sunday evening," may inspire to action more than a fifteen minute lecture. The ward teacher's duty is to see that all members do their duty.—*IE*, 41:200-201 (1938.)

BISHOPS TO BE SPECIFIC. Just a word to the bishops. I believe that teaching will be more effective in the Church if you will call your priesthood to you and point out to them in meeting, after prayer, in humility, what it means for them to go out from house to house as your representatives. Don't just call them somewhat indifferently from the pulpit and make an assignment in an indefinite way; but rather there in your bishop's meeting tell them individually what it means to be a teacher, ask them if they will stand by you in your efforts to uphold the standard of the Church. When you have occasion to release them, do it in a dignified and honorable manner, by telling them how you appreciate what they have done, and why they are at present released.—*CR*, October 1916, pp. 60-61.

THE OPPORTUNITY IN WARD TEACHING. I believe that in ward teaching there is one of the greatest opportunities in all the world to awaken in those who are negligent, discouraged, downhearted, and sad, renewed life and a desire to re-enter into activity in the Church of Jesus Christ. By such activity they will be led back into the spiritual atmosphere which will lift their souls and give them power to overcome weaknesses which are now shackling them.

To give help, encouragement, and inspiration to every individual is the great responsibility and privilege of ward teachers.—*IE*, 41:201 (1938.)

Chapter 15

Tithing and Welfare Practices

TITHING

LAW OF GOD. The law of tithing as now understood and practised by the Church of Jesus Christ of Latter-day Saints was given by revelation to the Prophet Joseph Smith in response to a prayer in which the Prophet sought the Lord to know "how much he required of the properties of the people for a tithing." The Lord answered saying, the "beginning" of tithing consisted first of "all the surplus property," and named the specific purposes for which this "surplus property" should be used. "After that" tithing consists "of one-tenth of all the interest annually; and this," he continued, "shall be a standing law unto them forever." (See D. & C. 119.)

To members of the Church of Jesus Christ, therefore, tithing is as much a law of God as is baptism. No one is compelled to obey the one any more than the other; and no one receives the blessing of either without obedience thereto. They who reject the law of tithing put themselves in the same class as the "Pharisees and lawyers" who in the days of John the Baptist, "rejected the counsel of God against themselves." To those who accept the system of tithing as a law of God, nothing more need be said to convince them of the virtue of paying one-tenth of their annual interest, for if sincere, they certainly acquiesce in what is God's will; but even to those who do not so regard it, tithing makes most worthy appeal.

MEANS OF REVENUE. Man is a social being. God designed him to be such. From infancy to old age, he is dependent upon others for his development, education, and happiness. In the right kind of social groups, the more a man gives, the more he receives; the more he teaches, the more he learns; the more happiness he bestows, the happier he becomes. Every group has its laws and standards of conduct, human society especially.

Now wherever there is an organization of human beings for any purpose whatsoever, there must be provision made

for the accomplishing of that purpose, and its achievement
implies some kind of contribution from members of the group.
Everybody should share in this contribution. Some can give
it in one way, some in another. Tithing is one means of
sharing social responsibility. It is a just means as well, for
every person gives proportionally as much as another. It is
God's plan of raising revenue for the Church. "There is no
such thing," said the late President Joseph F. Smith, "as an
organization of men for any purpose of importance without
provisions for carrying out its designs. The law of tithing
is the law of revenue for the Church of Jesus Christ of Latter-
day Saints. Without it, it would be impossible to carry on
the purposes of the Lord." (Joseph F. Smith, *Gospel Doctrine,*
p. 226.)

AN AVENUE OF SERVICE. In every family, every town,
every city, every state, every nation, there are members of
the social group who need the assistance of others. There
are children who are either fatherless or motherless or both;
there are widows in distress; there are the sick, the aged, the
infirm. Hospitals are to be built, properly equipped, and
maintained; schools to be supported, temples and churches
to be erected, ar.d social service of every description to be
carried on. Tithing is an adequate and proper method of
raising funds for the conducting of this essential and praiseworthy social service. It is well to remember, also, that the
Savior of men, who gave his life for the service of humanity,
said, " . . . whosoever shall give to drink unto one of these
little ones a cup of cold water . . . verily I say unto you, he
shall in no wise lose his reward." (Matt. 10:42.)

A SOURCE OF PROTECTION. Tithing should not be given
with a selfish end in view. A man who pays tithing just to
keep his name on the record will receive his reward, of course;
he will have his name on the record. "Verily, he hath his
reward," as the man who prayed to be seen and heard of
men. But he who gives because he loves to help others and
to further the cause of righteousness, who gives cheerfully
and with thanksgiving in his heart, also has his reward; for
in giving he is really obtaining. In losing his life for Christ's
sake, he finds it. If all would thus lose themselves unselfishly
in the law of tithing, there would be sufficient in the Lord's

storehouse to insure the comfort and education of every person in need in the Church. The Church would thus become the best, the safest insurance society in the world. The time will come when tithing as a sufficient means of protection will come to be more fully understood than it is today. There should be no need of members of the Church of Jesus Christ's joining secret societies either for fellowship, fraternity, or financial aid for their wives and children. The law of tithing properly lived means adequate protection for all.

Tithing Is a Source of Spiritual Power. But aside from these social and temporal benefits resulting from a compliance to this law as a social factor, tithing makes its greatest appeal to the sincere mind because of its spiritual significance. It is an unfailing source of spiritual power. True and constant obedience to this law will give as much spiritual development as will obedience to any other principle of the gospel. Inasmuch as one may not infrequently be compelled to practise self-restraint and self-denial in personal desires and perhaps personal needs, the paying of tithing develops self-mastery. Selfishness and self-love are thus supplanted by unselfishness and a love for others. "A man who loves only himself and his pleasures is vain, presumptuous, and wicked even from principle"; but, "he who reigns within himself, and rules passions, desires, and fears, is more than a king."

It is surprising how frequently the struggle between sordidness and generosity centers around one's pocketbook. Thus tithing teaches those fundamental elements upon which strength of character rests: viz., self-control, self-denial, generosity, love for fellow men, and love for God. It is impossible for a selfish soul to enter the kingdom of heaven. Paying an honest tithe is one of the very best means of overcoming these barriers to eternal happiness.

Faith in the Church of Jesus Christ is best manifested in little things performed in daily life. "Flights of heavenly fancy and longings to see the invisible" have their place in the world, no doubt; but the world is made better and happier by the practical deeds performed each day in that obedience to the laws of God which makes the wheels of society run smoothly, which comforts the fatherless and the widows in their affliction, which gives a secure heritage to our loved ones, and which gives one sufficient strength of character to keep oneself unspotted from the world. Such a faith is exemplified by the man who is honest with the Lord.—*MS*, 86:584-586 (1924).

THE CHURCH WELFARE PLAN

THREE UNDERLYING PURPOSES. The underlying purpose of the Church welfare plan is threefold, viz.:

1. To supply, in a helpful and dignified manner, food, clothing, and shelter to every person so in need.

2. To assist men and women who, through misfortune, ill luck, or disaster, find themselves without gainful employment, to become once again self-supporting.

3. To increase among the members of the Church the true spirit of the brotherhood of Christ, having in mind in all their service the divine saying, "Inasmuch as ye have done it unto one of the least of these my brethren, ye have done it unto me." (Matt. 25:40.)

THE PLAN BASIC TO THE PROGRAM OF THE CHURCH. The plan is not something new but rather a means of uniting along well-established lines quorum, auxiliary, and ecclesiastical groups in their efforts to serve one another and the Church. Presidencies of stakes, bishoprics of wards, quorum officials, Relief Society officers, now work unitedly instead of independently in giving relief and helpfulness to those who merit assistance. The only modification or addition in the ecclesiastical organizations of the Church is the uniting of several stakes into what is called a region.—*CR*, October 1941, p. 54.

A STATEMENT WHEN THE PLAN WAS INAUGURATED, APRIL 1936. During the last few years practically all the world has been passing through a critical period of depression. People in this intermountain region have been hit, in some respects, more severely than others. Mining, farming, and stock raising are our principal industries. When the mines closed, many men were thrown out of employment. When the springs and rivers dried, products of farms shriveled and died. The price of cattle dropped below the cost of raising them. As a result many people are worried and disheartened. They have lost not only their farms or business interests, but also their homes. Day by day men have vainly searched for honest work. After fruitless searching and inquiry, they return home almost with bitterness in their hearts. Wives with a fortitude sublime encourage their husbands even though it is more difficult for wives to struggle continually to keep up appearances and to supply food and nourishment for their children. It is embarrassing to such men and women, accustomed to independence, comfortable living, and even opulence, to accept help either from the government or the Church.

What, then, shall we do?

With resolute hearts, with courage to meet disaster with a smile, let us accept conditions as they are, rebuild, and with united effort regain financial and economic independence. —*CR*, April 1936, pp. 58-59.

The Importance of Agricultural Prosperity. Dr. John A. Widtsoe expressed a profound truth when he said, "No country can prosper unless the men who till the soil succeed." I do not know of anything else that we can do. We haven't sufficient factories to employ people who are out of work; the mines are not running to capacity. We can go back and with help buy a few cattle and some horses and retill our farms.

Here in this intermountain country we have a great obligation. The eyes of the world are turned toward us, not only because of the message we have, but also because there are scenic wonders here which attract men from far and near. When they drive past our farms and our houses, they should see the houses painted, the farms properly tilled, and the weeds along the road cut. In this we have a bounden duty that travelers might see evidence of neatness, thrift, and industry, fundamental principles of the Latter-day Saints.

In these efforts toward rehabilitation, all must co-operate. Let the money that is being given as a dole apply on the purchase of a team, chickens, or implements, and thus enable men and women to get back to a life of independence. Here is one field of endeavor in which I think our hearts need strengthening and in which we can manifest that courage and quality of mind which will enable us to meet difficulties that are ahead.—*CR*, April 1936, p. 59.

THE SPIRITUAL VALUE. Frequent reference has been
made, and appropriately so, to the plan inaugurated by the
General Authorities of the Church for the relief of those who
are unemployed. It is at present one of our greatest and one
of the most important concerns of the Church. I desire to
call attention to the spiritual value of this important and far-
reaching undertaking.

In the 29th section of the Doctrine and Covenants, we
are told that " . . . all things unto me [the Lord] are spiritual,
and not at any time have I given unto you a law which was
temporal; neither any man, nor the children of men; neither
Adam, your father, whom I created.

"Behold, I gave unto him that he should be an agent
unto himself; and I gave unto him commandment, but no
temporal comandment gave I unto him, for my commandments are spiritual; they are not natural nor temporal, neither
carnal nor sensual." (D. & C. 29:34-35.)

The development of our spiritual nature should concern
us most. Spirituality is the highest acquisition of the soul,
the divine in man; "the supreme, crowning gift that makes
him king of all created things." It is the consciousness of
victory over self and communion with the Infinite. It is
spirituality alone which really gives one the best in life.

It is something to supply clothing to the scantily clad,
to furnish ample food to those whose table is thinly spread,
to give activity to those who are fighting desperately the
despair that comes from enforced idleness, but after all is
said and done, the greatest blessings that will accrue from the
Church welfare plan are spiritual. Outwardly, every act
seems to be directed toward the physical: remaking of dresses
and suits of clothes, canning fruits and vegetables, storing
foodstuffs, choosing of fertile fields for settlement—all seem
strictly temporal, but permeating all these acts, inspiring and
sanctifying them, is the element of spirituality.—CR, October
1936, p. 103.

THE QUORUM TO IMPROVE HOME AND COMMUNITY EN-
VIRONMENT THROUGH THE WELFARE PLAN.[1] The Church
of Jesus Christ of Latter-day Saints is seeking, through its
welfare plan, through increased quorum consciousness and

---

[1]See Chapter 13 for relation of quorum activity to the welfare plan.

responsibility, to make both home and community environment better and brighter.—*CR*, April 1941, p. 108.

THE DYNAMICS OF THE PLAN

THE NECESSITY OF INDIVIDUAL ENTERPRISE. I believe in individualism as opposed to paternalism. In saying this I recognize the fact that a man's duties to himself and to his fellow men are indissolubly connected. Jesus taught that if a man is true to his own highest interests he cannot fail to discharge his obligations to his neighbors. Conversely, he taught that if a man is faithful to the interests of his fellow men, he cannot be faithless to his own. And as a man thinks, so he acts.

Within my experience there has never been a time when the doctrine of individual initiative and individual effort should be more generally taught and more earnestly put into effect than at the present day.

Too many men are claiming that the world owes them a living and are sitting effortlessly by, expecting the world to throw its luxuries into their passive laps. Too late they will learn that the earth rewards richly only the strenuous strugglers. Emerson quotes someone as saying that "the world is in a state of bankruptcy; that the world owes the world more than the world can pay, and ought to go into chancery and be sold." Such reputed insolvency involves all the population, and he who does not get out and rustle for himself is a contributor to the alleged bankruptcy.—*CR*, April 1938, p. 18.

No JUSTIFICATION FOR IDLENESS. Thousands, through no fault of theirs, are out of jobs and are vainly seeking a means of an independent livelihood. However, failure to find it is no justification for idleness. There are fences to rebuild, barns to repair, yards to clean up, houses to remodel and to paint, vicious and destructive weeds to destroy as they deface the highway and ravage crops. Instead of waiting expectantly for the government to find work for us, let us look around and see if there is not work near at hand. Such work will be a benefit not only to the individual but also to the community and the public generally.—*CR*, April 1938, p. 19.

WORK AND INDIVIDUAL SALVATION. I desire to say a word
about work as a means of salvation to the individual. Work!
O how often do we read in the scriptures about the blessings
that come from *doing!* Eternal life rests upon the knowledge
of God and his Son Jesus Christ. Now, note it, "And this is
life eternal, that they might know thee the only true God,
and Jesus Christ, whom thou hast sent." (John 17:3.) How
do you get that knowledge? In another place he says, "If
any man will *do his will,* he shall know of the doctrine, whether
it be of God, or whether I speak of myself." (*Ibid.,* 7:17.)
There you have the *doing,* the *work,* associated with the knowledge, and knowledge bringing eternal life—"To know thee is
eternal life." To *do* is to *know.*

In our physical being there is no development; there is
no growth without activity; in the intellectual world there
is no advancement without effort, work; and in the spiritual
world, in the development of our spirits, there is no growth
without effort. There is no salvation without work.

I do not mean redemption from death—Christ has done
that; he has given us all that we need to obtain salvation. The
doctrine of work does not rob him of any of his glory. "For by
grace are ye saved through faith; and that not of yourselves:
it is the gift of God." (Eph. 2:8.) But aside from that, the
individual growth and advancement, the individual knowledge,
the advancement in God's truth, depends upon the doing of
God's will. Let us teach ourselves that; let us teach our
children and give them something to do; let them know the
sin of idleness.—*CR,* October 1909, p. 90.

Joseph Smith, the Prophet, has repeatedly given us the
assurance that God will not support the idler, that the idler
has no place in this Church. The children should know it—
O these young men, some of whom belong to us, who are
looking forward to a life of ease, to clean clothes, soft white
hands—the result, they think of leisure or of wealth! These
young men should be warned of the danger of that kind of
life.—*CR,* October 1909, p. 90.

Work brings happiness, and that happiness is doubled
to him who initiates the work.—*CR,* April 1938, p. 20.

OPPORTUNITIES ARE ALWAYS AT HAND. Too many of us
fail to take advantage of opportunities near at hand. We

justify inactivity by nursing the impotent thought that success
cannot be obtained without influence, money, social or political
"pull."—*CR,* April 1938, p. 20.

THE NEED AND VALUE OF CO-OPERATION. In emphasizing
individual effort, I am not unmindful of the necessity of co-
operation—

> "There is a destiny that makes us brothers;
>   None goes his way alone:
> All that we send into the lives of others
>   Comes back into our own."
>   Edwin Markham, *"A Creed."*

A single, struggling individual may be stalled with his
heavy load even as he begins to climb the hill before him.
To reach the top unaided is an impossibility. With a little
help from fellow travelers, quorums, or wards, he makes the
grade and goes on his way in gratitude and rejoicing.

This, I think, is in harmony with the teachings of Jesus,
who "sought to perfect society, not by popular agitation or
by reorganization, but by perfecting the individual. He recognized the fatal fallacy in the dream of those who hoped to make
a perfect state out of imperfect individuals. The ideal social
state, which he described as the kingdom of God, is a commonwealth in which all men are united and governed by a
commanding love both for God and for their neighbors."

The present-day turmoil and bitter strivings threaten to
undermine basic foundations of Christian relationship. Liberty,
freedom of speech, self-government, faith in God, and particularly faith in the efficacy of the gospel of Jesus Christ are
facing a bombardment from the ranks of error such as the
world has seldom if ever witnessed.—*CR,* April 1938, pp. 20-21.

WHAT ONE WARD ACCOMPLISHED. The admonition to
work out your own salvation applies not only to persons but
also to the individual quorum, to the individual ward, to the
individual stake. Look around you, and you will find that
there is work for you in your own community. These suggestions are not impractical effusions of a dreamer, as Bishop
Lawrence B. Johnson of Randolph, Utah (Woodruff Stake),
has demonstrated. In that little village, ten or twelve more

houses are needed to meet the bare necessities of natural increase in population. People have not the money with which to pay for these houses. But there are certain resources which they do possess—health, brawn and muscle, and initiative and foresight on the part of leaders. Twelve miles from this town are groves of timber; trees that can be hewn into house logs.

Bishop Johnson presented his plan and called for volunteers from the ranks of the unemployed. He anticipated meeting five or six men with teams and axes. At the appointed hour one Monday morning twenty men responded.

With a little help a sawmill was obtained; and with the co-operation of the Forestry Service, 200 trees, the forest life of which was about ended, had been transformed into excellent housing material—25,000 scale feet of logs made ready for use, and the work still continues. For their labor the men were given work receipts, which are accepted at the regional storehouse in exchange for clothing, shoes, groceries, and other necessities.—CR, April 1938, pp. 19-20.

ANOTHER GROUP ENTERPRISE. An apt illustration of how the Church, through the welfare plan, may stimulate and enable the community, as well as individuals, to self-effort is shown by a little assistance rendered the people of Woodruff Ward about June 1936.

The depression had left this community practically without funds. They had no money with which to purchase even seed potatoes for spring planting. They were given a loan of $360.10 with which they bought the necessary amount of seed potatoes. In the fall the planters repaid this loan in full, had sufficient potatoes on hand for their families throughout the year, and an ample supply of seed for replanting.

The bishop of the ward reports that the cash income from sales of the surplus of the 1937 crop amounted to twenty-eight hundred dollars, notwithstanding the fact that each grower contributed to the ward security [welfare] committee one-third of what he raised. Bishop LeRoy D. Tingey also added this significant statement: "Not one of our people has been on relief."

A spirit of confidence has been awakened, which will be of lasting benefit to the community, for prior to 1936 not a

few of the families in Woodruff purchased their potatoes from
Bear Lake. It is an interesting observation that recently a
man from Bear Lake purchased his potatoes from Woodruff.
—*IE*, 41:39 (1938).

BUILDING THE CENTRAL STOREHOUSES. An important and
most commendable enterprise undertaken by the Church is
its welfare program. Of its value and significance much has
been said during the conference. I desire to commend, in
the presence of this large audience, the able and unselfish work
of the eleven members of the general committee chosen to
assist the General Authorities. These men are leaders in their
chosen occupations and professions. They, as you, give their
very best to the advancement of this great undertaking, contributing their time and ability without a cent of compensation. The reward of their effort lies in their love for the work.

Under the direction of this committee and the management of experienced and dependable contractors, the central
storehouse building project is being carried on at 751 West
Seventh South, (Salt Lake City), one of the pivotal centers
around which this entire plan revolves.

In your mind's eye, come with me momentarily and stand
outside those unfinished buildings. Here we see a worthy
example of co-operation. The steel lying there, being used
to reinforce the cement, has been furnished at cost by firms
not associated with the Church; so have the cement and the
lumber; so have the materials purchased from merchants in
this city; also the electric poles and the wire. The spirit of
co-operation is manifested by members and nonmembers.
Here are from forty to sixty men working daily—men otherwise
unemployed, each recommended by his bishop. Each receives
for his labor small amounts in cash; the balance in orders on
the storehouses.

UNION MEN COMMENDED. One of the most pleasing
things which you observe is the fact that union men work side
by side with non-union men. I wish to commend the brick-
layers' union particularly for their attitude toward this great
welfare movement in permitting their men to work side by
side with others in the spirit of true brotherhood.—*CR*, October 1938, p. 132.

THE "MORMON HANDICRAFT" PROJECT. I would ask you, too, to contemplate the Mormon handicraft project carried on by the Relief Society, a most commendable enterprise, in which 650 women have found employment while they remained at home with their families.—*CR*, October 1938, p. 132.

THE SPIRIT OF THE PLAN. Too many men quail under the impending onslaught and cry vainly, "What can we do?"

This we can do:

First: by self-effort attempt to initiate work around the home and in the neighborhood; quorums and groups rendering necessary aid whenever possible; and practise honesty; speak well of your neighbors; and if you cannot do this say nothing. Seek the best in life and thus give to your own soul and to your own environment a touch of the beautiful.

Second: by proclaiming, and, what is even more effective, by exemplifying in life the principles of the gospel of Jesus Christ as the only permanent panacea for the ills of mankind. —*CR*, April 1938, p. 21.

The willingness to serve others is ready for expression in the hearts of millions, if only nations or groups in nations will but point the way. Here is one illustration: September 19, 1937, the Salt Lake region of the Church welfare plan, finding itself in need of a new storehouse, held a special fast day for the purpose of raising funds with which to make the first payment. The committee asked the people to go without two meals on that day and contribute the equivalent in cash for the project. The leaders anticipated raising about four thousand dollars. The people contributed over fifteen thousand dollars—realization exceeding anticipation nearly four times!—*CR*, October 1937, p. 102.

FAST DAY OBSERVANCE

ORIGIN AND MEANING. The word *fast* is used to signify a self-imposed restraint with respect to the eating of food. Historians tell us that the custom of fasting dates back to the early history of the human race. They surmise that it was first practised because of the salutary influence that it has on the health and also because of the increased power such voluntary abstinence gives the spirit in holding under subjection the purely physical appetites of the body. It may be nearer the truth, however, to say that fasting originated when the Lord first revealed to man the gospel plan, thus antedating even the law of Moses, when an annual fast day was prescribed. (See Lev. 23:27-29.)

Whatever its origin, it is significant to note that several virtues are attached to the observance of the custom. Two of these are mentioned by those who seek to find a natural reason for its adoption; and of course it follows inevitably that these and other virtues are in it if the assumption be right that God prescribed it in the beginning as a rite to be observed by mankind. All the principles associated with fasting seem to point to the fact that it produces (1) physical benefits; (2) intellectual activity; and (3) spiritual strength.

It is generally conceded that most people usually consume more food than the body requires. Overeating clogs the system with deleterious waste products. When such a condition exists, a short fast is undoubtedly useful as a means of restoring the body to its normal, active state.

A clogged digestive system is but the inevitable forerunner of a clogged brain. Mr. Upton Sinclair, who has written a symposium on fasting, advocating particularly the "fasting cure," suggests that poets would write greater poetry if they but understood the merits of fasting and then adds, "The great thing about the fast is that it sets you a new standard of health." Of course, that eminent writer has in mind a longer period of abstinence from food than that prescribed by the Church, to be observed at regular intervals, but, as an eminent Scotch physician says, "Fasting for a longer or a shorter period is often a beneficial practice, especially in the case of those who have been living too freely."

But the struggle for existence is so keen with most of mankind that the majority find it necessary to live not too freely but too meagerly. This being true, what virtue in fasting is there for them? We answer: the greatest of all benefits—the spiritual strength derived by the subjection of physical appetite to the will of the individual. "He who reigns within himself, and rules passions, desires, and fears, is more than a king." As in eternal life, so in self-mastery, there is no one great thing which a man may do to obtain it; but there are many little things by observing which self-control may be achieved; and a subjecting of the appetite to the will, and a refusal to satisfy desire are two of these little things. It was with the thought in mind of gaining spiritual strength that James, the psychologist, made this suggestion: "To do each day something which you do not like to do." If there were no other virtue in fasting but gaining strength of character, that alone would be sufficient justification for its universal acceptance.

MODERN CHURCH PRACTICE. But associated with this practice in the Church of Jesus Christ of Latter-day Saints is the giving of a fast offering, the underlying purpose and far-reaching benefits of which make the monthly observance of fast day one of the most significant features of this latter-day work. There are in it, besides the benefits mentioned above, (1) all the spiritual uplift that comes from a Christlike desire to serve one's fellow man, and (2) an economic means, which, when carried out by a perfect and active organization, will supply the needs of every worthy poor person within the confines of the organized branches of the Church.

The regularly constituted fast consists of abstinence from food once each month, from the evening meal of Saturday to the evening meal on the following Sunday; that is, it means missing two meals on the first Sunday of each month. The value of those two meals given as a voluntary donation for the relief of those who are hungry or otherwise in distress constitutes the fast offering. Think what the sincere observance of this rule would mean spiritually if every man, woman, and child were to observe the fast and contribute the resultant offering, with the sincere desire of blessing the less fortunate brother or sister or sorrowing child! The great Tolstoy, sensing the need of this bond of sympathetic brotherhood in Christ, once wrote that he had no right to eat his crust of bread if his brother had none. Can you not see associated with this simple act the divine principle of service as expressed in the Master's words: "Inasmuch as ye have done it unto one of the least of these my brethren, ye have done it unto me"? (Matt. 25:40.)—MS, 85:424-425 (1923).

THE ECONOMICS OF THE FAST OFFERINGS

A VOLUNTARY CONTRIBUTION BASED ON PRINCIPLE. We
are asked, as a Church, to fast once a month—to refrain from
Saturday evening meal until Sunday evening meal. The requirement is that all members of the Church fast that day,
attend to their meetings, particularly sacrament meeting, and
in accordance with the revelation of God, give their oblations,
render their sacraments, and offer their prayers to God. We
are asked, further, to contribute in effect the amount of those
two meals for the benefit of the worthy poor in the ward. No
stated amount is given; each one is left to give voluntarily that
which he believes he ought to give, so that the bishop may
have in his hands sufficient funds to aid those who may be
in need.

Now, it is a little, simple thing, and at first thought it
does not seem to have much of the power of salvation in it,
but like all other principles and ordinances of the gospel of
Jesus Christ, it is associated with the fundamental principles
of life and salvation. That is why I desire to call the attention
of the presiding authorities as well as of all the Saints in
Israel, to the importance of living up to this requirement more
closely in the future than they have done in the past. Let us
see what it means.

If we contribute to the bishop the value of two meals
once a month, we are certainly no poorer financially than we
would be if we had consumed those meals as we regularly do.
There cannot be any loss to our own family in a financial
way, and we have given at least a mite towards alleviation of
hunger, perhaps distress, in some home that is less fortunate,
less blessed than we. There is no loss to us financially, no
man is poorer, no man is deprived of one blessing, no child
is deprived of anything that he would have had if he refrained
from giving that small contribution. Financially then, nobody
who gives it is any the poorer.

PHYSICAL BENEFITS. Physically, we are better off by refraining from eating at least once a month than we are when
we eat regularly three meals a day. I am reminded of having
read the opinion of one of our leading athletes who in his
training watched the effect of eating three regular meals,
then of eating two regular meals and finally of eating one meal

daily, regularly, and he concludes so far as he is concerned
that when he ate three meals a day he had been eating too
much, and when so doing found it necessary to fast at regular
periods in order to maintain his vitality to the standard possessed when he ate more sparingly. Physiology books will
give us the same lesson. So, generally speaking—each individual must take this for his own good—but generally speaking no person is injured in any way by his depriving himself
of those two meals on fast day, but, on the contrary he is
benefited physically.

SPIRITUAL STRENGTH AND SELF-MASTERY. There is still
another blessing, and here I believe is the most potent factor,
the most saving power in this fast-day requirement. What our
young people need, what every man and every woman in this
world needs in order to keep himself or herself free and unspotted from the sins of the world, is the power of self-mastery.
Each individual should studiously practise self-control. It
does not come all at once. Nature never makes cash payments
as a whole, says William George Jordan. Her payments are
always made in small instalments. Those who desire to win
self-mastery must do it by constant application. About the
only definite command, to fast as given in the Law, refers to
this principle as an "affliction of the soul." It is associated
with spiritual uplift, and therein is one of the greatest blessings
that come to those who will fast as God has asked them to.

Some may say, "Well, that isn't much, I cannot see how
the refraining from partaking of food once a month regularly
is going to give me any self-control." It does, however; it is
one of the best lessons that adults as well as children can
practise. Appetite is calling; there is a yearning, and the
natural tendency is to yield.

Teach the child to master appetite. Teach him, not
harshly, but kindly, with the Spirit of the Lord, with the
spirit in which the revelation was given, and you will find
that in childhood these little lessons in abstinence coming
daily to your boy, unconsciously are placing into his little
spirit power that may save him from falling in disgrace sometime when he is driven on by the fire of youth to the very
verge of the precipice of destruction. Then is the time that
he will need mastery of self, and he will have it. Men who

have studied this principle suggest that we need to take some such lesson as this not only weekly or monthly, but daily. —CR, April 1915, pp. 103-105.

A MEANS OF RELIGIOUS PRACTICE AND SOCIAL ADVANCEMENT. Do not think that there is not a spiritual significance in the little principle of fasting. Do not think, parents, that you are favoring your child when, out of compassion, you say, "Oh, give him his breakfast; oh, let us have breakfast; let us have dinner; I have a headache; the little boy is too young to go without his meal," and so on. You do not know what you are doing by such teaching as that. I want to tell you that the children of our Church can be so taught this principle of self-denial that they will set worthy examples to their parents in the observance of it. Your deacons particularly—there is a magnificent opportunity for teaching them one way of honoring the priesthood.

Now, what does obedience to this requirement mean in aiding those who might be in need? It means that money need not be taken from the tithing fund because some of us did not comply with the principle of fast offering! Think what it means, and particularly when we are aiding ourselves by doing it. We are losing nothing financially; we are blessing ourselves physically; and we are gaining greater spiritual power to withstand the temptations that we meet in life; and, best of all, we are practising the very essence of our religion; the true Christ spirit is manifest in that little offering.—CR, April 1915, pp. 105-106.

CHAPTER 16

SUNDAY SCHOOLS AND THE SPIRIT OF WORSHIP

THE SUNDAY SCHOOL MOVEMENT

A SACRED OBLIGATION. The proper training of childhood is man's most sacred obligation. Children at birth are the most dependent and helpless of all creatures, yet they are the sweetest and the greatest of all things in the world. They come from the Father pure and undefiled, their souls like stainless white paper on which is to be written the aspirations and achievements of a lifetime. Whether that scroll shall become the biography of a noble Christlike life, or a series of blots and blurs, depends largely, if not entirely, upon the guiding influence of parents, playmates, and teachers. "A creature undefiled by the taint of the world, unvexed by its injustice, unwearied by its hollow pleasures; a being fresh from the source of light, with something of its universal lustre in it—if childhood be this, how holy the duty to see that in its onward growth it shall be no other."

In the formation of character and guidance of childhood, parental influence is greatest; next comes the teacher's. Of the former, I cannot comment in this article; and of the latter, I must confine my reference only to a few of those who have sought to establish an environment in which children might be fired with an ambition to be useful and infused with a desire to be obedient, that thereby they might enjoy the first and foremost right of childhood; viz., to be happy. "There is true nobility in the soul of that man or woman who sincerely desires and strives to lead children out of contaminating influences into an environment of high ideals and lofty endeavor."

ROBERT RAIKES AND MODERN SUNDAY SCHOOLS. It was just such yearnings and strivings of honest minds and hearts that gave birth to our modern Sunday Schools. The first of these was established at Gloucester, England, over one hundred fifty years ago.

Robert Raikes, proprietor of the *Gloucester Journal,* a man noted for his deeds of philanthropy, saw from his window one day, "neglected, ragged children, playing, quarreling, cursing, and fighting and using language too coarse to repeat." These unfortunate children, neglected by their parents, were gathered in a private home, the charge of four women, "who were employed at a shilling a day."

The forenoon session was held from ten to twelve o'clock. Every Sunday afternoon the children were conducted to the parish church where they participated in worship and recited from the catechism.

Judging from the description given of this Sunday School in the *Gloucester Journal,* the public became interested, and the movement became popular, though some ecclesiastical authorities and "timid religionists" opposed it as a very dangerous innovation. Volunteer teachers supplanted those who were paid a shilling a day. It is true there are authentic records extant which prove that Sunday Schools existed before 1783, but Robert Raikes' Sunday School is generally considered the beginning of the modern Sunday School movement.

FIRST SUNDAY SCHOOL IN THE UNITED STATES. It is difficult to determine who merits the credit of organizing the first Sunday School in the United States. One such school was organized under the direction of Bishop Asbury at the house of the Cranshaws in Hanover City, Virginia, 1786. In December 1790, a meeting was called to consider the importance of this work, and in January 1791, a Sunday School Society was organized for the purpose of securing religious instruction for poor children on Sundays. The teachers, as those of Robert Raikes, were paid a small salary. Other schools followed and became the nucleus of the American Sunday School Union, a national organization formed in 1824.

SUNDAY SCHOOLS IN THE RESTORED CHURCH—AT KIRTLAND. The first Sunday Schools in the Church of Jesus Christ of Latter-day Saints were organized in Kirtland, Ohio. Unfortunately, we have very little record concerning their organization and conduct. In Helen Mar Whitney's memoirs we find the following:

"Among other pleasing recollections were our Sunday Schools, where I used to love to go and recite verses and whole

chapters from the New Testament, and we received rewards
in primers, etc., which I think were more highly appreciated
in those days than they are at the present time. At ten o'clock
we would form in line and march with our teachers up to the
temple. The thought that I could never see or enjoy them
again would make me sad, as a child, when we were driven
away from Kirtland to Missouri, and sometimes I would cry
bitterly."

IN THE EUROPEAN MISSION, 1840. I am indebted to Sister
Susa Young Gates for the following regarding Sunday Schools
organized in the European Mission as early as 1840:
"When Brigham Young was presiding over the European
Mission in 1840 and Parley P. Pratt was editor of the *Star,*
a number of questions propounded by Elder Joseph Fielding
were answered in the *Star.* Doubtless Brigham Young scruti-
nized both questions and answers before they came into print."
Among these questions was this:

" '10. Would it be well to establish Sunday Schools in
the Church?'
"Ans. Certainly; let the elders gather the people together,
old and young, every Sabbath day, in the streets, if no more
convenient place offers, and teach them the first principles
of the gospel of Christ, viz., faith, repentance, and baptism for
the remission of sins, for the first lesson; eating and drinking
at the table of the Lord, laying on of hands for the reception
of the Holy Ghost, the resurrection of the dead and eternal
judgment for the second lesson; and for the third lesson, let
parents teach their children obedience, and train them in the
way they should go; and finally let the elders, brothers, and
sisters, all with one accord, teach their friends and neighbors,
and make them wise unto salvation; and practise what they
preach on the Sabbath and six other days in each week, even
unto the end. They will find it a very profitable school, and
receive a glorious reward for their labors."

AT NAUVOO AND WINTER QUARTERS. Sister Annie Wells
Cannon informs me that she has heard her mother, Emmeline
B. Wells,
" . . . many times speak of holding a Sunday School in
Nauvoo and also at Winter Quarters. I have thought it was

officially organized by the priesthood, though I think it was held in the home of Presiding Bishop Newel K. Whitney, and must have been with his approval."

FIRST SUNDAY SCHOOL IN THE ROCKY MOUNTAINS. The credit and honor of organizing the first Sunday School in the Rocky Mountains is due Elder Richard Ballantyne, who was both teacher and superintendent of the first session held in the West. This was in a room of Brother Ballantyne's log house located on the corner of First West and Third South Streets, Salt Lake City.

The following are some of the original members of the thirty who first assembled to receive instructions from the noble soul who strove to keep the children of Zion under up-building influences: Richard Ballantyne, Lydia Phelps Thorpe, Sophronia E. Carter, Margaret O. Best, Angus M. Cannon, Leonora Cannon Gardner, Martha Van Cott Price, Samuel H. B. Smith, S. A. Whitney, Joseph S. Horne, George J. Taylor, Robert Frank Turnbow, David H. Cannon, John G. Turnbow, Henry I. Horne, Jacob Peart, Sarah J. Cannon, and Olive Peck.

In stating his reason for organizing this school, Elder Ballantyne said, "I felt that the gospel was too precious to myself to be withheld from the children; they ought to have the privilege of gospel teaching and that was the main purpose— to teach them the gospel."—*IE*, 33:480-481 (1930).

SUNDAY SCHOOL ADMINISTRATION[1]

CONTROLLING PRINCIPLES. In the best conducted Sunday Schools of the Church, self-government is manifest in every procedure, and fundamental principles of good conduct, worship, and devotion are exemplified in every exercise. That school approaches nearest the ideal, in which the superintendent finds it unnecessary even to say a word by way of direction from the moment when the bishop makes his announcements for the day until the classes march to their respective classrooms. Each participant in the opening exercises knows his duty and is prepared to perform it properly without either announcement or direction. This may be said also

---

[1]See also, chapter on "Education," for materials in religious education work and calling of teachers, etc.

of the school as a body. Thus is the fundamental principle of self-government encouraged. So in each succeeding exercise are emphasized, in one way and another, punctuality, courtesy, order, reverence, worship, respect for authority, consideration of the rights of others, responsiveness, self-control, obedience, etc.

In these and other ways does the Sunday School aid in the discharging of the most important and sacred obligations of man; viz., the proper training and instruction of childhood. In the most efficient schools every child and every adult senses the fact that he is an instructor as well as a learner, and to a certain extent, carries the responsibility of following the divine injunctions—"Suffer little children, . . . to come unto me: for of such is the kingdom of heaven." (Matt. 19:14.)—*IE*, 33:481 (1930).

TEACHER-TRAINING CLASSES. It is the bishop's duty to call the heads of all the auxiliary associations—at least the president of the Relief Society, the superintendent of the Sunday School, and Mutual Improvement, Primary, and Religion Class presidents, in council meeting—the express purpose being to choose by unanimous approval, by prayer, and under the inspiration of the Lord to which they are entitled, some man or woman in that ward who will stand as a leader, as a teacher trainer of the young men and young women who are going to take the course. It is the bishop's right, of course, to name him, but he will ask the others for suggestions.

THE TEACHER TRAINER—HIS QUALIFICATIONS AND DUTIES. In that connection, may I merely suggest that the teacher trainer be chosen from the ranks of those who remain more or less permanently in the ward. You may have some man who stands pre-eminently, perhaps, as an educator; but as soon as the school year closes, he may go to some other place. Then you are left; the result is that there may be a feeling that there is nobody else to succeed him, and your teacher training movement receives a setback which it may be difficult to overcome. Better have one even less experienced in the science of pedagogy and psychology, and who is permanently residing with you, and, above all, whose heart is in the work of the Lord and in the teacher-training organization established for the instruction and development of those who have to teach the youth of Israel.

After all, the technical learning is secondary, if we keep in mind the ultimate aim of the work. We must never lose sight of that. It is the Spirit which teaches the spirit. What you are is what will influence your children—not what you say. The Spirit of the Lord is what is going to reach those teachers and teach your children—and the world must come to it. So do not say you haven't somebody in your ward who can take the leadership of the class. You have some man who stands pre-eminently as a preacher, as a teacher of righteousness.

However, the teacher trainer should not be a preacher. The teacher-training organization is in every sense of the word a class. If you members depend upon the teacher trainer for giving the lesson, expounding it as he would expound a principle of the gospel from the pulpit, you will find that there will be little development on the part of the teachers. Expect preparation from all the officers and teachers from all auxiliary organizations, and all that the teacher trainer is to do is to guide in this and that elucidation of the lesson and topics of the lesson assigned. You may have preachers in these teacher trainers, but you will not have the development of the class. It is a class in every sense of the word.—*IE*, 22:901-903 (1919).

EMPHASIZE JOY. I commend the Deseret Sunday School Union Board for emphasizing joy in the life of Sunday School officers, teachers, and children. Joy is sweeter than pleasure. Joy is an emotion excited with the acquisition or expectation of good. Pleasure is a state of gratification of the senses or mind and may be sensuous. It may be self-indulgence. It is nearly always transitory. Joy and happiness are permanent. Joy is pleasure not to be repented of.

Children are entitled to joy.—*I*, 80:560-561 (1945).

PERSONAL INFLUENCE. As I look in restrospect upon three-score-and-ten years' association with Sunday School work, I am inclined to believe that that which is most potent in shaping a boy's life is personal influence.—*I*, 84:105 (1949).

THE SUNDAY SCHOOL LOOKS FORWARD

"Simon, son of Jonas, lovest thou me more than these?" Simon answered. "Yea, Lord; thou knowest that I love thee." Jesus said unto him. "Feed my lambs." (See John 21:15.)

Such was the divine injunction given by the risen Lord to Peter, his chief Apostle, emphasizing the fact that the proper training of childhood is man's most important and sacred duty.

There is true nobility in the soul of that man or woman who sincerely desires and strives to lead children out of contaminating influences into an environment of high ideals and lofty endeavors.

Next to eternal life, the most precious gift that our Father in heaven can bestow upon man is his children. Ideals that relate to God and to little children are indispensable elements to happiness and eternal life. An institution, therefore, that makes heaven its aim, and childhood its obligation, is one with which every loyal heart should desire to be associated. Such an organization is the Deseret Sunday School Union.

My topic is "Toward What the Sunday School is looking in the Future."

First: The Sunday School looks forward to the time when every girl and boy, every man and woman will be enrolled as a member.

The Sunday School in the West began in 1849 with one superintendent and teacher and thirty pupils. It required forty-seven years—from 1849 to 1896— for the Sunday School membership to reach the first one hundred thousand. The impetus of that one-hundred-thousand group added another one hundred thousand in eighteen years. With this multiple force of two hundred thousand, only seventeen years were required—1914 to 1931—to top the three-hundred thousand mark. Think what gains are possible in the future.

If every student, every pupil, will make it his or her obligation to bring in one new member, you will have, with the application of just this one means, nearly a million membership. Further than that, no teacher must be satisfied until she makes an effort to have every boy and girl enrolled who in age and ability belong to her class. The Sunday School looks forward to your accomplishing that duty. In handling these seemingly indifferent ones, fellow teachers, will you please keep in mind these three parables: The Lost Sheep, The Lost Coin, The Prodigal Son. The first was lost in his eagerness to seek daily sustenance and wandered too far from the flock. The coin was lost through carelessness of the house-wife. The prodigal son became lost because he desired his portion and spent it in profligacy. He did not get back until he came to himself and said, "I will rise and go to my father." Through study and prayer to the best of your ability counter-act those three enticing elements as you seek to bring back the lost ones.

Second: The Sunday School looks forward to the time when in every class in the Sunday School the principles of punctuality, courtesy, self-control, respect for authority, studiousness, responsiveness, and, particularly, reverence and worship, will so impregnate the atmosphere that even the dullard by absorption will be benefited. This is not dreaming; I am not being visionary. The Sunday Schools of the future may realize just that ideal atmosphere.

Third: The Sunday School looks forward to the time when every teacher will possess the qualities mentioned by these Sunday School children.[1] You say, "Well, that will be perfection." Granted, then, let us do our best to approach it, fellow teachers, for they named some practical qualities and attributes which impress childhood. In that connection, every Sunday School teacher should come prepared to give his les-son. The Deseret Sunday School Union looks forward to the time when no teacher will come unprepared to his or her class. That means that every teacher will have within his or her mind a sincere and prayerful desire to awaken within at least one heart every Sunday (and we hope in many hearts) the desire to achieve mastery over weak and selfish indulgences; to awaken even in childhood a hope in the boys to become noble characters; in the girls, to become modest, beautiful women. To awaken in their hearts the desire to become friends; also to look forward to the time when they will be worthy companions in loving homes, and, later in life, to be worthy of fatherhood and pure motherhood. These are true

---

[1]Preparation, presentation of material in the light of the restored gospel, sweet, spiritual, moral, uplifting influence, punctuality—in short, a real Latter-day Saint.

ideals of the gospel, but they are practical ones. Finally, the teacher will have in her heart the desire to awaken a love of the gospel of Jesus Christ, obedience to which brings happiness in this life and salvation throughout eternity.

Fourth: The great Sunday School of the future will have a teacher-training class in which not only the active teachers, but also prospective teachers may receive practical instructions in the preparation and presentation of lessons. That is an important factor. To reach the ideals I have mentioned, or even to approach them, the prepared teacher must see clearly the message she is to impart. You cannot give what you do not possess. You cannot awaken in the hearts of children a nobility which is not yours. She must know the details associated with the incidents of her lesson; must through keen observation, and further research and study, gather illustrative material; must organize logically the accumulated material that it may be presented impressively; must exercise discrimination and eliminate that which is irrelevant. This requires not only study, but also intelligent guidance which may be given in these teacher-training classes.

If a lesson thus prepared be developed in an atmosphere of cheerfulness, the child cannot help being interested and inspired, and the teacher is doubly blessed. To give a lesson well prepared is like mercy—it blesses him that gives and him that receives. It is true in teaching as in life—"Give to the world the best you have, and the best will come back to you."

Fifth: The Sunday School of this century—the beginning of this new century—looks forward to the time when, as a principal part of preparation, every teacher will pray sincerely and earnestly for God's guidance on the day she meets the children placed under her care.

There is a story told of General Charles George Gordon— that "each morning, during his journey in the Sudan country, for one-half hour there lay outside his tent a white handkerchief. The whole camp well knew what it meant, and looked upon the little signal with the utmost respect; no foot dared to pass the threshold of that tent while the little guard lay there. No message, however pressing, was to be delivered. Matters of life and death must wait until the little signal was taken away. Everyone knew that God and Gordon were communing together."

Prayer is just as important in times of peace as in war. Teachers, begin the preparation of your lessons in prayer. Teach your lessons with a prayerful heart. Then pray that God will enrich your message in the souls of your children through the influence of his holy Spirit.

Finally, the Deseret Sunday School Union looks forward to the time, and we hope it is beginning today, when nobility of character will be recognized as being greater than intellect; when faith in our Lord and Savior Jesus Christ, when loyalty to the standards and principles of his restored gospel will be the motivating ideals in the life of every child and youth in the Church. May God's nearness and his guidance, to which all pupils and teachers are entitled, hasten that day.—*IE,* 52:804, 805, 863 (1949).

REVERENCE

THE PRINCIPLE. A principle to which I wish to refer is reverence. I look upon reverence as one of the highest qualities of the soul. An irreverent man is not a believing man. I think a man cannot testify of his knowledge of the existence of God and take God's name in vain. He can do it by words, but as the king in *Hamlet,* his words will fly up, but his thoughts remain below.

I was deeply impressed with the lesson that Elder George Q. Morris taught his missionaries in the Sacred Grove. They have an entrance there now, a sort of fence and a gate leading into the sacred spot, where they hold the service.

There as you enter the gate is a sign, "Quiet, please." I wish everybody in the Church could experience that quiet attitude of several hundred missionaries in that Sacred Grove, and as soon as the amen of the benediction was given, these elders retired without consultation, without shaking hands, to the outside part of the grove.

APPLICATION IN SUNDAY SCHOOL WORK. In our meeting-houses today we have reverence just as soon as the hour comes for worship, but in Sunday Schools particularly, at the change of classes there is a hubbub. That is not educative to our children. They have done away with the marching we used to have when I was in the Sunday School work in Weber. They now think it undignified for older persons to march.

Well, superintendents, you may do this, at least—when you separate for classwork, let a class rise and pass out to the room, and then another class follow, without this careless, sometimes boisterous attitude of everybody's mingling and talking as he goes to his class.

Reverence indicates high culture and true faith in Deity and in his righteousness.—CR, October 1951, pp. 179-180.

Our classrooms are sometimes places of boisterousness. Here is where we need good teachers. A teacher who can present a lesson interestingly will have good order, and when he or she finds students who are rebellious, flipping papers, paying no attention, stumbling, kicking one another, he or she may know that the lesson is not being properly presented. Perhaps it was not even properly prepared.

One of our mothers recently went to a Sunday School class to try to find out why her son was losing interest. There was so much boisterousness, so much confusion, so much noise, that she felt heartsick; and as she arose to leave, she said to the teacher: "I thought this was a Sunday School class, not bedlam!"—CR, Sept.-Oct. 1950, p. 164.

In the classrooms children should be taught, should be free to discuss, free to speak, free to participate in classwork, but no member of the class has the right to distract another student by jostling or making light and frivolous remarks. And I think in this Church, in the priesthood quorums and classes and in auxiliaries, teachers and superintendents ought not to permit it. Disorder injures the child who makes it. He should learn that when he is in society there are certain things which he cannot do with impunity. He cannot trespass upon the rights of his associates.

Let children learn this lesson in youth because when they get out in society and try to trespass against the law, they will feel the restraining hand and probably suffer punishment.

Good order in the classroom is essential to instil into the hearts and lives of young men and young women the principle of self-control. They want to talk, and they want to whisper, but they cannot do it, because it will disturb somebody else. Learn the power and lesson of self-mastery.

Reverence should be particularly manifest in sacrament meetings, in quorum meetings, in Sunday School, in M.I.A., in Primary, yes, and in Relief Society. This is a missionary Church. People come here for light and knowledge, for instruction, and they have a right to find it when they come. —CR, Sept.-Oct. 1950, pp. 165-166.

REVERENCE AND RESPECT FOR LAW. Akin to the respect for law and a contributing factor toward it is reverence for sacred things. It has been truly said that reverence is the noblest state in which a man can live in the world. If that is true, then irreverent man has a crudeness about him that is repellent. He is cynical, often sneering, and nearly always iconoclastic.

Reverence and obedience to law should begin at home. Indeed, too much emphasis cannot be laid upon the responsibility of parents to teach their children reverence for God in all things sacred, and to honor and uphold the law.

The true expression of reverence is found in the Savior's admonition to love the Lord thy God with all thy might, mind, and, strength, and thy neighbor as thyself. (See Matt. 22:37-39.)

As a Church in our worshiping assemblies, we have much room for improvement in this regard. Stake officers, bishops, quorum presidents, auxiliary leaders should make a special effort to maintain more reverence during hours of worship. Children should be impressed with the inappropriateness of confusion and disorder in a worshiping assembly and should be made to realize that it is the height of rudeness to leave service before dismissal. Young people who ignore such proprieties are two hundred and fifty years behind the times. They should have lived in colonial days when just to make sure they stayed out the service, young men were locked in their pews by their superiors.—CR, April 1937, pp. 29-30.

REVERENCE AND CHARACTER. The principle of self-control lies at the basis of reverence and good order in classrooms. I do not know how to define reverence, but I do know how to classify or to place it as one of the objectives of nobility, indeed, one of the attributes of deity.

Love is the divinest attribute of the human soul. I am not so sure but sympathy is next to it—sympathy for the afflicted, for suffering animals, for our brethren and sisters. That is a Godlike virtue.

Kindness is also a sublime virtue. The first sentence in what is now known as the Psalm of Love is this: "Love suffereth long and is kind."

However, I am prompted to place reverence next to love. Jesus mentioned it first in the Lord's prayer: "Our Father which art in heaven, Hallowed be thy name." (Matt. 6:9.) *Hallow*—to make holy—to hold in reverence!

When Jesus cleansed the temple, he was filled with reverent indignation because men were desecrating his Father's house, selling doves and lambs to be offered as sacrifice. Money-changers were there for the convenience of those who came from other countries, so they could give in local currency their temple contributions. Seemingly, in their own eyes, they were justified, but they were doing these things in the house of God. We are told that he overturned the money-changers' tables and said to the sellers of doves, "Take these things hence; make not my Father's house an house of merchandise." (John 2:16.)

"Reverence," wrote Ruskin, "is the noblest state in which a man can live in the world. Reverence is one of the signs of strength; irreverence one of the surest indications of weakness. No man will rise high who jeers at sacred things. The fine loyalties of life must be reverenced or they will be foresworn in the day of trial."

Charles Jefferson, the author of *The Character of Jesus*, writes: "Men in many circles are clever, interesting, brilliant, but they lack one of the three dimensions of life. They have no reach upward. Their conversation sparkles, but it is frivolous and often flippant. Their talk is witty, but the wit is often at the expense of high and sacred things."—*CR*, Sept.-Oct. 1950, pp. 163-164.

SOCIAL SIGNIFICANCE. A great man is reverent. He reverences Deity; he reverences all things associated with Deity; and the great problem that is facing the world today is the attitude toward God, his Son, and the gospel of Jesus Christ.—*DNCS*, September 6, 1952, p. 15.

Not long ago we stood close to the iron curtain. You could feel the shadow hanging over great Berlin. Read the latest news from old China, and you will see how the effort is being put forth to crush Christianity and belief in Christ.

Irreverence and disbelief are pervading the minds of too many people in nations now conquered by the communists; and you need no further proof of the error of that ideology. Reverence in the home, reverence for God's name should be dominant in every home. It is wrong, it is irreverent, to take his name in vain. There is no provocation that will justify it. Let us apply that quality and that virtue here in this beautiful house. Even loud speaking should be avoided. —*DNCS*, September 6, 1952, p. 15.

AN APPEAL FOR LEADERSHIP. I am going to make one appeal for this vast audience of leaders. I believe there is one great need in the Church which you presidencies of stakes, bishoprics of wards, presidencies of quorums, and officers in auxiliaries, can supply. I have in mind the need of more reverence in our houses of worship, better order and discipline in our classrooms, in quorum meetings, and in auxiliary groups.—*CR*, Sept.-Oct. 1950, p. 162.

PREPARATION TO ENTER THE HOUSE OF WORSHIP—A LESSON IN ATTITUDES. If you were going to meet the queen of England today you would make great preparation in anticipation of going into her presence. When Helen Keller and her teacher were invited to meet the king of Belgium, Miss Keller, who I think in many respects is the most distinguished woman in all modern history, seemed somewhat agitated as she stood in the waiting room. Though she had stood before dignitaries before, she sensed a responsibility in meeting His Royal Highness.

What I am saying is that whenever you go into the presence of a dignitary, an earthly dignitary, you make preparation. You know that that is one fundamental reason why we put on our Sunday best to come here to the house of God, to come into his presence. Such preparation is in and of itself a virtue. It has a psychological effect, and that father who, in his eagerness to make money, will take his son out in the field to work on Sunday without giving that son an opportunity to take a rest, change his clothes, and come in cleanliness of body and of mind into the presence of his heavenly Father, deprives his son of a blessing, whether he is in the Church or out of it.

There is a fundamental virtue in coming to the house of worship. One of the fundamental conditions contributing to a person's right thinking and acting is a reverence for God. A growing disbelief among the masses of mankind in a Supreme Being is a principal cause of crime.—*DNCS*, April 30, 1952, p. 2.

CHAPTER 17

THE APOSTLESHIP IN THE ANCIENT CHURCH

THE ANCIENT CHURCH

MEANING OF APOSTLE. The word *apostle* means an "envoy" or "one who is sent." An Apostle is a "special witness of the name of Christ in all the world."

In all the accounts given of this important event, Peter's name is mentioned first, indicating that he was chosen as the chief Apostle and was undoubtedly appointed and set apart as the President of the Council of Twelve. The names of the Twelve whom Jesus ordained at that time were:

(1) Simon Peter, and his brother (2) Andrew; (3) James and (4) John, the two sons of Zebedee; (5) Philip of Bethsaida, and (6) Nathanael, also called Bartholomew; (7) Thomas, also called "Didymus," a name which means "a twin"; (8) Matthew, the publican, or tax gatherer; (9) James, the son of Alphaeus, called "James the Less"; (10) Lebbeus, who was also called Thaddeus, and also Judas, but not Judas Iscariot; (11) Simon, the "Canaanite," or "Simon the Zelotes," and (12) Judas Iscariot, who became the traitor.

These twelve men were, for the most part, Galilean fishermen, who labored at their trade on the shores of Galilee. Matthew, however, was a publican, and therefore despised by the Jews; and Judas was a Judean. Some of the leaders of the Jews thought that they were unlearned and ignorant men. (See Acts 4:13.) "Unlearned they were; but not ignorant; for by their wisdom and preaching, they overthrew the whole edifice of human wisdom, and led the world to the light of truth."—*AA*, pp. 25-26.

SIMON PETER—THE CHIEF APOSTLE

DESIRABLE CHARACTERISTICS OF AN APOSTLE. When Jesus called Simon *Peter* or "The Rock," he undoubtedly expressed in that name one characteristic which he desired to see in the faith of his disciples, and particularly in each of his Apostles. He desired them to possess a faith that was unwavering—a faith that would make them steadfast in the truth regardless of miracles or the acts of men—a faith that would trust the Lord at all times and under all circumstances, let those times and circumstances be what they may.

Jesus knew that the Jews were easily influenced; that a miracle performed today might awaken a feeling in them that he was the king for whom they had been waiting, and that a truth taught tomorrow might arouse in them a feeling that he was an impostor. He wanted to lead them to God and to his gospel. He longed to have them comprehend the truths of life so they would live them after he was gone from their midst.—*AA*, p. 34.

TESTIMONY AND REVELATION. At last Jesus discovers the assurance in Peter for which he has been laboring many months to develop. He now knows that Peter's spirit has received divine assurance that all these miracles and mighty manifestations have been wrought by the power of God through his only Begotten Son. He knows that the testimony borne by Peter comes not from men but from God, and no matter what men may think or do, Peter will stand firm as a rock on this testimony.

"And I say also unto thee," continued Jesus, "That thou art Peter, and upon this rock I will build my church; and the gates of hell shall not prevail against it." (Matt. 16:18.)

By that he meant that as Simon's name *Peter* means rock, so this testimony that comes by revelation shall be the rock upon which Christ's church shall be built because when one receives such divine assurance in his soul that the gospel is true, no views of men, nor waves of temptation, nor "the power of hell" can deprive him of it. You remember when Jesus first met Simon, he said he should be called "the Rock." Ever since then it would seem that Jesus has been waiting for the time when Peter's testimony would be like his character—expressive and firm. That time has come; and Peter is now prepared to receive a greater responsibility.

"And I will give unto thee the keys of the kingdom of heaven: and whatsoever thou shalt bind on earth shall be bound in heaven: and whatsoever thou shalt loose on earth shall be loosed in heaven." (*Ibid.*, 16:19.)

One *key* was to open the door of the gospel to the Gentiles, but it took quite a while before Peter knew how to use it.

It is one thing to know that the gospel is true; it is quite another thing to comprehend its purpose and significance. —*AA,* pp. 42-43.

LESSONS FOR YOUTH IN THE APOSTLESHIP OF PETER. Peter's experience is the experience that will come to nearly all the boys and girls who read these pages. The knowledge of truth, and the testimony of the gospel may come gradually to most of them. The one great lesson for them to learn even in youth is, that *purity of thought,* and a *sincere heart seeking* the Savior's *guidance daily* will lead to a testimony of the truth of Christ's gospel as sure and permanent as that which Peter possessed as he descended Mt. Hermon after seeing the Transfiguration of Christ, and hearing the voice of God testify to his divinity.

But *knowing* that Jesus is the Savior of mankind did not give Peter a comprehension of the gospel plan. In this regard, he had yet much to learn. And, it may be, that his strength of character, or shall we say his judgment, was not yet so sound as it should have been in a man whose whole life should be as firm as a rock.—*AA,* pp. 48-49.

INSTRUCTIONS TO THE FIRST CHIEF APOSTLE. It is said when Peter went out speechless from the face of all, and filled the silence, weeping bitterly, that his grief was so heavy that he remained alone all day during Friday and Saturday following the Savior's crucifixion. If so, his sorrow for what he had done was made all the more acute as he recalled the many kind words the Savior had spoken to him, and the many happy moments he had spent in the Lord's company. Every word and act and look associated with his Master would flash upon his mind with a new meaning. Perhaps for the first time in his life, he now fully realized why the Lord had desired his nature and faith to be as "the Rock." Through the mist of his bitter tears, he saw all the true attributes of manhood as they were personified in Jesus—reverence, brotherliness, patience, sincerity, courage.

These and many other noble traits made Jesus appear to him now more holy than ever. But the more clearly Peter

saw Christ's strength and holiness, the more clearly he realized
his own littleness and misery. This last manifestation of his
weakness, which led him to deny his Lord, made him see himself in a new light, and it had a decisive effect upon him. Out
of the "deep silence" of his suffering, those two days, there was
born that strength which Christ had urged upon him ever
since he called him *Peter.—AA,* pp. 66-67.

Several days after this, Peter and six other disciples were
back on the sea of Tiberias, fishing. They were in Galilee,
evidently waiting to meet the Lord there as he had promised.
One evening, as if Peter had almost despaired of waiting, he
said to the others, "I'm going fishing."

"We also go with thee," said they.

They entered into a boat immediately, and let down their
nets. They toiled all night and caught nothing, just as some
of them had done on a memorable occasion several months
before.

As morning dawned, they saw a man standing on the
shore, but in the distance, they could not tell who he was.
Suddenly the man cried, "Sirs, have ye any meat?"

"No," was their reply.

"Cast the net on the right side of the ship, and ye shall
find," said the man.

They did so, and caught so many fish that they could
scarcely draw in the net.

John, whose loving eyes were made more keen by a loving heart, rushed to Peter's side and whispered, "It is the
Lord."

Instantly, Peter knew John spoke the truth, and man of
action that he was, he put on his fisherman's coat, plunged
into the sea, and hastened to the feet of the Master. The
others came in the little ship, dragging the net of fishes.

Jesus had already started a fire and was cooking them
something to eat. After the greetings, he said, "Bring of the
fish which ye have now caught."

Peter was the leader in going to the net and in drawing
it to the land. While the fish were cooking, the disciples
counted the number caught, and found that in that one
draught there were 153; "and for all there were so many, yet
was the net not broken."

Jesus had shown them where to catch the fish; he had
started the fire on which to cook them; and now "he taketh
the bread and giveth them and the fish likewise." Surely these
little incidents would tend to impress them with the truth
that if they "would seek first the kingdom of God and his
righteousness all else will be added." At any rate, this is
the lesson taught on that great occasion: The Apostles were
not now to spend their lives seeking the things which perish,
but in searching for souls that will endure throughout all
eternity. Many are now together in the fold of Christ, and
the shepherd is called away. Henceforward Peter and his
associates must be the keepers of this flock.

When they had broken their fast, Jesus said to Simon
Peter, "Simon, son of Jonas, lovest thou me more than these?"

"Yea, Lord," answered Peter, "thou knowest that I love
thee."

"Feed my lambs." That is, Take care of the little ones
in my Church. Do not let them go astray in paths that will
lead them to sin and misery.

He saith unto him again the second time, "Simon, son
of Jonas, lovest thou me?"

"Yea, Lord, thou knowest that I love thee."

"Feed my sheep." Keep the older ones together and give
them the words of life as thou has received them from me.

A third time Jesus said, "Simon, son of Jonas, lovest thou
me?"

And Peter, somewhat grieved, answered, "Lord thou
knowest all things; thou knowest that I love thee."

"Feed my sheep."

And then the Savior admonished Peter not always to
follow his own inclinations and impulsive nature, but ever to
do his duty as the shepherd of the fold. When Peter was
young and did not have the knowledge and responsibility he
now possessed, he could go fishing and make money or study
or do whatever he wished, but now he must attend to his
duties in the kingdom of God no matter what might come
to him personally in doing so. Even though Peter's duty led
to the cross, the Savior said, "Follow me."

While this conversation was going on, Jesus and Peter
were walking alone a little ahead of the others. Peter turned
and saw John following close to them.

"Lord," said Peter, "what is John to do?"

"If I will that he tarry till I come, what is that to thee, follow thou me." As much as to say, Just attend faithfully to your duty, Peter; teach others to do the same; and all will be well. (See John 21.)

This is the last recorded word of Christ to Peter; but he was present, of course, when the Savior gave his final charge to the Twelve. (See Mark 16:16.)

From this time Peter's zeal in the work of the ministry was constant, and his boldness unsubdued.—*AA*, pp. 69-73.

OTHERS CHOSEN TO ASSIST THE APOSTLES. As the membership of the church increased, men were called and ordained to various offices in the work of the ministry. Besides the Apostles, there were evangelists, pastors, teachers, deacons, etc. Among the first to be chosen and ordained to a particular office of service in the Church were "seven men of honest report, full of the Holy Ghost, and wisdom." Their names were Stephen, Philip, Prochorus, Nicanor, Timon, Parmenas, and Nicolas. They are called deacons, and one of their chief duties was to oversee the distribution of food among the poor.—*AA*, p. 91.

PETER'S DIFFICULTY IN UNDERSTANDING HIS CALLING. Though only a few years had passed since the Apostles had received the final commission to "Go ye into all the world, and preach the gospel . . ." (Mark 16:15), yet, through their earnest and continuous labors, churches were established in all Judea, Galilee, and Samaria. As it was the duty of the Twelve to look after the interests of the whole church, it became necessary for them to travel throughout all the land of the Jews. Peter visited from place to place, organizing, ordaining, blessing, and preaching the gospel of Christ.—*AA*, p. 95.

It had been Peter's duty and privilege to preach the gospel first to the Gentiles. Please note that when the Lord desired the Gentiles to hear his word, he instructed the chief of the Twelve to turn the key that opened the gospel door to them. This is one of the special duties of the Apostleship.

Since that time, many Gentiles had become converted; and in some cities they met and worshiped together with the Jews. This was particularly true in Antioch, an important city of Syria where the followers of Jesus were first called Christians.

But there were certain men from Judea who went to Antioch and caused trouble. These were Jews who had accepted the gospel but who still believed that the Gentiles would have to do everything the Jews did before they could obtain salvation.

The question as to whether the Gentiles might receive the gospel and be saved, without conforming to every Jewish rite, came before the Twelve and other Church leaders in Jerusalem.

"And when there had been much disputing, Peter rose up, and said unto them, Men and brethren, ye know how that a good while ago God made choice among us, that the Gentiles by my mouth should hear the word of the gospel, and believe.

"And God, which knoweth the hearts, bare them witness, giving them the Holy Ghost, even as he did unto us;

"And put no difference between us and them, purifying their hearts by faith." (Acts 15:7-9.)

He then told them not to provoke God by passing some rule that would compel the Gentiles to do what the Lord does not require of them, for, he added, "But we believe that through the grace of the Lord Jesus Christ we shall be saved, even as they." (*Ibid.*, 15:11.)

There was a time when Simon, the Jewish fisherman, with all his Jewish prejudices, would have rather yielded to the Jewish side of this question; but now, it was not Simon, the fisherman, who spoke, but Peter, the chief Apostle of the Lord. What were prejudices to him in the light of the inspiration of truth! All that was necessary for him to know was whether the thing was right, and prejudice or no prejudice, favor or no favor, he would defend it.

It is true that once after this council, so Paul says, (See Gal. 2:7), Peter withdrew from the company of some Gentiles because some of the Jews came down from Jerusalem. Paul says he rebuked Peter for his actions on this occasion, but we have no record of what Peter said or did. Knowing Peter as we do, we are safe in concluding that he did not intentionally waver from the right. It seems more probable that Paul misunderstood Peter's motives. At any rate, we may rest assured that what Peter said and did was intended to help those who were influenced by his actions.

From that time, we know very little of Peter's travels. By reading his epistles, we get a little insight into the nature of his labors and travels during the last years of his life. Undoubtedly, he visited every country where there were organized branches of the Church, even to the "seven churches in Asia."

We do not know just where he died nor the kind of death he suffered, but it is evident that the end was not far off when he wrote his second epistle to the churches. That was about thirty-five years after he first met the Savior. He was in the ministry then, approximately thirty-five years, perhaps longer. —*AA*, pp. 108-110.

A LESSON FROM THE CHIEF APOSTLE. To the priesthood I quote the truth and the admonition given by the chief Apostle to the members of the priesthood over nineteen hundred years ago—that chief Apostle, my favorite, wrote this letter:

"The elders which are among you I exhort, who am also an elder, and a witness of the sufferings of Christ, and also a partaker of the glory that shall be revealed:

"Feed the flock of God which is among you, taking the oversight thereof, not by constraint, but willingly; not for filthy lucre, but of a ready mind;

"Neither as being lords over God's heritage, but being ensamples to the flock.

"And when the chief Shepherd shall appear, ye shall receive a crown of glory that fadeth not away.

"Likewise, ye younger, submit yourselves unto the elder. Yea, all of you be subject one to another, and be clothed with humility: for God resisteth the proud, and giveth grace to the humble.

"Humble yourselves therefore under the mighty hand of God, that he may exalt you in due time:

"Casting all your care upon him; for he careth for you.

"Be sober, be vigilant; because your adversary the devil, as a roaring lion, walketh about, seeking whom he may devour:

"Whom resist stedfast in the faith, knowing that the same afflictions are accomplished in your brethren that are in the world." (I Peter 5:1-9.)

Just one element I wish to emphasize. The instructions I give are nineteen hundred years old, yet new today and applicable as then to elders, from the chief elder. But he said, be "ensamples to the flock." (*Ibid.*, 5:3.) Ever keep in mind, fellow workers, that example should start at home. That is the best place to exercise the lofty ideals of the priesthood.—*CR*, April 1948, pp. 171-172.

JAMES, THE SON OF ZEBEDEE

When the Twelve were chosen, James was chosen next to Peter, and one of the three who constituted what we might call the Presidency of the Twelve. In this position, he became closely associated with the Redeemer and was an eyewitness to some of the most sacred incidents in his Lord's ministry. Thus, with Peter and John, he was present in the room when the little daughter of Jairus was restored to life.

He was also one of the favored three on the Mount of Transfiguration; and was one of those chosen to accompany the Master to the secluded place in the Garden of Gethsemane, when Christ suffered those bitter agonies preparatory to his betrayal and sufferings on the cross.

About forty-two or forty-four years after Christ, Herod Agrippa, as you have already learned, commenced a bitter persecution against the Saints. James was among the first to be arrested.

Sentence was passed upon him very soon after he was apprehended, yet, so remarkable were his faith and his courage during the trial that the officer who guarded him, (who, some say, was his accuser) repented of his sins, became converted, and declared his faith in Christianity.

As James was being led to the place of execution, this officer threw himself at the Apostle's feet, and humbly begged forgiveness for what he had said against him.

Putting his arm around the penitent man, James answered, "Peace, my son, peace be unto thee, and pardon of thy faults."

Both were then executed by order of the cruel Herod.

Thus James, the first martyr Apostle, partook of the cup
of which he had said to his Lord many years before he was
willing to drink.—*AA*, pp. 115-117.

JOHN, THE BROTHER OF JAMES

In the first chapter of the gospel according to John, we
read that two disciples of John the Baptist heard their master
bear witness to the divinity of Jesus. Said the Baptist, referring to Jesus walking alone in the distance, "Behold the
Lamb of God, which taketh away the sin of the world."
(John 1:29.) One of the two disciples who heard this testimony is named; he was Andrew, the brother of Simon Peter.
(See *ibid.*, 1:40.) The other is not named. Indeed throughout
the entire book, which, undoubtedly, was written by John
himself, the name of John, son of Zebedee, is never once
written. In the account of the Last Supper, we read of a
"disciple whom Jesus loved," who sat so near the Lord that
his head could rest on Jesus' bosom.

These two instances, and others that might be named,
indicate to us a prominent trait in John's character; viz., an
unassumed modesty that won him the respect and love of all
who knew him.

But John was the son of Salome and Zebedee, and the
younger brother of James, with whom he was called
"Boanerges," or Son of Thunder. This gives us a little insight
into another phase of his character. Like his brother James,
he was evidently fiery in his zeal in whatever he undertook
to do, and fearless in doing what he thought was right.

A modesty that made him shrink ever from praising
himself or unduly pushing himself forward; a fearlessness in
defending what is right, and a love for his Master that gave
him the highest place in the Savior's heart—these are three
traits of John's character which stand out distinctly in the
fragmentary accounts of his life.

He lived, and was probably born in Bethsaida, the home
of Peter and Andrew and Philip. He was a fisherman by trade
and worked with his father and brother James. His father,
Zebedee, owned his own ships, and employed servants; so we
conclude that he was well-to-do financially. (See Mark 1:20.)

He was a seeker after true learning and especially after those things which would tell him about God and the hereafter. He kept his mind and heart pure, so that he could appreciate the truth when he heard it.

When, therefore, John the Baptist came out of the wilderness preaching repentance and declaring that the kingdom of heaven was at hand, John was one of the fearless young men who believed the Baptist and followed him. Thus he was prepared to accept John's testimony of Jesus after the latter was baptized in Jordan, and was one of the two who had the first interview with the Savior of the world at the beginning of his ministry.

On the same occasion when Simon Peter and his brother were called as disciples of Jesus, James the son of Zebedee and John were with their father mending their nets, and when Jesus called them, they immediately left the ship and their father and followed him. (See Matt. 4:21-22; Luke 5:1-11.)

Luke tells us that John was present at the miraculous draught of fishes and was very much astonished at what he heard and saw on that occasion. It was one of the first lessons, if not the first impressive lesson, that taught him the great truth that obedience to Christ's words brings blessings.

ONE OF THE SPECIAL THREE. From this time on to the end of his eventful life, he was always in the ministry. When Jesus chose his disciples, John was chosen one of the special three, although he was the youngest member of the Twelve.

From that time, John was in the close companionship of Jesus, and witnessed some of the most remarkable and divine incidents recorded in the history of Christ's ministry. He was one of the three Apostles permitted to remain in the room when the little daughter of Jairus was restored to life. (See Luke 8:51.) He was on the Mount of Transfiguration when the Savior conversed with Moses and Elias and when a voice from heaven said, "This is my Beloved Son, hear him." (See Ibid., 9:28-35.)

With Peter, James, and Andrew, John was present on the Mount of Olives when Jesus taught them concerning the destruction of the temple and of Christ's second coming. How the memory of such occasions must have filled his soul in after years, with rejoicing and sweet content!

To him and Peter was entrusted the duty of making preparations for the Passover.

At the solemn moment when the Savior said, "One of you shall betray me," it was John, the "disciple whom Jesus loved" who received the answer indicating who the traitor was.

When the gloom of Gethsemane began to weigh heavily upon the spirit of Jesus, John was one of the three unto whom the Savior said, "My soul is exceeding sorrowful, even unto death: tarry ye here, and watch with me." (Matt. 26:38.)

Later that same night, when the traitor gave the kiss of betrayal, and the soldiers arrested Jesus and bore him away a prisoner, all the other disciples fled, but John accompanied his Master to the house of the high priest and later admitted Peter, who, you remember, had "followed afar off."

Though we are not told, yet we can imagine what this beloved disciple's feelings were as he listened to the false and wicked accusations against his Lord, and how his heart must have ached as he saw Jesus beaten and scourged, and a crown of thorns put on his head. If he had wanted to call down fire from heaven and consume the Samaritans who refused shelter and accommodations to his Lord, what must have been the state of his fiery soul when he beheld the Jews and their judges persecuting the Christ to death!

How his soul must have been rent in agony as he saw his Savior nailed to the cross, and yet what peace must have come to him as he received from the dying lips of his Master one of the dearest commissions ever given to mortal man. As the three Mary's and John stood by the cross, Jesus looked down upon them and said to his mother, "Woman, behold thy son!" and to John, "Behold thy mother!"

"And from that hour that disciple took her unto his own home." (John 19:27.)

On the Sunday morning following the crucifixion, John was with Peter when Mary Magdalene came running to them, saying: "They have taken away the Lord out of the sepulchre, and we know not where they have laid him." (Ibid., 20:2.)

As soon as the Apostles heard this, they ran for the spot where Jesus had been buried. John being the younger outran Peter and was the first to see the empty tomb; and " . . . looking in, saw the linen clothes lying; yet went he not in." (Ibid., 20:5.) A moment later, however, he followed

Peter into the tomb, made a careful examination of the linen clothes and napkin that was about the head; but not yet realizing that Christ was to rise the third day, each returned to his own home.

John was with the ten and later with the eleven when Christ appeared to them in the upper room. Of this and other glorious experiences he bears testimony in his gospel. " . . . that ye might believe that Jesus is the Christ, the Son of God; and that believing ye might have life through his name." (Ibid., 20:31.)—AA, pp. 118-123.

JOHN'S ACTIVITIES, CA. 35-50 A.D. For about fifteen years after the Savior's ascension it is believed that John continued at Jerusalem and remained a true son to Mary. During all that time, however, he was always active in the ministry.

He was with Peter going to the temple when the lame man at the Gate Beautiful asked them for alms.

With Peter he exercised his faith on that occasion to bless the poor man who had never walked.

John, undoubtedly, testified to the multitude who assembled at Solomon's porch on the day of this miracle; but no historian has told us what he said. We infer from what Luke says that John spoke at that time; but only Peter's sermon, and only a little of that, has been preserved.

While they were speaking, the captain of the temple arrested them and put them in prison.

When they were brought out before the council next day and told not to preach about Jesus any more, John was just as bold as Peter in declaring, "Whether it be right in the sight of God to hearken unto you more than unto God, judge ye,

"For we cannot but speak the things which we have seen and heard." (Acts 4:19-20.)

After they were released, they continued preaching to the people and praising the Lord for all his wonderful manifestations to them. The great spiritual feast that resulted from their labors must have filled John's soul with a divine peace such as he had never before experienced, for of all the Apostles, he was the most spiritual-minded.

During this period, he was imprisoned several times, but never once did he waver in his determination to let all the people know that Jesus Christ was the Redeemer of the world. He could suffer and be happy because he loved those whom he served. Thus in the beginning of his ministry his character shone out in true greatness; for he was "willing, patient, and strong to endure for others."

When the Samaritans received the gospel through the preaching of Philip, John accompanied Peter to Samaria, and conferred the Holy Ghost by the laying on of hands upon those whom Philip had baptized.

No doubt this was just one of many visits he made during those fifteen years that he remained at Jerusalem. The Twelve, the seventies, elders, priests, teachers, and deacons were out preaching in all the cities roundabout Jerusalem, and the three chief Apostles, Peter, James, and John would be required, and when not required would be invited, to organize the branches and to meet with the new converts and give encouragement in their glorious faith.

When the great question arose about what the Gentiles who joined the Church should be required to do, John was one who sat in the council held at Jerusalem. Paul, writing about this council, mentions James, Cephas, and John who "seemed to be pillars." In the light of the organization of the Church today, we know that Peter, James, and John were the men who presided at that time, although it was James who rendered the decision that was made effective throughout all the provinces.—*AA*, pp. 125-127.

JOHN AFTER THE COUNCIL OF JERUSALEM. An important council was held about fifty years after the birth of Christ (50 A.D.) During the next eighteen years John seems to have been hidden from view. Nothing is known about what he did or where he went. It is presumed that he left Jerusalem, and seldom, if ever, returned. If so, then we may rightly conclude that Mary, the mother of Jesus, had left Jerusalem also, and left it and all her loving kindred and friends on earth for a happy, glorious meeting with her Son in their heavenly home on high. The dutiful and loving attention John had bestowed upon Mary, he is now free to give to the Church which bears her Son's name.

Undoubtedly he visited nearly all, if not all the important places where Christians dwelt; but most of his latest years seem to have been spent in Asia Minor.

Tradition informs us that he made his home at Ephesus, a large and populous city of Iona, about forty miles from Smyrna. It was noted chiefly for its wickedness and the beautiful temple of Diana. Some claim that Jesus' mother Mary and Mary Magdalene went to Ephesus with John and died there. The tradition is a pleasing one; for with the devotion of a son to his mother, as shown by John, there is associated Mary Magdalene's love, which might well be expressed in the words of another beautiful woman, who said to her husband's mother, "Intreat me not to leave thee, or to return from following after thee: for whither thou goest, I will go; and where thou lodgest, I will lodge: thy people shall be my people, and thy God my God:

"Where thou diest, will I die, and there will I be buried: . . ." (Ruth 1:16-17.)

From Ephesus John visited all the branches of the church laboring, especially among the "seven churches in Asia."

When John had spent several years at Ephesus, a cruel Roman emperor, during his persecution of the Church, arrested him, had him carried to Rome, condemned him to death, and had him plunged into boiling oil. John's life being preserved through the power of God, he was then banished to Patmos. All that John says about it is that he was " . . . in the isle that is called Patmos, for the word of God, and for the testimony of Jesus Christ." (Rev. 1:9.) It is quite evident from this that he had been persecuted for his belief in the gospel and for his unwavering testimony of the life, death, and resurrection of Jesus Christ. He was probably the last living witness of the Savior's miracles and teachings. Perhaps that is why he was banished. But wicked men could not banish the testimony he had borne. That was planted in the hearts of thousands of sincere believers and, like seeds sown in fertile soil, would grow and bear rich harvests for ages to come.

Nor did banishment injure the aged Apostle, for he was not alone even on that uninhabited and barren rock. One

Sunday morning, or the "Lord's day," as he called it, he heard behind him a great voice, as of a trumpet that said to him, " .. What thou seest, write in a book, and send it unto the seven churches which are in Asia; ... " (Rev. 1:11.) He turned, and saw the Son of Man clothed with a garment down to the foot and bound with a golden girdle. As he beheld his Lord wrapped in such divine splendor, he fell at his feet as dead. But the Savior, John says, " . . . laid his right hand upon me, saying unto me, Fear not; I am the first and the last:

"I am he that liveth, and was dead; and, behold, I am alive for evermore." (*Ibid.*, 1:17-18.)   He was again commanded to write all he had witnessed and what would yet be shown him in vision.   Thus was given to the "seven churches of Asia," and subsequently to the world, what is now known as "Revelation," the last book in the Bible, but the first one written by its author.

Upon the death of Domitian, the cruel emperor who had banished him, the Apostle was permitted to return to Ephesus, where he continued his preaching, writing, and testimony.

Besides "Revelation," he wrote his gospel and his three epistles.

John's second epistle should be of special interest to the young.   From it we infer that there were two Christian homes, in each of which John took delight.   The mothers were sisters.   His letter is addressed to "The Elect Lady" or, as she is sometimes called, the Lady Electa and her children.   John tells of his love and that of others for them—mother and children—because of their Christian character.   He tells of his great joy because of the children walking in the truth, living as children should live who have learned of the teachings of Christ.

It is said that when he became so old and feeble that he could not walk to church nor preach to his people, his loving friends would carry him to the place of meeting.   On these occasions, he would repeat again and again, "My dear children, love one another."   One day some asked him, "Master, why dost thou always say this?"   He answered, "This is what the Lord commands you; and this, if you do it, is sufficient."

"Beloved, follow not that which is evil, but that which is good.   He that doeth good is of God: but he that doeth evil hath not seen God." (III John 11.)—*AA,* pp. 129-132.

THE ANCIENT APOSTLES AND THEIR PROBLEMS

"GOD IS NO RESPECTER OF PERSONS." You remember how difficult it was for the Lord to convince Peter that the Gentiles were worthy to be baptized into the Church of Jesus Christ. Peter saw in a vision a vast sheet descending from heaven in which there were unclean animals, and he heard a voice saying, "Arise, Peter; slay and eat." But Peter said, "Not so, Lord: for nothing common or unclean hath at any time entered into my mouth." (See Acts 11:7-8.)

When Peter realized the meaning of the vision, his whole Jewish nature was shocked; for to obey was to break the law of his forefathers by associating with Gentiles. The Jewish Christians who were with Peter from Joppa to Caesarea were "astonished" when they saw "the gift of the Holy Ghost poured out" on the "unclean" Gentiles. When Peter reached Jerusalem, he was accused of having not only associated but also having eaten with Gentiles, but Peter had learned by revelation that "what God has made clean" no one should "call common or unclean," that the Lord is "no respecter of persons" and that "every nation" that accepts him and "feareth him and worketh righteousness" may receive his blessings.

THE QUESTION AGITATED. But there were many Jews in the Church who did not believe this, and the only condition on which they would accept a Gentile was that he should obey the Jewish religion also. When this class of Christians heard that Paul and Barnabas had baptized hundreds of Gentiles, they became very much agitated in their feelings, and some of them went to Antioch and began to preach, first privately then publicly, that unless the Gentiles obeyed a certain Jewish rite, they could not be saved. Paul and Barnabas had told the Saints that obedience to the gospel of Christ would save the Gentiles as well as the Jews, and that the Gentiles did not have to become Jews. Now these men from the chief branch of the Church declared that Paul and Barnabas were wrong. No wonder "those who from among the Gentiles were turned unto God," were "troubled" and perplexed. Indeed, the controversy became so sharp that it threatened to lead some out of the Church.

MESSENGERS SENT TO JERUSALEM. So it was " . . . determined that Paul and Barnabas, and certain other of them, should go up to Jerusalem unto the apostles and elders about this question." (Acts 15:2.)

The church in Antioch evidently believed Paul and Barnabas to be in the right, for when they started on their journey they were escorted on their way by the church. As they passed through Syro-Phoenecia and Samaria, and told the Saints who greeted them how the Gentiles had been converted, they " . . . caused great joy unto all the brethren." (Ibid., 15:3.)

This was Paul's third visit to Jerusalem since his conversion. The first was three years after he joined the Church, when he spent two weeks with Peter, and then had to flee for his life. The second was when he accompanied the messengers who brought relief to the Saints in Judea during the famine. That was the time Peter was sentenced to be killed. Fifteen years had passed since he left Jerusalem for Damascus with papers to arrest all Christians whom he found! Now he enters the city as the defender of one of the greatest truths that the Christian Church or the world can know; namely, that God is no respecter of persons but will bless every nation as it obeys the principles of life and salvation.

PAUL IN COUNCIL WITH THE LEADERS. He first met in council with Peter, James, and John, and received for the first time, so far as we know, "the right hand of fellowship" from John, the beloved disciple. Titus was with Paul as an example of those who were Gentile converts.

This visit was really an appeal to the Presidency of the Twelve, and confirms the belief of the members of the Church today that Peter, James, and John were appointed leaders at that time just as three high priests are now chosen as the First Presidency of Jesus Christ's Church.

At length the great meeting was called at which was to be settled once and for all the standing of the Gentiles in the Christian Church. "It was a scene of earnest debate, and perhaps, in its earlier portion, of angry disputing"; but finally Peter addressed the assembly and told how God had revealed to him the fact that the Gentiles could accept the gospel without obeying all the Jewish ceremonies.

Then Paul and Barnabas spoke amidst great silence, while every eye was riveted upon these two great missionaries who had first organized branches of the Church among Gentile nations.

Finally, James, the brother of the Lord, who was known among the Jews as "James the Just," arose and gave the decision of the council, which established the union of the Jewish and the Gentile Christians.

PAUL RETURNS TO ANTIOCH. Thus the controversy ended, and Paul's mission to the Gentiles was authoritatively approved. When he started back to Antioch, he was accompanied by Judas, surnamed Barnabas, and Silas, "chief men among the brethren." It seems that John Mark went with them also. They carried with them the decree of the council to be read to the churches that had been so disturbed by the controversy.—*AA*, pp. 167-171.

MINISTRY AND AUTHORITY OF THE EARLY APOSTLES

CHOSEN BY INSPIRATION. The first important point to note is the prayerfulness with which Christ approached the choosing of his Twelve. If you will read in the sixth chapter of Luke from the twelfth to the sixteenth verses, you will find there a very brief account of Christ's choosing the Twelve. The twelfth verse, especially, is significant:

"And it came to pass in those days, that he went out into a mountain to pray, and continued all night in prayer to God." (Luke 6:12.) (There is a very clear exposition at once of two divine Personages in the Godhead—God the Father to whom Christ prayed, God the Son who had the responsibility of establishing the gospel in the Meridian of Time and throughout all ages.) "And when it was day, he called unto him his disciples: and of them he chose twelve, whom also he named apostles." (*Ibid.*, 6:13.)

SIGNIFICANCE OF THE NUMBER TWELVE. Some have asked whether the number twelve had any significance. Well, it has. The people to whom Jesus first came were the descendants of the twelve tribes of Israel. They were looking forward to an earthly king, as well as one who would stand at the head of these twelve tribes. Now it is not clearly stated anywhere in the scriptures whether Jesus chose the Twelve because there were twelve tribes of Israel, but the implication is that he did. We find in secular literature the following:

"The Apostles were twelve in number. The number was intended to be significant. Its import could not have been lost on the Twelve themselves when they were first called, or on the multitude who witnessed their election. Our Lord was evidently thinking of the twelve tribes of Israel. Though ten of the tribes had largely disappeared, the mission of the Messiah was to be to all the tribes of the nation. Hence the fitness of the number chosen by our Lord. There was one Apostle for each tribe. Nor should it be overlooked that the employment of this number was a fresh claim on the part of Jesus to be the Messiah. His disciples would argue this: 'Who but the Messiah could venture to create a body or group of twelve disciples only? Nobody had done so before, no prophet, not even the Baptist. Jesus then must be the Messiah.' "

Again we read: "Their number, corresponding to that of the twelve tribes, shows that they are destined primarily to work among the children of Israel, to whom, accordingly, they made their first appeal in Jerusalem."

Now, if that were all we had, I would hesitate about even mentioning this, associating the number twelve with the twelve tribes, but if you will turn to the Doctrine and Covenants, Section 29, verse 12, you will find the following:

"And again, verily, verily, I say unto you, and it hath gone forth in a firm decree, by the will of the Father, that mine apostles, the Twelve which were with me in my ministry at Jerusalem, shall stand at my right hand at the day of my coming in a pillar of fire, being clothed with robes of righteousness, with crowns upon their heads, in glory even as I am, to judge the whole house of Israel, even as many as have loved me and kept my commandments, and none else."

I think we need not pause longer on the significance of the number. It is a fact that that number was chosen, the group consisted of twelve, that it was so during Christ's ministry among men. As far as we can find in the Acts of the Apostles, it continued to be so. It is very difficult to find out whether every vacancy that occurred was filled, thus continuing the exact number of twelve, but we do know that the first vacancy made by Judas Iscariot was filled before the work was taken up, and we can readily infer that that policy was continued throughout the ministry of the Twelve, at any rate in this dispensation the Lord again chose twelve, and he also chose twelve from among the Nephites; so it would seem that there is some significance to the number as it relates to the Council.

APOSTLES ORDAINED AND QUALIFIED. Now what about the ministry of the Twelve? We are told that they were ordained and set apart. The inference in Matthew is that the Savior not only ordained them, or authorized them, but he also qualified them—note that—he qualified them to have power over unclean spirits, over diseases, over those spirits which were troubling the people, and sent them forth authoritatively commissioned to represent him, the Author of life. Two great objectives he set clearly before these Twelve. If you will read in Matthew, chapter ten, you will find there the instructions given to the Twelve when Christ first sent them out.

SPECIFIC AND GENERAL COMMISSIONS. Now here you will have to study carefully, and it might not be so interesting to you, but you who would like to follow it, I would suggest this: that you will note the first commission Christ gave related to a temporary mission, and that will be covered from the fifth to the fifteenth verses. "Go not into the way of the Gentiles, and into any city of the Samaritans enter ye not:

"But go rather to the lost sheep of the house of Israel." (Matt. 10:5-6.)

See how he circumscribed them! In effect he said: That is your mission now, only to the lost sheep of the House of Israel, not to the Samaritans who are looked upon with distrust by the Jews because they turned away from the teachings of Judah. No Samaritan was to receive the gospel under the first commission.

The second part is found from the sixteenth to twenty-third verses. This relates more to the gospel ministry of that time. Here Jesus refers to some of the principles general in application—one of them is "lose yourself for the good of others."

Then the third part from verses twenty-four to forty-two, Christ gave the wider application, "Go ye and teach all nations." This was given after his death and after his resurrection. Note the difference: First, an immediate mission, second, a gospel of general application, and third, a universal assignment with a promise. Upon them he placed the responsibility of carrying the gospel to the world. These instructions the Twelve carried out specifically, and at first held strictly to their calling that they must go only to the Jews and not to the Gentiles.

APOSTLES NOT OF THE TWELVE. I want to bring to your attention another testimony concerning the reality of the resurrection. It is given by Paul. He, too, was an Apostle, though you cannot find that he was ever sustained as one of the council. By the way, there are Apostles who are not members of the council. I think there were in that day, at least they were considered to be Apostles. In one instance, for example, Paul and Barnabas are referred to as "these Apostles." As far as we know, Barnabas was never an Apostle. The point I am making is that a man may be an Apostle but not one of the Council of the Twelve. We have had that in our day. John W. Young was ordained an Apostle February 4, 1864, but he was never a member of the Council of the Twelve from that time to the day of his death. Daniel H. Wells was sustained as a counselor to the Twelve Apostles, and I have heard President Grant say no wiser counselor ever lived in this Church or in the United States than Daniel H. Wells. He was not, however, sustained as a member of the quorum, nor as an Apostle, but just counselor to the Twelve. Brigham Young, Jr., was ordained as an Apostle by his father on February 4, 1864, but he did not become a member of the Council of the Twelve until October 1868, when he was chosen to fill the vacancy caused by George A. Smith. Elder Sylvester Q. Cannon was ordained an Apostle but was not sustained as a member of the Council of the Twelve for some time.

Now, whether Paul was a member or whether he was not, we are not going to say, but he was an Apostle of the Lord Jesus Christ and a witness of his resurrection. This is what he wrote deliberately to a group of Saints known as Corinthians: "For I delivered unto you first of all that which I also received, how that Christ died for our sins according to the scriptures;

"And that he was buried, and that he rose again the third day according to the scriptures:

"And that he was seen of Cephas [Peter], then of the twelve:

"After that, he was seen of above five hundred brethren at once; of whom the greater part remain unto this present, but some are fallen asleep.

"After that, he was seen of James; then of all the apostles.

"And last of all he was seen of me also, as of one born out of due time.

"For I am the least of the apostles, that am not meet to be called an apostle, because I persecuted the church of God." (I Cor. 15:3-9.)

AN APOSTLE'S DUTY.   An Apostle's duty as commissioned is to be a special witness of the Lord Jesus Christ, to bear witness to his doctrine, of its effect upon mankind.—*RSM*, 25:806-813 (1938).

CHAPTER 18

THE SPIRIT OF THE WORK IN THE MODERN CHURCH

THE SPIRIT OF THE WORK

EFFORTS OF PRIESTHOOD WORKERS. It is a source of real encouragement to contemplate the loyalty and energetic efforts of the priesthood of the Church, including, of course, the General Authorities, stake and ward officers, presidencies of missions, missionaries, officers, and members of branches throughout the world. I believe I can say in truth that the standard of efficiency in missions and in organized stakes has never been so high.—*CR*, April 1952, pp. 11-12.

ORGANIZATIONAL EFFICIENCY. When you go home to your ward, look around next Sunday and try to estimate how many of the Latter-day Saints are absent from the sacrament meeting. It may be that there are twenty percent, or fifty percent absent. Suppose your estimate is fifty percent; then there are that many people in the ward who are neglecting one of the duties of a Latter-day Saint.

Upon whom rests the responsibility of bringing in these brethren and sisters? First, in my opinion, it rests upon the bishopric. As the bishop sits there, let him look around and notice whether all the presidents of the various organizations in the ward are present. If the presidents of the priesthood quorums be absent, it is the duty of the bishopric, I think, to visit those officers and bring them. They may go further; it is their duty to visit the various families and members who are absent and endeavor to bring them in. But it is not the bishopric's meeting; this Church rests upon all and not upon a few.

If one of the seven presidents of the seventies' quorum in that ward is present, and he finds that some of the seventies are absent, the responsibility of bringing them to meeting rests upon him. If presidents of the various quorums of deacons are present, they should note what quorum members have absented themselves from that meeting, and let them assume the responsibility of visiting those members. And so throughout the various organizations in that ward. Where is the responsibility, then? It is divided as it should be, as God intends it to be, among the people composing the Church of Jesus Christ of Latter-day Saints; the responsibility does not rest upon the officers alone; it rests upon the members also. God has blessed them with—what? Wealth? No, probably not. With intellectual superiority? Possibly not, but he has blessed them with moral strength and with a knowledge of the gospel, or else they were not true to themselves when they went down into the waters of baptism. He has blessed them with a knowledge of the truth; and the knowledge of the truth is not enough unless it is expressed, unless it is bringing others to that knowledge. That is the spirit and responsibility of the Latter-day Saint, and it rests upon all.—CR, October 1906, p. 114.

THE BLESSINGS OF FRIENDSHIP AND FELLOWSHIP IN THE CHURCH. Among life's sweetest blessings is fellowship with men and women whose ideals and aspirations are high and noble. Next to a sense of kinship with God come the helpfulness, encouragement, and inspiration of friends. Friendship is a sacred possession. As air, water, and sunshine to flowers, trees, and verdure, so smiles, sympathy, and love of friends to the daily life of man! "To live, laugh, love one's friends, and be loved by them is to bask in the sunshine of life."

One of the principal reasons which the Lord had for establishing his Church is to give all persons high and low, rich and poor, strong and feeble an opportunity to associate with their fellow men in an atmosphere of uplifting, religious fellowship. This may be found in priesthood quorums, auxiliaries, sacrament meetings. He who neglects these opportunities, who fails to take advantage of them, to that extent starves his own soul.—CR, April 1940, p. 116.

I am happy in my love for my immediate associates, President George Albert Smith and President J. Reuben Clark, Jr., and for these noble men of the Council of the Twelve, the Patriarch, the Assistants to the Council of the Twelve, the Council of the Seventy, the Presiding Bishopric. I find it a joy to work with you loyal men who preside in stakes and wards and branches. It is a privilege to have the opportunity to labor with you, to recognize your unselfish devotion to the Church.—*CR*, October 1947, p. 115.

CONFIDENCE IN LEADERSHIP. My confidence in the First Presidency as noble men and inspired leaders is secure. My association with the Council of the Twelve, with members of the Deseret Sunday School Union board, with members of other general boards, with stake and mission presidencies, and with the priesthood generally throughout the Church is a constant source of inspiration and delight.

The teachings and life of the Master have never before seemed to me more beautiful, more necessary, and more applicable to human happiness. Never have I believed more firmly in the perfection of humanity as the final result of man's placement here on earth. With my whole soul I accept Jesus Christ as the personification of human perfection—as God made manifest in the flesh, as the Savior and Redeemer of mankind.—*CR*, April 1932, p. 62.

It is just twenty-eight years since I was called into the Council of the Twelve. I have looked introspectively into my own soul and thought this:

"Never before in my life have I felt so grateful for my membership in the Church of Jesus Christ of Latter-day Saints. Never before have I felt more intensively how beneficial the Church has been to me and my loved ones. Never before has my testimony been stronger. Never have I felt so deeply in every fiber of my being that this Church was established by God the Father and his Son Jesus Christ, and that the men who have guided its destiny have been inspired by the revelations of God to them."—*CR*, April 1934, p. 20.

A TRIBUTE TO PRESIDENT HEBER J. GRANT. I have never known a man who exemplified so completely the mastery of mind over matter—whose will could so masterfully bring under subjection physical whims and desires. Perseverance and self-mastery are qualities that will always be connoted with the name of Heber J. Grant.—*IE*, 48:334 (1945).

WE ARE NOT ALONE. One of the elements in the incident to Paul near Damascus is the great fact that Jesus, our Lord, is interested in his Church, and in the members. As he was interested then, so he is interested today.

I like to feel that he is watching over us, that he is grieved when we do not comply with the ideals and the standards he has given us in the gospel. He was grieved with Saul, a chosen servant, who was going about blindly to destroy the Church. He is delighted when he finds the brethren whom he has appointed doing their duty and trying to live clean, upright lives, living in accordance with the standards of the gospel.

I like to feel that his servants whom he has chosen in this dispensation are also interested, and I hope that President George Albert Smith, who was with us not long ago, is pleased with what we have done during the last six months. I am sure he is pleased with the dedicating of the temple site in Los Angeles because I know that was an enterprise that was dear to his heart.

I like to feel that President Heber J. Grant is near us, ready to help, especially pleased to see that the Church is growing. And President Joseph F. Smith, President Lorenzo Snow, President Wilford Woodruff—those men, I have met— President Woodruff, in our home, closely associated with President Smith, and as you know, with President Grant and President George Albert Smith.

I like to think that President John Taylor is equally interested, also President Young, and especially the Prophet Joseph. The work over on the other side is real, and the curtain sometimes between us and them is very thin. I hope the Lord will help us to go forward as these, his former representatives, would like us to go forward, that we shall always realize that this is the Church of Jesus Christ, who is our head. —*CR*, October 1951, p. 160.

THE WORK OF THE RELIEF SOCIETY. The responsibility of the Relief Society is to aid the priesthood in establishing the kingdom of God, in relieving the suffering and giving succor to the poor, and in many ways in contributing to the peace and happiness of the world. In no one way can these high achievements be better realized than in excelling in the art of home building..—*RSM*, 23:9-10 (1936).

One of the most encouraging promises ever given to people who love service is that made by the Savior in these words, "Inasmuch as ye have done it unto one of the least of these my brethren, ye have done it unto me." (Matt. 25:40.) It is because the Relief Societies of the Church include generally our mothers, and because they are devoted to the service of God's children, that this organization merits first place among the auxiliaries of the Church of Jesus Christ. I grew to manhood before I realized the significance of the service that is rendered by our sisters in this Church. In fact I had to go on my first mission before I had a glimpse of the magnitude and beauty of the service that is rendered by our sisters of the Relief Society.—RSM, 23:689 (1936).

THE TABERNACLE CHOIR AND ITS SERVICE. We must not close the conference without expressing appreciation to the Tabernacle choir, its leader, assistant, to the organists, and to every member. That singing group has attained, through merit, outstanding recognition as one of the great choral organizations of the world. It merits the gratitude of all members of this Church. I do not know of another choir in the world that gives so much time and means, financially, in their service, as the members of this choral group. In your behalf, I thank them with all our hearts for their unselfish devotion and continual attention to this great duty.—CR, October 1951, p. 157.

Music is truly the universal language, and when it is excellently expressed, how deeply it moves our souls!—IE, 48:309 (1945).

UNISON—AN IDEAL. The Lord has said: "For my soul delighteth in the song of the heart; yea, the song of the righteous is a prayer unto me, and it shall be answered with a blessing upon their heads." (D. & C. 25:12.)

Your unison in song in the national broadcast this morning deeply impressed me—yours were truly songs of the heart. I pray that they will be visited with blessings upon your heads, and that this choir in rendering such a wonderful service to the Church, to the state, and to the nation may receive added blessings. I would that the same oneness, unity, and harmony manifested in that congregational singing might characterize every righteous endeavor of the Church.—*CR*, October 1936, pp. 102-103.

UNITY IN CHURCH ORGANIZATIONS. In branches and wards, there is no virtue more conducive to progress and spirituality than the presence of this principle. When jealousy, backbiting, evil-speaking supplant confidence, self-subjection, unity, and harmony, the progress of the organization is stifled. —*CR*, October 1939, p. 102.

DETAILS OF CHURCH ADMINISTRATION

HIGH STANDARDS ENJOINED FOR CHURCH SOCIALS. I have in mind only one or two items to give at the conclusion of this impressive conference. One that I mention by way of caution is that in your carnivals which you hold in order to raise money for building purposes, you avoid those games which are unbecoming or that will in any way cast reflection upon our young girls or men who hold the priesthood. We know the difficulties that you have to raise fifty percent of the cost of these edifices, and we commend you highly, and our sisters, for the effort you put forth. But there are some games which are carried on in carnivals outside the Church which are unbecoming the recreation furnished by the Church officers.

One I will name is a feature in which young Bee Hive girls come out in public in bathing suits, sit on a springboard before young men who throw balls to hit a certain spot which will loosen the springboard and cause the young girl to drop into a tank of water.

I have seen colored and white men do that for so much money, but let us not have our young girls do it, nor men who hold the leadership in the priesthood.—*CR*, October 1951, pp. 178-179.

PURPOSES OF CONFERENCES. Reference to the Doctrine and Covenants will disclose the fact that there are four principal purposes of holding conferences of the Church:

First, to transact current Church business.

Second, to hear reports and general Church statistics.

Third, to " . . . approve of those names which I [the Lord] have mentioned, or else disapprove of them. . . . " (D. & C. 125:144.)

Fourth, to worship the Lord in sincerity and reverence, and to give and to receive encouragement, exhortation, and instruction.—*CR*, October 1938, pp. 130-131.

THE NEED FOR CHECK-UP. It is a good thing in the Church, as in business, to check upon ourselves to see whether we are succeeding or failing.

Organizations as individuals are either progressing or retrogressing; they seldom if ever stand still. To progress is to obey the law of life. If the Church or any part of it were not improving, you may rest assured that it would be deteriorating. No ward, stake, or branch of the Church can long remain stationary. It is a source of satisfaction to all of us to realize that we belong to a Church that is moving forward.—*CR*, October 1938, p. 131.

THE DANGERS OF UNAUTHORIZED DIRECTION. It is a little dangerous for us to go out of our own sphere and try unauthoritatively to direct the efforts of a brother. You remember the case of Uzza who stretched forth his hand to steady the ark. (See I Chron. 13:7-10.) He seemed justified, when the oxen stumbled, in putting forth his hand to steady that symbol of the covenant. We today think his punishment was very severe. Be that as it may, the incident conveys a lesson of life. Let us look around us and see how quickly men who attempt unauthoritatively to steady the ark die spiritually. Their souls become embittered, their minds distorted, their judgments faulty, and their spirits depressed. Such is the pitiable condition of men who, neglecting their own responsibilities, spend their time in finding fault with others.—*CR*, April 1936, p. 60.

IN CASES OF OFFENSE. Has somebody offended you in the Church? You may hold resentment if you wish, say nothing to him, and let resentment canker your soul. If you do, you will be the one who will be injured, not the one who you think has injured you. You will feel better and be far happier to follow the divine injunction: If you have aught against your brother, go to him. (See Matt. 5:23-24.)—*DNCS*, January 2, 1952, p. 3.

THE SELECTION OF PERSONNEL. Bishops, do not hesitate to ask the men and women whom you choose to teach our children the following direct questions:

Can you support the authorities of the Church? Are you in harmony with the bishopric? with the stake presidency? the General Authorities?

Do you keep the Word of Wisdom when you are out in society, on the street, or wherever you are?

Do you pay your tithing?

Do you keep the Sabbath day holy?

Are you honest in your dealings with your fellow men?

Do not hesitate to put these and other pertinent questions directly to teachers when you call them. Appeal to them and try to make them realize that to be a teacher is to be a leader, a co-partner with the Creator in molding souls. —*IE*, 47:721 (November 1944).

ASPECTS OF GENERAL CHURCH ADMINISTRATION

THE CALL TO MEMBERSHIP IN THE FIRST PRESIDENCY, OCTOBER 1934. My beloved brethren and sisters, if it were possible I would have you interpret my feelings this morning by looking into the depths of my soul and thus save me the seeming impossibility of describing them to you. Needless to say I am overwhelmed. During the past few days I have had difficulty in keeping my thoughts and feelings under control. The light heart, the buoyancy of spirit that should accompany the high appointment that has come to me has been somewhat counterbalanced by a heaviness incident to the realization of the great responsibility that comes with the call to the First Presidency.

I love President Heber J. Grant. He has been to me a true friend; more than that, since my father died, I have felt free to go to President Grant for help and counsel as I would go to my own father. His nature is as open, as pure and clear as a faultless crystal—open, loyal, true. I esteem it indeed the highest compliment and privilege to have this expression of his confidence. With all my soul I pray for strength that I may not disappoint him, and that I may be true to the trust that he and my heavenly Father have thus reposed in me.

I have known President Clark since my school days at the University of Utah. I admired him then. I considered him one of the choicest young men I had ever seen or had ever known. His ability was evident even to his schoolmates. He and the sweet girl who later became my sweetheart and wife, were graduated with their A. B. degrees on the same day. We have followed him in his work in Washington; we were thrilled when we learned of the responsibility that he carried there, and the trust which the members of the Senate of the United States placed upon him even before his name was generally known. I love him as a friend, and to be associated with him now in this high quorum, the highest in the Church, makes me feel very happy and thankful, but also very humble.

And so if you could look into my soul, you would see sincere gratitude and deep appreciation. You would find there also a regret that I am leaving the immediate association with the members of the Council of the Twelve. For twenty-eight and one-half years it has been my privilege to work side by side with these good and able men. President Clawson I love with all my soul. His worth and ability are not generally known. He is retiring, he is quiet in his labors, a perfect gentleman, genial, kind, and considerate. As the President of the Council he is prompt in attending to questions and problems referred to the group, as loyal and true in his testimony as the polar star, unwavering, undeviating in the discharging of duty and trust. It is not easy to disentwine my soul directly from his, my president. That entwinement is just as binding with the hearts of these brethren with whom I have worked daily, at times in committees, considering the welfare of the Church at large, and the welfare of individuals.

I want to bear witness today that you may travel the world over, you may read your histories of men devoted to great undertakings and noble problems, but you cannot find a group of men whose lives are more consecrated, whose desires are more noble in the interests, the happiness and peace of mankind, than are the lives and desires of these, my associates in the Council of the Twelve Apostles of this Church. You must live with them to know them. You must be in daily contact with the burdens they are carrying, with their concerns and anxieties for the youth, their willingness to go to the ends of the world at a moment's call if need be to establish better conditions, to make the world happier, more peaceful, more just, and bring about more amicable conditions and relationships in human society. And so it is not an easy task, I say, it is not without regret that I withdraw my membership in that Council.

I appreciate the trust you, my brethren and sisters, have manifested in me. It is a wonderful thing to be trusted. I agree with him who says that to be trusted is a greater compliment than to be loved. Love is the sweetest thing in the world, but to be trusted throws upon him who receives that trust an obligation that he must not fail to discharge. And so I pledge you here, my fellow workers in the First Presidency, you my brethren of the priesthood, in whose company I have spent so many happy hours in priesthood and auxiliary work, I pledge you, my brethren and sisters, to give my best in the service of God.

I uphold before you this morning the President of this Church as God's representative, divinely appointed, and say to all Israel, stand by your chief. Let that spirit of unity and oneness for which our Lord and Savior prayed on the night of his betrayal, be characteristic of this his Church: Father, keep them one, as thou and I are one.—*CR*, October 1934, pp. 89-91.

THE CALL TO SERVE AS PRESIDENT OF THE CHURCH. My beloved fellow workers, brethren and sisters: I wish it were within my power of expression to let you know just what my true feelings are on this momentous occasion. I would wish that you might look into my heart and see there for yourselves just what those feelings are.

It is just one week ago today that the realization came to me that this responsibility of leadership would probably fall upon my shoulders. I received word that President George Albert Smith had taken a turn for the worse and that the doctor thought the end was not far off. I hastened to his bedside, and with his weeping daughters, son, and other kinfolk, I entered his sickroom. For the first time, he failed to recognize me.

Then I had to accept the realization that the Lord had chosen not to answer our pleadings as we would have had them answered and that he was going to take him home to himself. He rallied again later in the day. Several days preceding that visit, as President Clark and I were considering problems of import pertaining to the Church, he, ever solicitous of the welfare of the Church and of my feelings, would say, "The responsibility will be yours to make this decision," but each time I would refuse to face what to him seemed a reality.

When that reality came, as I tell you, I was deeply moved. And I am today, and pray that I may, even though inadequately, be able to tell you how weighty this responsibility seems.—CR, April 1951, p. 157.

The Lord has said that the three presiding high priests chosen by the body, appointed and ordained to this office of Presidency, are to be "upheld by the confidence, faith, and prayer, of the Church." No one can preside over this Church without first being in tune with the head of the Church, our Lord and Savior, Jesus Christ. He is our head. This is his Church. Without his divine guidance and constant inspiration, we cannot succeed. With his guidance, with his inspiration, we cannot fail.

Next to that as a sustaining potent power come the confidence, faith, prayers, and united support of the Church.

I pledge to you that I shall do my best so to live as to merit the companionship of the holy Spirit, and pray here in your presence that my counselors and I may indeed be "partakers of the divine spirit."

Next to that, unitedly we plead with you for a continuation of your love and confidence as you have expressed it today. From you members of the Twelve, we ask for that love and sympathy expressed in our sacred Council. From the Assistants to the Twelve, the Patriarch, the First Council of the Seventy, the Presiding Bishopric, we ask that the spirit of unity expressed so fervently by our Lord and Savior when he was saying good-bye to the Twelve, may be manifest by us all.

You remember he said, as he left them: "And now I am no more in the world, but these are in the world, and I come to thee. Holy Father, keep through thine own name those whom thou hast given me, that they may be one, as we are. . . .

"Neither pray I for these alone, but for them also which shall believe on me through their word;

"That they all may be one; as thou, Father, art in me, and I in thee, that they also may be one in us: that the world may believe that thou has sent me." (John 17:11, 20-21.)

Brethren and sisters, brethren of the General Authorities, God keep us as one, overlooking weaknesses we may see, keeping an eye single to the glory of God and the advancement of his work.

And now to the members of the Church: We all need your help, your faith and prayers, not your adverse criticisms, but your help. You can do that in prayer if you cannot reach us in person. The potency of those prayers throughout the Church came to me yesterday when I received a letter from a neighbor in my old home town. He was milking his cows when the word came over his radio which he has in his barn that President Smith had passed. He sensed what that would mean to his former fellow townsman, and he left his barn and went to the house and told his wife. Immediately they called their little children, and there in that humble home, suspending their activities, they knelt down as a family and offered prayer. The significance of that scene I leave for you to understand. Multiply that by a hundred thousand, two hundred thousand, half a million homes, and see the power in the unity and prayers, and the sustaining influence in the body of the Church.

Today you have by your vote placed upon us the greatest responsibility, as well as the greatest honor, that lies within your power to bestow as members of the Church of Jesus Christ of Latter-day Saints. Your doing so increases the duty of the First Presidency to render service to the people. —CR, April 1951, p. 157.

THE METHOD OF CHURCH COUNCILS

To think independently! Men sit in council, but the value of that council is for each one to express what he feels, independently of whether it is going to please somebody else or not. That is the value of counsel and associated with that is the ability to yield that independent thought to the thought of the group—three members of a bishopric sitting there counseling, each one giving his best thought, his best judgment, and even the inspiration that comes to him. But when two decide, then the other says, "Then that becomes my view with yours."

I saw it in a council meeting one day when a question of grave importance came up. I was in harmony with my President in the Council, President Francis M. Lyman, and with other members of that Council, and we were united as we met the First Presidency that morning.

President Joseph F. Smith did not ask our view that day. Usually he asked the junior member to express his thoughts and give his best judgment. To our surprise the President did not ask that. He arose and said, "This is what the Lord wants."

While it was not wholly in harmony with what he had decided, President Francis M. Lyman, the President of the Twelve, was the first on his feet to say, "Brethren, I move that that becomes the opinion and judgment of this Council."

"Second the motion," said another, and it was unanimous. Six months did not pass before the wisdom of that leader was demonstrated.

Think independently, but be united with the majority of your associates in council.—*DNCS*, June 11, 1952, p. 3.

Book IV

THE CHURCH AND MODERN SOCIETY

"We should put forth every effort to supplant the aristocracy of wealth with the aristocracy of character and to awaken in the minds of the youth a realization that to be honest, to be dependable, to be a loyal citizen of the country, to be true to the standards of the gospel are the noblest ideals of life."

—David O. McKay
Conference Report
October 1930, p. 10.

CHAPTER 19

OUR CHANGING TIMES

DOMINANT INFLUENCES IN MODERN SOCIETY

THE ARISTOCRACY OF PHYSICAL FORCE AND BIRTH. To understand more clearly conditions as they exist, I think it is well to consider the dominant influences of society today. If we go back through history, we find that at one time the world was governed by the spirit of might; physical force was the aristocracy of the age. And naturally men chose to be strong in physical achievements. Later that period gave way to another aristocracy or ruling power. The sons of these physical men became the rulers, and so there developed an aristocracy of birth.

THE ARISTOCRACY OF WEALTH. You and I are witnessing and have witnessed the decay of this aristocracy. Thrones are crumbling; their power is diminished. Titles can be purchased by money. Supplanting the aristocracy of birth has come the aristocracy of wealth. Money, it is said, can buy anything.

We in this financial age need to realize this when we examine and study the conditions that are influencing the youth of today. Many of them are seeking to be wealthy. They are thinking that success lies only in the obtaining of the dollar, and with that unwise ideal they will sacrifice that which is higher and better than any material possession.

THE ARISTOCRACY OF CHARACTER. Do not misunderstand me, I would not underrate the value of wealth. I am cognizant of the fact that the second great commandment was to replenish and subdue the earth. I realize that one great purpose of life is to subdue matter, and I rejoice when I see the great reservoirs filled with water from which flows that element which will change the sagebrush flat into a waving wheat field, and that is wealth. I do not take second place to anyone in the realization of the good which this can do. I am merely emphasizing the thought that there is a nobler ideal in life than the accumulating of wealth.

When God gave us the command to subdue matter, he meant us to use the power derived therefrom, the power of material things, to realize something which is higher; and that is character, a life that will merit the inspiration of God. What the sunshine is to the field and to the flowers, the Holy Spirit is to the life of man, and the Holy Spirit does not abide with base characters. He will not dwell in unclean tabernacles.

My thought is that we should put forth every effort to supplant the aristocracy of wealth with the aristocracy of character and awaken in the minds of the youth a realization that to be honest, to be dependable, to be a loyal citizen of the country, to be true to the standards of the gospel are the noblest ideals of life. The important problem is how to instil these lofty principles into the minds of young people, and thereby make them worthy citizens.—CR, October 1930, pp. 9-10.

A REVOLUTIONARY PERIOD. We are living in what may well prove to be the most epoch-making period of all time. There is ample evidence on every hand that we are witnessing one of those tidal waves of human thought and emotion which periodically sweep over the world and change the direction of human endeavor. It is a time that demands clear thinking and sound judgment. Whether we are willing to admit it or not, this is a revolutionary period.

There is social and political upheaval. "Thoroughly tested, well-tried principles are being thrown into discard. Long accepted social theories," writes Charles Foster Kent, "have suddenly been rejected, and new ones are being adopted. Many of the moral standards of our fathers are being set aside in theory as well as practice. . . . Religious dogmas long regarded as the cornerstones of religion and the church are being disproved or supplanted by the discoveries of modern science."

It is not strange, therefore, that the majority of the men and women in this war-shattered and war-threatening world are unhappy, because they feel the foundations beneath them are tottering. As reported in the public press a year or so ago, an experienced United States congressman, reputably one of the best lawyers in Congress, said: "There isn't a person in this room now who can be certain that he can leave to his children the heritage of the privilege of being free."

CHARTING A TRUE COURSE. Today, if ever, is a time for young people who are not satisfied with merely building "birds' nests" or with temporary desires and pleasures of the moment, to get in mind eternal verities, fundamental truths, and make them life's guiding stars.

If in this unsettled sea of human perplexities, yearnings, disappointments, and despair, we would pause and eliminate from our minds our immediate demands and schemes for livelihood, if we would set aside our desires for personal pleasure resulting from indulgence in gratification of appetites and passions, if we would for an hour or two withdraw ourselves completely from the physical, the sensual, the political, and even the social influence of this human world, and let our souls commune with self and with the infinite—we should find that only in the recognition and adoption of eternal verities can the yearning of a sincere mind be satisfied and peace and happiness be realized.

REALITY IN PERSPECTIVE. The captain of the *Kon-Tiki*, when midway in the Pacific Ocean, experienced in reality what I am now suggesting you try to experience in imagination. Floating on a raft with his five companions, a thousand fathoms of water beneath them, a myriad of glittering, tropical stars in the firmament above, he writes: "Whether it was 1947 B.C. or A.D. suddenly became of no significance. We *lived*—and *that* we felt with alert intensity. We realized that life had been full for man before the technical age also—in fact, fuller and richer in many ways than the life of modern man. Time and evolution somehow ceased to exist: *All that was real and that mattered were the same today as they had always been and would always be.*"

The captain seemed to feel what our poet said about truth:

" . . . 'Tis the last and the first,
For the limits of time it steps o'er.
Though the heavens depart, and the earth's fountains burst,
Truth, the sum of existence, will weather the worst,
Eternal, unchanged evermore."

John Jacques, "Oh, Say What Is Truth."

If as I say, we could divest ourselves of all immediate wants and perplexities and talk with self in a serious sort of way, we should find ourselves giving value to like realities. Out of such soul communion would come a recognition that no matter what physical, material, political, industrial, and other changes may occur, no matter how theories of governments may change; how fashions, customs, and ideals may be accepted and abandoned, there remain unchanging verities eternally operative in the universe, ever contributing to the spiritual progress, to the peace, to the happiness of the individual and of the race.

FUNDAMENTAL CONSIDERATIONS. With this recognition would come certain fundamental questions, the answer to which can be found only by reference to eternal truth. A few of these vital problems might be as follows:

First—The ever-present reality and mystery of life and immortality of the human soul.

Second—The existence of God and our relation to him. Is it possible for man's spirit to be in harmony with that divine Being?

Third—These eternal verities accepted, the question arises what is the noblest aim in life—pleasure, wealth, or character?

Fourth—Every human heart yearns for love even more than the body yearns for food. Every normal person seeks a soul mate and recognizes the family as the true source of love's expression.

Such questions enter either in a fleeting or contemplative degree the mind of every thinking or contemplating person. —*DNCS,* June 6, 1951, p. 2.

THE KINGDOM OF GOD AND THE REVOLUTIONS OF THE TWENTIETH CENTURY

For nearly twenty centuries millions of Christians have prayed for the coming of the kingdom of God, and for more than twenty centuries, millions of people have persistently rejected the conditions indispensable to the realization of this era of peace and brotherly kindness.

Even though the essentials for a better world have not been generally accepted, yet mankind has ever striven for a better way of living. In every progressive age of the world's history, thinking people have been dissatisfied with their current social and economic conditions and have sought for remedial changes. Many of their hoped-for Utopias, however, though they have inspired men to action, have ended only as dreams and fantasies.

POLITICAL UPHEAVALS INSUFFICIENT. In response to this urge for change, the twentieth century is no exception. Indeed, during the last fifty years people have witnessed greater political unrest, more stupendous upheavals than have probably occurred in the same length of time in the history of the world. European monarchies have been overthrown. Democracy, as exemplified in Great Britain and her dominions and in the United States, has successfully withstood the battling horrors of a world war, and now, after only a quarter of a century, is again either actually participating in or standing on the brink of a second devastating conflict.

If, in the spirit of charity, we say that misguided men have brought all this about because of their desire for a better government, the fact still remains that civilization is encompassed by social upheavals that threaten to divert, if not entirely thwart, the progress and happiness of the present generation. —CR, October 1940, p. 101.

THE REVOLUTIONARY SWEEP OF WORLD WAR I. When I think or read of the horrors of the most wicked of wars now going on in Europe, when I picture young men who have been forced to carry the gun and slay their fellow men, running across a field, burrowing into the earth as animals, to protect themselves from their fellow men, when I read of these men lying heaped in trenches, and in fancy hear their groans as they turn their ghastly faces to heaven, when I think of the devastated towns and see fleeing from those towns husbandless women, dragging fatherless children, when I think of the thousands of human beings who are going to die of starvation and disease—because we are told that for every soldier that dies in battle five others at least will die of exposure, disease, and starvation—I say when I think of all these horrors that come in the wake of war, I try to find out the cause of it all.

Each nation is calling its people to "Come to the defense of the nation, because the war is forced upon us." It seems to have such right on its side that it is fighting for its life, for its country, its God. But the real causes are not evident; however, you will discover that one cause of the disastrous war lies deeply rooted in the fact that those highly so-called Christian nations have never applied the gospel of Jesus Christ.

FAILURE TO APPLY CHRISTIAN PRINCIPLES. The leaders and rulers who brought this war upon the people failed to apply the little, simple principles that Christ taught centuries ago. Why, if they had applied only one of his teachings, the whole war might have been averted; for example, if you bring your gift to the altar, and there rememberest that thou hast aught against thy brother; leave there thy gift upon the altar and go first to thy brother; first reconcile thyself to him, then come and offer thy sacrifice. (See Matt. 5:23-24.) If the first two nations that clashed, because of having misunderstood each other, had applied that little simple doctrine and lived it, maybe the whole thing would have been averted for a time.

But that is only one. The roots of the causes of this war lie deeply bedded in vanity, one monarch feeling above another, so far above him, in fact, that he would not arbitrate, would not go to his brother and have an understanding of the misunderstandings that had risen. Yes, the causes of war are vanity, selfishness, unjust commercialism, unrighteousness, and other things contrary to the spirit of the gospel of Jesus Christ. O if the people of the world could only apply the gospel in their nationalism! But they have considered it only as a thing apart from daily life—as something to be treated as a mere social function. They haven't felt that it is a vital force, the vital force in humanity

It may be that this dreadful carnage which is going on— the toppling of thrones, the destruction of monarchies, may be but a step to prepare the way for the preaching of the gospel of Jesus Christ, and the giving to the millions of honest souls in those countries the opportunity of accepting it. I, for one, believe it with all my soul. Upon whom, then, rests the responsibility of carrying this message to them after the way is prepared? Upon whom but those unto whom has been given the power and authority to represent God in this world?

That is you, my brother; that is you, my sister. How glorious
the gospel seems to us; but oh, how mighty the responsibility
upon the elders of the Church! The first step toward carrying
this responsibility is to apply our religion in our lives.—CR,
October 1914, pp. 88-89.

THE MORAL CRISIS OF OUR AGE. The world faces a crisis
—a terrible crisis. Opportunity is given for men to choose
wisely and live, or disregard the Master's teachings and die.
Down through the ages comes resounding the cry of Joshua—

" . . . choose you this day whom ye will serve; . . . but as
for me and my house, we will serve the Lord." (Joshua 24:15.)

And the thrilling words of Peter when commanded not to
speak at all, nor to teach in the name of Jesus:

"Whether it be right in the sight of God to hearken
unto you more than unto God, judge ye.
"For we cannot but speak the things which we have seen
and heard." (Acts 4:19-20.)

The choice today is between dictatorship with the atheistic teachings of communism, and the doctrine of the restored
gospel of Jesus Christ, obedience to which alone can make
us free.—CR, April 1948, p. 70.

THE NEW BARBARISM. "During the first half of the twentieth century we have traveled far into the soul-destroying land
of socialism and made strange alliances through which we
have become involved in almost continuous hot and cold wars
over the whole of the earth. In this retreat from freedom the
voices of protesting citizens have been drowned by raucous
shouts of intolerance and abuse from those who led the retreat
and their millions of gullible youth, who are marching merrily
to their doom, carrying banners on which are emblazoned
such intriguing and misapplied labels as social justice, equality,
reform, patriotism, social welfare.

"Intoxicated with pride in our achievement, enmeshed in
the interesting problems still unsolved, we have left unguarded
the gate through which are pouring the destructive hordes and
forces of a new invasion of barbarism."* Hearing the dangers
just enumerated, the nation is threatened with the disinte-

---

*W. C. Mullendore, president, Southern California Edison Co.

grating influence of moral turpitude; honesty seems to be out-moded; the stability of the family life is threatened; loyalty and patriotism have lost their order; crime and lawlessness, particularly among young people, are increasing alarmingly. —DNCS, October 18, 1952, pp. 2, 4.

"Men and Brethren, What Shall We Do?" Through-out the world generally today there is a spirit of unrest, a grasping for untried ideologies (and our community is no exception), and, what is worst of all, a tendency toward moral abandonment. It is all too apparent that "our spiritual culture lags far behind our material culture in its develop-ment."

Now is a time when peoples in all the world should pause and in all earnestness repeat the Pentecostal question pro-pounded to Peter and other Apostles:

"Men and brethren, what shall we do?" (Acts 2:37.)

The United Nations on Trial. Representatives of fifty nations are now assembled trying to find an answer. Com-munist nations, however, are clashing with Christian groups, and it looks as though the proverbial dove of peace, if not killed, might again be seriously crippled.

At the final plenary session of the United Nations con-ference when the charter was about to be signed, five great leaders invoked the Lord's aid to the end that the cause of peace would not fail.

Said Mr. Edward Stettinius [U. S. Secretary of State in 1945]:

"To the governments and peoples of the fifty nations here represented, this charter is now committed, and may Almighty God from this day on and in the months and years to come sustain us in the unalterable purpose that its promise may be fulfilled."

The Earl of Halifax, chairman of the delegation of the United Kingdom, said:

"Let us also, mindful alike of the world's need and of our own weakness, pray that, under God's guidance, what we have done here in these last weeks will be found worthy of the faith which gave it birth, and of the human suffering which has been its price."

His Royal Highness, Amir Faisal Ibin Abdiel Aziz, chairman of the delegation of Saudi Arabia, stated:

"As long as we are united together in a spirit of co-operation, the hands of Almighty God will lead us. We shall always have his aid so long as we help one another."

And Field Marshal Jan Christiaan Smuts of South Africa, said:

"May heaven's blessings rest on it."

And the President of our own United States prayed that under God's guidance the cause would succeed.

Unless such appeals were mere empty phrases, these leaders indicate the only safe and sure way in which wars may be averted and peace among nations established. Not through communistic theories, not by the manifestations of mistrust, suspicion, and hatred will the turbulency of national ills be quieted. Unless the spirit of Christianity permeate the deliberations of the United Nations, dire tragedies await humanity. —CR, October 1947, pp. 117-118.

AMERICA—A CHOICE LAND. The economic progress of our country during the past century has been phenomenal. So also has been her influence politically among the nations. Today America is reputedly the only nation in the world "capable of sustaining western civilization."

Opposed to her is Russia, which has renounced faith in God and in his overruling power in the universe.

The threatened impending clash between these two nations is more than a test of political supremacy, more than a fight between capitalism and communism—it is the ever-contending conflict between *faith* in God and in the gospel of Jesus Christ, and *disbelief* in the philosophy of Christian ideals. Faith in man is the power that leads to brotherhood; faith in God, the ladder by which men climb toward perfection. *Faith* is strength; doubt, weakness and disintegration.

There can be no question about the outcome of the anticipated ominous clash, which we earnestly hope and pray will never come, between these two great nations of conflicting ideals, if the inhabitants of America will but keep their faith in the Lord of heaven and earth, and in the principles of peace taught by his Son on the shores of Galilee two thousand years ago. Upon this is the promise of possession of this land and prosperity therein based:

"Behold," says the prophet, "this is a choice land, and whatsoever nation shall possess it shall be free from bondage, and from captivity, and from all other nations under heaven, if they will *but serve the God of the land, who is Jesus Christ,* . . . " (Ether 2:12. Italics author's.)—*IE*, 50:562-563 (1947)

CHAPTER 20

WAR AMONG NATIONS

THE CURSE AND PROBLEM OF ORGANIZED WARFARE

" . . . and they shall beat their swords into plowshares, and their spears into pruninghooks: nation shall not lift up a sword against nation, neither shall they learn war any more.

"But they shall sit every man under his vine and under his fig tree; and none shall make them afraid: for the mouth of the Lord of hosts hath spoken it." (Micah 4:3-4.)

So wrote the Prophet Micah, probably quoting Isaiah, seven hundred fifty years before Christ. Nearly twenty-seven hundred years have passed since the eye of prophecy visioned a time when "war shall be no more." During the intervening centuries, many nations have lifted up sword against nations; and war has continued to be one of mankind's greatest evils. Truly it seems that human beings are more prone to war than to peace.

WORLD WAR II IN RETROSPECT. The latest war (I wish we could say confidently the last) was one of the most devastating in the history of the world. What destruction, sorrow, and suffering it has caused! According to reliable estimates, its direct cost is over one trillion thirty billion dollars, not counting the destruction and damage of property. There have been over a million casualties in the United States, another million and a half in Britain, making a combined loss in these two countries alone of killed, wounded, missing, and prisoners, of two and a half million. The Russian and Chinese losses exceed those numbers by millions. Add the millions of dead, wounded, and missing by the Germans, the Japanese, and those of the crushed countries of Europe, and the cost in wealth and in human life becomes staggering. We are close enough to the tragedy to realize that war is "the greatest curse that can be entailed upon mankind." "Under its standards gather violence, malignity, rage, fraud, perfidy, rapacity, and lust."

We wonder how many more years will pass before " . . . they shall sit every man under his vine and under his fig tree; and none shall make them afraid: . . . " (Micah 4:4) when, in Alfred, Lord Tennyson's words:

"The war drums throbbed no longer, and the
        battle flags were furled
In the Parliament of man, the Federation of the
    world."

"Locksley Hall."
—*IE*, 48:638 (1945).

BASIC CAUSES OF ARMED CONFLICT

LIKE CAUSES PRODUCE LIKE EFFECTS. Approximately only a quarter of a century ago, the world listened to the clanging of arms of nations fighting in a world-wide war that was supposed to end war forever. Up to that time it was the bloodiest war in history.

Again, misguided leaders of nations, worshiping the god of materialism, have brought on World War II, and unless the nations avoid the evil things which caused this war, there will be a World War III even more destructive, more terrible than the present murderous conflict. Like causes produce like effects.

THE ANALYSIS—WITH A VIEW TO AVOIDING FUTURE CONFLICT. Now, while the trying exigencies of war are wringing our hearts, it would seem the part of wisdom for men to examine some of the basic causes that produce armed conflict with the view of avoiding them in the future.

I. *Development of Brutal Instincts.*

The seeds of war lie in man's nature. These seeds germinate at the first natural urge for self-preservation, self-perpetuation, or a desire for conquest.

The fruit of such seeds is hatred and brutality.

Knowing this, the world's chief gangster trained his youth to be brutal. In anticipation, indeed, in glorification of armed conflict, this man declared that he would train youth to be brutal. "In my great educative work," said he, "I am beginning with the young. . . . Weakness has to be knocked out of them. . . . A violently active, dominating, intrepid, brutal youth—that is what I am after. There must be no weakness or tenderness in it. I want to see once more in its eyes the gleam of pride and independence of the beast of prey."

It is significant that one hundred years before this egotistic leader began to poison the minds of youth, a German philosopher—Heinrich Heine—warned the German people that:

"Evils will follow the rise of 'Germanic pantheism,' because then there will awaken in him that fighting folly that we find among the ancient Germans, that fights neither to kill nor to conquer, but simply to fight. Christianity has—and that is its fairest merit—somewhat mitigated that brutal German lust for battle. But it could not destroy it; and once the taming talisman, the cross, is broken, the savagery of the old battlers will flare up again, the insane rage of which Nordic bards have so much to say and sing. That talisman is brittle. The day will come when it will pitiably collapse. Then the old stone gods will rise from forgotten rubble and rub the dust of a thousand years from their eyes; and Thor will leap up and with his giant hammer start smashing Gothic cathedrals ... and when you hear a crash as nothing ever crashed in world history, you'll know that the German thunder has hit the mark. At that sound the eagles will fall dead from the sky, and the lions in the farthest desert of Africa will put in their tails and slink away into their royal caves. A play will be performed that will make the French Revolution seem like a harmless idyll in comparison. . . .

"Beware! I wish you well; that is why I tell you the bitter truth. You have more to fear from a liberated Germany than from the whole Holy Alliance with all its Croats and Cossacks." (Heinrich Heine, *Works of Prose*, ed. by Herman Kesen, pp. 51-53.)

II. *The Collapse of Humanitarian Principles.*

The substitution of ancient gods for Christianity was followed by the collapse of humanitarian principles, and, as Will Erwin said in "An Appeal to Common Sense," men were back to the ethics of the barbarian hordes. Barbarians of the twentieth century before Christ killed in any manner which their imagination suggested. And so now do civilized men of the twentieth century after Christ. The barbarians of the twentieth century before Christ killed the women and children of the enemy as tribal self-interest seemed to dictate, and so now do so-called civilized men of the twentieth century after Christ. The barbarians of the twentieth century before Christ made slaves of the conquered people, or forced them to pay tribute; so virtually do civilized men of the twentieth century after Christ.

"A brutal youth," having in their eyes "the gleam of the beast of prey" harp back to the law of the jungle, as far from the teaching of Christ as hades from heaven! It is the doctrine of avarice, selfishness, and hate.

There are some things which man should hate—he should hate injustice; hate hypocrisy; hate wickedness in all its forms; but never hate mankind.

We hope and pray that this World War II will soon come to an end, and that war-weary, heavyhearted peoples may again have peace.

Peace will come and be maintained only through the triumph of the principles of peace, and by the consequent subjection of the enemies of peace, which are hatred, envy, ill-gotten gain, the exercise of unrighteous dominion of men. Yielding to these evils brings misery to the individual, unhappiness to the home, war among nations, with resultant misery and death.

Two thousand years ago Jesus wept over Jerusalem, the inhabitants of which were blind to the things which pertained to their peace. Today contention, strife, and hatred are manifest between capital and labor unions, and bitterness among advocates of nazism, fascism, communism, and capitalism. No matter how excellent any of these may seem in the minds of their advocates, none will ameliorate the ills of mankind unless its operation in government be impregnated with the basic principles promulgated by the Savior of men. On the contrary, even a defective economic system will produce a good result if the men who direct it will be guided by the Spirit of Christ.

Actuated by that Spirit, leaders will think more of *men* than of the success of a system. Kindness, mercy, and justice will be substituted for hatred, suspicion, and greed. There is no road to universal peace which does not lead into the heart of humanity.

III. *To Avoid Another War People Must Change their Way of Thinking.*

Men say that so long as human nature is as near to the animal nature as it is, that selfishness, suspicion, greed, chicanery will continue to pervade and govern human society. If that be true, then man must rise above the animal instincts, and strive for the higher and more abundant life. If this requires a change of human nature, then human nature must be changed.

IV. *Eliminate Arrogance of Superiority.*

With the Spirit of Christ in their hearts *no nation will arrogate to itself superiority over others but give to each nation, however small, however seemingly backward, the right of self-determination.*

V. *Seek Material Advancement as a Means to Spiritual Attainment.*

With the spirit of the gospel in men's hearts, nations will accept the truth that integrity is more to be desired than intellectual acumen or the accumulation of wealth. Men will then look upon material advancement not as an end in itself, but as a means to spiritual attainment. They will recognize the significance of "But seek ye first the kingdom of God, and his righteousness; and all these things shall be added unto you." (Matt. 6:33.) Statesmen, churchmen, schoolteachers, civic officers, newspapermen—all who in any way mold public opinion—must grapple intelligently with spiritual apathy and moral decay.

Some day men must realize that only true religion can satisfy the yearning soul.

VI. *Two Great Forces Point the Way to Peace.*

I see two great forces leading the way from the abyss of another world war into the realm of peace and progress— *America and the gospel of Jesus Christ.*

AMERICA'S OPPORTUNITY. America has the great opportunity to lead the world from political intrigue and cheap demogoguery, from national selfishness, from unrighteous usurpation of power, and from unholy aggrandizement. She must prove to the people of Europe and of all the world that she has no selfish ends to serve, no desire for conquest, no arrogance of national or race superiority. When these ideals are established, America can blaze the trail and lead the world to peace.

> "This is a land where hate should die—
> This is a land where strife should cease,
> Where foul, suspicious fear should fly
> Before our flag of light and peace."

But I repeat, permanent peace will be found only in the application of the principles of the gospel of peace. Christ came to earth to bring peace and good will. When he said: "I came not to send peace, but a sword," (Matt. 10:34) he perceived how the acceptance of eternal principles might render asunder the dearest ties, and how a man's foes may become those of his own household. Asserting the principles of the gospel over everything else, he added: "He that loveth father or mother more than me is not worthy of me: and he that loveth son or daughter more than me is not worthy of me." (*Ibid.*, 10:37.) Thus he but emphasized the great truth that acceptance of the principles of the gospel is the supreme purpose of life.

Again the Lord has revealed himself to man, and in that revelation may be found the answer to the perplexities and yearnings of the human soul.

Again in this age Christ has said:

"I am the light of the world: he that followeth me shall not walk in darkness, but shall have the light of life." (John 8:12.)

I feel that we can join with the poet in saying:

> "O Christ, who died to give men life,
> Bring that victorious hour,
> When man shall use for peace, not strife,
> His valor, skill, and power."

God grant that the nations of the earth will soon open their eyes and behold the light of the world and thereby accept in this day the things which belong unto their peace.—*IE*, 47:657-658, 708 (1944).

GOD NOT THE CAUSE OF WAR. I am not one of those who sees in this world catastrophe the hand of God as its cause. I do not believe that God has caused the misery, the famine, the pestilence, and the death that are now sweeping the war-torn countries of Europe. I do believe that the conditions of the world today are a direct result—an inevitable result—of disobedience to God's laws.—CR, April 1917, p. 46.

Commenting upon the unjustifiable attempts of strong nations to subdue weaker nations, one of our leading popular contributors to syndicated newspapers said:

"Out of all history you will find but one world conquerer who came with clean hands, and those hands the soldiers pierced with iron spikes as they nailed the Nazarene to the cross."

It was this same clean world conqueror who said:

"Therefore, whosoever heareth these sayings of mine, and doeth them, I will liken him unto a wise man, . . .

"And every one that heareth these sayings of mine, and doeth them not, shall be likened unto a foolish man, . . . (Matt. 7:24, 26.)—CR, October 1935, p. 97.

MAN BRINGS CONFLICT UPON HIMSELF. Man, through his littleness, through his rejection of the gospel, his selfishness and weakness, brings contention and strife upon himself.

But a wise Father will work out of men's mistakes and blunders greater blessings than they might have obtained with their own wisest foresight. Gloomy clouds often hang heavily about us, but the rains that descend from them often prove a blessing. So it may be with the ominous clouds lowering today over civilization.

I do not believe in the advocacy of discouragement and gloom; better, the gospel of hope. Remember, the Church of Jesus Christ is established nevermore to be thrown down or given to another people. The gospel has not yet been preached to every nation, kindred, tongue, and people, and I am sure that the Lord will open up the way for the consummation of his purposes.—CR, October 1941, p. 53.

Why this world-wide holocaust? Why this mad orgy of death? Because man is acting contrary to eternal principles of right!—CR, October 1942, p. 67.

VICIOUS WAR PROPAGANDA—A COMMENT ON KOREA (1951). At the moment there is being enacted a great world drama, the final act of which we can only dimly surmise. In Korea one of the bloodiest wars of modern times is raging. But here is a singular thing. Engaged in it are soldiers from South Korea, the United States, Great Britain, France, Turkey, Greece, the Netherlands, Australia, Canada, New Zealand, Thailand, the Philippines, South Africa, and one or two other nations—all enlisted under the United Nations' banner.

Political relationships leading up to their fighting as an international army need not concern us this morning, but there is one significant fact most worthy of attention: Battling for the same cause are Buddhists, followers of Confucius, Moslems, and Christians. Opposed to these are communists, openly avowed to be anti-Christ. Two hundred twenty-nine thousand casualties are already reported in this conflict!

More destructive to the spreading of Christian principles in the minds, particularly of the youth, than battleships, submarines, or even bombs, is the sowing of false ideals by the enemy. Particularly, during the last five years, communist Russia has gained for the time being conquests over the satellites under her domination, including China, and is now threatening Japan by sowing seeds of mistrust in the body politic.

Misrepresentation, false propaganda, innuendoes soon sprout into poisonous weeds, and before long the people find themselves victims of a pollution that has robbed them of their individual liberty and enslaved them to a group of political gangsters. Let us draw a lesson from this.

So it is with evil thoughts that may be permitted insidiously to enter and to find lodgment in the human mind. —CR, April 1951, p. 96.

CAN WAR BE JUSTIFIED? AN INQUIRY AND EXAMINATION AS AMERICA ENTERED WORLD WAR II

THE QUESTION RAISED. In the face of the tragic condition among mankind, honest thinking men and women ask how is it possible to reconcile the teachings of Jesus with the participation of the Church in armed conflict.

THE NATURE OF WAR. War is basically selfish. Its roots feed in the soil of envy, hatred, desire for domination. Its fruit, therefore, is always bitter. They who cultivate and propagate it spread death and destruction and are enemies of the human race.

War originates in the hearts of men who seek to despoil, to conquer, or to destroy other individuals or groups of individuals. Self-exaltation is a motivating factor; force, the means of attainment. War is rebellious action against moral order.

The present war had its beginning in militarism, a false philosophy, which believes that "war is a biological necessity for the purification and progress of nations." It proclaims that "might determines right," and that only the strongest nations should survive and rule. It says, "The grandeur of history lies in the perpetual conflict of nations, and it is simply foolish to desire the suppression of their rivalry."

War impels you to hate your enemies.

The Prince of Peace says, love your enemies.

War says, curse them that curse you.

The Prince of Peace says, pray for them that curse you.

War says, injure and kill them that hate you.

The risen Lord says, do good to them that hate you.

WAR THE ANTITHESIS OF CHRISTIANITY. We see that war is incompatible with Christ's teachings. The gospel of Jesus Christ is the gospel of peace. War is its antithesis and produces hate. It is vain to attempt to reconcile war with true Christianity.

In the face of all this, I shall seem inconsistent when I declare that I uphold our country in the gigantic task it has assumed in the present world conflict and sustain the Church in its loyal support of the government in its fight against dictatorship.

JUSTIFICATION OF THE POSITION TAKEN BY THE CHURCH— CHRIST'S TEACHINGS NOT TO BE PERVERTED. In justification of this seeming inconsistence, I shall not attempt to prove that there are occasions when Jesus would approve of a nation's starting a war. That he used force to drive from the temple the money changers and other desecrators of the house of

God is a fact; but only a misapplication of the text can make that incident a justification for one Christian nation's going to war against another. On that occasion, as on all occasions, Jesus opposed and denounced wrong. With the strength of fiery indignation and of his own moral force, and not merely with a whip of small cords, Jesus drove the self-convicted desecrators from the temple.

Neither shall I attempt to prove that he favored war when he said: "Think not that I am come to send peace on earth: I came not to send peace, but a sword." (Matt. 10:34.) They who would quote this saying as indicating that Jesus approves war surely put a strained interpretation on its true meaning, which refers most clearly to the incompatibility between truth and error. It clearly refers to the necessity of a choice, which has been made by thousands, between accepting the gospel or continuing in ease and comfort with relatives. There is not in that quotation any justification for one Christian nation's declaring war upon another.

Nor, again, would I try to justify my seeming inconsistency by referring to what he said on another occasion as follows:

"But now, he that hath a purse, let him take it, and likewise his scrip: and he that hath no sword, let him sell his garment, and buy one.

"And they said, Lord, behold, here are two swords. And he said unto them, It is enough." (Luke 22:36, 38.)

Without reading into the text something which is not intended or even implied, the most that one can get from this admonition is that henceforth the disciples going forth into an antagonistic world might supply themselves with necessary support and the usual means of defense.

None of these sayings of the Savior's can be taken to prove that he justifies war.

Tolstoy, in his *Christianity and Patriotism*, says:

"A Christian state, to be consistent, ought, on entering upon a war, not merely to remove the crosses from the churches, to turn the churches themselves into buildings for other purposes, to give the clergy other duties, and above all, to prohibit the gospel—but ought to renounce every precept of morality which follows from the Christian law."

Notwithstanding all this, I still say that there are conditions when entrance into war is justifiable, and when a Christian nation may, without violation of principles, take up arms against an opposing force.

Such a condition, however, is not a real or fancied insult given by one nation to another. When this occurs, proper reparation may be made by mutual understanding, apology, or by arbitration.

Neither is there justifiable cause found in a desire or even a need for territorial expansion. The taking of territory implies the subjugation of the weak by the strong—the application of the jungle law.

Nor is war justified in an attempt to enforce a new order of government, or even to impel others to a particular form of worship, however better the government or eternally true the principles of the enforced religion may be.

TWO PRIME CONSIDERATIONS—POSSIBLY A THIRD. There are, however, two conditions which may justify a truly Christian man to enter—mind you, I say *enter, not begin*—a war: (1) an attempt to dominate and to deprive another of his free agency, and (2) loyalty to his country. Possibly there is a third, viz., defense of a weak nation that is being unjustly crushed by a strong, ruthless one.

Paramount among these reasons, of course, is the defense of man's freedom. An attempt to rob man of his free agency caused dissension even in heaven. Scriptures tell us:

" . . . Michael and his angels fought against the dragon; and the dragon fought and his angels,

"And prevailed not; neither was their place found any more in heaven.

"And the great dragon was cast out, that old serpent, called the Devil, and Satan, which deceiveth the whole world: he was cast out into the earth, and his angels were cast out with him." (Rev. 12:7-9.)

In that rebellion Lucifer said in substance: "By the law of force I will compel the human family to subscribe to the eternal plan, but give me thine honor and power."

To deprive an intelligent human being of his free agency is to commit the crime of the ages.

So fundamental in man's eternal progress is his inherent right to choose that the Lord would defend it even at the price of war. Without freedom of thought, freedom of choice, freedom of action within lawful bounds, man cannot progress. The Lord recognized this and also the fact that it would take man thousands of years to make the earth habitable for self-governing individuals. Throughout the ages advanced souls have yearned for a society in which liberty and justice prevail. Men have sought for it, fought for it, have died for it. Ancient freemen prized it; slaves longed for it; the Magna Charta demanded it; the Constitution of the United States declared it.

"This love of liberty which God has planted in us," said Abraham Lincoln, "constitutes the bulwark of our liberty and independence. It is not our frowning battlements, our bristling seacoasts, our army, and our navy. Our defense is in the spirit which prizes liberty as the heritage of all men, in all lands, everywhere. Destroy this spirit, and we have planted the seeds of despotism at our very doors."

A second obligation that impels us to become participants in this world war is loyalty to government.

"We believe that governments were instituted of God for the benefit of man; and that he holds men accountable for their acts in relation to them, both in making laws and administering them, for the good and safety of society.

"We believe that no government can exist in peace, except such laws are framed and held inviolate as will secure to each individual the free exercise of conscience, the right and control or property, and the protection of life." (D. & C. 134:1-2.)

The greatest responsibility of the state is to guard the lives and to protect the property and rights of its citizens; and if the state is obligated to protect its citizens from lawlessness within its boundaries, it is equally obligated to protect them from lawless encroachments from without—whether the attacking criminals be individuals or nations.

We are informed by competent authority that twenty years ago the government of the United States entered into an agreement with Japan to maintain peace in the Pacific

Ocean, and "keep honorable hands off China." "Before the year was over," writes Mark J. Gayn, in an article *Prelude to Treachery*, "the ablest men on the Japanese naval general staff went to work blueprinting war on the United States and Britain."

From such treachery the state is in duty bound to protect itself, and its only effective means of doing so under present world conditions is by armed force. As a Church:

" . . . we believe that all men are justified in defending themselves, their friends, and property, and the government, from the unlawful assaults and encroachments of all persons in times of exigency, where immediate appeal cannot be made to the laws, and relief afforded." (D. & C. 134:11.)

Even though we sense the hellish origin of war, even though we feel confident that war will never end war, yet under existing conditions we find ourselves as a body committed to combat this evil thing. With other loyal citizens we serve our country as bearers of arms, rather than to stand aloof to enjoy a freedom for which others have fought and died.

One purpose of emphasizing this theme is to give encouragement to young men now engaged in armed conflict and to reassure them that they are fighting for an eternal principle fundamental to the peace and progress of mankind. —CR, April 1942, pp. 70-74.

CHAPTER 21

THE CONTROL OF WAR AND THE QUEST FOR PEACE

THE CONTROL OF WAR

POLITICAL PROPOSALS. Statesmen, men of science, thinking men in all nations, laymen everywhere sense the need of something definite to which to look forward, some clear beacon that will guide the stranded nations to a safe harbor or permanent peace. As practical steps toward that goal they say: (1) mete out just punishment to villains and murderers; (2) make restoration of sovereign rights to those who have been deprived of them by force; (3) secure equal enjoyment by all nations of world trade and materials needed for prosperity; (4) establish improved labor standards, economic advancement, and social security for all; (5) declare a peace assuring safety and tranquility the world over; (6) grant freedom of the seas to all; (7) exact promise of abandonment by all nations of the use of force, and of disarmament of aggressive nations pending the establishment of general security. These and other expressed aims are worthy ideals and point to the fact that generally in men's hearts there is a desire to treat fairly their fellow men.

THE INDISPENSABLE IDEA. In all such seeking, however, there is one idea indispensable to the establishment of a permanent peace which too many men and some nations have obliterated from their minds, but which now should be reburnished until it shines as the unclouded noonday sun. I call it an *idea*, having in mind the fact that "there is more dynamite in an idea than in many bombs." It is as old as the Lord's first message to man, and some of you listening in will call it trite—men in the past have entertained it for a time, have dallied with it, then without attempting to make it a reality have permitted it to drop below the plane of consciousness and even to sink into the abyss of unbelief. This idea, so frequently mentioned but so seldom practised, connotes things, which, if lost, civilization itself is lost. It connotes the right to live, to be treated decently, to be kindly spoken to, to enjoy home, to love, and to be loved. It connotes strength to defend the right—sympathy for those who, striving, have failed. It connotes justice and mercy. It turns the eye and the heart from beastly passions to noble aspirations.

It is Christ's plan of love and service.—CR, October 1942, pp. 68-69.

WORLD FEDERATION AND HUMAN NATURE. Individuals, groups, and nations viewing with alarm the many critical national, industrial, and moral problems are hoping that "some means will be found to turn our misdirected powers into new channels, leading to the establishment of new and prosperous conditions."

Radio and press commentators, contributors to magazines, editorial writers, and statesmen suggest various plans and policies as solutions of our difficulties and perplexities. One of the best is a plan for a world federation, supported by a sufficiently strong armament to enforce its laws and statutes.

One great objection to its adoption, however, is that "human nature is not spiritually ready" for such a federation.

It is of this "spiritual readiness" I wish to speak.

It is the duty of the members of the Church to hold aloft true spiritual standards. Then we shall be better prepared for any eventuality brought about by pagan aggression. These principles have been proclaimed in all ages. They are simple, easily understood, but all too generally ignored.—*CR,* April 1948, p. 65.

THE RULE OF LOVE MUST SUPPLANT THE RULE OF FORCE. If the world would be at peace, it must supplant the rule of force by the rule of love. The scriptures tell us that in the beginning Satan proffered to force all men into subjection to the will of God. By compulsion he would save every person, and for so doing he asked that the honor and the glory that are the Lord's should be his.

There is an example of dictatorship supreme!

In contrast to this, the Lord's plan was to give men their free agency. The Prophet Joseph Smith said:

"To every man is given an inherent power to do right or to do wrong. In this he has free agency. He may choose the right and obtain salvation, or he may choose evil and merit abomination."

A man may act as his conscience dictates so long as he does not infringe upon the rights of others. That is the spirit of true democracy, and all government by the priesthood should be actuated by that same high motive. We are told,

"That the rights of the priesthood are inseparably connected with the powers of heaven, . . .
"No power or influence can or ought to be maintained by virtue of the priesthood, only by persuasion, by long-suffering, by gentleness and meekness, and by love unfeigned; . . .
"Reproving betimes with sharpness, when moved upon by the Holy Ghost; and then showing forth afterwards an increase of love toward him whom thou hast reproved, lest he esteem thee to be his enemy." (D. & C. 121:36, 41, 43.)

Peace is not found in selfishness, but in striving to help make the world better and happier.—CR, October 1938, p. 134.

I know of no better way to bring about harmony in the home, in the neighborhood, in organizations, peace in our country, and in the world than for every man and woman first to eliminate from his or her heart the enemies of harmony and peace such as hatred, selfishness, greed, animosity, and envy.

"And why beholdest thou the mote that is in thy brother's eye, but considerest not the beam that is in thine own eye?" (Matt. 7:3.)

Pertinent to this thought, Charles Wagner, author of The Simple Life, makes this comment:

"Each person's base of operations is the field of his immediate duty; neglect this field, and all you undertake at a distance is compromised. First, then, be of your own country, your own city, your own home, your own church, your own workshop; then, if you can, set out from this to go beyond it. That is the plain and natural order, and a man must fortify himself with very bad reasons to arrive at reversing it."
—CR, October 1941, p. 57.

Confidence in Our Fellow Men. Essential to our peace of mind, and eventually to the peace of nations, is to keep confidence in our fellow men. You say, how can we keep confidence when men are so corrupt? I answer that even if two or three, or even a score of men prove themselves dishonest and wicked, we are not justified in losing confidence in all men. Most people are honorable and upright—I like to think that—and desirous to:

" . . . do justly, and to love mercy, and to walk humbly with thy God." (Micah 6:8.)

Even if international leaders of a nation or of five nations disavow their Creator, and that's what they are saying in their hearts, "my power and the might of mine hand have got me this wealth," and even deny the Christ who redeemed them, let us remember that ten times that number of nations still profess to believe in God and in individual freedom.

These three principles—faith in God—acceptance of Christ as the Savior of man—confidence in our fellow men— are summed up by the Savior as follows:

"Thou shalt love the Lord thy God with all thy heart, and with all thy soul, and with all thy mind.

"This is the first and great commandment.

"And the second is like unto it, Thou shalt love thy neighbour as thyself." (Matthew 22:37-39.)—CR, April 1948, p. 68.

Man's suspicion and lack of trust are among the greatest enemies of peace. Nations are distrustful of one another.

This lack of confidence in one's fellow man is even more of an individual than a national vice. We are prone to magnify weaknesses and to imagine vices in others that do not exist. We chew the cud of slander with satisfaction—slander, "whose whisper over the world's diameter, as level as the cannon to its blank, transports his poisoned shot." Talk about battles yet to be fought! Backbiting and evil speaking head the list!

"If any man among you seem to be religious, and bridleth not his tongue, . . . this man's religion is vain." (James 1:26.) —IE, 48:638, 1945.

THE QUEST FOR PEACE

WHAT THE WORLD NEEDS TODAY. The world has just emerged from the most gigantic war of history, as a result of which, it is suffering from the usual postwar maladies—unrest, dissatisfaction, financial stringency, underproduction, high cost of living. A superficial examination, then, seems to indicate that the world's trouble today is caused by the war, so we might hastily conclude that what it most needs is an antidote—an international tribunal or a League of Nations—to prevent even the recurrence of this calamity.

However, a more critical examination reveals the fact that the war was an *effect* as well as a *cause*. It was the result of a condition in which the root of all the world's ills finds nourishment. This condition was created by the warped judgment, the unspiritual, the anti-Christian ideals fostered by a coterie of individuals in whose hands had been placed the steering wheel of the German ship of state. Treitschke's and his kindred teachers' anti-Christian philosophy was the element in which the seeds of the war germinated. He taught that the "state is the highest thing in the external society of man," and renouncing the foundation of all moral standards declared that the "absolute sovereignty of the state cannot be bound by any obligation, even of its own making." "A state cannot bind its will for the future over against other states." Out of such doctrine sprang the warped judgment that declared an international agreement "nothing but a scrap of paper." He further taught that war is sanctified, that it should "be conceived as an ordinance set by God," and that "the living God will see to it that war shall always recur as a terrible medicine for humanity."

Instructed in such pernicious doctrine, it is no wonder men harbor the unchristianlike spirit.

The world needs today, the *application* in all phases of daily life of principles that are directly opposite to these debasing standards.

In other words the world needs *practical religion*—it needs *applied Christianity*. It needs not only to *pray*, "Thy kingdom come. Thy will be done in earth, as it is in heaven," (Matt. 6:10) but also to *work* for the "establishment of divine government among human beings."

This implies that religion among men must be not only a subjective feeling, an inward state, but also an expression of that feeling manifested in human associations and social relations.—*YWJ*, 31:386-387 (1920).

THE NEED FOR PEACE. The greatest need of this old world today is peace. The turbulent storms of hate, of enmity, of distrust, and of sin are threatening to wreck humanity. It is time for men—true men—to dedicate their lives to God, and to cry with the spirit and power of the Christ, "Peace, be still. . . . " (Mark 4:39.)—*MS*, 85:802 (1923).

A GUIDE TO PEACE. Jesus said on one occasion to his disciples who were somewhat worried and anxious because Jesus had told them he was going to leave them,

"Let not your heart be troubled: ye believe in God, believe also in me." (John 14:1.)

In that one sentence, Jesus gives both a comforting admonition and a guide to contentment and peace.—*CR*, April 1948, p. 64.

It is not an easy thing to make God the center of our being. To do so we must determine to keep his commandments. Spiritual attainment, not physical possessions, not the indulgence and the gratification of the body, must become the chief goal.

Only in the complete surrender of our inner life may we rise above the selfish, sordid pull of nature. We should seek first the kingdom of God, and his righteousness. (See Matt. 6:33.) What the spirit is to the body, God is to the spirit. As the body dies when the spirit leaves it, so the spirit dies when we exclude God from it. I cannot imagine peace in a world from which God and religion are banished.—*IE*, 48:639 (1945).

THE ATOMIC BOMB IS NOT THE THREAT. The most ominous threat to the peace and happiness of mankind in this the twentieth century is not the probable misuse of the atomic bomb, but the dwindling in men's hearts of faith in God. "Epochs of faith are epochs of fruitfulness; but epochs of unbelief, however glittering, are barren of all permanent good." —*IE*, 50:507 (1947).

DISREGARD FOR THE MORAL LAW—THE REAL THREAT. Declarations recently made by one or two rulers of nations indicate the unrest, political upheavals, and a tendency to barbarism, in which "might makes right." These things are in direct opposition to the life and teachings of him whose resurrection from the grave is being celebrated today.

One man recently said: "We must arm. The watchword is this: more cannons, more ships, more airplanes, at whatever cost, with whatever means, even if it should mean wiping out all that is called civil life.

"When one is strong, one is dear to one's friends and feared by one's enemies. Since prehistoric times the shout has come down on the wave of centuries and the series of generations, 'Woe to the weak.'"

During World War I such mad doctrine cost the lives of nine million men. Commenting upon that holocaust a recent writer says: "Why in the name of reason and sweet mercy had this iniquitous bedlam come to pass?" And then he answers: "The question is not new, yet it struck at me with fresh, relentless force, and across my mind flashed the endless explanation advanced by human ingenuity, the talk of economic stress, of boom and slump, of unemployment and the rest; of the rise and fall of nations; the need for colonies; the survival of the fittest; the whole bag of tricks. How fatuous, how futile they all seemed! For it was clear, acutely clear. There was only one reason, one basic explanation: *Man had forgotten God!* Millions now living were blind and deaf—dead indeed to the knowledge of their Creator. For countless human souls that name was nothing but a myth. For others, an inherited tradition to which lip service must be paid; for others a convenient oath; for others bland hypocrisy."

And so I say today, the line is sharply drawn between the teachings of Christ and the proclamations and practices of autocrats, who with radical disrespect for men and the human ideals of justice, liberty, equality, and fraternity, "relegate to the limbo of old superstitions, God, the soul, and moral law."—CR, April 1939, p. 111.

Let us hope that a time will soon come when men with such natures and aspirations will be so few that we shall not have to fight them as we do a pack of wolves. Let us strive to make real the dream that Christian nations will some day unite not for war but for the establishing of the kingdom of God which should be a real and not a mystical kingdom. —*DNCS*, December 25, 1943, pp. 1, 5.

THE BATTLE AGAINST SELFISHNESS. Another old battle still raging and one we must win before permanent peace is established on earth is the battle against selfishness.

Selfishness is the root from which spring most human ills and suffering. Selfishness promises satisfaction, but its fruit is disappointing and produces only ill will and unhappiness. Selfishness and enmity caused the first recorded murder and the first implied rejection of the great truth that man is his brother's keeper.

It was selfishness that caused the violation of the Munich Pact, which led, in September 1939, to the murderous invasion of Poland and the subsequent destruction of European nations with all its attendant horrors and human suffering. It was selfishness and inordinate ambition that caused the Pearl Harbor tragedy.

Unless the battle against selfishness is won at the peace table, our hopes for a permanent peace may be shattered, and the world again stricken in warfare.

Nature's law demands us to do everything with self in view. Self-preservation is the first law of mortal life. But Jesus says:

"He that findeth his life shall lose it: and he that loseth his life for my sake shall find it." (Matt. 10:39.)

Jesus on the Mount of Temptation triumphed over all appeals to selfishness and thereby set an example to all men who would strive for spiritual attainment. As Jesus resisted the tempter, so selfishness must be overcome by subjugation and resistance. There is no development of character without resistance; there is no growth of spirituality without overcoming.

"And he that overcometh, and keepeth my works unto the end, to him will I give power over the nations." (Rev. 2:26.)—*IE*, 48:639 (1945).

Intemperance goes hand in hand with lawlessness, and lawlessness is an enemy of peace.—*IE*, 48:699 (1945).

WHAT MEN MIGHT DO. If men and nations will hold their belief in God and accept the teachings of Jesus Christ, pilotless planes and other argosies of the air encircling the globe in a nightless world will carry not bombs of merciless destruction but gifts and blessings to what is now a groping, benighted world.—CR, October 1947, p. 121.

The soul is the fountain from which the peace of the world will spring. Centered in the heart also are the enemies to peace—avarice, ambition, envy, anger, and pride. These and other vices which bring misery into the world must be eradicated before permanent peace is assured. There shall have to be felt in the hearts of men more consideration for others—there shall have to be manifested around the coming peace table at least a little of the Christ spirit—do unto others as you would have others do unto you. (See Matt. 7:12; Luke 6:31.)—IE, 47:62 (1943).

True religion is today the world's greatest need—a sense by the individual of a relationship with God—that indefinable something which enters into the soul of man and which unites him with his Creator.

"The wind bloweth where it listeth, and thou hearest the sound thereof, but canst not tell whence it cometh, and whither it goeth: so is every one that is born of the Spirit." (John 3:8.)

A celebrated British statesman, Edmund Burke, in the latter half of the eighteenth century wrote: "True religion is the foundation of society. When that is once shaken by contempt the whole fabric cannot be stable nor lasting." —IE, 48:699 (1945).

THE GRAND DESIGN. Some day intelligent human beings will realize the importance and benefit of living in right relations one with another. When that time comes, the Savior's prayer will be in people's hearts—Make them one, as thou Father and I are one. (See John 17:21.)

This condition can be achieved not alone from mere belief, nor from oratorical exhortation, but by the application in business, social, and national life of the principles of the gospel of Jesus Christ.—CR, October 1937, p. 103.

Chapter 22

The Cause of Human Liberty

THE DOCTRINE OF FREE AGENCY

THE POWER OF CHOICE—A DIVINE GIFT. Man's greatest endowment in mortal life is the power of choice—the divine gift of free agency. No true character was ever developed without a sense of soul freedom. If a man feels circumscribed, harassed, or enslaved by something or somebody, he is shackled. That is one fundamental reason why totalitarianism is so diabolically wrong, and some day in the future must be defeated. God intends man to be free.—*IE*, 44:396 (1941).

" . . . remember, my brethren . . . ye are free; ye are permitted to act for yourselves; for behold, God hath given unto you a knowledge and he hath made you free." (Helaman 14:30.)

Next to the bestowal of life itself, the right to direct that life is God's greatest gift to man. Among the immediate obligations and duties resting upon members of the Church, and one of the most urgent and pressing for attention and action of all liberty-loving people is the preservation of individual liberty. Freedom of choice is more to be treasured than any possession earth can give. It is inherent in the spirit of man. It is a divine gift to every normal being. Whether born in abject poverty or shackled at birth by inherited riches, everyone has this most precious of all life's endowments—the gift of free agency, man's inherited and inalienable right.

Free agency is the impelling source of the soul's progress. It is the purpose of the Lord that man become like him. In order for man to achieve this it was necessary for the Creator first to make him free. "Personal liberty," says Bulwer-Lytton, "is the paramount essential to human dignity and human happiness."—*CR*, April 1950, pp. 32-33.

A FUNDAMENTAL GOSPEL PRINCIPLE. I refer to the fundamental principle of the gospel, free agency. References in the scriptures show that this principle is (1) essential to man's salvation; and (2) may become a measuring rod by which the actions of men, of organizations, of nations may be judged.

"Therefore, cheer up your hearts, and remember that ye are free to act for yourselves—to choose the way of everlasting death or the way of eternal life." (II Nephi 10:23.)

"For the earth is full, and there is enough and to spare; yea, I prepared all things, and have given unto the children of men to be agents unto themselves." (D. & C. 104:17.)

"Behold, here is the agency of man, and here is the condemnation of man; because that which was from the beginning is plainly manifest unto them, and they receive not the light." (Ibid., 93:31.)

"Therefore, it is not right that any man should be in bondage one to another.

"And for this purpose have I established the Constitution of this land, by the hands of wise men whom I raised up unto this very purpose, and redeemed the land by the shedding of blood." (Ibid., 101:79-80.)

Again:

"My independence is sacred to me—it is a portion of that same Deity that rules in the heavens. There is not a being upon the face of the earth who is made in the image of God, who stands erect and is organized as God is, that should be deprived of the free exercise of his agency so far as he does not infringe upon others' rights, save by good advice and a good example." (Brigham Young.)

It is true that faith is an essential principle in all progress, not spiritual progress only, but to all progress. But next to faith as an essential to man's advancement is free agency.

The history of the world with all its contention and strife is largely an account of man's effort to free himself from bondage and usurpation or to protect himself in the freedom he possessed.—CR, April 1940, pp. 116-117.

There exists an eternal law that each human soul shall shape its own destiny. No one individual can make happiness or salvation for another. "Even God could not make men like himself without making them free."—DNCS, June 8, 1935, p. 1.

I believe that God is love, that he is our Father and desires the happiness and eternal life of his children. Indeed, this is his glory, " . . . to bring to pass the immortality and eternal life of man." (Moses 1:39.) He has placed man upon earth and, as he revealed to the Prophet Joseph, as recorded in the twenty-ninth section of the Doctrine and Covenants, he gave to man that he might be an agent unto himself. (See 29:35.)

Men may choose the right or they may choose the wrong; they may walk in darkness or they may walk in the light; and, mind you, God has not left his children without the light. He has given them in the various dispensations of the world the light of the gospel wherein they could walk and not stumble, wherein they could find that peace and happiness which he desires, as a loving Father, his children should enjoy, but the Lord does not take from them their free agency.

The Prophet Lehi, in speaking to his son Jacob, bears testimony to that truth in unmistakable terms. He says: "Wherefore, the Lord God gave unto man that he should act for himself. Wherefore, man could not act for himself save it should be that he was enticed by the one or the other." (II Nephi 2:16.) And then, in the twenty-seventh verse: "Wherefore, men are free according to the flesh; and all things are given them which are expedient unto man. And they are free to choose liberty and eternal life, through the great mediation of all men, or to choose captivity and death, according to the captivity and power of the devil; for he seeketh that all men might be miserable like unto himself." (II Nephi 2:27.)—CR, April 1937, p. 47.

MAN WILL REBEL AGAINST TYRANNY. I do not know that there was ever a time in the history of mankind when the evil one seemed so determined to strike at this fundamental virtue of free agency.

But, thank heaven, there is innate in man a feeling that will rebel against tyranny. It has manifested itself throughout the ages; for example, in the days of King John men who resented dictatorship gathered at Runnymede and made the king sign a paper that a man has the right to be tried by his peers, and that the individual is not a mere pawn in the hands of a dictator. A few hundred years afterward came

the Declaration of Independence, and then the Constitution
of the United States, fundamental in which is the right of
the individual to worship God, to speak as he feels, to own
his property, to take care of his family—his home, his castle.
—*DNCS*, January 2, 1952, p. 3.

RESPONSIBILITY ATTACHES TO FREE AGENCY. With free
agency there comes responsibility. If a man is to be rewarded
for righteousness and punished for evil, then common justice
demands that he be given the power of independent action. A
knowledge of good and evil is essential to man's progress on
earth. If he were coerced to do right at all times or were
helplessly enticed to commit sin, he would merit neither a
blessing for the first nor punishment for the second.

Thus we see that man's responsibility is correspondingly
operative with his free agency.—*CR*, April 1950, p. 33.

Freedom of the will and the responsibility associated with
it are fundamental aspects of Jesus' teachings. Throughout
his ministry he emphasized the worth of the individual and
exemplified what is now expressed in modern revelation as the
work and glory of God. Only through the divine gift of soul
freedom is such progress possible.

Force, on the other hand, emanates from Lucifer himself.
Even in man's pre-existent state, Satan sought power to compel the human family to do his will by suggesting that the
free agency of man be inoperative. If his plan had been accepted, human beings would have become mere puppets in
the hands of a dictator, and the purpose of man's coming to
earth would have been frustrated. Satan's proposed system
of government, therefore, was rejected, and the principle of
free agency established in its place.—*CR*, April 1950, pp. 34-
35.

THE INTERACTION OF FREE AGENTS—SOCIAL CONSE-
QUENCES. There is another responsibility correlated and even
coexistent with free agency, which is too infrequently emphasized, and that is the effect not only of a person's actions but
also of his thoughts upon others. Man radiates what he is,
and that radiation affects to a greater or lesser degree every
person who comes within that radiation.—*CR*, April 1950, p.
34.

FREEDOM REQUIRES JUSTICE AND FAIR PLAY: ANECDOTE. I believe we ought to be influenced in this as a crowd of sailors was governed by one of their number many years ago. It was during the anti-slavery agitation, and a meeting was called in Faneuil Hall, Boston. Some sailors had been hired to break up the meeting. They went there in a body, danced around on the floor, sang, yelled, and in every way possible tried to prevent the orators from addressing the meeting. In vain were they appealed to. Their love of liberty, the memory of their old home, the honor of Massachusetts, all were invoked; but still they continued their disturbance and refused to be quiet.

Suddenly a man, evidently one of their number, arose. Quieted for a moment by his appearance, thinking they had found a champion, the mob ceased its noise. The man said, "Boys, I would not be quiet unless I had a mind to." Encouraged by this remark, the mob burst into loud applause, which lasted probably five minutes. When it ceased, because of the men's desire to hear more, the man continued: "No, I would not be quiet if I didn't have a mind to; but, if I were you, *I would have a mind to,* not because of the memory of this hall, not for the honor of Massachusetts, not for loyalty to her government only, but because you are men; and honorable men always stand up for the liberty of right, justice, and free speech." They were quieted; their manhood had been touched.—*CR*, October 1906, pp. 111-112.

FREEDOM OF WORSHIP. This principle of free agency and the right of each individual to be free not only to think but also to act within bounds that grant to everyone else the same privilege are sometimes violated even by churches that claim to teach the doctrine of Jesus Christ. The attitude of any organization toward this principle of freedom is a pretty good index to its nearness to the teachings of Christ or to those of the evil one; for example, I read recently the statement of a leading clergyman who claimed the divine right of his church, wherever it was in power, to prohibit any other church from promulgating its doctrine. And, "if religious minorities actually exist, they shall have only a *de facto* existence without opportunity to spread their beliefs."

He who thus tramples underfoot one of God's greatest gifts to man, who would deny another the right to think and worship as he pleases, propagates error and makes his own church in that regard as far as he represents it a propagator of evil.

Contrast this unchristian-like stand with the statement of the Prophet Joseph Smith:

"We claim the privilege of worshiping Almighty God according to the dictates of our own conscience, and allow all men the same privilege, let them worship how, where, or what they may." (Article of Faith No. 11.)—*CR*, April, 1950, p. 36.

THREATS TO POLITICAL LIBERTY

THREATS TO INDIVIDUAL FREEDOM. Individual freedom is threatened by international rivalries, interracial animosities, and false political ideals. Unwise legislation, too often prompted by political expediency, is periodically being enacted that seductively undermines man's right of free agency, robs him of his rightful liberties, and makes him but a cog in the crushing wheel of a regimentation which, if persisted in, will end in dictatorship.—*CR*, April 1950, p. 35.

THE THREAT FROM THE RULE OF FORCE. Force rules in the world today; consequently, our government must keep armies abroad, build navies and air squadrons, create atom bombs to protect itself from the threatened aggression of a nation which seems to listen to no other appeal than compulsion.—*CR*, April 1950, p. 35.

THE KIND OF POLITICAL LEADERSHIP NEEDED. Today there is a great need in the world for men of integrity, men of honor, men whose word is as good as their bond, leaders of nations who will consider international agreements sacred. —*CR*, October 1951, p. 11.

COMMUNISM AND OTHER "ISMS." Today there are in this country enemies in the form of "isms." I call them anti-Americanisms. Only a few of the leaders fight openly—most of the army carry on as termites, secretly sowing discord and undermining stable government. Of the truth of this statement recent investigations made by a committee of the United

States Senate bear ample evidence. Of the menace of one of these, Dr. William F. Russell, Dean of Teachers' College, Columbia University, in an address "How to Tell a Communist, and How to Beat Him," is one of the many authorities whom we might quote as to the pernicious activity of these groups.

Dr. Russell says:

"Communist leaders have steadily insisted that communism cannot live in just one country. Just as we fought to make 'the world safe for democracy,' so they are fighting to make the world safe for communism. They are fighting this fight today. Every country must become communistic, according to their idea. So they have sent out missionaries. They have supplied them well with funds. They have won converts. These converts have been organized into little groups called 'cells,' each acting as a unit under the orders of a superior. It is almost a military organization. They attack where there is unemployment. They stir up discontent among those oppressed. * * * They work their way into the unions, where they form compact blocks. They publish and distribute little papers and pamphlets. At the New York *Times* they pass out one called 'Better Times.' At the Presbyterian Hospital it is called 'The Medical Worker.' At the College of the City of New York, it is called 'Professor, Worker, Student.' At Teachers' College it is called 'The Educational Vanguard.' These are scurrilous sheets. In one issue I noted twenty-nine errors of fact. After a recent address of mine they passed out a dodger attacking me, with a deliberate error of fact in each paragraph. These pamphlets cost money—more than one hundred dollars an issue. The idea is to try to entice into their web those generous and public-spirited teachers, preachers, social workers, and reformers who know distress and want to do something about it. These communists know what they are doing. They follow their orders. Particularly they would like to dominate our newspapers, our colleges, and our schools. The campaign is much alike all over the world. I have seen the same articles, almost the same pamphlets, in France and England as in the United States.

"You see, when it comes to fighting communists I am a battle-scarred veteran. But after twenty years I cannot tell one by looking at him. However, only the leaders proclaim their membership. The clever are silent, hidden, anonymous, boring from within. You can only tell a communist by his ideas."

Their method of working their way to the seizure of power he describes as follows:

"Talk about peace, talk about social equality, especially among those most oppressed. Talk about organization of labor, and penetrate into every labor union. Talk on soap boxes, publish pamphlets and papers. Orate and harangue. Play on envy. Arouse jealousy. Separate class from class. Try to break down the democratic processes from within. Accustom the people to picketing, strikes, mass meetings. Consequently attack the leaders in every way possible, so that the people will lose confidence. Then in time of national peril, during a war, on the occasion of a great disaster, or on a general strike, walk into the capital and seize the power. A well-organized minority can work wonders."

I have been informed from several sources that some of these spurious political growths are sprouting here in our own midst, that members of these groups have even received instructions regarding what to do in case this country should become involved in war. The nature of these instructions savors very much of the diabolical gunpowder plot in the time of James the First of England.

Latter-day Saints should have nothing to do with secret combinations and groups antagonistic to the constitutional law of the land, which the Lord "suffered to be established," and which "should be maintained for the rights and protection of all flesh according to just and holy principles."

Of course there are errors in government which some would correct; certainly there are manifest injustices and inequalities; and there will always be such in any government in the management of which enter the frailties of human nature. If you want changes, go to the polls on election day. Express yourself as an American citizen, and thank the Lord for the privilege that is yours to have a say as to who shall serve you in public office.—CR, October 1939, pp. 103-105.

Do not let advocates of communism mislead you in their attempt to denounce capitalism. Fundamental in the belief and promulgation of communism is the denial of the existence of God and the desire to substitute for the belief confidence in the state. The state is not an organization to suppress people. The state should have no power but that which the people give it; and when the state becomes a director, a controller of the individual, it becomes despotism; and human nature has fought that since man was created; and man will continue to fight that false ideal.

Individual freedom is innate in the human soul. God has given us our free agency, and next to life itself that is our greatest gift from heaven, and you red-blooded men and women know that is true because of your own love of liberty. —*DNCS*, April 30, 1952, p. 2.

I wish to mention another condition that gives cause for concern and apprehension, and that is the insidious influences, as well as the blatant heralding of ideas that undermine century-tried principles of peace, of justice, and of advancement toward the day of universal brotherhood.

We are grieved when we see or hear men and women, some of whom even profess membership in the Church, looking with favor upon the pernicious teachings of these groups, especially communism. These credulous, misguided persons claim to be advocates of peace and accuse those who oppose them as advocates of war. They should remember that all of us should ever keep in mind that there are some eternal principles more precious than peace, dearer than life itself.

Our revolutionary fathers sensed this, and their innermost feelings were expressed in the words of Patrick Henry: "Is life so dear or peace so sweet as to be purchased at the price of chains and slavery?"

Free agency, for example, is a divine gift, more precious than peace, more to be desired even than life. Any nation, any organized group of individuals that would deprive man of this heritage should be denounced by all liberty-loving persons. Associated with this fundamental principle is the right of individual initiative, the right to worship how, where, or what one pleases, and the simple privilege to leave a country, if one chooses, without having to skulk out as a culprit at the risk of being shot and killed.

At heart communism is atheistic, and fascism is equally antagonistic to freedom and to other Christian principles— even denying the divinity of Jesus Christ and the existence of God.—*CR*, October 1951, pp. 10-11.

THE DANGERS OF DISUNITY. What really prompts me to emphasize this principle [unity] is the presence in our own United States of influences the avowed object of which are to sow discord and contention among men with the view of undermining, weakening, if not entirely destroying our constitutional form of government. If I speak plainly, and in condemnation lay bare reprehensible practices and aims of certain organizations, please do not think that I harbor ill-will or enmity in my heart towards other United States citizens whose views on political policies do not coincide with mine. But when acts and schemes are manifestly contrary to the revealed word of the Lord, we feel justified in warning people against them. We may be charitable and forbearing to the sinner but must condemn the sin.

There is a danger even more menacing than the threat of invasion by a foreign foe. It is the unpatriotic activities and underhanded scheming of disloyal groups and organizations within our own borders. This country is so situated geographically that there need be little fear of invasion by an outside enemy. Furthermore, the government, knowing who and where the enemy is, can make ample preparation to meet his attacks. But the secret, seditious scheming of an enemy within our own ranks, hypocritically professing loyalty to the government, and at the same time plotting against it, is more difficult to deal with.

Disintegration is often more dangerous and more fatal than outward opposition; for example, an individual can usually protect himself from thunder showers, and even from tempests, from freezing weather or intense heat, from drought, or floods, or other extremes in nature; but he is often helpless when poisonous germs enter his body or a malignant growth begins to sap the strength of some vital organ.

The Church is little if at all injured by persecution and calumnies from ignorant, misinformed, or malicious enemies;

a greater hindrance to its progress comes from faultfinders, shirkers, commandment breakers, and apostate cliques within its own ecclesiastical and quorum groups.

So it is in government. It is the enemy from within that is most menacing, especially when it threatens to disintegrate our established form of government.—*CR*, October 1939, pp. 102-103.

THE DEFENSE OF LIBERTY

FOR WHAT DO WE STAND? We have cause for apprehension. I refer to the efforts to deprive man of his free agency—to steal from the individual his liberty.

The two most important documents affecting the destiny of America are the Declaration of Independence and the Constitution of the United States. Both these immortal papers relate primarily to the freedom of the individual.

Founded upon that principle of free enterprise fostered by these documents, the United States of America in less than two centuries has achieved a greatness that exceeds that of any other country in the world.

Our national standards are threatened. Add to this the increasing tendency to abandon ideals that constitute the foundation of the American home, and you will agree with me that there is cause for apprehension.

Now what shall we do about it? That concerns us.

When Paul was a prisoner in Rome, he sent a letter to Timothy, saying: "Preach the word; be instant in season, out of season; reprove, rebuke, exhort with all longsuffering and doctrine.

"For the time will come when they will not endure sound doctrine; but after their own lusts shall they heap to themselves teachers, having itching ears;

"And they shall turn away their ears from the truth, and shall be turned unto fables." (II Timothy 4:2-4.)

It is as important today as when Paul wrote that farewell message to Timothy that officers and teachers in the Church "preach the word; be instant—that is, eager, earnest—in season and out of season."

THE WORD TO PREACH. Today, in the midst of the world's perplexity, there should be no question in the mind of any true Latter-day Saint as to what we shall preach. The answer is clear.

In the year 1830, there was given to the people of this land and of the world, a divine plan whereby individuals can find security and peace of mind and live in harmonious accord with their fellow beings. In all man's theories and experiments since history began, human intelligence has never devised a system which, when applied to the needs of humanity, can even approach this plan in effectiveness.

In simple words, then, this is the word which we should preach—the gospel plan of salvation.

The founders of this great republic had faith in the economic and political welfare of this country because they had faith in God. Today it is not uncommon to note an apologetic attitude on the part of men when they refer to the need of God governing in the affairs of men. Indeed, as has already been said, the success of communism depends largely upon the substitution of the belief in God by belief in the supremacy of the state.

Preach in season and out of season belief in God the eternal Father, in his Son Jesus Christ, and in the Holy Ghost.

Second: Latter-day Saints proclaim that fundamental in this gospel plan is the sacredness of the individual, that God's work and glory is " . . . to bring to pass the immortality and eternal life of man." (Moses 1:39.)

Under this concept, it is a great imposition, if indeed not a crime, for any government, any labor union, or any other organization to deny a man the right to speak, to worship, and to work.

Third: Preach that the plan involves the belief that governments were instituted of God for the benefit of man. Man was not born for the benefit of the state. Preach " . . . that no government can exist in peace," and I quote from the Doctrine and Covenants, "except such laws are framed and held inviolate as will secure to each individual the free exercise of conscience, the right and control of property, and the protection of life." (D. & C. 134:2.)

Fourth: Preach the sacredness of family ties—the perpetuation of the family as the cornerstone of society.

Fifth: Proclaim the necessity of honesty and loyalty, doing an honest day's work for an honest day's pay. Preach that honesty in government is essential to the perpetuation and stability of our government, as it is necessary to the stability of character in the individual. "We believe in being honest, true, chaste, benevolent, virtuous, and in doing good to all men; . . . If there is anything virtuous, lovely, or of good report or praiseworthy, we seek after these things." (Article of Faith No. 13.)

To summarize: Let us be instant in season, and out of season, declaring that a kind and loving heavenly Father is as ready and eager today as ever to bless and to guide all his children who will sincerely seek him, and I bear you witness to that truth.

Proclaim that his beloved Son, the Redeemer and Savior of mankind, stands at the head of his Church that bears his name—that he guides and inspires those who are authorized to represent him here on earth—authorized by the priesthood when heavenly messengers bestowed upon the Prophet Joseph Smith and others associated with him divine authority.

Preach that the responsibility of declaring this plan of life, this way of life, this plan of salvation rests upon the entire membership of the Church, but most particularly upon those who have been ordained to the priesthood and who have been called as leaders and servants of the people.

To them today, as Paul said to Timothy, we give the admonition:

"Preach the word; be instant in season, out of season; reprove, rebuke, exhort with all longsuffering and doctrine." (II Timothy 4:2.)

> "In Zion let God's name be praised
> Who has a feast prepared,
> The glorious gospel standard raised,
> The ancient faith restored.
> Swift heralds, the glad news to bear
> O'er land and ocean fly;
> And to the wondering world disclose
> The message from on high."

God gives us power to fulfil this destiny of the Church, and to perform our duties.—*CR*, April 1952, p. 13-16.

Chapter 23

Political Liberty

GOVERNMENT AND LIBERTY

FREE AGENCY—THE KEY DOCTRINE REPEATED. In the light of the principle of free agency, it is not difficult to distinguish between the right and the wrong system of government. It is not difficult to tell when an organization transcends its bounds and becomes despotic.—*CR*, April 1940, p. 117.

POLITICAL FREEDOM. Man's free agency is an eternal principle of progress, and any form of government that curtails or inhibits its free exercise is wrong. Satan's plan in the beginning was one of coercion, and it was rejected because he sought to destroy the agency of man which God had given him.

When a man uses this God-given right to encroach upon the rights of another, he commits a wrong. Liberty becomes license, and the man a transgressor. It is the function of the state to curtail the violator and to protect the violated.—*CR*, April 1940, p. 118.

It is well ever to keep in mind the fact that the state exists for the individual, not the individual for the state. Jesus sought to perfect society by perfecting the individual, and only by the exercising of free agency can the individual even approach perfection.—*CR*, April 1940, p. 118.

POLITICAL ATTITUDES. Knowledge of God and his laws means stability, means contentment, means peace, and with that a heart full of love reaching out to our fellow man offering the same blessings, the same privileges. Love will beget tolerance and kindness. Now I bespeak that during the next month or so, when our towns and cities and states will be more or less stirred up by political contention, that we remember to have charity and love for one another. Oh, let us not deal in personalities and tear down a brother's reputation and hurt his feelings! We are striving to establish the kingdom of God; let us hold to that fact as the anchor of our soul and then breathe forth charity and love to those who may not see just as we do. I mean that while we are urging our particular political beliefs, that we avoid dealing in personalities; we cannot afford to hurt a brother's feelings and wound him.—*CR*, October 1912, p. 122.

THE VOTING FRANCHISE. Our community is a great factor in the teaching of our children. Our officers, public servants, are teachers of the youth, and they carry the responsibility of teachers. It is our duty, therefore, as citizens of this great republic, to exercise our right at the ballot box. It is our duty to see that men in both our great parties are chosen who will teach not only by precept, but also by example, obedience to law; that these men so elected will appoint men under them who will not scoff at the law, or who will not in any way protect those men or women who violate moral laws.

I said that the greatest obligation upon society is the proper training of youth. The home, our quorums, our officers in the community are three great educational factors, and all three are subject to our sentiment, our approval. —*CR*, April 1928, pp. 105-106.

The philosopher Thoreau said, "It matters not half so much what kind of ballot you drop into the ballot box once a year, as what kind of man you drop out of bed into the streets every morning."—*CR*, October 1951, p. 11.

GOOD GOVERNMENT DEFINED. "Government represents the authority of the group, usually exercised in an external coercive way, to enforce the will of the group upon its individual members." That government is best which has as its aim the administration of justice, well-being, and the promotion of prosperity among its members.—*CR*, April 1930, p. 80.

RIGHTS OF LABOR AND UNION MEMBERSHIP. Latter-day Saints should avoid affiliation with any committee, any group, any union that would, through coercion or force, deprive a person of the free exercise of his or her freedom of choice. It is understood, of course, that any person is free to join a union, when to do so favors his best interests; but no one should be compelled to join, or be deprived of any right as a citizen, including the right to honest labor, if he chooses not to become a member of a union or specially organized group. —*CR*, April 1940, p. 118.

THE CONSERVATION OF RESOURCES. We have heard, during the last year, a great deal about the necessity of conservation. We have been admonished from pulpits and by the press to conserve our resources, and in a measure the people have responded nobly to that appeal. On every hand you can see evidences of the desire on the part of the people to conserve the products of the earth and to utilize them for the blessing of the people who are in distress. There is more care taken on the farm to reap the harvest with which God has blessed the people; there is more thought given in the kitchen, and the foodstuff is being conserved and more economically used, perhaps, than ever before. Economy and thrift are fundamentals in the social organization and in the teachings of this Church.—*CR*, October 1917, p. 55.

THE CONSERVATION OF HUMAN WELL-BEING. This conservation and care is in keeping with the example which Jesus gave his disciples. You remember on one occasion he fed the multitude and commanded them to sit on the ground and with five barley loaves and two fishes fed the five thousand, after which he said, "Gather up the fragments that remain, that nothing be lost." (John 6:12.)

All this conservation of material things, I say, is most commendable and pleasing to God, but the greatest conservation that mankind can engage in is the conservation of youth, the conservation of manhood, and the protection of womanhood. I appeal to the Latter-day Saints today to give more thought to the protection, to the consideration of the dearest possession you have—your sons and daughters.—*CR*, October 1917, p. 56.

AMERICA: THE PROMISED LAND OF FREEDOM

THE WESTERN HEMISPHERE "NEW WORLD." America, and this includes Canada and the southern republics, was a choice land when the Jaredites left the land of Shinar approximately four thousand years ago. So was it fourteen hundred years later when Lehi and his colony formed the nucleus of a nation, prospered on the bounty of the country, and after a thousand years perished because of transgression.

America was a great land when the stately Indian chiefs ruled their tribes, which thrived from the Bering Sea in the north to the Panama and the towering Andes in the south.

THE HOPE OF CIVILIZED MAN. Today, yielding to the demands of the greatest economic era since the dawn of her creation, America is demonstrating the vastness of her resources and the extent of her natural possibilities as never before. This country is not only the choicest of all lands, but now also the preserver of true liberty, and the hope of civilized man!

God has made America fruitful; man must make and keep the nation great.—*CR*, April 1943, p. 17-18.

THE CHURCH, GOSPEL PRINCIPLES, AND AMERICAN FREEDOM. The Church of Jesus Christ of Latter-day Saints believes with the Prophet Lehi that America is a "land of promise, a land choice above all other lands"—a land of liberty unto those who keep the commandments of God. But " . . . if the day shall come that they will reject the Holy One of Israel, the true Messiah, their Redeemer and their God, behold, the judgments of him that is just shall rest upon them." (II Nephi 1:10.) The Church believes, also, that before the end of wickedness shall come, and wars shall be no more, this gospel of the kingdom must be preached to all the world. (See Matt. 24:14.)

The Constitution of this government was written by men who accepted Jesus Christ as the Savior of mankind. Let men and women in these United States then continue to keep their eyes centered upon him who ever shines as a Light to all the world. Men and women who live in America, "the land of Zion," have a responsibility greater than that yet borne by any other people. Theirs the duty, the obligation to preserve not only the Constitution of the land but also the Christian principles from which sprang that immortal document.

With the appeals for freedom that you transmit to your fellow countrymen across the sea, send also in messages that connote a sincerity never before expressed, an avowed conviction that Christ is the way, the truth, the life, the only safe guide to that haven of peace for which men and women the wide world over are earnestly praying. (See John 14:6.)

To this end let members of the Church, and honest men in every clime accept, not as an abstract, inapplicable saying, but as an eternal and guiding truth, the declaration of the Redeemer: "I am the light of the world: he that followeth me shall not walk in darkness, but shall have the light of life." (John 8:12.)—*CR*, October 1942, p. 70.

THE AMERICAN HERITAGE OF FREEDOM. As precious as life itself is our heritage of individual freedom, for man's free agency is a God-given gift. In sensing our responsibility to preserve it for ourselves and our posterity, let students and patriotic people ever keep in mind the warning voice of James Russell Lowell proclaiming: "Our American republic will endure only as long as the ideas of the men who founded it continue dominant."

There is a crying need today to have this truth heralded throughout the land that youth especially may appreciate and hold the freedom of the individual as sacred as did our revolutionary fathers.

Into the soul of every student I would have instilled the patriotic fervor of Patrick Henry: "Were my soul trembling on the wing of eternity, were this hand freezing to death, were my voice choking with the last struggle, I would still, with the last gasp of that voice, implore you to remember the truth: God has given America to be free."

Already there are insidious influences working termite-like to destroy this basic principle of true democracy.

As reported in the public press a year or so ago, an experienced United States Congressman, reputably one of the best lawyers in Congress, said: "There isn't a person in this room now who can be certain that he can leave to his children the heritage of the privilege of being free."—*DNCS*, June 20, 1951, p. 3.

To live in a land in which each individual has the right to life and liberty is a glorious privilege.

If any man in this country prefers a government ruled by a dictator, he should go where the dictator rules; but here in the United States of America the people believe in a government as Abraham Lincoln declared, "of the people, by the people, and for the people."—*CR*, April 1940, p. 118.

A LAND OF PLENTY AND OUR OBLIGATIONS. Approximately thirty-five centuries ago Moses, "the human transmitter of the greatest human conduct code of all time," warned the people of Israel as follows:

"Therefore thou shalt keep the commandments of the Lord thy God, to walk in his ways, and to fear him.

"For the Lord thy God bringeth thee into a good land, a land of brooks of water, of fountains and depths that spring out of valleys and hills;

"A land of wheat, and barley, and vines, and fig trees, and pomegranates; a land of oil olive, and honey;

"A land wherein thou shalt eat bread without scarceness, thou shalt not lack any thing in it; a land whose stones are iron, and out of whose hills thou mayest dig brass.

"When thou hast eaten and art full, then thou shalt bless the Lord thy God for the good land which he hath given thee.

"Beware that thou forget not the Lord thy God, in not keeping his commandments, and his judgments, and his statutes, which I command thee this day:

"Lest when thou hast eaten and art full, and hast built goodly houses, and dwelt therein;

"And when thy herds and thy flocks multiply, and thy silver and thy gold is multiplied, and all that thou hast is multiplied;

"Then thine heart be lifted up, and thou forget the Lord thy God, which brought thee forth. . . .

"And thou say in thine heart, My power and the might of mine hand hath gotten me this wealth.

"But thou shalt remember the Lord thy God: for it is he that giveth thee power to get wealth, that he may establish his covenant. . . .

"And it shall be, if thou do at all forget the Lord thy God, and walk after other gods, and serve them, and worship them, I testify against you this day that ye shall surely perish." (Deut. 8:6-14, 17-19.)

All that Moses wrote in praise of the richness and productivity of the promised land, and more than he wrote, can be applied to this great land of America—a land of corn, wheat, barley, and all other kinds of grain—a land of milk and honey

—a land where we eat bread without scarceness—a land whose stones are gold, silver, and iron, and out of whose hills we dig copper—a land aptly called the "granary of the world."

His words of admonition are equally applicable—

"When thou hast eaten and art full, then thou shalt bless the Lord thy God for the good land which he hath given thee." (Deut. 8:10.)—CR, April 1948, pp. 65-66.

THE CHURCH'S OBLIGATION TO BE EXEMPLARY. We learn from authentic sources that communistic countries, operating from behind the "iron curtain" accuse democratic countries, and particularly the United States, of virtually every political and moral crime under the sun. Our democracy is described as an instrument to enslave people.

Such slander has been compared to slugs that crawl over our cabbages. You may kill them, but there is still the slime.

"The surest method against such slander is to live it down in perseverance in well doing, and by prayer to God that he would cure the distempered mind of those who traduce and injure us."

To the Church today are applicable the words of the Savior:

"Let your light so shine before men, that they may see your good works, and glorify your Father which is in heaven." (Matthew 5:16.)

If we would face the future, no matter what it may be, with calmness of spirit, with an assurance that God governs in the affairs of men, let us as individuals and as a group live exemplary lives.—CR, April 1948, p. 69.

America is a land of boasted liberty, but liberty may be either helpful or fatal according to the use made of it. Is it liberty when a group of men with threats of violence prevent an employer from entering his own property? No! Liberty is shackled and violence rules! "Liberty is an atmosphere of the higher life, and it is only by a slow and patient inward transformation that one becomes capable of breathing it.

"Liberty?—it is respect; liberty?—it is obedience to the inner law; and this law is neither the good pleasure of the mighty, nor the caprice of the crowd, but the high and impersonal rule before which those who govern are the first to bow the head. Shall liberty, then, be proscribed? No; but men must be made capable and worthy of it, otherwise public life becomes impossible, and the nation, undisciplined and unrestrained, goes on through license into the inextricable tangles of demogoguery."—*CR,* April 1937, p. 29.

CONSTITUTIONAL GUARANTEES OF LIBERTY

THE CONSTITUTION OF THE UNITED STATES. If we would make the world better, let us foster a keener appreciation of the freedom and liberty guaranteed by the government of the United States as framed by the founders of this nation. Here again self-proclaimed progressives cry that such old-time adherence is out of date. But there are some fundamental principles of this republic which, like eternal truths, never get out of date, and which are applicable at all times to liberty-loving peoples. Such are the underlying principles of the Constitution, a document framed by patriotic, freedom-loving men, who Latter-day Saints declare were inspired by the Lord.—*CR,* October 1940, p. 104.

Next to being one in worshiping God, there is nothing in this world upon which this Church should be more united than in upholding and defending the Constitution of the United States.—*CR,* October 1939, p. 105.

THE LAND OF THE FREE. Many years ago the Lord said to the prophet, speaking of America, that no king shall ever rule this land. (See II Nephi 10:11.) It is the land of the free; and it has become an ensign to the whole world. In this land was first revealed in this dispensation, the gospel of Jesus Christ. As thrones topple and monarchies crumble, we will see that the people who are given their free agency will begin to appreciate the principles of self-government, preparatory to their accepting the gospel of Jesus Christ, which is the perfect law of liberty. I can see in all this a step toward a truer brotherhood—a preparation for the millennium. It may yet be far in the future, no one knows, but I can see divine influence overruling the destiny of nations, at least preparatory to the preaching of the gospel of Jesus Christ. —*CR,* April 1917, p. 49.

I am grateful for this republic and for the individual freedom vouchsafed by the Constitution of the United States and the Bill of Rights. I observed firsthand on my recent trip the evils of communistic dictatorship. It leaves no doubt in my mind of its evils.—*DNCS*, September 6, 1952, p. 3.

CONSTITUTIONAL PRIVILEGES TO BE UPHELD. I repeat that no greater immediate responsibility rests upon members of the Church, upon all citizens of this republic and of neighboring republics than to protect the freedom vouchsafed by the Constitution of the United States.

Let us, by exercising our privileges under the Constitution—

(1) Preserve our right to worship God according to the dictates of our conscience.

(2) Preserve the right to work when and where we choose. No free man should be compelled to pay tribute in order to realize this God-given privilege. Read in the Doctrine and Covenants this statement:

" . . . it is not right that any man should be in bondage one to another." (D. & C. 101:79.)

(3) Feel free to plan and to reap without the handicap of bureaucratic interference.

(4) Devote our time, means, and life, if necessary, to hold inviolate those laws which will secure to each individual the free exercise of conscience, the right and control of property, and the protection of life.

To sum up this whole question: In these days of uncertainty and unrest, liberty-loving people's greatest responsibility and paramount duty is to preserve and proclaim the freedom of the individual, his relationship to Deity, and, (repeating the message of our President, to which I subscribe with all my soul) the necessity of obedience to the principles of the gospel of Jesus Christ—only thus will mankind find peace and happiness:

"If ye continue in my word, then are ye my disciples indeed;

"And ye shall know the truth, and the truth shall make you free." (John 8:31-32.)—*CR*, April 1950, p. 37.

CHAPTER 24

THE CHURCH AND THE TRANSFORMATION
OF SOCIETY

THE TRANSFORMATION OF SOCIETY

THE MISSION OF THE LATTER-DAY SAINTS. The mission of the Latter-day Saints may be considered in two great aspects; one, the proclamation to the world of the restoration of the gospel of Jesus Christ—the declaration to all mankind that God the Father and his Son Jesus Christ appeared in this dispensation to the Prophet Joseph Smith. That in itself is a wonderful message.

The other great purpose of the Church is to translate truth into a better social order, or in other words, to make our religion effective in the individual lives of men, and in improving social conditions.—*CR*, October 1927, p. 11.

The other day I read, in a very carefully written book, on the life of Christ—a summary of his teachings to the world. The eminent writer said:

"Christ came to the world and gave to the world a message, which consists, first, *in giving to men a true conception of God;* second, in teaching men how *to attain a larger and freer life.*"

Then, basing the message, or the third lesson, upon the fact that a man's actions depend upon his motives, he draws this conclusion,

"*Christ's message meant the ultimate development of God's kingdom or rule upon earth,* which is *destined to transform society.* Loyalty to the divine King—the common Father of all mankind, is the strongest and only universal bond that can bind all men together. His teachings, therefore, have a large social, as well as individual significance, for they contemplate a universal brotherhood or democracy in which all men are united in the common desire to do the will of God."

I think this is a good summary of the message that your sons and daughters are giving to the world. They teach to all men a true conception of God. They invite the world to investigate the great declaration that God and his beloved Son have appeared in person in this dispensation. What a glorious message! Second: they are teaching men the means of attaining a higher and freer and diviner life. Say what you will, that is their only purpose, and they prove their sincerity in it by leaving their loved ones, leaving their vocations, spending their own money, or the hard earnings of their beloved parents, in trying to induce men to hear that message. Third: they can stand before the people of the world and say that the gospel of Jesus Christ does contemplate, in its ultimate consummation, the transformation of society; and who, conversant with world conditions today, will say that the time is not ripe for society to be transformed!—*CR*, October 1922, p. 77.

THE RIGHT LEADERSHIP. Truly, the time has come as perhaps never before when men should counsel together, and in wisdom determine how the world may be made a better place in which to live.

To achieve this desired end, the first and most important step is to choose as leader one whose leadership is infallible, whose teachings when practised have never failed. In the present tempestuous sea of uncertainty, the pilot must be one who through the storm can see the beacon in the harbor of peace.

The Church of Jesus Christ of Latter-day Saints proclaims that there is but one such guiding hand in the universe, but one unfailing Light, and that the Light of Christ who said: "I am come that they might have life, and that they might have it more abundantly." (John 10:10.) An active, sincere faith in the basic teachings of Jesus of Nazareth is the greatest need of the world. Because many reject this truth is all the more reason why sincere believers should proclaim it.—*CR*, October 1940, p. 102.

When the people who call themselves Christian militantly enlist under the leadership of the One to whom they refer as King of the world; when they accept as facts and not as theories his moral and spiritual teachings; when for selfishness they substitute kindness and thoughtfulness for others; when they aggressively defend the principles of true liberty, then may we begin to realize the hope that wrong may be abolished, righteousness be enthroned in human hearts, and honest relations and justice become the daily practice of society. Then, and not until then, will the kingdoms of this world become the kingdoms of our God.—CR, October 1940, p. 105.

THE GOSPEL DESTINED TO TRANSFORM SOCIETY. Missionaries are preaching that the gospel is destined to transform society. We believe it and we believe that from an economic standpoint, from a social standpoint, from a spiritual standpoint, we can offer to the world today such practical ideals in organized society, that if applied to the world, would alleviate much of the suffering and misery in this poor war-ridden, famine-stricken, selfish world. Take for example the little simple work of the fast day contribution to the poor.

I remember mentioning that before an audience in New Zealand, at Auckland, about six hundred nonmembers being present. We took that as the theme because a day or two before the meeting a paper had published the fact that citizens had discovered some suffering women and children about whose condition nobody seemed to be aware.

Following the meeting, a man said: "Do you really mean to say that every member of your Church is visited every month by some officer?"

"Yes, that is the plan."

"And that the amount contributed once a month on your fast day is sufficient to meet all the needs of the poor?"

"Yes, that is the fact. All do not do it, however," I confessed.

Ah, that is it. Don't you see—all do not comply. All do not come up to the standard. O fathers and mothers, what an example to the world in economic salvation if we could only live up fully to this economic principle!—CR, October 1922, p. 79.

CONTRIBUTING TO SOCIAL TRANSFORMATION. All should take pride in making Mormonism a synonym for trustworthiness, temperance, chastity, honesty, justice—these are fundamental principles of the Church of Jesus Christ of Latter-day Saints, and by exemplifying them in our lives we contribute to the transformation of society, we translate our religion into better social conditions and bring salvation and peace to men here and now.—*CR*, October 1927, p. 14.

NEED OF GOSPEL PRINCIPLES FOR SOCIAL WELL-BEING. The battle against godlessness must still be fought. Nietzsche, even before World War I, denounced Christianity as a cunningly devised system that has "debauched and undermined and sapped the vigor of the modern European world, and is the most powerful instrument of racial degeneration ever devised by the common herd."

Nietzsche is dead, but the poisonous seeds that he and others like him have sown in blindness and bitterness still produce fruit of skepticism and unbelief. In charity we can say that the Christianity Nietzsche condemns is not the gospel of Jesus Christ as taught by the Redeemer of man. But egotists and misled people who cannot discriminate between truth and error still find themselves wavering with respect to the divine mission of Jesus Christ.

Every true Christian, and especially every faithful member of the Church of Jesus Christ, should be militant in defending the principles of the gospel as given by our Lord and Savior, for, in the words of Mark Hopkins, true Christianity "promotes industry, honesty, truth, purity, kindness. It humbles the proud, exalts the lowly, upholds law, favors liberty, is essential to it, and would unite men in one great brotherhood. It is the breath of life to social and civil well-being here, and spreads the azure of that heaven into whose unfathomed depth the eye of faith loves to look."—*IE*, 48:638-639 (1945).

If you are now thinking that the application of Christ's teaching is impracticable under modern conditions, let me ask you to bring to mind a few specific examples of people who have devoted themselves to the common good. Recall the life of Florence Nightingale, and a million others like her, unheralded and unsung. Think of the Red Cross, a comparatively recent organization among Christian nations. Think of Abraham Lincoln, consecrating his life to his country.

If still you are doubtful, consider the humble life and great achievements of Dr. George Washington Carver, "who has done more than any other living man to rehabilitate agriculture in the South." He refused a proffered salary of

$100,000, preferring to devote his talents and energy to the benefit of his fellow men.

Christianity applied to daily life!—*CR*, October 1937, p. 102.

MEN MUST CHANGE THEIR THINKING. Because of terrible forces, newly discovered, scientists and military experts are now saying that all present means of defense are inadequate, are in fact already antiquated, and must be changed if the world is to be protected from future devastation.

I would that these men of reputed wisdom and foresight would lay equal emphasis on the fact that the future safety of the world depends not so much upon the changing of defenses as upon the changing of men's way of thinking and acting. Men and nations must have a change of heart. Hate, envy, suspicion, and greed must be supplanted by sympathy, forbearance, tolerance, and justice before peace comes.—*IE*, 48:638 (1945).

A CHANGE IN HEART NOTED. Today as we behold nations grasping at one another's throats, the strong crushing the weak, we are prone to think that righteousness among nations is waning. In our own country, we know that the struggle is still rife between capital and labor; that enemies to our democratic institutions are becoming more blatant; we see political demagogues more seemingly successful, drunkenness and immorality still flauntingly defiant; and we wonder whether mankind is growing better or worse. In private life unemployment, disappointments, adversity, sickness, and sorrow make us discouraged and sometimes despondent.

Still I am confident that truth will yet prevail, and in that confidence say with the Psalmist:

"Be of good courage, and he shall strengthen your heart, all ye that hope in the Lord." (Psalm 31:24.)

We may take courage in what I believe is a fact, that in the hearts of more millions of honest men and women than ever before in the history of the world, war is abhorrent. War has lost its false glamor and boasted glory. Such an attitude at least keeps alive our hope for the dawning of that day when men " . . . shall beat their swords into plowshares, and their spears into pruninghooks: nation shall not lift up sword against nation, neither shall they learn war any more." (Isaiah 2:4.)—*CR,* April 1940, p. 114.

OPTIMISM FOR A REVOLUTIONARY AGE. Please do not think me a pessimist. I love life. I think it is a joy to live in this age. Every morning, as I greet the sun as he ushers in these unexcelled autumn days, I feel the joy of living. I realize the accomplishments, to a certain degree, of this wonderful mechanistic age. Today time and distance are practically annihilated. Fifty years ago neighbors fifty miles apart were comparatively strangers. Today you can go to your telephone and in a few minutes talk to a friend seven thousand miles away. When Charles A. Lindbergh reached the American Embassy in Paris, after having flown from New York to Paris in thirty-three hours, he went to the telephone and within an hour told his mother that he had reached his destination in safety. If we were in tune at this moment, we could hear Big Ben striking over Westminster Abbey.

Millions of people in the world heard Admiral Richard E. Byrd at the South Pole. Men are penetrating the stratosphere and hoping for the nearby day when they will eat breakfast in New York and luncheon in Paris.

Yes, it is a glorious age in which we live, but no thinking man will doubt that this age is fraught with limitless perils as well as with untold possibilities. It is because of threatening dangers that the world should become anchored in the eternal truths of Jesus Christ, and realize that there are eternal verities in this changing world.—*CR,* October 1935, p. 98.

THE MODERN EFFORT TO SAVE THE WORLD

FROM WHAT DOES THE WORLD NEED SAVING? During my [European] visit reporters have asked me in one way and another, this question: "In what respects is Mormonism attempting to save the world?"

I have answered by asking another question. "What does the world need saving from?" And they have hesitated to say.

But we do not hesitate to answer that the world needs saving, first, from a shrinking faith in the existence of God;

and second, from ignorance of our relationship to God, and from their own sins and weaknesses; and third, from fear of oppression by their neighbors, and fear of the hatred of mankind.

REBUILDING FAITH. Now, think of the first: Mormonism declares to the world that our Father in heaven is a real person; that he can appear as a personal being to his children even today as he did in ancient times. That is a glorious message to the world; there is nothing more important since the Savior walked the earth. It declares to the world that God is not just a force permeating all the universe—but that power may express itself and manifest itself as a person. Those who hesitate to believe that and who say, "Why, you are too practical in trying to personalize God," lose sight of this great fact, that no matter how much greater God may be than a person, he is greater than the greatest of his works. The greatest of his creations is man, a personal being. As one man has said: When we visualize God as a spirit, we are looking at him through the clearest lens by which the human mind can comprehend the infinite. We can visualize his Son, Jesus Christ, who walked as a person on the shores of Galilee, and he said, If ye have seen me, ye have seen the Father also. (See John 14:9.)

And so the Church declares to the world that our Father in heaven is real, that we may get in communication with him if we live properly.

REPENTANCE — THE WAY OUT. That brings us to the second plan that the Church has of saving the world. Let me here repeat that passage of James describing pure religion: "Pure religion and undefiled before God and the Father is this, To visit the fatherless and widows in their affliction, and to keep himself unspotted from the world." (James 1:27.)

Let us consider that second part. The message of Mormonism is to help men recognize their weaknesses and to help man overcome those sins and weaknesses. Here we have not time to discuss what sin is, but John Wesley's mother reputedly has given us this:

"Would you judge of the lawfulness or unlawfulness of pleasure? Take this rule: Now note—whatever weakens your reason, impairs the tenderness of your conscience, obscures your sense of God, takes off your relish for spiritual things, whatever increases the authority of the body over the mind, that thing is sin to you, however innocent it may seem in itself."

The message of these young men who are going in all parts of the world, the message of the Church to all the world is: Repent of those things which contribute to the superiority of the physical senses over our love for spirituality. That is why they cry repentance! What does repentance mean? A *change* of life, a *change* of thought, a *change* of action. If you have been angry and hateful, change that hatred and enmity to love and consideration. If you have cheated a brother, let your conscience smite you and change that, and ask his forgiveness, and never do it again. In thus changing your life from those things which are on the animal plane, you repent of your sins. If you profane Deity, never do it again! Instead of profaning his name, worship him! And once that feeling of change comes to the soul, you desire to be born again, to have a new life.

A NEW BIRTH—A CHANGED LIFE. Then what is the next step in the gospel? Burying the old man with all that hatred and jealousy and sin.

This changing of life, this repenting is what the world needs. It is a change of heart. Men must change their way of thinking! Change their way of feeling! Instead of hating and fighting and crushing one another, they should learn to love!

Some men say you cannot change the lives of men, you cannot change their hearts.

We proclaim that God has restored the gospel of Jesus Christ and made himself known again to man. We whisper to all the world, repent of the evils of your heart. Give your hearts to God instead of yourself, in selfishness. And then we proclaim, serve your fellow men instead of exploiting them. That is what James had in mind when he said, " . . . visit the fatherless and widows in their affliction. . . . " (James 1:27.) Serve one another; make your livelihood, subdue nature, yes; cultivate your fields of beets, fields of potatoes, rye six feet tall, rectangular fields of wheat and of oats. In all these missions of Europe we have seen just such products. We commend that.

The Lord has said, subdue nature, but not just for ourselves, not just to make our own comfort. Provide for our loved ones, yes, educate them and give them comfort, but use all that God gives us in the earth for his glory and his kingdom. "Inasmuch as ye have done it unto one of the least of these my brethren, ye have done it unto me." (Matt. 25:40.)

God help us all to proclaim to the world the necessity of repentance, the importance of baptism, first to fulfil all righteousness, second as the entrance into the kingdom of God, the doorway into his Church, and third to bury our old life and be guided by his holy spirit.

I know the gospel is divine, and the world needs it. When God's will shall be done on earth as it is done in heaven, then there will be hastened that universal brotherhood of man for which we are all praying. May the Latter-day Saints in Germany, and in every other mission in Europe, keep their faith and live in accordance with the teachings of the gospel, I humbly pray in the name of Jesus Christ. Amen. (From the text of an address given by President David O. McKay at Conference of the West German Mission held in the Palm Gardens, Frankfurt, Germany, July 2, 1952.)—*DNCS*, July 30, 1952, p. 7.

THE ELIMINATION OF EVIL. On the night of Gethsemane, in the Upper Room, before Jesus and the Apostles left for the garden, he prayed:

" . . . I am no more in the world, but these are in the world, . . .

"I pray not that thou shouldest take them out of the world, but that thou shouldest keep them from the evil." (John 17:11, 15.)

The mission of the Church is to minimize and if possible eliminate evil from the world. The need of such a unifying force is expressed by a leading writer (Samuel Z. Batten) as follows:

"The world has many good people in it today, more who are ready to believe than ever before, but these people possess no unifying ideals, no organic principles, no coherent view of life, no synthetic program of action. Society is coming to self-consciousness, and is beginning to take note of its troubles and needs, but it has no clear sense of direction, no organizing impulse, no all-inclusive ideals, no mighty impulsion. . . . Is there anything by which our nature can gain its unity; our race acknowledge its brotherhood, our humanity order its affairs as a whole?"

We answer, yes—such a uniting force, such an ideal is the gospel of Jesus Christ as restored through the Prophet Joseph Smith. It explains man's life and its purpose, and has within it the vital saving elements, noble ideals, and spiritual uplift for which the heart of man today is yearning.—*CR*, April 1941, pp. 107-108.

THE DOCTRINE OF INDIVIDUAL EFFORT. Present-day difficulties and perplexities call for individual as well as co-operative effort. To paraphrase Lord Nelson's famous statement: Now is the time for every man to accept responsibility and to do his duty.

Undoubtedly there are many causes contributing to these untoward conditions, chief of which is failure to adopt the teachings of Jesus.

Well, what can we do about it? Sometimes when we think how little we can do, we almost despair of attempting to do anything. But there are a few simple but fundamental things which everyone can do.

One of these is for each individual to work out his own salvation.

An outstanding doctrine of the Church is that each individual carries this responsibility, and that the salvation of man is a process of gradual development. The Church does not accept the doctrine that a mere murmured belief in Jesus Christ is all that is essential to salvation. A man may say he believes, but if he does nothing to make that belief or faith a moving power to do, to accomplish, to produce soul growth, his protestation will avail him nothing. "Work out your own salvation" is an exhortation to demonstrate by activity, by thoughtful obedient effort the reality of faith. But this must be done with "fear and trembling"; that is, with a consciousness that absolute dependence upon self may produce pride and weakness that will bring failure. With fear and trembling we should seek the strength and grace of God for inspiration to obtain the final victory.

However, to work out one's salvation is not to sit idly by dreaming and yearning for God miraculously to thrust bounteous blessings into our laps. It is to perform daily, hourly, momentarily, if necessary, the immediate task or duty at hand, and to continue happily in such performance as the years come and go, leaving the fruits of such labors either to self or to others to be bestowed as a just and beneficent Father may determine.—CR, April 1938, pp. 16-18.

THE CONQUEST OF SOCIAL EVILS

Elements that Promote Social Disintegration. Right thinking, upright men and women everywhere are desirous of eliminating from our communities evil elements that are constantly disintegrating society—the liquor problem with its drunkenness, poverty, and misery; immorality with all its attendant evils; war, which is literally hell on earth.

What should be our attitude towards these social conditions? First, see to it that as individuals we do not by our acts contribute to their existence, and second, put forth every righteous effort to eradicate them from our communities.—CR, April 1941, p. 108.

Criminal Law Enforcement. It is from within, morally speaking, that our cities become corrupt; not from outward, open assaults on virtue, but from insidious, corrupt actions of trusted individuals. Our government, as you know, has recently uncovered a gambling ring that covers a twenty billion dollar business in vice. Many large cities in the United States are connected with it and contaminated by it.

Too many of these city officials license darkened rooms wherein men and women, and not infrequently teen-age boys and girls, may guzzle beer and whiskey and indulge in other vices sought by persons of low ideals. For the permission and perpetuation of such dens of iniquity in our cities, the public is not entirely free from blame. However, those who are elected to office—commissioners, peace officers, trusted servants of the people—are most directly responsible.

Generally speaking, these men are honest in their intentions and actions to enforce the laws and if possible to eradicate, at least to reduce to a minimum, the evils upon which the underworld thrives. One or two, or a half a dozen unprincipled men, however, can frustrate the most earnest efforts of the upright officials; for example, officers informed that minors are permitted to enter a certain "joint" will find when they get to the place that the proprietor has been "tipped off," and seemingly everything is within the law.

If and when appreciation for such "tip-offs," and other favors, is expressed in secretive payments of money, those participating in the graft may meet in a room, a club, or in a private residence, ostensibly to play a social game of poker, and under this guise divide their ill-gotten gains. Thus do our cities, as individuals, become corrupt from within.—*CR,* April 1951, p. 97.

STEMMING CRIMINALITY. There are two ways to stem criminality. One is by united, concentrated public opinion. The other, and more effective, is by personal contact. There are many in this audience who can look back with gratitude to the visit of some kind man, somebody who put his hand on your shoulder and said: "Don't do that," or "I commend you for not doing this, my boy." Some word of commendation, some gentle hand led you back into the path that has given you the success which you have attained. Personal influence—we must not lose sight of it! That organization which can supply that personal influence with the least waste of effort, and with the highest degree of efficiency, is the most potent organization in the world.

You have before you, bishops, the following means in your hands: the priesthood, Relief Society, Sunday School, Young Men's and Young Women's Mutual Improvement, and Primary Associations, not to name the Church schools and seminaries. I say bishops, because the bishop is the head of these organizations, and if the bishop will accept the responsibility of formulating and of assigning the list, as I am going to outline it, there need not be a boy or girl who within two months may not have had a personal visit from an efficient officer or teacher.

So we find in each group there are one or two, three or four, who need special care, special guidance. How best can we reach them? In this way: Let every teacher in the quorums, every teacher in these auxiliaries have before him the list of these potential delinquents. Be not satisfied with the good class you have Sunday morning or Tuesday night, but feel that the work is not done until you have carefully considered that other list which you hold in your hand, in regard to which you will report to your bishop at least once a month your success in reaching those whose names are found thereon.

We know you can't bring them all in. We have tried it. But you can bring some, "And if it be so that you should labor all your days . . . " says the Lord through the Prophet, "and bring, save it be one soul unto me, how great shall be your joy with him in the kingdom of my Father!" (D. & C. 18:15.) And who knows what that soul may be in that kingdom? Through loving effort you might discover some "inglorious Milton."—CR, April 1931, pp. 82-83.

RAISING MORAL STANDARDS. It is charged that "one of the distinctive traits of modern society in every country is the sinking of the moral ideal in the minds and life of the people." Manifestly, then, an essential in world betterment is the raising of the moral standard.

If anyone says, "This is trite," then I say such a thought itself justifies the call for men who will rededicate themselves to the principles of honesty, justice, tolerance, and love, and who will practise these virtues in their business and professional activities. "And this life is possible," as someone has declared, "in social conditions the most diverse, and with natural gifts the most unequal. It is not fortune, or personal advantage, but our turning them to account that constitutes the value of life."

"Nothing," says Emerson, "can bring you peace but the triumph of principles."—CR, October 1940, p. 103.

THE BUILDING OF ZION

A MODERN ZION. " . . . Zion shall flourish, and the glory of the Lord shall be upon her." (D. & C. 64:41.)

Zion means literally a "sunny place," or "sunny mountain." It first designated an eminence in Palestine on which

Jerusalem is built. In the Doctrine and Covenants, Zion has three designations: first, the land of America; second, a specific place of gathering; and third, the pure in heart.

As the Zion in Jerusalem was distinct as it stood wrapped in the clear sunshine, so I like to think of modern Zion as enveloped in heavenly light, because of merited divine favor. In considering how best to build Zion today let us, as wise and able architects do, see clearly first what we are going to build. Let us draw some plans and specifications.

If we have in mind the physical Zion, then we must strive for more fertile acres; bring from the mountains gold and silver in abundance; found factories to furnish more employment; extend in length and width our concrete public highways; build banks to protect, or to dissipate, as has been the case recently, the wealth we accumulate; transform our vast coal fields into electricity that will furnish light, heat, and power to every family; improve the means of communication until with radio in our pockets we may communicate with friends and loved ones from any point at any given moment.

Is it these physical phases of Zion which we are to build? Certainly it is difficult to picture the city of Zion without at least some—if not all—such modern necessities and luxuries. On the other hand, it is possible to have all these things and instead of reaping the blessings of Zion, suffer the very torments of hell. If the wealth, for example, from the wide acres be obtained by the oppression of the poor; if the gold and silver be obtained at the expense of human happiness and even of life itself; if in the palatial offices men sit and scheme how to prey upon their fellows, plan to extort money by kidnaping, or other unholy efforts, then all of these advantages will be but a means of making life miserable and unhappy.

It is well, therefore, for us to realize at the outset that "the greatness of a nation is measured, not by its fruitful acres, but by the men who cultivate those acres; not by great forests, but by the men who use those forests; not by its mines, but by the men who work them." America was a great land "choice above all other lands" when Columbus discovered it. Men of America have made it a great nation.—IE, 38:229 (1935).

ZION, THE PURE IN HEART. The Zion we build will pattern after the ideals of its inhabitants. To change men and the world we must change their thinking, for the thing which a man really believes is the thing which he has really thought; that which he actually thinks is the thing which he lives. Men do not go beyond their ideals; they often fall short of them, but they never go beyond them.

Victor Hugo said: "The future of any nation can be determined by the thoughts of its young men between the ages of eighteen and twenty-five." Thus it is easy to understand why the Lord designates Zion as ". . . the pure in heart . . ." (D. & C. 97:21); and only when we are such, and only when we have such shall Zion " . . . flourish, and the glory of the Lord shall be upon her." (Ibid., 64:41.)

The foundation of Zion then will be laid in the hearts of men; broad acres, mines, forests, factories, beautiful buildings, modern conveniences, will be but means and accessories to the building of the human soul and the securing of happiness.

THE FOUR CORNERSTONES. Let us then as we draw our plans for Zion today choose what we may call the "four cornerstones of Zion's inhabitants."

First: A firm belief and acceptance of the truth that this universe is governed by intelligence and wisdom, and, as Plato said, " . . . is not left to the guidance of an irrational and random chance."

The second cornerstone is that the ultimate purpose in God's great plan is the perfecting of the individual.

It is his desire that men and women become like himself.

The third cornerstone is a realization that the first and most essential thing in man's progress is freedom—free agency. Man can choose the highest good, or choose the lowest good and fall short of what he was intended to be.

The fourth cornerstone is a sense of responsibility toward other individuals and the social group.—IE, 38:229, 254 (1935).

TRANSFORMING SOCIETY—LOCAL COMMUNITY PRIDE. One of the best ways of building up our home, be it a domicile, a city, a state, or a nation, is to speak well of that home, city, state, or nation. Let the tongue be under contr   and speak well of the home. I have rejoiced time and again, when visiting the different stakes surrounding Utah, to hear our brethren tell about the advantages of some particular town. "Why," they would say, for example, "we are blest with the purest air, we have the best water that can be found in the world"; and they will enumerate, one after another, the benefits and blessings of that particular locality.

I recall now how the brethren in Canada were eager to impress those who were with them with the resources of that country. Why, the advantages were innumerable; for example, one visitor said, "But you haven't the scenery we have in Utah." "Yes, we have," persisted President Edward J. Wood. "We have even better scenery than you have in Utah." "Where?" "I will show you," and then a ride forty miles from Cardston took us to one of the most beautiful mountain scenes in the world—the Switzerland of America.

He felt that there was nothing that could make him feel dissatisfied with his home there. "Even the winds in Canada," he said, "are blessing us, because they blow the snow off, so the cattle can eat the grass." This is the point—he could see good in everything. There was contentment—not a spirit of tearing down, finding fault, complaining. I believe it is a good lesson; let us speak well of our home city; let us see the advantages of it.—CR, April 1910, p. 107.

PRIDE IN THE STATE. Let us speak well of our home state. But we cannot speak well of the state unless we speak well of the men who have founded the state. There is no other state in the union that can boast of stronger, truer, more virtuous, upright, God-fearing citizens and men of God than can the state of Utah. Let the young men throughout Zion realize this fact, and let their tongues proclaim it, and let them not encourage the company of those who would use this unruly member to vilify the men who founded this empire.

I overheard a conversation the other day which in effect was as follows: A prominent man and his wife evidently had been entertaining an eastern visitor who had been interested in the history and in different places of Salt Lake City. I judged that he was profoundly impressed, as every honest thinking man is when he sees the results of the labor and industry of the pioneers of our state. Among other things, he mentioned his going to church.

"I was at church last Sunday," I heard him say.

"Oh, were you?" answered his host, followed by some remark that I did not catch. "Well, where did you go to church?"

"At the Tabernacle."

And the sneer on that woman's face made my blood boil. With the sneer came some remark about not dignifying the Tabernacle as a church.

I saw the shadow of disappointment creep over that eastern visitor's face. He had dignified it, and he had been profoundly impressed, but when our own people, citizens of this state, though not members of the Church, spoke evil of something in our midst, the shadow of disappointment darkened his countenance. It will always be so.

O let us speak well, when we can do it truthfully—and we can in this case. Let us speak well of our city and state, to all who come within our borders; let us speak of the advantages and growth of our state.

SPREAD "GLAD" TIDINGS—NOT BAD. Let us speak well of those within our Church. Brethren and sisters, Christians have the responsibility of giving good news to the world—not bad news. Latter-day Saints have the responsibility of carrying glad tidings to the world. Let us not wait until we go abroad to carry it; let us give the good news today—good news of our neighbors, good news of our bishops, good news of our stake workers, good news of all whom we meet and whose company we may chance to be thrown into. If we cannot speak well of them, truthfully, let us refrain from speaking at all.—CR, April 1910, p. 108.

POSITIVE SOCIAL CRITICISM. Then say you, would you not speak of evil conditions? Must we not raise our voice in denouncing conditions and men who are bringing evil upon us? Yes, speak of conditions; but it is unnecessary to revile the character of men. We cannot do it as true Latter-day Saints; we must rise above it. Though we are *in* the world, we must not be *of* the world. There is a trait in the hearts of the world to pick at their fellow men. Emerson says that so pronounced is this tendency that an accident cannot happen in the street without the bystanders becoming animated with a faint hope that the victim will die. We cannot encourage that tendency. As James says, it is from the earth—sensual, devilish. We must not pick out that which will tear down a brother's character, nor the character of the city, the state, or the nation.—CR, April 1910, p. 109.

BOOK V

THE IMPROVEMENT OF MAN
IN SOCIETY

*"The responsibility is upon
each individual to choose the
path of righteousness, of
faithfulness, and of duty to
fellow men. If he chooses
otherwise and as a result
meets failure, misery, and
death, he alone is to blame."*

—DAVID O. MCKAY
Conference Report
April 1938, p. 18.

Chapter 25

The Nature of Man

THE CONDITION OF MAN

FIRST CONSIDERATIONS. Adam and Eve chose to take upon themselves mortality, and they were banished from God's presence. They were driven from the garden, and in their humiliation, their judgment or their memory was taken from them.

Now, imagine, young men and women, in what condition were those first people when they were placed upon this earth to gain their livelihood by the sweat of their brow, not remembering as the years passed, their spiritual state in the garden.

I picture them subject to the earth. If their bodies became cold, it was the sun that warmed them. If their throats became thirsty, it was a stream that quenched that thirst. If they wished to have a soft bed, it was a skin, or the leaves of the trees that furnished it. In a word, the earth produced that which satisfied their wants and needs and the mysteries of Nature would stir their souls.

They were subsisting upon what the earth gave them, and if, in that condition, ten, fifteen, twenty, one hundred, five hundred years passed, if no voice had come from "toward the garden," what condition would they have been in? They would naturally be grateful for the sun, for the moon and the stars that gave light by night; for the streams and other gifts of nature. The book of Moses says that under that condition some of them became, "carnal, sensual, and devilish by nature."

There is a passage in the Bible which says, "For by grace are ye saved through faith; and that not of yourselves: it is the gift of God." (Eph. 2:8.)

There are several good explanations of that, but to me here is one of the best illustrations of the grace of God to man. Adam heard the voice of God "toward the garden." And the Lord gave him commandments and said: " . . . offer the firstlings of their flocks . . . unto the Lord." (Moses 5:5.) By inference we conclude, the best that you raise in the garden and the field. See what that means in developing spirituality?

Selfishness, the animal nature, would say, "I want that." But God, knowing that the highest purpose of man is to develop the spirit within him, said, Give the firstlings to God, thinking not of self, but of something higher. What a sublime purpose! What an essential purpose! It was as if the Lord said: You who live in the earth need the experience to know good from evil, and to live not for yourself, but for God. Whatever you do—do in his name.—*DNCS*, January 2, 1952, pp. 2, 3.

MAN, HIS KNOWLEDGE AND BELIEFS. I should like to take as text that remarkable passage: "But there is a spirit in man: and the inspiration of the Almighty giveth them understanding." (Job 32:8.)

Man is a dual being. This fact I have accepted, it seems, since childhood, although I was a little shaken regarding it when I took psychology. James, the psychologist, however, recognized that the field of spirituality was beyond him. His honest attitude helped me during the period of doubt and hasty conclusions characteristic of youth.

This we do know: that we are here, and that we come in contact with things which our senses disclose. I am conscious of everything I see or hear. There are animals which receive these impressions in a different manner from that through which we receive them. A snake, for example, has no visible ear, but he hears and interprets vibrations through his skin, or possibly through his tongue. There are very few things which we do know, even with these five physical senses. An Indian philosopher classified all things into the following four groups:

"*Things we know.*
"*Things we assume to know.*
"*Things we believe.*
"*Things of which we are wholly ignorant.*"

As illustrations of the first class he listed:

"We know that we exist.
"We know that other people exist.

"We know that other things besides ourselves also exist.

"We know that fire burns and that water quenches thirst.

"We know that snow is soft and white and that ice is hard and cold to our senses.

"We know that flowers bloom and that birds sing.

"We know that certain things we call food, water, and air are necessary to what we name the life of our physical bodies.

"We know when we are happy and we know what sorrow is.

"We know these things," he explained, "because they fall within the radius of our own individual experience."

As illustrations of the second class he recorded:

"We assume to know that the earth is round.

"We assume to know how old we are . . .

"We assume to know about Columbus . . . Washington . . . Moses . . . Benjamin Franklin . . . Newton, etc."

Of *"things we believe,"* he wrote:

"Many there are who believe in a God in the sense that the Great Creative Intelligence is a distinct and definite personality . . .

"There are also those who believe in the absolute, inherent immortality of all mankind." .

Of *"things we do not know, or assume to know,"* he wrote:

"We neither know, nor assume to know, nor can we formulate a well-defined belief as to when time began or when, if ever, it will end; where space begins, how far it extends, or where, if at all, it ends; . . . when . . . matter first came into existence . . . how many suns, moons, and stars there are throughout all the universe of space; . . . the number of fishes or other living things in all the waters of the earth, the insects which pervade the atmosphere. . . ."

According to the statements thus set forth, how limited is that first class! We know only the things which come within the limit of these five senses. Yet, I must challenge that statement because there are other things which we know, as assuredly as we know those which we are seeing at this moment. I can see—I know that book [book raised up in evidence.]

If I take that and get its dimensions, I still find that I do not know it. I don't know the story of that binding, whether it goes back to the woods and the subsequent progress it has made. In other words, I don't know that which I say I know. If I take a thread and dissect it and split it up into molecules, then atoms, then electrons, and attempt to analyze it, I shall finally get to the point where I see I do not know it. But what I *think* about that book or that desk, I know, as I know nothing else in the world. *The most real thing to me in all my existence is my thought.*

And what you are thinking, whatever it may be, is the most real to you in this world at this moment. You can analyze your brain and catch the explosion in the brain which seems to produce the thought, but the thought is yours, as literally as the coat you are wearing or any physical part of your being.

Now what is that something which claims the thought? My thesis is based on the claim that that which claims the thought is the *spirit,* and that this spirit within may become aware of fact independently of these five senses—perhaps through vibrations, perhaps independent of them, I don't know.

I know that thought or feeling of awareness may be sensed independently of these five senses. The spirit in man controls this physical body just as the driver of an auto may control that machine. Just so, may man be controlled. Furthermore the spirit may become cognizant of an event prior to its happening or which is beyond the limit of these five senses.

What I am going to say now you may be inclined to question.

I am wondering if in early times when men walked and talked with God, if they were not more responsive spiritually than they are today. Adam, Enoch, Moses, Peter, John the Beloved, Abraham, all had this gift of spiritual response. Christ had it in perfection. Joseph Smith possessed the gift— but there is a remnant of it in everyone's soul, and particularly everyone who holds the priesthood. If you haven't had the experience that was given by the Lord through Joseph Smith to Oliver Cowdery, let me read this passage from the Doctrine and Covenants 9:7-9: "Behold, you have not understood; you

have supposed that I would give it unto you, when you took
no thought save it was to ask me.

"But, behold, I say unto you, that you must study it out
in your mind; then you must ask me if it be right, and if it is
right I will cause that your bosom shall burn within you;
therefore, you shall feel that it is right.

"But if it be not right you shall have no such feelings,
but you shall have a stupor of thought that shall cause you to
forget the thing which is wrong; therefore, you cannot write
that which is sacred save it be given you from me."

There are certain parts of the body known as "vestigial
organs"; for example, the tonsils, after a certain age; the ap-
pendix is another example. Sometimes I wonder if the spirit
nature of man today hasn't been restricted in its manifestations
and expressions—its responses feeble but not wholly lost.

Wordsworth said:

> "Our birth is but a sleep and a forgetting;
>   The Soul that rises with us, our life's Star,
> Hath had elsewhere its setting
>   And cometh from afar:
> Not in entire forgetfulness,
>   And not in utter nakedness,
> But trailing clouds of glory do we come
>   From God, who is our home."
>
>   "Intimations of Immortality."

And so in finding and trailing this spiritual contact with
the Infinite, God is pulling us back into his presence. If you
have ever felt the touch of inspiration, you will know that what
I say is true.

You know that you love, and love is not part of your
physical body but a definite and divine attribute of the human
soul. There is an eternal part of us which will outlive the sun,
the moon, and the earth itself.—*DNCS*, August 8, 1936, p. 1.

FREEDOM OF THE INDIVIDUAL. The power of choice is a
God-given gift, and the purpose of life is happiness. Things
which pertain to the physical nature are so easily obtained
and the pleasure so immediate that many spend most of their
time seeking them and neglecting the permanent joys of the
spirit.—*DNCS*, June 6, 1951, p. 2.

THE PRINCIPLE OF CHOICE. The principle of choice came
to Adam and Eve and to Cain and Abel. Let me refer to the
account of those two boys. They, too, heard the doctrine,
". . . offer the firstlings of their flocks, for an offering unto
the Lord." (Moses 5:5.) They, too, heard, bring the best
product the earth gives. And one of those boys gave the
firstlings of his flock, and gladly gave them. But the other kept
the best to himself.

When the Lord rewarded Abel, on natural principles,
Cain became jealous. He became so envious that in anger
he slew his brother. God asked Cain, "Where is Abel, thy
brother?" " . . . Am I my brother's keeper?" answered the
guilty man, sullenly. Said the Lord, "If thou doest well,
shalt thou not be accepted? and if thou doest not well, sin
lieth at the door." (See Gen. 4:9, 7.)

Thus briefly were eternal principles promulgated in the
first stages of man on earth, and applicable today.

The choice is given, whether we live in the physical
world as animals, or whether we use what earth offers us as
a means of living in the spiritual world that will lead us back
into the presence of God.

This means specifically:

Whether we choose selfishness or whether we will deny
ourselves for the good of others;

Whether we will cherish indulgence of appetite, passion,
or whether we will develop restraint and self-control.

Whether we choose licentiousness or chastity;

Whether we will encourage hate or develop love;

Whether practise cruelty or kindness;

Whether be cynical or sanguine—hopeful;

Whether we be traitorous—disloyal to those who love us,
to our country, to the Church or to God—or whether we will
be loyal;

Whether we be deceitful, or honest, our word our bond;

Whether a slanderous or a controlled tongue.—*DNCS,*
January 2, 1952, p. 3.

INDIVIDUALISM. We are not saved as a state. We are not
saved as a group. Man is saved as an individual, and as an
individual he lived in the life of the Savior, the Son of Man.

No person was too humble, no person was too simple to receive his attention, and to have the right to live. The story of Jesus is the story of his dealings with individuals.—*DNCS*, June 11, 1952, p. 15.

The responsibility is upon each individual to choose the path of righteousness, of faithfulness, and of duty to fellow men. If he chooses otherwise, and as a result meets failure, misery, and death, he alone is to blame.—*CR*, April 1938, p. 18.

THE SACREDNESS OF PERSONALITY. There is an unchanging truth in an unchanging world which should be an anchor to the soul of every person in it: the sacredness of personality. The least child was sacred to Jesus. It is not the will of your Father in heaven that one of these little ones should perish. That simple truth in the world, what would it mean?

"Inasmuch as ye have done it unto one of the least of these my brethren, ye have done it unto me." (Matt. 25:40.)

And in this modern day he said:

"Remember the worth of souls is great. . . . " (D. & C. 18:10.)

A proper conception of this divine principle would change the attitude of the world to the benefit and happiness of all human beings. It would bring into active operation the Golden Rule: Do unto others as you would have others do unto you. (See Matt. 7:12.)—*CR*, October 1935, p. 101.

RESPECT FOR ALL RACES. What a different world this would be if men would accumulate wealth, for example, not as an end but as a means of blessing human beings and improving human relations. A Christian conception of the right and value of a human soul, even though his skin be dark, would have prevented the slaughter that at this moment is being perpetrated in Ethiopia.—*CR*, October 1935, p. 101.

MAN AND HIS NATURE

DUAL ASPECTS. Man has a dual nature: one, related to the earthly or animal life; the other, akin to the Divine. Whether a man remains satisfied within what we designate the animal world, satisfied with what the animal world will give him, yielding without effort to the whim of his appetites and passions and slipping farther and farther into the realm of indulgence, or whether, through self-mastery, he rises toward intellectual, moral, and spiritual enjoyments depends upon the kind of choice he makes every day, nay, every hour of his life.—*CR*, April 1949, p. 13.

THE BODY. The body with its five or more senses, with its appetites and passions, is essential to life and happiness, but in the ultimate analysis it is only a means to a higher end. When man makes its gratification an end in itself, he frustrates the purpose and descends to sensuality. Therefore, ". . . choose you this day whom ye will serve; . . ." (Joshua 24:15.)—*CR*, April 1949, p. 16.

A SPIRITUAL BEING. Man is a spiritual being, and at some period of his life everyone is possessed with an irresistible desire to know his relationship to the Infinite. He realizes that he is not just a physical object that is to be tossed for a short time from bank to bank, only to be submerged finally in the everflowing stream of life. There is something within him which urges him to rise above himself, to control his environment, to master the body and all things physical and live in a higher and more beautiful world.—*CR*, October 1928, p. 37.

Those who choose to remain in this material world and who close their eyes to the promise and possibility of a higher life, merely acknowledge that our purpose here is to be born, to live, breathe, prepare in a general way for those who follow after us, and then to die.—*DNCS*, June 8, 1935.

CHAPTER 26

THE BUILDING OF HUMAN CHARACTER

MAN AND CHARACTER DEVELOPMENT

THE UPWARD CLIMB. Since man's first advent on earth, God has been urging him to rise above the selfish, groveling life of the purely animal existence into the higher, more spiritual realm. After several thousand years of struggling, mankind even now but dimly recognizes the fact that the greatest of the world's leaders are those who most nearly approach the teachings of the Man of Galilee. This is psychologically sound because the thoughts a man harbors determine the realm in which he serves. "Be not deceived", writes Paul to the Galatians, "God is not mocked: for whatsoever a man soweth, that shall he also reap.

"For he that soweth to his flesh shall of the flesh reap corruption; but he that soweth to the Spirit shall of the Spirit reap life everlasting." (Gal. 6:7-8.)—CR, April 1951, pp. 95-96.

THE POWER OF THOUGHT. What a man continually thinks about determines his actions in times of opportunity and stress. A man's reaction to his appetites and impulses when they are aroused gives the measure of that man's character. In these reactions are revealed the man's power to govern or his forced servility to yield.—CR, October 1951, p. 8.

THE POWER OF ACTIONS. Actions in harmony with divine law and the laws of nature will bring happiness, and those in opposition to divine truth, misery. Man is responsible not only for every deed, but also for every idle word and thought. Said the Savior:

" . . . every idle word that men shall speak, they shall give account thereof in the day of judgment." (Matthew 12:36.)

As a boy I questioned that truth when I first heard it expressed by my father. I remember saying to myself, "Not

even the Lord knows what I am thinking now." I was very
much surprised, therefore, when later as a student in the university, I read the following in William James' *Psychology*
about the effect of thought and action on human character:

SPINNING OUR OWN FATES

"We are spinning our own fates good or evil, and never
to be undone. Every smallest stroke of virtue or of vice leaves
its ever so little scar. The drunken Rip Van Winkle, in
Jefferson's play, excuses himself for every fresh dereliction by
saying, 'I won't count this time.' Well! he may not count it,
and a kind Heaven may not count it; but it is being counted
none the less. Down among his nerve-cells and fibers the
molecules are counting it, registering and storing it up to
be used against him when the next temptation comes. Nothing
we ever do is, in strict scientific literalness, wiped out. Of
course, this has its good side as well as its bad one. As we
become permanent drunkards by so many separate drinks,
so we become saints in the moral, and authorities and experts
in the practical and scientific spheres, by so many separate
acts and hours of work. Let no youth have any anxiety about
the upshot of his education, whatever the line of it may be.
If he keep faithfully busy each hour of the working day, he
may safely leave the final result to itself. He can with perfect
certainty count on waking up some fine morning, to find
himself one of the competent ones of his generation, in whatever pursuit he may have singled out. Silently, between all
the details of his business, the *power of judging* in all that
class of matter will have built itself up within him as a possession that will never pass away. Young people should know
this truth in advance. The ignorance of it has probably
engendered more discouragement and faint-heartedness in
youths embarking on arduous careers than all other causes
put together." (*Psychology*, Henry Holt and Co., N. Y. 1892,
p. 150.)—CR, April 1950, pp. 33-34.

GIVING GOD THE GLORY. A willingness to give God the
glory is a sure means of subduing selfishness. Faith, therefore, is a foundation element in true character building; for
an upright character is the result of continued effort and right

thinking, the effect of long-cherished associations with God-like thoughts. He approaches nearest the Christ spirit who makes God the center of his thoughts and acts, and who can say in his heart, " . . . not my will, but thine, be done." (Luke 22:42.)—*IE*, 47:13 (1943).

THE ROLE OF IDEALS

THE EFFICACY OF STRIVING. I never hear one of our brethren bear testimony to the divinity of this work, without feeling that the strength and growth of his character depends upon a consistent life with that testimony; and it makes character to live in harmony with man's ideals, or at least to strive to live in harmony with them.

I can illustrate what I mean by relating an incident concerning two of our boys at college. They had been taught as you boys and I have been taught, that next to life itself, we should cherish chastity.

One of these boys noticed that there was a laxity among his classmates, and after a few months at college, he partook of a different spirit from the one he had in his home, and one night he said to his companion, who was older than he, "I am going out tonight with those fellows."

"Well, you'd better not," said his companion.

"Oh," he said, "I do not know! Those fellows have a good time, take their wine, have their cigarets and their cigars, they enjoy themselves; and here we are restrained. They get their lessons; they are doing just as well in college as we are; and I am going out with them. I am not so sure that our ideals are necessary, anyhow."

The older one walked up, put his hand on his companion's shoulder, and said, "Those boys may be getting along all right in school; they may do these things to which you refer with impunity; but you can't."

"Why?"

"Because you know better. And once you break through that ideal, your character is broken."

It was the best lesson he learned in college, and I am very glad that he learned it and lived it.—*CR*, October 1918, pp. 137-138.

Resist the devil, and he will flee from you. Court him, and you will soon have shackles, not on your wrists, but on your soul.—*DNCS*, August 8, 1951.

IDEALS AND CHARACTER. I shall never forget the picture of an Arizona mother's parting with her son. It was about a year and a half ago, when we first entered the war. He was one of the first to go. The mother, with her heart almost breaking, went with him to the recruiting office, and in the presence of a United States officer, when she was taking her last good-bye, said, "John, I want you to come back to me just as clean and sweet as you are now, or do not come back at all."

And the officer said, "Why, madam, you must not expect that of your boy."

"I do expect it of him," she returned, "and every Mormon mother expects it of her boy. I do expect it of you, John, and I know you will." With that she gave him a caress and went back to her home, and he to fight for his country.

Don't you think that boy will strive for righteousness, for the ideals of home, and the ideals of his character? He knows what is right; and if he is going to be a man of strong character, he must maintain those ideals.—*CR*, October 1918, p. 138.

THE SPIRITUAL LAW OF CHARACTER. Is the truth of the paradoxical statement, *losing oneself to find oneself*, so elusive that mankind cannot grasp it? Or is it so in conflict with the struggle for existence that men consider it impractical? Even so, the fact remains that He who is " . . . the way, the truth, and the life" (John 14:6) has herein set forth an immutable law, obedience to which will ameliorate those social and economic conditions in which

> "Man's inhumanity to man
> Makes countless thousands mourn."
> Robert Burns, "Man Was Made to Mourn."

Specifically stated, this law is: *We live our lives most completely when we strive to make the world better and happier.* The law of pure nature, survival of the fittest, is self-preservation at the sacrifice of all else; the law of true spiritual life is *deny self for the good of others.—I,* 80:567 (1945).

MANHOOD AND WOMANHOOD

THE GLORY OF CREATION. We want men. There is nothing in life so admirable as true manhood; there is nothing so sacred as true womanhood. Manhood! Oh, what that means—to be a man, to be worthy of the honor that Anthony gave to Brutus, when he pointed and said:

> "This was the noblest Roman of them all:
> All the conspirators, save only he,
> Did that they did in envy of great Caesar;
> He only, in a general honest thought
> And common good to all, made one of them.
> His life was gentle, and the elements
> So mix'd in him that Nature might stand up
> And say to all the world 'This was a man!' "
>
> Shakespeare, *Julius Caesar.*

Wordsworth's heart leaped up when he beheld a rainbow in the sky. Burns' heart wept when his plowshare overturned a daisy. Tennyson could pluck the flower from the crannied wall, and see, if he could read in it the mystery, all that "God and man is." All these, and other great men, have shown to us, in the works of nature, the handiwork of God. Shakespeare could find "tongues in trees, books in the running brooks, sermons in stones and good in every thing." All, I say, are expressions of goodness, and praises to God invite; but the glory of creation, "the beauty of the world," says Shakespeare, "the paragon of animals," is man. "An honest man is the noblest work of God." (Pope.)

We delight in associating with true men; it is good to be in their presence. "They are living light fountains," says Carlyle, "which it is good and pleasant to be near." I often think that it is easy to be honest; and to be honest means that we are in harmony with divine law, that we are in keeping with the noblest work of God.—CR, October 1908, p. 108.

TRUE TO CONSCIENCE. All men who have moved the world have been men who would stand true to their conscience—not only James, not only Paul, Peter, and all those ancient Apostles, but all other great men in history. I often admire Luther; I cannot help feeling better when I read his words to the assembly at the Diet of Worms, all the Catholic Church opposing him, and all the powers of the land staring him in the face:

"Let me then be refuted and convinced by the testimony of the scriptures or by the clearest arguments, otherwise I cannot and will not recant, for it is neither safe nor expedient to act against conscience. Here I take my stand; I can do no otherwise, so help me God!"

It was Joseph Smith who, after having a testimony of the Lord Jesus in his bosom, declared to the men who said, "It is from the devil"—ministers who had influence with him before, men whom he respected as, at least, attempting to teach the word of God—to them he said: "I had seen a vision; I knew it, and I knew that God knew it." And he was true to this testimony to the last. When he was going to his death, he declared to all the world: "I have a conscience void of offense toward God and toward all men." Why? Because he had been true to it; he was a man possessing divine manhood, for true manhood is divine.

It was that spirit that prompted our leader (President Joseph F. Smith) to say to the world: "I will be true to those who have trusted me; I cannot do otherwise." That is the manhood the Latter-day Saint should possess, in defending the truth.—*CR*, October 1908, pp. 110-111.

MANHOOD SUSTAINS TRUTH. The man who is true to his manhood will not lie against the truth. We are told that we can crucify the Lord afresh. If that be true, we can *betray* the Lord afresh. There is that within every man which is divine, a divinity within every man's soul. It cannot die. God renews it, inspires it, works to keep it alive. The man who will be true to the divine within, is true to his Lord, and is true to his fellow men. The man who betrays that, the man who is untrue to that which he knows to be right, is wavering, is weakening. God pity him; he may go so far that he will step out of the light, out of that divine presence; and woe be unto him when he does; God help him.—*CR*, October 1908, p. 110.

FOUR PICTURES OF IMPORTANCE AND BEAUTY. There are four pictures upon which I always love to look. The first of these is the picture of Christ before Pilate when that Roman official said to the angry mob, "Behold the man!" (John 19:5.) As he said it, he pointed to Jesus, crowned with thorns, bearing upon his shoulders the purple robe. He pointed to one at whom the angry mob sneered, condemned as a felon and blasphemer, and yet when he said, "Behold the man!" he described one who was perfect in character, who was conqueror over weaknesses and temptations, and who could say, as he did to his fellow workers, "These things I have spoken unto you, that in me ye might have peace . . . be of good cheer; I have overcome the world." (John 16:33.) He is our pattern.

The other picture is Christ in his youth. Have you not admired the paintings of the best artists who have tried to picture purity and strength in that young boy of twelve years? I have, and I never look upon one of the choicest of these without feeling that I am looking upon one who is the embodiment of youthful strength, vigor, and purity.

The third is the picture of the boy who, as Hawthorne describes him, looked upon the great stone face, and, while thinking of the ideals and virtues characterized in that great work of nature, developed those same virtues in his own life.

The fourth is a picture in real life, a youth whose clear eyes picture the strength of young manhood and the purity of the life he has led. What more beautiful thing can one see in nature than that? We love beauty in womanhood; we also love handsomeness and strength in young manhood; and that strength and handsomeness come as a result of true living.—CR, October 1926, p. 112.

THE CONTROL OF APPETITE

NATURE OF THE PROBLEM. Appetite is a God-given quality. Blessed are they who have a good appetite. But to gormandize is injurious. And that brings me to one general statement, that most of our troubles here in this life in trying to subdue nature and subduing our appetites all come within the question of limitation. Many things are right, up to a certain point, and beyond that they become evils or vices.

A THREEFOLD CLASSIFICATION. Latter-day Saints should learn to control, to live within that proper limit; for example, and I shall just state it briefly, all evils may be classified into three groups, the first designated by those of which Paul says, "Let him that stole steal no more." (Eph. 4:28.) Exclude them from life entirely; stealing, lying, sinning sexually, murder, all those sins which should never be committed constitute this class. Never do them—there is no justification.

In the second group are jealousy, hatred, envy, animosity —all such evils you must overcome by suppression. That is where your control comes in. Suppress that anger! Suppress that jealousy, that envy! They are all injurious to the spirit anyhow.

Then there is a third, and in that third group we find nearly all our difficulties, those things which are virtues up to a certain point, and beyond that point they become vices. I mentioned one—appetite. It is a virtue. It is a guide to you, but if you gormandize in food, you injure your body, you frustrate God's plan. Your appetite becomes depraved, corrupt, and it becomes an enemy to you. Our passions are virtues to perpetuate life. Prostitute them, and you have the vilest of sins!

So the whole lesson is one of subduing, not just physical matter, that you might realize the ideal, but subduing your own passions and appetites, and conquering them. Some of you say we hear too much about keeping the Word of Wisdom. Why, it is one of the best lessons for the young in all this world, and for the old! You reach out to indulge in certain things. Resist, avoid creating an appetite for that which creates an appetite for itself. But beyond that, you develop the power to say, "No, thank you." And the strength that comes to the character more than compensates for any immediate pleasure.—*DNCS*, September 6, 1952, p. 15.

SELF-MASTERY. I commend to you, young man and young woman, the virtue of self-mastery, if you would fulfil the true measure of your life in subduing, in order to realize the ideal, the spiritual development of your soul.—*DNCS*, September 6, 1952, p. 15.

COURAGE. It is easy enough to do right when in good company, but it is not easy to defend the right when the majority of the crowd are opposing it; and yet, that is the time to show true courage.—*AA*, p. 185.

CHARACTER BUILDING—THE PURPOSE OF RELIGION

THE DEVELOPMENT OF CHRISTIAN CHARACTER. What is the end and purpose of religion, swaying the lives of men the centuries through? The Latter-day Saints answer in the words of the Lord revealed through the Prophet Joseph, that the end and purpose of true religion, which is the work of God, is " . . . to bring to pass the immortality and eternal life of man." (Moses 1:39.)—*CR*, October 1926, p. 111.

The house is not the family. The wind may tear the roof off, blow out the windows; the hurricane may even sweep the house away; but the family remains, that which makes the home. Nor is the body the life itself. It is but the house in which the spirit lives. Sickness may waste the body, but the true life is the spirit within, that which thinks and feels and loves and suffers and wills and chooses, aspires, and achieves. The purpose in life is to beautify, ornament, develop that something within. To develop a more radiant and lovely character is the true purpose in life.—*FS*, ms., Mrs. Emma Nelson Felt, December 19, 1945.

THE TWO METHODS. There are two ways in which character is built in our Church. One is positive. In that positive development we ask young men and young women to participate in the various organizations and the quorums of priesthood.

Now there is alongside these positive means a negative means. All through life the Latter-day Saint child is asked to refrain from indulgence in things that will tend to weaken character.—*CR*, October 1926, pp. 112-113.

RELIGIOUS CHARACTER AND CIVILIZATION. Pure religion gives one power to rise above the selfish, sensual, sordid life of what Eucken calls pure nature, and enables one to "experience a divinity in life above and beyond the world of sensible reality."

"Without this religion," this philosopher continues, "no true civilization is possible. A civilization declining all contact with a supernatural life and refusing to establish those mysterious inner relations, gradually becomes a parody of civilization."—*CR*, October 1937, pp. 100-101.

How THE CHURCH CONTRIBUTES TO CHARACTER BUILDING. In the changing of men's lives the Church recognizes certain fundamental factors so essentially important that they are constantly called to our attention; for example, recognizing the reality of the divine edict "visiting the iniquity of the fathers upon the children unto the third and fourth generation . . . " (Ex. 20:5) the Church emphasizes the necessity of moral and physical fitness for parenthood. Hence, the constant plea that young men and women live clean, chaste lives prior to their assuming the responsibility of marriage, and their remaining true to that sacred covenant. Hence is constantly held before us the ideal of temple marriage, where the sanctity of the marriage covenant is sealed and ratified by the highest divine authority given of God to man. Hence, the emphasis laid upon the Word of Wisdom wherein tobacco, stimulants, and narcotics are eschewed, and temperance and obedience to the laws of health encouraged and admonished. Hence the belief from childhood in being " . . . honest, true, chaste, benevolent, virtuous, and in doing good to all men." (Articles of Faith No. 13.)

The Church, recognizing the potency of other influences besides the home in the growing child's life before he reaches self-determination, offers a religious environment almost from the time of birth. The Sunday School, the Primary, the Mutual Improvement Associations arrange suitable instruction, entertainment, and proper guidance from the cradle roll to maturity.—*CR*, April 1941, pp. 106-107.

IT IS THE LITTLE THINGS THAT COUNT. There is no one great thing which we can give a child which will determine his future any more than there was any one great thing which the rich young ruler could do to obtain eternal life, but there are many little things. As a child grows physically by eating regularly at intervals, by breathing fresh air constantly, by resting at stated intervals, so character is built by little things, by daily contacts, by an influence here, a fact or truth there. —*I*, 81:161 (1946).

HONESTY AND GENUINE CONVERSION. The man or woman who keeps the Word of Wisdom is true to himself or herself. The man who is honest with his God in paying his tithes and offerings is usually honest with his fellow men.—*IE,* 47:720 (1944).

Man's greatest need is real conversion to the eternal truths of the gospel—to the truth that Jesus Christ came to give life and light to the human family. I feel that with all my soul.—*CR,* October 1951, p. 11.

The real test of any church or religion is the kind of men it makes.—*CR,* April 1949, p. 11.

Chapter 27

The Word Of Wisdom

HEALTH OF BODY AND SPIRIT

THE RAVAGES OF PHYSICAL DISEASE. There are many things that attack the vitality of the body. We expose ourselves to disease; it gets into an organ that is somewhat impaired; then the ravages of disease weaken that and impair other organs, the result being that the body succumbs to the attack. Only the other day, a brother and I were called to administer to a woman, a mother. Two weeks ago she was healthy and strong, a beautiful young woman. She exposed herself—not needlessly, either—by going to a place where the water was impregnated with typhoid germs. Those germs entered her system and attacked the organs of her body. One organ after another became impaired and deranged, and when we reached her bedside, we found that she was literally poisoned by the ravages of that disease. If you had heard her husband's prayer, as he knelt by the bedside, pleading with God to abate that fever, to restore his wife to him and to the two little children, your hearts would have been touched as ours were, and your faith would have been exercised, as ours was, that she might be restored, the ravages of the disease be counteracted, that she might again enjoy good health and strength.

THE PERIL OF SPIRITUAL DECAY. Bodily ailments deprive us of the full exercise of our faculties and privileges and sometimes of life itself. It is necessary, therefore, to take care of the body. But, great as is the peril of physical decay, greater, far greater, is the peril of spiritual decay. The peril of this century is spiritual apathy. As the body requires sunlight, good food, proper exercise, and rest, so the spirit of man requires the sunlight of the Holy Spirit; proper exercise of the spiritual functions; avoiding of evils that affect spiritual health, which are more ravaging in their effects than typhoid fever, pneumonia, or other diseases that attack the body. These diseases may stop the manifestations of life in the body, but the spirit still lives. When disease of the spirit conquers, the life dies eternally. Such an extreme spiritual disease would, of necessity, be an unpardonable sin.

SYMPTOMS OF SPIRITUAL DISEASE. When men get spiritually sick, they do not care much for religion. They think it not necessary for them to attend to their spiritual wants. Dissatisfied with themselves, they find fault with those who do enjoy the true life of spirituality. Why? Because they don't know what real spiritual life is. Their bodies are succumbing to the diseases that are attacking the spirit. How? Why, in many ways. Those boys who sat in the rear room of a saloon, playing cards for hours, drinking whiskey or beer, profaning the name of God—invited into their souls a malady that is more fatal than typhoid fever or any other disease that can attack the body. Their spiritual life was being deranged; it is deranged. Though the mothers did not detect, when their boys came home that night, just how deeply imbedded were the germs of that spiritual disease, the germs were there, and those boys' spirits were poisoned. This condition keeps them from Sabbath school the next Sunday; it keeps them from their quorum meetings during the week; it keeps them from the Mutual Improvement Association; they have not the life, the moral strength to go to these places for spiritual sunlight and the healthful exercise of the spirit.

The man who hates his brother, and kneels down for prayer with that hate in his heart, has in his spirit a disease that will impair his spiritual life. The man who cheats his neighbor—I care not whether anybody knows it or not, he knows it (remember it is the real growth we are speaking of)—the man who takes advantage of a brother is weakening his spirituality. He cannot enjoy true growth in this Church, so long as he harbors that dishonest sentiment. The man who steals is inviting into his soul that which will prevent him from growing to the perfect stature of Christ. The man who fails in any way to live up to that which God and conscience tell him is right is weakening his spirituality—in other words, is depriving himself of the sunlight in which his spiritual nature will grow.

REPENTANCE—THE GREAT REMEDY. Let us then, as individuals, grow from within; be men of God, pure within, repentant; for no man can gain salvation unless he repents of his sins. No matter where we are, no matter what people outside of this Church may think of us, no matter what the ministers of the world may say, we are what our inner life makes us, what God knows we are.—CR, October 1907, pp. 61-63.

STRENGTH AND BEAUTY OF BODY. To boys I would say, that if they want to live physically, if they want to be men strong in body, vigorous in mind, if they want to be good sports, enter the basketball game, enter the football game, enter the contest in running and jumping, if they want to be good Scouts, if they want to be good citizens, in business, anywhere, avoid tobacco and live strictly the religious life. I am not afraid to call it the religious life to them. It is not a thing that will make them gloomy and sad. Live the gospel of Jesus Christ, for it is the science of life revealed from on high.—CR, October 1920, p. 45.

How much more beautiful is that woman who has natural beauty because of true growth, because of the working harmoniously together of all the organs of the body to foster and build up the demands, the needs of nature, than she who, plastering the outside, tries to get beauty from without. The latter cannot be compared to that beauty which comes from true growth and which results from the healthy condition of every organ of the body. How strong is that man, how admirable in structure, who has health throughout his body, whose organs are in good condition! The healthy man, who takes care of his physical being, has strength and vitality; his temple, if you please, is a fit place for his spirit to reside in.—CR, October 1907, p. 61.

HUMAN USE OF TOBACCO AND ALCOHOL

"EVILS AND DESIGNS." One of the most significant statements in the Doctrine and Covenants, one which carries with it evidence of the inspiration of the Prophet Joseph Smith, is found in the 89th section:

"In consequence of evils and designs which do and will exist in the hearts of conspiring men in the last days, I have warned you, and forewarn you, by giving unto you this word of wisdom by revelation." (D. & C. 89:4.)

"Evils and designs which do and will exist in the hearts of conspiring men. . . . " The purport of that impressed me in the twenties and the thirties of this century. I ask you to recall the methods employed by certain tobacco interests to induce women to smoke cigarets.

You remember how insidiously they launched their plan: First, by saying that it would reduce weight. They had a slogan: "Take a cigaret instead of a sweet."

Later, some of us who like the theater noticed that they would have a young lady light the gentleman's cigaret. Following this a woman's hand would be shown on billboards lighting or taking a cigaret. A year or two passed, and soon they were brazen enough to show the lady on the screen or on the billboard smoking the cigaret.

I find here a clipping which I set aside in the early thirties, which corroborates this idea. This is 1931:

"It is well-known that the cigaret manufacturers are after the young women and girls, now. They say there are twenty-five million of these in the United States, and if they can popularize smoking among them, they will be able to increase their sales from three billions, six hundred million dollars annually to six billion dollars. This is their claim and their aim."

Now, it is common to see beautiful young women depicted on billboards and in the popular journals advertising certain brands of cigarets.

I may be wrong, but I thought I saw an indication recently that *conspiring* men now have evil designs upon our youth. Keep your eyes and ears open, to observe if they are not taking the same steps now to get our young men as they did to entice women to use that vile weed.—*CR*, Sept.-Oct. 1949, pp. 185-187.

"STRONG DRINK . . . IS NOT GOOD." On the 27th of February, 1833, the Prophet Joseph Smith received the revelation recorded in the eighty-ninth section of the Doctrine and Covenants. I want to read a few paragraphs from that section:

"Behold, verily, thus saith the Lord unto you: In consequence of evils and designs which do and will exist in the hearts of conspiring men in the last days, I have warned you, and forewarn you, by giving unto you this word of wisdom by revelation—

"That inasmuch as any man drinketh wine or strong drink among you, behold it is not good, neither meet in the sight of your Father, only in assembling yourselves together to offer up your sacraments before him.

"And, behold, this should be wine, yea, pure wine of the grape of the vine, of your own make." (D. & C. 89:4-6.)

The particular sentence to which I wish to call attention is this: " . . . inasmuch as any man drinketh wine or strong drink . . . behold *it is not good,* neither meet in the sight of your Father." That is the word of God to the people of this generation. It stands with just as much force as the words of the Savior, "If any man will do his will, he shall know of the doctrine, whether it be of God, or whether I speak of myself." (John 7:17.) Latter-day Saints, you know this statement of the Savior's is true; we testify that if any man will do the will of God he will get the testimony, in his heart and in his life, that the gospel of Jesus Christ is true. We accept the words of the Savior, " . . . except ye repent, ye shall all likewise perish." (Luke 13:3.) Those eternal truths, so tersely expressed, we accept as true. We may not live up to them wholly, but as a people we accept them, because they are the word of God. Just so strong, just so eternal stands this truth: Strong drink is not good for man. Yet many years have passed, and during that time this doctrine has been preached every week, if not every day, in some congregation of Israel, and still we find in our midst a few who say, by their acts, it is good for man.

I am glad when I study this passage, to find that the Lord did not say, "Strong drink *to excess* is not good"; nor "Drunkenness is not good." Suppose he had weakened that expression by modifying it and saying, "Strong drink in excess, or when taken in large quantities, is not good," how soon we should have justified ourselves that a little drink is good. But like other eternal truths it stands unqualified; strong drink is not good.

I have met men, particularly during the agitation that is now manifested against the liquor evil, who have said: "I do not want to be deprived of the privilege of taking a little, if I want it. When I think it is going to do me good, I want to take it." Others, I rather think, would say that the Church is a little too strict in regard to the Word of Wisdom: "A little beer," they say, "does not harm anyone; a little wine is not injurious." Well, it is sufficient for me to know that God has said, "Wine, strong drink, is not good for man"; and I wish that all members of the Church would accept that divine statement and prove in their lives to the whole world that they accept this as a revelation from God. That is the best way to close saloons in your towns. It is the most effective.—CR, April 1911, p. 61.

"TOBACCO . . . IS NOT GOOD FOR MAN." I think tobacco is a vice which should be shunned as the bite of a rattlesnake. When I say that, I am not unaware of the fact that though seemingly there are some young men who can use tobacco without serious injury, there are many others who are poisoned, their characters weakened, and their health undermined by the ingredients of the cigaret. The Lord has said that tobacco is not good for man. That should be sufficient for Latter-day Saints.

Too many of our boys are tampering with cigarets. I do not like to hear tobacco programs on the radio. Young people say: "Well, they are the best we have." Of course they are, because tobacco interests can pay the highest salaries and get the best actors and singers to further their evil designs.—CR, September-October 1949, p. 188.

TOBACCO AND LUNG CANCER. Recently there came to this city a gentleman who has been specializing on cancer, Dr. E. L. Winder, Department of Surgery, Washington University School of Medicine, St. Louis, Missouri. He is attached to the National Cancer Foundation and is one of the most eminent men in cancer treatment in the country.

He came to the laboratory in which Dr. George R. Hill, Jr., works, because the company who employs him had published a paper on arsenic content of tobacco smoke. This gentleman stated that he had come to Utah to make a study of lung cancer since he had heard that cigaret smoking is appreciably lower in Utah than in any other state, "because

Mormons do not smoke." He reports that lung cancer, virtually unknown a hundred years ago, and occurring only rarely in 1912, is today taking the lives of more men than any other type of cancer. More than twenty percent of the cancers attributed to men are lung cancers. They have been endeavoring to determine why this increase in lung cancer and have found the answer—cigaret smoking.

He has personally investigated over five hundred cases of lung cancer and says that in every case but four, these men have been smoking cigarets, from one pack to two packs a day, for some twenty to thirty years. And then he adds: "That percentage is far too great to be meaningless."

He says that the average patient of lung cancer dies at fifty-two years of age and that the average lung cancer lasts only thirteen months before proving fatal.

He interviewed eleven or twelve Mormons who call themselves "Jack-Mormons," having lung cancer, and found them in every case but one, a man seventy-four years of age, to be heavy smokers.

Dr. Hill asked him if he had found similar cases among women. The doctor answered, "No, but I look for a very great increase in lung cancer among women in the next ten or fifteen years."—*CR*, September-October 1949, p. 189.

TOBACCO, LIQUOR, AND DELINQUENCY. I have been favored recently in receiving a monthly report of the young people who are arrested in Salt Lake County. Note from the following how many delinquents are users of tobacco:[1]

January there were ninety-four fingerprinted. Eighty of these were tobacco users, and sixty-eight used liquor.

February there were seventy-one fingerprinted. Fifty-six used tobacco, and fifty-one drank liquor.

March, eighty-eight. Seventy-eight tobacco users, and seventy-four drinkers.

April, there were 104. Eighty-seven used tobacco, eighty-six used liquor.

May, ninety-three. Seventy-five tobacco, sixty-seven liquor.

---

[1] 1949.

June, ninety-four.   Ninety-two tobacco users, eighty-six liquor.

July, 106.   Ninety-four tobacco users, eighty-eight liquor.

Out of the 650, 562 used tobacco; 520 drank liquor.—*CR,* September-October 1949, pp. 188-189.

RESULTS OF ALCOHOLISM.   A young man who, addicted to drink, became an alcoholic and finally took his own life in a New York hotel, left his last will and testament as follows:

"I leave to society a ruined character.   I leave to my parents as much misery as they can bear.   I leave to my brothers and sisters the memory of a misspent life.   I leave to my wife a broken heart.   I leave to my children the memory of a drunkard's name."

James L. Gordon, by whom this is quoted, says this ought to be written on the memory of every youth who is prone to say to himself, "I can drink, and I can let it alone." —*CR,* September-October 1949, p. 190.

TOBACCO AND HUMAN EFFICIENCY.   I have faith in our boys, because most of them are going out from homes radiating the principles of life and salvation.   Boys who hitherto have been somewhat indifferent before they enlisted have said, "Father, I am going to get a blessing from the patriarch," thus filling the father's heart with joy, for he knew that in that blessing the admonition would be renewed for him to conserve his manhood by keeping the Word of Wisdom and by keeping his body unstained by grosser evils.

Why, isn't it folly, when you think of it, for men to be starting a campaign to send out tobacco to our soldiers, when in 1900, the nation of Japan passed a law prohibiting the use of tobacco among the young people, principally because America had proved its injurious effects upon youth?   Why did the parliament at Tokyo pass such a law and send it as a decree from the emperor?   Because about twelve years preceding that, a professor of Yale University had made some interesting examinations among his students.   He had measured their height when they came; he had measured their chest girth and taken their weight.   He asked their age and found out, best of all, how many of them used tobacco and how many did not. Then he watched their development, and after nine years he published the results. In the first place he learned that the smokers were about fifteen months older than the nonsmokers. Second, notwithstanding that older age, the average height of the nonsmokers was about one-third of an inch more than the smokers. Then at the end of nine years he tabulated the following, based upon his observations among three classes: (1) The smokers who had smoked one year or more, (2) those who had smoked irregularly, and (3) those who had not used tobacco. In weight, those who had not used tobacco were 10.4 percent more than those who had used it a year or more; 6.6 percent more than those who had used it irregularly; in height, the nonsmokers had gained 24 percent over those who smoked one year or more; 11 percent over those who smoked irregularly. In girth, 26.7 percent more than those who smoked a year or more; 22 percent more than those who smoked irregularly. The lung capacity, 77 percent increase over those who smoked a year or more; 49 percent over those who smoked irregularly. Such were the physical gains. In intellectual gain he discovered that out of every one hundred of the students who had stood at the head of their classes, only five were smokers, ninety-five, nonsmokers, although sixty out of every hundred used tobacco. That is in keeping with the tests made in Harvard, where the examination of the records for fifty years proved that during those fifty years, not one smoker had stood at the head of his class, although 83 percent of the boys who entered Harvard were indulging in the use of tobacco. Eighty-three percent in the smoking group, and 17 percent in the nonsmoking group, and during that fifty years the heads of the classes were chosen from the 17 percent group.

Such facts were sufficient to influence the members of the parliament of Japan to pass a law in March 1900, to be effective April 1, 1900, as follows: "The smoking of tobacco by minors under the age of twenty is prohibited."—CR, October 1917, pp. 59-60.

"NATION-WIDE NUISANCE NUMBER ONE." It is not uncommon now to see bureaus, dressing tables, desks, mantels, and other pieces of furniture in first-class hotels marred by cigaret burns. Ashes litter costly carpets. Railroad stations, theater and hotel lobbies are littered with burnt-out matches, stubs of cigarets, and cigars. Smoking has become our nation-wide nuisance number one. If men and women must smoke, and it seems that many are now slaves to that habit, then for the sake of cleanliness and neatness and pride of our country, as well as of consideration for others, let them refrain from marring furniture and from strewing ashes and burnt-out matches and cigaret stubs in buildings where people assemble either for pleasure or instruction. Because of thoughtlessness in this regard, many of our public places are as littered as unkept barns.

I appeal to young men and women of the Church to refrain from this obnoxious habit. To bishops, I would say: Choose no person to act either as an officer or teacher in your quorums or auxiliaries who is guilty of using tobacco. If teachers cannot teach by example, their precepts will be " . . . as sounding brass, or a tinkling cymbal." (I Cor. 13:1.) —CR, April 1943, p. 20.

How to Stop Smoking. I heard today of a man who would like to join the Church, and he is going to as soon as he can overcome that habit of smoking. Surely he can overcome it. He can do as Brother Eli did, the first man with whom I went teaching. I heard him tell Harvey Brown, "I put my pipe upon the shelf, and I said 'I'll never touch it again.'" Then he added, "I never have."—DNCS, August 8, 1951.

PROHIBITION AS PUBLIC POLICY

The Question of Repeal of the Eighteenth Amendment (1933). I should like to say a few words regarding a great question that is related to the general theme of this conference. Our nation is facing it, and we as part of that nation must express ourselves regarding it. I have in mind the question of the repeal of the Eighteenth Amendment to the Constitution of the United States.

"Once to every man and nation comes the moment to
decide,
In the strife of Truth with Falsehood, for the good or
evil side;
Some great cause, God's new Messiah, offering each
the bloom or blight,

> Parts the goats upon the left hand, and the sheep
>   upon the right,
> And the choice goes by forever 'twixt that darkness
>   and that light."
>
> James Russell Lowell, *The Present Crisis.*

When James Russell Lowell wrote those lines, he had
in mind the great problem of slavery—"The earth-born
Cyclops, fellest of the giant brood." In that issue the people
of the United States chose sides, and the struggle, though
bitter and tragic, ended in driving one form of slavery from
our shores forever.

Today the liquor question, another earthborn giant,
stalks through the land, and the question of how best to
shackle him is now put squarely before the people.

Fewer than fifteen years have passed since the Eighteenth
Amendment was ratified by the largest number of states and
by the largest percentage of states that ever ratified any amendment to the Constitution in the entire history of our country.

That action was taken as the cumulative result of several
hundred years' experience with the evils of the liquor traffic.
Now after a little more than a decade of prohibition, because
of a few difficulties in enforcement, many people cry for a
return to old conditions. It was just such sudden changes
in the public opinion and acclaim that made James Fitz James
cry out:

> "Thou many-headed monster thing,
> O who would wish to be thy king!"
> Sir Walter Scott, *Lady of the Lake.*

This reversal of sentiment is due in general to one of two
conditions—perhaps both. Either prohibition has failed to
achieve the results anticipated, or the people finding themselves in such desperate financial straits are being swept off
their feet in their eagerness to grasp anything which offers
relief.

When the world war broke out, many men cried, "Christianity has failed." Just as they now cry, "Prohibition has
failed." Others answered then that Christianity had never
been tried, that it was the violation of Christian principles

that brought on the war. So we answer today: Prohibition has not failed; it has not been sufficiently tested. If public sentiment is against it, prohibition cannot be enforced, but if the majority of people favor it, it can be enforced. Now we are engaged in the struggle to test that sentiment.

THE CASE FOR PROHIBITION. Three reasons why the Eighteenth Amendment should not be repealed:

Because prohibition is the most effective means of dealing with the liquor evil. I believe that the results of honest investigation and unbiased observation prove the truth of this assertion; for example, arrests for drunkenness in fifty leading cities, statistics of which were collected by a judge of the Municipal Court of Chicago, fell from 302,071 in 1917 to 110,149 in 1920—a decrease of 63 percent.

Mr. Robert Carradini made a survey of 185 cities, the complete statistics of which show that the average annual number of arrests for intoxication per thousand of population in the four years preceding 1917 was 23.4 percent and that number in 1920 had fallen to 8.7 percent, a reduction of 62 percent.

Figures presented before the sub-committee of the Committee on Judiciary, United States Senate, April 1926, showed data covering statistics in 626 cities from 1917 to 1920. The number of arrests for drunkenness in all these 626 cities was less than 36 percent as great in 1920 as in 1917. From the same authority we learn that prison commitments decreased 59 percent, and there was a decrease of crime of over 40 percent.

It is true that since that time anti-prohibitionists can cite statistics showing: (1) an increase of arrests for drunkenness since 1920, (2) an increase of deaths from alcoholism since 1920, (3) an increase in insanity since 1920. They can show further that in 1924 the arrests for drunkenness were double what they were in 1920, but even then they were less than three-fourths of what they were before prohibition.

MORAL AND ECONOMIC BENEFITS OF PROHIBITION. Early in 1922 the Manufacturers' *Record* sent a questionnaire to hundreds of leading men of affairs including large manufacturers, employers of labor, bankers, and university professors asking their judgment about prohibition. Ninety-eight and one-half percent favored prohibition in some form. Some of the moral and economic benefits as they appeared to these men follow:

Happier homes with more contentment. Cleaner and better social life.

Increased purchasing power of homes, food, and clothes for women and children.

A change in the habits and expenditures of the workers. Men are buying their own homes, have savings accounts, and own automobiles.

A tendency toward thrift, contentment, comfort, and happiness. Families better cared for, and increased savings deposits.

More and cleaner recreation. Picture shows, parks, outdoor excursions.

Less loss of time. Fewer accidents, less incompetence, less carelessness, less inefficiency, better work, better homes.

Children and young people getting a better education. School attendance improved. Public and Sunday School. Improvement in community morale.

An incalculable economic and moral blessing to millions of our people and to the nation as a whole.

THE FUNDAMENTAL PRINCIPLE IN INDIVIDUAL GOVERNMENT. In my advocacy for prohibition I keep ever in mind the importance of that great principle which Joseph Smith enunciated when he was asked how he governed his people so well. He answered: "I teach the people correct principles, and they govern themselves." That is the fundamental principle in the United States in individual government, and when an individual becomes converted to a condition, he can live up to it. When we get the majority of the people converted to a condition that will favor temperance, the law will be enforced.

But there is another condition, also. We are living in a democracy. The majority of the people determine the kind of laws by which the people should be governed. That being true we are now facing a proposition to determine what the majority of the people desire. I believe that the American people desire temperance. I have given one reason why I think that the retention of the Eighteenth Amendment will foster and favor temperance.

REPEAL A STEP BACKWARD. There is a second reason which I will just name and that is the proposed amendment offers no new remedy for existing evils. If the Twenty-first Amendment is ratified, the question of prohibition is thrown back upon the states and is one step backward in the cause of temperance. The smaller the prohibitive area, the greater the difficulty of enforcement; the wider the area, the more effective the enforcement.

You who were on the firing line in this prohibition fight will remember how we first began to make towns dry, then counties, then states, and finally the question was made nation-wide. Now to change and go into the states as proposed by the Twenty-first Amendment is merely to take a step backward.

NEED OF MORE SPIRITUALITY. A third reason for my opposing the repeal of the Eighteenth Amendment is this:

The world today perhaps as never before needs more spirituality. Booze and depravity mingle together harmoniously, but booze and spirituality, never.

In an excellent editorial one of our daily papers impressively said: "Excessive materialism stands indicted in the minds of men. There needs to be inaugurated a new era of mutual accord, a return to an appreciation of the finer things of life, to the basic principles of human existence."

No one will contend that intoxicating liquors contribute spirituality either to the individual or to the nation. Nearly everyone concedes that intoxicants develop the baser, not the finer, things of life.

Sixteen years ago there was a terrific battle being waged at Verdun. On June 7, 1916, the French vacated the city Damloup under the hill on which Fort Vaux was situated. The defense of this fort was one of outstanding heroism, and Major Raynal, the commander, was treated with every honor as a prisoner of the Germans.

Fort Vaux had fallen, and other outer lines were broken through, but there was an inner circle of defense that was invincible. The words of General Petain, "They shall not pass," thrilled the heart and nerved the arm of every French soldier. For more than two long months the Germans hammered and battered at that inner defense in the most terrific conflict in the annals of war. In the last desperate assault of the Crown Prince, 40,000 German soldiers were slaughtered in a hopeless effort to break through the French curtain of fire. The inner circle of defense was impregnable. The main line held.

Today we witness the legalization of beer by the United States government. One of our outer defenses has fallen, and the enemy spurred on by victory will attack others. But the inner defense, the Eighteenth Amendment, must be defended at all costs. Let the words of General Petain, "They shall not pass," strengthen every heart and nerve every hand in defense of this part of the Constitution of the United States.

In addition to the fact that we believe that prohibition is the best means of fighting the evil, that the proposal of the Twenty-first Amendment offers no other remedy which we do not have, and that the cause of spirituality demands that we retain it, I will add in conclusion this thought:

Out of the high plane of spirituality comes the message from the President of the Church given to the world that intoxicating liquors, strong drink, and tobacco are not good for man. That is God's word given authoritatively, and on that truth we stand.—CR, April 1933, pp. 90-94.

OBSERVANCE OF THE WORD OF WISDOM

THE STATEMENT OF HYRUM SMITH IN 1843. In the early history of the Church, there were members who tried to justify the use of tea and coffee by the fact that these beverages are not specified in the revelation, and even today there are people who sing this same lullaby to their conscience. On these points the statement of Hyrum Smith, the Patriarch, is most pertinent. In a sermon on the Word of Wisdom, delivered in the year 1842, he said:

" . . . Tobacco is a nauseous, stinking, abominable thing, and I am surprised that any human being should think of using it. For an elder especially to eat, or smoke it, is a disgrace to him;—he is not fit for the office, he ought first to learn to keep the word of wisdom, and then to teach others.

God will not prosper the man who uses it. And again, 'hot drinks are not for the body, or belly.' There are many who wonder what this can mean, whether it refers to tea or coffee, or not. I say it does refer to *tea* and *coffee*. . . . "*

HIGH COUNCIL MINUTES OF 1834. For the benefit of those who might still seek cover under the fact that these were Hyrum's and not the Prophet's words and also for the information of those who harp on the *non-commandment* theme, we submit the following extract from the minutes of a meeting of the high council, held at Kirtland February 20, 1834. President Joseph Smith (the Prophet) presided, and opened the council by prayer.

"At a Church meeting, held in Pennsylvania, Erie County . . . some of the members of that Church refused to partake of the sacrament, because the elder administering it did not observe the Word of Wisdom to obey it. Elder Johnson argued that they were justified in so doing, because the elder was in transgression. Elder Pratt argued that the Church was bound to receive the Supper under the administration of an elder, so long as he retained his office or license. . . .

"The council then proceeded to try the question, whether disobedience to the Word of Wisdom was a transgression sufficient to deprive an official member from holding office in the Church, after having it sufficiently taught him. . . .

"After the Councilors had spoken, the President proceeded to give the decision:

"No official member of this Church is worthy to hold an office, after having the Word of Wisdom properly taught him, and he, the official member, neglecting to comply with or obey it; which decision the council confirmed by vote." (*History of the Church*, Vol. 2, pp. 34-35.)

MODERN LAXITY. Members of the Church who have formed either the tobacco habit or the tea and coffee habit, or both, are prone to seek justification for their indulgences in things which the Lord has said plainly are not good for man. Whenever they try to do so, they only parade the weakness of their faith in the Lord's words, which were given as

---

*President Hyrum Smith, *Times and Seasons* III:800 (Issue of June 1, 1842).

admonition and "wisdom," and obedience to which will bring
blessing as certain and sure as if he had said, "Thou shalt not."

Furthermore, priests and elders addicted to the use of
tobacco or to tea and coffee, who administer the sacrament
of the Lord's supper, almost make a mockery of that sacred
ordinance.   How inconsistent it is for a man to "witness
before God the Eternal Father" that he is willing to take
upon him the name of the Redeemer, and "always remember
him," then within an hour or so after making such a solemn
statement and promise go and do that which the Lord says
he should not do! "And why call ye me, Lord, Lord, and do
not the things which I say?" (Luke 6:46.)

PRESIDENT HEBER J. GRANT'S TESTIMONY.   In the organized stakes of Zion, as well as in the mission field, there is al-
together too much laxity in regard to the observance of the
Word of Wisdom.   Too many members move along the lines
of least resistance and yield to a craving of appetite developed
by disobedience to the Word of Wisdom of God, thus depriving
themselves of spiritual as well as physical strength.   To the
prevalence of such indulgence President Grant referred in his
opening address at the recent semi-annual conference of the
Church.   He warned the people against such practices, emphasized the blessings promised to those who observe the Word
of Wisdom, and concluded that part of his sermon by the
following testimony:

"I wish to bear my witness here that I believe with
all my heart and soul that if I had not obeyed the Word of
Wisdom, if I had not kept these commandments, that I would
not be standing before you this day as the President of the
Church of Jesus Christ of Latter-day Saints."

There is a substance in tea and coffee which when taken
into the human system, tends to increase the beating of the
heart; which in turn increases the rapidity of the circulation
of the blood and of breathing.   This causes the body to become
warmer and more exhilarated.   After a time, however, this
temporary enlivenment passes off, and the body is really in a
greater need of rest and recuperation than it was before the
beverage was taken.   Stimulants are to the body what the
lash is to the lagging horse—it causes a spurt forward but
gives no permanent strength or natural nourishment.

Frequently repetitions of the lash only make the horse more lazy; and the habitual use of strong drink, tobacco, tea, and coffee, only tends to make the body weaker and more dependent upon the stimulants to which it is addicted.

The Lord has said in unmistakable words that these things are not good for man. Science declares the same. God's word alone should be sufficient for every true Latter-day Saint. —MS, 85:712-714 (1923).

TEACHING THE WORD OF WISDOM TO THE WORLD. From two or three different sources comes the information that a few members of the Church are not upholding wholeheartedly the high standard of the mission in regard to the Word of Wisdom. Some seem to think that the elders would do better to preach less about the blessings following abstinence from the indulgence in tea, coffee, and narcotics and to give more emphasis to other equally important principles of the gospel. There are even officers who arrogate to themselves the justification of continuing in office while they persist unreservedly in the obnoxious use of tobacco. "Would it not be better," writes one, "if the elders said less about the Word of Wisdom, and preached more about love, repentance, and the consequences of sin?"

The answer to this is very simple. These, they ought to teach, but not leave the other untaught. Neither the Church nor the world at large can hear too much about the Word of Wisdom. It is a doctrine given to man for man's happiness and benefit. It is part of the philosophy of living. It should be observed not only by every elder but also by every member of the Church. The elder who hesitates to teach it is shirking his duty. He who fails to live it robs himself of strength of body and strength of character to which he is entitled. Truth is loyalty to the right as we see it; it is courageous living of our lives in harmony with our ideals; it is always power. With the ideals of right living before him, no Latter-day Saint can continually violate the Word of Wisdom with impunity.

In this old world, the easiest way seems to be the indulgent way. If a person have the least desire or inclination to drink tea and coffee or to smoke tobacco, temptations to indulge the appetite are on every hand. At parties, during social calls, at chance introductions or friendly visits, in restaurants or trains, indulgence in these stimulants and narcotics is not only encouraged but also too often urged. Under such influence and environment, the easy way is to yield and become one of the crowd. But that is not the best way. One never develops character by yielding to wrong. "To him that *overcometh* will I give to eat of the tree of life. . . ." (Rev. 2:7.) Strength comes by resisting.

We are living not only in the commercial age, but also in the nicotine age, and viciously the cigaret habit is fastening itself upon the human race. Government statistics occasionally give us glimpses of the enormous strides that this insidious enemy to health and morals is making; but we little realize how active and potent are the forces at work to foster this and kindred vices—all for commercial gain. In "Habits that Handicap," Charles B. Towne explains how "salesmen and demonstrators," a few years ago, were employed by manufacturers to go throughout China "to show the people how to smoke cigarets." It is estimated that as a result of this campaign, one half of the cigaret consumption in the world is in China. It is little wonder, when we learn that because of cheap labor, twenty cigarets could be sold for a penny! The author also makes this remarkable statement:

"I consider that cigaret smoking is the greatest vice devastating humanity today because it is doing more than any other vice to deteriorate the race."

The voice of the Church will ever be raised against the increasing tendency among men and women to stain their lives with nicotine. Especially does it deplore this growing evil among women. Heretofore, virtuous Anglo-Saxon womanhood has been above this evil indulgence and has therefore been a restraining and uplifting influence on men. Now, this influence is being subjected to the insidious lure of the cigaret; and mothers of men, around whom center the sweetest, purest, noblest sentiments of our lives, are contaminating their sweetness and purity by indulgence in one of man's vices. The more woman becomes like man, the less he will respect her; civilization weakens as man's estimate of woman lessens.

True Latter-day Saint women never even think of smoking cigarets! That it is woman's *right* to indulge in this habit, we do not question; yet, we lose some of that sweet respect and admiration for women when we see them walk deliberately into mire holes that have heretofore besmeared only men. It is difficult to conceive proud and happy sons whose mothers' lives are stained with tobacco.

Elders hold their peace? Never! The Word of Wisdom is a vital part of the gospel, which is "the power of God unto salvation"—physical salvation as well as spiritual salvation.

The Church of Jesus Christ of Latter-day Saints stands committed unequivocally to the doctrine that tea, coffee, tobacco, and intoxicants are not good for man. True Latter-day Saints refrain from indulgence in tobacco and drink, either of stimulants or of intoxicants, and by example and precept, teach others to do the same.—*MS,* 86:648-649 (1924).

MAINTAINING STANDARDS. You know that too many of our girls today are indulging in nicotine. Designing men, by attractive, insidious advertising, are leading youth astray. Recently several young girls, some of whom are members of the Church, were playing cards, and nearly all of those present were smoking. One of the girls, who herself was smoking, said during the game while a cigaret was in her hand: "Next Sunday I begin to teach a Sunday School class. I am going into religion!"

A Catholic girl said to a Mormon girl who was not smoking: "I do not understand that. Your Church does not believe in smoking. Why is she appointed to teach a Sunday School class?"

"Well," said the Mormon girl, "you smoke."

"I know, but I am not teaching."

When that young girl was asked to teach a Sunday School class, I think some bishop erred! Young men and young woman whom we appoint to teach our children should be asked specific questions regarding their attitude toward the standards of the Church. I should not like to have any little grandchild of mine sit in a class Sunday morning and listen to a girl teach the Word of Wisdom, or any other principle of the gospel, and then have that grandchild see her teacher smoking a cigaret. A girl who accepts the responsibility of teaching, and who indulges in smoking and drinking, is guilty of hypocrisy, dishonesty of the worst kind.—*IE,* 47:720 (1944).

CHAPTER 28

OBEDIENCE TO LAW

THE TWELFTH ARTICLE OF FAITH

TEXT OF THE ARTICLE. Our twelfth Article of Faith says:

"We believe in being subject to kings, presidents, rulers, and magistrates, in obeying, honoring, and sustaining the law."

LAW AND THE COMMUNITY. Law, particularly in a democracy, is a system of social order established and enforced by society.

Divine law has its origin in deity; social law sprang primarily from the moral sense of the community. In a democracy in which the will of the people is sovereign, law is successfully operative only to the extent that the moral sense of the community is in sympathy with it.

The three significant words used in the twelfth Article of Faith express the proper attitude of the membership of the Church toward law. These words are *obey, honor,* and *sustain.*

SUSTAINING THE LAW. The article does not say we believe in submission to the law. Obedience implies a higher attitude than mere submission, for obedience has its root in good intent; submission may spring from selfishness or meanness of spirit. Though obedience and submission both imply restraint on one's own will, we are obedient only from a sense of right; submissive from a sense of necessity.

Honor expresses an act or attitude of an inferior towards a superior. When applied to things, it is taken in the sense of holding in honor. Thus, in honoring the law, we look upon it as something which is above selfish desires or indulgences.

To sustain signifies to hold up, to keep from falling. To sustain the law, therefore, is to refrain from saying or doing anything which will weaken it or make it ineffective.

We obey law from a sense of right.

We honor law because of its necessity and strength to society.

We sustain law by keeping it in good repute.—*CR*, April 1937, pp. 27-28.

THE LAW OF LIFE

Intelligent Obedience. We are all here to enjoy life in its fullest and most complete sense; but the message of the gospel of Jesus Christ is this: *that to live one must live in obedience to law, physical law, intellectual law, spiritual law. Transgression of law always brings unhappiness;* it always brings death when carried to the ultimate end.—*CR*, October 1920, p. 42.

Recently, a group of friends presented one of their number with a valuable, practical gift. In accepting it, the man said that wherever he might travel, the possession of that gift would be a constant reminder of his friends' affection and regard.

Brethren and sisters, all life is a gift of God. Appreciation of that fact should inspire us with a desire to live daily exemplary lives, that others, seeing our good deeds might be led to glorify our Father in heaven, of whose existence and inspiration I testify before you, and of the divinity of whose Church I bear testimony, in the name of Jesus Christ, our Redeemer.—*CR*, October 1951, p. 11.

Compensation and Retribution. Conformity to the Lord's word or law will invariably contribute to man's happiness and salvation. Those who do not what the Lord commands, we are told, will be subjected to justice and judgment. In other words, there is eternally operative in the moral world a law of compensation and retribution—compensation commensurate with conformity to law; retribution in actual degree to the extent of disobedience.

In this sense I use the word *law* as having a deeper significance than a rule or dictum prescribed by authority for human actions. It means, rather, a uniform order of sequence as operative and unvarying as the law of the inclined plane, or the law of falling bodies.

Confirmation of this may be found in the Lord's statement to Cain, the first disobedient son in history. "If thou

doest well, shalt thou not be accepted? and if thou doest not
well, sin lieth at the door. . . . " (Gen. 4:7.)

It is also stated by the Prophet Joseph Smith, "There is
a law, irrevocably decreed in heaven before the foundations of
this world, upon which all blessings are predicated—

"And when we obtain any blessing from God, it is by
obedience to that law upon which it is predicated." (D. & C.
130:20-21.)

It is said, parents, boys, and girls, that "the soul in the
formative period of youth, while it is yet unspotted from the
world, may be likened to a block of pure, uncut Parian marble,
in which lie boundless possibilities of beauty or of deformity.
From the crude marble one will chisel a form of exquisite
grace and symmetry; another, a misshapen monstrosity, each
visualizing in the formless stone the conception of his brain.
Thus we are molded by our ideals."

Thoughts are the seeds of acts and precede them. Mere
compliance with the word of the Lord, without a corresponding
inward desire, will avail but little. Indeed, such outward
actions and pretending phrases may disclose hypocrisy, a sin
that Jesus most vehemently condemned.

"O generation of vipers," he exclaimed, "how can ye,
being evil, speak good things?" (Matt. 12:34.) The Savior's
constant desire and effort were to implant in the mind right
thoughts, pure motives, noble ideals, knowing full well that
right words and actions would eventually follow. He taught
what modern physiology and psychology confirm—that hate,
jealousy, and other evil passions destroy a man's physical
vigor and efficiency. "They pervert his mental perceptions
and render him incapable of resisting the temptation to commit
acts of violence. They undermine his moral health. By
insidious stages they transform the man who cherishes them
into a criminal."

AN EXAMPLE FROM LITERATURE. Charles Dickens makes
impressive use of the above fact in his immortal story, *Oliver
Twist*, wherein Monks is introduced first as an innocent,
beautiful child; but as "ending his life as a mass of solid
bestiality, a mere chunk of fleshed iniquity. It was thinking
upon vice and vulgarity, that transformed the angel's face
into the countenance of a demon."

That great writer says this: "It is almost impossible to believe that such a devilish nature as Bill Sikes, depicted in the same book, could be found in human form," but Dickens says: "I fear there are in the world some insensible and callous natures that do become, at last, utterly and irredeemably bad. But whether this be true or not, of one thing I am certain—that there are such men as Sikes, who, being closely followed through the same space of time, and through the same current of circumstances, would not give by one look or action for a moment the faintest indication of a better nature. Whether every gentler human feeling is dead within such bosoms, or the proper chord to strike has rusted and is hard to find, I do not know, but the fact is so, I am sure."

I am trying to emphasize that each one is the architect of his own fate, and he is unfortunate, indeed, who will try to build himself without the inspiration of God, without realizing that he grows from within, not from without.——*CR,* October 1951, pp. 6-7.

No man can disobey the word of God and not suffer for so doing. No sin, however secret, can escape retribution. True, you may lie and not be detected; you may violate virtue without its being known by any who would scandalize you; yet you cannot escape the judgment that follows such transgression. The lie is lodged in the recesses of your mind, an impairment of your character that will be reflected sometime, somehow in your countenance or bearing. Your moral turpitude, though only you, your accomplice, and God may ever know it, will canker your soul.—*IE,* 44:395 (1941).

SELF-CONTROL. The lesson of self-control should begin in childhood, in the home. Little children should have a sense of freedom to do as they wish up to a certain point. Beyond that point they cannot go, and that is when that freedom interferes with the rights, comfort, or convenience of another member of the family.—*CR,* September-October 1950, p. 165.

PRACTICAL PROBLEMS

DISRESPECT FOR LAW. One of the principal functions of religion is to develop a sense of confidence in man and faith in God as the Father of men. If the Church of Jesus Christ cannot do these things, then it will have failed in fulfilling its

divine destiny. However, in efforts to establish confidence in
man and social institutions, we must not shut from our minds
certain unpleasant facts which tend to undermine confidence
and disintegrate the very foundation upon which society
is built.

Disrespect for law is among the worst of such evils. It is
regrettable that the United States today has the reputation
of being one of the most lawless of nations. This unsavory
reputation is attributed largely to the shattering during World
War I of long-cherished ideals and the lowering of moral
standards; and it is true that the war was in every respect a
vast school of demoralization. Every rule of morality, public
and private, was openly infringed.

There are those who blame prohibition for the wave of
lawlessness that has been sweeping over the country, but since
the repeal, the illicit traffic in booze still continues unabated.
Drunkenness is increasing, and so is the number of intoxicated
drivers who imperil the lives of innocent people on the public
highway. In the use of tobacco the law is flagrantly violated
and dishonored.

Note the following: "Any person who sells, gives, or
furnishes any cigar, cigaret, or tobacco in any form, or any
opium or other narcotic in any form to any person under
twenty-one years of age is guilty of a misdemeanor." And
again, "Any person under the age of twenty-one years who
buys, accepts, or has in his possession any cigar, cigaret, or
tobacco in any form, or opium or any other narcotic in any
form is guilty of a misdemeanor or shall be deemed a delinquent child as the case may be."

VIOLATIONS BODE ILL FOR SOCIETY. It augurs ill for society when in the face of such a law on the statute books,
many high school boys from fifteen to nineteen years of age
indulge openly in this pernicious habit. That such violations
occur constantly in our own community, none can deny.

Petty thefts, holdups, and robberies of various kinds and
degrees are all too common.

Illegal possession of corporate property is a new menace.
Millions of dollars are being lost to laborers, and bitter animosities engendered by sit-down strikes, a new weapon in the
hands of unionism which may prove a boomerang to honest

labor. If lawlessness or even disregard for the rights of employees on the part of employers is the cause of sit-down strikes, then the menace of such strife to the stability of society is only increased.

These things which I have merely named indicate the trend to disregard law and order. Of all crushing taxes that impede the economic recovery of the American people, the crime tax is the greatest.—CR, April 1937, pp. 28-29.

THE MANUFACTURE AND SALE OF LIQUOR. There is much being said now about the law prohibiting the manufacture and sale of liquor. Latter-day Saints should uphold that law everywhere, at socials, at banquets. Civil officers, members of clubs who are contributing to the formation of public opinion ought to be proud to uphold that law. It is a constitutional law, and it is time that the leaders of this country, the politicians, the statesmen, the leaders in civic affairs in the state and in the cities should so speak of this law, so act towards it, that public sentiment would be turned in favor of its enforcement.

Latter-day Saints, we are expected to uphold it and to uphold every other law which contributes to the advancement and peace of mankind. And these laws against the manufacture and sale of intoxicating liquors are such laws, and conditions now in society — with millions of automobiles, the drivers of which must be at their very best, active mentally, quick to respond physically in emergency—make it necessary that we eliminate from society anything that will becloud the brain or leave the driver's hand unsteady. We are living in a condition in which we cannot with impunity foster traffic in intoxicating liquors. God said long ago that they were not good for man. Our boys and girls, from the standpoint of integrity and consistency, should take a stand against the use thereof.—CR, October 1927, p. 14.

Chapter 29

Spirituality

THE NEED FOR SPIRITUAL RENAISSANCE

To Change the World.   Never before in the history of the world has there been such need as today of spiritual awakening: not that man is more depraved, not that he is less religious, but that he has in his grasp such seemingly unlimited mechanized power. If you put bombs into the hands of an inexperienced child, he is likely to blow himself to pieces; and, to a degree, that is just what we are witnessing in the world today.—*DNCS*, April 30, 1952, p. 3.

"Spiritual Renaissance and Improvement of Human Character."   I wonder if all these inventions during the past century have contributed to an increase in character, in honesty, in upright living, in a more sacred and reverent devotion to Christ and his gospel. I wonder whether the character of the men who are profiting by these wonderful inventions is any stronger and better than the character of the man who carried that hay on his back.

Are the men any better than the tall, handsome, upstanding young Swiss, who graciously stood by his cow and cart to let my son take his photograph, a young man in whom I thought I saw reflected the pride of the Swiss, the love of freedom and independence. After all, it is what is within the man that counts!

"For what is a man profited, if he shall gain the whole world, and lose his own soul?" (Matt. 16:26.)   Recently, on the deck of the Battleship *Missouri,* in Yokohama Bay, when Japan surrendered, General Douglas MacArthur said:

"If we do not now devise some greater and equitable system, Armageddon will be upon us. The problem is basically theological and involves a spiritual renaissance and improvement of human character. It must be of the spirit if we are to save the flesh."

I do not know that the problem is basically theological; we can have a study of theology without having character, without having religion; but the true meaning of that great general's utterance is in the following words, it "involves a spiritual renaissance and improvement of human character."

And more recently, a man teaching physical science in one of our leading universities, studying, evidently, the same great problem as it applies to humanity today, said, "I have come to three conclusions. The first is that salvation is not to be found in science. Second, we must have a moral revival. Third, we can have no moral revival without a living religion."—*DNCS*, September 6, 1952, p. 4.

THE STRUGGLE FOR SPIRITUAL POWER

EARTH THE PROVING GROUND. Man's earthly existence is but a test as to whether he will concentrate his efforts, his mind, his soul upon things which contribute to the comfort and gratification of his physical instincts and passions, or whether he will make as his life's end and purpose the acquisition of spiritual qualities.—*RSM*, 28:364 (1941).

In the hands of undeveloped, spiritually dead people has been placed the power of explosives, the radio, the airplane, the submarine, all the concentrated power of electricity, and even that of the breaking up of the atom. Unless there is a spiritual awakening, civilization is threatened. The carnal-minded in the world are causing heartaches and threatening the extinction of the race.

But the sun of hope is rising. Thinking men and women are recognizing the need of man's looking up toward the heavens instead of groveling in response to the animal instinct. One man, commenting on this, said that if all the destroyers of civilization could be eliminated, and the traits of the rest of us that come from destructive strains could be eliminated, an approach to the millennium some hundred years hence is by no means inconceivable.

Spiritual awakening in the hearts of millions of men and women would bring about a changed world. I am hopeful that the dawning of that day is not far distant. My faith in the ultimate triumph of the gospel of Jesus Christ assures me that a spiritual awakening must come. It will come through

the acceptance of Jesus Christ and obedience to his gospel.
—*RSM*, 28:367 (1941).

CIVILIZATION ON TRIAL. Civilization has grown too complex for the human mind to visualize or to control. Unless man comes to a speedy realization that the higher and not the baser qualities of man must be developed, then the present status of civilization is in jeopardy. Life on the animal plane has as its ideal the survival of the fittest—kill or be killed, crush or be crushed, mangle or be mangled. For man, with his intelligence, this is a sure road to anguish and death.

The spiritual road has Christ as its goal. The individual lives for something higher than self. He hears the Savior's voice saying: "I am the way, the truth, and the life. . . . " (John 14:6.) Following that voice, he soon learns that there is no one great thing which he can do to attain happiness or eternal life. He learns that "life is made up not of great sacrifices or duties, but of little things in which smiles and kindness and small obligations given habitually are what win and preserve the heart and secure comfort."—*RSM*, 28:366 (1941).

THE SPIRITUAL LIFE. "For what is a man profited, if he shall gain the whole world, and lose (forfeit) his own soul (life)? or what shall a man give in exchange for his soul (life)?" (Matt. 16:26.)

In quoting this passage, I have in mind to emphasize the dual nature of man—physical and spiritual. Joseph Smith's Revised Version, substituting as it does, the word *life* for *soul* makes justifiable the conclusion that preserving one's physical life is deemed more precious than the acquiring of any earthly emoluments, or the possession of the wealth of the world.

However, that Jesus had in mind the soul as a spiritual entity is confirmed by Mark who, recording this incident, adds: "Whosoever therefore shall be ashamed of me and of my words in this adulterous and sinful generation; of him also shall the Son of man be ashamed, when he cometh in the glory of his Father with the holy angels." (Mark 8:38.)

Luke confirms this thought as follows: "For what is a man advantaged, if he gain the whole world, and lose himself, or be cast away?

"For whosoever shall be ashamed of me, and of my words, of him shall the Son of man be ashamed, when he shall come in his own glory, and in his Father's and of the holy angels." (Luke 9:25-26.)

If we accept the spirit entity of man as real and eternal, how utterly foolish to ignore or to neglect its development by giving most, if not all, of our attention to physical needs, pleasures, and passions!—*DNCS,* June 6, 1951, p. 2.

THINGS WHICH STIFLE THE SPIRIT. There are some things which stifle spiritual contact. This old earth has tended to stifle spirituality right from the beginning. In the history of creation man was banished from the presence of God. Every one of us born here was so banished, and in our humiliation our judgment was taken from us. Man who once basked in the presence of God was later left to find his own way with nature. In his struggle for existence, he would go hungry, thirsty, cold, and nature would satisfy his wants. He would strike down a wild beast, and its meat would be his. Another man, seeing him, would try to get it. Then followed the combat of primitive man. Thus man "began from that time forth to be carnal, sensual, and devilish." (P. of G. P., Moses 5:13.) Such was the experience of man in his primitive state. In the struggle for physical necessities, higher spiritual values were either negative or forgotten.

So, today, a man who will unleash his passions and win his success at the expense of his fellows, develops selfishness— perhaps sensuality at the expense of spirituality.—*DNCS,* August 8, 1936, p. 1.

It is said that one Roman emperor offered a reward to anybody who would invent a new pleasure. Nero set Rome on fire for the mere pleasure of a new form of diversion. Rome fell because of extravagance, luxury, and dissipation. In personal, as in national life, these are unfailing signs of decline and decay. Truly,

" . . . he that soweth to his flesh shall of the flesh reap corruption; but he that soweth to the Spirit shall of the Spirit reap life everlasting." (Gal. 6:8.)—*CR,* April 1949, p. 14.

THE TRAGEDY OF FALSE IDEALS. The real tragedy of following false ideals is that by so doing we stifle and sometimes choke out spirituality completely.—*CR*, April 1949, p. 16.

As in the days of old, so there are today some who prefer to revel in what I have heard President George Albert Smith designate as the devil's territory rather than to strive for the higher and better things of life. Persons who condemn their will to the service of their appetites suffer the penalties.—*CR*, April 1949, p. 14.

ADVERSITY'S USES. There are those who have met disaster, which almost seems defeat, who have become somewhat soured in their natures, but if they stop to think, even the adversity which has come to them may prove a means of spiritual uplift. Adversity itself may lead toward and not away from God and spiritual enlightenment; and privation may prove a source of strength if we can but keep a sweetness of mind and spirit.—*CR*, October 1936, p. 103.

THE SOUL MUST BE IN TUNE. It is said that all the music we hear is that which the soul itself produces when it responds to the myriad voices from without. These sounds and voices from nature, God's great orchestra, must be reproduced by the soul's response before they can become music to us. It is not the music without that we hear, but the spirit's imitation of it.

If then, the soul be tuned to the same key so as to give a true response, rest assured that our lives will be filled with harmony and joy, for God's hand never strikes a discord. —FS, ms., Emma Lucy Gates Bowen, May 3, 1951.

THE ATTRIBUTES OF SPIRITUALITY

TOWARDS THE COMPANIONSHIP OF THE HOLY GHOST. Spirituality is the consciousness of victory over self, and of communion with the Infinite. Spirituality impels one to conquer difficulties and acquire more and more strength. To feel one's faculties unfolding and truth expanding the soul is one of life's sublimest experiences.

Being "honest, true, chaste, benevolent, virtuous, and in doing good to all men" are attributes which contribute to spirituality, the highest acquisition of the soul. It is the

divine in man, the supreme, crowning gift that makes him
king of all created things, the one final quality that makes him
tower above all other animals.

Divine is that admonition and promise given to the
Prophet Joseph Smith:

" . . . let virtue garnish thy thoughts unceasingly; then
shall thy confidence wax strong in the presence of God; and
the doctrine of the priesthood shall distil upon thy soul as the
dews from heaven.

"The Holy Ghost shall be thy constant companion, and
thy scepter an unchanging scepter of righteousness and truth;
and thy dominion shall be an everlasting dominion and without compulsory means it shall flow unto thee forever and ever."
(D. & C. 121:45-46.)—*CR*, April 1949, p. 17.

THE TRUE LIFE OF MAN. After all, the spiritual life is
the true life of man. It is what distinguishes him from the
beasts of the forests. It lifts him above the physical, yet he is
still susceptible to all the natural contributions that life can
give him that are needful for his happiness or contributive
to his advancement. Though in the world, he is not of the
world. (See John 8:23.)

Jesus taught that men and women fail to live truly,
unless they have spirituality. In the *Life and Teachings of
Jesus*, we read that the spiritual force underlies everything,
and without it nothing worth while can be accomplished.
"Spiritual needs can be met only by spiritual means. All government, laws, methods, and organizations are of no value
unless men and women are filled with truth, righteousness,
and mercy. Material things have no power to raise the
sunken spirit. Gravitation, electricity, and steam are great
forces, but they are all powerless to change the motives of
men and women." "Except a man be born again, he cannot
see the kingdom of God." (John 3:3.)—*CR*, October 1927,
pp. 120-121.

THE FOUNDATIONS OF SPIRITUALITY. Spirituality and
morality as taught by the Latter-day Saints are firmly anchored
in fundamental principles, principles from which the world
can never escape even if it would, and the first fundamental is
a belief—with Latter-day Saints a knowledge—in the existence

of a personal God. Latter-day Saint children have been taught to recognize him and to pray to him as one who can listen and hear and feel just as an earthly father can listen, hear, and feel, and they have absorbed into their very beings, from their mothers and their fathers, the real testimony that this personal God has spoken in this dispensation. There is a reality about it.—*CR*, April 1934, pp. 22-23.

Four Guiding Principles. The guiding principles to the realization of the higher life are not many or complex. Indeed, they are few and simple, and can be applied by everyone in any phase of life.

I. Recognition of the reality of spiritual values.

II. Sense of obligation to the social group.

III. Power of self-denial and the resultant self-mastery.

IV. A consciousness that the ultimate purpose of life is the perfecting of the individual.—*DNCS*, June 8, 1935, p. 6.

Giving. There is more spirituality expressed in giving than in receiving. The greatest spiritual blessing comes from helping another. If you want to be miserable, just harbor hate for a brother; and if you want to hate, just do your brother some injury. But if you would be happy, render a kind service, make somebody else happy.—*CR*, October 1936, pp. 104-105.

THE SPIRITUAL LIFE

A Sound Philosophy. Jesus said, " . . . Consider the lilies of the field, how they grow; they toil not, neither do they spin:

"And yet I say unto you, That even Solomon in all his glory was not arrayed like one of these." (Matt. 6:28-29.) I have heard skeptics say, "How impractical! How impractical such teaching! Taking no thought for tomorrow!" Some critics are judging without understanding what the Great Teacher had in mind.

Even from our scanty knowledge and power of analysis, let us consider the lilies of the field, how they grow. Down deep in the soil the lily sends its roots, seeking sustenance from the earth, not as an end; from that sustenance received, there comes through the earth a little plant, weak at first, but it grows into a stock.

All that sustenance is being produced for one purpose, that that lily might bloom in the sunshine and reproduce its kind. So we, with our tentacles, our roots, which we call hands and muscles and brain, bring our sustenance from the earth—not as an end, but that the spirit might so live that it may bask in the sunshine of the Holy Spirit. That is not impractical! That is sound philosophy, and true, as every saying of Christ is true.—*DNCS*, September 6, 1952, p. 4.

MATERIAL MEANS AND SPIRITUAL ENDS. That we must make a living is clearly manifest on every side. We are placed here to deal with the earth and earthly problems. Multiply, replenish, subdue, have dominion over the earth— these were the original commands given to man. Nature's first law is self-preservation, and efforts to gratify the flesh, satisfy the appetites, gain physical comfort and physical enjoyment, occupy the attention and time of the majority of the people of the world.

He that will not provide for his loved ones is worse than an infidel, and so it is a virtue to provide for loved ones; it is a necessity to preserve life. Too many people make this the sole purpose of life; but that is only a means—it is not an end in itself! Make it an end, and we are still on the animal plane, for that is the aim and purpose of every beast that creeps on the earth.

Man has a higher purpose. I remember reading, many years ago, "The purpose of life may be summed up in one sentence, *to subdue matter, that we might realize the ideal!*" I liked it! Conquer! Conquer the earth! Conquer the roaring streams that come out of the canyons in the springtime. Harness them. Instead of letting them destroy the land below by floods, hold back that mighty torrent and bring it down to irrigate the orchards and the fields, and thus furnish livelihood for thousands, tens of thousands, and millions. Subdue and conquer, yes! That we might realize the ideal. And what is that ideal? I cannot think of any higher and more blessed ideal than so to live in the Spirit that we might commune with the Eternal. Can you?—*DNCS*, September 6, 1952, p. 4.

The true aim of life is seeking the spiritual development rather than physical enjoyment or the acquisition of wealth. *DNCS*, September 6, 1952, p. 4.

CHAPTER 30

MAN AND SPIRITUAL PROGRESS

FUNDAMENTAL FACTS OF LIFE

MAN A DUAL BEING. Man is a dual being, and his life a plan of God. That is the first fundamental fact to keep in mind. Man has a *natural* body and a *spiritual* body. In declaring this fact the scriptures are very explicit:

"And the Gods formed man from the dust of the ground, and took his spirit (that is, the man's spirit), and put it into him; and breathed into his nostrils the breath of life, and man became a living soul." (P. of G. P., Abraham 5:7.)

Man's body, therefore, is but the tabernacle in which his spirit dwells. Too many, far too many, are prone to regard the body as the man, and consequently to direct their efforts to the gratifying of the body's pleasures, its appetites, its desires, its passions. Too few recognize that the real man is an immortal spirit, which "intelligence or the light of truth," animated as an individual entity before the body was begotten, and that this spiritual entity with all its distinguishing traits will continue after the body ceases to respond to its earthly environment. Said the Savior:

"I came forth from the Father, and am come into the world: again, I leave the world, and go to the Father." (John 16:28.)

As Christ's pre-existent Spirit animated a body of flesh and bones, so does the pre-existent spirit of every human being born into this world. Will you keep that in mind as the first basic truth of life?

The question, then, is: Which will give the more abundant life—pampering our physical nature or developing our spiritual selves? Is not that the real problem?

INDULGENCE LEADS TO UNHAPPINESS. Another basic fact to keep in mind is indulgence. Indulgence in appetites and desires of the physical man satisfy but for the moment and may lead to unhappiness, misery, and possible degradation; spiritual achievements give "joy not to be repented of."

In his epistle to the Galatians, Paul specifically enumerates the "works of the flesh," as he calls them, and the "fruits of the Spirit." Note this classification: The works of the flesh are manifest as these:

" . . . Adultery, fornication, uncleanness, lasciviousness,

"Idolatry, witchcraft, hatred, variance, emulations, wrath, strife, seditions, heresies,

"Envyings, murders, drunkenness, revellings, and such like: of the which I tell you before, as I have also told you in time past, that they which do such things shall not inherit the kingdom of God.

"But the fruit of the Spirit is love, joy, peace, longsuffering, gentleness, goodness, faith,

"Meekness, temperance: against such there is no law.

"And they that are Christ's have crucified the flesh with the affections and lusts.

"If we live in the Spirit, let us also walk in the Spirit." (Gal. 5:19-25.)

SPIRITUAL PROGRESS DEMANDS EFFORT. From the forty days' fast on the Mount of Temptation to the moment on the cross when he cried in triumph: "It is finished," Christ's life was a divine example of subduing and overcoming. Full of significance are his words spoken in his farewell address to his disciples:

"These things I have spoken unto you, that in me ye might have peace. In the world ye shall have tribulation: but be of good cheer; I have overcome the world." (John 16:33.)

"Moral law"—I am quoting now from a scientist who has glimpsed these eternal truths I have named—

"Moral law imposes disinterestedness; it orders that which is disagreeable, hard, and painful. Its requirements often revolt the flesh whose sole ambition is to persist and to enjoy. It demands the throttling of selfish sentiments for the sake of something which is still obscure to those who do not have faith, but which is even more powerful than the instinct of self-preservation: human dignity imposes a highly moral existence and paves the way to spirituality. And the greatest miracle is that this cruel law has won the universal respect of man who sometimes uses his intelligence to combat it, thus affirming its reality.

"The joys it procures compensate for the sacrifice it demands. The sentiment of duty accomplished is accompanied by a kind of total satisfaction which alone gives true peace of soul. The moral man—in olden days one would have said the virtuous man—spreads happiness and good will around him, or, if happiness is impossible, the resignation which takes its place." (Lecomte du Noüy—*Human Destiny.**)

There are thousands, millions of men and women who have high standards, and we do not have to yield to the few who fail.

THE CHALLENGE OF EIGHT DIFFICULTIES. Now, having in mind these four fundamental facts of life—the dual nature of man; his freedom of choice and his responsibility therefor; indulgences contrary to one's conscience leave heaviness of heart and unhappiness while spiritual achievements always give joy; spiritual progress demands effort. Let us consider these eight difficulties:

The First Problem: The Sabbath Day. Is it better to cherish Church ideals on Sunday, or indulge in Sunday sports? This is simply a question of *physical pleasure* or *spiritual development*, and in that we should keep in mind the following: First, Sunday is a day of rest, essential to the true development and strength of the body, and that is a principle which we should publish more generally abroad and practise. A second purpose for keeping holy the Sabbath day is: " . . . that thou mayest more fully keep thyself unspotted from the world. . . . " (D. & C. 59:9.) That is a glorious phrase.

Third, keeping the Sabbath day holy is a law of God, resounding through the ages from Mount Sinai. You cannot transgress the law of God without circumscribing your spirit.

Finally, our Sabbath, the first day of the week, commemorates the greatest event in all history—Christ's

(*Permission granted by Longman's Green & Co., Copyright, 1947 by Lecomte du Noüy.)

resurrection, and his visit as a resurrected being to his assembled Apostles.

Now if you want to indulge in bodily exercises and amusements, you cannot do it on the Sabbath day with impunity.

The Second Problem: Choosing Companions. Having in mind our basic truths, this question is a simple one— Whether you will choose companions who appeal to your baser nature, or those who inspire you always to be at your best.

Recently, I was thrilled and thankful when I heard a young Latter-day Saint woman say that she felt she would have to give up her sweetheart. She likes him, and he likes her, but lately he has chosen the way of the world. He likes a cigaret; he speaks disparagingly of the ideals of the Church. Fortunately, she is wise enough to observe that tendency, and she has "given him up." I say with all my heart: God bless her, because she knows that companionship leads to love. It is from such companionship that you find your companion for the future. If she joins her life with his, her ideals are going to be lowered; and she would rather take a little suffering now than much suffering later.

Choose good companions, and find among them those with whom you would like to go through life and eternity.

The Third Problem: Observing the Word of Wisdom. I am merely going to add one thought: Obedience to the Word of Wisdom develops greater spiritual power, that spiritual power which comes from resistance.

It is better for you in youth to say, "No, thank you," when offered to indulge in things which create an appetite for themselves. Be master, not a slave. Look around you and you will see the slaves to appetite—unfortunately now, increasingly among women—slaves! Where is the spiritual power in these future mothers?

The Fourth Problem: Does Active Membership in the Church Inhibit or Enhance One's Freedom and Development? Can you think of any organization in the world in which you can serve more effectively in an organized way than in the Church of Jesus Christ? Now, I mention service and character because those are the only two things which we can take with us in a few years when we leave this world.

" . . . shew me thy faith without thy works, and I will shew thee my faith by my works." (James 2:18.)

The Fifth Problem: Chastity. The dominant evil in the world today is unchastity. I repeat what appeared over the signature of President Joseph F. Smith while he was living:

"No more loathsome cancer disfigures the body and soul of society today than the frightful affliction of sexual sin. It vitiates the very fountains of life and bequeaths its foul effects to the yet unborn as a legacy of death."

The question is: What have you made of yourself—your character; and what service have you rendered to others?

He who is unchaste in young manhood is untrue to a trust given to him by the parents of the girl, and she who is unchaste in maidenhood is untrue to her future husband and lays the foundation in the home of unhappiness, suspicion, and discord. Do not worry about these teachers who say something about inhibitions. Just keep in mind this eternal truth, that chastity is a virtue to be prized as one of life's noblest achievements. It contributes to the virility of manhood. It is the crowning virtue of womanhood, and every red-blooded man knows that is true. It is a chief contributing factor to a happy home; it is the source of strength and perpetuity of the nation.

The Sixth Problem: To Be in the World But Not of the World. There is no loss of prestige in maintaining in a dignified way your standards. And when I hear girls expressing the thoughts that young women have that they are afraid that they might lose the influence or the respect of their sweethearts, I thought of a great illustration in literature wherein a Jewish maiden won the respect even of a profligate.

Read the story of Rebecca, that beautiful character in Sir Walter Scott's *Ivanhoe,* who was the prisoner of Brian de Bois-Guilbert. He had chosen her for base reasons. Others of his crowd chose the old father to rob him of his wealth. When Brian de Bois-Guilbert came in to take charge of his prize, Rebecca "had already unclasped two costly bracelets and a collar, which she hastened to proffer to the supposed outlaw, concluding naturally to gratify his avarice was to bespeak his favor." "Take these," she said, "and be merciful to me and my aged father! These ornaments are of value, yet they are trifling to what he would bestow, to obtain our dismissal from this castle, free and uninjured."

"Fair flower," replied the outlaw, "these pearls are orient, but they yield in whiteness to your teeth; the diamonds are brilliant, but they cannot match your eyes; and ever since I have taken up this wild trade, I have made a vow to prefer beauty to wealth."

"Thou art no outlaw," said Rebecca; "no outlaw had refused such offers. . . . Thou art a Norman—a Norman, noble perhaps in birth—Oh, be so in thy action, and cast off this fearful masque of outrage and violence!"

"I am not an outlaw, then, fair rose of Sharon. . . . And I am one who will be more prompt to hang thy neck and arms with pearls and diamonds, which so well become them, than to deprive thee of these ornaments."

"What would'st thou have of me," said Rebecca, "if not my wealth? We can have nought in common between us— you are a Christian—I am a Jewess—our union were contrary to the laws alike of the church and the synagogue."

"It were so, indeed," replied Brian de Bois-Guilbert, laughing: "wed with a Jewess—not if she were the Queen of Sheba!"

And then Rebecca knew his purpose. She threw open the latticed window, and an instant later stood on the verge of the parapet, with not the slightest screen between her and the tremendous depth below, and exclaimed: "Remain where thou art, proud Templar, or at thy choice, advance!—one foot nearer, and I plunge myself from the precipice; my body shall be bruised out of the very form of humanity upon the stones of that courtyard, 'ere it become the victim of thy brutality!"

As she spoke thus, she clasped her hands and extended them toward heaven, as if imploring mercy on her soul before she made the final plunge. The Templar hesitated, and a resolution which had never yielded to pity or disgrace gave way to his admiration of her fortitude. "Come down," he said, "rash girl!—I swear by earth, and sea, and sky, I will offer thee no offense."

And the reprobate for the first time in his life was taught respect for womanhood.

You can be in this world and "not of the world." Keep your chastity above everything else.

The Seventh Problem: The Value of Doing Right Though None Might See Me. "Tell me what you think about when you do not have to think, and I will tell you what you are."

Temptation does not come to those who have not thought of it before. Keep your thoughts clean, and it will be easy to resist temptations as they come.

The Eighth Problem: Getting Back on the Moral and Spiritual Highway. I, too, have mentioned the prodigal son who first "came to himself" before he turned his face homeward. Come back home, back to the path of virtue, but sense your own evil, and remember that there might be many who have been hurt on your way down.

When a man was asked how he could help those he had injured, particularly in slander, a good, wise, old man took a sack of feathers, scattered them, and then he said: "Now, try to gather them up."

He said: "Oh, I cannot!"

That is just it. Let us be careful that we have not wounded people and hurt them as we have been going down selfishly on the road of indulgence.

Young people: Is it the body you are going to serve and be a slave to or is it the spirit you are going to develop, and live happily in this life and in the world to come?

"I pray not that thou shouldest take them out of the world, but that thou shouldest keep them from the evil." (John 17:15.)

God give us power as young people and as parents to live in the world but be above the world.—*IE*, 52:558-560, 600-602 (1949).

CHAPTER 31

REACHING YOUTH

OUR GREATEST SOCIAL OBLIGATION

THE YOUTH OF THE LAND. An eminent statesman in the United States once wrote:

"If we work upon marble it will perish; if upon brass, time will efface it. If we rear temples they will crumble into dust. But if we work upon immortal minds, imbue them with principles with a just fear of God and love of fellow men, we engrave upon those tablets that which time cannot efface and which will endure through all eternity."

That thought, impressively expressed, gives us an idea of the theme I should like to stress. We are deeply perturbed, in these days, about great social questions. The best minds of the nation are now struggling with problems associated with one of the greatest financial crises that have ever swept this nation and the world. Important as this is, and other social and political questions, I believe that the most profound problem which this country faces, indeed the greatest obligation upon the government today, national, state, and local, is to determine how best to guide, protect, and educate properly, childhood and youth. This may seem commonplace to many of you, so commonplace that you will wonder why I take the time to speak of it.

Be that as it may, I believe all agencies interested in child welfare could cooperate in this great work to the great good of our state and nation. There are phases of this problem which affect the happiness and peace of mind of every father and mother in the land. The question of child health and guidance goes to the very root of our national life.—CR, October 1932, pp. 64-65.

THREE PARABLES AND THEIR APPLICATION. In the fifteenth chapter of Luke there is recorded a very significant message from Christ, relative to the lost and found. That message is embraced in three remarkable parables: one, the parable of the lost sheep; another, the lost coin; and a third, the prodigal son.

In the first the straying one seems to have become lost through stupidly wandering away for the necessary things of life. Perhaps the wandering was prompted by just a desire to seek the necessary things of existence.

The second, however, relates to a different kind of lost one—one that seems to be wholly unconscious of having wandered away; and the third, to another class, one who deliberately and wilfully become estranged from God.

I am not sure that I have applied these parables properly, but certainly there are just such classes of young men and young women who wander away and become lost. There are those in the world who become so absorbed in gaining a livelihood, and so interested in the material things of life, that they lost sight entirely of the religious ideals.

Of the second class, those who are unconscious of being in the dark, there are many such—speaking of the nation at large. It is admitted that in the United States there are twenty-seven million children who, though nominally Protestant, are not receiving any religious instruction. There are eight million children, if I remember rightly, less than ten years of age, who receive absolutely no religious instruction. I think we may consistently place this large group in the second class named—little children growing up in darkness, unconscious of the light. They are like an Easter lily before it blooms. They have an existence but are struggling out of the darkness of humanity. They may never bloom into the sunlight of the Holy Spirit. Now that is a tragedy.

Of the third, we see around us every day young men who wilfully and deliberately choose the pathway of indulgence, which leads them away from the Holy Spirit and leads them away from the testimony of the gospel of Jesus Christ. It is a great mission, the greatest in the world, to reach out after these young people, to extend a hand to the child, following Jesus' injunction to Peter to bring the lambs into Christ's fold. Indeed, there is nothing greater.

I think Herbert Hoover, when President of the United States, expressed the importance of such a mission most impressively when he said:

"These questions of child health and protection are a complicated problem, requiring much learning and much action, and we need have great concern over this matter. Let no one believe that these are questions which should not stir a nation, that they are below the dignity of statesmen or government. If we could have but one generation of properly born, trained, educated, and healthy children, a thousand other problems of government would vanish. We would assure ourselves of healthier minds in more vigorous bodies, to direct the energies of our nation to yet greater heights of achievement. Moreover, one good community nurse will save a dozen future policemen."—*CR*, April 1931, pp. 79-80.

PROPER ACCOUNTING. How may we reach these youth? In some of the organizations of the Church every boy and girl should be enrolled. His name or her name should appear on some record, if not on several records, throughout the Church, and some teacher or some officer has the obligation of coming in contact with that individual boy or girl.—*CR*, April 1931, pp. 81-82.

THE POWER OF PERSONALITY. You are not going to bring back erring youth unless you first let them know that you are interested in them. Let them feel your heart touch. Only the warm heart can kindle warmth in another. Wayward boys and girls are sometimes suspicious of people around them. Others get the idea that they are not wanted. The kind hand or the loving arm removes suspicion and awakens confidence. Your own experience bears ample evidence of the value of personal companionship.—*CR*, October 1932, pp. 67-68.

CHURCH SERVICE TO YOUNG WOMEN AWAY FROM HOME. A few years ago there appeared in one of our magazines, the story of a little lad who wandered from his mother's lap in the Badlands of the Dakotas and was lost. As night came on, the mother was distracted and the neighbors alarmed. The next morning, on the public square of the town near there, the sheriff met a group of farmers, teachers, office men, citizens of all ranks. He organized them for a systematic search. Before they started out he said, "Little Ronald is somewhere out in those Badlands. We must organize and search every bush, every crevasse, every water hole. We must not come back without that little boy. Pray God that we are not yet too late." They started out that Wednesday, but it was not until Thursday, and at about three o'clock in the afternoon that a mighty shout went up. They had found the boy.

Brethren, a few years ago you received a letter stating that a committee had been appointed by the Council of the Twelve to look after some of our girls who had wandered into the "badlands" of the city. They did not intend to get caught in the meshes of sin, but they had wandered from home and the protecting influence of home surroundings. You were asked if you would not kindly send to this committee the names and the addresses of those girls who came away from your town, just so that members of this committee could see that they became associated with some ward, with some young people here of good reputation, and in some cases, in all cases if possible, could see that they found suitable employment.

Later, you were asked from this pulpit if you would not please give closer attention to that phase of salvation of our youth. Only a few, comparatively speaking, have responded to that call. Well, if they were lost and faced physical death, you would not hesitate, the whole town would not hesitate to go out and rescue the lost girl or the lost boy. I want to tell you, from direct reports from our police officers who cooperate, in several instances some of these fine girls have suffered things worse than death.

Now we ask you once again please to send the names of those girls who legitimately, who unknowing what awaits them, some of them, leave their homes and come to Salt Lake City or Ogden or Provo, or some center, seeking employment, seeking to better themselves. Please cooperate with this committee or enable the members thereof to cooperate with you, so that these choice young people may not be ensnared by vicious men who lie in wait, not only to deceive, but to ruin.

Now, be careful, if the parents are sending them in, that you do not offend those parents; that is not necessary. This is merely a means of cooperating with parents in helping young people to start out from home to better their conditions.
—*CR*, April 1952, pp. 85-86.

YOUTH AND ITS ASPIRATIONS

A THREEFOLD CLASSIFICATION. I invite your attention for a few minutes to aspirations. Aspiration means "a desiring ardently; a strong wish, a longing for the realization of high ideals."

Just by way of emphasis, let us consider youth as grouped into three classes—

(1) *The infusorian class* into which fall the listless, drifting youth.

Down among the lowest types of living creatures, there is a little animal that moves about aimlessly. It "swims randomly about, moving apparently by flailing stimuli in its medium; and in its course it comes now in contact with some nutritive substance which it absorbs, and now into the neighborhood of some creature by which it is swallowed and digested. Lacking those developed senses and motor powers which higher animals possess, ninety-nine in the hundred of these minute animals seldom live but for a few hours, disappearing either by innutrition or by destruction." The infusorians enter upon life aimlessly, and ninety-nine out of one hundred of these animalculae perish in consequence.

Now you see what I mean by the infusorian group. One writer refers to them as that "great under class of men, content to creep, and without thought of wings for rising. Mere drifters are they, creatures of circumstances, indifferently remaining where birth or events have started them, having food and raiment, therewith they are content. No inspirations fire them, no ideals rebuke them, no visions of possible excellence or advancement smite their vulgar contentment. Like dead leaves swept forward upon the current, these men drift through life. Not really bad, they are but indifferently good, and therefore are the material out of which vicious men are made. In malarial regions, physicians say men of overflowing health are safe because the abounding vitality within crowds back the poison in the outer air, while men who live on the borderline between good health and ill, furnish the same conditions for fever that consume away the life. Similarly, the men who live an indifferent, supine life, with no impulses upward, are exposed to evil and become a constant menace to society."

(2) *The firefly youth.* Higher in the scale of intelligence and moral uplift, there are those who may be classed as the firefly men.

Often on a summer's evening, you students as children have observed what we used to call the "lightning bug." These flying creatures seemed most active just before a shower. The light from each would shine but for an instant, then the thing would be absorbed in the darkness. Another momentary flash, then blackness again!

Such is the firefly youth with respect to the noble aspirations. He has luminous hours in which his soul ardently desires to rise above all things mean and sordid and to bask in the realm of enlightenment and beauty. He would be valiant and courageous in defending virtue and the right under all circumstances. If he could only obtain strength and power, he would use them to help his fellow men and to make the world better! But when a few hours later he associates with companions unfired by such noble ideals, the light of his aspirations fades; the fires of enthusiasm die; and his soul is absorbed in the darkness of indifference and indulgence.

Good intentions must be carefully cherished or they will soon perish.

However, it is better to have hoped and yearned for better things, and had the hopes fade than never to have yearned at all. The flicker at least shows the presence of a light that might be fanned into a constant flame. That is better than damp driftwood from which will come not even a spark.

(3) *The conifer youth.* Then there is the third group, which I call the conifer youth. In using this term, I have in mind not just the ordinary cone-bearing tree of the conifer group, but particularly, the Giant Sequoia or "Big Tree" of the Sierra Nevadas. It grows from two hundred to three hundred and forty feet in height. The diameter is ordinarily ten to fifteen feet, and sometimes reaches twenty-five to thirty-five feet! There is a grove of these ancient trees in the Sequoia forest of the Yosemite Valley. One, "The General Sherman," is estimated to be 3500 years old. One cannot stand in the presence of this oldest living thing in existence without sensing a feeling of awe akin to reverence. It was

probably alive as a mere twig when the pyramids of Egypt were being built. It was young and vigorous when Greece was in its glory; it was just a young tree when Rome ruled the world. Empires have risen and fallen. Millions of men have lived and died during the tree's lifetime. It has withstood lightning, floods, fire, and still lives on!

It has survived because it has within it the powers of resistance.

The conifer youth senses the fact that man is not a mere animal, a creature of the flesh which profiteth nothing, but a spiritual being, a soul. He realizes that he is more than a physical object that is tossed for a short time from bank to bank, only to be submerged finally in the ever-flowing stream of life. There is something within him which urges him to rise above himself, to control his environment, to master the body and all things physical, and to live in a higher and more beautiful world. "These are the soul-architects who build their thoughts and deeds into a plan; who travel forward, not aimlessly, but toward a destination; who sail, not anywhither, but toward a port; who steer, not by the clouds but by the fixed stars. High in the scale of manhood these who ceaselessly aspire toward life's great Exemplar."

The great Exemplar is Jesus Christ, the Son of the living God, who in material possessions had "nowhere to lay his head," yet, as one writer has said more impressively than I, "a man of truly colossal intellect, incomparable as he strides across the realm and ages, yet always thinking the gentlest, kindliest thoughts; thoughts of mildness as well as majesty; thoughts of humanity as well as divinity. His thoughts were wings to all the low-flying; his thoughts freed those who had been snared in the thickets; his thoughts set an angel down beside each cradle; his thoughts of the incarnation rendered the human body forever sacred; his thoughts of the grave sanctified the tomb. Dying and rising, his thoughts clove an open pathway through the sky. Taught by him, the people have learned to think—not only great thoughts, but good ones, and also how to turn thoughts into life."—Newell Dwight Hills, "The Mind and Right Thinking."

THOUGHTS OF YOUTH DETERMINE CHARACTER. " . . . as he thinketh in his heart, so is he: . . . " (Prov. 23:7.)

The thoughts that a youth harbors during the formative period in his life will determine into which class he falls— whether he is a listless *infusorian,* a *firefly* youth with regards to good intentions, or an outstanding *Sequoia* in the realm of character.—*DNCS,* May 8, 1943, pp. 1-4.

DANGERS TO AVOID

In their yearning for a good time, young people are often tempted to indulge in the things which appeal only to the baser side of humanity, five of the most common of which are: first, vulgarity and obscenity; second, drinking and petting parties; third, unchastity; fourth, disloyalty; and fifth, irreverence.

VULGARITY AND OBSCENITY. Vulgarity is often the first step down the road to indulgence. To be vulgar is to give offense to good taste or refined feelings. A young man who would tell a vulgar joke in the presence of ladies discloses a nature leaning towards that which is low and coarse. A girl who would encourage it and laugh at it is taking a step toward that which is crude and unrefined.

Most of you have read David Starr Jordan's denunciation of this vice. He concludes it by saying:

"We find the corrosion of vulgarity everywhere, and its poison enters every home. The billboards of our cities are covered with its evidence; our newspapers are redolent with it; our story books reek with it; our schools are tainted by it; and we cannot keep it out of our homes, or our churches, or our colleges."

It is only a step from vulgarity to obscenity. The executive secretary of a committee appointed to curtail the distribution of obscene literature put on my desk only recently a most vile plaque, covertly cast reportedly here in our city, and sold to our young people at a nominal price. The best way to rid society of such baseness is for parents, businessmen, and especially every decent young person, to refuse to tolerate it and to report the vendors to the officers of the law.

DRINKING AND PETTING PARTIES. It is right, indeed essential, to the happiness of our young people that they meet in social parties, but it is an indication of low morals when for entertainment they must resort to physical stimulation and debasement. Such indulgence weakens one's character, discredits one's family name, robs one's future wife or husband of a priceless treasure, and sows seeds that may ripen into bitter fruit of marital suspicion, unhappiness, and divorce. A girl who sacrifices self-respect for social popularity debases true womanhood.

A spotless character, founded upon the ability to say no in the presence of those who mock and jeer, wins the respect and love of men and women whose opinion is most worth while. Drinking and petting parties form an environment in which the moral sense becomes dulled and unbridled passion holds sway. It then becomes easy to take the final step downward in moral disgrace.

UNCHASTITY. The test of true womanhood comes when woman stands innocent at the court of chastity. All qualities are crowned by this most precious virtue of beautiful womanhood. It is the most vital part of the foundation of a happy married life. There is a general idea throughout the world that young men may sow their wild oats, but that young women should be chaperoned and guarded. But even in this matter of chaperonage, there is too much laxity on the part of parents, if recent reports are to be relied upon.

In the Church of Jesus Christ there is but one standard of morality. No young man has any more right to sow his "wild oats" in youth than has a young girl. He who comes to his bishop to ask for a recommend to take a pure girl to the altar is expected to give the same purity that he hopes to receive.

A woman crowned with virtue is the "highest, holiest, most precious gift to man," excepting only salvation offered in the gospel, and that forms part of it. But a woman who barters her virtue "is not one of the least of man's shames."

DISLOYALTY. When, instead of high moral principles, a life of immoral indulgence is chosen, and man or woman gets far down in the scale of degeneracy, disloyalty is an inevitable part of his or her nature. Loyalty to parents becomes quenched; obedience to their teachings and ideals abandoned; loyalty to wife and children smothered in base gratification; loyalty to Church impossible and often supplanted by sneers at its teachings, and that means the perpetrator is "left to himself to kick against the pricks and to fight against God."

Irreverence. At this stage, irreverence is an inevitable consequence, a pretty sure sign of moral weakness. No man will rise high who jeers at sacred things. It is said that when Mr. Melville D. Landon (Eli Perkins) was preparing his volume on *Kings of the Platform and Pulpit,* he wrote to Colonel Robert G. Ingersoll for a copy of his most famous lecture. In a letter which accompanied the manuscript, Mr. Ingersoll said:

"Whatever you do, do not put anything into the book against Christ. I may have said silly things about him when a boy in Peoria, Illinois, but I now regard him as the one Perfect Man."—*CR,* April 1949, pp. 14-16.

The Temptation of False Popularity. Young men and women sometimes yield to indulgence for the sake of popularity. One who persistently bids for popularity at the expense of health and character is a foolish man. "A man who stands behind a bar and swallows drink after drink for the sake of sociability is paying a high price for a miserable product. Social popularity purchased in such a way and at such a price is not good enough for an honest man to wipe his feet upon." Indeed, men who yield to temptation to seek popularity among friends lose the very thing they desire, while the boy who maintains his standards wins their respect. Let me illustrate:

A year or so ago the president of one of the leading fraternities at the University of Utah, who maintained the standards of his Church under all conditions, was present with a group of students when one of his fraternity treated his comrades with cigarets. He passed the president of the fraternity without offering him a cigaret. Facetiously, the young Mormon boy said: "What's the matter, Bill, aren't you offering me one?" Bill, even though a smoker himself, replied: "Jack, if I ever saw you with a cigaret in your mouth, I would knock you cold!" The more the Mormon boy maintained his standards, the greater respect he won from his non-Mormon associates.—*DNCS,* January 25, 1947, p. 8.

Vain Shortcuts. We need not shut our eyes to the fact that too many of our young folk respond to the call of the physical because it seems the easy and natural thing to do. Too many are vainly seeking shortcuts to happiness. It should always be kept in mind that that which is most worth while in life requires strenuous effort.

"Enter ye in at the strait gate: for wide is the gate, and broad is the way, that leadeth to destruction, and many there be which go in thereat:

"Because strait is the gate, and narrow is the way, which leadeth unto life, and few there be that find it." (Matt. 7:13-14.)—*CR*, April 1949, pp. 13-14.

THE DANGER OF UNSTABLE OPINIONS. Now what are the sinful influences around us that tend to divert young people's minds from this right channel? We are living in an age which, measured by the standards of the gospel, is full of unstable opinions; and into that world of shifting uncertainty our young people are thrown. Think for a moment how their thoughts are diverted from our standards as they read some of the articles in current magazines.

From a leading magazine I have culled, just at random, this, in relation to religion:

Academic scholars who are shaping the thoughts of youth are declaring that one religious faith is just as good or just as useless, according to the professor's particular viewpoint, as another. "Buddhism, Hinduism, Judaism, Christianity, all spring from the same source, and in the ultimate analysis mean the same thing."

That is one of the things which I call unstable, and which threaten young people with an influence that will throw them into the fatal channel of wrong thinking. In customs and fashions, what was considered bad taste yesterday has become quite acceptable today.

In regard to the ideals of success and the standards that lead to success, I quote this surprising statement:

"Success is not the result of hard work, clean living, and personal integrity. The vulgar, proud, and haughty, not the meek, inherit the earth."

Young men and young women read those things, and their minds are diverted from the channel of right thinking and right living. Unstable opinions, shifting uncertainties!

Again, the wholesomeness of our ancestral home life is questioned. That thought, too, is leading our young people to think in a wrong direction.

Modesty, "that diamond setting to female beauty," is in some circles considered prudish, puritanic; and the influence is leading astray some of our girls who are susceptible to the influence of society.

Ride along the highway, see the obnoxious and sometimes obscene advertisements, how they flaunt themselves in the face of every traveler; and even obnoxious advertisements enter our homes over the radio.

COUNTERACTING SUPERFICIAL NONSENSE. Now, the important question with us today is, what are we doing to counteract this tendency towards fatal wrong thinking? I am going to name only three common phases of our Church which are fundamental toward right thinking and right living.

I should like to name, first, the duty that rests upon every parent and upon every teacher within this Church to arouse within the mind of the child a sense of responsibility toward other individuals and toward society.

I wish to name as the second principle a little simple thing which even in the naming will indicate to you perhaps how many have wandered from it, the simple principle of prayer. There are men in our midst who say that prayer is not efficacious. Unfortunately, some of our young people believe such fallacious remarks. Prayer is a fundamental principle of religion, the Christian religion particularly, and prayer is a force for good. A praying man is a growing man.

A third principle that contributes to right religious attitude is reverence—reverence for the Sabbath day and all things sacred. Reverence directs thought toward God. Without it there is no religion. Let us not make Sunday a holiday. It is a holy day, and on that day we should go to the house of worship and seek our God. If we seek him on the Sabbath day, get into his presence on that day, we shall find it less difficult to be in his presence the following days of the week.

There should be more reverence for the house of worship. I am offended when I see in Sunday School, or perhaps in Mutual, members leave the service after having rendered a musical number. Undoubtedly, they go to some other place to render the same service. Even that is not sufficient justification for the mark of seeming irreverence in leaving a worshiping assembly. Better secure somebody who can stay throughout the service, for the assembly in a dedicated chapel is in the presence of God. All are supposed to have come to meet him and worship him, and there should be present that spirit of order and reverence which will direct the worshipers' thoughts in the right channel.—CR, April 1929, pp. 99-102.

ANCHOR TO THE TRUTH. I know of no greater blessing you young folk can receive than to be anchored to the truth, and by that I mean three things: first, always to feel a surety that this Church is divinely guided; second, that the Lord has authorized his servants and placed upon them the duty to proclaim to the world the restoration and truth of the gospel of Jesus Christ; third, and most applicable to us all, that inspiration from the Lord is a reality, just as real as the love each one of us has for his loved ones.—CR, April 1950, p. 32.

BUILDING CONFIDENCE IN YOUTH

To BUILD CONFIDENCE A BASIC OBLIGATION. One of the paramount duties, I might say the paramount duty, of parents is to win and merit the confidence and respect of their children. Equally paramount in the life of a bishopric of a ward is to win and merit the confidence of the people of their ward. Too few parents have the confidence of their children. There are too few officers in the Church who have the confidence of the members, particularly of the young people of wards and stakes.—CR, April 1944, p. 107.

THE POISON OF UNJUST JUDGMENT. I feel impressed to say a word about something which destroys that confidence. The Savior on one occasion said:

"Judge not, that ye be not judged.

"For with what judgment ye judge, ye shall be judged: and with what measure ye mete, it shall be measured to you again.

"And why beholdest thou the mote that is in thy brother's eye, but considerest not the beam that is in thine own eye?" (Matt. 7:1-3.)

Then in strong condemnatory terms he said:

"Thou hypocrite, first cast out the beam out of thine own eye; and then shalt thou see clearly to cast out the mote out of thy brother's eye." (Matt. 7:5.)

The context of that scripture plainly indicates that the sin the Savior is condemning is the disposition to look unfavorably on the character and actions of others, which leads almost invariably to the pronouncing of rash, unjust, judgments upon them. Very often these judgments are formed on insufficient evidence and after superficial observations, and people who form them and express them in the presence of children put poison into those children's minds. Parents who speak at the table against the bishopric, against a teacher, stake president, or any other officer of the Church are, unwittingly, perhaps, but most assuredly, lessening in their children's minds the respect and confidence in Church authorities.—CR, April 1944, pp. 107-108.

THE POISON OF SLANDER. One of the most deadly weapons of warfare is the poison gas. Slander is to a child's confidence in Church authorities in undermining character what poison gas is to the physical body. Now, that is putting it strongly, but I believe it is true. We should avoid as poison "Slander whose whisper over the world's diameter, as level as the cannon to its blank, transports its poison shot."—CR, April 1944, p. 108.

THE STRENGTH OF WORTHY YOUTH. We hear a good deal of talk about our young people these days. Some say that they are indifferent, that they are losing their interest in the Church. I do not agree with this accusation. My experience with the young leads me to believe that there was never a time when youth more sincerely sought the truth, when they were more responsive to assignments made in the Church, when they were more observant of the ideals for which this Church stands.

Oh, I am not blind to the fact that there are those who are wavering. I also know that there were young people during our youth who wavered. I realize that there are those who stand on the sidelines and, arrogating to themselves superior wisdom which they do not possess, would fain guide and dictate, but there have always been such. The great majority of our young people are desirous of living the truth.

I realize the temptations were never stronger than they are today; but the young people who resist these temptations deserve all the greater credit. We hear about young boys and young girls who indulge in things contrary to the teachings of their parents and the officers of the Church, and contrary to the ideals of the gospel, but we too seldom hear about the much larger group who are exerting an influence for good upon their fellow workers and upon their associates.

If time permitted, I might narrate several specific instances in which our girls have wielded an influence upon their associates and led not only members of the Church but also people outside of the Church to lay aside violations of the Word of Wisdom and to conform to the ideals and principles of purity of life.—CR, April 1934, pp. 21-22.

Generally speaking, youth are anchored. Sometimes they seem to waver and digress from the standards. Some of them, it is true, lose their virtue, the most benighting and cankering condition that can contaminate young people's lives. I know that there is a looseness in sexual morality which is dangerous, which is threatening. I know too that such breaking down of moral standards is manifested not alone among the young people, and I warn the Church to guard against unchastity. Keep yourselves unspotted from the world, the fundamental element in pure religion.

No, we are not shutting our eyes to the dangers, but I want to tell you we must not shut our eyes to the virtues of the tens of thousands of those who are true and valiant.—CR, April 1934, p. 22.

A SIGNIFICANT MEDICAL PROOF. I am very happy and deeply grateful for the high type of young manhood and womanhood being reared in the Church as indicated recently by a report of 6,556 prospective missionaries in their medical examination including serological tests preparatory to their going on missions.

In 1946 there were 2,263 so examined. In 1947, 2,134; likewise in 1948, 2,159, or a total, as I say, of 6,556. Negative tests were shown by 6,554; only one in 1946 and one in 1947 were positive—one in more than three thousand.—*CR*, April 1949, p. 11.

EVIDENCE FROM THE MILITARY. Speaking generally, I have confidence in our young people. This confidence springs primarily from my intimate associations with hundreds of returned soldiers and others who have gone on missions, particularly during the last three years. While our young men were in the army, most of them (there were exceptions, of course) conducted themselves creditably. They met as regularly as possible for sacred service. As an illustration: During the war in the Pacific when the conflict was at its height, a chaplain one day accosted a colonel, saying: "Are you going to conference tomorrow?"

"What do you mean, conference?" answered the colonel.

"The Mormon soldiers in New Britain are holding a conference tomorrow."

I heard that same colonel say, upon his return from the army, "Those soldiers are among the best missionaries that the Church has ever had."—*CR*, October 1948, p. 118.

THE NOBILITY OF CLEAN LIVING. As I recall the influences upon my young life, I believe the greatest was the memorizing of that important saying: "My spirit will not dwell in an unclean tabernacle."

Then there were others, and they were all in the form of warnings. The first came to me as a boy as I sat on a spring seat by the side of my father as we drove into Ogden. Just before we crossed the bridge over the Ogden River, a man came out from a saloon, which was just on the northern bank of the river. I recognized him. I liked him because I had seen him on the local stage. But on that occasion he was under the influence of liquor, and had been for, I suppose, several days.

I did not know he drank, but as he broke down and cried and asked Father for fifty cents to go back into the saloon, I saw him stagger away. As we drove across the bridge, my father said: "David, he and I used to go ward teaching together."—*CR*, April 1949, pp. 180-182.

RETROSPECT AND PROSPECT. If there is concern about the recalcitrance of boys and girls, this generation is no exception

to those which have preceded it. Our great-grandfathers and
their great-grandfathers worried about the forwardness and
recklessness of their children and the bleakness of their future
just as we do today.—*CR*, October 1948, p. 118.

YOUTH AND THE SOCIAL ENVIRONMENT

A DUTY OF CITIZENSHIP. It is the duty of every law-
abiding citizen to see to it that our children have a wholesome
community environment in which to live during their tender
and impressive years.—*CR*, October 1948, p. 121.

It is my purpose to say a few words about the effect of
environment upon youth and the responsibility of adults to
make home and civic environment a contributing factor to
their right living.

The following is pertinent to what I have in mind:

"It is the age that forms the man, not the man that
forms the age. Great minds do indeed react on the society
which has made them what they are, but they only pay with
interest what they have received." (Macaulay.)

So also is this ancient proverb applicable:

"If there is righteousness in the heart, there will be beauty
in the character. If there is beauty in the character, there will
be harmony in the home. If there is harmony in the home,
there will be order in society. And if there is order in society,
there will be peace in the world."—*CR*, October 1948, p. 117.

SOCIAL ACTIVITY UNDER PROPER ENVIRONMENT. I think
it is almost a tragedy to have young girls and young boys
grow up without opportunity of social activity under the proper
environment, and recreational halls will be dedicated as fitting
places for these young folk to come and meet one another, to
meet the older ones, to participate in literature, in the art of
dancing, in the drama, in music, and all other features that
offer opportunity for development to our young boys and
girls.

I am sorry that the latest custom among young people is
to have a young man and his young sweetheart dance together
all evening. I should rather see them exchange partners as
was formerly the practice.

Some of our girls come, properly chaperoned, but they
do not get the opportunity to participate in the dances. The

recreation hall should be a place for cordiality where all young people may have an opportunity to mingle and to meet their mates. That means something in this day of divorces due to hasty marriages where they do not understand each other, where they marry not for ideal homes and the rearing of children, but for reasons lower than those which should actuate the idealism of proper marriage.—*DNCS*, April 30, 1952, p. 3.

THE HUMAN FACTOR. With the great masses of sensationalism and artificial stimulation to which the child of today is subjected in this age of mechanical wonders, it is of the gravest importance that society realize that it is only in the example of sincere living upon the part of the individual members of society that the child finds a dynamic impulse for his own wholesome development.

If we are sincere in our desire to reduce this delinquency among youth, let us look to ourselves as members of the community and as leaders and officials in civic circles.—*CR*, October 1948, pp. 120-121.

ADULT DELINQUENCY IN THE COMMUNITY. That there is a threatening increase in delinquency in our communities, particularly among boys and girls of high school age, is all too apparent to anyone who will open his eyes to see and his ears to hear; and steps should be taken to curtail this delinquency.

It is with this purpose in mind that I refer not to the delinquency of youth but to the delinquency of adults.

Youth is influenced by example and environment. Dominating groups exerting this influence are the home, the church, the school, social circles, and civic conditions.

There are too many delinquent fathers and mothers. Our homes are the centers that determine the type of our citizenry. To dignify home and parenthood is one of the noblest aims of human society. The greatest responsibility given to woman is the divine gift to be a mother. She thus blessed, who has health and opportunity, and shirks the responsibility for social prestige and pleasure, is recreant to her duty as wife and mother. The father, particularly, if he be a member of the Church and holds the priesthood, who fails to set a proper example before his children is a delinquent and is a contributor to child delinquency.

Upon the responsibility of parents to have proper home environment, modern revelation is most explicit:

"And again, inasmuch as parents have children in Zion, or in any of her stakes which are organized, that teach them not to understand the doctrine of repentance, faith in Christ the Son of the living God, and of baptism and the gift of the Holy Ghost by the laying on of the hands, when eight years old, the sin be upon the heads of the parents.

"For this shall be a law unto the inhabitants of Zion, or in any of her stakes which are organized.

"And their children shall be baptized for the remission of their sins when eight years old, and receive the laying on of the hands.

"And they shall also teach their children to pray, and to walk uprightly before the Lord." (D. & C. 68:25-28.)

Quarreling among parents and children, faultfinding, backbiting, smoking cigarets, drinking intoxicating liquors, using profane language, make a home environment that contributes to delinquency. No parent can consistently teach faith in Christ who profanes the name of Deity. Profanity is never heard in the well-ordered home. Swearing is a vice that bespeaks a low standard of breeding. Blasphemous exclamations drive out all spirit of reverence. Irreverence is always a mark of delinquency.—*CR*, October 1948, pp. 118-119.

SPENDING TO SAVE, IMPORTANT. One man estimates that we are spending ten billion dollars a year in the punishment of criminals; yet each year crime is eating more deeply into the vitals of our civilization.

I suggest that we expend some of that vast sum of money to better advantage by putting forth more effort to stop the source of crime by giving a little more attention to the young, for, mind you, the average age of the criminal in the United States today is under twenty-one years. That is something which challenges our attention. We are not spending proportionately the amount in preventing lawlessness among our youth that we are spending in punishing those who become entangled in the meshes of the law.—*CR*, October 1930, p. 9.

WHAT HAPPENS OUTSIDE OF SCHOOL. I am concerned about the child when he is not in school, about what he is doing after school. The leisure time of youth is the dangerous time. That is when he needs the training, and yet in some of our states we have compulsory education up to fourteen years of age, and in those same states have laws prohibiting a boy from working until he is sixteen. There you find a two-year period in which the boy is left practically to go his way. And what is his way? He will find the gang, and gangs are often the breeding grounds of bootleggers and organized vice squads.

Young boys who are going their own way should be guided, no matter what it costs, along the paths of better citizenship. In Utah we have a law that compels the young man and the young woman to be in school until he or she is eighteen years of age. However, it is one thing to force a boy into school, it is another thing to arouse in his life an ideal or a desire to emulate the best in life.—CR, October 1930, p. 11.

BISHOPS, THE AARONIC PRIESTHOOD, AND COMMUNITY ENVIRONMENT. But now, brethren of the Church, do you realize that we have in the organization of the Church the best means in all the world of training youth? Your deacon quorums, what are they but opportunities for the young boys to meet together and satisfy that spirit of brotherhood? Bishop, what is your priests' quorum but an opportunity for you as a president of that quorum to get those young men around you as your bodyguard, young men who carve the social atmosphere of the ward, and whom you may lead in paths of honor, trustworthiness, and faith?—CR, October 1930, p. 13.

Some of our foolish girls, in the cities particularly, are becoming addicts to nicotine. We should warn them, labor with them—not drive them from us—bring them into our Mutuals, our Sunday Schools, and into our socials where they may mingle with those who cherish higher ideals. I want to tell you, brethren, that we cannot with impunity sit by and be satisfied with having the best of our boys and girls come to auxiliary and priesthood meetings and let the others go unvisited.

If parents are failing in guiding the youth, then it is the duty of ward teachers and priesthood quorums and auxiliary teachers to supplant in the lives of these children the love which they are losing perhaps because of broken homes.—*CR*, September-October 1949, p. 190.

I look upon the organization of the Church as the greatest opportunity ever given to man for the proper training of youth. —*CR*, October 1930, p. 13.

I tell you the time has come for the nation, for the state, for the home, for the Church, to look more directly and particularly after the boys and girls and train them in the way they should go, and when they are old, few will depart from it. —*CR*, October 1930, pp. 13-14.

"Simon, son of Jonas, lovest thou me?"

"Yea, Lord; thou knowest that I love thee."

"Feed my lambs."

Jesus said to him the second time: "Simon, son of Jonas, lovest thou me? . . . Feed my sheep." (See John 21:15-16.)

This was one of the last and one of the most important injunctions that Jesus gave his Apostles following the resurrection. The Savior's charge to watch over the flock and to feed the lambs is as applicable at the present time as it was in the days of Peter. The Church of Jesus Christ must particularly accept this responsibility.—*CR*, April 1931, p. 79.

THE YOUNG MEN'S AND YOUNG WOMEN'S MUTUAL IMPROVEMENT ASSOCIATIONS

The ultimate aim of Mutual Improvement work is to aid in bringing to pass, under the inspiration and guidance of the Lord, the immortality and eternal life of man.

DIRECT AIM AND PURPOSE OF THE M.I.A. We have as the direct and immediate purpose, the establishing in the hearts of the young men and young women a testimony of the divinity of God's work, without which eternal life cannot be obtained— for " . . . this is life eternal, that they might know thee the only true God, and Jesus Christ, whom thou hast sent." (*Ibid.*, 17:3.)

MEANS OF ACCOMPLISHMENT. As a means of accomplishing this end, we have placed at our disposal and use the records of God's revelations to men, also the record of his hand-dealings with mankind. This includes, as you readily see, not only that which we have in sacred literature, known as the fundamental works of scripture, but also God's records in creation. Associated with these fundamental works of creation and revelation, we have access to all man's relationships with each other as social beings, and his attitude in relationship toward God and his work.

It is the records of God's hand-dealings with man that we are to consider now for a few moments. We call them lessons. We take from these records in scripture, in nature, or in life, some chapter, some incident, some paragraph, upon which we build a lesson, which we present to the young men and young women with the special purpose of convincing them of the truth—and having once convinced them, of moving them, if possible, to action to introduce that truth into their lives.

COMMANDED TO TEACH. We are definitely instructed by the Lord to devote special attention to this phase of our work. In section eighty-eight of the Doctrine and Covenants, we find the following commandment:

"And I give unto you a commandment that you shall teach one another the doctrine of the kingdom.

"Teach ye diligently and my grace shall attend you, that you may be instructed more perfectly in theory, in principle, in doctrine, in the law of the gospel, in all things that pertain unto the kingdom of God, that are expedient for you to understand;

"Of things both in heaven and in the earth, and under the earth; things which have been, things which are, things which must shortly come to pass; things which are at home, things which are abroad; the wars and the perplexities of the nations, and the judgments which are on the land; and a knowledge also of countries and of kingdoms—

"That ye may be prepared in all things when I shall send you again to magnify the calling whereunto I have called you, and the mission with which I have commissioned you." (D. & C. 88:77-80.)

Can you get in all literature a more comprehensive statement of the field into which teachers must enter for the purpose of being prepared to teach the word of God than in that revelation?

THE GREAT OBLIGATION IS PREPARATION. We are a Church of teachers. The Mutual Improvement Associations are two organizations of teachers. Even the young men and women whom you leaders teach are themselves in turn teachers. In the Latter-day Saint home the father and mother are required to be teachers of the word—expressly required so by the revelations of the Lord. Every auxiliary organization, every quorum, is made up of a body of men and women or of men, who are in the ultimate sense of the word, teachers; therefore, this revelation refers to all.

Now, the great obligation upon a teacher is to be prepared to teach. A teacher cannot teach others that which he himself does not know. He cannot make his students feel what he does not feel himself. It is ridiculous to attempt to lead a young man or a young woman to obtain a testimony of the work of God, if the man or woman who is attempting to lead does not have that testimony himself or herself.

HOW TO PREPARE. There are three things which must guide all teachers: First, get into the subject—any subject taken from this universe of facts mentioned in the revelation I quoted; second, get that subject into you; third, try to lead your pupils to get the subject into them—not pouring it into them, but leading them to see what you see, to know what you know, to feel what you feel.—IE, 22:899-900 (1919).

YOUTH AND THE RELIGIOUS LIFE

THE REALIZATION OF JOY—A RELIGIOUS DUTY. It is a mistake for young people to become imbued with the feeling that anything associated with religion is unpleasant or depressing. Youth is the happy time of life; all the colors of the future are bright. Their hearts are hopeful. It is our duty to see that those hopes are realized.

I hope to say a word that will lead some of the young men and the young women to feel that those hopes are best realized within the confines of the religious life.—DNCS, July 4, 1936, p. 1.

CHURCH AND PARENTS TO DEMONSTRATE JOYOUS LIVING. It is the duty of parents and of the Church not only to teach but also to demonstrate to young people that living a life of truth and moral purity brings joy and happiness, while violations of moral and social laws result only in dissatisfaction, sorrow, and, when carried to extreme, in degradation.—CR, April 1949, p. 12.

I know that if our young people will accept the teachings and live the standards they will be the happiest, most joyous persons in all the world, and I know if they do not, they will bring sorrow upon themselves and upon their wives and children in the future.—CR, April 1949, p. 182.

YOUTH'S DEVOTION TO THE CHURCH. Every week I sit with my brethren and hear recommends from bishops of young men and young women to go on missions. While there are some who we think should not have been recommended, the great majority of these young men and young women are the noblest in the land.

The young men, even the boys in Sunday School, particularly those in the deacons' quorums, teachers, and priests, and girls of corresponding age, are a credit to the parents, a credit to the Church. As an illustration, out in Uintah recently, I had the privilege of dedicating three church edifices. I learned from the president of the stake that many people had "given their all."

I have heard that expression in other places, and took it at first that it was just an exaggerated expression of devotion. But when I learned on this occasion of a widow who had given all she could possibly give—others, each of whom had sold their last cow, and others who had taken the tax money that had been saved, then I began to realize that there was something in that phrase. And the whole thing was climaxed by the following incident.

The ward was putting forth every effort to finish the meetinghouse, but it was unpaid for. They needed more money. I am not sure that young boy's father is in the Church. I think he is, but he would not contribute, and I have to imagine the devotion of his mother. But this young boy, about fourteen, had saved money by shining shoes, washing automobiles, doing odd chores, and had saved a hundred and fifty-nine dollars.

He had heard of a recent call for more contributions and said to the president of the stake who was cashier of the bank: "I need the nine dollars, but I wish you would take the hundred and fifty and give to the bishop to help pay the cost of that meetinghouse."

"But," said the president, "you cannot afford it."

"Yes, I can."

He gave his hundred and fifty dollars as a contribution. Several months passed, and the ward needed more money, and that young boy out of his meager savings gave a total of two hundred and twenty-five dollars.

An entire group of the Lesser Priesthood taking turns in shifts carried every brick from one old meetinghouse over to the new.

Well, I could multiply incidents of the devotion of the youth, so I have not lost confidence in them, but we must not close our eyes to the approaching wolves who would ravish the flock. We must not close our eyes to the fact that there are conspiring men who would pollute young boys, and girls of corresponding age, for sake of increasing profits. —*CR*, September-October 1949, pp. 187-188.

YOUTH MUST BE COURAGEOUS TO MAINTAIN THE CHRISTIAN LIFE. I appeal to youth to be courageous in maintaining the moral and spiritual values of the gospel of Jesus Christ. After all, "For what is a man profited, if he shall gain the whole world, and lose his own soul? or what shall a man give in exchange for his soul?" (Matt. 16:26.)—*CR*, April 1936, p. 61.

Courage to maintain our ideals is another field in which we can manifest courage and merit the approval of God in whom we trust. These are times when men should keep their heads and not be swept from their moorings by every will-o'-the-wisp theory that is offered as a panacea of our present ills. The times call for courageous youth to hold aloft the moral standard. In that field we can find the truest moral courage. It is said that heroism is concentrated courage. Well, our greatest heroes are not always found on the battlefield. I think we find them also among our youth: young men and

young women who, when put in social groups, will stand up
fearlessly and denounce those things which we know sap the
character, the very life energy of youth.—*CR*, April 1936,
pp. 60-61.

YOUTH AND ITS TESTIMONY

The Law of Faith. A testimony comes from several
sources, one of which I feel impressed to mention briefly.

One way of gaining a testimony is through miracles. I
heard, during my brief stay in Palmyra at the Bureau of Information, of a nurse who had been told that a patient would
die so far as the skill of doctors was concerned, for physicians
had so concluded. Two of the elders administered to the
patient, and she or he recovered. Observing the result of
the administration, the nurse had said to somebody, "I know
now that this is the true gospel." But did she?

What she really did know was that that young man or
woman was healed by a blessing. Whether that patient was
cured through his or her own faith or the faith of the elders
or the power of the priesthood, she does not know. Such a
blessing is a result of the gospel, and of the power of faith.
Such blessings follow obedience to the law of faith.—*DNCS*,
September 12, 1951, p. 2.

The Growth and Development of Testimony: Revelation to the Individual Soul. Let me say to you young
brethren, don't you be discouraged if a testimony does not
come all at once. It did not come suddenly to Peter. Let
me call your attention to one instance.

After feeding the five thousand, you remember, the
Savior crossed over to Capernaum on that tempestuous sea.
Some of the five thousand walked around the northern shore
and were in Capernaum to meet him the next day. Whether
the Savior gave his address in the streets of Capernaum or in
the synagogue, he delivered a masterful message, in which
he said to the assembled multitude, "Ye seek me, not because
ye saw the miracles, but because ye did eat of the loaves, and
were filled." (John 6:26.) They had seen the miracle, but they
had missed something deeper, more significant.

Then Jesus delivered that remarkable sermon on the
bread of life, but its symbolism they could not understand

and began to walk away. Those who had followed him began to leave him and turn their backs upon him, and finally only the Twelve were left, unto whom he said, "Will ye also go away?" Peter, the impulsive leader, practical and sound spokesman (I love him!), said unto him: "Lord, to whom shall we go? thou hast the words of eternal life.

"And we believe and are sure that thou art that Christ, the Son of the living God." (See John 6:67-69.)

I linger on *believe* and *are sure* because I think that is the way Peter would have said it. It seemed that at that time Peter's testimony was not strong and definite. I may be wrong and do not ask you to accept that interpretation if you do not believe it, but of this we may be sure, on that occasion he did not get the word *blessed.*

Jesus took the disciples from Capernaum and went up into the mountain close by to teach them further, and it was while he was up there during that week that he asked the question, "Whom do men say that I the Son of man am?" They answered and said: "Some say that thou art John the Baptist: some, Elias; and others, Jeremias, or one of the prophets. " Then he said: "But whom say ye that I am?" And Peter answered without hesitation, "Thou art the Christ, the Son of the living God."

"Blessed art thou, Simon Bar-jona: for flesh and blood hath not revealed it unto thee, but my Father which is in heaven.

"And I say also unto thee, That thou art Peter (Peter saw this testimony or revelation from God), and upon this rock I will build my Church; and the gates of hell shall not prevail against it." (See Matt. 16:13-18.)

Inspiration, revelation to the individual soul, is the rock upon which a testimony should be built, and there is not one living who cannot get it if he will conform to those laws and live a clean life which will permit the holy Spirit to place that testimony in him.—*DNCS,* September 12, 1951, p. 4.

CHAPTER 32

EDUCATION

TRUE EDUCATION: THE PARAMOUNT PURPOSE OF A FREE PEOPLE[1]

Our nation is facing stupendously critical problems, not the least of which is the present-day indifference toward the need of better training and proper education of youth—America's most precious asset, her greatest safeguard, her most important, most potentially profitable enterprise!

EDUCATION FOR A LIVELIHOOD. Students enter school primarily to gain economic or social advantage. But this aim is not always achieved, nor is it, nor should it be, the highest purpose of education. However, we must not underestimate the value of obtaining an education for a livelihood. Education for economic advancement is a good investment for the individual as well as for the state. The United States as a nation is still young, but its brief history is replete with striking examples of the value of its free public school system even as a financial investment.

THE EXAMPLE OF DR. GEORGE WASHINGTON CARVER. Here, for instance, was a son of a slave entering Iowa State College, having worked his own way through the grades, high school, and three years at Simpson College. Four years later, he took his degree in agriculture. His work so impressed the authorities that they appointed him a member of the college faculty. Soon thereafter he refused a tempting offer of one hundred thousand dollars a year. As a child, frail and undernourished, he earned a living by doing odd household chores. His adopted parents wanted him to get an education but offered him no money. The handicapped boy's primary purpose was the same as that of every other child in America; namely, to gain economic and social betterment—to broaden his means of gaining a livelihood. Experts say that this man (Dr. Washington Carver) has done more than any other living

---

[1]From the address delivered by President David O. McKay at Commencement Exercises, University of Utah, U. of U. Stadium, Saturday, June 9, 1951, 6:30 p.m.

man to rehabilitate agriculture in the South. Since 1898 the industry which he fostered has grown until it now runs into more than sixty million dollars a year.

No, I do not in the least disparage this aim nor criticize our public school system for planning to make possible its realization. But education for a livelihood is not the highest purpose of education.—*CAUU*, June 9, 1951, pp. 4-5.

THE PARAMOUNT EDUCATIONAL IDEAL, SPIRITUAL RATHER THAN ECONOMIC. After all is said and done, the most potent force for training youth in the United States today is our public school system. But let us face clearly and forcefully the fact that the paramount ideal permeating all education in the grades, the high school, through college and the university, should be more spiritual than economic.

I am but repeating what we all know and feel when I say that our country's greatest asset is its manhood. Upon that depends not only the survival of the individual freedom vouchsafed by the Constitution and Bill of Rights, and all other ideals, for which the founders of the republic fought and died, but also the survival of the best that we cherish in present-day civilization throughout the world.

The preservation of these must come through education. Lest you think that I am merely an idealist, appealing for something which cannot be attained practically through the curriculum of our public schools, let me say that if the *purpose* be properly emphasized and the *desire* to achieve it be generally sensed, the coming generation and adults of the present time can be influenced within the next ten years. Still fresh in our memory is the fact that a paranoiac, with a native ability to influence the masses, demonstrated through concentrated, continued effort by specially-trained instructors and leaders, how the minds of youth could be directed within two decades to accept even a perverted ideal. How near he came to this realization of his aim within a few short years is now a matter of history. If youth can be so influenced to degenerate to the jungle, it can also be trained by united purpose to ascend the path of spiritual attainment.

Only through proper education can these fundamental principles become fixed and guiding influences in the lives of human beings. Our educational system will radiate such principles just to the extent that we employ in our public schools, high schools, colleges, and universities men and women who are not only eminent in their particular professions but also loyal to the Constitution of our land, influential as leaders, noble in character.

EDUCATIONAL IDEALS AND THE PERSONALITY OF THE TEACHER. Imagine what it would mean to the national integrity of America if every one of the half million graduates, in addition to his having earned his diploma, could cherish the memory of a noble character of whom throughout the years he could say as a Chief Justice of the Supreme Court of the United States said of one who influenced his university career: "I admired him for his learning, loved him for his goodness, profited greatly from both. He believed that scholastic attainments were better than riches, but that better than either were faith, love, charity, clean living, clean thinking, loyalty, tolerance, and all the other attributes that combine to constitute that most precious of all possessions—good character."

In his appreciation of the instructor who wielded the most influence in his life, this leader of men is but echoing the sentiments expressed by Ralph Waldo Emerson, reputedly the wisest American—"Character is higher than intellect: . . . A great soul will be strong to live, as well as to think." The most potent influence in training our youth to cherish life, to keep their word of honor, to have increased respect for human kind and love of justice, is the life and personality of the teacher.

GENERAL EDUCATION AND THE INDUSTRIAL AGE. The contribution of general education to the industrial and commercial greatness of the country is obvious on every hand— in research laboratories, in increased productivity of farms, in achievements of electrical, physical, chemical, engineering sciences, in harnessing, either for the benefit or destruction of man, the boundless force of atomic energy. But what true education has done, and may do to awaken in the human heart a sense of the end and aim of human existence on this earth, what it has done to raise the standard of citizenship, how it has helped to make living happier by contributing to the prosperity, peace, and security of our country, are beyond evaluation!

Stockholders—the people of the United States—must make this greatest of industries in our republic pay dividends in character and true citizenship or face inevitable failure and possible catastrophe.—*CAUU,* June 9, 1951, pp. 9-10.

A FREE PEOPLE MUST STRIVE FOR THE HIGHEST AND BEST EDUCATION. Southey tells us that, in his walk one stormy day, he met an old woman, to whom, by way of greeting, he made the rather obvious remark that it was dreadful weather. She answered philosophically, that, in her opinion, "Any weather is better than none!" So we may say that any education is better than none, but a free people to remain free must ever strive for the highest and best.

To the members of the graduating class, I extend sincere congratulations upon your having completed the prescribed courses of study in your respective chosen professions, but, more than that, upon your increased ability to preserve the liberties of your country, and to be of greater service to your fellow men—for whatever your future successes or seeming failures, I still look upon all recipients of true education as individuals and groups radiating an influence that makes less dense and ineffective the darkness of ignorance, of suspicion, of hatred, of bigotry, avarice, and greed that continue to envelop in darkness the lives of men. Of course, to quote Newel Dwight Hillis: "Not all men are of equal value—not many Platos—only one, to whom a thousand lesser minds look up and learn and think. Not many Dantes: one, and a thousand poets tune their harps to his and repeat his notes. Not many Raphaels; one, and no second. But a thousand lesser artists looking up to him are lifted to his level. Happy the town blessed with a few great minds and a few great hearts. One such citizen will civilize an entire community."— *CAUU,* June 9, 1951, pp. 10-11.

A FREE PEOPLE'S BEST INVESTMENT

THE FOSTERING OF FULL ECONOMIC FREEDOM. I should like to say a few words on "Education—A Free People's Best Investment."

The fostering of full economic freedom lies at the base of our liberties. Only in perpetuating economic freedom can our social, political, and religious liberties be preserved. However, that is a theme in itself.

There are many who believe sincerely that the liberties of the individual as vouchsafed in the Constitution of the United States are in dire jeopardy. There are some who doubt it, thinking that humanity will weather this crisis as it has surmounted others in the past; for example:

"The world is passing through troublous times. Young people of today think of nothing but themselves. They have no reverence for parents or old age. They are impatient of all restraint. They talk as if they alone know everything. As for girls, they are forward, immodest, and unwomanly in speech, behavior, and dress."

When was that written? In the year 1274!

"My grandad, viewing earth's worn cogs,
Said things are going to the dogs.
His grandad in his house of logs,
Said things are going to the dogs.
His grandad in the Flemish bogs,
Said things are going to the dogs.
His grandad in his old skin togs,
Said things are going to the dogs.
There's one thing I have to state,
The dogs have had a good long wait!"

Such expressions of experiences of the past lead some to wonder whether present-day apprehensions of impending world catastrophe may not pass as have forebodings of other generations.

Let us today be appreciative of the fact that in the United States everybody has the right to express his or her own interpretation of impending events and that we can think and speak as we please without fear of oppression or punishment.

However, students, we must not let complacency blind our eyes to the real dangers threatening to destroy us. Judging from the written and expressed opinion of many of our leaders, our government is facing the greatest crisis in its history.
—DNCS, March 12, 1952, p. 2.

EDUCATION AN INVESTMENT, NOT AN EXPENSE. I wish to say that education is an investment, not an expense.—*DNCS,* March 12, 1952, p. 14.

INVEST IN OUTSTANDING TEACHERS. If the people of the United States would have the highest returns for their financial investment in education, they must as a matter of sound business judgment have, in all our schools, teachers of outstanding leadership and wholesome influence.—*DNCS,* March 12, 1952, p. 14.

THE NOBLEST PURPOSE IN EDUCATION. In my opinion, the highest, noblest purpose in all our education from the grades to the university is to teach citizenship and noble character. I believe that the thousands of students who have entered these halls have been made to sense, by absorption and by inference, that a man's character is greater than intellectual attainments or social privileges; that "every thought creates character; that every act is an incarnation of character; that every decision is a revelation of character; that habit is a pillar in the edifice of character."—*DNCS,* March 12, 1952, p. 14.

MORAL INSTRUCTION AND THE CURRICULUM. From *The Child, His Nature and His Needs,* a publication of the Children's Foundation, pages 102 and 106, I will read this question: "Should moral instruction receive a definite place in the school curriculum?" I want to tell you students, who will be leaders in a few years in scholastic fields and business, that unless we do make morality and ethics and spirituality and religion our direct aim this nation will not be prepared to counteract the evil influence of the teaching behind the iron curtain, the leaders of which are purposely, designedly, you take my word for it, teaching youth corrupt ideals and principles.

Now, our public schools, recognizing that, are setting forth ethical principles to be taught. But, note this, moral instruction is of the greatest usefulness where teachers are in earnest, where they possess the necessary skill, where they see that moral instruction is only one item in the general program of moral education, and where all the moral forces in the school are called into play together.

Now, I pause long enough to ask the leaders of this nation, how is it possible to get leaders in our schoolrooms, hold them, have men of influence and women of superior ability to teach our children unless we are willing to compensate them properly in their efforts so to teach their children? It is folly for this nation to expect more teachers throughout the land to forsake other and more lucrative opportunities if they do not give to our teachers, our professors in the universities, in the high schools, and in day schools a compensation that their position merits. We'll have to face it, giving only five billion dollars for education in the United States and expending at the same time twenty billion dollars to take care of crime is inconsistent. It takes us back to that old story: Which will you have—a fence around the cliff or an ambulance down in the valley ?

*   *   *   *   *

Here are some of the ideals recommended by our public school officers in our morality code which are very commendable: self-control, kindness, sportsmanship, self-reliance, duty, reliability, good workmanship, teamwork, loyalty, obedience to duty and to constituted authority. That is very commendable: obedience to all is necessary to protect the fundamentals of our government — freedom, justice, and equality, moral ideals—but unless we have teachers who will inspire the students and become as it were, heroes, ideals at least, in the minds of those students, these ethical principles will not become very impressive. Now admitting all that is necessary, pleading with our government, our state officials as well, and local boards, rightfully and respectably to compensate our teachers, there is something higher and greater which our public school system cannot teach; that which the church school is unhampered in teaching.

To live an upright life, to conform to high ethical standards is the responsibility and duty of every teacher in the land. Greater even than this is the responsibility of the religious teacher. His profession is higher than that of the teacher in the common school, for in addition in his belief in the efficacy of ethical and moral precepts, a religious teacher assumes the responsibility of leading the youth into the realms of spirituality. His duty comporting with his pretensions and profession is to open the eyes of the blind that they may see God. What is there in man so worthy of honor and reverence as this, that he is capable of contemplating something higher than his own reason, more sublime than the whole universe, that spirit which alone is self-subsistent, from which all truth proceeds without which there is no truth? Leading youth to know God, to have faith in his laws, to have confidence in his fatherhood and to find solace and peace in his love—this is the greatest privilege, the most sublime opportunity offered the true educator.—*DNCS*, October 18, 1952, p. 4.

THE IDEA AND MEANING OF A UNIVERSITY

A university is not a dictionary, a dispensary, nor is it a department store. It is more than a storehouse of knowledge and more than a community of scholars. University life is essentially an exercise in thinking, preparing, and living. Without further comment, I give you this definition: The aim of education is to develop resources in the child that will contribute to his well-being as long as life endures; to develop power of self-mastery that he may never be a slave to indulgence or other weaknesses, to develop virile manhood, beautiful womanhood that in every child and every youth may be found at least the promise of a friend, a companion, one who later may be fit for husband or wife, an exemplary father or a loving intelligent mother, one who can face life with courage, meet disaster with fortitude, and face death without fear.—*DNCS*, October 18, 1952, p. 2.

THE TEACHER AND THE TEACHING PROFESSION

THE NOBLEST PROFESSION. Teaching is the noblest profession in the world. Upon the proper education of youth depend the permanency and purity of home, the safety and perpetuity of the nation. The parent gives the child an opportunity to live; the teacher enables the child to live well. That parent who gives life and teaches his child to live abundantly is the true parent-teacher. However, today the customs and demands of society are such that the responsibility of training the child to live well is largely, and in too many instances, shifted entirely from the parent to the teacher.

In the ideal state, the teacher would be but the parents' ally, training the mind and encouraging worthy habits, and fostering noble traits of character inculcated by wise parental teaching and example, but in reality, the teacher, instead of being merely an ally must become the foster parent in training the child in the art of living. If that were all, his responsibility would be great enough; but it is not all. Often he faces even the greater task of overcoming the false teaching and improper training of unwise, irresponsible parents. In the light of such self-evident facts, I think it must be apparent to every thinking mind that the *noblest* of all professions is that of *teaching*, and that upon the effectiveness of that teaching hangs the destiny of nations. "All who have meditated on the art of governing mankind," says Aristotle, "have been convinced that the fate of empires depends upon the education of youth."—*RSM*, 21:722 (1934).

OBJECTIVES IN THE PUBLIC SCHOOLS. The general objectives in our public schools should be to assist the individual in the proper development of his physical, intellectual, and spiritual nature, that he may become of value to his country and of service to his fellow man. This objective can be accomplished only on the basis of true education.

And what is true education? "It is awakening a love for truth; giving a just sense of duty; opening the eyes of the soul to the great purpose and end of life. It is not so much giving words, as thoughts; or mere maxims, as living principles. It is not teaching to be honest, because 'honesty is the best policy'; but because it is right. It is teaching the individual to love the good, for the sake of the good; to be virtuous in action because one is so in heart; to love and serve God supremely not from fear, but from delight in his perfect character." No one can successfully controvert the fact that upon the teacher rests much of the responsibility of lifting society to this high ideal.—*RSM*, 21:723 (1934).

The responsibility of the teacher, however, does not end in his duty to teach truth positively. He enters the realm of what-not-to-do as well as the realm of what-to-do. In the garden of the human soul, as well as in the fields of human endeavor, there are thorns and thistles as well as flowers and useful plants. Thrice deserving of condemnation is he who would crush in a boy's mind a flower of truth and sow in its stead the seed of error! Hence, the importance of the teacher's knowing what she is teaching, conscientiously believing that it is in harmony with God and truth. I merely throw out the thought because you can go down on your knees in your home and ask God to give you the power to speak truth.

Wise parents and leading educators in the nation today realize that good citizenship can be attained only through character development. The sincere teacher realizes that hers is the opportunity to inculcate the virtues that contribute to the building of true manhood and womanhood. Hers is the sublime task to lead children and youth to believe that compliance with high moral standards leads to success and happiness.—*RSM*, 21:723-724 (1934).

THE GREAT RESPONSIBILITY OF THE RELIGIOUS TEACHER. To live an upright life, to conform to high ethical standards is the responsibility and duty of every teacher in the land. Greater even than this is the responsibility of the religious teacher. The religious teacher's profession is higher than that of the teacher in the common school; for, in addition to his belief in the efficacy of ethical and moral precepts, the religious teacher assumes the responsibility of leading the youth into the realm of spirituality.—*RSM*, 21:725 (1934).

Not long ago I noticed a young girl in her teens put forth a special effort to address the little boy who was by my side. I did not know her, cannot call her name today, but I could see she wanted to recognize the lad, and I noticed that he was glad when he saw her reciprocate or to return her salutation. As we passed, I said, "Who is she?"

"She is my Religion Class teacher."

"What is her name?"

"I don't know what her name is, but, oh, she is a *dandy!*"

He used an incorrect word, evidently did not know its true meaning, but the significance he gave the word I knew, and the expression on his face I read, and in my heart I thanked the young girl for the influence she has over that boy. Only in her teens, but what that girl will say to him in his Religion Class, he will accept as gospel truth; what she does in her life, he will emulate; and that young girl carries the responsibility, in a way, of molding my son's character; and the hun-

dred thousand teachers in this Church carry the same responsibility.—*CR*, April 1914, p. 89.

The most cherished opportunities of the religious teacher
should be to lead the child to see, through the trouble and
turmoil of a physical world, that "in all his dispensations
God is at work for our good. In prosperity he tries our gratitude; in mediocrity, our contentment; in misfortune, our submission; in darkness, our faith; under temptation, our stead-
fastness; and at all times, our obedience and trust in him."
—*RSM*, 21:726 (1934).

HOW TO SATISFY A CLASS. I have said to teachers on more
than one occasion: If you will give your classes a thought,
even *one* new thought during your recitation period, you will
find that they will go away satisfied. But it is your obligation
to be prepared to give that new thought.—*DNCS*, April 30,
1952, p. 3.

THE AWARENESS OF INDIVIDUALITY. From birth to death
men differ. They vary as much as do flowers in a garden. In
intellect, in temperament, in energy, and in training some
rise to one level and some to another.

The successful teacher is one who, with a spirit of discernment, can detect to a degree at least, the mentality and
capability of the members of his class. He should be able to
read the facial expressions and be responsive to the mental
and spiritual attitudes of those whom he is teaching. The
great Teacher had this power of discernment in perfection
as is well illustrated in his conversation with the woman of
Samaria whose interests he not only interpreted, but whose
soul he also read by virtue of her past deeds. Too few teachers
have this gift, even to a limited degree, but every teacher has
the responsibility of determining how best to approach the
members of the class in order to make appeals that will be
lasting.—*RSM*, 21:722 (1934).

It is written that "he who governs well leads the blind,
but he that teaches gives them eyes."—*CR*, April 1914, p. 86.

SEEK THE BEST. The lives of men become signposts to us,
pointing the way along roads that lead either to lives of usefulness and happiness or to lives of selfishness and misery. It

is important then that we seek, both in life and in books, the companionship of the best and noblest men and women. —*AA*, p. 2.

THE CHURCH AND EDUCATION

WE ARE FREE "TO LAUNCH INTO THE REALM OF THE INFINITE" IN SEARCH OF TRUTH. The Church stands for education. The very purpose of its organization is to promulgate truth among men. Members of the Church are admonished to acquire learning by study, and also by faith and prayer, and to seek after everything that is virtuous, lovely, of good report, or praiseworthy. In this seeking after truth they are not confined to narrow limits of dogma or creed, but are free to launch into the realm of the infinite, for they know that

> "Truth is truth where'er 'tis found,
> Whether on Christian or on heathen ground."

Indeed, one of the fundamental teachings of the Church is that salvation itself depends upon knowledge; for, says the revelation, "It is impossible for a man to be saved in ignorance," (D. & C. 131:6) and again, " . . . if a person gains more knowledge and intelligence in this life through his diligence and obedience than another, he will have so much the advantage in the world to come." (*Ibid.*, 130:19.)

KNOWLEDGE AND THE USE OF KNOWLEDGE. But gaining knowledge is one thing and applying it, quite another. Wisdom is the right application of knowledge; and true education—the education for which the Church stands—is the application of knowledge to the development of a noble and Godlike character.

A man may possess a profound knowledge of history and of mathematics; he may be authority in psychology, biology, or astronomy; he may know all the discovered truths pertaining to geology and natural science; but if he has not with this knowledge that nobility of soul which prompts him to deal justly with his fellow men, to practise virtue and holiness in personal life, he is not a truly educated man.

Character is the aim of true education; and science, history, and literature are but means used to accomplish the desired end. Character is not the result of chance work but of continuous right thinking and right acting.

SOME DEFECTS OF MODERN EDUCATION. True education seeks, then, to make men and women not only good mathematicians, proficient linguists, profound scientists, or brilliant literary lights, but also honest men, combined with virtue, temperance, and brotherly love—men and women who prize truth, justice, wisdom, benevolence, and self-control as the choicest acquisitions of a successful life.

It is regrettable, not to say deplorable, that modern education so little emphasizes these fundamental elements of true character. The principal aim of many of our schools and colleges seems to be to give the students purely intellectual attainments and to give but passing regard to the nobler and more necessary development along moral lines. This is particularly noticeable along the lines of self-control. Notwithstanding the study of hygiene in our public schools and the hundreds of books written in condemnation of the use of tobacco and alcoholic beverages, thousands of our school children are sapping their intellectual strength and blunting their moral sensibilities by the pernicious use of the cigaret and other forms of tobacco. The small percentage of these who reach college add to the tobacco the drinking habit, and to this sexual indulgence that leaves them stranded as moral wrecks before they are scarcely launched on their life's journey.

FAITH IN THE DISSEMINATION OF NEW IDEAS. I think every progressive age of the world has had intellectual and socially-minded leaders who have sought a better way of living than that which was theirs. The good life, so important to man's happiness, has been the quest of the ages. To sense the need for reform has been easy, but to achieve it has been difficult and often well-nigh impossible. Ideas suggested and proposed by the wisest of men have too often been impractical, often fantastic, yet in most cases the world in general has been made better by the dissemination of new ideas, even though the experiments proved failures at that time.—*IE*, 45:12 (1942).

THE SCHOOL TENDS TO SUPERSEDE THE CHURCH AS AN INSTITUTIONAL SOCIAL INFLUENCE. If the reports be true, with reference to the indifference of the country as a whole toward

Christian churches, we shall have to place next to the home, not the church, but the public school, as the most influential factor in lessening delinquency.—*IE*, 49:740 (1946).

DUTIES OF CHURCH AND SCHOOL. A potent factor in character development is the public school.

To these democratic institutions come children from all kinds of homes, including the delinquent. All I can say is that every teacher in church and in school should realize that he has the moral as well as the assigned responsibility to impress upon his students the true value of the highest and noblest things in life.—*CR*, October 1948, p. 120.

Schools and churches should radiate the fact that there are in life certain fundamentals which never change and which are essential to the happiness of every human soul. —*I*, 81:168 (1946).

TEACHERS AND ICONOCLASTS. You know there are occasionally men in the profession of teaching—as that is my profession I can speak plainly—who pride themselves on being iconoclasts; but unfortunately, when such teachers break their so-called images, they supply nothing to replace them. They destroy ideals but offer no others, thus leaving the young boy in doubt and uncertainty. Such a one seems to me to be heaving anchor and starting out on the ocean of life before his course is even charted.—*CR*, April 1932, p. 64.

TRUE EDUCATION INVOLVES THE DEVELOPMENT OF CHARACTER. True education does not consist merely in the acquiring of a few facts of science, history, literature, or art, but in the development of character. True education awakens a desire to conserve health by keeping the body clean and undefiled. True education trains in self-denial and self-mastery. True education regulates the temper, subdues passion, and makes obedience to social laws and moral order a guiding principle of life. It develops reason and inculcates faith in the living God as the eternal, loving Father of all.—*CR*, April 1928, p. 102.

There is true nobility in the soul of that man or woman who sincerely desires and strives to lead children out of contaminating influences into an environment of high ideals and lofty endeavors.—*I*, 84:620 (1949).

A PROPOSAL FOR GENERAL EDUCATION. General education would be much more effective in producing true manhood and pure womanhood if it gave more attention to the virtue of self-control and self-denial. The student who learns to control his appetites and desires, and to deny himself for the comfort and well-being of others, is more truly educated than the selfish, self-indulgent pedant. This self-mastery comes as the result of continuous overcoming—resisting a temptation of appetite this hour, overcoming a tempting desire the next.

"It is impossible," says Charles Wagner, "to be brotherly, to love, to give one's self, unless one is master of himself." If this one element in true education were emphasized by teachers and practised in early life by resisting even only those temptations that appeal to the appetite, our school system would be open to less severe censure than it is today.

In the meantime, let the Church continue its work in the interest of true education; and the Church schools and Sunday Schools ever keep before them the fact that only in true education lies the safety of the home, the state, and the nation, and that "In God's word we have a perfect standard both of duty and character, that by the influence of both, appealing to the best principles of our nature, we may be roused to the noblest and best efforts."—*I*, 46:584-585 (1911).

CHARACTER IS HIGHER THAN INTELLECT. Present-day conditions emphasize the fact (and I believe it with all my heart) that the most paramount objective of the public school system from kindergarten to the university should be character building and the evolving of true, loyal citizens of the republic. The teaching of the three "R's" of the arts and the sciences, even the delving into research work, should be but a means to the development of true manhood and noble womanhood. Education for loyal citizenship!—*IE*, 49:740 (1946).

MATERIAL AND CULTURAL SUPPLEMENTS. In teaching children, it should ever be kept in mind that "Behavior is caught, not taught." Example is more potent than precept. Parents have the duty to be what they would have their children become in regard to courtesy, sincerity, temperance, and courage to do right at all times.

It is true that

> "We need not power or splendor,
> Wide halls, or lordly dome,
> The good, the true, the tender—
> These form the wealth of home."

The fact remains, however, that there are certain material and cultural needs which are indispensable to successful home life. During the present crisis, to prevent the breaking up of homes, these material needs must be furnished by the group, either through the Church or the state. Here is where the complete organization of the Church should function most adequately. The material as well as the spiritual needs of every family in the Church should not only be known as I have already stated, but also supplied by the bishopric of the ward, either directly or indirectly. In a superior and effective manner the Church can also and does supply cultural needs such as education, social opportunities, music, etc. These may be obtained by every child, every youth, every person in the Church who will avail himself or herself of the opportunities offered. I wonder if parents generally are doing all they can to see to it that their boys and girls are members of quorums and auxiliaries, organized for the express purpose of supplementing the home in the training of youth.—*CR*, April 1935, pp. 114-115.

EDUCATION FOR BALANCED LIVING. Insinuations made to the young who are yet undecided as to what are the most important things in life may shake the faith of youth, and "Youth without faith is as day without sun."

I cite that instance to bring home to us today the necessity of parents and officers in the Church teaching more earnestly and diligently the principles of life and salvation to the youth of Zion and to the world in order to keep the latter properly balanced through the formative period of their lives.

"Our civilization is imperiled today," writes an American statistician, "simply because it is ill balanced. Our spiritual culture lags so far behind our material culture, in its development, that we have no adequate control over the latter. Our science, our education, and our government can do much to help correct this lack in our spiritual development, but in the main this must be done, if done at all, by religion and by the Church, for religion is the creator and the conservator of our social ideals, and the church is their chief propagator."

The confidence and faith I have expressed in the First Presidency, the Twelve, and others of my associates, as well as in the gospel and especially in the Savior, applies also to the tenets and teachings of the Church. Every one when properly interpreted and applied has in it a saving power and blessing for all who will accept it.—CR, April 1932, pp. 63-64.

THE CHURCH EDUCATIONAL SYSTEM

BRIGHAM YOUNG UNIVERSITY. From its beginning, Brigham Young University has had the revelation in the Doctrine and Covenants that "Intelligence, or the light of truth, was not created or made, neither indeed can be.

"All truth is independent in that sphere in which God has placed it, to act for itself, as all intelligence also; otherwise there is no existence." (D. & C. 93:29-30.)

What an impressive example of inspiration to the Prophet Joseph Smith! When answering your students' questions on "intelligence" or the origin of life, you teachers are not hampered or hesitant when you give these revelations as eternal verities.

Thus we have the glorious truth that uncreated, ever-existent intelligence animated spiritual bodies,

"For man is spirit. The elements are eternal, and spirit and element, inseparably connected, receive a fulness of joy;

"And when separated, man cannot receive a fulness of joy.

"The elements are the tabernacle of God; yea, man is the tabernacle of God, even temples; and whatsoever temple is defiled, God shall destroy that temple." (Ibid., 93:33-35.)

Thus may be found in this Church university without wonderment or equivocation the source not only of life, but also of intelligence, and the answer to the question of human immortality.

I heard your president say on an important occasion that this school is destined to be the greatest university in the world, and if we maintain these ideals, nothing can prevent its becoming so.

Another thought in this connection: When President Brigham Young called Brother Karl G. Maeser into his office and said, "We want you to go to Provo to organize and conduct an academy to be established in the name of the Church— a Church school," he implied that our Lord and Savior Jesus Christ would be kept in mind as the head, center, and life of this institution. How could it be otherwise when the school was to be established in the name of the Church, which is the Church of Jesus Christ!—*DNCS*, June 6, 1951, p. 3.

God bless you, teachers of this faculty, you students, that you may lift this school, if it has not yet attained it, to that height wherein it may be an example to all higher institutions in the world, that we may contribute to the new trend of thought of educational leaders that the great need of the world today is more spirituality, less atheism, more love for God, and for one's fellow men!—*DNCS*, October 17, 1951, p. 7.

PARAMOUNT OBJECTIVES OF THE SEMINARY TEACHER. Two paramount objectives of a seminary teacher are:

1. To establish the reality of a divine spirit.

2. To attain spiritual response.

Your work is to see into the boy's soul. There may be doubt and wonderment and questioning in him, so that he will come to you and say, "I don't believe you," and then you must lead him to the point where he will believe you. It is not enough to know youth by name but know their doubts and their wishes and their desires. Get over to the youth the fact that the physical part of their beings is but a machine, but the spiritual part is eternal.—*DNCS*, August 8, 1936, p. 8.

BOOK VI

A PHILOSOPHY OF FAMILY LIFE
AND RELIGIOUS LIVING

"The highest ideal for our young girls today, as for our mothers who crossed the plains, is love as it may be expressed in marriage and home building, and this virtue in which love finds true expression is based upon the spiritual and not the physical side of our being."

DAVID O. McKAY
The Improvement Era
Volume 23:473.

CHAPTER 33

WOMANHOOD AND MOTHERHOOD

WOMANHOOD

CREATION'S MASTERPIECE. A beautiful, modest, gracious woman is creation's masterpiece. When to these virtues a woman possesses as guiding stars in her life righteousness and godliness and an irresistible impulse and desire to make others happy, no one will question if she be classed among those who are the truly great.—FS, ms., Emma Lucy Gates Bowen, May 3, 1951, p. 1.

IDEALS FOR YOUNG WOMANHOOD. The highest ideal for our young girls today, as for our mothers who crossed the plains, is love as it may be expressed in marriage and home building, and this virtue in which love finds true expression is based upon the spiritual and not the physical side of our being. If marriage and home building be based upon physical attraction alone, love will sooner or later become famished and home life a heavy, disheartening existence.—IE, 50:686 (1947).

WOMANHOOD SHOULD BE INTELLIGENT AND PURE. Womanhood should be intelligent and pure because it is the living life-fountain from which flows the stream of humanity. She who would pollute that stream by tobacco, poisonous drugs, or by germs that would shackle the unborn, is untrue to her sex and an enemy to the strength and perpetuity of the race. —RSM, 27:21 (1940).

TRUE BEAUTY

TRUE BEAUTY IS CHASTE. A young lady was once deploring the frequency of the changes in styles, when a young man to whom she spoke said, "Well, why do you women permit it? You don't have to adopt every suggestion of the fashion plate."

"If it were not for you men," she replied, "we wouldn't."

"For us men! How is that?"

"Yes, for you men; for, after all, to make an honest confession, one of the reasons for all this style in dress and complexion is to bring forth the admiration of you selfish 'lords of creation.' "

The conversation was carried on in a jocular vein and continued for some time. The thought that this opinion influenced the girl to make herself beautiful seemed to tickle the young man's conceit; and he unconsciously tipped his hat backward, seemingly to make room for the expansion. The girl was the young man's superior and called forth his admiration, not merely by her outward beauty, but by a quality a thousand times more powerful and admirable.

The reason given for some of the girl's efforts towards outward adornment reminds me of Pope's lines,—

"Fair tresses man's imperial race ensnare,
And beauty draws us with a single hair."

Yes, men are attracted by beauty, and thousands are ensnared by it. There are thousands of men who look for nothing else and who desire nothing else but to have their senses pleased or their passions gratified. These outward adornments will satisfy and only outward adornment will retain. When beauty fades, the passion seeks for gratification elsewhere. "Beauty is only skin-deep," and when outward adornment is all a girl possesses, the admiration she calls forth is even more shallow than her beauty.

"Beauties in vain their pretty eyes may roll;
Charms strike the sight, but merit wins the soul."

It is not my purpose to discourage efforts to enhance physical beauty. When given by birth, it should be nurtured in childhood, cherished in girlhood, and protected in womanhood. When not inherited, it should be developed and sought after in every legitimate and healthful manner.

But there is a beauty every girl has—a gift from God, as pure as the sunlight, and as sacred as life. It is a beauty that all men love, a virtue that wins all men's souls. That beauty is *chastity*. Chastity without skin beauty may enkindle the soul; skin beauty without chastity can kindle only the eye. Chastity enshrined in the mold of true womanhood will hold true love eternally.

In the last paragraph, I have said that chastity is a beauty that all men love. Well, I will not change it, for he who does not is not a man, "He should be sent back to nature's mint and reissued as a counterfeit on humanity's baser metal." Such a one is not worth a pure maiden's scorn, not to say smile.

The flower by the roadside that catches the dust of every traveler is not the one to be admired and is seldom if ever plucked; but the one blooming away up on the hillside, protected by a perpendicular cliff is the flower with the virgin perfume, the one the boy will almost risk his life to possess.

Mere outside adornment may please the senses of many superficial admirers; the adornment of the soul and the chastity of true womanhood will awaken in the soul of true manhood enduring life, that eternal principle which some day will redeem the world.—*YWJ*, 17:360-362 (1906).

BEAUTY OF SPIRIT AND CHARACTER. I hope our sisters will resist all the temptations of the world that may come under the heading—vanity. I hope that we may have strength to resist all the allurements that come with wealth and worldly position, when we make those two things an end in themselves.—*CR*, April 1907, p. 12.

A SOBERING LESSON. One of the first great lessons that I ever had in my life was when I was attending the University of Utah. Mother came down to visit four of us children who were here as students. I remember on one occasion as we returned home from the theater, we were aroused by the screaming of a woman in a neighboring house. I thought a man was beating his wife and ran over and tapped on the window, protesting against the attack, although I confess I was a little afraid he might come out and beat me. My brother ran over to the fire station and telephoned for the police. The landlady came before the officers. As she opened the door, I saw for the first time in my life, a drunken woman. I shall never forget the shock that I received. There in the doorway were two little girls crying. With the memory of the shock, however, I treasure the kindly love of my mother, who, though somewhat timid, walked into the house and put her arms around the two little girls. Enough of that scene!

Several years afterward I had occasion to teach a class in the State Industrial School of Utah. In the girls' department were two beautiful young women, whom I did not recognize, either by features or by name, until a little boy who had grown up on that same lot to which I have referred, went with me one day to the class, and one of these girls recognized him and came up and told about the time when she lived on that lot. They were the little girls whom my mother comforted in the presence of a drunken woman; both now in the reform school! They were not to blame—victims of an evil environment into which the mother had led them. —*RSM*, 18:349-350 (1931).

MOTHERHOOD

THE GREATEST POTENTIAL INFLUENCE IN HUMAN LIFE. Motherhood is the greatest potential influence either for good or ill in human life. The mother's image is the first that stamps itself on the unwritten page of the young child's mind. It is her caress that first awakens a sense of security; her kiss, the first realization of affection; her sympathy and tenderness, the first assurance that there is love in the world. True, there comes a time when Father takes his place as exemplar and hero of the growing boy; and in the latter's budding ambition to develop manly traits, he outwardly seems to turn from the more gentle and tender virtues engendered by his mother. Yet that ever-directing and restraining influence implanted during the first years of his childhood linger with him and permeate his thoughts and memory as distinctively as perfume clings to each particular flower.

In more than one instance in the life of fiery youth, this lingering influence has proved a safeguard in the hour of temptation—an influence greater in its restraining power than the threat of the law of the land, the ostracism of society, or the fear of violating a command of God. In a moment of youthful recklessness the youth might defy one or all of these forces, and do what his hot blood bade, but at the critical moment, the flash of a mother's confiding trust, the realization of her sorrow if he fail to be true to it have given him power to refrain from indulgence that might blight his entire career. —FS, ms., Lydia Elizabeth Spencer Clawson, February 5, 1941, pp. 5-6.

GROUP INFLUENCE. I shall never forget, as long as I live, the impression my mother gave me when she told the story of those two thousand sons who went to battle under the leadership of Helaman. Think of those boys. Hold them as a pattern, you priests, teachers, and deacons, yes, and high priests, seventies, and elders. If two thousand men in that ancient time could live such lives, two thousand, nay ten thousand and a hundred thousand, men can live it today. These were their principles, founded upon the principle of faith, inculcated into their hearts by their mothers, who taught them in their youth that if they prayed to God nothing doubting, their prayers would be answered. Such is their testimony; such was the result of their mothers' teachings, showing the influence of home on boys' lives.—*CR*, October 1911, p. 60.

PRIMARY ATTRIBUTES OF MOTHERHOOD. Motherhood consists of three principal attributes or qualities: namely, (1) the power to bear, (2) the ability to rear, (3) the gift to love.

Some women there are who possess only the first, and who, therefore, are unworthy the name of mother. Selfishly, passionately, they have expressed themselves, as others of their kind, on the low plane of physical life, scorning the responsibility to sacrifice for and to rear their offspring, choking the fountain of love by selfish and wilful neglect of their children.

In contrast, there are other women, who, denied the power to bear children, adopt some as their own, rear them with an ability characteristic of and inherent in true womanhood, and fill the lives of their darlings with a love that only the yearning soul of such a mother can know. Such are true mothers, indeed, though part of the experience of motherhood be denied them!

This ability and willingness properly to rear children, the gift to love, and eagerness, yes, longing to express it in soul development, make motherhood the noblest office or calling in the world. She who can paint a masterpiece or write a book that will influence millions deserves the admiration and the plaudits of mankind; but she who rears successfully a family of healthy, beautiful sons and daughters, whose influence will be felt through generations to come, whose immortal souls will exert an influence throughout the ages long after paintings shall have faded, and books and statues shall have decayed or shall have been destroyed, deserves the highest honor that man can give, and the choicest blessings of God. In her high duty and service to humanity, endowing with immortality eternal spirits, she is co-partner with the Creator himself.—*IE,* 39:269 (1936).

MOTHER—A TRIBUTE. (In 1914 Congress authorized the President of the United States to designate by annual proclamation the second Sunday in May to be observed as "Mother's Day.")

A few nights ago I dreamed of Mother. She seemed as happy and beautiful as when, years since, she comforted and guided four girls and four boys in the cherished home of our childhood. The dream is mine. What it was is not here pertinent. But the joy I experienced at being once again in her company seemed so real that I could scarcely believe it was only a dream. I wish that I might dream of her oftener, for only in dreamland can we now hold converse over the incidents of my youth and early manhood, now treasured because of her association with them.

Fortunate the man who may go to his mother, at pleasure, and share her joy in reminiscence, or again receive her blessing in reality. Thrice fortunate the boy whose living mother's companionship is a daily guide and inspiration! Thrice blessed that girl into whose life radiates constantly the pure, self-sacrificing influence of a loving mother!

But this blessing, like all others that come to us without effort on our part, is too seldom appreciated until after it is gone. Children accept mother's and father's attention, care, and devotion as they accept the pure air and the glorious sunshine—just as a matter of course—as something which is their due in this workaday world.

Until "Where's Mother?" receives no sweet response do the childish minds realize how much Mother has been to them! Not until her smile and loving presence are but sacred memories do the children know that Mother held a place in their hearts that no one else can fill! It's an unfortunate phase of human nature that it is always inclined to undervalue its present blessings, that of Mother's and Father's presence being no exception.

It is most fitting, therefore, that our attention should be called to the fact that we are prone not only to undervalue mother's presence and love, but also, in consequence of this unconscious indifference, to neglect to express the appreciation and love we do feel for her. This is one purpose of Mother's Day. On this occasion we may recall memories of mothers who are gone, send loving messages to mothers too far away to visit, and make happier and more cheerful the lives of those who are near. The badge of the day is the white carnation, emblem of purity and enduring fidelity and love.

Throughout Christendom there is no married woman who may not be entitled to this tribute to motherhood. It is true that some wives have never been privileged to bear children, but it does not follow that they are not entitled to every honor due to the best of mothers.

Not only on one day, then, should we pay tribute to our mothers; but rather make that day the means of increasing our determination and ability to make every day of the year a day in which to honor Mother in particular and every woman who desires to be like Mother.—MS, 85:296-297 (1923).

THE GREATNESS OF MOTHERHOOD. The sweetness as well as the greatness of motherhood lies in the overcoming of self-love by Mother for her children. By nature the true mother is self-sacrificing. She is ever giving something of her life to make another either happier or better. Dying and giving—giving and dying—the two great elements that make the truly heroic—these are the Christlike virtues that make motherhood sublime.

The beginning of motherhood is but the entrance into the valley of the shadow in order to bring life to another. Herein is manifest love supreme; for "Greater love hath no man than this, that a man lay down his life for his friends." (John 15:13.) That some women enter into this realm impelled by less lofty motives or uninspired by any self-sacrificing thought, there can be no doubt; but this fact cannot rob the truly heroic soul of the honor due her any more more than the recreant soldier forced to the conflict can deprive of undying fame the hero who gloriously offers his life for his country.

Motherhood is the one thing in all the world which most truly exemplifies the God-given virtues of creating and sacrificing. Though it carries the woman close to the brink of death, motherhood also leads her into the very realm of the fountains of life and makes her co-partner with the Creator in bestowing upon eternal spirits mortal life. Artists may make new visions real; poets express thoughts never known before or dress old ones in a more becoming garb; engineers may transform deserts into bounteous fields and fill them with prosperous towns and thriving villages; scientists may discover new elements and by various combinations thereof create means contributive either to progress or destruction—all these are in a measure revealers of unknown things; but the mother who, in compliance with eternal law, brings into the world an immortal spirit occupies first rank in the realm of creation.

Motherhood is just another name for sacrifice. From the moment the wee, helpless babe is laid on the pillow beside her, Mother daily, hourly, gives of her life to her loved one. It has been aptly said that babes draw strength at first from her bosom but always from her heart. All through the years of babyhood, childhood, and youth, aye, even after her girls themselves become mothers and her sons, fathers, she tenderly, lovingly sacrifices for them her time, her comfort, her pleasures, her needed rest and recreation, and, if necessary, health and life itself! No language can express the power and beauty and heroism of a mother's love.

For all this consecrated devotion, she asks nothing in return. If her love is reciprocated, she is content; but if not, and her wayward child with poisoned feelings turns heedlessly from her, she still loves on, giving in yearning and solicitude far more than the recreant deserves. No, she asks nothing in return; nothing for the roses she has transplanted from her own cheeks to those of her darling; nothing for the hours of vigilance during days and nights of sickness; nothing for the thousand self-denials and sacrifices that had to be made that the children in their "teens" might receive proper schooling and "appear well" with their comrades; nothing for the heartaches caused by thoughtless word or act of wayward youth.

No, for all this and a thousand other things incident to motherhood, Mother asks nothing; but she deserves much. For kindness she deserves kindness; for tenderness, she should be given tenderness; for self-sacrifice, a little self-denial on the part of the children; for love, she should in return have love.

In the most agonizing moment of his life, Christ thought of his mother. In this as in all other things, the Savior of men has given us an example. As Mother gave us our life "at the peril of her own," so we should be pleased, no matter what our desires, our condition, or our pains to give such of our time, our thought, our words, our means, as may be necessary to Mother's contentment and peace.

To each mother's son or daughter, we would say: you need no suggestions on how to make your mother happy on Mother's Day as on every day in the year. If you order a white carnation to be given her, she will be pleased; if you tell her in a letter of your appreciation and love, she will shed tears of happiness; but if you keep the spotless character and purity of soul she has given you, she will rejoice as the most blessed of mothers.—*MS*, 86:296-297 (1924).

CHAPTER 34

COURTSHIP AND MARRIAGE

COURTSHIP: THE ROAD TO HAPPY MARRIAGE

THE IMPORTANCE OF SKILLS, ACTIVITIES, ASSOCIATIONS. The achievement of a happy marriage begins in childhood and youth. The opportunity of marriage begins in the early days in school. The young girl who learns to play the violin is more likely to find a good mate than one who sits at home, refusing to go out in society.

The boy who participates in athletics is more likely to find a mate than one who sits by the radio. In other words, associations are conducive to happy marriages because one becomes acquainted, one with another. One has more opportunities for choice.

In this connection, think for a moment what the Church offers to its members, particularly to the young boys and girls. —*DNCS*, February 7, 1952, p. 3.

THE PHILOSOPHY OF COURTSHIP. With the divinity of our marriage covenant, and the responsibility of parenthood ever in our minds, with temple marriage as an ideal for every worthy couple in the Church, we associate with courtship and marriage the most sublime ideals that influence human relations.—*CR*, April, 1935, p. 115.

Happiness does not begin at the altar; it begins during the period of youth and courtship. These seeds of happiness are sown by one's ability to master his driving passion. Chastity should be the dominant virtue among young people—the ideal which the world has not accepted and which many in the world will not believe exists or is cherished in the hearts of youth.—*IE*, 41:139 (1938).

"DATING": THE RESPONSIBILITY OF YOUNG MEN. Young man, always remember when you take your girl out to a party that her father and mother trust her to you. She is their most precious possession. If they gave you in trust a thousand dollars, you would not think of misusing it or spending it. They are giving into your keeping something which cannot be priced in money, and you are base indeed if you become disloyal to that trust. May I give you a heart petal here? I remember my father's admonition when I started in my teens to court a young girl: "David, you treat that young lady as you would have any young boy treat your sister." Young men, follow that advice and you will go through life with your conscience clear, and later in life you can say truthfully that with all your mistakes, you have never wronged a woman.—*IE*, 41:191 (1938).

Choosing a Companion: How Can You Be Sure? In choosing a companion, it is necessary to study the disposition, the inheritance, and training of the one with whom you are contemplating making life's journey. You see how necessary it is to look for the characteristics of honesty, of loyalty, of chastity, and of reverence. But after having found them— "How, then," you ask, "may you tell whether or not there is any consanguinity, that something which will make you at least congenial in each other's company?" "Is there," you ask, "some guide?" Though love is not always a true guide, especially if that love be not reciprocated or is bestowed upon a surly creature or a brute, yet certainly there is no happiness without love. "Well," you may ask, "how may I know when I am in love?"

That is a very important question. A fellow student and I considered that query one night as we walked together. As boys of that age frequently do, we were talking about girls. Neither he nor I knew whether or not we were in love. Of course I had not then met my present sweetheart. In answer to my question, "How may we know when we are in love?" he replied: "My mother once said that if you meet a girl in whose presence you feel a desire to achieve, who inspires you to do your best, and to make the most of yourself, such a young woman is worthy of your love and is awakening love in your heart."

I submit that as a true guide. In the presence of the girl you truly love you do not feel to grovel; in her presence you do not attempt to take advantage of her; in her presence you feel that you would like to be everything that a "Master Man" should become, for she will inspire you to that ideal.

And I ask you young women to cherish that same guide. What does he inspire in you—to feel as Portia did when she loved? She was wealthy; she was beautiful; but for Bassanio she wished she were a thousand times more beautiful, ten thousand times richer—that is what true love does. When a young man accompanies you after a meeting, or after a dance, and he shows an inclination to use you as a convenience or as a means of gratification, then you may put it down that he is not prompted by love.

Under such circumstances, no matter how fascinated you may be, young woman, no matter how confident you may feel that you love him, let your judgment rule and be master of your feelings. It may grieve you not to follow the inclination of your heart, but you had better be pained a little in your youth than to suffer pangs of torture later.—*IE*, 41:138-139 (1938).

A RULE FOR YOUNG WOMEN. Never marry a man who would deceive you, who would tell you a lie.—*IE*, 41:138 (1938).

AN HONEST PROPOSAL. Young man, if the girl with whom you are in love lives in a home of comparative luxury, and you hesitate to propose to her because you cannot offer her luxuries to which she has become accustomed, I suggest that a frank and open presentation to her of your problem might reveal the fact that you are misjudging her. You might discover that she will willingly share your poverty and help to build your home. If you enter into home building with a spirit of love and sacrifice, some day you will say as Henry Ward Beecher said: "We have a lovely home; it is fairly well-furnished; but I would like to live again those first two years when we rented one room in an attic and struggled together to make a picnic of our life."—*IE*, 41:191 (1938).

AN ANECDOTE. The problem of choosing a proper, congenial mate is most vital. In regard to this I suggest in general that you follow the advice of Sandy, the Scotchman, but not his example. His friend MacDonald came to Sandy and said, "I'm verra much worried, Sandy. I dinna ken whether to marry a rich widow whom I do not love, or marry a puir lass of whom I'm verra fond."

And Sandy said, "You'd better follow the promptins o' yer heart, MacDonald."

"All right," said MacDonald, "I'll do it. I'll marry the puir lass."

"In that case," said Sandy, "would you mind giving me the address of the widow?"—*DNCS*, February 27, 1952, p. 3.

CAREFUL OBSERVATION, SERIOUS AND PRAYERFUL THOUGHT NEEDED. No couple should enter into matrimony without careful observation and serious, prayerful thought. Everyone desires to live happily in married life. It is the natural, it is the normal life. The stability of government and the perpetuation of the race depend upon it. The happiness of mankind is not complete without congenial marriage.—*IE*, 41:138 (1938).

THE IMPORTANCE OF INTELLIGENCE. In Greek mythology there is a story of the three fates. In Rome these three fates were painted, presumably by Michelangelo, as three old women who control the destiny of mortals. They are three sisters. *Clotho*, the youngest, holds the distaff of life. *Lachesis*, the second sister, spins the thread as the years come and go. *Atropos*, the eldest, stands by with large open shears ready to cut the thread of life. If she cuts it short, the infant dies. If she permits the thread to unwind a little more, life is cut off in youth. But ofttimes she permits the thread of life to lengthen to old age. The mythical story implies that we are all subject to those three fates.

Applying this myth to our modern age, one writer on eugenics says: Science and the wide dissemination of knowledge have given us three fundamental things which determine our lives. These are heredity, environment, and self-effort, or what we make of ourselves by our own determination. These three modern fates should be kept in mind as we consider courtship and marriage.

What we are by heredity is determined; we cannot change it. We, who spring from families that have observed the gospel teachings, have inherited good qualities as well as good names. The least we can do is to transmit the same inheritance to our children. We are recreant to our obligation to society if we do not give to our progeny all the nobility bequeathed to us by our ancestors.

In our early youth, our environment is largely determined for us, but I wish to refer to the thought that in courtship and marriage we can modify, aye, can control to a very great extent, our environment. Morally speaking, we can carve the very atmosphere in which we live.

But the most important of these elements now is personal effort—that which we make of ourselves.—*IE*, 41:136-137 (1938).

THE PHILOSOPHY OF MARRIAGE. The exalted view of marriage as held by this Church is given expressly in five words found in the 49th section of the Doctrine and Covenants, "Marriage is ordained of God." That revelation was given in 1831 when Joseph Smith was only twenty-five years of age. Presiding officers in stakes, wards, quorums, and auxiliaries, it is your duty and mine to uphold the lofty conception of marriage as given in this revelation and to guard against encroaching dangers that threaten to lower the standard of the ideal home.

It is said that the best and noblest lives are those which are set toward high ideals. Truly no higher ideal regarding marriage can be cherished by young people than to look upon it as a divine institution. In the minds of the young such a standard is a protection to them in courtship, an ever-present influence inducing them to refrain from doing anything which may prevent their going to the temple to have their love consummated in an enduring and eternal union. It will lead them to seek divine guidance in the selecting of their companions, upon the wise choice of whom their life's happiness here and hereafter is largely dependent. "Our home joys," says Pestalozzi, "are the most delightful earth affords, and the joy of parents in their children is the most holy joy of humanity. It makes their hearts pure and good; it lifts them up to their Father in heaven." Such joys are within the reach of most men and women if high ideals of marriage and home be properly fostered and cherished.

And yet, if I mistake not the signs of the times, the sacredness of the marriage covenant is dangerously threatened. There are too many thoughtless, hasty marriages entered into without enough time taken to consider the temporal or eternal consequences. There are too many places where the marriage ceremony may be performed at any hour of the day or night without any previous arrangement—the license issued and the ceremony performed while the couple waits. Such marriages too often end in disappointment and sorrow; and, oh, how far they fall below the true ideal! As far as lies within our power, we must warn young couples against secret and hasty marriages.—*IE*, 56:221 (1953).

It is vital also to counteract the insidious influences of printed literature that speaks of the "bankruptcy of marriage," that advocates trial marriages, and that places "extra-marital relations" on a par with "extra-marital friendships."

I need say little about the growing evil of divorce and the resultant broken homes. You know that it is almost as easy to get a divorce as it is to get married. One of the peace officers in Salt Lake reported recently that eighty-six percent of the delinquent cases came from such broken homes. America seems to be drifting toward a low level as regards the law of family and home, with the result that sin and crime are increasing to an alarming extent among the youth of our fair land.

I mention these things not in the spirit of pessimism nor as a crier of impending calamity, but with the desire to call attention to the necessity of our maintaining the high standard of marriage set forth in the revelations of the Lord.—*CR*, April 1935, pp. 110-111.

ETERNITY OF THE MARRIAGE COVENANT. The eternity of the marriage covenant is a glorious revelation, giving assurance to hearts bound by the golden clasp of love and sealed by authority of the Holy Priesthood that their union is eternal.

Other covenants also continue with eternal progress throughout the ages of eternity.—*IE*, 45:55 (1942).

And now a word about the eternity of the marriage covenant. Some people question that, too. But let's look at the principle of it. Will you name for me in your minds the most divine attribute of the human soul? It isn't sympathy. And, girls, be careful not to be misled by sympathy. True, sympathy is next to love, but it is not love. Love is the most divine attribute of the human soul, and if you accept the immortality of the soul, that is, if you believe that personality persists after death, then, you must believe that love also lives. Isn't that sound? And I ask you this: Whom shall we love when we recognize those personalities in the next world?

True, we are admonished to love everybody. Yes, we should love everybody now; but you and I know that we love those whom we know best. I love her whom I have seen sacrifice her life for the little loved ones—her by whose side I have sat and together prayed and yearned over our little darling. I shall love my mother who I know offered her life that I might have being. When we meet these personalities in the eternal realm, we shall recognize them and know them because of these experiences in this life. And that union of loving hearts will be perpetuated after life. That is why we are married—sealed—for time and eternity. It isn't just a mere dogma of the Church—it is a truth fundamental to the life and happiness of all humanity. It is the part of wisdom to choose the house of the Lord in which to plight your love and to consecrate your vows.

Let me give you a glimpse of the significance of such a marriage. The bridegroom kneeling at the altar has in his heart the dearest possession that a husband can cherish—the assurance that she who places her hand in his, in confidence, in marriage, is as pure as a sunbeam—as spotless as newly fallen snow. He has the assurance that in her purity and sweetness she typifies divine motherhood. Now, young man, is not that complete faith and confidence worth everything else in the world?

And equally sublime is the assurance the young girl has that the man whom she loves, to whom she gives herself in marriage, comes to her with that same purity and strength of character which she brings to him. Such a union will indeed be a marriage ordained of God for the glory of his creation.

This is your heritage, youth, as you contemplate an eternal partnership, and I pray that you may realize it and find the true joy and happiness of such a cherished ideal.—*IE*, 41:191 (1938).

THE MEANING OF MARRIAGE IN THE TEMPLE. Temple marriage is basically appealing; it is scientifically sound; and any young man who takes his sweetheart to a temple should go there with the understanding that their union is to be just as eternal as the love that has brought them to the altar, and there is no question about it.

Before you can get married in the temple, it is required that you have lived a clean life. You have the assurance, young lady, that the man whom you are about to marry is bringing to you a clean body. Each of you has the assurance that the source of life is unpolluted.

To summarize: Young men and young women who would live the happiest lives would do well to prepare themselves to be worthy of that form of marriage which God has ordained— the union of a man and woman worthy to have their marriage solemnized in the temple of the Most High. There as true lovers kneel to plight their troth, each may cherish the assurance of the following:

First, that their married course begins in purity. The children who come to bless the union are guaranteed a royal birth so far as inheriting a clean body is concerned.

Second, that their religious views are the same. The difficulty of rearing children properly is aggravated when Father and Mother have divergent views regarding doctrine and church affiliation. (Another great advantage of seminaries, auxiliaries, Sunday School, etc., you meet those of your own Church!)

Third, that their vows are made with the idea of an eternal union, not to be broken by petty misunderstandings or difficulties.

Fourth, that a covenant made in God's presence and sealed by the Holy Priesthood is more binding than any other bond.

Fifth, that a marriage thus commenced is as eternal as love, the divinest attribute of the human soul.

Sixth, that the family unit will remain unbroken throughout eternity.

Boys and girls, God bless you to keep your lives unpolluted, that you may go in prayer to God and ask him to guide you in choosing your mates, and when chosen, that you will both so live that you can enter the house of God, and if he were present and asked you about your lives, you could answer him honestly, "Yes, we are clean."

A marriage begun on that basis, will bring you the happiness, the sweetest joy known in this life, or throughout eternity. —*DNCS*, February 27, 1952, pp. 4-5.

Marriage in the light of revelation is an institution with the stamp of divinity upon it, and no person and no state can deprecate that institution with impunity.—*DNCS*, February 27, 1952, p. 3.

THE PURPOSE OF MARRIAGE

REARING OF FAMILIES. Some young couples enter into marriage and procrastinate the bringing of children into their homes. They are running a great risk. Marriage is for the purpose of rearing a family, and youth is the time to do it. I admire these young mothers with four or five children around them now, still young, happy.—*DNCS*, June 11, 1952, p. 3.

The principal reason for marriage is to rear a family. Failure to do so is one of the conditions that cause love to wilt and eventually to die.—*IE*, 46:657 (1943).

INTELLIGENCE AND MUTUAL CONSIDERATION. Seeking the pleasures of conjugality without a willingness to assume the responsibilities of rearing a family is one of the onslaughts that now batter at the structure of the American home. Intelligence and mutual consideration should be ever-present factors in determining the coming of children to the household. When the husband and wife are healthy and free from inherited weaknesses and diseases that might be transmitted with injury to their offspring, the use of contraceptives is to be condemned.

The Lord has told us that:

" . . . whoso forbiddeth to marry is not ordained of God, for marriage is ordained of God unto man.

"Wherefore, it is lawful that he should have one wife, and they twain shall be one flesh, and all this that the earth might answer the end of its creation." (D. & C. 49:15-16.)

By direct revelation, in this passage we have stated in a few words, the purpose of marriage. It is to bear children and rear a family. Let us keep that in mind. Hundreds are now saying, and hundreds more will say— "How can I marry and support a bride in a manner with which she has been accustomed? How can I get an education and support a family? I cannot even find a place in which to live."

These are practical questions, and our boys and girls are facing them. I am willing to recognize these and other difficulties and meet them, keeping in mind what the Lord has said that "marriage is ordained of God for man." And I repeat that the very purpose of marriage is to rear a family and not for the mere gratification of man or woman. Keeping this thought uppermost in married life, we shall have fewer difficulties and more readily find content.

OVERCOMING ECONOMIC DIFFICULTIES. How are we going to overcome some of these present-day difficulties? Postponement of marriage is not the answer. I know that there are many parents whose sons and daughters are struggling for an education who say it would be better if young couples postponed marriage until after they gained an education. I am not so sure about it. Each case must be considered on its merits. The principal thing is to be sure the couple love each other. Marriage without love will bring misery. But if they are sure they are mated and have the same ideals, generally early marriages are best.

There was a time in the beginning of this country—it goes back before the beginning of this country—when every girl was given a dowry, and we still have the practice of a girl's preparing a trousseau, which is a commendable practice. I think where parents can help they should help young couples, especially those who have five or six years ahead in getting a college degree. We still retain also the bridal shower, at which, in some countries, people give money.

I think the government is doing a good thing in giving our returned servicemen a few dollars to help them get a start after their having been discharged from the service. Recently I heard a most interesting report on this subject. The incident happened in Logan at the dedicatory service of a quonset house dedicated for worship on the campus of the Utah State Agricultural College. There were present a number of young married couples, young wives with babes in their arms. At the beginning of the dedicatory services, the presiding officer said, "We have many babes here today. If there be people present who do not like the crooning of babies, we will wait a few minutes now for these people to leave." To encourage thus the rearing of families is most commendable. That house was built expressly for young folk rearing families, young G.I.'s who have started out to build their homes even while they are getting an education.—*IE*, 51:618 (1948).

BIRTH CONTROL

Any effort or desire on the part of a married couple to shirk the responsibility of parenthood reflects a condition of mind antagonistic to the best interests of the home, the state, and the nation. No doubt there are some worldly people who honestly limit the number of children and the family to two or three because of insufficient means to clothe and educate a large family as the parents would desire to do, but in nearly all such cases, the two or three children are no better provided for than two or three times that number would be. Such parents may be sincere, even if misguided; but in most cases the desire not to have children has its birth in vanity, passion, and selfishness. Such feelings are the seeds sown in early married life that produce a harvest of discord, suspicion, estrangement, and divorce. All such efforts, too, often tend to put the marriage relationship on a level with the panderer and the courtesan. They befoul the pure fountains of life with the slime of indulgence and sensuality. Such misguided couples are ever seeking but never finding the reality for which the heart is yearning.

Depriving themselves of the comfort and happiness of the companionship of children, the barrenness of their lives drives the young couple to seek the hollow fads and fascinating excitements of "society," many of which pursuits are as antagonistic to the real purpose of life as the influence of evil can make them.

As I write these lines, I have in mind a young girl who has substituted for the reality of home and family, the froth of week-end parties and midnight carousals, including the most degrading but fashionable habit of cigaret smoking. She began her married life in honor and is the mother of two beautiful children; but she was caught in the whirlpool of pleasure and passion, and though flaunting daily the latest fashions, is sinking from respectability to degradation. "O what a falling off were here!" I cannot look upon such actions of young husbands and wives without a feeling of pity mingled with contempt. There is comfort only in the thought that in our communities such cases are exceptional.

Love realizes his sweetest happiness and his most divine consummation in the home where the coming of children is not restricted, where they are made most welcome, and where the duties of parenthood are accepted as a co-partnership with the eternal Creator.

In all this, however, the mother's health should be guarded. In the realm of wifehood, the woman should reign supreme.

Man, not woman, is the chief cause of this evil of race suicide now sweeping like a blight through the civilized nations.

Marriage is ordained of God that children might be so trained that they may eventually be worthy of Christ's presence; and that home is happiest in which they are welcomed, as God and nature intended they should be.—*RSM*, 3:366-377 (1916).

PROBLEMS OF DIVORCE AND FAMILY DISORGANIZATION

MISUNDERSTANDING BRINGS TRAGEDY. When we refer to the breaking of the marriage tie, we touch upon one of the saddest experiences of life. For a couple who have basked in the sunshine of each other's love to stand by daily and see the clouds of misunderstanding and discord obscure the lovelight of their lives is tragedy indeed. In the darkness that follows, the love sparkle in each other's eyes is obscured. To restore it, fruitless attempts are made to say the right word and to do the right thing; but the word and act are misinterpreted, and angry retort reopens the wound, and hearts once united become torn wider and wider asunder. When this heartbreaking state is reached, a separation is sought. But divorce is not the proper solution, especially if there are children concerned. —*IE*, 46:657, 704 (1943).

DIVORCE UNDER EXTREME CONDITIONS ONLY. Except in cases of infidelity or other extreme conditions, the Church frowns upon divorce, and authorities look with apprehension upon the increasing number of divorces among members of the Church.—*IE*, 46:657 (1943).

GUIDANCE FROM THE SCRIPTURES. In all the problems and perplexities of human existence, Jesus Christ is the one safe guide to whom we can go for guidance and comfort. Mark's account of Jesus' answer to the Pharisees on divorce sets forth the Savior's attitude toward this vital question.

A careful study of this text and other references that he made to marriage and divorce leave little doubt that Jesus set forth the lofty ideal that marriage is of divine origin and that the marriage bond should be held sacred.

When the Pharisees, seeking to justify the granting of divorce, cited the fact that "Moses suffered to write a bill of divorcement and to put a wife away" on the ground of "some uncleanness," Jesus answered:

"For the hardness of your heart he wrote you this precept.
"But from the beginning of the creation God made them male and female.
"For this cause shall a man leave his father and mother, and cleave to his wife;
"And they twain shall be one flesh: so then they are no more twain, but one flesh.
"What therefore God hath joined together, let not man put asunder." (Mark 10:5-9.)

In the light of scripture, ancient and modern, we are justified in concluding that Christ's ideal pertaining to marriage is the unbroken home, and conditions that cause divorce are violations of his divine teachings.

To look upon marriage as a mere contract that may be entered into at pleasure in response to a romantic whim or for selfish purposes, and severed at the first difficulty or misunderstanding that may arise, is an evil meriting severe condemnation, especially in cases wherein children are made to suffer because of such separation.

Marriage is a sacred relationship entered into for purposes that are well recognized—primarily for the rearing of a family.—*IE*, 48:238 (1945).

Maintaining Family Integrity: Advice to the Priest-hood. I am going to venture to enter into a discussion of home life. I would rather enter into it as it should be, rather than what it sometimes is. But we find that the following conditions seem to be contributive to the separation of husband and wife, and the breaking up of the home: unfaithfulness on the part of either or both—(do you know what that means, those of you who have been through the temple?)—drunkenness, physical violence; in some cases imprisonment has brought disgrace to the family; the union of an innocent girl to a reprobate; some cases disclosed sordid, licentious, brutal actions of covetous men. I know you think those are harsh words, but you can read in some of these applications reports of treatment that has wrung women's hearts.

I know that the woman is to blame in some cases, and particularly young women who married young boys in a hurry when World War II broke out.

May I now suggest that we unite for just a few minutes as bishops, presidents of stakes, as fathers, and as young men contemplating marriage, to consider some things which will avoid the breaking up of the family, which will avoid this breaking of women's hearts, this turning out of children from what should be loving homes or throwing them entirely upon the responsibility of mothers. Let us instruct young people who come to us, to know that a woman should be queen of her own body. The marriage covenant does not give the man the right to enslave her or to abuse her or to use her merely for the gratification of his passion. Your marriage ceremony does not give you that right.

Second, let them remember that gentleness and consideration after the ceremony is just as appropriate and necessary and beautiful as gentleness and consideration before the wedding.

Third, let us realize that manhood is not undermined by the practising of continence, notwithstanding what some psychiatrists claim. Chastity is the crown of beautiful womanhood, and self-control is the source of true manhood, if you will know it, not indulgence. Sexual indulgence whets the passion and creates morbid desire.

Let us teach our young men to enter into matrimony with

the idea that each will be just as courteous and considerate of a wife after the ceremony as during courtship.

And we have the ideal in this Church, I hope, today as ever, that a young man keep himself clean and pure during his courtship days, so that he can kneel at the altar and give just the same purity of life to that sweet girl as he exacts from her. I submit to you that that is a glorious ideal. I know the world thinks we cannot live it, but you and I know that we can and do so live.

Fourth, minimize the faults, commend virtues. After the first thrill of the honeymoon is worn off, couples begin to see frailties, idiosyncrasies which they had not noticed before. Responsibilities of motherhood come to the woman. Difficulties in paying debts come. And so we become prone to find fault. Let us learn to control ourselves in that respect.

I do not know who wrote this, but it is good advice: "In the first solitary hour after the ceremony, take the bridegroom and demand a solemn vow of him (this is to the girl) and give a vow in return; promise each other sacredly never, not even in jest, to wrangle with each other, never to bandy words, or indulge in the least ill-humor. Never—I say never! Wrangling in jest, putting on an air of ill-humor, merely to tease, becomes earnest by practice! Mark that!

"Next, promise each other, sincerely and solemnly, never to keep a secret from each other, under whatever pretext, and whatever excuse it might be. You must continually, and every moment, see clearly into each other's bosom. Even when one of you has committed a fault, wait not an instant, but confess it. And as you keep nothing from each other, so, on the contrary, preserve the privacies of your house, marriage state, and heart, from father, mother, brother, sister, aunt, and from all the world. You two, with God's help, build your own quiet world. Every third or fourth one you draw into it with you will form a party and stand between you two. That should never be. Promise this to each other. Remember the vow at each temptation. You will find your account in it. Your souls will grow, as it were, to each other, and at last will become as one. Ah, if many a pair had, on their marriage day, known the secret, how many a marriage were happier than, alas, they are!"

I regard it as an incontrovertible fact that in no marriage circle can true peace, love, purity, chastity, and happiness be found, in which is not present the Spirit of Christ, and the daily, hourly striving after loving obedience to his divine commands, and especially the nightly prayer expressing gratitude for blessings received.

God help us to build homes in which the spirit of heaven on earth may be experienced. You and I know that that is possible; it is not a dream; it is not a theory. We may have that sweet companionship between husband and wife which grows dearer and dearer as troubles of life come on. We can have homes in which children will never hear Father and Mother wrangle or quarrel. God help us as men of the priesthood, to build such homes, and to teach young men and young women who are anticipating home life, to cherish such an ideal.—CR, April 1952, pp. 86-87.

A man who has entered into a sacred covenant in the house of the Lord to remain true to the marriage vow is a traitor to that covenant if he separates himself from his wife and family just because he has permitted himself to become infatuated with the pretty face and comely form of some young girl who flattered him with a smile. Even though a loose interpretation of the law of the land would grant such a man a bill of divorcement, I think he is unworthy of a recommend to have his second marriage performed in the temple. A separation because of infidelity is another matter.—IE, 46:647 (1943).

As teachers, we are to let the people know, and warn these men—and this is not imagination—who, after having lived with their wives and brought into this world four and five and six children, get tired of them and seek a divorce, that they are on the road to hell. It is unfair to a woman to leave her that way, merely because the man happens to fall in love with some younger woman and feels that the wife is not so beautiful or attractive as she used to be. Warn him! Nothing but unhappiness for him and injustice to those children can result.—CR, April 1949, pp. 182-183.

CHASTITY TO BE MAINTAINED. No one can transgress the laws of chastity and find peace. That is the message to our boys, to our girls. No matter what the opportunity, no matter what the temptation, let the young man of Israel know that to find happiness he must hold sacred his true manhood; let him know that he is going to live and live completely by refusing to yield to that temptation. Then he is happy; he is *happy*. There is peace instead of turbulency in his soul.—CR, October, 1920, pp. 43-44.

ONE STANDARD OF MORALITY. In the Latter-day Saint Church there is but one standard of morality. In the world many people protect their girls and daughters, irrespective of religion. They know what it means for young girls to be treated as slaves, as playthings, and they shield their own daughters from the ravages of men. But their boys are too often left free to prey upon helpless creatures who are not so protected.

Thus in the world you have the double standard, but in the Church of Jesus Christ there is but a single standard. It applies to the boys as well as to the girls. If you follow that standard—indeed, if you will listen to the promptings of your best self, your clearest judgment, the whisperings of your own true heart, you will learn this lesson: That self-mastery during youth and the compliance with the single standard of morality is (1) the source of virile manhood; (2) the crown of beautiful womanhood; (3) the foundation of a happy home, and (4) the contributing factor to the strength and perpetuity of the race!—IE, 41:139 (1938).

THE PROSTITUTION OF LOVE. Man is endowed with appetites and passions for the preservation of his life and the perpetuation of his kind. These, when held under proper subjection, contribute to his happiness and comfort; but when used for mere gratification, lead to misery and moral degradation.

Associated with these natural instincts, young folk, is a sin that always seeks seclusion. It is the prostitution of love. God has instituted marriage and the family as the proper condition of expressing in our lives this divine virtue. But sometimes men and women with low ideals and weakened wills permit their passions, like unbridled steeds, to dash aside judgment and self-restraint and to cause them to commit sin that may sear their conscience and leave in their hearts an everlasting regret.

In this day when modesty is thrust into the background, and chastity is considered an outmoded virtue, I appeal to you to keep your souls unmarred and unsullied from this sin, the consequence of which will smite and haunt you intimately until your conscience is seared and your character sordid.

Remember, too, the significance of the Savior's saying that if any shall commit adultery even in his or her heart, he shall not have the Spirit but shall deny the faith and shall fear.

Resist evil, and the tempter will flee from you. If you keep your character above reproach, no matter what others may think or what charges they may make, you can hold your head erect, keep your heart light, and face the world undauntedly because you, yourself, and your God know that you have kept your soul untarnished.—CR, October 1951, pp. 8-9.

HIGH THINKING AND FIDELITY. "My spirit," says the Christ, "will not dwell in unclean tabernacles." The corruption that is in the world through lust, as mentioned in one of Peter's epistles, has its source in thoughts and schemes harbored in the individual mind. A man who takes advantage of his neighbor in a business deal when the opportunity offers has prepared himself for the occasion by dishonest thinking. Young couples do not lose their chastity, named by the Book of Mormon as "precious above all things," without their having previously in thought justified the act.

The husband who coolly turns from a loyal wife and family and seeks illicit relationship elsewhere, perhaps with a disloyal wife of a neighbor, has previously poisoned his soul with immoral ideas. Disgruntled members of society, faultfinders, in wards and stakes, do not become such merely because of some offense, real or imagined. What they say and do have been preceded by selfish desires or unattained ambition.—CR, April 1951, pp. 96-97.

Bearing tragic witness to the lessening regard for purity in marriage is the large number of so-called war brides whose husbands have returned to face broken promises and tragic instances of infidelity.—IE, 49:690 (1943).

Appreciation is a great virtue, and if husbands and wives expressed it more frequently in our homes, wives would be happier, and husbands would probably be more kind.

I am glad to hear the presiding brethren express their love for their wives and appreciation for what the women have done in the building of this Church.—*DNCS*, January 2, 1952, p. 2.

KINDNESS OF HUSBANDS TO WIVES. I mention this now, because I think we are sometimes cruel to our wives. I have here two letters, one anonymous, another signed by a woman. They are asking "What shall we do? Our husbands are cruel to us."

Says one, "My husband has a terrible temper. He comes home and scolds the children. He is cruel to me. At first he seemed to be a good, loving husband, but when my first baby was born, then were born my troubles."

I cannot imagine a man's being cruel to a woman. I cannot imagine her so conducting herself as to merit such treatment. Perhaps there are women in the world who exasperate their husbands, but no man is justified in resorting to physical force or in exploding his feelings in profanity. There are men, undoubtedly, in the world who are thus beastly, but no man who holds the priesthood of God should so debase himself.—*CR*, October 1951, p. 181.

CHAPTER 35

THE HOME AND FAMILY LIFE

PARENTHOOD

A SACRED OBLIGATION. Equal in importance to the high conception of the marriage covenant is the teaching of the Church in regard to the responsibility of parenthood.

Parenthood and particularly motherhood should be held as a sacred obligation. There is something in the depths of the human soul which revolts against neglectful parenthood.

Parents cannot with impunity shirk the responsibility to protect childhood and youth.—CR, April 1935, pp. 112-113.

RESPONSIBILITY OF PARENTHOOD. You may think me extreme, but I am going to say that a married woman who refuses to assume the responsibilities of motherhood, or who, having children, neglects them for pleasure or social prestige, is recreant to the highest calling and privilege of womankind. The father, who because of business or political or social responsibilities, fails to share with his wife the responsibilities of rearing his sons and daughters, is untrue to his marital obligations, is a negative element in what might be and should be a joyous home atmosphere, and is a possible contributor to discord and delinquency. Herbert Hoover, a former president of the United States, once said:

"Our country has a vast majority of competent mothers. I am not so sure of the majority of competent fathers."

Fathers may and should exercise a helpful, restraining influence, where a mother's tenderness and love might lead to indulgence on the part of the children. In this respect, however, every father should ever keep in mind that he was once a mischievous youngster himself and deal with his boy sympathetically.—IE, 49:691 (1946).

UNITY IN THE HOME. I can imagine few if any things more objectionable in the home than the absence of unity and harmony. On the other hand, I know that a home in which unity, mutual helpfulness, and love abide is just a bit of heaven on earth. I surmise that nearly all of you can testify to the sweetness of life in homes in which these virtues predominate. Most gratefully and humbly, I cherish the remembrance that never once as a lad in the home of my youth did I see one instance of discord between Father and Mother and that good will and mutual understanding have been the uniting bond that has held together a fortunate group of brothers and sisters. Unity, harmony, good will are virtues to be fostered and cherished in every home.—CR, October 1939, p. 102.

THE ART OF HOME BUILDING

By the art of home building, I mean the inculcating in the lives of children a nobility of soul that leads them instinctively to love the beautiful, the genuine, the virtuous, and as instinctively to turn from the ugly, the spurious, and the vile.—RSM, 23:4 (1936).

Six Elements of True Home Building:

1. Let us substitute the present tendency toward a low view of marriage with the lofty view which God gives it. Yesterday I stood at the altar of the temple, as I have stood many a time, and saw two hearts—two souls—slipping into one, as two dewdrops on the stem of a rose when the sun comes out in the morning, one slipping into the other, the two becoming one. That high view of marriage in the mind of that young bridegroom, and the appreciation of the sacredness of marriage by the bride, I think is one of the sublimest things in all the world. They had the high view of marriage, not a low view of it as a means of gratifying passion. Let us look upon marriage as a sacred obligation and a covenant as possibly an eternal one.

2. Teach the young of both sexes in the responsibilities and ideals of marriage so that they may realize that marriage involves obligation and is not an arrangement to be terminated at pleasure. In this regard it is the duty of parents to set an example in the home that children may see and absorb, as it were, the sacredness of family life and the responsibility associated therewith.

3. Instruct young girls in the fundamental arts of housekeeping, so that when responsibilities of wifehood come, they may be free from the difficulties and perplexities which arise from ignorance and inexperience.

4. Marriages should be solemnized, as far as possible, in the house of God. This will minimize the evils that follow runaway marriages.

5. Keep religion in home life. We should make it obvious, both by our actions and our conversation, that we are seriously interested in religious things and believe in them ourselves: faith in God, in the divine mission of Jesus Christ, and in the restoration of the gospel. Our religion should also take the form of honesty in our dealings with our family, our neighbors, and all with whom we come in contact; of kindness to our employees, or fair play to our employers; and good measure to our customers. Talk about these intangibles should become as common practice in our homes and offices as talk about golf, parties, and profits if we want to succeed in solving the family problems.

To give young people the right start in life, we must discuss with our children and friends questions of motive and subjects like birth, love, marriage, death, and destiny. Babson says: "One of the best things that could happen to America today would be a return to family prayers; the getting together after breakfast or in the evening for five or ten minutes for simple family worship! The saying of grace before meals would be a step in this direction." I am glad that that practice is general, I hope, throughout the Latter-day Saint homes.

6. Teach the young that the foundations of a happy home are laid before even the bride and bridegroom kneel at the marriage altar.—*RSM*, 23:9-10 (1936).

When our children are given us, and that admonition "Suffer them to come back to me" is given, three means of developing them are at hand: The first is home influence; the second, activities—avenues of action, including vocations and avocations ;and third, social environment. In all three of these there must be the predominating element of salvation—I mean physically, intellectually, spiritually. And what is it? Work! Work in the home! Work; legitimate work, in the avenues of life! Work, legitimate work in the social world! —*CR*, October 1909, pp. 89-90.

It isn't enough to say that we believe in home building and in the purity of the home. What are we doing? Go into the homes of true Latter-day Saints, and there see if the most substantial part of the nation—the home—is not the best that can be found. The family tie is an eternal one; it is not one of experiment; it is not one of satisfying passion; it is an eternal union between husband and wife, between parents and children. That eternal bond is one that must be held sacred by the man as well as by the woman. Is it a source of safety? Is it a blessing to humanity to have such homes? The safety of our nation depends upon the purity and strength of the home; and I thank God for the teachings of the Church in relation to home building, and the impression that kind parents have made, that the home must be the most sacred place in the world. Our people are home builders, and they are taught everywhere, from childhood to old age, that the home should be kept pure and safe from the evils of the world. —CR, April 1909, pp. 65-66.

THE PHYSICAL ENVIRONMENT. A good home requires good health habits through parents' instruction and example in eating, sleeping, and proper exercise. I need not dwell upon this phase of the fundamental conditions of a good home; if we can have properly ventilated homes, if we know what kind of food to give to the children, we are contributing to the health and happiness of the home.

THE CULTURE OF THE HOME. Parents must lead in the cultural development and show a willingness to answer questions. A child that is asking questions is contributing happiness to your life. Fortunate the child whose parents can leave their work occasionally to encourage the child in constructive play or spend a few hours in nature study!

UNDERSTANDING INDIVIDUAL DIFFERENCES. You wonder why one child is so different in disposition from another. Besides inherited tendencies, he has had different influences operating upon him. The first babe had no brothers to tease him; the tenth babe perhaps had nine.—RSM, 18:349 (1931).

A PHILOSOPHY OF FAMILY LIFE

THE SPIRITUAL ENVIRONMENT OF THE HOME. Every home has both body and spirit. You may have a beautiful house with all the decorations that modern art can give or wealth bestow. You may have all the outward forms that will please the eye and yet not have a home. It is not home without love. It may be a hovel, a log hut, a tent, a wickiup, if you have the right spirit within, the true love of Christ, and love for one another—fathers and mothers for the children, children for parents, husband and wife for each other—you have the true life of the home that Latter-day Saints build and which they are striving to establish.

No matter what they may be without, are your homes pure within? Are morning prayers offered there regularly? Or do the things of this world take you away from your homes and make you deprive yourself of morning prayers with the children? "Woe to that home where the mother abandons her holy mission or neglects the divine instruction, influence, and example—while she bows, a devotee at the shrine of social pleasure; or neglects the essential duties in her own household, in her enthusiasm to promote public reform."

We must consider the home; it is the spring of life, if you please, of our social conditions today. It is no wonder, when we think of some home pictures that are shown to us, that millions and billions of dollars are spent trying to purify streams made impure by the unholy fountains of home life in the world.

From such homes as these come the men who are trespassing upon the rights of others, come women who are degraded, and who are dragging their virtue and that of others in the mud. It is such homes from which springs much of the evil in society today. I wish the money now spent in police and detective work could be used in purifying those homes. What the world needs today is good parents. Where parents are incapable of rearing their children properly, the state should assist by means of guardians of the young who should be required to do individual work.—CR, October 1907, p. 63.

AN ILLUSTRATION. One day a young son, just married, invited his father to visit him and his bride in their new home. The young son took the father from room to room and showed him the furnishings, the paintings on the walls and so forth, and the father said, "This is lovely. I congratulate you, but,

Son, I have looked in vain for anything that indicates that you have a place here for God."

In writing about it later, the young man said, "I went through the rooms later, and I found that Father was right."

Let us go back to our homes and see whether the spirit of our homes is such that if an angel called, he would be pleased to remain.—CR, October 1951, pp. 160-161.

To every sincere follower of Christ, religion should denote not only a sense of relationship to God, but also an expression of that feeling in actions with respect to right and wrong and obligation to duty.

This was undoubtedly the kind of religion Patrick Henry had in mind when, in the closing scene of his life, he said: "I have now disposed of all my property to my family. There is one thing more I wish I could give them, and that is the Christian religion. If they had that, and I had not given them one shilling, they would be rich; and if they had not that, and I had given them all the world, they would be poor." —CR, October 1937, p. 100.

"And they shall also teach their children to pray, and to walk uprightly before the Lord." (D. & C. 68:28.)

This command leaves no question as to the responsibility of parents to teach their children—a responsibility too frequently shifted to the shoulders of the church, public schools, and officers of the law.—IE, 46:656 (1943).

THE IMPORTANCE OF EXAMPLE. I believe that parents generally are teaching their children the gospel, yet I am convinced that there is still much opportunity for improvement in this regard. I am not thinking of the set hours in which you sit down to teach these doctrines to your children, but of the example fathers and mothers give to their children regarding the faith that is dear to your hearts. Your example will teach these principles more effectively than what you say. Out of our homes come the future leaders of the government. If our homes were all they should be, the nation would be safe.—CR, October 1932, pp. 66-67.

THE HOME AND FAITH IN THE EXISTENCE OF GOD. If you ask me where I first received my unwavering faith in the existence of a God, I would answer you: in the home of my childhood—when Father and Mother invariably called their children around them in the morning and at night and invoked God's blessing upon the household and upon mankind. There was a sincerity in that good patriarch's voice that left an undying impression in the children's souls; and Mother's prayers were equally impressive.

I ask today that every father in the Church see to it that, in all sincerity, he impress his children with the reality of the existence of God, and with the reality that God will guide and protect his children. You carry that responsibility. Home is one of the units—the fundamental unit of society. Let the sincere investigators who believe more from what they see than from what they hear, find, upon investigation, that Mormons prove by example in the home, by devotion, and in their service to God, that they believe and know that God is their Father.

I knew before I heard my father testify that he had heard a divine voice, that he lived near to his Maker; and I know, by a nearness to that same Eternal Father since, that Father told the truth when he said he received in answer to prayer this admonition given in audible tones: "Testify that Joseph Smith is a prophet of the living God." Such is the reality of the true Latter-day Saints' conception of God the Father. —*CR*, October 1922, p. 78.

SOME FUNDAMENTAL PRINCIPLES OF FAMILY LIFE. There are a few fundamental principles which we should ever keep in mind. First, the eternity of the marriage relation. Oh, may our youth throughout the land realize that they have within their grasp the possibilities of that form of marriage which will contribute more to their happiness in this world and their eternal union and happiness in the world to come than can be obtained anywhere else in the world.

Second, let us hold to that first word in the second part of the fundamental law of humanity, the Ten Commandments. Those first few commandments refer to our relationship to God. The last few to our relationship to humanity. The second part begins with the word honor—"Honour thy father and thy mother." Let us cherish in our homes as we cherish the lives of our children themselves that word *honor* with all the synonyms—respect, reverence, veneration; honoring mother, honoring father, having them honor us as we honor and revere God our Eternal Father. Let the element of honor, devotion, reverence permeate the home life.

Third, let us never lose sight of the principles of obedience. Obedience is heaven's first law, and it is the law of the home. There can be no true happiness in the home without obedience—obedience obtained, not through physical force, but through the divine element of love. There is no true home when love does not abide.—*CR*, April 1919, pp. 77-78.

The inspiration of God is seen in requiring the Latter-day Saints to keep their homes intact, and to teach their children the principles of the gospel of Jesus Christ. I mean that the gospel of Jesus Christ should be offered up in sincerity, that the children daily would realize that we desire in our home the presence of God. If we can invite the Savior there, we may know that the angels will be not only willing but eager to protect our boys and girls.

I believe that in most homes boys and girls are taught to pray before retiring for the night. I believe, however, that, too generally, the morning prayers are neglected. When we come to think of it, though, it is during the waking hours that our boys and girls need the protection of God, and the guidance of his Holy Spirit, more even than when they are asleep.

The dangers surrounding our boys and girls today are the dangers that come to them out in society, out in the darkness of the night, when they are away from the parental influence. I plead with the parents of the Church to know where your boys and girls are at night between the hour of sunset and the hour of retiring. I plead with you to know where they are during the day. Keep your minds upon them. Let your thoughts go with them.

Homes are made permanent through love. Oh, then, let love abound. If you feel that you have not the love of those little boys and girls, study to get it. Though you neglect some of the cattle, though you fail to produce good crops, ever study to hold your children's love.—*CR*, October 1917, pp. 57-58.

Is FAMILY LIFE A PERMANENT FORM OF SOCIAL ORGANIZATION? We are living in a most momentous age. We see on every hand manifestations of commotion. The world seemingly is stirred as it has never been stirred before. Political institutions are crumbling. Old forms and methods are fast giving way to new ones. Political organizations are being revolutionized, some for better and some for worse. Old fundamental principles of government are tottering. Some have even been replaced by theories that are not tenable, others not practicable, and some that are infamous. In the midst of this world commotion the home, the fundamental institution of society, is also threatened.

Latter-day Saints, the responsibility of saving this sacred institution devolves largely upon you, for you know that the family ties are eternal. They should be eternal. There is nothing temporary in the home of the Latter-day Saint. There is no element of transitoriness in the family relationship of the Latter-day Saint home. To the Latter-day Saint the home is truly the cell-unit of society; and parenthood is next to Godhood.

The relationship of the children to the parents should be one which would enable those children to carry out ideal citizenship as they become related to the state and to the larger forms of society. The secret of good citizenship lies in the home. The secret of instilling faith in God, faith in his Son, the Redeemer of the world, faith in the organizations of the Church, lies in the home. There it is centered.

God has placed upon you parents the responsibility of instilling these principles into the minds of children. Church schools, Sunday Schools, Mutual Improvement Associations, and Primary, are all helps in government, established here to assist in the upbuilding and guidance of the youth, but none of these—great and important factors as they are in the lives of our youth—can supplant the permanence and the influence of the parents in the home.—*CR*, April 1919, pp. 76-77.

Oh, I praise God for the instructions he has given his people regarding the sacredness, the sanctity, and permanence of the family relationship. Let us impress these instructions upon our children.—*CR*, October 1917, p. 56.

RECREATION IN THE HOME. I wish to emphasize the fact that our homes should be more attractive and that more of our amusements should be in the home instead of out on the streets.—*I*, 80:562 (1945).

THE HOME AND SOCIETY

A PLACE TO TEACH. The home is the best place in the world to teach the highest ideal in the social and political life of man; namely, perfect liberty of action so long as you do not trespass upon the rights and privileges of another.—*IE*, 49:691 (1946).

THE STATE HELPLESS WHEN THE HOME FAILS. The safety, the perpetuity of our government, or of any republican form of government, depends upon the safety and permanency of the home. Herein we get a glimpse of one thing in which this people may be the saviors, in a way, of this great nation. The home is the place where the perpetuation of the principles of liberty as well as the instructions in the gospel of Jesus Christ should be given to the children. When the home breaks up, then the children begin to wander off into sin. Then the law must reach out to bring them back and try to teach them some principles of service, and principles of true government; but, oh, how helpless, how helpless the state, when the home has failed!—*CR*, October 1917, p. 57.

THE SOURCE OF NATIONAL STRENGTH. The real source of security of our nation rests in the well-ordered, properly conducted homes.—*IE*, 48:239 (1945).

The character of the child is formed largely during the first twelve years of his life. It is estimated that in that period the child spends sixteen times as many waking hours in the home as in school and more than a hundred times as many hours in the home as in the church. Every child is, to a great degree, what he is because of the ever constant influence of home environment and the careful or neglectful training of parents.—*CR*, April 1935, p. 113.

I desire to call attention to the fact that the united, well-ordered American home is one of the greatest contributing factors to the preservation of the Constitution of the United States. It has been aptly said that "Out of the homes of America will come the future citizens of America, and only as those homes are what they should be will this nation be what it should be."—*CR*, April 1935, p. 110.

HOME BUILDING PARAMOUNT. Would you have a strong and virile nation? Then keep your homes pure. Would you reduce delinquency and crime? Lessen the number of broken homes. It is time that civilized peoples realized that prevention is more profitable than punishment and that the home is the incubator either of children of high character or of criminals. Home building, therefore, should be the paramount purpose of parents and of the nation.—CR, April 1935, p. 115.

One of the highest ideals of life is to keep secure and free from sorrow the homes of the Church and of the nation. —IE, 46:704 (1943).

Infidelity and sexual immorality are two principal evils that threaten to weaken and to wreck present-day civilization. Unfortunately, the trends of modern life are tending to disintegrate the very foundation of the Christian home. Sexual laxity among young people, birth control, and intemperance are its insidious and vicious enemies. When family life disintegrates, the foundation and bulwark of human society is undermined.—CR, October 1947, p. 119.

THE PRECIOUS GIFT OF CHILDREN

Next to eternal life, the most precious gift that our Father in heaven can bestow upon man is his children.—I, 84:620 (1949).

Our country's most precious possession is not our vast acres of range land supporting flocks and herds; not productive farms; not our forests; not our mines nor oil wells producing fabulous wealth. Our country's greatest resource is our children.—CR, October 1951, pp. 5-6.

THINGS TO WHICH EVERY CHILD IS ENTITLED. There are three fundamental things to which every child is entitled: first, a respected name; second, a sense of security; third, opportunities for development.

The family gives to the child his name and standing in the community. A child wants his family to be as good as those of his friends. He wants to be able to point with pride to his father and feel an inspiration every time he looks at his mother. It is a mother's duty so to live that her children will associate with her everything that is beautiful, sweet, and pure. And fathers, even the poorest of us, from a financial standpoint, may so conduct our lives as to be able to give our sons a good name.

THE SENSE OF SECURITY. In regard to the sense of security, every child is entitled to food, shelter, and raiment, and he should feel in his home a safe and comfortable protection from the outside world.

In this phase of family life the Church can render excellent service. No other organization in the world is so well prepared to know the physical and economic condition of each person as is the Church of Jesus Christ of Latter-day Saints. Now is an opportune time for the Church to demonstrate its efficiency not only in knowing the needs of the destitute but in supplying their needs.—CR, April 1935, pp. 113-114.

CHILDREN DESERVE TO BE TAUGHT INTELLIGENT OBEDIENCE. Unhappiness in the child's life, as in the adult life, springs largely from nonconformity to natural and social laws. The home is the best place in which to develop obedience, which nature and society will later demand.—I, 81:166 (1946).

It is my opinion, and my opinion is confirmed by experience, that the best time for the child to learn the rules of conformity is between the ages of three and five.—I, 81:166 (1946).

Home is the center from which woman rules the world. It is there she teaches her child self-restraint, develops in him the confidence and strength that spring from self-control. It is there the child learns respect for the rights of others. It is in a well-directed home that men and women first develop a consciousness that true happiness lies in conforming one's life to the laws of nature and to the rules of social conduct. —IE, 50:641 (1947).

MUTUAL LOVE AND RESPECT

"HONOUR THY FATHER AND THY MOTHER." It is a dangerous sign when home discipline breaks down, and the loving advice of a wise father and a loving mother is defied. We are told by an elderly American explorer that among the Iroquois Indians "the crime which is regarded as most horrible, and which is without example, is that a son should be rebellious toward his mother"— an ideal that might be well cherished today among men who esteem themselves high in the scale of civilization.—*CR*, October 1951, p. 5.

PARENTS TO TEACH FILIAL PIETY. A great Chinese philosopher, as a minister of crime, is reported to have set free a son who had offended against the canon of filial behavior, on the ground that the father who had so ill-taught him was the one to blame. Said he:

"When superiors fail in their duty, should inferiors die? This father never taught his son to be filial. To act upon this charge would be to kill the innocent."—*CR*, October 1948, p. 120.

FIDELITY TO PARENTS. Love is the highest attribute of the human soul, and fidelity is love's noblest offspring. To be the worthy son or the worthy daughter of noble parents is one of the greatest responsibilities of youth, one of the important duties of life. Disloyalty to righteous parents is as reprehensible as disloyalty to God. There is a sacred trust in sonship which should never be violated.—*IE*, 43:395 (1940).

FATHER AND SON. One evening, about five o'clock, four brethren were riding down Main Street in an automobile. Just as they passed First South Street, they heard a little plaintive cry, "Papa! Papa! Papa! wait" The father was the driver, and his ready ear recognized his son's voice. He brought the machine instantly to a standstill. As the men looked out, they saw coming out of that bustling, jostling crowd of humanity, a little nine-year-old boy, out of breath, panting, crying, because of his effort to overtake the machine.

The father said, "Why, where have you been, my son?"

"I have been looking for you."

"Well, did you leave the place where we agreed to meet?"

"Yes, I went up to see where you were."

The boy understood that they were to meet in front of the Tabernacle. The father evidently meant to meet the child farther down the street. Through this misunderstanding the son had become separated from his parent, and the little child was thrown into that vast throng, unprotected.

I believe that illustrates the keynote of warning that has been sounded frequently. Fathers, is there a misunderstanding between you and your sons? Is there one wandering amidst the throngs of life, surrounded by all kinds of temptations, and you expecting to meet him at an appointed place which he does not know? He may not come out from that throng and cry, "Father, Father!" and if he should, your ears might be deaf to that call, because of the concentration of your mind upon the affairs of life. So you might speed by him and leave him in the midst of evil, to find his own way home. Take your sons with you along this road of life, that you may have them with you in that eternal home where there is everlasting peace and contentment.—CR, October 1909, p. 89.

"Charity suffereth long, and is kind; . . . " (I Cor. 13:4.) The spirit of kindness is as enduring as love itself. Let us go home, and if we have been cruel, either by treating our wives with indifference, or by scolding or loud talking, if we have been cruel to our children by neglect or by striking them, let us see if we cannot repent and look introspectively and see whether or not we are to blame for some of the conditions that arouse these passions.—CR, October 1951, p. 182.

CONTROL THE TONGUE! He is a weak man who will curse or condemn some loved one because of a little accident. What good does it do him? He would be a man if he would develop his spirit and control that anger, control his tongue. A little thing? Trace it, and you will find that not yielding and not controlling it bring many an unhappy hour in your home. —DNCS, September 6, 1952, p. 15.

A PICTURE OF HEAVEN. I have but one thought in my heart for the young folk of the Church, and that is that they be happy. I know of no other place than home where more happiness can be found in this life. It is possible to make home a bit of heaven; indeed, I picture heaven to be a continuation of the ideal home.—IE, 51:618 (1948).

CHAPTER 36

A PHILOSOPHY OF HAPPINESS

HAPPINESS AND THE POWER TO CHOOSE

THE NATURE OF MEN AND NATIONS DETERMINED BY CHOICE. Man's success or failure, happiness or misery, depends upon what he seeks and what he chooses. What a man is, what a nation is, may largely be determined by his or its dominant quest. It is a tragic thing to carry through life a low concept of it.—*CR*, September-October 1950, pp. 108-109.

FREE AGENCY REQUISITE TO HAPPINESS. There cannot be happiness without free agency. If the soul feels circumscribed, harassed, or enslaved by something or somebody, there cannot be true progress. That is why some of the nations today are wrong and some day in the future will have to change their policy. God intends men to be free.—*IE*, 42:459 (1939).

Choosing the right with unvarying and unwavering determination, resisting temptations from within and from without, cheerfulness in the face of difficulties and experiences, reverence for God and respect for your fellow men, willingness to assist in the establishment of the kingdom of God—these, though you might miss some of the emoluments of the world, will bring peace and happiness to your soul, and through obedience to the principles and ordinances of the gospel, bring immortality and eternal life. Your soul will rise in ecstasy and clearer understanding of that great word of God given in modern revelation: " . . . this is my work and my glory— to bring to pass the immortality and eternal life of man." (Moses 1:39.)—*CR*, September-October 1950, p. 112.

THE GOSPEL AND CHOICE. Happiness consists in mastering evil tendencies, not in indulging them, and the gospel of Jesus Christ enables us to master those evil tendencies—*DNCS*, August 8, 1951.

DISTINGUISH BETWEEN JOY AND PLEASURE. Let us in life distinguish between the joy that the Prophet Lehi had in mind when he said, "men are, that they might have joy," and the pleasure that the world is seeking by indulging in appetites and passions, vainly hoping to find happiness. Happiness springs from within.

The significance of pleasure is well expressed by the poet Burns in these words:

"But pleasures are like poppies spread:
    You seize the flower, its bloom is shed;
Or like the snow falls in the river,
    A moment white—then melts forever;
Or like the borealis race,
    That flits ere you can point their place;
Or like the rainbow's lovely form,
    Vanishing amid the storm."

Burns, *Tam o'Shanter.*

Pleasure is not the purpose of man's existence. Joy is. —*DNCS,* August 8, 1951.

SIN IS NEVER HAPPINESS. "The more I know intimately the lives of other men, to say nothing of my own," said Aldous Huxley in a letter to Charles Kingsley, "the more obvious it is to me that the wicked does not flourish nor is the righteous punished.

"The ledger of the Almighty is strictly kept, and every one of us has the balance of his operations paid over to him at the end of every minute of his existence. The absolute justice of the system of things is as clear to me as any scientific fact. The gravitation of sin to sorrow is as certain as that of the earth to the sun, and more so, for experimental proof of the fact is within the reach of us all, nay, is before us all our lives, if we had but the eyes to see it."

Associate with that the saying in the Book of Mormon, sin is never happiness. (See Alma 41:10.)—*CR,* October 1951, p. 8.

THE SEARCH FOR HAPPINESS

THE SEEDS ARE WITHIN US. There are seeds of happiness planted in every human soul. Our mental attitude and disposition constitute the environment in which these seeds may germinate. There is as much need for sunshine in the heart as for sunshine in the world. Today as perhaps never before, mankind needs encouragement and cheer.

It is a duty to seek to acquire the art of being cheerful. "A cheerful spirit is one of the most valuable gifts ever bestowed upon humanity by a kind Creator. It is the sweetest and most fragrant flower of the spirit that constantly sends out its beauty and fragrance and blesses everything within its reach." I think the writer goes to a little extreme. Cheerfulness is but one quality, but it is a wonderful strength in time of distress.—*CR*, October 1934, p. 92.

Happiness Has Social and Economic Ingredients. I am happy when I know that my associates are happy. We cannot be happy if our loved ones are discouraged or ill. We are social beings, and our lives are intricately woven one with another, and we progress as a body when individuals in the body progress.

I have noted recently something which has given me great concern. I have thought that I have detected in men and women who have called upon me and whom I have met in my travels just a little evidence of discouragement, and yet it is our right to be happy. It is the destiny of man to have joy.—*CR*, October 1934, p. 91.

But the Quest Is Unfulfilled in the Search for Material Treasure. If the experience of the past few years has taught us anything, it has taught us that it is unwise to seek happiness in worldly possessions only. I say "only" because I do not minimize the value of the material things of the world as contributing factors to man's peace, joy, and contentment. The Lord himself has said that if we worship him with rejoicing and prayer, with glad hearts and cheerful countenances, the fulness of the earth is ours.

In the Doctrine and Covenants he says plainly:

" . . . the fulness of the earth is yours, the beasts of the field and the fowls of the air, and that which climbeth upon the trees and walketh upon the earth;

"Yea, and the herb, and the good things which come of the earth, whether for food or for raiment, or for houses, or for barns, or for orchards, or for gardens, or for vineyards;

"Yea, all things which come of the earth, in the season

thereof, are made for the benefit and the use of man, both to please the eye and to gladden the heart;

"Yea, for food and for raiment, for taste and for smell, to strengthen the body and to enliven the soul.

"And it pleaseth God that he hath given all these things unto man; for unto this end were they made to be used, with judgment, not to excess, neither by extortion." (D. & C. 59:16-20.)

However, to seek happiness or even contentment in the acquisition of these worldly things alone is to lose sight of the higher purpose of life. And that is one reason why there is discouragement and why there is despair generally in the world. The seeking of these material things has been the end, and now that they seem to be suddenly wiped away, men are distracted.—CR, October 1934, pp. 92-93.

PROPER EVALUATION OF BLESSINGS. Brethren and sisters, with debts piled upon you, with difficulty to pay your taxes, with the loss of your home pending, if you would still be happy, look to yourself and count your blessings, and keep confidence in your God and in your fellow man.

Another source of joy within your reach is the proper evaluation of blessings. You have your health. Next to life itself that is one of the greatest blessings that can come to you—the second blessing that we mortals are capable of receiving, a blessing that money cannot buy. If you have it, thank the Lord night and morning that he has given it to you.

In addition to this he has given you ability to appreciate his glorious gospel, the sunshine, the voice of nature speaking to you. Do you open your eyes and see it? I have rejoiced during this conference to hear the brethren acknowledge the blessing of our environment, the products of the field, scanty as they are, in some sections of the country, the flowers blooming, the sunsets, and above all the realization that we are living in God's world and that he is the Creator of it. If you stop to think, you still have the power and ability to appreciate and to enjoy things which no one, no depression can take from you.

There is something else which we sometimes do not properly evaluate. That is our family. I know it hurts us if we see our loved ones hungry. There is no need of any child's being hungry in this Church. Let us thank God for the organization and say we will buckle to and make our contributions so that these conditions will be removed, and thank him for our loved ones, ours for time and all eternity.

Finally, you have the opportunity for association with others, an ever present condition of happiness. If you affiliate with your quorum and other organizations, meeting regularly with your fellow men, you will know what that brotherhood is to which I have referred in my association with these brethren in the Council of the Twelve, a brotherhood which is eternal, a family relationship and social contact which will drive sorrow away under any conditions. You have, too, the realization that even if death should come you have the assurance that death is not victorious but has been overcome in the resurrection of our Lord Jesus Christ. Count these blessings. They are within the reach of every soul, no matter how humble or how great.—CR, October 1934, pp. 94-95.

KNOWLEDGE IS FUNDAMENTAL TO HAPPINESS. There are signposts along life's highway which, if followed, will lead any man to do the Lord's will, to know his Son, the Redeemer of the world, to know whom is eternal life. And while we are gaining this great knowledge which leads to immortality, we find the greatest joy in mortality that can be experienced by the human soul.—CR, September-October 1950, pp. 110-111.

No greater gift or blessing can come to man in this life than a knowledge that God lives, that Jesus is the Savior of the world, and that these two personages did actually appear to the Prophet Joseph and restore, through him, the gospel of Jesus Christ.—CR, October 1910, p. 47.

THE CONDITIONS OF HAPPINESS

THE SECRET OF HAPPINESS. So many people have lost the proper sense of values and have sought peace and happiness in vain in the acquisition of wealth at the expense of spiritual growth.

Wherein then does the secret of happiness lie? The Savior gives us the key to it when he says: "The kingdom of God is within you." The power is within man to choose the right or to choose the wrong. Happiness is not an external condition, it is a state of the spirit and an attitude of the mind.

FUNDAMENTAL GOALS—WORTHY OBJECTIVES. Let us consider conditions in which we can always find happiness, conditions which are to the little seeds of joy in our souls what the ray of light and moisture are to the flowers and growing plants.

To have faith that God is our Father is the safest anchorage of the soul and brings peace and solace under any condition; and the second is confidence in our fellow men. You note at once, of course, how these go back to those two great commandments: " . . . love the Lord thy God with all thy might, mind, and strength, and thy neighbour as thyself." (See Matt. 22:37, 39.)

Now let us not consider these merely as orthodox principles. They are fundamental in our happiness and salvation here. I know that it is a little difficult today to keep confidence in certain groups of men. It is dreadfully discouraging to lose confidence in an associate. When we see and read about human jackals who are preying upon society, we find it hard sometimes to keep our poise and let the sunshine of confidence enter our souls, and yet I believe it is true that mankind generally are growing better. This I do know, that often when we misjudge a brother and seem to lose confidence in him, if we will go to him and find his point of view, our confidence will be restored.—CR, October 1934, pp. 93-94.

HEALTH, WORK, AND HAPPINESS. One condition of happiness is health, though we may be comparatively happy without it. I have seen cheerful, radiant people who have not enjoyed good health, but their joy and radiance result from patient endurance. A kind Providence seems to reward them.

To most of us who must be actively performing our duties, good health is essential to success and happiness. And obedience to the gospel of Jesus Christ contributes to both. It is glorious, glorious, to have the body respond to what the active spirit within would like it to perform. Compliance with the Word of Wisdom contributes to health and vigor of body and mind.

When Orlando, in *As You Like It*, was banished by his unscrupulous brother, his old servant, Adam, who had at-

tended him from boyhood, proffered to go with him, saying,
"Let me be your servant: Though I look old, yet I am
strong and lusty."

Then he gave as a reason,
"For in my youth I never did apply hot and rebellious
    liquors in my blood,
Nor did not with unbashful forehead woo
The means of weakness and debility;
Therefore my age is as a lusty winter,
Frosty, but kindly: . . ."

(Act II, iii, 17-68.)

Next to health as a means of giving happiness I think I
would name work. That is why Latter-day Saints are so
happy. They have so much to do they have not time to think
of their troubles, but better than that, they are thinking of
others. They are not seeking happiness, but when they give
others joy, happiness is their reward.

For example, I have seen young girls who have spent
the entire day serving people on Old Folks' Day, seeking the
comfort and happiness of somebody else. I remember on one
occasion when one of those young ladies came home in the
evening she suddenly realized she was weary, threw herself on
the cot, and said, "My, I am tired, but do you know this has
been one of the happiest days of my life." She had found joy
in work that gave joy to others.—DNCS, August 8, 1951.

Learn to like your work. Learn to say, "This is my work,
my glory, not my doom." God has blessed us with the privilege
of working. When he said, "Earn thy bread by the sweat of
thy brow," he gave us a blessing. Men and women have
accepted it. Too much leisure is dangerous. Work is a divine
gift.—DNCS, August 8, 1951.

"Sermons in Stones, Books in Running Brooks. . . ." Another contributing factor to happiness is to be able to enjoy
the gifts of nature.

The poorest man living can enjoy these because God gives
all his blessings free:

" 'Tis Heaven alone that is given away,
'Tis only God may be had for the asking."
    Lowell, "The Vision of Sir Launfal."

Everybody can enjoy a glorious sunset. You would have to pay a great sum for a painting by a skilled artist. Only the wealthy can afford it, but almost any evening we can look at a brilliant western sky, and each one of us can say, "That's mine."

Too few of us appreciate what this means.—*DNCS*, August 8, 1951.

HAPPINESS, CONSCIENCE, AND THE SENSE OF FREEDOM. The first condition of happiness is a clear conscience. No man who does wrong or who is unvirtuous will be happy. No unvirtuous woman can ever be happy unless he or she fully repents. Uprightness of character, honesty in dealing with your fellow men, honor bright, your word as good as your bond, then when your head touches your pillow at night, and you contemplate your actions during the day, you sleep with a good conscience.

Daniel Webster said, "Weighed against conscience, the world itself is but a bubble, for God himself is in conscience lending it authority."

Happiness is the end and design of life, for man is that he might have joy; but I repeat, it does not come from without.

The second factor I name as contributing to happiness is a sense of freedom. It is sweet to contemplate that word. It is glorious to think of the liberties that we enjoy as citizens of this great republic. We love to look back to the heroes who offered their lives, their fortunes, and their sacred honor in defense of individual liberty.

"God is endeavoring to make men like himself. To do this he must first make them free." The philosopher who wrote those words got a glimpse of an eternal gospel truth. Man can choose the highest good or choose the lower good and fall short of what he was intended to be.

I leave this fundamental to happiness with the admonition to you to be true to the Constitution of the United States, to the Bill of Rights. Do not let any theories of misguided politicians induce you to do anything that will deprive us of our liberties as vouchsafed by that immortal document.

SELF-MASTERY EMPHASIZED AGAIN. A third contributing factor to happiness I name as the confidence of self-mastery.

No one wishes to be a slave to other human beings; no one willingly bows down to a dictator. But some are slaves to themselves, to their appetites, and passions. They are not free. They have deprived themselves of freedom and of individual liberty. Instead of being kings and masters of self, they are slaves.

That is one reason why the Lord has given us the Word of Wisdom, one reason why he has told us to control our passions, to control anger, not to speak evil of one another, but to control that tendency of human nature to slander or to rejoice in a brother's faults.

Any physiology book will tell you how nicotine may harm the body, particularly how injurious is its effect upon the young. Science demonstrates that, too, but there is a greater reason why young people especially should not indulge in cigaret smoking or in habit-forming drinks—because as children of God they should not be slaves to an appetite.—*DNCS,* August 8, 1951.

THE GOSPEL OF JOY

I think it is highly fitting to say a few words to refresh our own minds regarding the purpose of preaching the gospel. It is illustrated in the song "Joy, praise, exaltation of the soul." It is expressed in the scripture, "men are, that they might have joy." (2 Nephi 2:25.)

Happiness is the aim of the gospel, not pain nor grief, not gloom, not mere pleasure. There is a difference between pleasure and joy, between pleasure and happiness.

THE PROPHET'S TEACHING. The Prophet Joseph said that "Happiness is the object and design of our existence, and will be the end thereof if we pursue the path that leads to it." And this path is virtue, uprightness, faithfulness, holiness, and living all of the commandments of God. But we cannot live the commandments without first knowing them, and we cannot expect to know all or more than we now know unless we comply with or keep those we have already received. One purpose of proclaiming the gospel is to declare to the world what these commandments are as recorded in the gospels giving the account of Jesus' teachings and those of the Twelve who followed him.

THE GRAND PRINCIPLE OF APPLIED GOSPEL "SCIENCE":
UNSELFISH SERVICE. All mankind desires happiness. Many
also strive sincerely to make the most and best of themselves.
Surprisingly few, however, realize that a sure guide to such
achievement may be found in the following declaration by
Jesus of Nazareth: "For whosoever will save his life shall lose
it: and whosoever will lose his life for my sake shall find it."
(Matt. 16:25.)

This significant passage contains a secret more worthy of
possession than fame or dominion, something more valuable
than all the wealth of the world.

It is a principle, the application of which promises to
supplant discouragement and gloom with hope and gladness;
to fill life with contentment and peace everlasting. This being
true, its acceptance would indeed be a boon today to this
distracted world. Why, then, do men and nations ignore a
thing so precious?

Is the truth in the paradoxical statement, losing one's
life to find it, so elusive that mankind cannot grasp it? Or
is it so in conflict with the struggle for existence that men
consider it impractical?

Even so, the fact remains that He who is "The way, the
truth and the life" has herein set forth an immutable law,
obedience to which will ameliorate those social and economic
conditions in which

> "Man's inhumanity to man
> Makes countless thousands mourn."
>
> Burns, *"Man Was Made to Mourn."*

Specifically stated, this law is, "We live our lives most
completely when we strive to make the world better and
happier." The law of pure nature, survival of the fittest, is
self-preservation at the sacrifice of all else; but in contrast
to this the law of true spiritual life is, deny self for the good of
others.

The Church of Jesus Christ of Latter-day Saints accepts
as fundamental this law of life. Faithful members thereof
are convinced that only in its application can true happiness
be found or a truly great character be developed; and they

believe with Emerson that "character is higher than intellect—a great soul will be fit to live as well as to think." To them, also, the safety and perpetuity of our nation depend upon the character-building, law-abiding individual.

With this end in view, a virtual army of men and women, serving willingly without salary, offer every week to a whole generation of children and youth instruction and guidance in character-building and spiritual growth. In addition to this army of officers and teachers, men ordained to the priesthood have accepted the obligation to devote their time and talents as far as possible to the scattering of sunshine, joy, and peace among their fellow men.

In all such efforts these men and women are but actuated by the high ideals of the prophet of the nineteenth century who, exemplifying the teachings of Christ, said, "If my life is of no value to my friends, it is of no value to me."

Never was there a time in the history of the world when the application of this principle was more needed. Therefore, let sincere men and women the world over unite in earnest effort to supplant feelings of selfishness, hatred, animosity, greed, by the law of service to others, and thereby promote the peace and happiness of mankind.—*CR*, April 1936, pp. 45-46.

There is one thing needful for joy to which man is entitled, and it is the greatest of all. It is the service we render mankind.

There is something we can take home to God, in achieving which we find true happiness, and that is *character*—what you have made of yourself during this mortal existence. Character—it may be weak; it may be strong. You must decide, but whatever you make it during the twenty, thirty, fifty, seventy, eighty, one hundred years that you spend here will be what you take back there. Character and the service you have rendered will determine your position and place in the next world.—*DNCS*, August 8, 1951.

The Results are Visible. A number of years ago, President Edward J. Wood, his counselors, and I were about to enter the temple at Cardston when an automobile stopped at the west gate. None of us recognized the travelers—a man, his wife, and two children, if I remember rightly. They came toward us, and then the gentleman introduced himself as a minister from Iowa.

He said, "We have just driven through Utah, and the first building that impressed us was the temple at St. George. We came north, and we saw the Manti Temple, a beautiful structure. We continued farther north, and visited the Temple grounds and the Tabernacle in Salt Lake City. Everybody around there seemed to radiate joy, and we heard the congregation sing 'Come, Come, Ye Saints.' Now in Canada we see this temple. There is something about the people whom we have met from St. George to Canada which has impressed us greatly. It is the happiness you seem to radiate. I am going to teach my congregation to sing that song, 'Come, Come, Ye Saints.' "

He was impressed with something which to him was indefinable. We are a happy people.—*DNCS*, August 8, 1951, p. 2.

THE REWARD OF CLEAR CONSCIENCE. It is glorious when you can lie down at night with a clear conscience, knowing you have done your best not to offend anyone and have injured no man. You have tried to cleanse your heart of all unrighteousness, and if you put forth precious effort, you can sense as you pray to God to keep you that night that he accepts your effort.

You have a sense that you are God's child, not a mere cog of the state, but a person whose soul God wants to save. You have the strength, the sense of resistance to evil, to keep from evil. You also have the realization that you have made the world better for having been in it. These and a hundred other virtues and conditions are all wrapped up in the gospel of Jesus Christ.—*DNCS*, June 18, 1952, p. 3.

"THE MEASURE OF THE STATURE OF THE FULNESS OF CHRIST." True happiness is found in living the Christ's life—on Monday as well as on Sunday. He who is virtuous only at intervals proves that his pretended virtue is but a sham. Such a person lacks sincerity, the foundation of a true character, without which happiness is impossible. He who seeks for happiness alone seldom finds it, but he who lives, that is, who loses himself to give happiness to others, finds that a double portion has come to himself. Membership in the Church of Jesus Christ of Latter-day Saints carries with it the responsibility to overcome temptation, to battle error, to improve the mind, and to develop one's spirit until it comes to the measure of the stature of the fulness of Christ. — MS, 85:9, 1923.

THE GRAND KEY. If you would be happy, obey the principles of the gospel.—DNCS, January 2, 1952, p. 4.

Book VII

SELECTED ESSAYS AND ANECDOTES

"I wish I could say to every young man in the Church, that if you would be successful, if you would be happy, if you would conserve your strength, intellectual, physical, and spiritual, you will resist temptation to indulge your appetites and your passions."

David O. McKay
The Improvement Era
Volume 48:310

Chapter 37

Lessons From Life

I

BUILDING FOR ETERNITY

There is a mythical Greek tale that Charon was permitted once upon a time to visit the earth to see what men were doing. From a lofty eminence he looked over the cities, palaces, and other works of men. As he turned to resume his assigned task, he exclaimed: "These human beings are spending their time in building just birds' nests. No wonder they fail and are ashamed."

Men today to far too great an extent not only are spending their time with things which have no permanent value but also are ruthlessly destroying much that they have built throughout the centuries. War is making the earth a shambles. Churches, palaces, cottages, hospitals in many parts of the globe lie in ruins as if shaken by a terrible earthquake. As accompaniment to this destruction there is a pall of night which seems to be enveloping nations as an impenetrable fog—a darkness that springs from hate; for, " . . . he that hateth his brother is in darkness, and walketh in darkness, and knoweth not whither he goeth, because that darkness hath blinded his eyes." (I John 2:11.)—CR, October 1942, p. 67.

All the truly great men of the world have built something besides "birds' nests." Out of the deep longing of their minds and hearts, they have brought forth gems of truth that have made the world richer. They have wrought deeds of love and sacrifice that have inspired millions. In so doing, they might have suffered; many indeed have met untimely death; but all who thus gave their lives, saved them. That which we do for God and our fellow men lives forever; that which we do just for ourselves cannot endure.—AA, p. 3.

II

SHIPWRECK REPENTANCE

In August 1899, the steamship *City of Rome* collided with an iceberg just off the coast of Newfoundland. There was panic aboard the vessel, and for a time passengers wondered whether they would have to take to the lifeboats. Among those passengers was one who professed belief in God and in the restored gospel but had actually not conformed to his belief. He would not participate in worship; he violated the Word of Wisdom and assumed generally a careless attitude toward things religious. Every morning from the time that boat left Glasgow harbor until the morning of the collision this gentleman had taken his coffee at breakfast. At the moment of the collision he was at the bar. Strange as it may seem, in the hour of imminent danger he was the first of his group to suggest that they retire for prayer and seek God's protection. The vessel made no progress that night, a sleepless one for this particular passenger. Next morning he ordered neither tea nor coffee, and, seeing this, one of his companions said. "What's the matter, 'Doctor'? Aren't you going to have your coffee this morning?"

"No, sir," came the prompt reply. And then seemingly in all earnestness he added: "I am not going to taste another drop of tea or coffee until we get to New York!"

No self-denial, no outward act, no pretense can conceal from the Lord an insincere heart.—*IE*, 48:69 (1945).

III

DANGEROUS REEFS

Twenty-four years ago when the steamship *Marama* dropped anchor outside the coral reef that surrounds the island of Rarotonga, a passenger desiring to go ashore asked the captain why he did not sail nearer to the wharf. In answer, the experienced seaman mentioned treacherous waters and pointed to an engine of one ship, the *Maitai*, and to the bow of another, still protruding out of the water—both carrying mute evidence of the danger of anchoring too close to the shore of this coral-bound island. "We anchor here," said the captain, "because it is safer to avoid being dashed to pieces, as were those two vessels, hulls of which lie on those dangerous reefs."

A flippant attitude toward marriage, the ill-advised suggestion of "companionate marriage," the base, diabolical theory of "free sex experiment," and the ready-made divorce courts are dangerous reefs upon which many a family bark is wrecked.—*IE*, 48:238-239 (1945).

IV

THE NETTLES

Jean Val Jean as Monsieur l'Mayor—you will remember, in that great work of Victor Hugo's (*Les Miserables*)—came one day upon some laborers who were very busy pulling up nettles. The nettles were lying there—thrown out to die. The great leader picked up one and said: "This is dead, but it would be well if we knew how to put it to some use. When the nettle is young, the leaves make excellent greens, even when old it has filaments and fibers like hemp and flax. Cloth made from the nettle is worth as much as that made from hemp. Chopped up, the nettle is good for poultry; pounded, it is good for horned cattle."

He named some other uses and added, "If we would take a little pain, the nettle would be useful; we neglect it, and it becomes harmful, then we kill it."

He then paused and said: "How much men are like nettles! My friends, remember this, that there are no bad herbs and no bad men; there are only bad cultivators!"

I think the man or woman who stands before a class to teach the standards of the Church who himself or herself does not live up to those standards is a "bad cultivator."—*IE*, 47:720-721 (1944).

V

"THANK YOU"

Whenever we receive a favor or a gift, the least we can do is to express appreciation by saying "thank you." Very often those words seem very feeble in expressing the feeling we have of a favor bestowed.—*CR*, October 1951, p. 157.

VI
KINDNESS TO ANIMALS

It is a good thing to teach our boys to be kind. A man who was working for me once on the farm came home about sundown, and said, "I have just killed a porcupine over there."

I said, "Why did you kill it?"

"Oh," he said, "just for fun." And I said, "Did you kill it or is it over there suffering?"

"Oh, I killed it." Well, I wondered, so I just took time to cross those two creeks and go over to the little hill. He had not killed it. The poor creature was just stunned; its head was beaten, and it was struggling. What fun can there be in treating dumb animals in that cruel way?—CR, October 1951, pp. 180-181.

VII
WISDOM AND "MONKEY BUSINESS"

This is an incident that occurred in a zoo. It is simple, and some probably may think we should not go to the monkeys for lessons. I think they can teach us something. Sister McKay and I stood one day, I believe it was at San Diego, watching a mother monkey with a newborn babe. She was guarding it, her quick eye watching the other monkeys in the cage; but the little babe was free to do just as it pleased, hopping around, weak in its infancy, getting hold of the bars, starting to climb. When it would reach a certain place, the mother would reach up and bring it back. When it got into a danger point, that mother instinctively guarded it and by action, said, "Back this way." And then the babe was free again, but only within certain limits.

I said to Sister McKay, "There is a lesson of life in guiding children. Teach children early in life that they are free to do as they please so long they do not get into danger or interfere with the actions and rights of others. Freedom has its limitations.—CR, September-October 1950, p. 165.

VIII
MAUDLIN SENTIMENT

I am reminded of a circumstance of the Russian woman who felt sympathy; she knew how to sympathize with the poor heroine on the theater stage. This Russian lady sat in her box, comfortable in her furs and silks, and as she looked at the performances she wept in sympathy with the heroine who was suffering imaginary torments; and while that Russian woman was sympathizing with the stage heroine, her own coachman froze to death on the carriage seat outside, because of insufficient clothing. It is not enough to *feel;* we must *act,* so that it will benefit somebody.—*CR,* October 1906, p. 113.

IX
"HIDE YOUR FACE, GEORGE, AND BLUSH"

There are instances in history where little simple acts have expressed the spirit of the entire nation. One comes to my mind now. At one time during the Revolution, General Greene had been defeated; he was alone, penniless, hungry, footsore. He went into an inn, and the proprietor said: "Hello, General Greene! All alone?"

"Yes, alone, hungry, and penniless."

The lady of the house set before him a warm breakfast— plain, but the best she had, and then, shutting the door quietly behind her, she brought and put into the general's hand, a purse.

"There!" she said; "it is all I have, but you are welcome to it; take it."

There was hanging just over the fireplace of that humble inn, the picture of King George III. General Greene arose, turned the picture to the wall, and on the back of it wrote this line: "Hide your face, George, and blush."

Why?

Because that little simple act had within it the expression of the spirit of the Revolution. The spirit of freedom was expressed by that woman in a little deed of service to her country. That is why General Greene said: "Hide your face, George, and blush."

So it may be in this Church; some little act by a deacon, a teacher, a priest, an elder, a seventy, a high priest, an Apostle, or anyone—some little act may manifest a young man's service to his Church and express that loyalty which he feels, which every young man desires to express, and which can best be manifested by service in the work of the Lord.—*CR*, April 1908, p. 96.

X

"THE RAPIDS ARE BELOW YOU"

I am reminded of an old story that appeared in one of our early schoolbooks. Many of you will remember it. You remember, the author pictures some people sailing down the river towards Niagara Falls, and the man on the shore cries:

"Young men, ahoy, the rapids are below you!"

But they went on laughing and carousing. Later he cried: "Young men, ahoy, the rapids are below you!"

But they heeded not his warning call until they suddenly realized that they were in the midst of the rapids, and with all the power at their command they failed to turn their boat upstream, so shrieking and cursing over they went!

Well, it is a very impressive picture. The lesson left an indelible impression upon me, but today it seems incomplete. It is one thing to stand on the shore and cry: "Young men, ahoy, there is danger ahead"; and it is another thing to row into the stream, and, if possible, get into the boat with the young men and by companionship, and by persuasion, by legitimate force, when necessary, turn the boat from the rapids. Too many of us stand on the shore and cry: "Young men, ahoy!" Let us get into their lives, let us touch their personality by our personality, and let them feel that there is something real in this religion; that it is the greatest thing in life, that nothing else can make them live as the true religious life.—*CR*, October 1920, pp. 41-42.

XI

A GENTLEMAN'S WORD

I like to think of that English gentleman who, finding himself distressed financially, borrowed from a friend, to whom he gave his written note; but before the gentleman received his competence, he was again in financial distress and borrowed from another friend, to whom he gave only his promise. Both these lenders knew when the gentleman received his money, and both called for the return of their money. The first who held the gentleman's note was surprised to hear the gentleman say, "I will pay the second first." The first one protested saying, "I lent you that money first, your lordship."

"Yes, that is true," replied the English gentleman, "but you hold my note. This friend has only my word of honor. I will redeem my promise first."

The first man taking the note from his pocket, tore it into pieces, threw it into the wastebasket, and said, "There, your lordship, I have only your promise."

"Since you place it upon that basis, you shall have your money first."

A mere incident emphasizing the importance that a gentleman places upon his word of honor.—CR, October 1929, pp. 13-14.

XII

THE EMPEROR'S PALACE AND THE CARVER OF IVORY

I am reminded of an incident that happened in front of the Japanese emperor's palace in Tokyo. Three or four of us Mormon missionaries were there, and with us a Japanese convert, a carver of ivory, wearing the cloak of the ordinary working man. As we stood there, I noticed the obeisance this Japanese, though a member of the Church, paid the grounds and particularly the palace. I turned to him and said: "Do you know, Brother Watanabe, that you have something which is of more value than all the wealth you are looking at, and something which the emperor cannot have unless he follows the same road that you have followed?"

The man looked up in surprise to think that he, a humble carver, would have something which was of more value than the emperor's palace or all his possessions. And through the interpreter, Brother Stimpson, he said: "What is it?"

"Why," I said, "it is the priesthood of the Almighty. You are an elder in the Church of Jesus Christ, and that is of more worth to you than all the wealth you are now looking at."
—CR, October 1948, pp. 173-174.

XIII

EYES THAT SEE NOT

Fifteen miles from Vernal, Uintah County, stands a hill over which people walked and rode at intervals for years without seeing anything unusual about it. They noticed two great rocks uniform in size, but to men bent upon pioneer duties they were only rocks. One day a man from the Carnegie Institute walked over the same hill. The nature of the rocks suggested to him that they probably belonged to the Jurassic period of the world's history. He knew that in these strata are sometimes found fossils of huge animals that once roamed over parts of the earth. What were only common rocks to the farmer, the cattleman, and the pioneer were to the trained mind of the scientist, fossilized remains of two vertebrae of a gigantic creature that had been extinct for centuries. In the course of a short time this discoverer had a force of men carefully uncovering these fossilized remains, and the people of the surrounding valley looked on with interest and amazement, as a dinosaur, sixty-five feet long and thirty-five feet high was uncovered. Following indications as he perceived them, this educator in the realm of science, by great effort and expense, unearthed one of the finest specimens perhaps yet discovered. Others have since been unearthed, one of which is on display in the University of Utah, and others are still lying in their original position in the quarry.

So men go through this life, catching occasional glimpses of a higher, a spiritual world; but unfortunately, they remain satisfied with but a glimpse and refuse to put forth the effort required to uncover the beauties and glories of that spiritual realm. They sense it blindly. Crowded by temporal demands, some there are who lose sight of even the indications. The game of life is fascinating, and when men enter it, they enter to win. To win becomes the sole aim of life. The merchant, for example, wishes to succeed, no matter what it costs, though it be honor itself. The politician (not the statesman) enters the political world to satisfy his ambition, regardless of serving the community or his country. Thus, men lose sight of the high things of life; worldly things crush the spiritual light flickering within the soul. Some follow the will-o-the-wisp of indulgence, of passion, become dupes of an illusion, they soon begin to grovel. Truly as Wordsworth says:

"The world is too much with us; late and soon,
Getting and spending, we lay waste our powers.
Little we see in nature that is ours;
We have given our hearts away, a sordid boon."
—*RSM*, 21:725-726 (1934).

XIV
THE PHENOMENON OF PRE-VISION

A number of years ago President Francis M. Lyman and President B. H. Roberts had attended a quarterly conference at Loa, Wayne County, Utah. In those days traveling was by team and whitetop. The brethren had started early that morning to catch the train at Sigurd—fifty or sixty miles distant. They stopped for breakfast at Koosharem. While they were eating, a very singular incident occurred. A young man, seeing the whitetop, knowing the elders were in the house, dismounted from his horse, entered, and eagerly asked: "How long are you brethren going to stay here?"

"Just long enough to finish our breakfast. Why?" queried Elder Lyman.

"Because I should like to bring my uncle here and have you administer to him."

Before the brethren had finished their breakfast, there entered the living room of the house a man who was led in his physical blindness by his wife and this young, outstanding rancher. As the elders entered the living room, Brother Lyman, in his bighearted way, putting his hand on the man's knee, said: "Well, so you want to be administered to, do you?"

"No, I do not," was the surprising reply.

"Well, then," said President Lyman, "why are you here?"

"Because my wife and my nephew put me in the wagon and brought me here," was his frank statement.

"How long has it been since you lost your sight?" asked President Lyman. The man told him. And Brother Lyman said: "Well, you believe the Lord can heal you, do you not?"

The man answered, "Well, I think he can. I don't know if he will."

There seemed to be an absolute absence of faith so far as the man was concerned.

"Do you belong to the Church?" asked President Lyman.

"No, I do not," was the reply.

"Well, if the Lord heals you, you would be glad to acknowledge his power, should you not?"

"Yes, if he did, I think I should."

Let me tell you at this point now what seemed to me in that instance to be most significant, and then I will finish the story. That young man had seen in a dream or vision the night before two men who had administered to his uncle, and the latter had received his sight through that administration. That is what prompted him to dismount from his horse, and make the request.

President Lyman and President Roberts performed the administration. The man, his wife, and nephew returned to their home. Presidents Lyman and Roberts resumed their journey to Salt Lake City.

Two or three months later, President Lyman was attending a conference in Blackfoot, Idaho. Among those who greeted him, walking unaided, was this man to whom they had administered. "Do you remember me?" the man asked.

President Lyman said, "Yes, and I see you have received your sight."

"Yes, I have," said the man; "I can read a newspaper as well as you can."

During the brief interview that followed, President Lyman remarked: "I remember our conversation—how do you account for your having received your sight?"

"Well," said the skeptic, "I believe that the medicine I was taking had just begun to work."

There was a miracle, but its effect in converting the man to the power of God was nil.

To me a most important phase of the story is the pre-vision of that young rancher, for I know that pre-vision is an actual fact in life, and it was through his faith that the man had been blessed.

You young men who pass through periods of doubt about the reality of the spirit in man, and of the possibility of its being in contact with divine influence, should ponder earnestly on the fact that there is something within you which can become cognizant of happenings or incidents that are entirely beyond the limit of any one or all of your five physical senses. —*DNCS*, September 12, 1951, p. 2.

XV
INTEGRITY

There is a virtue—I shall call it a principle—which I wish to emphasize as worthy of our thought and increased effort to establish it among men. That principle is integrity. While visiting in one of the stakes of Zion, in a neighboring state to Utah, I listened to one part of a conversation carried over the telephone. The president of the stake was called from the dinner table to the telephone, and this conversation followed— I was told that which I did not hear, so I can give it to you in full:

"Do you know," said the stranger, a non-member of the Church, to the president of the stake, "do you know Mr. So and So?"

"Yes."

"Is he a member of your Church?"

"He is."

"Well, is he in good standing in your Church?"

"Yes."

"All right; thank you. He is here in our office desiring to borrow some money to make an investment. He referred us to you and said he was a member of your Church. If he is in good standing, we will lend him the money."

Oh, that confidence! My heart rejoiced, and it rejoices today that, so far as honesty and integrity are concerned, the Church of Jesus Christ is a light. You and I grieve most deeply when we hear of a member who forgets himself and destroys, by his dishonesty, that confidence.—*CR*, October 1910, pp. 47-48.

XVI
THE CHURCH AND THE OAK: AN ALLEGORY

I picture the Church as a mighty oak, against which little boys throw mud, covering the bark, and sometimes injuring the leaves; they even use their penknives in an attempt to chop down the tree. At worst, they only riddle a few leaves and besmear the bark. In a few days, the mud is all gone; the rains have washed it off. The life of the oak has pushed out new bark and new leaves; and the mud, which defaced only the outward part, is all gone. Why? Because the life of the oak was untouched, and it had the power within it to throw off those excrescences thrown upon it by thoughtless boys or malicious youths. So it is with the Church—calumny cannot hurt it if it is pure within.—CR, October 1907, p. 60.

XVII

"DANDY": AN IMPULSIVE COLT

Recently I had great pleasure in training a well-bred colt. He had a good disposition, clean, well-rounded eye, was well proportioned, and all in all, a choice equine possession. Under the saddle he was as willing, responsive, and co-operative as a horse could be. He and my dog Scotty were real companions. I liked the way he would go up to something of which he was afraid. He had confidence that if he would do as I bade him he would not be injured.

But Dandy resented restraint. He was ill-contented when tied and would nibble at the tie rope until he was free. He would not run away; he just wanted to be free. Thinking other horses felt the same, he would proceed to untie their ropes. He hated to be confined in the pasture, and if he could find a place in the fence where there was only smooth wire, he would paw the wire carefully with his feet until he could step over to freedom. More than once my neighbors were kind enough to put him back in the field. He learned even to push open the gate. Though his depredations were provoking and sometimes expensive, I admired his ingenuity.

But his curiosity and desire to explore the neighborhood led him and me into trouble. Once on the highway he was hit by an automobile, resulting in a demolished machine, injury to the horse, and slight, though not serious, injury to the driver.

Recovering from that, and still impelled by a feeling of wanderlust, he inspected the fence throughout the entire boundary. He even found the gates wired. So, for awhile we thought we had Dandy secure in the pasture.

One day, however, somebody left the gate unwired. Detecting this, Dandy unlatched it, took Nig, his companion, with him, and together they visited the neighbor's field. They went to an old house used for storage. Dandy's curiosity prompted him to push open the door. There was a sack of grain. What a find! Yes, and what a tragedy! The grain was poisoned bait for rodents! In a few minutes Dandy and Nig were in spasmodic pain, and shortly both were dead.

How like Dandy are many of our youth! They are not bad; they do not even intend to do wrong; but they are impulsive, full of life, full of curiosity, and long to do something. They, too, are restive under restraint, but if they are kept busy, guided carefully and rightly, they prove to be responsive and capable; but if left to wander unguided, they all too frequently find themselves in the environment of temptation and too often are entangled in the snares of evil.—*DNCS*, February 23, 1946, p. 8.

Chapter 38

Outlooks At Religion And Religious Practices

I

A MISSIONARY EXPERIENCE IN SCOTLAND

One gloomy, misty morning a young elder was distributing tracts in Stirling, Scotland. He had been away from his home in Utah only a few months, but he had already encountered the opposition that prejudice and bigotry were hurling against the Church. For the first time in his life he had felt the sting of ostracism. He was in the land of his father's birth, in the home country of his ancestors, as far back as records could trace them. He spoke the same language as those around him. He was somewhat conversant with the history of the old Stirling Castle, with its romances and tragedies. He had read several of Scott's historical novels and could read and quote from Burns' love songs with appreciation. He thought he was the worshiper of the same God as the professing Christians with whom he associated. He was not at a loss, therefore, for material for conversation on topics interesting to Scotchmen when opportunities for conversation presented themselves. Gradually, however, there had crept over him the realization that he and his companion were in no manner a part of the social or religious element of that city.

This ostracism was because of their religion.

Their Church was considered as unwholesome, as something to be despised. Was it? Yet, after all, was it really worth the seeming sacrifices that he, his companion, and thousands of others were making for it? Most surely someone was deceived. Either he was wrong or the people were. They seemed sincere in their opposition to his Church. He was sincere in his advocacy of it. Were they right or was he?

With these thoughts and feelings and many others associated with them, he took his tracts that morning and entered a "close," distributing them from door to door from the ground floor to the top. When he came down, a half dozen or more housewives were assembled at the entrance to the "close." As he passed them, one sneeringly remarked, "Ye can gang awa' hame; ye canna hae ony o' oor lassies!"

Scarcely four months had passed since the sweetest girl in all the world had led him to hope that she would give her hand, as well as her heart, to him upon his return from his mission; so nothing could have been farther from his mind that morning than a desire to win the favor of any other girl. So the woman that sneered was deceived. But her taunt had in it such a vile accusation; viz., that he was there to traffic in the virtue of women and to cover such traffic with the garb of religion!

The most real thing to him in all the world were his own thoughts and feelings, and he knew as he knew nothing else that those women, and all who thought as they, though the number might run into millions, were deceived.

A few days later his companion and he met a minister, who accused them of not being Christians because they believed in the Book of Mormon. Again the elder knew, knew beyond a shadow of doubt, that, in company with all his associates, he accepted Christ and him crucified. The very purpose of his being in Stirling was to bear witness that the living Christ had again spoken to man; to testify that there is no other name given under heaven whereby mankind may be saved.

As he knew his own soul, so he knew that the minister was either deceived or dishonest, in either case, an unsafe guide to the people. That minister's attitude toward his church was typical of the attitude of nearly every minister in the so-called Christian churches.

On that one point, at least, the young elder knew absolutely that those professing Christian leaders were in error and were teaching the people falsehoods.

His familiarity with the New Testament had convinced him that the ministers were not teaching the principles and ordinances of the gospel as Christ and his Apostles taught and practised them; so it was a simple matter for him to decide in his own mind as to who were in error—he and his companion, or, all the rest of the people in Stirling, ministers included!

False accusations thus became a means of clarifying his mind regarding Mormonism and the world as no other experience in his life had clarified it. Study, devotion to duty, and the inspiration of the Lord later made clearer his vision of the glorious principles of salvation and gave him communion with his Friend and Savior, the Redeemer of the world.—*MS*, 85:24-25 (1923).

II

WHICH, THE CHRISTIAN?

In Adelaide, Australia, there lived a man who had lost his sight. Several years after his affliction came upon him he became converted to the gospel of Jesus Christ as revealed through the Prophet Joseph Smith. He was self-supporting, succeeding financially, seemed happy and contented, and was in many ways a remarkable man. His brother-in-law, a minister in the Church of England, refused even to talk to him, on the sole ground that the sightless man was a Latter-day Saint. With the utmost compassion for his brother-in-law, he said one day, "Physically I am blind; but spiritually I know that I see the truth. As my brother-in-law thinks I am spiritually blind, I have kindly asked him to lead me into the light, but he has turned against me because I have joined the Church. I understand why he does so, and, therefore, can forgive him for choosing to ignore me."

Measured by the standard of kindly feelings, which one of these men is the true Christian?

Near Newcastle, England, an elder was distributing gospel tracts from door to door. His motives were pure. He sincerely believed that he had a message of vital importance to every person in the world. Important or unimportant, it certainly could do no one any harm. But whether his message did or did not possess virtue, his thoughts and feelings toward his fellow men were in keeping with Christ's teachings regarding man's duty toward his neighbor. Seeing the elder tracting, a gentleman—I shall call him such, though he does not deserve the title—said:

"What are you doing?"

"I am distributing gospel tracts," was the reply.

"Are you a Mormon elder?"

"Yes."

Without the least provocation the man, pale with rage, then raised his cane and assaulted the elder, whose first impulse, naturally, was to knock the offender down, which he could readily have done. However, he controlled himself and received several blows without retaliating. He wisely held his ground, however, and continued his tracting. The would-be defender (?) of Christian principles walked away, his heart still filled with a bitterness made only more intense by his unjustified attack.

Judged by Christ's standard of right thinking, which one of these men is the true Christian?—MS, 85:41 (1923).

III

THE SPIRIT OF SLANDER AND THE SPIRIT OF THE GOSPEL

It is easy to distinguish between the spirit of slander and the spirit of the gospel. I remember an instance in England during my late mission that may illustrate my meaning. Two elders had gone to great expense, for them, in procuring a hall, and in announcing their meeting and distributing literature. Their hopes were high on Sunday morning when, as they approached their hired hall, they saw a goodly number of persons accepting their invitation. One gentleman who was dressed in the garb of a Christian divine approached the hall and was greeted by the elder who was standing at the door. The latter extended his hand, but the minister refused, saying contemptuously, "I did not come here to shake hands with you."

"Very well," said the elder, "you are welcome," and invited him into the hall.

When the elder reported this to me, he said: "I felt somewhat discouraged and gloomy."

I said: "You ought to be very thankful for the experience that came to you that morning. That gentleman misjudged you. You know he misjudged you. You know your sincerity. You know what you had in your heart. You know also that he was wrong in his accusation and in his feelings towards you and your people. Test that spirit and see if you have not more confidence in the work in which you are engaged than you ever had before."—*CR*, October 1931, pp. 10-11.

IV

THE EFFICACY OF PRAYER

Since childhood it has been very easy for me to believe in the reality of the visions of the Prophet Joseph Smith. What I am going to say may seem very simple to you, but to me it is a heart petal.

When a very young child in the home of my youth, I was fearful at night. I traced it back to a vivid dream in which two Indians came into the yard. I ran to the house for protection, and one of them shot an arrow and hit me in the back. Only a dream, but I felt that blow, and I was very much frightened, for in the dream they entered the house, a tall one, and a smaller one, and sneered and frightened Mother.

I never got over it. Added to that were the fears of my mother, for when Father was away with the herd, or on some mission, Mother would never retire without looking under the bed; so burglars or men who might enter the house and try to take advantage of Mother and the young children were real to me.

Whatever the conditions, I was very much frightened. One night I could not sleep, and I fancied I heard noises around the house. Mother was in another room. Thomas E. by my side was sleeping soundly. I became terribly wrought in my feelings, and I decided to pray as my parents had taught me.

I thought I could pray only by getting out of bed and kneeling, and that was a terrible test. But I did finally bring myself to get out of bed and kneel and pray to God to protect Mother and the family. And a voice, speaking as clearly to me as mine is to you, said, "Don't be afraid; nothing will hurt you." Where it came from, what it was, I am not saying. You may judge. To me it was a direct answer.

I say it has been easy for me to understand and believe the reality of the visions of the Prophet Joseph. It was easy for me in youth to accept his vision, the appearance of God the Father and his Son, Jesus Christ, to the boy praying. I thought of nothing else. Of course that is real. It was easy for me to believe that Moroni came to him there in the room. Heavenly Beings were real from my babyhood on, and as years came those impressions strengthened by reason and strengthened by the inspiration of God directly to my soul.

I know that those visions were real, and that Joseph Smith was a prophet of God, and when we say this, it means that we know that Jesus lives, that Christ is our Redeemer, and that this is his Church. We are merely his representatives. When we accept that, then the reality of God the Father, Father of our spirits, is easy to accept.

These things being real, brethren, we cannot do anything else but try our utmost to do what Jesus Christ, our Redeemer, asks us to do, for he has given us the gospel that bears his name, and in the words of Peter, . . . "there is none other name under heaven given among men, whereby we must be saved." (Acts 4:12.)—CR, October 1951, pp. 182-183.

V

THE REALITY OF THE UNSEEN WORLD

One day in Salt Lake City a son kissed his mother good morning, took his dinner bucket, and went to City Creek Canyon where he worked. He was a switchman on the train that was carrying logs out of the canyon. Before noon his body was brought back lifeless. The mother was inconsolable. She could not be reconciled to that tragedy—her boy just in his early twenties so suddenly taken away. The funeral was held, and words of consolation were spoken, but she was not consoled. She couldn't understand it.

One forenoon, so she says, after her husband had gone to his office to attend to his duties as a member of the Presiding Bishopric, she lay in a relaxed state on the bed, still yearning and praying for some consolation. She said that her son appeared and said, "Mother, you needn't worry. That was merely an accident. I gave the signal to the engineer to move on, and as the train started, I jumped for the handle of the freight car, and my foot got caught in a sagebrush, and I fell under the wheel. I went to Father soon after that, but he was so busy in the office I couldn't influence him—I couldn't make any impression upon him, and I tried again. Today I come to you to give you that comfort and tell you that I am happy."

Well, you may not believe it. You may think she imagined it, but you can't make her think so, and you can't make that boy's father think it. I cite it today as an instance of the reality of the existence of intelligence and environment to which you and I are "dead," so to speak, as was this boy's father.—FS, ms., James H. Douglas, Ogden, 1943.

VI

NO MAN CAN SERVE TWO MASTERS

Brethren and sisters, we must choose whom we will serve. I say we cannot go on serving, part of the time, the enemy, and part of the time, the Church. We cannot do this. The Lord has said plainly,

"No man can serve two masters: for either he will hate the one, and love the other; or else he will hold to the one, and despise the other. Ye cannot serve God and Mammon." (Matt. 6:24.) These words are true; and I believe we should take them as literally as did the Prophet Joseph Smith take the words of James:

"If any of you lack wisdom, let him ask of God, that giveth to all men liberally, . . ." (James 1:5.)

The Prophet believed these words and took them for their meaning. So I believe we should take Christ's words and know that we cannot serve two masters. Let us choose today whom we shall serve.

The truth that we cannot serve two masters is emphasized in Byron's *Cain*, and I feel to mention it here for emphasis. Cain is tempted by Lucifer; and after the devil has led him on, telling him that the gospel is nothing, that Adam was deceived, that the Lord is only a cruel God, Cain says:

"Wilt thou teach me all things?"

"Aye," says Lucifer, "upon one condition."

Cain: "Name it."

Satan: "That you fall down and worship me, the lord."

Cain: "Thou art not the Lord my father worships?"

Satan: "No."

Cain: "His equal?"

Satan: "No. And have naught in common with Him. No; nor want anything to do with Him. I would be aught above, beneath, I would rather be anything than subject to His power. I dwell apart; yet am I strong, and many there are who follow me, and many yet who shall. Be thou among the first."

Cain answered: "I have never yet bowed to my father's God, though my brother, Abel, oft implores that I should offer sacrifices with him."

Lucifer quickly catches him: "Hast thou not bowed to Him?"

Cain: "Have I not said it? Need I say it? Dost not thy mighty knowledge teach thee that?"

Then these words, and Byron never uttered a greater truth:

Satan: *"He who bows not to Him has bowed to me."* He who bows not to God has bowed to Lucifer.

"But," says Cain, "I will bow to neither."

"Ne'ertheless," answers the tempter, "thou art my worshiper; he who worships not Him is mine the same."

This truth harmonizes with the scripture. "No man can serve two masters: for either he will hate the one, and love the other; or else he will hold to one, and despise the other." (*Ibid.*, 6:24.)—CR, April 1908, pp. 94-95.

VII

THE PIONEERS—BENEFACTORS OF HUMANITY

When I recently visited Omaha, being a few miles from Florence, I was forcibly reminded of the early experiences of our parents at that place, and at Des Moines, Iowa, then on the frontier. I have heard them tell how they prepared their teams, hitching up a cow with an ox, sometimes a cow with a horse, making ready to take that thousand mile journey; where? Out into the barrenness, out into the wilderness!

What was their purpose? What was the motive? As a prominent educator in Chicago said, the other day: "Not for the golden California, but that they might worship God Almighty according to the dictates of their conscience; and I admire them for it." Such was their motive—to build the Church and to save the principles revealed to man. They had risked all; they had risked life and everything they had and were willing to endure any hardship. Wives walked every step of the way on this long journey, mothers carrying their babes.

On the 24th of July, 1847, they were here in this valley. What did they see? You try to picture what they saw. These words will call up the barren picture in the minds of pioneers who are with us today—God bless them and preserve them long with us for what they have done, that we might at least express our appreciation of their devotion to the truth. They saw sagebrush; they heard the howl of the coyote; they saw in the distance the smoke of the Indian fire and the salt sea in the west reflecting the beautiful sunlight; but there was no apparent place for a home. There was nothing inviting; in fact, they had been warned that nothing would grow; a thousand dollars had been offered for the first ear of corn that they would produce. Yet, within a few feet of where we meet today, the prophet of the Lord said, "Here we shall build a house to God."

Now what do we see? Just look at our city today, its climate modified, its fruit unexcelled, substantial and comfortable homes everywhere, towns and cities flourishing. To whom are we indebted for all this? The people of the Mormon Church, the pioneers of 1847 and of subsequent years. They were builders, colonizers, benefactors to our nation, benefactors to humanity. Did they tear down anything? Did they destroy? Did they find fault? No. They protected themselves, with a motive that they might continue to bless.—CR, April 1909, p. 65.

VIII

THE MEANING OF "THIS IS THE PLACE" MONUMENT

Monuments are links that unite one generation to another. We assemble here today to unveil and dedicate one of the great monuments of the world. In some respects it is most unique and outstanding. It is a monument designed by a sentence.

In our country we have the Washington Monument, the Lincoln Memorial, the Thomas Jefferson Memorial, the Brigham Young Monument, and others erected to individuals. This monument is designated as "This is the Place" Monument.

Every sentence or phrase serves two purposes; it denotes a certain thing; it also connotes, sometimes, many things. Abraham Lincoln, for example, denotes a long, tall, angular individual, but his name connotes the preservation of the union and other historical events that are cherished by every true citizen of the United States. Let us consider for a moment or two what the phrase, "This is the place," connotes.

A hundred years ago today the great leader, President Brigham Young, looked over this valley and said: "This is the right place. Drive on." What did he have in mind when he said: "This is the place"?

By reading the reports of his sermons we find that he had in mind, first, the prophetic utterance of the man whom he loved, the Prophet Joseph, who said the Saints would go to the West, build cities, and become a mighty people in the midst of the Rocky Mountains.

Secondly, when that great leader uttered the sentence, "This is the place," he had in mind that here they would find a place of refuge and peace.

Thirdly, he had in mind that from this center there would radiate to all the world a message of truth, insofar as it would be possible for that little band and those who followed them to declare that truth to the world, to establish brotherhood, peace, and above all, faith in God, our Father.

Fourthly, he had in mind to establish in this place worship, industry, education, and mutual service.

Regarding the importance of education, President Young said on one occasion soon after they entered the valley:

"First build your fort and protect yourselves from depredations. As soon as you have built your log house, let a sufficient number of rooms be appropriated for schools, furnished by the best teachers, and give every child among you an opportunity of continuing his education anew and see that he attends to it. That individual who has an opportunity to educate his children and does not, is not worthy to have children. Teach your children the principles of the kingdom that they may grow in righteousness."

Fulfilment of prophecy—a place of refuge and peace—a center from which would radiate the message of truth—a place wherein to establish true worship, industry, education, and service—these are some of the thoughts connoted in the mind of Brigham Young when, a century ago, he said: "This is the place!"—*IE*, 50:573 (1947).

IX

AN OPEN AIR MEETING

An incident that occurred one night on City Road, in old Glasgow, about the last night that I was in the mission field, has been called to mind.

We were met, as we approached the place of meeting, by a motherly woman, whom I had never seen before, and have never seen since, who said, "The minister wi' a' his congregation is here the nicht, to break up your meetin'. Stand close thegither, so he canna get in the circle." And she and some of her friends joined in that circle and helped us keep it.

When the first speaker began to testify to the restoration of the gospel, this alleged minister cried out, "These men are Mormons," and the elder, who at that time was giving his first address in public out in the field, became somewhat confused, said a few more words, and stepped back in the ring. Then this interrupter had the crowd, and among other things said, "These men come from Salt Lake City; they are after your daughters, and they want to take them out there and hitch them to the plow and make them work and make slaves of them."

Well, we called on Brother Leggatt, who was a resident of Glasgow, and he stepped out in the ring and said, "Fellow Townsmen," which gave the lie right at once to the minister's statement that we were all from Salt Lake City, and then Brother Leggatt bore his testimony in an excellent address. Well, that man continued his railing until our meeting was about half over, at which time the crowd began to realize that his heart was filled with animosity, and they silenced him and listened to the message which the elders had to give.— *CR*, October 1916, pp. 69-70.

X

FACING THE TABERNACLE CONGREGATION

It is always more or less an ordeal for me to face an audience, and particularly a congregation in this historic Tabernacle. I've been in hopes for years that I would outgrow that feeling, but I still think, study, and pray in anticipation; I tremble as I stand before you with the sense of inadequacy to give a timely message as it should be given; and after it's over, worry in self-reproachment for having failed to do justice to the cause. I suppose you brethren have all sensed these same feelings; so I ask for your sympathy, your help this morning. I particularly pray for guidance of the Holy Spirit.—*CR*, Sept.-Oct. 1949, pp. 116-117.

XI

THE PRIMARY BIRTHDAY PENNIES

Generosity is benevolence in action, and Carlyle says benevolence "is the minister of God." This edifice is the result of true benevolence—one of the most precious of the spiritual attributes of man.

The birthday penny contribution touches every little boy, every little girl who participates. Childhood is being trained in this fundamental spiritual quality every time February comes, and children count their years in pennies for blessing those in need.

I saw an illustration of how real such a contribution is to a child one day at our home in Ogden. I needed some material from the store, looked at my watch, and noted that it was near closing time for business. I asked one of my boys to hurry down town before the stores closed.

As he was a little late returning, I said, "What made you so long returning?"

He answered, "I thought I would run down and back instead of taking the streetcar and save the money because next Sunday is dime Sunday."

Only a little thing, but the boy earned his dime to be one with his classmates in making his class one hundred percent successful in that contribution.

I noticed in the program today a letter from one of the little children here in the hospital. "I like this hospital. I

gave my pennies on my birthday to the Primary, and I am glad
all the children give theirs so I can come here and get well
with the other children. We do so many nice things here."
    Benevolence! Generosity!
    May the spiritual significance of this reach to the outer-
most parts of the world. These contributions come from
Canada, Mexico, all over the United States, wherever the
Church has a branch. And all little children are welcome who
need assistance rendered by this hospital. If they can pay,
then contributions are received. If they cannot, the children
receive the blessings just the same.—*DNCS,* March 5, 1952,
p. 3.

XII

THE PRIMARY HOSPITAL

    The Primary Hospital is a blessing to thousands of chil-
dren in need of medical skill and careful nursing. It is
a monument to all who believe in doing gracious deeds to their
fellow men.—*DNCS,* March 5, 1952, p. 3.

XIII

DIVINE AUTHORITY BY DIRECT REVELATION: AN INCIDENT

    A young girl came to Sister McKay not long ago and
said she was asked to give the fundamental beliefs of our
Church, and she said, "Do you know, I was at a loss to do it."
We were surprised to hear her say that. No young man or
young woman in this Church, in his or her teens, should ever
be at a loss to say what the fundamental truths of this so-called
Mormonism are.
    Let me just illustrate. Suppose young man, young
woman, that a person were to ask you to name three, just three
distinguishing features of the Church. What should you
answer? Every young man or young woman who follows a
course of study from the Primary and Sunday School up to
the missionary department should be able to answer that
and give not only three, but a half dozen, distinguishing
features of this Church.
    Let me particularize. I was asked that question one time
on board a ship that left the northern part of Australia for

Singapore. A man and his wife from California met two Mormon elders aboard that vessel, and the woman, after a few minutes' introduction, said, "Would you mind if I ask you a personal question?"

I said, "Certainly not, and I will answer before you ask it. I have only one wife."

"How did you know I was going to ask that?"

"Because that is the false idea that many have regarding Mormonism."

"Then," she said, "if that (meaning plural marriage) is not the fundamental purpose of your religion, what is?"

I said, "We are Christians."

She said, "So are we." Then she gave that question. "What are the distinguishing features of your Church as compared with ours?"

"I will state them briefly," I answered. "The first distinguishing feature of the Church of Jesus Christ of Latter-day Saints is divine authority by direct revelation." I hesitated.

"What do you mean?"

"Just that. I do not say 'divine authority.' There are others who claim divine authority. The Roman Catholics claim it direct from Peter. The Greek Orthodox claim it direct from the five Apostles who survived Peter. We claim that that authority was lost during the Dark Ages, as Roger Williams stated in substance when he resigned as pastor of the oldest Baptist Church in America, that he resigned because he did not have the authority to represent the Savior. And there was no man living who had that authority nor can there be until new Apostles are sent for whose coming he said he was waiting. That was one hundred and fifty or more years before the Prophet Joseph said he had received a revelation that the churches had lost their authority, and he was divinely commissioned to organize this Church and given the priesthood by direct descent from our Savior to represent God on earth.

"That is what we mean by divine authority by direct revelation."—*DNCS*, April 30, 1952, p. 3.

XIV

THE PROSTITUTION OF WORTHY PRINCIPLES

I often find my mind occupied by an ever-recurring thought suggested by a conversation I had recently with some students, more particularly with one student, who came to inquire for guidance and to seek possible help.

This particular young man was very much perturbed in his feelings. He had heard in one of his classes several imputations that seemed to conflict with his ideas of religion. One of the latest, for an illustration, was this: His teacher had said that the principle of "fasting is a relic of asceticism." I immediately asked him if he had ever thought that asceticism as related to fasting might be the prostitution of a worthy principle. He said he had never considered that phase of the question.—CR, April 1932, pp. 61-62.

XV

THREE PARABLES

There are three very remarkable parables recorded by Luke in the fifteenth chapter. They are called the parables of the lost and found. Usually whenever they are referred to, the principles of repentance and forgiveness are emphasized, and the rejoicing over the lost because the lost has been found. To that phase of the parable I am not going to refer tonight, except to say that I think that part of these parables is sometimes misinterpreted or at least misapplied. There is another phase of these parables which appeals to me even more than the rejoicing, and that is what I want to speak about tonight. I desire to refer to the conditions that contribute to their being lost.

The scene is a gathering of publicans and sinners who have assembled, it seems, in quite large numbers to hear the message of Jesus. Standing out are pictured Pharisees and Sadducees who are sneering at the Man of Nazareth who is speaking to these publicans and sinners, and the Pharisees and Sadducees are judging him, I suppose, by the company he is keeping. By the Sadducees, the publicans and sinners are looked upon as lost. To the multitude Jesus speaks three parables. The first, the parable of the lost sheep:

"What man of you, having an hundred sheep, if he lose one of them, doth not leave the ninety and nine in the wilderness, and go after that which is lost, until he find it?" (Luke 15:4.)

I ask you tonight, how did that sheep get lost? He was not rebellious. If you follow the comparison, the lamb was seeking its livelihood in a perfectly legitimate manner, but either stupidly, perhaps unconsciously, it followed the enticement of the field, the prospect of better grass until it got out beyond the fold and was lost.

So we have those in the Church, young men and young women, who wander away from the fold in perfectly legitimate ways. They are seeking success, success in business, success in their professions, and before long they become disinterested in Church and finally disconnected from the fold; they have lost track of what true success is, perhaps stupidly, perhaps unconsciously, in some cases, perhaps willingly. They are blind to what constitutes true success.

Jesus gave an apt definition of success, I think, when he spoke of Mary Magdalene, saying, "She hath done what she could." (Mark 14:8.) True success is reaching the level of our best in our association with our fellow men. Many of these wandering away as the lost sheep are seeking success for selfish purposes, not for the benefit of their fellow men. See the difference?

Over twenty years ago we had a truly excellent group of missionaries in the European Mission. I have been interested in watching them during the intervening years. One of these was a brilliant missionary, and he was faithful. He came home, completed his education, and succeeded in obtaining a high position in his profession. For twenty years now he has been following that profession. He is successful in it, but he has gone so far and has so little contact with the flock, the body of the Church, that he hesitates about affiliating himself with it.

There was another missionary who came home about the same time who also started out to succeed, and he has succeeded; he is a prominent businessman in this city, highly successful; but he has always kept in touch with the Church. I think he is a success. He has succeeded in his business, but he has used his means to help the Church of Jesus Christ; he is in the fold. There is no need of striking out in selfishness, thinking you have to leave the Church in order to succeed. In the Church we can ask God's help to guide us.

You remember the story of the businessman who went into his private office in the morning and closed the door, and one of his agents came and said to the secretary: "I want to see the manager."

The secretary answered: "He is in conference."

"I have come a long way to see him. I want to see him this morning. I cannot wait."

"Well, he is in conference."

The man arrogantly pushed by the secretary, opened the door of the manager's office, and then quietly closed it, and apologetically said: "I did not know that he is that kind of man."

Said the secretary: "I told you that he was in conference."

The man was on his knees asking God's aid that day in his business.

I ask our young men at home who are striking out in legitimate enterprises to remember that the true success is not just in achieving that one aim, but in keeping in touch with the organization in which they can serve their fellow men, in which they can live to the level of their best.

The second parable is the parable of the lost coin. A woman lost it, and, looking in vain to find it, called in the neighbors to help her search for it.

In this case the thing lost was not in itself responsible. The one who had been trusted with that coin had, through carelessness or neglect, mislaid it or dropped it. There is a difference. Our charge is not only coins, but also living souls of children, youth, and adults. They are our charges. Some of them may be wandering tonight because of the neglect of the ward teachers whose duty it is to "... watch over the church always, and be with and strengthen them;

"And see that there is no iniquity in the church, neither hardness with each other, neither lying, backbiting, nor evil speaking." (D. & C. 20:53-54.)

Let us see that each one does his duty. Someone may be wandering because of the careless remark of a girl of her age in Mutual (and I have in mind a case), and the president of the Mutual lets her go, fails to follow her next Tuesday night and invite her to come. Another may be lost because of the inactivity of the Sunday School teacher or the indifference of the Sunday School teacher who is satisfied with the fifteen people there that morning, instead of thinking of the fifteen who are wandering because of neglect.

Our responsibility is to keep the trust that God has reposed in us, calling us to guard these precious souls.

The third parable is the prodigal son, the "younger son," we are told, so he was immature in his judgment. He was irking under the restraint, and he rather resented the father's careful, guiding eye. He evidently longed for so-called freedom, wanted, so to speak, to try his wings. So he said, "Father, give me the portion of goods that falleth to me." (Luke 15:12) The father gave him his portion, and out the lad went.

Here is a case of volition, here is choice, deliberate choice. Here is, in a way, rebellion against authority. And what did he do? He spent his means in riotous living; he wasted his portion with harlots. That is the way they are lost.

Youth who start out to indulge their appetites and passions are on the downward road to apostasy as sure as the sun rises in the east. I do not confine it to youth; any man or woman who starts out on that road of intemperance, of dissolute living will separate himself or herself from the fold as inevitably as darkness follows the day.

"My spirit shall not always strive with man, . . . " (Gen. 6-3), says the Lord. His spirit will not dwell in an unclean tabernacle, he has told us. He who tries to live a double life, who does live a double life in violation of his covenants, to quote one author, "is either a knave or a fool." Often he is both, because he himself is using his free agency to gratify his passions, to waste his substance in riotous living, to violate the covenants that he has made in the house of God.

In such cases there is little we can do but warn and plead until the recreant, as the prodigal son, at last "comes to himself." I am simply trying to picture how these three different parables can be applied to our own groups.

I wish I could say to every young man in this Church, that if you would be successful, if you would be happy, if you would conserve your strength, intellectual, physical, and spiritual, you will resist temptation to indulge your appetites and your passions. That is gospel truth—indulgence does not strengthen youth or manhood; restraint and self-control do. That is psychologically sound, because, instead of expending your energy as animals, self-control gives you more power and energy to expend intellectually and spiritually. Chastity strengthens manhood.

He is unwise who starts out as the prodigal son to waste in riotous living the substance which God has given him in physical manhood and intellectuality.

God help us that we as leaders may try to guide those who are wandering away from the flock. God give us power to inspire them with the true ideal of success as contained in another saying of our Savior, "But seek ye first the kingdom of God, and his righteousness; and all these things shall be added unto you." (Matt. 6:33.)—*IE*, 48:309-310 (1945).

XVI

THE WAGES OF SIN

The young man sat before me downhearted, self-reproachful, discouraged. Evidently, he had reached that dangerous point in his life when the spirit of abandonment cries out, "O what's the use!" and where the spirit of youth, weakened by indulgence, turns the sharp corner and stumbles and shambles heedlessly, recklessly along the road of indulgence and sin. His voice was somewhat husky, his eye rather lusterless. He looked dejected and sad; nor did his looks belie his feelings. A few years ago, he had faced the future with fond anticipations and bold aspirations. His castles in the air were stately, and his chances of occupying them assured. With youth and all the buoyant energy of young manhood he was fortified, and with glorious opportunities he was favored.

But now he sat, still a youth, with ambition blunted, with hopes crushed though not killed, with energy dissipated, and with his heart heavy in the realization of having failed—sick, self-condemning, sad.

What was the matter, you ask? In answer to that question he himself had said that he lacked "manhood"; by which he meant he had lacked self-mastery. He had started in hopefulness to build his castles; then temptations came to him; and he had yielded. He had given himself to indulgence and sin and was then and is now reaping the wages thereof. His looks, feelings, demeanor—all bore mute witness to the fact that " . . . the wages of sin is death." (Rom. 6:23.)

Death in the literal sense means extinction or cessation of life. It also means "spiritual lifelessness" and a failure to respond to one's environment. Death is the opposite of life. It is in reality the result of ignorance of God and of his laws; for knowledge of the only true God and Jesus Christ whom he has sent is eternal life. To the extent that one breaks the law governing physical growth, to that extent one impairs one's health, and thereby deprives oneself of so much opportunity to live.

To violate a law governing intellectual attainment is to weaken to a degree the intellect, and to transgress the laws governing spiritual attainment is to lose to a certain degree spiritual life. "An extreme violation may bring total cessation or death; that is, may make it impossible for the physical man to respond to physical environment. Every little transgression, then, has a tendency to produce, and does to a limited extent produce death."

In *Every-day Ethics*, sin is defined as a "wilful abandonment of any chosen purpose, it is disloyalty to your own ties, *it is your own power used to destroy you*. Laziness, selfishness, cowardice, blindness, always hurt you in carrying out that life for which you were meant." Thus we see how the youth to whom we refer had in blindness and weakened will, impaired the only forces he possessed with which to build the sterling character he at one time dreamed himself to become.

We are in a world of inexorable law. If we obey the laws of sin, we reap the reward of sin; if the laws of righteousness, we reap the reward of righteousness. How clearly the Prophet Joseph Smith set forth this truth in the revelation that says, "There is a law, irrevocably decreed in heaven before the foundations of this world, upon which all blessings are predicated—

"And when we obtain any blessing from God, it is by obedience to that law upon which it is predicated." (D. & C. 130:20-21.)

How great, how glorious is the gospel of Jesus Christ that sets forth in clearness and simplicity the laws of life. Mormonism, so-called, embraces all these laws, and is, therefore, truly the philosophy of living. How tragic that end which comes through disobedience to these laws. Such an end is marked by physical debility, heartaches, discouragement, self-condemnation, sadness, abandonment, despair, death; "For the wages of sin is death; but the gift of God is eternal life through Jesus Christ our Lord." (Rom. 6:23.)—*MS*, 86:664-665 (1924).

XVII

TWO WAYS OF LIFE

There is a most significant story of two boys—one who heeded God's commandment and offered sacrifice, paid his devotion to Deity in accordance with the command of the Lord. The other failed to do it because his heart was centered upon the things of the earth. As a consequence he became grasping and selfish and murderous. He choked his soul with greed. He stifled his spirituality. He became jealous and envious and finally murdered his brother.

In that simple account of Cain and Abel we find the story of the race. The man who sets his heart upon the things of the world, who does not hesitate to cheat a brother, who will lie for gain, who will steal from his neighbor, or who, by slander, will rob another of his reputation, lives on a low, animal plane of existence, and either stifles his spirituality or permits it to lie dormant. To be thus carnally minded is death. No truer word was ever spoken or written.

On the other hand, the man who tills the soil, garners his fruit, increases his flocks and his herds, having in mind making better the world in which he lives, desiring to contribute to the happiness of his fellows, and who does all things for the glory of God, will, to the extent that he denies himself for these ideals, develop his spirituality. Indeed, only to the extent that he does this, will he rise above the plane of the animal world. —*RSM*, 28:365 (1941).

CHAPTER 39

ESSAYS FROM EUROPE
AT QUARTER CENTURY

I

PERSONS AND PRINCIPLES

In the month of August 1897, among the passengers aboard the S. S. *Belgenland,* sailing from Philadelphia to Liverpool, was a group of colored people known as "The Fiske Jubilee Singers." Just as the vessel was leaving the harbor, some of the white passengers made slighting remarks about these Negroes. Undoubtedly the taunts reached the ears of some of the singers and wounded their feelings; but they neither showed resentment nor deigned to reply.

However, at a concert given about a week later, one of the sopranos sang most beautifully and impressively a solo that seemed to contain a sufficient answer as well as a gentle rebuke to those who in rudeness had given offense. I do not remember the song; but the chorus was something like this:

> "If you want to know a Christian,
>   Just watch his acts and walks;
> If you want to know a Christian,
>   Just listen how he talks."

That simple rhyme expresses the true philosophy of practical religion. Of what value are the lofty principles of Christianity if they are not introduced into our daily lives? What good does it do, for example, to preach universal brotherhood, and then to step from the pulpit to the street and rail against and denounce any who should be included in this brotherhood? Race, creed, color, position, training—all contribute to the difficulty of making practical the universal charity taught by Christ and which pseudo-Christians profess to believe; but such profession without the practice only emphasizes the hypocrisy lurking in the heart of the pretender. It is not easy, I know, but the true Christian is he who exemplifies in his "acts," his "walks" and his "talks" that which his tongue says he believes.—*MS,* 86:72 (1924).

II
THAT REMARKABLE INFLUENCE

Many years have passed since that morning in June when the emigrant ship *Amazon* lay "broadside-on to the wharf" in the London docks. On that morning, Charles Dickens "went on board their ship to bear testimony against the Mormons if they deserved it," and he "fully believed they would"; but to his "great astonishment, they did not deserve it"; so he concluded his testimony as an "honest witness" by saying: "I went over the *Amazon's* side, *feeling it impossible to deny that, so far, some remarkable influence had produced a remarkable result, which better known influences have often missed.*" Intervening years have given ample opportunity for the world to study the results of that remarkable influence.

Before this article can appear in the *Millennial Star*, there shall have been held in various parts of the world, and particularly in the state of Utah, fitting celebrations commemorative of the entrance of the first Pioneer band into the valley of the Great Salt Lake. Some remarkable influence had carried them over a thousand mile pilgrimage, "which," said an English writer in 1852, "has not been paralleled in the history of mankind since Moses led the Israelites from Egypt."

From July 24th, 1847, to June in the early 60's, when Charles Dickens as the *Uncommercial Traveller* went aboard the *Amazon*, Mormon emigrants by thousands and tens of thousands, had crossed seas and plains, and "gathered with the Saints" in the Rocky Mountains. Each company—we might almost say with accuracy, each individual—was impelled to take the journey by the same remarkable influence which had actuated the original Pioneers.

This same influence produced such remarkable results among every emigrant ship under control of the Latter-day Saints that "The Select Committee of the House of Commons on emigrant ships for 1864," after having summoned the Mormon agent and passenger-broker before it, "came to the conclusion that no ships under the provisions of the 'Passenger Act' could be depended upon for comfort and security in the same degree as those under his (the Mormon agent's) administration." "The Mormon ship is a family under strong and accepted discipline with every provision for comfort, decorum, and internal peace," they reported.

From the day of the organization of the Church, that remarkable influence has impelled men, women, and children who had reached majority, if necessary—and often it has been—to leave comfortable homes and to endure privations and hardships. It has succored them in distress and comforted them in sorrow. It has enabled them to endure the significant shrug and the contemptuous sneer of their one-time friends and associates.

That remarkable influence gave men and women strength not only to walk a thousand miles but also to pull handcarts on which were piled their scanty supplies of utensils and clothing. It inspired women with unwavering faith in the overruling power of God, as with heartstrings stretched to the breaking point, they stood by open graves on the prairies and saw their husbands, who had succumbed to the rigors of fatigue and starvation, rudely covered with cold and pitiless clay. Elder John Walsh, now a missionary in Great Britain, when but four years of age, buried his little face in the folds of his mother's dress, while his weak and frail body shook with sobs, as he stood fatherless and she husbandless with a babe in her arms, by the side of a grave in which their husband and father found his final rest with nine others who had died the same night!

That mother is still living, still true to the Church, still testifying that some remarkable influence has sustained her and has blessed her and her children. And her son, with a rich experience of three score and ten years, is now testifying to the British nation that remarkable results follow the adherence to that remarkable influence which inspired his parents and tens of thousands of other Englishmen to embrace the gospel of Jesus Christ as restored through the Prophet Joseph Smith.

What is this influence which made eight hundred emigrants so orderly and contented; which merited the commendation from a select committee from the House of Commons; which sustained pilgrimages that are scarcely paralleled in the history of mankind; which seems stronger than lovers' vows and mightier even than death?

It is the living testimony that God lives, that he is verily our Father, that Jesus Christ, the Only Begotten of the Father, is our Lord and Savior, and that the gospel, the "power of God unto salvation," has been restored in this age, through the instrumentality of the boy Prophet Joseph Smith.

Blessed is he who is inspired by this testimony, ". . . for flesh and blood hath not revealed it unto thee, but my Father which is in heaven." (Matt. 16:17.)

This remarkable influence and testimony is the "rock" upon which the Church of Jesus Christ is built.—*MS*, 86:504-505 (1924).

III
ROBERT BURNS

On January 25, men in every civilized nation will pay tribute to the memory of Robert Burns, who has achieved in the world of poetry an unexcelled distinction. In the art of "singing the soul into song and setting the heart to music" the Scottish bard has no rival. Such a man is truly a "living-light fountain," which it is ever pleasant and profitable to be near, especially during that season when his worldwide admirers are celebrating the anniversary of his birth. His poetry has been described as "pure passion." "Other lyrists are literary at their best; when Burns is literary, he is at his worst. His note falls like the note from the lark, straight from the heart. It is not an imitation of life but life itself running into laughter and tears."

Wherein lies the secret of his spontaneous outburst of song? What elements in his nature entered into his poetry to give it immortality? The creator, ever greater than the thing created, must give part of himself to that which he creates, if he desires it to live, whether it be thoughts, feelings, personality, or being. What qualities of Burns' soul have entered into his poetry to give it such ever increasing life and vigor among men?

In a general way it may be said that a person is governed by his intellect, his emotion, and his will. When these three are strong there is usually found greatness and leadership. When these are weak, there is found mediocrity or a nature unbalanced. With the intellect, we see; with the emotion, we feel; with the will, we guide and control. The truly great as well as the truly educated man possesses the power "to see clearly, to imagine vividly, to think independently, and to will nobly."

Unfortunately, in the case of his will Burns was deficient; or if not deficient, then defiant. This weakness of will, or defiance of the accepted standards of moral conduct, led him into many humiliating experiences and disastrous conditions. For these actions his friends offer neither denial nor palliation. How deeply in his better moments his own soul regretted having yielded to temptations that beset his pathway can be inferred from the letters of apology that followed his indulgences. His open, honest life, however, as well as the divine injunction to judge not," will justify us in "scanning gently" this side of his nature.

But in the ability to think clearly and independently, to imagine vividly, and to sympathize sincerely may be found the secret of Burns' greatness. His power to see clearly places him in the front ranks of the thinking men of the world. This power, it is true, was not evident in the management of his personal affairs, but it is very apparent in his estimate of the false religious and social standards of his time. Cant and hypocrisy he despised. Indignantly he cries out against ministers whose lives were inconsistent with their preaching:

> "But I gae mad at their grimaces.
> Their sighin', cantin', grace-proud faces
> Their three-mile prayers, and half-mile graces,
>   Their raxin' conscience,
> Whose greed, revenge, an' pride disgraces
> Waur than their nonsense."

But sincerity and the true worship that springs therefrom, he admired and praised.

> "Compar'd with this, how poor Religion's pride
>   In all the pomp of method, and of art;
> When men display to congregation's wide
>   Devotion's ev'ry grace, except the heart!
> The Power, incens'd, the pageant will desert,
>   The pompous strain, the sacerdotal stole;
> But haply, in some cottage far apart,
>   May hear, well-ples'd, the language of the soul;
> And in His Book of Life the inmates poor enroll."

How he scores those who are only outwardly righteous, we sense from such poems as "an Address to the Unca Guid," or "Holy Willy's Epitaph," etc.

With charity in his heart for the weaknesses of his fellow men he discerned clearly the effect of social forces and environment upon the lives of those around him.

"I have observed," he said, "in the course of experience with human life that every man—even the worst—has something good about him; though very often nothing else than a happy temperament of constitution inclining him to this or that virtue. For this reason, no man can say in what degree any other person besides himself can be, with strict justice, called wicked. Let any of the strictest character for the regularity of conduct among us examine impartially how many vices he has never been guilty of, not from any care or vigilance, but for want of opportunity, or some accidental circumstances intervening; how many of the weaknesses of mankind he has escaped, because he was out of the line of such temptation; and what often, if not always, weighs more than all the rest, how much he is indebted to the world's good opinion, because the world does not know all; I say, any man who can thus think will scan the failings, nay the faults and crimes of mankind around him, with a brother's eye."

This clear introspective insight reveals the true Burns in the relation to himself and to his fellows. His careful study of man's inhumanity to man led him to summarize his conclusions as follows:

"Then gently scan your brother man,
   Still gentler sister woman;
Tho' they may gang a kennin' wrang,
   To step aside is human:
One point must still be greatly dark
   The moving *why* they do it;
And just as lamely can ye mark
   How far perhaps they rue it.
Who made the heart, 'tis he alone
   Decidedly can try us.
He knows each chord its various tone,
   Each spring its various bias;

> Then at the balance let's be mute,
>   We never can adjust it;
> What's done we partly can compute,
>   But know not what's resisted."

That he thought independently, even disregardingly of his fellows' opinions, is evident to all who are in the least degree acquainted with his philosophy and his manner of expressing it.

But Burns' greatest power lay in the breadth and depth of his sympathetic soul. From this source his poetry flowed to immortality as from an inexhaustible and over-flowing fountain. In the realm of sympathy with inanimate, as well as with animate nature, Burns is supreme. His poems "To a Daisy" and "To a Mouse" are gems. His sympathy for animate nature has, fortunately for the world, found expression in many individual poems. Hear him say in the "Twa Dogs":

> "My heart has been sae fain to see them
> That I for joy hae barkit wi' them."

Besides this great poem, which is in reality an interpretation of Scottish peasant life, this fundamental trait has impelled him to give, out of the fulness of his emotion, other immortal poems, among which are, "Poor Mailie," "Auld Mare Maggie," "The Wounded Hare," etc. In the stormy winter night he thinks of the "silly" sheep, and the "ourie cattle," and words come "like tears of infinite compassion" as he writes:

> "Ilk happin bird, wee helpless thing
> That in the merry months o' spring
> Delighted me to hear thee sing
>   What comes o' thee?
> Where wilt thou cower thy chitterin' wing,
>   And close they ee?"

His sympathy with man brought him in touch with nearly all classes, from the humblest peasant to the leaders in society, in politics, and in literature. He entered, too, the field of political life, and in sympathy "Joined hands with Washington across the Atlantic, and the French Revolutionists across the Channel." His soul responded to the message of the angels that heralded, with the birth of the Savior, "Peace on earth, goodwill toward men." The appreciation of this message is what his soul prayed for when it sang:

"Then let us pray that come it may,
   As come it will for a' that.
That sense an' Worth o'er a' the earth
   Shall bear the gree an' a' that.
For a' that and a' that,
   It's coming yet for a' that,
That man to man, the world o'er,
   Shall brithers be for a' that."

To pray for power to see things as they are, not as others imagine them to be; to cherish charity in our hearts for our fellow men; to realize that, "next to love, sympathy is the divinest attribute of the human soul," and to manifest it for "all things, both great and small"; to strive by righteous endeavor to hasten the day when men of all nations shall live as brothers—these are some of the ideals of life which should be emphasized when the world commemorates the anniversary of the poet Burns.—MS, 85:56-59 (1923).

IV

THE GOSPEL OF INTELLIGENT EFFORT

One day a group of small boys were swimming. Perhaps it would be more accurate to say, they were learning to swim, for none could take more than a few strokes. Just below them a short distance down the stream was a treacherous hole much beyond their depth. Into this, either through bravado or accident, one daring youngster either plunged or fell. He became helpless to save himself, and for a moment his companions were powerless to aid him. Fortunately, one with presence of mind and quick action, jerked a long stick from a willow fence and threw one end of it to the drowning lad. The latter grasped it, held on tightly, and was saved.

All the boys declared that the venturesome lad owed his life to the boy who furnished the means of rescue.

This is undoubtedly the fact; and yet in spite of the means furnished him, if the lad had not taken advantage of it, if he had not put forth all the personal effort at his command, he would have drowned, notwithstanding the heroic act of his comrade.

In this old world of ours, children of men are playing, swimming, struggling in the sea of life. There are those who claim that no one will sink and be lost if he will look to Jesus on the shore and say, "I believe." There are others who declare that everyone must by his own efforts swim to the shore or be lost forever. The real truth is that both of these extreme views are incorrect. Christ will not save men who will put forth no effort themselves, any more than the young rescuer on the river bank could have saved the drowning lad if the latter had not seized the means provided him. Neither can man save himself without accepting the means provided by Christ for man's salvation.—*MS*, 85:760 (1923).

V

CHRISTMAS CUSTOMS

The most widely commemorated date throughout the lands of Christendom is December 25, on which the followers of Jesus Christ, the Savior of mankind, celebrate his birth. This almost universal celebration is carried on, too, and will probably continue to be carried on indefinitely in future years, notwithstanding the pretty generally accepted fact, now confirmed by revelation, that Jesus was not born on that day, nor even in that month.

The celebration as we have it today is a combination of Christian worship and the pagan celebration of the winter solstice. The 21st of December is the shortest day of the year. From that time the sun recommences its upward course, announcing that midwinter is passed and spring and summer are approaching.

The Romans celebrated this change, under the title of "Saturnalia," by universal license and merrymaking. This Roman "festival of Saturn" is really the celebration which was adopted by the early Christians and is now known as Christmas. With it have been accepted also ancient customs and superstitions from other nations.

For example, the mistletoe bough is a remnant of an old ceremonial rite performed annually by the Druids, by whom the mistletoe was not only held in reverence but also believed to possess wondrous curative powers. The ceremony consisted in the people's marching to the forest and gathering around the oak on which the mistletoe grew. The chief Druid, clothed in white, climbed the tree and with a golden knife cut the plant; another priest standing with outstretched mantle caught it as it fell. Two white bulls brought for the purpose, and sometimes human beings as well, were then sacrificed as a propitiation to the savage god of the Druids.

The mistletoe cut by the priest was afterwards divided into small portions and distributed among the people, who hung the sprays over their doors to please and to protect their deities during the winter.

The custom of burning the yule log has been transmitted from Scandinavian ancestors who kindled huge fires to their god *Thor*.

The origin of the Christmas tree is not definitely known, but it is believed to have come down to us from the Roman "Saturnalia," having been carried into Germany by the legions of Drusus, whose great exploits established Roman supremacy in Germany about 15 B.C. Thus we see that even the Christmas tree with its glittering pendants and pretty toys antedates the birth of the Savior.

Good old St. Nicholas or "Santa Claus," as the American first christened him, was a real person who lived in Russia about the time that old Diocletian was persecuting the early Christians. It is probable that St. Nicholas was imprisoned by this cruel emperor.

St. Nicholas had the true spirit of Christmas and went about giving comfort to the people and making children happy. He gave gifts but concealed the identity of the giver. It is a glorious thing to have old St. Nicholas in our hearts and in our homes today, whether he enters the latter through the open door or creeps down the chimney on Christmas eve. To bring happiness to others without seeking personal honor or praise by publishing it is a most commendable virtue.

Festivity and gaiety, the elements in the Roman "Saturnalia," are still features of Christmas; but the dominating spirit of pagan license has been supplanted by the noble impulse and desire to give joy and blessing. The mistletoe bough still hangs in our houses, but the heathen superstitions of sacrificing animals and men to propitiate angry gods has been supplanted by the realization of the significance of Christ's great sacrifice. The yule-log fire that formerly burned out old wrongs and consumed bitter feuds, now glows in the grates of loving homes, where hearts beat in thanksgiving and praise for the sacredness of home ties that bind the family circle. Glittering ornaments and brilliant decorations are still hung upon the Christmas tree, but no images of Bacchus hang thereon, and jolly hymns in which

> "They praised the god of wine,
> Whose earthen image adorned the pine,"

are replaced by the heavenly anthem, "Glory to God in the highest, and on earth peace, good will toward men." (Luke 2:14.) Good old St. Nicholas has long since gone the way of all mortals, but the joy he experienced in doing kindly deeds is now shared by millions who are learning that true happiness comes only by making others happy—the practical application of the Savior's doctrine of losing one's life to gain it. In short, the Christmas spirit is the Christ spirit, that makes our hearts glow in brotherly love and friendship and prompts us to kind deeds of service.

It is the spirit of the gospel of Jesus Christ, obedience to which will bring "peace on earth," because it means—good will toward all men.—MS, 85:808-809 (1923).

CHAPTER 40

THE WORLD VIEW:
BRETHREN IN OTHER LANDS

THE GIFT OF INTERPRETATION

THE GIFT OF INTERPRETATION—The occasion was a conference held at Huntly, New Zealand, a thousand people assembled. Before that time I had spoken through interpreters in China, Hawaii, Holland, and other places, but I felt impressed on that occasion to speak in the English language. In substance I said, "I have never been much of an advocate of the necessity of tongues in our Church, but today I wish I had that gift. But I haven't. However, I am going to speak to you, my brothers and sisters, in my native tongue and pray that you may have the gift of interpretation of tongues. We will ask Brother Stuart Meha who is going to interpret for me, to make notes, and if necessary he may give us a summary of my talk afterwards."

Well, the outpouring of the gift of tongues on that occasion was most remarkable. Following the end of my sermon Brother Sid Christy, who was a student of Brigham Young University, a Maori, who had returned to New Zealand, rushed up and said, "Brother McKay, they got your message!"

Well, I knew they had by the attention and the nodding of their heads during the talk. I said, "I think they have but for the benefit of those who may not have understood or had that gift, we shall have the sermon interpreted."

While Brother Meha was interpreting that or giving a summary of it in the Maori language some of the natives, who had understood it, but who did not understand English, arose and corrected him in his interpretations.

President George Albert Smith and Brother Rufus K. Hardy visited New Zealand several years after that event, and Brother Hardy, hearing of the event, brought home testimonies of those who were present, and he took the occasion to have those testimonies notarized. So it is the gift of interpretation rather than the gift of tongues, that was remarkable.—DNCS, October 18, 1952, p. 2.

REFLECTIONS FROM THE WORLD TOUR 1920-1921

When we left home, December 4, 1920, we looked forward with no little misgiving and anxiety to the trip ahead of us. It was no simple matter to contemplate traveling to the Orient, thence to the Antipodes, much of that distance to be spent on the water. The distance itself made us realize that we were undertaking a great responsibility. Absence from our loved ones was keenly felt by both, but greater than these two, and other incidental things that made us hesitate about accepting this responsibility, was the realization that we were going on a first visitation to our people to represent the General Authorities. The keen sense of our responsibility adequately to fulfil the desires of President Grant and his counselors and the Twelve who had honored us with that call, made us seek the Lord as I had never sought him before in my life, and I wish to say this afternoon that the promise made by Moses to the Children of Israel just before they crossed the Jordan River into the Promised Land has been fulfilled in our experiences. As we sought the Lord with all our souls, he came to our guidance and assistance.

It may be that the realization of our dependence upon him made more prominent what seems to me to be a deplorable tendency of the world to disregard, even to disown, their relationship to our heavenly Father. It was our privilege to hear educators and other prominent men speak in different places and upon different occasions, and to mingle with different classes of men and women on boats, for we spent a total of five months on the water, sailing in about twenty-three different vessels, every vessel well crowded with all classes of tourists, most of whom were professed Christians. Frequently, we were grieved to note the attitude of apology that these Christian men and women assumed toward God, their Creator, and his Son, Jesus Christ.

I have been in mixed gatherings here in the state and out of the state, in which some men, when speaking of the early pioneers of Utah, would refer in a rather apologetic way to Brigham Young, and on some occasions I have felt that the speakers even hesitated to name him and give him the credit due him in the settlement of this great intermountain commonwealth, and in the founding of institutions that since have become centers of influence and might. Just such an attitude I have seen manifest among so-called Christians when they would begin to talk about God. He did not seem to be real to them. He did not seem to be in very deed their Father in heaven.

There is a tendency, it seems to me, among Christian nations to move toward a conception of God very much similar to the conception of the Buddhist who say: "There is no personal God-Creator on whose mercy and good will the universe is dependent. Everything owes its origin and development to its own inherent vitalism, or, what comes to the same, to its own will to live. Human ignorance it is which alone invented a personal God-Creator." The Buddhist utterly rejects the belief in a personal God. So do many in the Christian world. In opposition to this false conception of God, I wish to declare that today I feel as I have never felt before in all my life that God is my Father. He is not just an intangible power, a moral force in the world, but a personal God with creative powers, the Governor of the world, the Director of our souls. I should like to have the young men of Israel feel so close to him that they will approach him daily, not in public alone, but in private.

*   *   *   *

Inspiration was given to us on this trip. That is why I touch this theme.

I want to testify to you that God was with us when we stood beneath that tree in old China when we dedicated that land to preaching of the gospel. My words may not convince you of the fact, but no disputant can convince us that our souls were not filled to overflowing with the Spirit of God on that occasion.

Again the veil was thin between us and departed friends, when we stood in prayer on the side of old Haleakala, the largest extinct volcano in the world, and poured out thanksgiving to God for what he had done for Presidents Joseph F. Smith, George Q. Cannon, Elders Francis A. Hammond, James Hawkins, and their wives, and other missionaries who carried the gospel message to the Hawaiian people.

I knew of his protecting care in the Tongan Islands; for when the vessel was submerged by a mountainous wave, we felt peace and security.

At Papeete, Tahiti, we knew his guiding hand and acknowledged his overruling providence, when replacing our judgment by his inspiration, he moved us to do something which our own judgment had told us not to do, subsequent events proving that the inspiration came in rich abundance in the priesthood meetings with your boys. God bless them wherever they are today, for they are God's servants, as long as they will keep themselves pure and spotless from the sins of the world; and I testify to you that his Spirit is guiding them, magnifying them in their youth, making them a power in preaching the gospel of Jesus Christ.

Again, when among the Samoans, we felt his presence on several occasions, especially in that memorable farewell at Sauniatu. May I take this occasion to say, brethren and sisters, that we are not sufficiently close to the Tahitians, the Maoris, the Tongans, the Samoans, and the Saints in Australia and New Zealand. In distance they are a long way off, and visitations of General Authorities are all too infrequent. They need things which they do not get—sometimes, I think, just because of the great intervening distance; but their hearts are as true and genuine and their faith just as sincere as yours and mine.

Another memorable example of God's guiding hand was experienced when we met Joseph Wilford Booth at the very time and place that we should have met him in order to make our mission to the Armenians successful. He did not know where we were, and we knew not where he was. He was praying that the hope of President Grant, expressed in a letter, might be realized; (for the President of the Church, too, was praying that Brother Booth would meet us and that we three would go to Armenia together); we were praying that we might meet him, so that our mission there would not be a failure; and God answered our prayers. If I narrated the details, most of you, too, would be convinced that there was some power above chance that brought about that meeting.

RESTORATION OF THE JEWS IN PALESTINE. Now, I say that one result of approaching God, our Father, is inspiration. Now, may I take sufficient time to give one circumstance in which the inspiration of the Lord to the Prophet Joseph was fulfilled in part at least, right before our eyes. You will recall the words of Moses as recorded in Deuteronomy:

If they (Israel) "shall corrupt yourselves, and make a graven image, or the likeness of any thing, . . .

"I call heaven and earth to witness against you this day, that ye shall soon utterly perish from off the land whereunto ye go over Jordan to possess it; ye shall not prolong your days upon it, but shall utterly be destroyed.

". . . even in the latter days," continues Moses, "if thou turn to the Lord thy God, and shalt be obedient unto his voice;

". . . he will not . . . forget the covenant of thy fathers which he sware unto them." (Deut. 4:25-26, 30-31.)

You remember also, in the Book of Mormon, which was published before the organization of the Church, that there is a passage referring to the Jews as follows: "Nevertheless, when that day cometh, saith the prophet, that they no more turn aside their hearts against the Holy One of Israel, then will he remember the covenants which he made to their fathers." (1 Nephi 19:15.)

If you will turn to the tenth chapter of Second Nephi, you will see what that promise is, ". . . they shall be restored in the flesh, upon the earth, unto the lands of their inheritance." (2 Nephi 10:7.)

And another significant remark, that ". . . the Gentiles shall be great in the eyes of me, saith God, in carrying them forth to the lands of their inheritance." (2 Nephi 10:8.) That prophecy revealed to the Prophet Joseph is very significant in view of current events, in the light of the attitude of the Jews toward Christianity, and toward Christ.

A SIGNIFICANT EXPERIENCE IN JERUSALEM. All this, however, I must leave by mere reference and carry you now to Jerusalem on the second day of November 1921. On the previous day, Jerusalem had been all bustle and business. David Street was lined with little shops in which Jews and Mohammedans were carrying on their trade. Little donkeys heavily laden with the goods of commerce were walking up the rough stone steps of David Street. We saw no camels on that street, it being too narrow. Camels were lying down depositing their burdens at Damascus Gate.

On November 1, 1921, Jerusalem was a typically busy oriental city; but on the following day all things were changed.

David Street, so far as business was concerned, was quiet. Shop windows were closed, so were the shops outside of the wall. By the Allenby Hotel every shop window was boarded. No autos stood as usual in front of the hotel ready to carry tourists down to the Dead Sea and to Jericho. Our guide, Michael, a Greek Christian, seemed to radiate a foreboding feeling. I rather jocularly approached him and wondered what was the matter with him. He remained silent, his attitude portending evil, and he indicated to us to be quiet. We had scarcely reached the Jaffa Gate where, by the way, is seen the "eye of the needle," when he broke his silence.

"Don't you see that all business houses are closed?" said he.

"Yes," I replied, "what does it signify?"

"It means," he continued, "that today the Mohammedans and the Christians are uniting in protest against Mr. Balfour's declaration that Palestine shall be set aside as a Jewish State."

Well, it was like a thunderclap from a clear sky. I had not dreamed that there would be opposition to that movement. We had seen the Jews present in the city carrying on their trade evidently in peace, without molestation. We had looked up a few statistics and knew that in 1914 it was estimated that eighty thousand people were in Jerusalem, fifty thousand of whom were Jews, most of whom had come there but recently; for fifty years before that there were only twenty thousand people in Jerusalem all told. Now to hear from our guide, who seemed to know what he was talking about, that the Mohammedans and Christians were opposed to the Jews' coming back, was an astonishment to me.

I haven't time to take you through that day, but I just call your attention to this fact, that at eleven o'clock, when we came back to the street leading to the Jewish quarter, Brother Hugh J. Cannon and I expressed a desire to confer with the Jews regarding the opposition so strongly manifest that day.

"Don't go there," cried Michael.

"Why?" we asked.

"Because there is danger."

"No," I replied, "I think there is no danger."

"If you go there, you go alone," said our guide.

I said: "All right, Michael, here is where you and we part company. We will meet you at two o'clock."

So, alone we went into the Jewish quarter, to hear their side of it. We will never forget that scene! Groups of Jews from foreign countries, Russia, Rumania, and Orthodox Jews, who had been in Jerusalem a number of years talked together in subdued tones. From windows and balconies women peered at us, evidently suspicioning us as spies — children looked from behind shutters, and doorways. We finally found a young Jew who could speak English; and in answer to our question as to what all this meant, he said:

"The Mohammedans and the Christians are uniting in protest against Mr. Balfour's declaration that Palestine shall be set apart as a home for the Jews."

As we walked back, we again passed through a group of British soldiers in full uniform, including steel helmets, muskets in hand, bayonets fixed, guarding the Jews. We knew how necessary their presence was; for, as we had come up David Street we had seen several Jews and two Jewesses, one of whom clasped a baby to her breast, stoned by Mohammedans and so-called Christians, their only offense being that they were Jews, who had come back to their promised land.

As we passed these British soldiers, I said: "Boys, we hope you will keep them (the Moslems) straight."

"Oh, I think we can," answered one of the "Tommies"; and as we went back to our hotel, we commented upon this scene and the significant passage which I have read: ". . . and the nations of the Gentiles shall be great in the eyes of me, saith God, in carrying them forth to the lands of their inheritance.

"Yea, the kings of the Gentiles shall be nursing fathers unto them, and their queens shall become nursing mothers." (2 Nephi 10:8-9.)

On the tower that now marks the spot of the tower of David, British officers were waving signals over the city, giving orders to keep the peace; armored cars, bearing British soldiers were driven through the streets to subdue the threatened uprising. Notwithstanding these precautions, eight men lost their lives on the streets of Jerusalem that day.

At five o'clock the order was given by Acting Governor General Samuels, the first Jew to rule in Palestine for 1600 years, that no person should be on the street after five o'clock. The order was obeyed absolutely.

We were witnesses that day of the beginning of the fulfilment of that prophecy which refers to the time, now near at hand, when the Jews will "no more turn aside their hearts from the Holy One," and when the Gentiles shall be the means of restoring them to their own land.

IF WE ONLY KNEW THE READINESS OF CHRIST TO HELP. The next day we crossed the Brook Kedron, passed the Garden of Gethsemane, and ascended the Mount of Olives, to the spot, as nearly as we could determine, where Christ stood when he looked at Jerusalem and wept over her. In the light of the opposition to his purposes to which we were witnesses, I thought that he would weep again if he were standing there today. "If thou hadst known," cried he, "even thou, at least in this day, the things which belong unto thy peace! but now they are hid from thine eyes." Neither do they who are now opposing his purposes know the things which belong unto their peace. "If they only knew!"

I desire to say to the children of Israel today, in these valleys of the mountains, to the boys and girls especially: If you only knew that Christ is ever ready to give you help in time of need, and comfort and strength, you would approach him in purity, simplicity, and faith.—CR, April 1922, pp. 65-69.

"HUI TAU"

Oberammergau has its Passion Play; Salt Lake City, its great annual and semi-annual conferences; and New Zealand, its *Hui Tau*. The first has awakened international interest; the second, inter-state; and the third, only inter-conference; yet in proportion to the people participating, the third serves a purpose of sufficient importance to give it rank among the significant gatherings of the world.

The *Hui Tau* is the annual conference of the members of the Church of Jesus Christ of Latter-day Saints, in New Zealand. Unlike the other two notable gatherings named, it is not held successively at the same place; but before the close of each conference, the district chosen for the succeeding one is named; thus giving the people so favored one year in which to prepare for this important event.

Members and non-members cooperate in this preparation; for it is a recognized fact that the district in which the *Hui Tau* is held must bear most of the expense. Suitable grounds must be supplied; outbuildings erected; accommodations for a thousand visitors or more provided; and a sufficient number of women and girls found who will cook, wash dishes, and serve at tables where hungry hundreds will sit three times a day during the entire conference. Besides all this, a considerable sum of money must be forthcoming. Judging from the eagerness shown by residents of different cities to secure the favored decision, these conditions are met without much difficulty.

At 3:30 p.m., Friday, April 22, 1921, President Hugh J. Cannon and I had our first introduction to a *Hui Tau*. In company with President George S. Taylor, who, with several of his associates, had welcomed us at Wellington, a number of elders, and about eighty Maoris, we had alighted from the train at Huntly Station and were driven immediately by auto across the Waikato River to a little settlement "in the heart of Maoriland." As we neared our destination, we beheld, in an open field on our right, two large tents, and a number of smaller ones, nestling around them. The same scene at home would have been proof sufficient that a three-ringed circus had come to town. And, truly, the tents seemed sufficiently large to house the entire menagerie and army of actors and acrobats that go with this world-wide form of entertainment.

Hundreds of people were already assembled in the open space between us and the two largest tents; and what we saw and participated in during the next two hours contributed to make that day one of the most unique and interesting of this extensive tour.

Sister Taylor, Miss Miriam, and others from the Mission House had joined us. Brother Sid Christy had come bounding to extend greetings, and, fortunately for us, put us at our ease by timely suggestions and explanations. As our party began to walk slowly toward the assembled multitude, our ears were greeted by a shrill cry from a score of women's voices: "*Haere Mai! Haere Mai.*" and other terms of welcome, accompanied by such wild gesticulations, jumping, dancing, and grimacing that, had it not been for the assurances of Brother Christy, I should have thought we were about to be attacked instead of welcomed.

This welcome cry was followed by the *Haka* or war dance by a dozen men or more in front of the crowd, urged enticingly on by the dancing of two women, one at each end of the row of warriors. How they wriggled and writhed, rolled their eyes until only the whites were visible, lolled their tongues, and made unsightly grimaces! I was fascinated and yet worried because surely some acknowledgment must be made of this most demonstrative welcome.

However, when within a hundred yards of the dancing group, we were told to stand still. The representative of the "king" of the district, an uncle, we were informed, stepped forward, and flourishing a cane (*mere*) in his hand, and walking briskly forward and back, delivered an impassioned address of welcome. He was followed by the next man in rank, and he by several others, each expressing his joy and gratitude for the visit of those who had traveled so far to meet them.

At this point we should have replied in true Maori fashion; but as the crowd were waiting to shake our hands, it was suggested by our host that they would "accept a *Hongi* as a gracious reply." And so, beginning with the woman on our left, we clasped hands and pressed noses with the entire assembly!

Even during the first experience we learned that the *Hongi* varies in a degree and intensity as does our kiss, though perhaps not with the same significance.

As we took our places in the seats provided for us, we saw entering the grounds a group of visiting Maoris.

"*Haere Mai! Haere Mai!*" again cried the women! And again the gesticulating, dancing, and speech making!

Then we saw the reciprocal performance. At the conclusion of the addresses as mentioned above, both sides remained silent, and all heads were bowed. Soon we heard moans, and we noticed that men and women were crying. It was not make-believe, either, for tears were flowing. This was the *Tangi* part of the welcome. They were expressing sympathy for those who had lost loved ones during the past year. Following this, the leading man among the visitors, flourishing his cane, responded to the welcome, and told why they had come. He was followed by others, and then the group retired to give place for other groups to follow. Thus the home people welcomed the visitors all through the day!

The next morning, we received evidence, and each succeeding day confirmation that the *Hui Tau* is a well-disciplined organization. Every person on the grounds was expected to respond with promptness and dispatch to the following signals:

At 6:15 a.m. a clanging bell drove Morpheus to his sunless cave and bade his subjects get up!

At 7 a.m. it called to *Karakia,* or morning service; at 8 a.m. to *kai,* (breakfast); at 10 a.m. to *Karakia,* or first session of conference; 1 p.m. to *kai,* (lunch); 2 p.m. to *Karakia,* second session of conference; 5 p.m. to *kai,* (dinner); 6:30 p.m. to *Karakia,* evening service; 7 p.m. to *Karakia,* evening session of conference.

Rongo Pai, or Scripture Service

Twice a day as intimated above, everybody excepting the women folk preparing the breakfast, assembled in the large tent, and participated in devotional service, consisting of (1) singing, (2) prayer, (3) repeating in concert passages of scripture, and (4) questions and discussion. The quotations were selected from the *Ready References,* and chanted in unison. It was significant that only the older Maoris participated in this memory work; the younger ones who joined them read from the book. This is explained by the fact that when the gospel first came among the Maoris, very few could read, so they memorized what was taught them. The chant or song was given as an aid to memory. There were those present who can repeat every passage in the *Ready References,* under its appropriate subject. The meaning of the passages was made clear and their applicability to the Latter-day work shown during the discussion that followed. It was plainly evident that the Maoris *had assembled to learn more of the gospel of Christ and not merely to be entertained.*

Following the service, as many as could be seated at the first tables, answered the call to *kai.* Under a canopy, fully as large as that in which services were held, were arranged eight long tables each with a seating capacity of forty persons. Four well-organized and thoroughly disciplined corps of women and girls furnished these tables and served the guest, each group taking charge of eighty people at every sitting.

Each group, too, had its own boiler for cooking, its own tanks for dishwashing, and its own cupboards for the dishes, and every plate, cup and saucer, knife, fork, and spoon was accounted for.

Boiled meat, potatoes, spinach, butter, jam, and cheese made the principal eatables; but cake, watermelons, and other fruit and delicacies were also served. Some of the meat and potatoes were prepared in the *hangi*, that is, cooked in a pit in the good old Maori fashion, except that chains were heated instead of rocks. And we must admit that meat thus cooked is far more tender and delicious than that boiled in the more modern manner.

As the women peeled the potatoes, it seemed by the ton, or washed the dishes, literally by the hundreds, they worked in unison to the rhythm of some song, hummed as gleefully as though they were having a jamboree. Sometimes the young girls having "finished the dishes" would wind up with a bit of the *kani kani* or *hula hula*.

How efficient this organization and how effectively it worked may be partly realized when I tell you that during the four and one half days of the *Hui Tau* approximately ten thousand meals were served! And that, too, without any apparent extraordinary effort!

Sleeping Accommodations

Some of the best homes in the district were given over entirely to the accommodation of the visitors, Elder Cannon and I each having a room and a bed as comfortable as one could wish. The fifty elders, however, did not fare so well. They slept on mats laid on straw on the floor of the Church. It was truly a community bedroom!

But the greatest and most interesting sleeping apartment was the large assembly tent. Every four feet around its entire circumference constituted a bedroom; and a similar double tier extended from the speaker's stand down the middle to the opposite end. Thus feet to feet hundreds of heads pointed toward the outside and hundreds of others toward the middle of the tent, a passageway being left open all around this combination bedroom and assembly hall; beds remained intact, and were sat upon or reclined upon during each service.

For the convenience of those people who like to sleep in Church, I recommend this combination scheme most highly.

Entertainments

While the religious purpose of the *Hui Tau* is evident on every hand, and gospel conversations and discussions are carried on with almost every group between meetings, there is no dearth of amusement and legitimate entertainment. Chief among these I think I shall name the *Poi Dance* as given on two different occasions by fifteen young Maori maidens dressed in native costume. Combining as it does, rhythm, beauty, grace, and skill, the *Poi Dance* easily ranks among the most beautiful dances in the world. I have never seen any that excel it.

If the *Poi* is the most beautiful, the *Haka* is the most thrilling! After seeing this native war dance, one can readily understand how the ancient warriors, aroused to the highest pitch of enthusiasm, if not frenzy, rushed so madly into battle, or stormed with bare hands and naked bodies almost impregnable *pas!*

We were given a glimpse, too, of the *whaka ropiropi;* but one of the native brethren suggested that they "go slow on that"; and a "hint to the wise" was in this case "sufficient."

Too much credit cannot be given to the *Hui Tau* committee composed of all native men, who have so successfully managed these *Hui Taus* for many years.

Brother William Duncan is chairman, and a more able, loyal Church worker than he is seldom found anywhere in the world! He is a man among men, a worthy example of what Mormonism will do for those who will accept it and live it. He has been ably assisted by four others, equally worthy of commendation and esteem.

This year, the committee was enlarged by the addition of more members.

Though each annual gathering costs between $2500 and $3000, the committee is free from debt and has a fair balance in the bank. Besides this, they have accumulated considerable property, such as tents, a dynamo, electrical appliances, stoves, etc.

Electric lights illuminated the grounds and tents to the entire convenience and delight of all.

But the things mentioned above are only adjuncts to the principal features of this notable gathering! The glory of the *Hui Tau* is seen and felt in the twelve or fourteen worshiping assemblies, which, during the one recently held, culminated Tuesday forenoon in a wonderfully inspirational priesthood meeting. The earnestness, faith, and devotion of the audience; the manifestation of the inspiration of the Lord upon the speakers, native as well as European, the excellent music, and the confidence, sympathy, and brotherly love that flowed from soul to soul, all combined to make every service a supreme joy.

Not the least remarkable feature of this memorable event was the skill, the intelligence, the accuracy, and the inspiration with which Elder Stewart Meha interpreted the addresses of the visiting brethren. His interpretation was simply marvelous! Truly he was remarkably blessed.

The spirit, intelligence, and earnestness of the threescore elders and lady missionaries were distinct contributions to the success of each session. No more devoted, self-sacrificing men and women can be found anywhere in the world. I could not help thinking how proud and happy the parents and wives of those young men would be if they could have seen these missionaries in the glory of their work as we met them!

Success and long life to the *Hui Tau!* May each succeeding one be more successful than the last! May its influence extend until it becomes a power not only to cement the love and increase the faith of Church members, as it does even now, but also to break down the barriers erected by the ignorant and vicious to impede the progress of the Church of Jesus Christ.

Our tour of inspections of missions has been replete with many wonderful, interesting, and inspirational experiences; but to date, there are four which stand out like brilliant gems in a coronet, and not the least of these is the *Hui Tau* in Maoriland. Brother Cannon joins in love to all our friends. (En route to Tonga, May 4, 1921).—*IE*, 24:769-777 (1920-1921).

AH CHING

"For great and low there's but one test,
'Tis that each one shall do his best.
Who works with all the strength he can
Shall never die in debt to man."

Confucius once said, "All my knowledge is strung on one thread;" and on that "one connecting thread," we learn from his disciple, Tsang Tsu, were hung the principles, *self-control and charity to one's neighbor*. These are certainly two fundamental elements in character building, without which no man can justly claim true nobility.

I thought I saw the fruits of these two principles exemplified in the life of Ah Ching as I listened to him one day, when he and his wife, his son Arthur, and Telese (Mrs. Arthur Ah Ching), acted as hosts and hostesses to a number of missionaries. That Saturday afternoon and evening, July 4, are numbered among the most pleasant of the many delightful days and nights spent in "dear old" Samoa. Every hour seemed rich in fruition of profitable intercourse and valued friendships or inspirational experiences, not the least interesting of which was Ah Ching's narration of his early life in these islands. I wish my pen could reproduce his accent and his nervous, animated facial expression as he spoke, in his "pidg'n" English mixed with Samoan words, of the trials and reverses and service of those struggling years.

Ah Ching is small of stature, about five feet, five, I should say, and rather lightly built at that. His muscular movement, like his thoughts, indicates a highly nervous temperament. I fancy his temper in his early youth was of the gunpowder type; when touched off, it would go with a flash; and yet, today, I believe he can endure imposition and ignominy, if necessary, as patiently as any of his brethren.

If you were to meet him on the street or could see him move unobstrusively into a rear or side seat of the church, you would think him, if you gave him even a passing thought, one of the most humble of Chinese. I'm not sure that your opinion would change, either, if you chanced to see him in his modest three-roomed house in the rear of his little store in Apia; and yet, if you were to offer him a cashier's check of $50,000 for his property interests, he would undoubtedly smile at you, shake his head, and turn to his busy, unassuming life with a view of adding a few more pounds sterling to his comfortable fortune.

This prosperous little businessman "no can lead," he "no can lite;" but he can "speakee China, and speakee Samoa." He keeps no books and has never kept an account in his business transactions, but he had never purchased an article in his life without paying spot cash for it. He has never "owed a man a penny." He quickly remarked, "If any man no payee me, please himself, me no care."

Now, undoubtedly, in this old workaday, business world, which in many of its aspects seems a long way from the anticipated time when every man will esteem his neighbor as himself and there shall be no rogues to defraud and to steal, an X-ray examination into Ah Ching's business might reveal the fact that not a few men have "pleased themselves" not to "payee" all they owe him. At any rate there was one who deliberately planned to defraud him, and whose dastardly treachery was the means of testing Ah Ching in life's crucible. Had his character not possessed more pure gold than dross, he would perhaps even now be deprived of life or be still wearing the stripes of a condemned felon.

Ah Ching was a young man in his teens when he left Pu Chow, Fukien Province, China, and enlisted as one of the crew of a small vessel sailing for the South Seas. True to his thrifty nature, acquired by heredity and necessity, he saved nearly every penny of his fair wage. Thus after ten years constant service with the ship's company, he had accumulated a thousand pounds sterling or more. A business friend, whom he had met during his not infrequent visits to Apia, induced him to invest his hard-earned savings in a hotel and store, he to furnish the money, his friend to furnish the brains and business acumen required, and the two to divide the profits upon a proportionate basis acceptable to both. Ah Ching invested his money, only to discover in a year or two that he had been robbed of every penny of his hard-earned savings. In certain transfers of the property, it seems his friend had appropriated everything to himself. Trusting Ah Ching couldn't "leadee," couldn't "litee," so he became an unsuspecting victim to the treachery of one to whom he had entrusted practically his life; for "you take one's life, when you take away the means whereby one lives," and up to that time Ah Ching had had but one object and that was to make money, though he had always made it honestly.

When he realized that he had been robbed of all the savings of his young life, when he sensed the villainy of the dishonest scoundrel whom he had called friend, all the fire in his

Chinese nature flashed forth and showed him but one more
thing for which to live, and that one thing, revenge. He truly
wished that his enemy "had forty thousand lives—one was too
poor, too weak, to satisfy his revenge."

"He cheatee me all my money: I killee him;" he hissed
in his rage, "I sharpee a knife like a lacee," he narrated, indicating the length of the knife by touching with his right hand
the elbow of his left arm, which he stretched full length. His
knife sharpened, he cried in his agonized rage:

"Me killee him!"

"Something insidee me say, 'No killee him;' I stop; and
it say again 'no killee him.' "

"Then I know God, he helpee me, so I no killee him. I
cly, that is all—just cly." (Cry.)

Who can deny that God did "helpee" him in this great
crisis of his life? Whether that help sprang from an unsullied
conscience or gave strength in a moment of weakness to a will
that once more assumed the mastery of a passion, or whether
his spirit responded to the promptings of the infinite—the fact
remains that his frenzy was overpowered, his spirit subdued,
and he just "clied."

It was not an easy matter for Ah Ching to cry "down" to
his injured and revengeful spirit; but once he became victor,
he felt, though he did not then know, that,

"Vengeance is mine; I will repay, saith the Lord."
(Romans 12:19.)

It was a real joy to all who heard him relate his experience to see his face light up as he said:

"Me gladee from that day to this."

Truly, the fruits of that spirit are love, joy, and peace.

"Well, how did the man prosper with his stolen money,
Brother Ah Ching?" I asked.

"That house he burnee down," he answered, "man in
the stleet—all bowed down—nobody likee him—die poor."
This intimation that God had avenged his enemy, recalled the
lines:

"I know that each sinful action, as sure as the
sun brings shade,
Is somewhere, sometime punished ahead of him,
though the hour be long delayed."

With prospects of success ahead of him, Ah Ching had married a chieftain's daughter. Now they were homeless and penniless, except for the money earned day by day at odd jobs. To add to his difficulty, he had voluntarily proffered support to two of his fellow countrymen, one of whom was sickly and unable to supply the least of his necessities. I do not now recall whether I learned what claim the other man had.

"Were they your relatives?" I inquired knowing the strong ties of family relationship in the Chinese mind.

"No," was his reply, "no lelation—just Chinamen, that's all—needee help, and I give him—I findee wolk sometimee; my woman she takee in washing. Sometimee me have no lice for all (rice), but me givee Chinamen lice alle samee."

Sharing his last kernel of rice with a fellow man in need, and that, too, without any recompense or desire for reward—is not that true service? No doubt the gratitude whispered by the sick and dying man fully repaid Ah Ching for his years of gratuitous food and shelter; but there will be further recompense when one who takes note of all such kindnesses will some day say,

"These deeds shall thy memorial be—
Fear not thou didst them unto me."

It is no wonder that the sound of the gospel struck a responsive chord in this humble man's heart—conscientiousness, self-mastery, and service among its principal themes.

His Church record like his life is marked not in words but in deeds. You may know his annual income by his tithes and offerings which are freely and thankfully given as expressions of his gratitude for the manifest goodness of God to him.

His rise from poverty to opulence began about the time that he joined the Church, the turning point being marked in his mind, as undoubtedly it was in reality, by a singular dream that came to him.

"I dleamed one night," he narrated, "that the Lord, he say to me, 'Plenty money in the stleet, why you no pick him up?' Next morning I got up, lookee the stleet—no money. I could see no money in the stleet. Then I thought; I sellee things in stleet, and makee money."

With the little savings he and his wife had hoarded, he purchased by paying cash in full, one case of salmon, one sack of sugar, one gross of matches, five plugs of Samoan tobacco, one hundred pounds of Samoan kava, and 900 pounds of flour. When this was sold, he purchased more. Thus began his little business, which today includes three separate stores, and a bakery, all free from encumbrances, and carrying on a thriving trade.

His faithful wife, who shared his struggles in poverty, lived to share only a part of his prosperity. A year or so after her death he married her sister, who evidently is an excellent helpmeet and companion to him and in whom we thought we could detect the same admirable qualities of womanhood as those elements of manhood which have contributed to the commendable life of her husband. Through her lineage he now holds the title of chief among her people.

Of his sons and daughters, we learned but little. His son Arthur, who is now a partner in the business, was educated in China where his father supported him seven years. He and his wife, Telese, are also members of the Church, and seem to hold the confidence and esteem of the mission authorities and elders who know them. They are certainly as bounteous in their desires to please and to serve others as their father, Ah Ching; for after eighteen or more feasted that afternoon with all the delicacies Samoa produces, all the Sauniatu band boys were feted to their appetites' content.

As we sat in his flower-bedecked home in Tulaele, with evidences of thrift and opulence on every hand, as we thought of the number of men and women whom it is in his power now to bless, as we heard him express his gratitude for what the gospel has brought him and for what it means to him, there passed quickly in my mind, in striking contrast to this scene of success and sweet contentment, a picture of a possible felon's cell with all its associated misery and ignominy.—*IE*, 24:992-996 (1921).

FAST DAY AND THE MIDDLE EAST: AN INCIDENT IN CHURCH HISTORY

When Brother Hugh J. Cannon and I were visiting the missions of the Church, we were asked to meet the Armenian Saints over in the Near East. Nobody knew definitely their whereabouts, they were so scattered. We had their names, but we could not even pronounce them correctly. During that time, you members at home were asked to hold a special fast day for the benefit of the European Saints, including the Armenians.

Do you remember that you collected $115,000 that one day? Do you remember that Elder J. Wilford Booth was chosen by the Authorities to take part of that over to the Armenian Saints? We were coming west from one side of the world. Brother Booth was traveling east, hoping to meet us. We got a letter in Jerusalem from President Heber J. Grant saying: "Brother Wilford Booth is sent to meet you somewhere with money for relief of the Saints in Armenia."

He sent one copy to Cairo and another to Jerusalem, but he did not know where we would meet. We sent a cable to Brother Whitney in England. He answered, "Brother Booth on his way. Will meet you *somewhere*."

We sent a cable to the United States Consul in Beirut asking if he had heard from President Booth, and he wired back, "Booth on his way. Whereabouts unknown."

How we met is an interesting and faith-promoting story. The point I am making is that every cent that you contributed in that special fast day was delivered to those Saints in the Near East, without one cent of expense being taken from your contribution—because of the complete organization of the Church.—*DNCS*, April 30, 1952, p. 3.

FAITHFUL UNTO DEATH: AN IMPORTANT EPISODE

In the bright sunshine of a January forenoon in the year 1924, at a customs house on the coast of old Tyre and Sidon, I last shook hands with my beloved brother and esteemed friend, President Joseph Wilford Booth, of the Armenian mission. Little did I realize, as we bade each other good-bye, that we should never in this life see each other again! That that was our final earthly parting, however, is attested by a cablegram from President John A. Widtsoe, announcing the sudden and wholly unexpected death of Elder Booth on December 5, 1928.

At that farewell, just before I entered the auto bus that was to take me to Haifa, my friend and I embraced each other, and exchanged a mutual "God bless you!" "I'm sorry to have you leave me, Brother McKay," said he, as his eyes, became tear-dimmed, and his countenance became saddened by a shadow of sorrow. That sentence was the nearest to a complaint that I ever heard Elder Booth utter. Through that remark, however, and the look that accompanied it, I caught a glimpse of a noble heart longing for companionship—the companionship and strength of a fellow missionary who could help solve perplexing questions and share the heavy burdens incident and peculiar to that far-off mission. A few minutes, thereafter, I was speeding on my return journey toward England to rejoin the five hundred other elders then laboring in the seven missions of Europe. Brother Booth returned to Aleppo alone, for Elder Earl B. Snell, his only missionary companion, had been honorably released to return home, and no other missionaries had as yet been called to the Armenian mission. Fortunately, President Booth's wife had joined him just ten days before. Back to Sister Booth and to the Saints he loved, he wended his solitary way, to work out, under God's guidance, the destiny of the mission over which he had been called to preside.

More than two years before this parting, President Hugh J. Cannon and I had miraculously met Brother Booth at Haifa, when we were all three on our way to gather and to succor the scattered Armenian Saints. That memorable meeting was about 2 p.m., November 4, 1921. Brother Booth's first desire, following greetings and explanations, was to take us to visit the graves of Elders Adolph Haag and John A. Clark, who sleep in what is known as the German cemetery, just outside Haifa. Later, in Aleppo, we visited the grave of Elder Emil J. Huber, who laid down his life there. Elder Edgar A. Simmons lies buried in Aintab, but we had no opportunity of visiting his resting place. None of us imagined then that President Booth, himself, would also end his earthly labors in that far-away land.

In Volume 12 of *The Improvement Era,* under the title "Four Heroes Far Away," Brother Booth has written an account of these brethren and their heroic deaths. He, himself, now brings the number to five.

The three of us left Haifa for Beirut, a few hours later, where we stayed that night.

At 2:30 p.m., November 8, 1921, we reached Aintab. The alacrity with which the Saints, who, like hunted hares, were living in caves and ruined houses, became informed of our coming, is still an unexplained mystery to me; but at five p.m. seventy-four grateful people, including some who were not yet Church members, assembled in a fairly commodious place to greet us. Only those who beheld the heartfelt welcome which that people gave President Booth can realize what his return to them meant. One kind woman, whose countenance reflected deep and sincere appreciation, expressed the feeling of all when she said: "For seven years we've been in hell, but today we are in heaven."

That evening it was decided that the members of the Church and their near associates should leave Aintab at the first opportunity. They would have started that night, if possible.

Upon Brother Booth's return to Aleppo, he took up his abode among the refugees and began to make preparations for the exodus from Aintab, eighty miles distant.

What difficulties he encountered in accomplishing this duty, perhaps no one can now realize. There were carts and horses and other transportation facilities to secure. There was permission of a not too-favorable government to obtain. There were winter rains and cold weather to endure, and muddy roads to traverse.

How he was impressed to seek the aid of General De La Mathe of the French army, who issued an order for passports for fifty-three Mormons to come out of Aintab; how Lieutenant A. P. Guitton conveyed President Booth from Aleppo to Aintab, furnishing food, bedding, and protection free of charge; how the little colony packed household furniture and personal belongings on the mule-drawn vehicles that made up the train that started from Aintab to Aleppo on a wet December day; how much of the poor but treasured household articles were abandoned by the roadside to lighten the mud-bedraggled wagons; how the Saints endured the exposure in comparative cheerfulness because they were going to safety; the difficulties of housing them after their arrival in Aleppo—all these experiences, though unpleasant and full of anxiety, were cherished memories, during his lifetime, in the man's mind who alone carried the worry and responsibility of it all! They constitute also a bit of Church history that merits proper recognition and which reflects the great outstanding fact that the intrepid, unselfish missionary, Joseph Wilford Booth, literally gave himself to relieve, comfort, and cheer a people whom he loved.

From November 1921, Elder Booth labored constantly for the alleviation and betterment of the members of the mission over which he presided. For over a year he labored alone. In April 1923, Elder Earl B. Snell joined him, and together they worked diligently in securing more commodious quarters for the colony, in teaching, and in making more effective for good the organizations in the Aleppo branch. In the renovating and the remodeling of the large house rented, these two dauntless missionaries not only directed the efforts of carpenters, masons, plasterers, and cement mixers, but also became themselves workers in these trades.

But the greatest results of this devoted service are seen not in material things but in the development of the members of the branch. To one who saw them in their discouragement and distress in 1921, the change wrought is wonderful. It is true that from a financial standpoint many are still dependent and are yet longing for the day or opportunity to come when they can earn their own livelihood and become permanently assured of being placed beyond the reach of dire want; but in the joy of association in surroundings of safety, in the assurance of proper care and skill in times of sickness; in opportunity for mutual helpfulness and for spiritual growth and enlightenment, the change which was brought about by their mission president is little short of a transformation.

No wonder the people loved him, for he loved them and had demonstrated that love throughout eleven years of faithful service, to which he has since added over seven years more —faithful and ever solicitous, even unto death!

No man in the Church could have been truer to his trust, no one less complaining, no one more hopeful, no one more self-denying, no one more willing to sacrifice personal comforts and convenience to give aid to the poor and unfortunate, no one more ready to give his life for his friends and in the service of his God than was President Joseph Wilford Booth.

I know what fond wishes and fervent prayers he had in his heart as he left me, at the coast of Tyre and Sidon, to return to the little branch at Aleppo. During the nearly five intervening years, he and his faithful wife, Sister Mary R. Booth, have labored unceasingly and uncomplainingly to make real their cherished hopes and desires for the Armenian Mission.

Every day, this faithful, intrepid missionary, following in the footsteps of his Master, "went about doing good." His noble soul was actuated by this high motive even when death called. It was truly with an upright heart that President Booth met this relentless visitor, whose final summons he would answer as he had answered every other worthy call to responsibility, by saying cheerfully and resolutely: "I am ready."

With the passing of President Booth, closes another important and tragic episode in the history of the Church.—*IE*, 32:179-184 (1929).

A RETURN TO SCOTLAND 1952

Very few who are present can realize what this moment means to me. With appreciation of your welcome I associate in a reminiscent mood events that have led to my standing before you in the position I now occupy.

Before I tell you how thankful I am for the hearty welcome extended to Sister McKay, our son and daughter, and me in Glasgow and in Edinburgh, let me just briefly state that it has been over a hundred years since my grandfather, William McKay, and grandmother, Ellen Oman McKay, left Thurso, Scotland, having become converts to the Church of Jesus Christ of Latter-day Saints.

They settled in Ogden, Utah, and so in the same year did the Powells and the Evans families from Wales. William McKay's second son, David, met a little girl sixteen years of age, Jennette Evans, who became David's wife.

About 1877 William McKay, my grandfather, came back to his native land as a missionary and went up to Wick, Thurso, and Aberdeen, bearing witness that the gospel had been restored and that he knew it to be true.

About 1882, his son David, my father, came over here as a missionary. He, too, labored in Glasgow, Dundee, Aberdeen, and in Thurso, and he was president of the Scottish Conference.

In 1897 I was called as a missionary, an unmarried man, young, earnest, and eager as these young missionaries. I was assigned to come to Scotland and labor. After a few months the presidency of the European Mission, then President Rulon S. Wells, James L. McMurrin, and Joseph Parry appointed me president of the Glasgow Conference.

An elderly woman in Thurso whom I visited in 1898 was the playmate of my grandmother. She remembered when William McKay and Ellen Oman were married. She remembered when they were baptized, in referring to which she said, "I remember when they dipped them i' the Burn; do you do that noo?" I assured her that we did. "And are ye Willie's grandson? Ach a' ne, ach a' ne, I am gettin' auld!" She felt then as I do tonight, as expressed by Sir Walter Scott:

"Years rush by as like the wind,
We see not whence the eddy comes,
Nor whitherward it is tending,
And we seem, ourselves, to witness their flight,
Without a sense that we are changed.
Yet time is beguiling man of his strength
As the winds rob the trees of their foliage."

Though time dims our youthfulness and affects the physical body, it cannot touch the spirit. And so, as I look back in reminiscent moods upon these events and many others that have crowded my mind, I stand before you with gratitude in my heart that a humble elder a hundred years ago knocked at a door in Thurso, or really in Janetstown near Thurso, and testified that the gospel of Jesus Christ had been restored. I am thankful that my grandfather and grandmother believed him because that was the beginning of all the events that have happened in the century leading to this moment.

Grateful, am I?—words are too feeble to express my gratitude! Your welcome tonight, your beautiful presents, mean more than just a greeting, mean more than just an expression of friendship and goodwill—they mean a recognition that all of us in the Church have been inspired and led by a high and guiding hand.—*DNCS*, June 18, 1952, p. 2.

GOSPEL LIGHT IN FINLAND

The text in which the Savior says, "I am the Light of the world," was suggested by the experience we had last evening. For the first time in my life I heard about John's Day. I had seen the midnight sun before—thirty years ago—but I did not know that a whole nation celebrated the time, the night when the sun reaches the farthest point north and starts back south.

I saw the bonfires lighted—even in the rain. Usually rain puts fires out over in the West, but here they burn just the same. We saw a city of four hundred thousand people practically deserted—citizens out celebrating John's Day. I thought how appropriate to pay tribute to the light, and at the same time to express less enthusiasm for darkness.

Six months from now, about December 21, the people particularly above the Arctic Circle will see very little light. They will have plenty of darkness. I learned today, however, that they have electricity, so they have artificial light. But the land generally will be in darkness.

I thought—that is typical of life. Many of us walk in darkness in regard to our judging others; for example, this morning I received three beautiful roses from a sister, and I heard that that good woman is the only member of the Church in her town. And I heard that her neighbors, when they learned that she had joined the Mormons, turned their backs upon her. They had potatoes in her cellar, and they took the potatoes out.

Now, if a person said to you that you had done something wrong, and you had not done something wrong, you would know that that person was misjudging you. That person, so far as you are concerned, is in darkness. You may condemn him if you wish or you may pity him. But you know within your own soul that that person is misjudging you. Your conscience is clear, for it is in the light of truth; and that person is walking in the darkness because he is misled in that misjudgment. And so I would like to say regarding this good sister and others in Finland and in other places who have joined the Church and have been condemned by your neighbors—you remain true to the light that is in your soul, and, as your Savior of old, ask the Lord to forgive those who accuse you wrongfully.

Yes, it is a great thing to celebrate the light. And the great light that the world needs today is the light of Jesus Christ. We may cry, "Peace"; we may legislate for peace; we may have to contend with the enemies of peace; but, my dear brethren and sisters in Finland and all the world, I bear you the testimony that Peter gave to the Sanhedrin when they had imprisoned Peter and John for bearing the same truth. He said, "If we this day be examined of the good deed done to the impotent man, by what means he is made whole;

"Be it known unto you all, and to all the people of Israel, that by the name of Jesus Christ of Nazareth, whom ye crucified, whom God raised from the dead, even by him doth this man stand here before you whole.

". . . for there is none other name under heaven given among men, whereby we must be saved." (Acts 4:9-10, 12.) Thus the chief Apostle added his testimony that Jesus Christ is the light and Savior of the world.

God bless you, my dear friends. I was happy to see the number who came from way up north, closer to the midnight sun than we are. Well, you have seen the light of day shining for twenty-four hours at a time. May the light of the Savior shine in your hearts forever, and keep alive that testimony you have that the gospel of Jesus Christ is true.—*DNCS*, July 23, 1952, p. 3.

THE CHURCH IN EUROPE 1952

On May 29, 1952, accompanied by Sister McKay, my son David L., as secretary, and Mildred, his wife, I left for an important mission to Europe.

It is marvelous how much closer in time modern transportation has brought the nations of the earth; for example, Sunday, June 1, at 6:30 in the evening, we left New York. Owing to unfavorable weather conditions, the plane landed at Sydney, Newfoundland, instead of at Gander, and did not leave for Glasgow until Monday, 1:30 a.m. After fifteen hours of actual flying time we were at Prestwich Airport, in Ayrshire, Scotland, and later that same evening, Monday, we participated in the dedication of the first chapel owned by the Church in Scotland.

Wednesday, the evening following, we dedicated another in Edinburgh, and there is a suitable place in Aberdeen now ready for dedication. For these and other chapels in Great Britain, much credit is due to Elder Stayner Richards, who, with his associates, has manifested wisdom and economy.

If I followed my inclinations, I would pause here long enough to tell you of my feelings upon returning to Scotland after twenty-nine years, my latest visit, and after fifty-four years since I labored there as a young, unmarried missionary. What a flood of memories filled my soul as a Mrs. O'Hara, living in the apartment, graciously showed Sister McKay, two elders, and me the old 52 Holmhead Street headquarters of the Scottish Conference fifty-four years ago!

Beginning with the meetings in Scotland, we carried your love and greetings to the approximately 40,000 members of the Church in the ten missions in the nine European countries. June 2 to July 4, they met us in Europe to receive your greetings. July 26, you met us here to receive their thanks. And now, this morning, I express again to you in Zion the loving greetings of the Saints in Europe.

One impression I received right at first, and it became more and more pronounced as we came in contact with people in all walks of life, was a more tolerant attitude than I experienced a half century ago. It was a joy to mingle with intelligent people radiating a spirit of goodwill.

One beneficial result of the tour was a keener realization on the part of members of the Church that they are not detached entities but are in reality part of the Church as a whole. Nearness in time contributed to this feeling, but more especially their meeting one of the Sunday School general superintendency[1] and a member of the general board of the Primary,[2] hearing incidents, items of instruction, that happened or were given, as it were, but a week before, awakened a sense of belonging that was satisfying and encouraging.

It was truly a joy and inspiration to see the loyalty and feel the responsiveness of members of the Church in every mission. There was no exception. To greet those eagerly expectant, graciously warmhearted people gave a joy almost inexpressible. We sensed to a small degree, at least, the truth of the saying: "To love and to be loved is the greatest happiness of existence." This was especially true so far as our love for those faithful people is concerned.

I should be remiss, indeed downright unappreciative, if I did not take this occasion to refer appreciatively to the instances of goodwill manifested on this recent presidential tour of the European missions.

[1]Elder David Lawrence McKay.
[2]Sister Mildred C. McKay.

Our Church knows full well what it means to be misjudged, scoffed at, and persecuted. It can appreciate, too, in full value, tolerance, and a sense of justice and fair play.

The mission presidencies, missionaries, members of the Church, and their friends were most gracious in their greetings and manifestations of deference to the office of President. Everywhere their welcome was most generous. To all these we shall ever be grateful for the distances they traveled, for the sacrifices they made, for their wholehearted, radiant gladness—all of which contributed so much to the success of a very important mission.

I wish to refer especially to the good will shown by prominent businessmen, representatives of the press, hotel managers, government officials, and others whose interest and courtesy were shown without reserve.

It is unwise to attempt to mention a few because of possibly showing partiality and failing to mention deserving persons, but I will name the Honorable Charles U. Bay, American Ambassador to Norway, who not only by proffered words, "If there is anything I can do for you, please let me know," but also by direct action with the assistance of his undersecretary, Leon Cowles, rendered invaluable service in securing rightful privileges for our missionaries in Norway. He said that was his first official act as ambassador. Other ambassadors and ministers, including Honorable John M. Cabot of Finland and Honorable James C. Dunn of Paris, were equally considerate in proffering help and cooperation. Their courtesy was unbounded.

Others who did not hesitate to inconvenience themselves to render favors were Colonel Tooler and General Wood of the American Army, through whose graciousness, at the intercession of President Stayner Richards and A. Hamer Reiser, special favors were granted to us visitors in attendance at the Queen's Garden Festival at the Buckingham Palace.

I mention appreciatively, also, the service rendered by the Consul General J. D. van Karnebeek, here in the United States, whom we happened to meet before we left, who arranged for a most cordial visit to Her Majesty, Juliana, Queen of the Netherlands.

I wish to mention President Juho K. Paasikiivi of Finland, a dignified, princely gentleman, conference with whom, accompanied by President Henry A. Matis, I shall remember with satisfaction and pleasure. For exceptional courtesies shown by Mr. Sholz, the manager of the Palace Hotel near The Hague, Holland; to passport officials at Berlin, who finding us without visas, gave special considerations and, out of courtesy, obtained the necessary papers without delay, we mention appreciatively.

We are mindful also of the outstanding consideration shown by eleven policemen who were at the Mercedes Palast, at North Berlin, where an audience of twenty-six hundred persons crowded to overcapacity that large theater. How their favorable attitude stood out in contrast with the action of police when some members of the Twelve and others who sit here in this audience this morning were hunted and arrested a half century ago!

I wish to name appreciatively, also, Elder William Zimmer, and two real estate men, Mr. Hans Jordi and Mr. Hermann Schulters, who assisted President Samuel E. Bringhurst in choosing prospective temple sites in Switzerland.

For his having built suitable houses in Berlin, I wish to commend President Walter Stover, whose devotion to the German Saints was outstanding and whose generosity and wisdom will ever be cherished by the thousands whom he blessed. Included in this expression of appreciation are officials who aided President James L. Barker and President Golden L. Woolf in their securing official recognition of the Church in France.

An outstanding feature of our visit in Germany was the attendance of American servicemen. In the West German Mission they gathered as groups that compared favorably with our groups of missionaries. And how proud we were of these choice young men and women, a credit to their parents, to the Church, and to our nation. Whether they participated in concerts or attended to the details of conference, greeted strangers, or looked after the welfare of Saints and investigators, their ability was manifested, their dignity commendable, and their sincerity in their work most outstanding.

Well, fellow workers, all these and a hundred other instances that I might name are evidences of friendship and good will that will contribute to the peaceful relationships that should exist between this country and the free countries of Europe.

I am sorry that I must now sound a note of discouragement, for I cannot refrain from referring to the attitude of selfishness, distrust, and hatred manifest by the leaders of communism. How they hate America and everything American!

They are not only anti-American—they are anti-Christian! By every means possible—newspapers, billboards, documents, radio—they try to inculcate hatred in the hearts of the youth.

By the iron curtain they scheme to keep Western influence out of Russia and prevent Russians from becoming acquainted with the West. A distinguished sociologist once wrote, "Give us the young and we will create a new mind and a new earth in a single generation." That is one aim and purpose of the Russian dictators.

Largely because of their nefarious schemes and false ideologies, civilization is facing a crisis. We are in a period of uncertainty, of international tension. Not infrequently we see manifest among people a feeling of impending crisis in which is fear that the atom bomb might bring to a tragic end present-day civilization. Articles in the daily press and in magazines give unmistakable evidence of this condition. You can pick up any magazine or any daily paper and read such headings as: "Our Democracy in Danger" — "Communism—a New Kind of Threat" — "Foundations of our Republic Threatened" —"The World Cannot Exist Half Slave and Half Free."

These are some I have taken at random.

"Look at the map of the world," says one. "The iron curtain of Soviet communist control has descended over vast areas and over hundreds of millions of people in Eastern Europe and in Asia, since the close of World War II. It is unspeakably tragic that this should be the case, when it need not have been." Another: "We Face a Spiritual War." Then, last: "Red China's War against God."

Well, brethren and sisters, let us not despair. A man's comfort in time of ease and peace, as well as in times of stress and danger, will be found in the depths of the sincerity of his belief in an eternal Being, his faith in the gospel of Jesus Christ. Commenting upon the need of sincerity, of faith, one writer once asked this vital question, and I give it to you:

"Is Jesus to you only a legendary figure in history; a saint to be painted in the stained glass of Church windows; a sort of sacred fairy not to be approached and hardly to be mentioned by name, or is he still what he was when he was in the flesh—a reality, a man of like passions with ourselves, an elder brother, a guide, a counselor, a comforter, a great voice calling to us out of the past to live nobly, to die bravely, and keep up our courage to the last?"

Notwithstanding the threatening conditions that exist in the world today, members of the Church of Jesus Christ need not fear nor be perturbed, if they will but anchor their souls in unchanging truths revealed by our Father in heaven.

If communists attempt to poison the minds of youth, as they are doing, against God the Father and his Beloved Son, if they pervert the gospel of peace and good will, if they continue to sow the seeds of mistrust and hatred, we must more guardedly protect our youth, more militantly instruct them in the principles of the restored gospel, implant in their hearts the truth that ". . . there is none other name under heaven given among men, whereby we must be saved." (Acts 4:12.) Let them realize that without Christ the world is lost.

James L. Gordon is right when he declares: "A cathedral without windows, a face without eyes, a field without flowers, an alphabet without vowels, a continent without rivers, a night without stars, and a sky without a sun—these would not be so sad as a world without a Bible or a soul without Christ."

He is the Son of "God in the Highest" as proclaimed by the heavenly hosts, the Prince of Peace, our Elder Brother, our Redeemer, our Savior.

"His purposes fail not, neither are there any who can stay his hand.

"From eternity to eternity he is the same, and his years never fail.

"For thus saith the Lord—I, the Lord, am merciful and gracious unto those who fear me, and delight to honor those who serve me in righteousness and in truth unto the end.

"Great shall be their reward and eternal shall be their glory." (D. & C. 76:3-6.)—DNCS, October 11, 1952, pp. 2-3.

I have an entirely different viewpoint of these countries now than when I went over to Europe before. Today I realize the responsibility of this Church to proclaim the gospel is world-wide, now that the means of transportation and communication are such we are only a day, in time of travel, from the European nations.

The members of our Church in Europe, as in the isles of the sea, sense their importance as members and their responsibility as representatives of the Church in those distant lands. The members of the Church here at home should realize more clearly the loyalty and devotion they owe to their fellow members in Europe.—*DNCS*, September 6, 1952, p. 1.

God bless the Church. It is world-wide. Its influence should be felt by all nations. May his spirit influence men everywhere and incline their hearts toward good will and peace. May divine guidance be given the priesthood, who hold the responsibility of declaring to an indifferent world the restoration of the gospel of Jesus Christ, I pray in the name of Jesus Christ. Amen.—*DNCS*, October 11, 1952, p. 3.

INDEX

CHURCH OF JESUS CHRIST OF

Latter-Day Saints

San Leandro Ward

SCHEDULE OF MEETINGS

Priesthood	Sunday	8:45 A.M.
Sunday School	Sunday	10:30 A.M.
Sacrament Service	Sunday	5:30 P.M.
Relief Society	Tuesday	10:00 A.M.
M.I.A.	Tuesday	7:30 P.M.
Genealogy	Thursday	7:30 P.M.
Primary	Thursday	4:00 P.M.

EVERYONE WELCOME

SUNDAY SCHOOL PROGRAM
October 6, 1957

Services Conducted by - - - Clarke B. Murphy

Opening Hymn - - - - - - - - - - - - -Page 171
    "Now to Heaven Our Prayer"

Opening Prayer   Elwood Randall

Practice Hymn - - - - - - - - - - - - -Page 36
    "God of Power, God of Right"

2½ Minute Talk - - - - - - Kenneth Hunsinger
2½ Minute Talk - - - - - - - George Bohannon

Sacrament Song - - - - - - - - - - -Page 218
    "We'll Sing All Hail to Jesus Name"

Sacrament Gem - - - - - - - - -Linda Painter
    "If any of you lack wisdom, let him ask
    of God, that giveth to all men liberally,
    and upbraideth not, and it shall be given
    him." James 1:5

ADMINISTRATION OF SACRAMENT

SEPARATION FOR CLASS

Closing Hymn - - - - - - - - - - - - - Page 38
    "Each Cooing Dove"

Closing Prayer - - - - - - - -Wilford Snyder

ANNOUNCEMENTS

Your Bishopric extends to all members of the ward an invitation to next Sunday's Sacrament Service to listen to a very interesting and important subject, The Great Apostasy, to be presented by Brother Melvin D. Danielson and Brother Mal Duke. This principle is greatly misunderstood by a confused world today. Plan to be present.

Correlation Meeting will be held Thursday, October 24, 1957, at 7:30 P.M. All officers and teachers are expected to be present.

The Los Angeles Temple Excursion bus will leave Next Friday P.M. Plan to take advantage of this opportunity. The cost is small. Contact Bishop Lauper for details.

Fathers & Sons Outing on Friday and Saturday, October 11th and 12th, at Redwood Park. Free Supper and Breakfast will be served.

Senior Saints - a free dinner will be served at the chapel on Friday, October 18th. It promises to be a very pleasant evening. Contact Brother & Sister Smithen for transportation.

WARD TEACHERS: Plan now to make your calls early this month. We should not fail to bring our percentage up.

LADIES: Relief Society Opening Party and Luncheon will be held Tuesday, October 8th at 10:00 A.M. All ladies are cordially invited.

SAN LEANDRO WARD OFFICERS

Bishop	Marcel F. Lauper	LO 8-0229
1st Counselor	LaRue B. Duffin	TR 2-1414
2nd Counselor	Harold P. Hansen	SW 8-2740
Ward Clerks:		
Membership	C. LeRoy Bauer	LO 8-4313
Historical	Gordon Belnap	
Finance	Robert C. McHenry	LO 8-7920
Asst. Ward Clerk	J. Fred Berger	SW 8-7088
Ward Teaching	Elton J. Flaner	TR 2-6362

SUNDAY SCHOOL

Superintendent	Clarke B. Murphy	TR 2-0786
1st Assistant	Robert F. Bundy	LO 8-8185
2nd Assistant	Russell V. Heath	EL 1-3805
Secretary	Goldie Murphy	TR 2-0786
Jr. Sunday School	Winifred Heath	EL 1-3805

OTHER AUXILIARY HEADS

YMMIA Superintendent	William F. Callahan	EL 7-0695
YWMIA President	Viola Schipper	LO 2-4890
Relief Society	Nelle Christensen	LO 9-0256
Primary	Geneva Griggs	LO 9-1432
Genealogy	Daniel Canning	TR 2-9743

MELCHIZEDEK GROUP LEADERS

High Priests	Wilford L. Nelson	TR 2-8954
Seventies	John S. Dutson	LO 8-7033
Elders	John R. McDonald	LO 8-4514

AARONIC PRIESTHOOD COMMITTEES

Sec. Senior Aaronic	Edward H. Painter	LO 8-8847
Sec. Aaronic under 21	Anthony T. Bozich	EL 7-0216
Asst. Sec. Aaronic under 21	Kenneth L. Frye	SW 8-6269

★ ★ ★

Bulletin Editor	Dolores Bednar	LO 9-3105
Messenger Reporter	Marilyn Nelson	TR 2-8954

DAVID O. McKAY'S BIRTHPLACE